A LOWER LADAKHI VERSION OF THE KESAR SAGA

A LOWER LADAKHI VERSION OF THE KESAR SAGA

TIBETAN TEXT; ENGLISH ABSTRACT OF CONTENTS; NOTES AND VOCABULARIES; AND APPENDICES

A. H. FRANCKE

GYAN

Published by

Gyan Publishing House
5, Ansari Road
Daryaganj, New Delhi-110002
Phone: 011-47034999, 9811692060
E-mail: books@gyanbooks.com

Distribution Network
gyanbooks.com
India, USA, Canada, UK, Australia, France

ISBN : 978-81-2123-731-4 (PB)
First Published, Calcutta, 1905

2nd Impression 2020

Printed at: Gyan Press, Delhi.

A Lower Ladakhi Version of the Kesar Saga
Author: A. H. Francke

གཤམ་ཡུལ་ན་བཤད་པའི་
ཀེ་སར་གྱི་སྒྲུངས་བཞུགས་སོ །

A LOWER LADAKHI VERSION
OF THE
KESAR SAGA

TIBETAN TEXT; ENGLISH ABSTRACT OF CONTENTS; NOTES AND VOCABULARIES; AND APPENDICES

BY
A. H. FRANCKE, PH.D.,
Moravian Missionary

INTRODUCTION
BY
SUNITI KUMAR CHATTERJI,
M.A. (Calcutta), D.LIT. (London), F.R.A.S.B.,
Professor, University of Calcutta,
Philological Secretary to the Royal Asiatic Society of Bengal

PRINTED AT THE BAPTIST MISSION PRESS
PUBLISHED BY THE ROYAL ASIATIC SOCIETY OF BENGAL

CALCUTTA
1905–41

CONTENTS

FOREWORD

The legend of the Tibetan King Kesar (or Gesar) is the most widely known hero-myth of Central Asia and holds the same position as the story of Rama in this country. Numerous versions of this legend in songs, lyric poems and prose romances exist in Tibet, Mongolia and China, and a vast mass of literature has grown around this theme in these countries. As far as is known the earliest accounts of the Saga were published in Europe in 1836 in the form of German renderings of portions of the Kalmuck text written in Pekin in 1716 by the command of the Emperor Kang-hsi. Since then other versions have been published including the French and English translations of a Tibetan prose work by Madame David-Neel in 1933. These recensions seem, however, to be later and much coloured by the ideas of Lamaistic Buddhism. At the beginning of the present century Dr. A. H. Francke, a Moravian missionary in Ladakh, discovered two versions of the Kesar story current there which he succeeded in getting written down. The Leh version, collected by Dr. Francke together with text, translation, notes, etc., was published in the *Memoirs* of the Finno-Ugrian Society of Helsingfors in 1900. The second version, from Khalatse of Lower Ladakh, appears to be the oldest and the most important corpus of the Kesar legend so far found, and developed wholly in the horizon of the pre-Buddhistic Bon religion and free from all Lamaistic taints. The Royal Asiatic Society of Bengal undertook to publish the original text of this version with an English summary and notes, etc., in the *Bibliotheca Indica Series*, and during the period from 1905 to 1909 four fascicles were printed. The last fascicle containing the Title-pages, Preface, Contents and Index was sent by the author in 1925, but the period of quiescence that followed in the Society's activities must have been responsible for the non-publication of the work. In the meantime, the author passed away in 1933. After the re-organization of the work of the Society was undertaken in 1939, the last fascicle of the Kesar Saga, left partly in proof and partly in MSS. by Dr. Francke, was entrusted to Dr. S. K. Chatterji, D.Lit., Philological Secretary, for early publication. Dr. Chatterji has contributed a general introduction containing the history and a dissertation on the place of the Saga in the life and literature of Central Asia, and at his suggestion six articles on the Kesar Saga already published by Dr. Francke in the

Indian Antiquary, *Mem. Finno-Ugrian Society*, and *J.P.A.S.B.*, between 1901–1907, which have now become rare, have been included as appendices in the present work for the benefit of scholars. These six articles are as follows:—

1. The Spring Myth of the Kesar Saga.
   (The *Indian Antiquary*, Vol. XXX, 1901, pp. 329–341; Vol. XXXI, 1902, pp. 32–40.)
2. The Winter Myth of the Kesar Saga.
   (This English version is published for the first time. A few of Francke's notes are incorporated. The Tibetan Text and Francke's German Translation appeared in the *Suomalais-urgrilaisen Seuran Toimituksia XV* (*Memoirs* of the Finno-Ugrian Society XV), Helsingfors, 1902.)
3. A Ladakhi Bon-Pa Hymnal.
   (The *Indian Antiquary*, Vol. XXX, 1901, pp. 359–364.)
4. Ladakhi Songs.
   (The *Indian Antiquary*, Vol. XXXI, 1902, pp. 304–311.)
5. The Ladakhi Pre-Buddhist Marriage Ritual.
   (The *Indian Antiquary*, Vol. XXX, 1901, pp. 131–149.)
6. The Paladins of the Kesar Saga.
   (*Journ. Proc. Asiat. Soc. Bengal*, N.S., Vol. II, 1906, pp. 467–469.)

The Society is indebted to Dr. Bata Krishna Ghosh, Ph.D., for having kindly supplied us in collaboration with Prof. Chatterji with an English translation (Appendix 2) of Dr. Francke's original German account of the Winter Myth of the Kesar Saga published in the *Memoirs* of the Finno-Ugrian Society of Helsingfors.

It is to be hoped that the completion of this very important work will remove a long-felt desideratum of scholars interested in the linguistics, religion and social institutions of ancient Tibet.

B. S. Guha,
General Secretary,
Royal Asiatic Society of Bengal.

Calcutta,
November 15, 1941.

INTRODUCTION

THE SAGA OF KING KESAR

I. The Bod or Tibetan People, and the Bon Religion.

Tibet is now recognised as one of the Buddhist countries. A good deal if not almost all of what is noble and beautiful and indicative of high culture in present-day Tibet came with Buddhism, and it was largely India and to some extent China which gave to Tibet its civilisation. The Tibetans are the kinsmen of the Burmese, the Siamese and the Chinese in language, if not wholly in race. This group of peoples, to which the name *Sino-Tibetan* or *Tibeto-Chinese* has been given, had developed its distinctive speech and the bases of its characteristic culture near the head-waters of the Yang-tsze-Kiang (or it may be in North China, in the valley of the Hwang-Ho) several thousand years before Christ.

One branch of them went north-east into North China and settled there, or stayed on in their original home in the Hwang-Ho valley, long before 2000 B.C., and there it became the ancient Chinese people, who built up a very high and original type of civilisation before 1500 B.C., which independently of any other cultures reached its highest point during the first year-thousand before Christ, and attained still further development through contact with Buddhism and Indian civilisation during the first year-thousand after Christ. Two other groups of the same primitive Tibeto-Chinese people, who later came to be known as the *Dai* (or *Thai*) and as the *Mran-mā*, descended from their original homeland further to the south, and were settled in Northern Burma, Southern China and Northern Indo-China—the Mran-mā in Northern Burma, and the Dai in South China and Northern Indo-China. Central and Southern Burma and Southern Indo-China in ancient times were inhabited by the *Rmañ* people (later known as *Mon* or *Mun*, through modification of the word) in *Rāmañña-dēsa* or Suvarṇa-bhūmi, i.e. South and Central Burma and Dvārāvatī, i.e. South Siam, and by the *Khmer* people in Cambodia. These Rmañ (Mon) and Khmer peoples were Austro-Asiatic by language, distinct from the Tibeto-Chinese, and had already, during the early centuries of the Christian era, Indianised themselves in religion and culture by adopting Brahmanism and Buddhism and Indian ways of life, with Sanskrit as their sacred language. The Mran-mā, later known as the *Byammā*, conquered the Rmañ or Mons, and absorbed them and adopted their Indian culture, and became the Burmese people: the history of Burma has been the history of a long conflict between the Mran-mā and the Rmañ, between the Sino-Tibetan Burmans and the Austro-Asiatic Mons, and it ended in a final triumph of the Northern Sino-Tibetan invaders, the Mons dying as a people but profoundly influencing the Burmans in almost everything except language. The Dai or Thai similarly assimilated a large Mon element in Siam and adopted the Indian culture of the latter, and were further profoundly modified by the Khmers, Austro-Asiatic kinsmen of the Mons, who still live as a separate people. Thai tribes now occupy Eastern Burma (as the *Shans*), Siam, and part of French Indo-China (as the *Laos*); while masses of them were transformed into South Chinese people through the cultural influence of North and Central China. One branch of the Thai, the *Ahoms*, penetrated into Assam during the first half of the 13th century, and supplied the ruling house in that part of India, giving to it their name (*Aham* or *Asam*), and ultimately becoming completely Hinduised.

A fourth band of the Tibeto-Chinese are the Tibetans. They appear to have mingled racially with cattle-raising Central Asian tribes of Mongoloid and Indo-European origin (like the Mongols, the Turks and the Śakas or Scythians), for the Tibetans are the only people of the Tibeto-Chinese linguistic group who adopted milk and milk-products like butter and cheese as an important article of food. They settled in Tibet, according to a later Buddhist tradition, or reconstruction of past history, of very doubtful historical value, sometime during the middle of the first year-thousand before Christ, when Buddha lived and preached in India. This group of Tibeto-Chinese called itself *Bod*, a name which was current at least as early as the middle of the first millennium A.D.; and this name has survived to our day, although in a modified form, as *Pö* or *Phö*. The Indians who came in touch with this group of the Sino-Tibetans, probably for the first time during the early centuries of the Christian era, changed the name *Bod* into *Bhōṭa*, which is the Sanskrit and other North Indian term for Tibet and the Tibetans. (Was the voiced aspirate *Bh-* heard dialectally in this word in ancient Tibet—so that a variant **Bhod*, or **Bhot*, gave the Indian form of the word? We should note the aspirated modern Tibetan *Phö*.) This Bod-Bhōṭa-Pö people, i.e. the Tibetans, were for a long number of centuries in a barbarous or semi-civilised state. Some groups of these Tibetans, or tribes allied though not exactly identical with them, penetrated into the foothills of the Himalayas and so came into India, advancing well enough even into the plains of North Bengal. Others settled in Assam and the Indo-Burmese frontier: but these were tribes rather distinct from both the Tibetans and the Burmese.

There is no record of the first contact between the Tibetans and the Indians. Before the acceptance of Buddhism by the powerful King of Tibet Srong-btsan-sgam-po in the seventh century, this contact, it can be assumed, was sufficiently long and close. Srong-btsan-sgam-po (who reigned c. 630–650 A.D. and was thus a contemporary of Emperor Harsha-vardhana of North India) maintained political relations (which, according to tradition, were cemented by marriage) with India (Nepal) and with China. (In the seventh century A.D., it is likely that Nepal was already inhabited, as now, by an Indianised and mixed people with primitive Mongoloid elements.) The Tibetan scholar Thon-mi Sambhoṭa was sent by this king to India, and he adapted the Indian alphabet for the Tibetan language, which was first written down during this century. The final affiliation of Tibetan culture to those of India on the one hand and China on the other was effected during the reign of Srong-btsan-sgam-po; the traditional story of his marriage with a princess of Nepal and a princess of China (Buddhist legend saw in them the incarnations respectively of *Śyāmā-Tārā* or 'Dark Tārā' and *Sitā-Tārā* or 'White Tārā', two forms of *Tārā*, the *Śakti* of *Lōkēśvara*, i.e. the Bōdhisattva *Avalōkitēśvara*) may be looked upon as a symbolisation of this event, if its historicity is doubted.

The religion which the Tibetans followed before their acceptance of Buddhism is known as the *Bon* religion. It was originally a form of primitive *Shamanism*—a belief in unseen powers which were either harmless or harmful for man, and which could be controlled by man through magical rites and incantations (the name being from the word *Shaman*, a Mongol transformation of the Sanskrit *Śramaṇa*, which is applied to the priests of Central Asian Buddhism, and, by extension, to the priest-magicians of the pre-Buddhist religion of the Mongol world). Such a religion appears to have developed not only among the primitive Tibeto-Chinese, but also among their kinsmen of the Mongol or Yellow race—the Uralic peoples (Lapps, Finns, Esths, Voguls, Ostyaks, Magyars, etc.), the Altaic peoples (Mongols, Manchus, Turks, etc.), and others, and the Red Men of the two Americas. One of the noteworthy characteristics of this Shamanism, including the Bon religion, is the faith in the power of the magical word, which, by constant repetition with the prescribed ritual, can compel supernatural powers, gods, devils or spirits, to come under the control of man. Penances of various sorts and offering of sacrifices were considered efficacious to bring the favour of the gods and spirits. As in most religions (even the so-called monotheistic ones), the world was believed to be full of spirits, and people were encouraged to believe in their presence and potency, and in magic. There are numerous points of agreement between Bon Shamanism and certain forms of Hindu Tantricism, in ideas as well as in ritual. Like the Hindu conception of *Puruṣa* and *Prakṛti*, or *Śiva* and *Śakti*, like the similar Chinese conception of *Yang* or the Male Principle and *Yin* or the Female Principle, operating in the creation and maintenance of the universe, the Tibetans also have the idea of *Yab-Yum* or 'Father and Mother', of the Male and Female Principles. It may be permissible to assume that both the Chinese idea of Yang-Yin and the Tibetan one of Yab-Yum originated in some common ideology of an analogous nature among the primitive Sino-Tibetan ancestors of both the peoples: the Chinese conception shows (so far as the Chinese characters for *Yang* and *Yin* in their composition reveal) the presence of the ideas of light and darkness, of heat and cold, in nature, emanating from the Male and Female Principles underlying all existence. Among the Tibetans, there is ample evidence of the presence of the conception of a 'King of Heaven' and a 'Queen of Heaven', which is based, like our Indian figures of *Śiva* and *Umā*, on the idea of Yab-Yum, of 'Father and Mother'. The ancient Chinese also conceived of their great Mother Goddess, *Si-wang-Mu* or 'the Queen Mother of the West', as an embodiment of Yin or the Female Principle, and her male counterpart was *Tung-wang-Kung* or 'the Just King of the East', who represented Yang or the Male Principle. The Hindus of course developed a mystic philosophy, as the basis of this mythological conception, of *Brahman* and *Māyā*, of the Supreme Spirit (*Puruṣa*) and Nature or Matter (*Prakṛti*), of *Sat* (that which exists—the Positive Principle) and *Asat* (that which does not exist—the Negative Principle), of the Unmanifest (*Avyakta*) and the Manifest (*Vyakta*), etc., which is not found in the case of the Tibetan Yab-Yum and the Chinese Yang-Yin, at least in such deep and wide ramifications: nevertheless, the occurrence, probably independent occurrence, of this conception among these two distinctive peoples of the Middle and Far East, namely, the mixed Austro-Asiatic, Dravidian and Aryan Hindus, and the Sino-Tibetans, is noteworthy. It may be imagined that the Yab-Yum idea belonged to the native Bon religion of the Tibetans, and it was adopted into the Mahāyāna Buddhism of Tibet, itself modified by Śākta Tantric ideas and practices on the soil of India.

It may also be asked if the Bon religion of the primitive Tibetans is not connected with the religion of the ancient Chinese as it manifested itself, e.g., in the ritual and mythology of Tao-ism, and in the popular side of the religion which was officialised by Confucius. As two important branches of the same race or speech-group, they may be expected to have preserved some common inheritances.

In the racial sensitiveness of the Tibetans, there appears to be present a predilection for the apprehension of the wonderful and the spiritual through the intermediacy of the terrible rather than the beautiful; and, as a consequence, both in the Bon religion and in Tibetan Buddhism gods and goddesses of a frightful aspect were as much or perhaps more in evidence than those of a benign and gracious form. The wild and desolate natural background of Tibet, with its snow-capped mountains and its desert plains, devoid generally of the softness and beauty of greenery, was probably responsible for this mentality of the Tibetans, in their mythological conceptions and imaginings.

From the seventh century onwards, right down to recent times, attempts were frequently made to strengthen Buddhism in Tibet and at the same time to suppress entirely the Bon religion; but the Bon faith never died out. What has happened in other lands has also happened in Tibet. Mahāyāna Buddhism with its Tantric colouring from India, and the native Bon religion of Tibet—these two have influenced each other, and influenced profoundly. The Buddhism of Tibet is full of Tantric practices and ideas, and many of its theories and practices appear to be nothing but Bon ideas and practices which were but submerged and not destroyed by Buddhism. The Buddhism of Tibet, *Lamaism*, thus received its distinctive colouring from the earlier Bon religion. Tibetan life retains a good deal of its Bon bases. And the Bon religion, too, in the form in which it survives in Tibet, has been profoundly modified by Indian Buddhistic notions and practices such as developed in Bengal, Bihar and Nepal during the closing centuries of the first millennium A.D. Buddhist ideas, Buddhist mythology, Buddhist practices and Buddhist monastic organisation—all these have inextricably commingled with the Bon religion of the present day. Although the Buddhistic ruling classes of Tibet do not officially recognise the Bon religion, it still persists as a faith suppressed or overlaid, particularly in Eastern Tibet. There are Bon priests, Bon temples and Bon monasteries, fairly well-organised; and Bon hagiologies imitate the Buddhist 'Golden Legends' of Tibet. But it would be impossible to find the Bon religion in its pristine purity anywhere—it does not exist in life, though vestiges of it may be expected to survive in the older literature of Tibet.

The mixed Bon religion which is still current in Tibet is known as *Bsgyur Bon* or 'modified Bon'. Śarat Chandra Dās gave an account of the philosophy and mythology of this Bsgyur Bon (or *Gyur Bon*) in the pages of the *Journal and Text of the Buddhist Text Society*, Calcutta, for 1893 (Vol. I, Part I, January 1893, Appendix, pp. 1–7: 'A Brief Sketch of the Bon Religion of Tibet—Gyur Bon or the Modified Bon', translated from *Mdo Sermig* and *Ḥdus-pa Rin-poche*, life of *S̲h̲en-rab mi-wo* [=*Gśen-rab-mi-bo*], the Bon teacher, and Śen-rab's great exploit; Vol. I, Part II, May 1893, Appendix II, 'The Bon Religion: Bon Deities', pp. 11–14, with plate giving figures of Bon gods; Vol. I, Part III, November 1893, Appendix I, 'The Principal Deities of the Bon Pantheon', pp. 1–3, with plate similar to that in Part II). On the ideal plane, this Bsgyur Bon presents us with some conceptions of a high order. The highest aim of a Bon devotee is to attain to the position of the Eternal called *Gyung Drung* (=*Sanātana* in Sanskrit), and at the same time to retain his personality, with a view to work for the good and welfare of all living beings of the world. Whoever endeavours to gain that supreme position must perform two kinds of good work on this earth, viz., those of ordinary usefulness, and those of supreme usefulness. In these two there are said to exist two kinds of hindrances, one called *Bgegs-kyi Bar-chad*, i.e. 'obstruction caused by evil spirits', and the other called *Dug-gis Bar-chad*, i.e. 'obstruction to virtue by *dug*, i.e. poison, or moral corruption'. By the word *bgegs*, according to Bon mysticism, is understood the co-operating cause (=Sanskrit *pratibandhaka*, *vighna*), and *dug* (=*viṣa* in Sanskrit), i.e. poison, is the *rgyu* or the original cause (*hētu* in Sanskrit). The *dug* consists of attachment to worldly objects, anger, stupidity—or darkness, pride or vainglory, envy and jealousy—in short, all moral sins and vices. The way to remove these obstructions is twofold: to train up the mind in wisdom, in the first instance, to rid it of the *dug*,—and to perform religious and magical ceremonies and incantations to remove the *bgegs*. In practical Bon, greater weight appears to be placed on the second way. Bon deities are either wrathful in spirit, or mild and peaceful. Goddesses (*Lha-mo*) take precedence over the gods. The Bon pantheon has not been systematised, and it is apparent from the meagre details available about the Bon deities that they present a good deal of agreement with the Buddhist Lamaistic pantheon of Tibet. The pictures that Sarat Chandra Das has given in the Buddhist Text Society's papers give a number of dancing figures, naked except for the loin cloth, with heads of fanciful and frightful animals.

From the epic stories about the Tibetan Hero-King Kesar, and from popular songs collected in Ladakh by Dr. A. H. Francke (which are republished in the present volume), Dr. Francke himself attempted to deduce and describe a Bon pantheon, which as he suggested represented the Bon god-world in its primitive form, unmixed by the notions of Lamaistic Buddhism (Tantricism and Mahāyāna). Because this pre-Buddhistic religion and pantheon as deduced from the Ladakh poems and the Kesar tales differed in certain important respects from the later, systematised Bon religion and pantheon—that of the Bsgyur Bon—as in Bon-po MSS. published by Dr. B. Laufer, Dr. Francke qualified what may be called the Bon religion of Ladakh by the term *Gling-Chos*, i.e. 'Mythology of Gling'—Gling being the name of the country over which the hero Kesar ruled, and originally the word '*Gling*' probably meant 'the Earth'. Mr. Johan van Manen has an informing paper on the Bsgyur Bon god *Sgang-ba* (*Journal and Proceedings of the Asiatic Society of Bengal*, New Series, Vol. XVIII, 1922, pp. 195–222). In that article Mr. van Manen mentions some papers by Dr. B. Laufer on Bon in the *Toung P'ao* and other journals, and these, together with Sarat Chandra Das's work, and that of Francke, exhausts all that is available on *Bon-Chos* or the Bon Religion, pure or mixed.

The nature of the primitive or original Bon religion—its ideas and its mythology—cannot be said to have been clearly and fully made known to us, despite the very valuable work of Francke with the Ladakh Kesar Saga. But it may be permissible to assume that the kernel of much of what is found in the Bsgyur Bon (possibly the conception of the Gyung Drung), and the pantheon of the Ladakhi Kesar Saga, together with certain ideas analogous to Indian Tantricism including the leaning towards sorcery and mysticism, are derived from the primitive Bon religion. It was doubtless a religion with some organisation, claiming the homage of the masses: that is why Indian Buddhism could not wholly stamp it out, and had to make a good deal of compromise with it. One thing appears clear: in the Bon faith the Tibetans appear to have found some support for their language and for the culture that is associated with language: for the Tibetans accepted Buddhism from India, but not the Indian vocabulary (Sanskrit, Prakrit, or 'Bhāshā') of Buddhism. This suggests a well-formed literary tradition (although as yet unwritten), a habit of taking recourse to the native language for philosophical and other ideas. Like some other peoples—the Arabs, the Uralic Finns, and the Polynesians—the primitive Tibetans appear to have possessed the gift of the word, and to have lacked the cunning of the hand—the plastic skill. Excepting what was connected with their language, it would seem that they had no art traditions, and they were content to accept *in toto* the art of India as it came to them from Bengal and Bihar, directly and through Nepal; and, excepting for slight imitations of the art of China, they kept the Indian tradition intact for some thirteen centuries, adding scarcely anything of their own.

II. Kesar (Gesar), King of Gling, and the Kesar Saga.

Like the story of Rāma and of Arjuna and the Pāṇḍavas in India, throughout the whole of Tibet, including Ladakh or Western Tibet which is now a part of the State of Jammu and Kashmir. there is a popular story or legend, that of King Kesar (or Gesar). Professor Sylvain Lévi has called the Kesar story 'the Iliad of Central Asia': we should add, it is the Odyssey also. It forms, in fact, the combined Rāmāyaṇa and Mahābhārata of the Tibetan people. The Mongols and the Manchus have adopted Kesar as a national hero. He is honoured in China; and it has been supposed that his personality has contributed to the creation of Kuan-ti, the Chinese God of War. It is now impossible to trace the historicity of this hero: we do not know when he was born, and in which part of Tibet he flourished. He is claimed by the East, by Khams; he is claimed by the West, by Ladakh: and the Mongols in the North think he was a Mongol hero. Dr. A. H. Francke considered him entirely mythical—a humanisation of the Sun; the Kesar Story he thought was a Solar Myth. It is not unlikely: but it may be just equally possible that like the heroes in many another legend cycle, like a Roland or an Arthur, a Cuchulainn or a Sigurd, Kesar was partly historical and partly legendary.

In Tibet a mass of literature of various types have been found on Kesar: (1) songs or lyrics, which are sung on special occasions; (2) short lays or narratives in prose and verse, which are just told as tales; (3) long narrative works in prose and verse which are chanted by trained reciters taking several days or weeks; and (4) huge works, mainly in verse, which are comparable to the Indian Purāṇas. Of these (1), (2) and (3), until they were written down by European scholars and translated into German, English and French, formed part of the oral popular literature of the Tibetans; and (4) form written compositions in Tibetan, esteemed for their romantic and edifying value. They show a progressive elaboration of the original story. The short songs and short narratives in prose and verse as under (1) and (2) have been found in Ladakh or Western Tibet; the late Dr. A. H. Francke, member of the Moravian Mission in Ladakh, discovered and published these some forty years ago. At least one long narrative as under (3) has been found in Khams or Eastern Tibet by Mme. Alexandra David-Neel. She heard it chanted in the Khams dialect by a sort of rhapsodist at Jakyendo (Kyirku or Lcher-ku), a village in Eastern Tibet: he took over six weeks to sing it through, giving two recitals of three hours each every day. She also heard other rhapsodists sing the same story, and she had MS. works on the epic to consult. On the basis of these, taking the story in its most commonly accepted version in Eastern and Central Tibet, Mme. David-Neel brought out French and English versions of it, in collaboration with Lama Yongden, in 1933. (Cf. *The Super-human Life of Gesar of Ling, the legendary Tibetan Hero, as sung by the Bards of his Country*, by Alexandra David-Neel and the Lama Yongden: with Preface by Sylvain Lévi: London, Rider & Co., 1933.) The long compositions as under (4) are exceedingly long indeed, and Mme. David-Neel makes mention of one manuscript in her possession 'which treats of the single episode of Gesar's (i.e. Kesar's) struggles against King Satham, and is seven hundred and forty-eight pages long'. Mr. Johan van Manen's similar long MSS. of episodes of the Kesar story have been noted by Dr. Francke in his *Preface*.

The Mongols received their Lamaistic Buddhism from the Tibetans, during the 13th–14th centuries, and by that time the Kesar story had taken up a Buddhist or Lamaist colouring, if it were really pre-Buddhistic originally, and was passed on to the Mongols as a Buddhist story. Then the Manchus, who are immediately related to the Mongols, came to know it, and from the Manchus, the Chinese, after the former had conquered the latter in the 17th century. It may be said that in a way the Kesar story, emanating from the Tibetans, has become the common property of the Mongolian peoples of Central and Eastern Asia.

Because of its romantic charm and its special flavour, the Kesar Saga fully deserves to be regarded as a noteworthy literary heritage for the whole of humanity.

It has been said before that nothing is known about the historicity of Kesar. He may belong to the centuries before King Srong-btsan-sgam-po, some of whose achievements and qualities as a national hero who established his people in their culture may have been transferred to an earlier, pre-Buddhistic Kesar. He might have been later in time. Whatever his historicity, there is no doubt that he has become *the* National Hero of the Tibetans: in him have become incarnate as it were the Tibetan conception of the Ideal Man, Ideal Warrior and Ideal King. He is a National Hero of the type of Rāma and Arjuna of India, Rustam of Persia, Gilgamesh of the Assyrio-Babylonians, David of the Jews, Hēraklēs and Akhilleus of ancient Greece, Sigurd-Siegfried of the old Germanic world, King Arthur of the British (Welsh), and Cuchulainn and Finn of the ancient Irish: an embodiment of the highest ideals and aspirations of a whole people for centuries. The Tibetans, as well as the Mongols and the Manchus, have almost made a cult of King Kesar: they believe and hope that Kesar, who is now living in the Buddhist heaven, will come down on earth once again, and will lead the peoples of Central Asia to a glorious destiny.

Of the various forms in which the story of Kesar has been found, the poems and the short prose and verse narratives (in two recensions) which Dr. A. H. Francke obtained in Ladakh, present unquestionably the shortest and the most beautiful versions of the story, and possibly also the oldest; certainly these versions show the least admixture of Buddhistic notions and mythology. The other versions—the long narratives as recited by the minstrels, and the voluminous written texts—show a very great elaboration and accompanying deterioration of the story. Besides, in these bigger versions the Kesar legend has been very closely interwoven with Lamaistic ideas and mythology. The longer narratives have a different atmosphere altogether, when compared with the poems and the shorter recensions obtained from Ladakh. The Lamaistic atmosphere in these long versions in fact has enabled the story to win the approval of the Buddhist scholars, and, consequently, to continue in popular favour. But the Ladakh poems and recensions, as Dr. Francke has made it clear, appear to be totally lacking in the Buddhist or Lamaistic spirit, popular or hieratic. Of course, references to Buddhism, the religion established for over a thousand years, could not be eschewed in this mass of popular literature: but its religious and cultural background is that of the pre-Buddhistic Bon world. In other words, it becomes quite clear from the simplest and most beautiful form in which the Kesar Saga has been found in the poems and recensions discovered by Dr. Francke in Ladakh, that the Saga took its rise within the lap of the Bon religion, before the general acceptance of Buddhism by the Tibetans.

The songs which Dr. Francke found in Ladakh were published in the original with English translation in the *Indian Antiquary* for 1901 and 1902. Of the two versions of the Kesar story, one (in two recensions) was obtained from the village of Sheh, and the other from Khalatse. The Sheh version was published in the original Ladakhi Tibetan with translation and notes by the Finno-Ugrian Society of Helsingfors in Finland in 1901 and 1902. This Sheh version is in two parts, which Dr. Francke called *the Spring Myth of the Kesar Saga* and *the Winter Myth of the Kesar Saga*. The *Spring Myth* portion was published in an English rendering, with notes and an analysis of the Bon pantheon which can be deduced from it and from the poems, in the *Indian Antiquary* for 1901 and 1902. The Khalatse version in the original Tibetan, with English abstract of the various episodes and notes on the Tibetan text, was taken up by the Asiatic Society of Bengal for publication years ago. The text and the English abstract, etc., were printed and made available to the public in four fascicles during 1905–1909; and now it is being brought out in its complete form in the present volume, which is considerably augmented with Notes and Appendices giving all that Francke obtained from Ladakh relating to the Kesar Saga—the Poems (in the original Tibetan and Francke's English translation), and the Sheh Recension (the whole of it, both the *Spring Myth* and the *Winter Myth*) in English, as well as the Supplementary Stories about the Paladins of the Kesar Saga. Dr. Francke's *Preface* was written in 1925, and he sent a *List of Personal and Local Names and other Proper Nouns in the Kesar Saga* as well as an *Index to the Words explained in connexion with the Kesar Saga*; but before any of these could be printed, he passed away in 1933. So that Dr. Francke's *Lower Ladakhi Version* (i.e. *the Khalatse Version*) *of the Kesar Saga* remained to be completed by printing the *Preface* from the author, and the *List of Personal Names* and the *Index of Words* as prepared by him. In printing this *Preface* and the *List of Personal Names*, it was thought that the other Ladakhi Version of the Kesar Saga, that from Sheh, in English translation, and the Ladakhi Poems connected with Kesar and with the Bon religion, as well as the Stories of the Paladins, might advantageously be reprinted in the present book; which will thus give in one volume all the mass of Western Tibetan (Ladakhi) materials collected, translated and commented upon by Dr. Francke bearing on the Kesar Saga, and that in its simplest and most primitive form. Only the Tibetan texts of the Sheh Version and of the Stories of the Paladins are not given: these will be found respectively in the *Memoirs of the Helsingfors Finno-Ugrian Society*) as noted above, and in the *Journal and Proceedings of the* (*Royal*) *Asiatic Society of Bengal* for 1906 and 1907. The *Index* of (Tibetan, Words in the Ladakhi Kesar Saga texts is not included, as it can have only a very specialised interest.

The value of these Francke texts for the study of the Kesar Saga and of the Bon religion and pantheon cannot be over-estimated. As Francke himself suggested in his *Preface* to the Khalatse Version about these oral versions of the Kesar Saga, 'it is highly probable that they will be of a similar usefulness for a thorough understanding of the Kesar-epic as are the Norse Versions of the Nibelungen Saga for the understanding of the Nibelungen epic'. We have here a mass of additional material in following the development of the romance and the epic from the earlier lyric, ballad and tale in prose and verse, such as has been seen in the case of heroic and romantic story cycles among other peoples.

In 1836 I. J. Schmidt published from St. Petersburg a German translation of a romance of Kesar from the Mongol language. The Kesar story was noted by others, but no definite text or translation was available, before Dr. Francke procured the Ladakh recensions and poems about 1900. Thus Sir Charles Bell in his *People of Tibet* (Oxford, 1928) notes (p. 10): 'It is to this legendary period that the great Tibetan Saga or epic belongs. It tells of Ke-sar, the King of Ling, a country in Tibet or on the eastern border. The King of Hor, a neighbouring land, carried off Ke-sar's wife. A war ensued to recover the queen, in which Ke-sar was eventually victorious. The whole epic is full of tales of fighting and miraculous prowess. In his difficulties King Ke-sar is aided by a goddess, A-ni Gung-men Gyal-mo, his aunt, who helps him in his difficult undertakings, just as the Grecian and Trojan heroes are protected and guided by their gods and goddesses. The epic is a long one, and is divided into three parts. There are no printed copies of it in Tibet, and but few manuscript copies. It is recited orally by both men and women, especially among the pastoral tribes. There are many who can recite it for days together without repeating themselves.'

It would thus appear that quite a number of different recensions of the Kesar epic are current—in oral versions, in manuscripts, and also in printed books: for Dr. Giuseppe Tucci discovered in a monastery in Spiti a Kesar epic, block-printed in the style of Buddhist books (Giuseppe Tucci and E. Ghersi, *Cronaca della Missione Scientifica Tucci nel Tibet occidentale, 1933*, Rome, 1934, p. 62). Before some of these are available in modern printed editions, or before their contents at least are known, it will not be possible to initiate a critical study of the Kesar legend. The voluminous MSS. in the possession of Mme. David-Neel and of Mr. van Manen are but part of the entire epic, probably in its latest literary form: their collection and publication, and much more their translation, would be a Herculean task which it does not seem likely will be taken up by any scholar in the immediate future.

The Kesar Saga has also given a subject for Tibetan artists. In Tibetan pictorial and sculptural art, Buddhist themes all but monopolise the entire field. Images of Bon deities are found, and they are not so uncommon. But Bon *thaṅkas* or scroll paintings are comparatively rare. There are some twelve specimens of Bon *thaṅkas* in the Musée Guimet, some of which have already been described and reproduced (*Guide-Catalogue du Musée Guimet: Les Collections Bouddhiques: Inde Centrale et Gandhara, Turkestan, Chine Septentrionale, Tibet*, by J. Hackin, Paris and Brussels, 1923, pp. 116–118; cf. also *Mythologie Asiatique illustrée*, Librairie de France, Paris, 1928: Mythologie du Lamaisme, by J. Hackin, pp. 158–162).

The Musée Guimet has one very highly interesting *thaṅka* on the Kesar story. It is Buddhistic in at least its outward affiliation, as it has as its central figure a picture of the benign Lamaistic goddess *Mthing-gi zal bzang-ma*, an attendant of the fierce *Lha-mo* (=*Śrī-dēvī*), carrying an arrow and a mirror and riding on a mule. A number of episodes in the Kesar story surround the central figure, among which is one of Kesar's playing practical jokes with ʼBruguma before their marriage, and other scenes depict his prowess in many adventures, and his final beatification in the Buddhist heaven. Kesar is shown always in a white dress, the long Tibetan gown, and in a plumed cap with four flaps (cf. *Mythologie Asiatique illustrée*, op. cit., pp. 158–160). There might be other similar pictures, and possibly also bronze and terracotta statuettes representing the main characters in the story.

III. The Story of Kesar according to the Ladakh Recensions.

Don-grub, the third son of the King of Heaven *Dbang-po-rgya-bzhin*, became incarnate on earth to rule over the land of Gling. The circumstances necessitating his birth, and the events connected with it, are described at length, but these appear to be later additions to the story, after Kesar had become to some extent deified. Don-grub was born on earth and became known as Kesar. (This name is found in Central Tibet as *Gesar*, and among the Mongols the form of the name is *Geser*. In Ladakh, apart from *Kesar*, the form *Kye-sar* also occurs, which is in Classical Tibetan *Skye-gsar*, meaning 'Newly-born' or 'Born again'. *Kesar* and *Gesar* mean in Tibetan 'anther or pistil of a flower,' and also 'saffron': in both these senses we have in Sanskrit the word *kēsara*: it is not known which is the original word—the Sanskrit or the Tibetan, although Sanskrit *kēsa* 'hair' is Indo-European. Dr. Francke thought that the Tibetan name *Kesar* was derived from the Sanskrit.) Kesar became perfect in all the arts in his youth, and gave evidence of his bravery and prowess in a number of adventures.

At that time there was a beautiful maiden named *'Bruguma* (*'aBruguma*), the daughter of a rich man of Gling. (*'Bru-gu-ma* means 'a Broken Fragment of Grain'. In Central Tibet, the name occurs as *Śes-lcaṅ 'Brug-mo*, now pronounced *Shéchang Ḍugmo*. The Mongols know her as *Rogmo*. A variant of the name found in Ladakh is *'Briguma*, which means 'Young Yak Cow', or 'Yak Heifer'.) Kesar wanted to marry 'Bruguma There was a rich and powerful rival of Kesar for 'Bruguma's hand, but he was put out of court by Kesar with his superior qualities. Kesar at first concealed his identity before 'Bruguma and her people by taking the garb of a 'street-boy'. He teased 'Bruguma by some rude horseplay and practical jokes befitting a primitive society, and ultimately his claims to 'Bruguma's hand were accepted by her parents, and he married 'Bruguma. After that they began to live together in Gling, and the chiefs of the land of Gling recognised in Kesar a true hero and made him king. Sometime after this Kesar went to China, and there he performed some wonderful acts. He married the daughter of the Emperor of China and returned home with her, and for a time lived happily with his two wives. (In the Kesar Saga, this second wife of Kesar, the Chinese Princess, has no further place.)

At the suggestion of the goddess *Ane-bkur-dman-mo*, Kesar went to quell the Giant or Devil of the North. This goddess was none other than the Queen of Heaven, the mother of Kesar when he was staying in heaven as Don-grub. In the Kesar Saga she is always present, helping Kesar and saving him whenever he is in danger. Kesar took leave of his beloved wife 'Bruguma. (There are one or two beautiful lyrics on this parting of the hero and his wife.) Kesar, after great difficulties, arrived in the North land. The wife of the giant, whose name was *Dzemo-Bamza-bum-skyid*, fell in love with Kesar, and through her help Kesar was able to attack the giant when he was asleep and to kill him. Dzemo made Kesar take charmed food and drink, and so made him lose his memory. Forgetting his wife and his land of Gling, Kesar stayed on with Dzemo. A daughter was born to them.

In the meanwhile, during Kesar's absence from home, 'Bruguma had to suffer from a terrible mishap. The King of the land of *Hor*, *Gur-dkar*, finding that Kesar was absent from his country for a long time, attacked Gling, and wanted to carry off 'Bruguma. 'Bruguma tried her best to save herself, and concealed herself from the invader, but ultimately she was captured and taken to Hor. Kesar and 'Bruguma had a son, and the King of Hor killed the child. After 'Bruguma had stayed in Hor for some time, during which she tried to put off her marriage with her captor, her feelings gradually changed towards the latter—more so as her husband Kesar was not heard of for such a long time. She had to marry the King of Hor; and finally she came even to love him.

Kesar was living with Dzemo, forgetful of everything. His memory was restored miraculously at the sight of some birds which had brought tidings of his reverses at home: he remembered his beloved wife and his home. He vomited out the magic food and drink given to him by Dzemo. Leaving Dzemo and her daughter, he tried to ride back home to Gling. At this Dzemo in a frenzy killed her little daughter. Returning home, Kesar found that another chief had taken possession of his land and castle, and that his wife was with the King of Hor. He gathered his men and got his kingdom back, and then went to Hor to punish the abductor and to bring back his wife.

When in the land of Hor, he took up apprenticeship under a blacksmith there, and began to watch the King of Hor and 'Bruguma. Here he showed his prowess and his magic power in many ways. 'Bruguma recognised him, but instead of helping Kesar she supported Gur-dkar, to whom in the meanwhile she had borne two children, a son and a daughter. Ultimately Kesar, with the help of the goddess Ane-bkur-dman-mo, attacked Gur-dkar in his room, and in spite of his prayers killed him as the goddess directed him. In this way Kesar recovered his wife and returned with her to Gling. The two children of 'Bruguma by Gur-dkar were slain by Kesar.

'Bruguma, according to the Khalatse version, was made to undergo penances and punishments for her unfaithfulness, and after some years when she was cleansed from her guilt Kesar took her back as his wife, and they lived the rest of their life happily, until, according to the longer Buddhistic versions, his translation to heaven.

IV. Literary and Cultural Importance of the Kesar Saga.

The above is a brief *résumé* of the Ladakh versions of the Kesar Saga, which undoubtedly form the most primitive recensions of it. The other versions obtained in Tibet and in Mongolia have a strong Buddhistic colouring, and they are very elaborate; and although there are numerous points of difference in detail, the main outlines of the story are everywhere the same—Kesar's early life, his marriage with 'Bruguma (or 'Brugmo), Kesar's victory over the Giant of the North with the help of the latter's wife, Kesar's forgetfulness, abduction of 'Bruguma by Gur-dkar the King of Hor, faithlessness of 'Bruguma to Kesar, and killing of Gur-dkar and his children by Kesar and recovery of 'Bruguma.

The story must be admitted to be great, quite epic in its conception, and at par with that of the Iliad and of the Odyssey, of the Rāmāyaṇa, of the Niblung Saga, and with some of the Old Irish tales. As in all epic and romantic tales, there is plenty of the supernatural in it: but nevertheless, the tale has a very great human interest, because it is ultimately a reflex of the life of the people among whom it grew up. Human passions, human sufferings and triumphs are there in plenty; and the supernatural accretions have not been able to blur the bold outlines of the main characters. Kesar has some primitive qualities, in spite of his innate nobleness worthy of a hero-king who has come to establish a kingdom of God on earth. Kesar's wife, 'Bruguma, is not an immaculate heroine: one feels the contrast with such ideal characters as Sītā, and Pēnelopē, and Derdriu the wife of Noisi in the Old Irish legend. One is rather reminded of Helen in the Greek story, of Gwenhwyfar the wife of Arthur in the British legend, and to some extent of Gudrun in the Sigurd Saga; but still, 'Bruguma is very human, and we feel like commiserating with her in her sufferings and her weakness, although we would have liked her to have remained constant to Kesar. Viewed from all aspects, it can be justly claimed for this Saga that it is highly romantic, and highly dramatic, and quite a distinctive source of romantic wonder and romantic pleasure. As such it possesses a literary value of its own.

Moreover, this appears to be the one great epic tale with a consistency of plot and character which originated among the peoples of the Mongolian race—Tibeto-Chinese, Altaic and Uralic, and American. The immediate kinsmen of the Tibetans—the Chinese, the Thai, the Burmese, and the other tribes of South China, Burma and Assam—have not produced any epic story of the magnitude of the Kesar Saga. The Meithei (Manipuri) story of the lovers, the Princess Thoibi and the Hero Khamba, is late, and but a slight thing beside the Kesar epic. The well-known Burmese legend of Maung-Tin-De (*Moṅ-Taṅ-Tay*) and his sister Shwe-myat-hna (*Rhwe-myak-hnā*) who are worshipped as *Nats* or godlings among the Burmans cannot be compared with the story of Kesar. Ancient and medieval China produced fine romances, but no hero tale of national significance. One or two Thai folk-tales are attractive, but the Thai people, like the Burmese, have been captivated by the imagination of India. But the genius of Tibet in spite of its allegiance to the literature of Buddhism, kept true to its national hero. The Turks, the Mongols and the Manchus have no such hero tale of their own. The Uralic Finns of course have the *Kalevala* ; but in spite of its great qualities, and its being a repository of early Finnish life, legend and wisdom, it lacks coherence, it lacks a well-knit story, and above all, it lacks romance—the true romance that we associate with the deathless love between man and woman. The same may be said of the Esthonian epic *Kalevipoeg*. The Japanese in spite of their *Kojiki* and *Nihongi* have produced no real epic tale, although they have some delicately woven romances. The same thing is to be said of the Koreans. And the members of the Mongol race in America, even the civilised Toltecs, Aztecs, and Mayas, and the rest of the Mexico and Yucatan and Central America peoples, and the Quechuas and Aymaras and other peoples of South America, are equally lacking in the matter of a great hero tale. We cannot of course seriously take Longfellow's *Hiawatha* as a genuine native American production, the story-part of which moreover of 'Red Indian' origin is not in any way 'epic' in character.

Like many other great stories, the Kesar story has had its appeal for other peoples who came to know it. The Mongols and the Manchus have made it their own. And it penetrated from Ladakh into the State of Hunza-Nagyr, in Kashmir, among the Burushaski people, from whom a folk-tale version has been recovered (*The Burushaski Language*, by Lt.-Col. D. L. R. Lorimer, Institutet for Sammenlignende Kulturforskining, Oslo, 1935, Vol. II, Texts and Translations, No. IV, pp. 100–179). It may be that versions in other languages in tracts contiguous to Tibet may still be forthcoming. National in origin, it has become an international tale, although within a restricted area, taking into note the situation of the Tibetan people.

The Kesar Saga thus takes its stand beside the great epic tales of the world. As such, lovers of literature cannot ignore it: particularly in its Ladakhi forms, with their simple style of narration and their primitive atmosphere.

Moreover, we get from it glimpses of the soul of the Tibetan people before it was transformed by Buddhism. In spite of the Ladakhi versions presenting a world rather different from that of the later Bon religion, these do give us valuable sidelights, as Francke has shown, into the pre-Buddhist religion of Tibet. A good deal of primitive religion and mythology is hidden behind the divine, the demoniac and the human characters of the Kesar Saga—although foreign influences (from the Indian world, from the Iranian and Græco-Roman worlds, and may be even from the Germanic world) might have helped it to acquire its present form. To find out the bases of the religion and culture of the primitive Tibeto-Chinese people, the Kesar Saga, specially in the old Ladakhi form, is sure to furnish valuable material.

From all these aspects the Saga cannot be neglected by students of anthropology and sociology, of religiology and of comparative literature.

SUNITI KUMAR CHATTERJI.

ROYAL ASIATIC SOCIETY OF BENGAL,
CALCUTTA,
March 1, 1941.

[NOTE.—In the Appendices as reprinted in this volume, Francke's system of transliteration of Tibetan is retained without change. This system uses no letters with diacritical signs, employing digraphs (like **sh, zh, ts, dz, ng,** ny), and ignores the ḥ (or ') in the middle of words, and uses the Greek γ for a silent **g**-.]

PREFACE

As far as we can see at present, the first European who makes any mention of the existence of the Kesar Saga among Mongolian peoples, is a German, Peter Simon Pallas, born at Berlin 1741. He heard of it during his travels in Russian service among the Kalmuks of the Russian steppes.

Not much later the travellers, B. Bergmann and I. J. Schmidt, published parts of the legend in German, being translations from the Mongolian. B. Bergmann's translation is in metrical form and is to be found in his work *Nomadische Streifereien unter den Kalmucken.* "The underlying Kalmuck text appears not to have become known. I. J. Schmidt translated from a Mongolian edition which had been made in 1716 at Pekin by command of the emperor Kang-hsi. The work bears the title *Die Taten Bogda Gesser-Chan's*". According to Schmidt's statement, Gesser-Chan stands in high honour among the Chinese, and the then reigning dynasty (the Manchus) even recognized him as their tutelary genius. He further says: " Since Gesser-Chan is named in the legend as ruler of the three Tibetan tribes of the Tussa, Dongsar, and Lik, this has given occasion to the Chinese to interweave him in their history of the three kingdoms, and to assign him an epoch in their chronology, being the beginning of the third century."

As long as only the Mongolian version of the Kesar Saga was known, it had to remain undecided whether the saga be of Mongolian or Tibetan origin. Nevertheless, Schmidt already drew attention to the circumstance that the theatre for the scenes acted in it is to be found in Tibet.[1] The first European, who brought tidings of a Tibetan Gesar Epic, was Csoma de Körös, the great investigator of the Tibetan language.[2] Thereupon efforts were made to find manuscripts of the epic, and H. A. Jäschke succeeded in discovering such a one at *Byams-pa* near Leh in Ladakh. He had this copied, and the copy was sent to St. Petersburg, where it still lies. Up to the present day, it seems not to have been possible to translate this version of the saga.

---

[1] See Schmidt's translation, Preface, p. IX.

[2] Grammar of the Tibetan Language, p. 180.

In the meantime, I had noticed in Leh that popular forms of the Kesar Saga are at home in Ladakh, and I succeeded in getting one such text written down. This text, together with translation and notes, was then published from Helsingfors.[1] Antithetical with I. J. Schmidt's Gesser-Chan, that is entirely written in prose, the composition of the Kesar Saga in the Tibetan versions is for the most part metrical. At least, the speeches are almost always written in verse.

When I was transferred from Leh to Khalatse in Lower Ladakh in 1900, I found a man in the latter village who was noted for his astonishing knowledge of the popular Kesar Saga. His name was *dKon-mchog-bkra-shis-rgya-mthso-pa.* (The last three syllables of his name had been added on his marrying into the family of *rGya-mthso-pa* in Khalatse.) However, he was a native of Lerdo (*Lai-rdo*), and this village is situated opposite to *sKyur-bu-can* on the Indus in Lower Ladakh. Therefore he may have brought his version of the saga from Lerdo. Now I closeted this bard (for the metrical parts of the saga are sung during the recital) for several weeks with *Ye-shes-rig-'adzin*, clerk and schoolmaster at Khalatse, and in this way gained the Lower Ladakhi version of the Kesar Saga, so named by me on its publication in the *Bibliotheca Indica*, in the numbers 1134, 1150, 1164, and 1218.

But herewith *dKon-mchog-bkra-shis's* material was by no means exhausted. He continued his story-telling, and related the adventures of the principal heroes of the saga. These last sections I published in J. & P. ASB., under the title, "The Paladins of the Kesar Saga"[2].

Through these publications, the question was now opened up, how the hitherto unknown literary versions of the Kesar Saga and the recently published popular versions were to be reconciled with each other. Do they depend upon one another? Or does each go its own way independently of the other? The first thing necessary was to obtain such literary versions. I myself succeeded in buying copies of parts of the *Byams-pa* manuscript, i.e. of the very same work that had been sent to St. Petersburg. Copies of the same book, made before that by Dr. Karl Marx in Leh, appear to have passed into Dr. B. Laufer's possession. In addition to the above, I found a manuscript of the *lTang* war episode of the Kesar Saga, in the Museum für Völkerkunde in Berlin.

---

[1] Mémoires de la Société Finno-ougrienne, No. XV, 1900, 1902.

[2] Vol. II, 1906, No. 10, pp. 467 ff.; Vol. III. 1907, Nos. 2, 3, pp. 67 ff. and pp. 261 ff.

In consequence of the skilful quest of Mr. J. van Manen, General Secretary of the Asiatic Society of Bengal, a much greater quantity of material has been brought to light, and we are astonished on hearing of what extraordinary volume the literary settings are. Mr. van Manen writes as follows in his letter of June 23rd, 1925: "What will be certainly of interest to you is to hear that I have obtained a very interesting complete Umed (*dbu-med*) ms. of the *Hor-gling* in its written recension, and also a similar complete copy in Uchen (*dbu-can*) of the *Lho-gling*. The former I have had now copied out in Uchen (*dbu-can*) also.

"They record the wars against, respectively, the *Shing-khri rgyal-po*, the *Gur-dkar rgyal-po*, the *Sa-tham rgyal-po*, and the *rMa-bdud rgyal-po*.

"These four seem not to have been ever printed, but exist only in ms. The two which I have are very bulky. My Uchen (*dbu-can*) *Hor-gling* covers 1,300 pages of 17 lines each, foolscap. The *Lho-gling*, 1,000 such pages. The text is mostly metrical. Only the connecting passages between the *glus* (songs) are in prose.

"The four works are described as the *a-ma* (mother), but there seems quite a literature grouped around them, described as *yan-lag* (limbs)."

Although the literary settings of the Kesar Saga are extremely voluminous, according to these communications, yet there remains nothing further to be done, than that the scientific world tackle their translation. The immediate result of such work will mean a due inflation of the Tibetan dictionaries. But then we may hope to gain clearer insight into the comparative relations of the various Tibetan versions, as well as to the versions in Mongolian, Chinese, Turkish, and other languages.

Let me mention one thing. In his criticism of my "Frühlingsmythus der Kesarsage," Dr. B. Laufer said that this oral version of the legend was to be accepted as the repetition of some or other literary setting of the saga that a story-teller of fairy-tales had read; just as in India the tales from the great epics are repeated for public entertainment by persons who have read them themselves. Although at the first glance this explanation seems feasible, yet I have given to consideration that in Ladakh from one village to another there are deviations in the oral versions of the saga which are never given in prose, but always in verse, and that just these verses variate with the villages. Who would believe that it would occur to a man reciting a literary work in all the villages to remodel into new verses those he had just been reading in the book, instead of telling his story in prose?

No: the more obvious acceptance is that in Ladakh we are in the home-land of the Kesar Saga, and that here every village feels it has the right to possess its own version of the Kesar Saga and to hand it on to posterity. But the importance of such possession comes from the fact that in this country the mythology, forming the background of the Kesar Saga, has not yet quite died out, but continues to exist as a kind of religion. The heroes of the Kesar Saga are in this country still deities whose festivals are celebrated, and in whose honour songs are sung (the so-called *gling-glu*).[1]

Till now I have published only a few of these songs. It will be of value for the study of the Kesar Saga to collect also the interesting marriage songs [2] of the Tibetans, as well as the hymns sung at the spring festival. All this literature is full of the mythology of the oral versions of the Kesar Saga. Whether the same mythology will be found in the background of the literary forms of the Kesar Saga is a question the answer to which I shall await with interest.

Just now I mentioned Ladakh as the home-land of the saga. That is perhaps somewhat premature; but it is permissible to mention what points to Tibet as the homeland in general, and to Western Tibet in particular. As Schmidt already observed, the names of places in the saga, as far as cognoscible, are to be sought for on Tibetan and not on Mongolian territory. In the oral versions, one district stands out with special distinctness as Holy Land. That is the district around the sacred Lakes Manasarowar and Rakas Tal, and the sacred mountain Kailāsa situated there. This sacred circuit originally belonged to the West Tibetan kingdom with its capital Leh (*Sle*); and consequently the saga has evidently kept firm footing specially in the Western kingdom. The entire Western kingdom is called *Khrom-ge-sar-gdan-ma* in inscriptions as well as in folklore. That means "market, Gesar's throne". The rulers of Leh, who possessed the country previous to the dynasty descended from Langdarma, named themselves the descendants of Gesar.

The so-called wars of the saga (actually only bridal expeditions) are made on countries in the closest proximity of Ladakh or Tibet. Such

---

[1] Compare *Indian Antiquary*, Vol. XXX, 1901, p. 359 ff.—*A Ladakhi Bon-Po Hymnal* and *Ladakhi Songs*, Nos. 21 to 30.

[2] Compare my publication, *Die tibetischen Hochzeitslieder*, Folkwang Verlag, 1923.

warlike expeditions are undertaken against *Hor* (Turkestan); *rGya-nag* (China); *'aGro-yul* (compare *'aGro-shod*, "wheat country"), a province of Tibet; *Lho-yul* (probably the Tibetan province which is written *Lho-bo*, *Glo-bo*, or *Blo-bo*). As all these countries actually exist, one could readily believe that the saga contains historic elements. But the study of the oral versions destroys this belief. Here everything melts into mythology. However, it is beyond doubt that also many of the other names of places occurring in the saga are the names of places actually existing that could probably still be found in the district around the Sacred Lakes.

As far as the name of the hero in the saga is concerned, it occurs in two different forms, of which the one (*K[y]e-sar*) is peculiar to the oral versions from Ladakh, while the other (*Ge-sar*) is found in the literary settings. As to the name *Ge-sar* (= *Gesser* of the Mongolians) I. J. Schmidt says that the Tibetan word *Ge-sar* means "the pistil of a flower".[1] Jäschke confirms this in his Dictionary. At the same time, the Indian word *Kesara* is brought in as comparison, and as a further meaning "filament", "anther" is given. So far the word could be of Indian origin, and then the form with *G* would not be so primitive as that written with *K*. I can remark to this that in Ladakh the Indian name *Kesara* is specially used to designate "saffron" and saffron is called *King Kesar's flower*. Also Sarat Chandra Das confirms that *Gesar* is a name for saffron. The juice of the yellow saffron is, besides, used to decorate the Gesar manuscripts. I have seen such in which important lines, or entire pages, were painted over with saffron.

K[y]e-sar, the form of the verbal versions, has given occasion to a popular etymology among the Ladakhis that I have formerly alluded to.[2] According to this, the word *Ke-sar* is said to have been evolved out of *skye-gsar*, "new-born". However, this name has nothing to do with the Buddhist doctrine of re-incarnation. It is said to have been given only in connection with the story of the hero's birth on earth, after his death in heaven. This popular etymology has one particular support in the fact that in Lower Ladakh the name is actually sometimes pronounced *Kye-sar*.

Lastly, Professor Grünwedel's opinion is to be mentioned, viz. that the name Kesar could be a form of the Latin *Caesar* = *Kaiser*. Just as well as the name of Charlemagne, *Karl*, has travelled as far as Russia

---

[1] Schmidt's Introduction, p. IX.

[2] See *Frühlingsmythus*, p. 29.

(*Korol*, *Krol*-" king "), so could the word *Caesar* finally have been carried to Tibet.

I personally incline most to the hero-king's name being derived from the Indian word *Kesara*, " saffron, or anther ". Kesar is without doubt a god of spring, and the saffron is one of the earliest spring-flowers. Besides, Kesar is also a god of generation, and the word Kesara, in its meaning of " pistil " or "anther" points to this.

(1925.) A. H. FRANCKE.

Fasc. No. I.

དཔའ་བོ་ཙོ་བརྒྱད་ཀྱི་སྒྲུངས་བཞུགས་སོ།

THE STORY OF THE EIGHTEEN HEROES

(PREFACE TO THE KESAR-SAGA).

EDITED BY

A. H. FRANCKE,

Moravian Missionary.

Published for the Bibliotheca Indica by the Asiatic Society of Bengal.

CALCUTTA:

PRINTED AT THE BAPTIST MISSION PRESS.

1905.

PREFACE.

My sincerest thanks are due to the Council of the Asiatic Society for allowing me to edit for the Bibliotheca Indica a Lower Ladakhi Version of the Kesar-saga. The plan of the work is the following:

Prologue to the Kesar-saga. Birth of Kesar. Wooing and marriage to *a'Bruguma.* Kesar's journey to China and marriage to a Chinese Princess. Kesar's journey to the North. Capture of *a'Bruguma* by the king of Hor. Kesar's defeat of the king of Hor.

Accompanying the Tibetan text will be given a vocabulary of the new words and an abstract of contents.

In criticising one of my former papers on the Kesar-saga, one of my critics makes the following remark with reference to the line *Sangs rgyasla btangbai gri zhig dgos,* 'you must have a knife to stab Buddha': "if this line occurs at all!" This means no less than suspecting me of introducing new lines into the saga, simply to suit a certain purpose of my own. I must say that it would be very unwise of me to do so. I could easily be exposed. There is not only a British Joint Commissioner at Leh, who could find out a great deal with the help of Urdu, as well as any of the visitors to Ladakh, numbering about 50 in a year, but there is also a whole staff of missionaries at Leh, some of whom have just as critical a mind as any German professor.

What I have to do with regard to the Tibetan text is to correct orthographical mistakes, if they are due to carelessness of the writer. In all doubtful cases I shall give, as I have always done, the word in the doubtful spelling as well; this refers especially to the names In this edition I shall not even attempt to reconstruct incomplete verses, but leave them as I find them.

As regards the value of the oral versions of the Kesar-saga, it is highly probable that they will be of a similar usefulness for a thorough understanding of the Kesar-epic, as are the Norse versions of the Nibelungen-saga for the understanding of the Nibelungen-epic. With regard to my former publication of the birth-story of Kesar, I was told that it was an abridged repetition of the Kesar-epic. This cannot possibly be said of the present version of the saga, because it is entirely different from the former. A whole chapter like the "Prologue to the Kesar-saga" does not appear to occur in the epic at all.*

* Also the Mongolian version of the Kesar-saga (Schmidt's translation) does not contain it, bnt starts with the birth-story of Kesar.

But also of the latter there may exist several recensions. The oral versions of the Kesar-saga are interesting also from another point of view. They show what the Ladakhis hold of the Kesar-religion at the present day. For that this mythology has not yet ceased to exercise the power of a religion, is shown most plainly in the marriage ritual and in the *g Ling glu.*

The following version of the Kesar-saga was dictated slowly by an inhabitant of *Khalatse,* who was brought up in *Lerdo* near *Tagmacig.* This version is probably the one which is current at *Lerdo.* The name of the dictator is *dKon mchog bKrashis rgya mthsopa.* The name of the writer is *Yeshes rig 'adzin,* munshi of *Khalatse.*

A. H. FRANCKE.

༄༅། །གླིང་གི་དཔའ་བོ་བཅོ་བརྒྱད་ཀྱི་སྐྱེ་རབས་སྒྲུངས་ཡིན།

ཡོད་ཚུག།

No. 1.

ཡུལ་ཀ་ལ་ཀོལ་ཟེར་བའི་ཡུལ་ཞིག་ཡོད་ཚུག། དེ་ཡུལ་པོ་ལ་མི་རྒད་པོ་
ཞིག་དང་རྒད་མོ་ཞིག་ཡོད་ཚུག། ཁོང་གཉིས་ཀ་ལ་གཉེན་འཁོར་མེད་མཁན
ཡིན་པས། ཞག་ཅིག་ཁོང་གཉིས་ཀ་ས་ཁྲུད་ཡན་པ་ཞིག་ལ་སོང་སྟེ། ཐོང་རོས་
རྒྱ་ཅན་ཞིག་བཅོས། དེ་ནས་ཡུལ་མི་ཚང་མ་དབྱིད་ལ་ཞིང་རྨོ་ཐོ་བསླེབ་སྟེ། ཁོང་
གཉིས་ཀ་ལ་དེ་ཞིང་པོ་ལ་ས་བོན་ཞིག་མེད་པ་ཡིན། གཞན་མ་མི་ཞིག་ནས་བུ
ལོན་ཟུམ་སྟེ་ཁྲིངས། དེ་ནས་ཚང་མས་ཞིང་རྨོ་ཟ་ན། ཁོང་གཉིས་ཀྱས་ཡང་
དེ་ཞིང་པོ་ལ་ས་བོན་བཏབ་སྟེ་རྨོས། དེ་ནས་ཚང་མས་ལྷུར་རྒྱ་བཏང་ཅན། དེ་ཨ
བི་ཡང་སོང་སྟེ་རྒྱ་བཏངས་པ། དེ་ཞིང་གི་དཀྱིལ་ལ་ལྗོང་པ་གཅིག་ཅིག་མེད་པ
སྐྱེས་དེ་མེད་ཚུག། དེ་ནས་ཨ་བི་ཡ་མཚན་སོང་སྟེ་རྒྱ་མ་བཏང་བ། ཁང་པ་རུ
ལོག་སྟེ་ཡོང་སྟེ་ཨ་པོ་ལ་ཟེརས་པ། ལྷ་ཨ་པོ། ཚང་མའི་ཞིང་དེ་སྔོན་པོ་སོང་
སྟེ་འདུག། ང་རང་གི་ཞིང་རྒྱ་ཅན་པོ་ལ་ལྗོང་པ་གཅིག་ཅིག་མེད་པ་མི་འདུག།
ངས་རྒྱ་མ་བཏང་བ་ཡོངས་ཟེརས་པ། དེ་ནས་ཨ་པོས་ཟེརས། ལྗོང་པ་གཅིག
མེད་ནའང་། ཁོ་རང་གི་རྩ་ལ་རྒྱ་སྐྱིལ་དེ་ཡོང་ ཟེརས་པ། ཡང་ཨ་བི་ལོག་སྟེ་

སོང་སྟེ་ཆུ་ཞིག་སྐྱིལ་དེ་ཡོངས། དེ་རྫུག་གིས་ཆུ་བདང་གིན་བོརས་པ་སང་། སྔོན་ལ་ཚང་མ་རི་ཞིང་ཛ་རན་ཚུག་པ། དེ་ལྡོང་པ་གཅིག་ཅིག་པོ་ཆེན་མོ་སོང་སྟེ། ཤིང་ཀྱིལ་ཞིག་ཟམ་སོང་། དེ་ནས་མི་ཚང་མས་ཞིང་ཛ་ཅན། ཨ་པོ་ཡང་སྟུ་རི་ཞིག་ཁྱེར་ནས་སོང་སྟེ། དེ་དྲིམ་གྱི་རྩ་ལ་སོང་སྟེ་བདུངས། ལན་གཉིས་གསུམ་བརྡུངས་པ་སང་། དེའི་ཁ་ཐོག་ནས་གྲོ་ནས་ཁ་ཅིག་འབུད་དེ་ཡོངས། དེ་ནས་ཨ་པོ་འཕྲད་གྱིན་ཞིག་ཁང་པ་ལ་ལོག་སྟེ་ཡོང་སྟེ་ཨ་བི་ལ་ཟེར་ས་པ། ལྷ་ཨ་བི། ང་དང་གི་ལྡོང་པའི་བུ་དྲ་དེ་ལ་ངས་ བརྡུངས་པ། ཁ་ཐོག་ནས་ནས་ཁ་ཅིག་འབུད་དེ་ཡོངས་པ། པོ་རིན་ཟེད་རི་འདུག་ཟེར་ས་པ། དེ་ནས་ཨ་བི་དང་ཨ་པོ་གཉིས་ཀ་སོང་སྟེ། ལྡོང་པའི་བུ་དྲའི་རྩ་ལ་ཡུལ་ཐག་ཆེན་མོ་ཞིག་བཅོ་སྟེ། དེ་ལ་ཛལ་ལ་བདང་སྟེ་བདེ་མོ་བཅོས། དེ་ནས་ཨ་པོ་དང་ཨ་བི་གཉིས་ཀས་སྤྲོ་རེས་ངདང་གིན་ཞིག་ལྡོང་པའི་དྲིམ་པོ་ལ་བརྡུངས། དེ་ནས་ཁ་ཐོག་ནས་འབྲུ་མང་པོ་ཆེན་མོ་པོ་རིན་ཟམ་རི་ཆུ་ཡོང་བ་ཚོགས་ལ་བབས། ཁོང་གཉིས་ཀས་ཁང་ཚུ་ལ་སྐྱུ་སྟེ་ནང་མིག་ཚང་མ་གང་སོང་། ཁང་ཚུའི་ནང་དུ་མ་ཤོང་བས། ཞིང་དེ་ཁ་བང་པ་ཆེན་མོ་ཞིག་བཅོ་སྟེ། དེའི་ནང་དུ་བདངས།།

No. 2.

དེ་བང་བ་བཀང་སྟེ། དེ་ཁ་ལ་རྗོ་བ་ཞིག་བཀབ་སྟེ། ཀ་ལག་བདང་སྟེ་ཨ་པོ་དང་ཨ་བི་གཉིས་ཀ་ཁང་པ་རུ་ཡོང་སྟེ་ཁོང་མང་པོ་འཐད་སོང་། དབྱིད་ཁ་རུ་མི་ཚང་མས་བང་བ་ནས་ཕིང་ཟ་ན། ཨ་པོ་ཡང་ཕད་ཅིག་ཁྱེར་དེ་བང་བ་ཕིང་བ་སོང་། ཁོས་བང་བའི་ཁ་རྗོ་ཕྱེ་སྟེ་བལྟས་པ། འབྲུ་ཚང་མ་འབུ་རྙིག་ལ་གྱུར་དེ་བང་བ་གང་སྟེ་ཡོད་ཚུག། དེ་ནས་ཨ་པོ་ཡ་མཚན་སོང་སྟེ་ལོག་སྟེ་ཁང་

ཏུ་ལ་ཡོང་སྟེ་ཨ་བི་ལ་ཟེརས་པ། ཕྲ་ཨ་བི། ང་དངགི་བང་བའི་ནས་ཚང་མ་འབུ་རྟིག་ལ་གྱུར་དེ་འབུ་རྟིག་དང་བང་བ་གང་སོང་སྟེ་འདུག་ཟེརས། དེ་ནས་ཨ་པོ་དང་ཨ་བི་གཉིས་ཀ་ལ་ཆོར་ཀ་ཡོང་སྟེ་ཟེརས་པ། ཁང་ཏུའི་ནང་དུ་ཡོད་མཁན་གྱི་ནས་པོ་ཟ་ཚར་འདུག། ད་ཅི་བཅོ་ཡིན་ཟེར་རིན་ཞིག་འདུགས། ཞག་བདུན་སོང་བ་དང། ཁོང་བདེན་མ་ཆེས་པར་ཨ་པོ་ཡང་བལྟ་ལ་སོང་སྟེ། བང་བའི་ཁ་ཕྱེས་དེ་བལྟས་པ། འབུ་རྟིག་གཅིག་དང་ཅིག་གིས་བཟོས་དེ། འབུ་རྟིག་ཆེན་མོ་གཅིག་ལ་གྱུར་དེ་ཡོད་ཚུག། ཨ་པོས་ཁ་རྡོ་དེ་བཀབ་སྟེ་ལོག་སྟེ་ཨ་བི་ལ་ཟེར་བ་ལ་ཁང་པ་རུ་ཡོངས། ཕྲ་ཨ་བི། བང་བའི་ནང་གྱི་འབུ་རྟིག་ཚང་མ་ཚར་དེ་འབུ་ཆེན་མོ་གཅིག་ལ་གྱུར་དེ་འདུག་ཟེརས། དེ་ནས་ཡང་ཞག་བདུན་སོང་སྟེ། ཡང་ཨ་པོ་བལྟ་ལ་སོང་སྟེ་ཁ་ཕྱེས་དེ་བལྟས་པ་སད། འབུ་རྟིག་པོ་སྤྲུ་གུ་བདེ་མོ་ཞིག་ལ་གྱུར་དེ་ཡོད་ཚུག། ཉི་མ་ལ་བདང་ན་ཞུ་ཅེས། གྲིབ་འཁྲུགས་ལ་བོར་ན་འཁྱུངས་ཅེས། གསེར་རི་ཆུན་ཆུན་པོ་བྲང་འཁོར་ལ། དཔལ་ལི་ཅོ་རི་སྐྱིད་འཁོར་ལ་ཡོད་མཁན་ཞིག་ཡོད་ཚུག། དེ་ནས་ཨ་པོས་ཁ་རྡོ་མགྱོགས་པ་བཀབ་ཀབ་སྟེ་ཕྱིར་ལོག་སྟེ་ཁང་ཏུ་ལ་ཡོང་སྟེ་ཨ་བི་ལ། ཕྲ་ཨ་བི། དེ་བང་བའི་ནང་ན་སྤྲུ་གུ་སྐྱི་འདྲ་ཅེས་བདེ་མོ་ཞིག་འདུག་ཟེརས་པ། ཨ་བི་འཐད་དེ། ཕྲ་ཨ་པོ། ང་དང་གཉིས་ཀ་ལ་ཟླ་མཁན་ཅིག་རག། ཀྱལ་ལ་སོང་། ང་དང་ལ་སྤྲུ་གུ་མེད་ཟེརས། ཁོང་གཉིས་ཀ་མགྱོགས་པ་སོང་སྟེ་བལྟས་པ། བདེན་པ་ཡོད་ཚུག། དེ་ནས་སྤྲུ་གུ་ཁང་ཏུ་ལ་ཁུར་དེ་ཁྲིད་སྟེ། དྲི་དོན་ཐོག་དོན་བདང་སྟེ་དཀོན་མཆོག་ལ་མང་པོ་བཅོལ་ནས། ཁོང་གཉིས་ཀ་མང་པོ་འཐད་གྱིན། འདུགས།

No. 3.

ཞག་བདུན་སོང་སྟེ་ཕྲུ་གུ་ལ་མིང་བདག་ཅེས་སི་ཐི་ལ། ཨ་པོ་གྱང་ཅི་ལྡུང་པའི་ནང་དུ་མེ་མེ་སློབ་དཔོན་རྩེ་དགུ་ལ་ཞུ་བ་ལ་སོང་སྟེ། མེ་མེའི་དགོན་པའི་རྩར་སོང་སྟེ་གླུ་འདི་ལྟར་བཏངས།

མེ་མེ་སློབ་དཔོན་གྱིས་ཨ་པོ་ངའི་དངོས་ལ་གསན་ལོ།
སློབ་དཔོན་རྩེ་དགུས་འང་བཀྲ་ཤིས་ཀྱི་བདག་ལ་གསན་ལོ།
ཨ་པོ་ང་རང་ལ་ཚ་བོ་ཞིག་ཐོབ་ལོ།
བཀྲ་ཤིས་ང་རང་ལ་བུ་ཚ་ཞིག་འབྱོར་ལོ།
ངའི་ཚ་བོ་ལ་མིང་ཞིག་སྐུལ་ལོ།
ངའི་བུ་ཚ་ལ་མིང་ཞིག་སྐུལ་ལོ།
ཨ་པོས་མེ་མེ་ལ་དེ་ཟུག་ཞུས་པ་སང། མེ་མེ་སློབ་དཔོན་རྩེ་
དགུས་ལན་དུ་གླུ་འདི་ལྟར།།
གླིང་གི་ཨ་པོས་ངའི་དངོས་ལ་ཉེན་དང།
གླིང་གི་བཀྲ་ཤིས་ངའི་བདག་ལ་གསན་དང།
ཨ་པོ་རང་ལ་བུ་ཞིག་འབྱོར་ཏེ་ཡོད་ན།
བཀྲ་ཤིས་རང་ལ་ཚ་བོ་ཐོབ་སྟེ་ཡོད་ན།
བླ་མ་ང་ཡིས་མིང་ཞིག་བདག་ཡིན།
སློབ་དཔོན་ང་ཡིས་མིང་ཞིག་བདག་ཡིན།
བུ་ཚ་དེའི་མིང་ལ་དོང་གསུམ་མི་ལ་སྟོན་མོ་དོག།
ཚ་བོ་དེའི་མིང་ལ་དོང་གསུམ་མི་ལ་སྟོན་མོ་དོག།།

No. 4.

མེ་མེ་སྐྱོབ་དཔོན་གྱིས་དེ་ཟུག་ཟེར་པ་སང། ཨ་པོ་ཕྱིར་ལོག་སྟེ་རང་གི་ཁང་དུ་ལ་ཡོངས། ཁྲིམ་མཆོས་པ་ལ་ཁྲི་ཞིག་ཡོད་ཚུག། དེ་ཁྲི་ལ་ཁྲི་ཕྲུག་གཉིས་སྐྱེ་སྟེ་ཡོད་པས། དོང་གསུམ་མི་ལ་སྟོན་མོས་དེ་ཁྲི་ཕྲུག་གཉིས་ཀ་གསོ་སྟེ་ལིངས་ཁྲི་བཅོ་སྟེ་ཡོད་ཚུག། ཁོས་དེ་ཁྲི་ཁྲིད་དེ་ཞག་དང་ལིངས་ལ་སོང་སྟེ། སྐྱིན་དང་གྲོང་མང་པོ་ཁྲོང་སྟེ། ཨ་པོ་དང་ཨ་བི་གཉིས་ཀ་ལ་.ཤ་མང་པོ་ཁྲོང་སྟེ་བཏངས། ཞག་ཅིག་ཁྲི་གཉིས་ཀ་སྔོན་ལ་འབུད་དེ་སོང་། དོང་གསུམ་མི་ལ་སྟོན་མོས་ཁྲིའི་རྗེས་པོ་བཅད་དེ་སོང་པ་སང། གྲང་ངི་ལྷུང་པའི་སྤུ་ལ་སོང་། བསླེབ་པ། མེ་མེ་སློབ་དཔོན་རྩེ་དགུ་འདུག་སའི་མཚམས་ཀྱི་ལྷག་ལ་བྲག་ཆེན་མོ་ཞིག་ཡོད་ཚུག། དེ་བྲག་གི་དཀྱིལ་ལ་ཁྲི་གཉིས་ཀས། སྲིན་པོ་མགོ་དགུ་ཡོད་མཁན་ཞིག་སྐར་དེ་ཡོད་ཚུག། དོང་གསུམ་མི་ལ་སྟོན་མོ་དེར་བསླེབ་སོང་། སྲིན་པོ་དེས་ཀླུ་འདི་ལྟར་བཏངས།།

ཀྱེ་མ་གསན་དང་ཨ་ཙོ་ལེ།
ཀྱེ་མ་གསན་དང་ལིངས་མི་ལེ།
ཨ་ཙོ་བའི་ཁྲིས་ང་སྐར་དེ་ཡོད།
ལིངས་པའི་ཁྲིས་ང་བཀག་སྟེ་ཡོད།
ང་མ་བསད་ན་ཉིད་ཀྱི་དམག་གཡོག་བཅོ་ཡིན།
ང་མ་བསད་ན་ཉིད་ཀྱི་ལིངས་གཡོག་བཅོ་ཡིན།
ང་མ་བསད་ན་ཉིད་ལ་ཕན་ཐོགས་.ཞིག་ཡོང་ཡིན།།

No 5.

སྲིན་པོས་དེ་ཟླུག་ཟེརས་པ། དེ་ནས་དོང་གསུམ་མི་ལ་ཕྱོན་མོས་བསད་ཅེས་ལ་ཡང་མ་ཤེས། ཕྱུད་ཅེས་ལ་ཡང་མ་ཤེས་པར། མི་མེ་སློབ་དཔོན་རྩེ་དགུ་ལ་ཞུ་སྟེ་སྒྲུ་འདི་ལྟར་བཏངས།།

ངའི་མི་མེས་དངོས་ཤིག་ལ་ཉེན་དང།
སློབ་དཔོན་རྩེ་དགུས་བདག་ཅིག་ལ་གསན་དང།
ཨ་ཡི་བྲག་བཟངས་པོའི་ནང་ན་སྲིན་པོ་མགོ་དགུ་ཞིག་འདུག་ལོ།
བྲག་བཟངས་པོའི་ནང་ན་ངའི་ལིངས་ཁྲིས་བཀགས་དེ་འདུག་ལོ།
དེ་སྲིན་པོ་བསད་ད་ཕྱུད་དེ་རིག་བཏང་ལོ།
དེ་མགོ་དགུ་བསད་ད་ཕྱུད་དེ་རིག་བཏང་ལོ།

དོང་གསུམ་ཤི་ལ་སྟོན་མོས་དེ་ཟླུག་ཞུས་པ། མི་མེས་ལན་དུ་སྒྲུ་འདི་ལྟར་བཏངས།

གླིངས་ཀྱི་ཕྲ་གུས་འང་ངའི་དངོས་ལ་ཉེན་དང།
དོང་གསུམ་མི་ལ་སྟོན་མོས་ངའི་བདག་ལ་གསན་དང།
དེ་སྲིན་པོ་དེ་ཁྱེད་ཀྱིས་བསད་པ་རིག་དགོས་སུག།
དེ་མགོ་དགུ་དེ་ཁྱེད་ཀྱིས་བསད་པ་རིག་དགོས་སུག།
དེ་ཀུན་བསད་དེ་ཁྱེ་རང་ཕི་ལོག་ལ་ཞོན་པ་རིག་དགོས།
ཕི་ལོག་ལ་ཞོན་དེ་སྨོན་ལམ་ཞིག་བཏབ་དགོས།
ཀྱཻ༔ གི་མཐིལ་ནས་དཀོན་མཆོག་ལ་སྨོན་ལམ་ཞིག་ཏོབ་ལོ།
སྲིན་པོའི་མགོ་བཞི་བཅད་དེ་འཕང་ན།
གླིང་མཁར་ཀྱི་རྩིག་ལྷན་པོ་ལྷན་ཆེན།

སྲིན་པོའི་མགོ་བཞི་བཅད་དེ་འཕང་ན།

གླིང་མཁར་རྩེ་དགུའི་ཀྲུ་བཞི་ལྷན་ཆེན།

སྲིན་པོའི་མགོ་གཅིག་བཅད་དེ་འཕང་ན།

གླིང་མཁར་རྩེ་དགུའི་ས་སྐང་ལྷན་ཆེན།

སྲིན་པོའི་རྐང་པ་བཅད་དེ་འཕང་ན།

གླིང་མཁར་རྩེ་དགུའི་ས་གདུང་ལྷན་ཆེན།

སྲིན་པོའི་ལག་པ་བཅད་དེ་འཕང་ན།

གླིང་གི་ཐུ་གདུང་ལྷན་ཆེན།

སྲིན་མོ་བཅད་དེ་འཕང་ན།

གླིང་མཁར་གྱི་གྲལ་ཆད་ལྷན་ཆེན།

སྲིན་པོའི་རྩི་བ་མ་བཅགས་ཏེ་འཕང་ན།

གླིང་མཁར་གྱི་ཐོག་ཀྲབ་ལྷན་ཆེན།

སྲིན་པོའི་ཤང་ཚ་ཕིང་སྟེ་འཕང་ན།

གླིང་མཁར་གྱི་ཕ་མར་རི་ཐོག་ས་ལྷན་ཆེན།

གློ་བ་དེ་ཕིང་སྟེ་འཕང་ན།

གསེར་པོའི་གསེར་རི་ལྷན་ཆེན།

སྙིང་པོ་བཅད་དེ་འཕང་ན།

དཀར་པོའི་དངུལ་རི་ལྷན་ཆེན།

གྲོད་པ་དཅད་དེ་འཕང་ན།

གྲོ་མ་ཐང་གི་ཐང་འགོ་ལྷན་ཆེན།

ཀྲུ་མ་བཅད་དེ་འཕང་ན།

ཀྲུ་མ་རོང་གི་རོང་འགོ་ལྷན་ཆེན།

ཆེའི་ཕོ་བ་བཅད་དེ་འཕང་ན།

སྤྱི་མགྲོ་ནང་མའི་ལིངས་ས་ལྷན་ཆེན།

སྤྲིན་པོའི་མིག་གཉིས་ཀ་ཕིང་སྟེ་འཕང་ན།

ཆུ་མིག་ཚང་ཡ་ལྷན་ཆེན།

སྣ་ཁྲུང་གཉིས་ཀ་བཅད་དེ་འཕང་ན།

སྐད་སྙན་གླིང་བུ་ལྷན་ཆེན།

མཁལ་མ་གཉིས་ཀ་བཅད་དེ་འཕང་ན།

ཀྲུབ་རྟེན་ཕོ་ལོང་ལྷན་ཆེན།

No. 6.

དེ་ཚང་མ་བཅད་དེ་འཕང་འཕང་ཚུགས་པ་ཞག་བདུན་སོང་། ཞག་བདུན་པ་ལ་ཁྲི་དང་མི་ཚང་ཀ་ལྷོགས་སེན་ཞིག་དང་ཁང་པ་རུ་བསྐྱེབ། ཁོང་བསྐྱེབ་ཟ་སྐྱེབ་ཚུགས་པ་ཨ་པོ་དང་ཨ་བི་གཉིས་ཀ་ལ་ཇོར་ཀ་ཆེན་མོ་སོང་། དེ་ནས་ཕྲུ་གུ་བསྐྱེབ་པ་དང་ཁོང་འཕྲད། ཨ་པོས་ཁོ་ལ་བག་མ་མ་ཁྲོངས་པ་སང་། ཀོ་སྤྲོ་བཅོ་སྟེ་རི་ལ་སོང་། ཞག་དེ་ཟམ་ཞིག་འདུགས་མཁན་ཡིན་ནོག་ཟེར་དེ། ཨ་པོ་མེ་མེ་སྐྱོབ་དཔོན་རྩེ་དགུ་ལ་ཞུ་བ་ལ་སོང་། མེ་མེའི་སྒོ་ལ་སོང་སྟེ་གླུ་འདི་ལྟར་བཏངས།

མེ་མེ་སྐྱོབ་དཔོན་ངའི་དངོས་ལ་ཉོན་དང་།

སྐྱོབ་དཔོན་རྩེ་དགུ་ངའི་བདག་ལ་གསན་དང་།

ངའི་བུ་ཚ་ལ་མཐའ་མ་ཞིག་འདྲི་བར་རན་ལོ།

དོང་གསུམ་མི་ལ་སྨོན་མོ་ལ་བག་མ་འདྲི་རན།

ཁོ་ཁ། མཛེས་པའི་མནའ་མ་ཞིག་ག་ན་འདུག་གཟིགས་འང།

དོང་གསུམ་མི་ལ་སྨོན་མོ་ལ་བག་མ་ག་ན་འདུག་གཟིགས་འང།

མོ་དཔེ་ཡིང་སྐྱེ་མོ་ཞིག་དོབ་ལོ།

ཕྱིས་དཔེ་བཏིང་སྐྱེ་ཕྱིས་ཤིག་སྐོར་ལེ།

ཤར་ན་འདུག་ག་ནུབ་ན་འདུག་གཟིགས་འང།

བྱང་ན་འདུག་ག་ལྷོ་ན་འདུག་གཟིགས་འང།

དེ་ཟླུག་ཞུས་པ་སང། སེ་སེ་སིས་གདམ་ལན་ལ་ཨི་ཟླུག་གླུ་བཏངས།

གླིང་གི་ཨ་པོས་འང་ངའི་དངོས་ལ་ཉེན་དང།

ཨ་པོ་བཀྲ་ཤིས་འང་ངའི་དངོས་ལ་ཉེན་དང།

ཁྲིད་ཀྱི་ཚ་བོ་ལ་མནའ་མ་ཞིག་འདྲི་ན།

དོང་གསུམ་མི་ལ་སྨོན་མོ་ལ་བག་མ་ཞིག་འདྲི་ན།

ཡུལ་གྱི་སྣང་ཕྱོགས་ཤིག་ནས་ལུག་ལོ་མ་བཅོ་བརྒྱད་ཁྲིད་ལོ།

དེ་ནས་ཨ་པོ་ལོག་སྐྱེ་ཡོང་སྐྱེ་ཨ་བི་ལ་དེ་གནས་ཚུལ་ཚང་མ་ཟེརས་དེ། ཨ་པོ་དང་ ཨ་བི་གཉིས་ཀས་སྣང་ ཕྱོགས་གཅིག་ནས་ལུག་ལོ་མ་ བཅོ་བརྒྱད་མི་ཐོབ་ཟེར་ནས། ཁོང་གཉིས་ཀས་གླབས་ཤིག་བཅོ་སྐྱེ། ང་དང་ངེ་ཚ་བོ་ལ་བང་རི་ཞིག་བཏང་ཡིན། དེ་ནས་མི་མང་པོ་ཞིག་འཛོམ་ན། དེའི་ནང་ནས་ལུག་ལོ་མ་བཅོ་བརྒྱད་བིང་ཡིན་ཟེར་དེ། ཁོང་གཉིས་ཀས་བང་རི་ཞིག་བཏངས། ཡུལ་ཚོ་གཉིས་ལ་ཏྲན་བཏང་སྐྱེ། ཨ་པོ་བཀྲ་ཤིས་ལ་དོང་གསུམ་མི་ལ་སྨོན་མོ་ཟེར་མཁན་ནི་ཚ་བོ་ཞིག་འགྱུར་བས། ཁོ་ལ་བང་རི་ཆེན་མོ་ཞིག་བཏང་ཆེན། དེའི་

ཡི་ལ་ཚང་མ་ལྷན་མོ་ལ་ཡོང་དགོས་ཟེར་དེ་བོས་མཁན་མི་ཞིག་བཏངས། ཕྱུལ་གཉིས་ཀྱི་བུ་ཆ་དང་བུ་མོ་ཚང་མ་ཡོང་ཟ་ན། ཨ་པོ་ཁོ་རང་གི་སློ་ལ་འདུག་སྟེ། བུ་མོ་ཚང་མ་ལ་འདྲི་སྟེ་ལུག་ལོ་མ་སུ་སུ་ཡིན་ཟེར་དེ། ལུག་ལོ་མ་ཡིན་མཁན་ཚང་མའི་མིང་འབྲི་འིན་ཞིག་ནང་མིག་སོ་སོ་ཞིག་ལ་བོར་སོང་། དེ་ནས་དོང་གསུམ་མི་ལ་སྤྱོན་མོ་ཡང་དེ་ནང་མིག་གི་ནང་དུ་འཇུར་དེ། འདི་བུ་མོ་ཚང་མ་ཁྱེ་རང་ལ་བག་མ་ཁྱོངས་པ་ཡིན་ཟེར་དེ། ཁོ་ཡང་ཁོང་སག་དང་མཉམ་པོ་བོར་སོང་།

No. 7.

དེ་ནས་དེ་བུ་མོ་ཚང་མ་ལ། དོང་གསུམ་མི་ལ་སྤྱོན་མོ་མཐོང་བ་ཟམ་ཞིག་ལ་སྐྲི་ཅེས་འཁུར་སོང་བས། ཟླ་དགུ་དངོས་བཅུ་འི་ཞག་ལ་སྤྱོན་ལ་རང་རིགས་ངན་ར་པོའི་མགོ་འཁུར་མཁན་ཞིག་སྐྱེས་པ་སང་། དོང་གསུམ་མི་ལ་སྤྱོན་མོ་དེ། མེ་མེ་སློབ་དཔོན་རྩེ་དགའི་རྩར་ཕྲུ་གུ་ལ་མིང་བཏག་པར་སོང་། མེ་མེ་འི་སློ་ལ་སླུ་འདི་ལྟར་བཏངས།

མེ་མེ་སློབ་དཔོན་ཉིས་ངའི་དངོས་ལ་ཉེན་དང་།
སློབ་དཔོན་རྩེ་དགུས་འང་ངའི་དངོས་ལ་ཉེན་དང་།
བུ་ཆང་རང་ལ་རིགས་ངན་ར་པོའི་མགོ་འཁུར་མཁན་ཞིག་སྐྱེས་ལོ།
དོང་གསུམ་མི་ལ་སྤྱོན་མོ་ལ་ར་མགོ་འཁུར་པ་ཞིག་སྐྱེས་ལོ།
དེ་ཕྲུ་གུ་ལ་མིང་ཞིག་རང་དགོ་ལོ།
དེ་བུ་ཆ་ལ་མིང་ཞིག་རང་དགོ་ལོ།

དེ་ནས་མེ་མེ་སློབ་དཔོན་རྩེ་དགས་གདམ་ལན་དུ་སླུ་འདི་ལྟར་བསླངས།།

གླིང་གི་དཔའ་བོས་འང་ངའི་དངོས་ལ་ཉེན་དང་ལེ།

ནོང་གསུམ་མི་ལ་སྨོན་མོས་ངའི་བདག་ལ་གསན་དང་ལོ།

ཁྱེད་ལ་བུ་ཆ་ཞིག་སྐྱེས་ལོ་ཟེར་ན་ལི།

ར་པོའི་མགོ་འཁོར་པ་ཞིག་སྐྱེས་ཟེར་ན།

ལུས་ངན་ཡང་དུ་གྱུར་ཏེ་པ་སང་ལྡན་རྣ་སྐྱེས་དོག།

དེ་ནས་ཁོ་ཕྱིར་ལོག་སྟེ་ཁང་པ་རུ་བསླེབ་སྟེ། ཡང་བུ་མོ་ཞིག་ལ་ལུངས་པོའི་མགོ་འཁོར་མཁན་ཞིག་སྐྱེ་སྟེ་ཡོད་ཚུག། ཁོ་ཡང་གཟུང་ངེ་ལྦུང་པའི་སྦུ་ལ་མེ་མེའི་རྩར་སོང་སྟེ་གླུ་འདི་ལྟར།

མེ་མེ་སློབ་དཔོན་ཉིས་ང་འི་དངོས་ཤིག་ལ་ཉེན་དང།

སློབ་དཔོན་རྗེ་དགུས་འང་ངའི་བདག་ཅིག་ལ་གསན་དང།

བུ་ཚ་ང་རང་ཁང་པ་ལ་བསླེབ་པ་དང་སྦྲུ་གུ་ཞིག་སྐྱེས་འདུག།

རིགས་ངན་ལུངས་པོའི་མགོ་འཁོར་མཁན་ཞིག་སྐྱེས་ལོ།

རིགས་ངན་སྦྲུ་གུ་དེ་ལ་མིང་ཞིག་རང་སྟུལ་ལོ།

ལུངས་པོ་འཁོར་མཁན་དེ་ལ་མིང་ཞིག་རང་སྟུལ་ལོ།

མེ་མེས་ལན་དུ་གླུ་འདི་ལྟར་བསླངས་སོ།

གླིང་གི་དཔའ་བོས་འང་ངའི་དངོས་ལ་ཉེན་དང།

ནོང་གསུམ་མི་ལ་སྨོན་མོས་ངའི་བདག་ལ་གསན།

རིགས་ངན་ལུངས་པོའི་མགོ་འཁོར་མཁན་ཞིག་སྐྱེས་ན།

རིགས་ངན་ཡང་དུ་སྒྱུར་ཏེ་ཨང་གར་ལུངས་པ་དོག།

དེ་ནས་མེ་མེ་སེས་ཁོ་ལ་ཟེར་ས་པ། ཁྱེ་རང་གི་ཨ་ནེ་ཚང་མ་ལ་གླིང་གི་དཔའ་བོ་བཅོ་བརྒྱད་འདི་རིང་སྐྱེ་ཆེན། ཁྱེ་རང་འདིར་མིང་བདག་ཅས་ལ་མ་ཡོང་།

ཁྱིད་ཀྱི་ཕྲུ་གུ་སྐྱེ་ཅེས་ཅན་ཚང་མ་ལ་མིང་ངས་བཏགས་དེ་བཏང་ཡིན་ཟེར་དེ། ཡི་གེ་གསལ་པོ་བྲི་སྟེ་ཁོ་ལ་བཏངས། ཡི་གེ་ནང་དུ་ཨི་ཧྲུག་བྲིས་ཡོད།

སྐྲ་དང་སྨང་ར་དཀར་པོ་ཡོད་མཁན་ཞིག་སྐྱེ་ཆེན།
དེ་ལ་ཁ་རྒན་དགའ་ནི་བདག་དགོས།
ཁྲའི་མགོ་འཁོར་མཁན་ཞིག་སྐྱེ་ཆེན།
དེ་ལ་ཁྲའི་མགོ་ཁྲ་ཐུང་བདག་དགོས།
ཤིང་སྐྱུའི་མགོ་འཁོར་མཁན་ཞིག་སྐྱེ་ཆེན།
དེ་ལ་སྐྱུ་བ་རྒོད་པོ་བདག་དགོས།
ཀླ་བའི་མགོ་འཁོར་མཁན་ཞིག་སྐྱེ་ཆེན།
དེ་ལ་ཀླ་བ་བཟང་པོ་བདག་དགོས།
མདའི་མགོ་འཁོར་མཁན་ཞིག་སྐྱེ་ཆེན།
དེ་ལ་མདའ་དཔོན་གོང་མ་བདག་དགོས།
ཨ་ལའི་མགོ་འཁོར་མཁན་ཞིག་སྐྱེ་ཆེན།
དེ་ལ་ཨ་ལ་ཅོང་གོལ་བདག་དགོས།
འབྲུའི་མགོ་འཁོར་མཁན་ཞིག་སྐྱེ་ཆེན།
དེ་ལ་འབྲུ་དམར་ལམ་བསྟན་བདག་དགོས།
ཤེལ་ལི་མགོ་འཁོར་མཁན་ཞིག་སྐྱེ་ཆེན།
དེ་ལ་ཤེལ་ལི་བུ་ཞུང་བདག་དགོས།
གོན་ཅེས་སི་གོང་བ་འཁོར་མཁན་ཞིག་སྐྱེ་ཆེན།
དེ་ལ་དགའ་ནི་གོང་བ་བདག་དགོས།

ལག་པ་རིང་མོ་འཁྲུར་མཁན་ཞིག་སྐྱེ་ཆེན།
དེ་ལ་ལག་ལག་རིངས་བདག་དགོས།
རྐང་པ་རིང་མོ་འཁྲུར་མཁན་ཞིག་སྐྱེ་ཆེན།
དེ་ལ་རྐང་རྐང་རིངས་བདག་དགོས།
བོང་བུའི་མགོ་འཁྲུར་མཁན་ཞིག་སྐྱེ་ཆེན།
དེ་ལ་བོང་ནག་ལྷུམ་བུ་བདག་དགོས།
མིའི་མགོ་འཁྲུར་མཁན་ཞིག་སྐྱེ་ཆེན།
དེ་ལ་བཀའ་བློན་ལྡན་པ་བདག་དགོས།
མི་རྒན་གྱི་མགོ་འཁྲུར་མཁན་ཞིག་སྐྱེ་ཆེན།
དེ་ལ་དཔལ་ལེ་རྒོད་པོ་བདག་དགོས།
གཡུའི་རངས་འཁྲུར་མཁན་ཞིག་སྐྱེ་ཆེན།
དེ་ལ་རྣ་གཡུ་རྣ་རྩ་ལ་བདག་དགོས།
དུང་གི་རངས་འཁྲུར་མཁན་ཞིག་སྐྱེ་ཆེན།
དེ་ལ་བླ་བ་དཀར་པོ་བདག་དགོས།

No. 8.

དེ་ནས་ཁོས་དེ་ཡི་གེ་ཁྲུར་དེ་ལོག་སྟེ་ཁང་པ་ལ་ཡོངས། དེ་ཡི་གེ་ནང་ལྟར་ཞག་གཅིག་གི་ནང་དུ་ཕྲུ་གུ་ཚང་མ་སྐྱེས། དེ་ནས་མི་མིས་བསླབས་མཁན་ནང་ལྟར་མིང་ཡང་ཚང་མ་ལ་བཏགས། ཕྲུ་གུ་སྐྱེའི་ཚོར་དང་ཕི་སྟ་རུ་བིང་སྟེ་སོང་སྟེ། རང་རང་གིས་ཁང་པ་རེ་རྩིགས་སོང་། དེ་ཨ་མ་ཚང་མ་ཡང་དེར་མ་འདུག་པར། རང་རང་གི་ཁང་པར་སོང་། དེ་ཕྲུ་གུ་ཚང་ནས་རང་རང་གིས་ཨ་ནེ་རེ་རེ་ཁྲིད་སྟེ།

ཁོང་ལ་ནོར་རི་མེད་པའི་ཕོ་ལ། ཁོང་ཚང་ཀུས་གྲུབས་བཅོས། པ་ཆི་དཔལ་དོང་མཁར་ལ་ནོར་ཡོད་ཟེར་འདུག། དེ་ནས་ང་དང་ཚང་མ་མཁར་བཅག་སྟེ་ནོར་འཁྱེར་བར་ཆེན་ཟེར་དེ་སོང་། དེའི་ནང་ན་དཔལ་ལེ་རྒོད་པོ་ཟེར་མཁན་པོ་ཁའི་ཨ་མ་བོ་མགར་མོ་ཞིག་ཡིན་པས། གྲིབ་ལོག་སྟེ་འགྲུལ་མ་ཐུབ་པར། གྲང་ངེ་ལྷུང་པའི་ཕྲུ་ལ་མེ་མེ་བསྐྱོབ་དཔོན་རྩེ་དགུའི་རྩར་ཁྲུས་བཏང་གིན་ཞིག་ཡོད་པིན; ཞག་ཅིག་ཁོ་ཡང་པ་ཆི་དཔལ་དོང་མཁར་ལ་ནོར་འཁྱེར་བར་ཆེན་བསམ་སྟེ། རྟ་ཞིག་ལ་ཞོན་དེ་སོང་བར། རྒྱ་ཆེན་མོ་ཞིག་གི་མདུན་ལ་བསླེབ། དེ་ཙུ་ལྷ་ཅོ་ཞིག་རྒྱ་ནས་མ་ཐར་བ་ཡོད་རྫུག། དེ་ལྷ་ཅོས། ལྷ་ཨ་ཅོང་ཡང་རྟམ་ཕོངས་ལ་བཏང་ན། ངས་ཕན་ཐོགས་ཤིག་བཅོ་ཡིན་ཟེརས། ཁྱེད་ཀྱིས་ང་ལ་ཕན་ཐོགས་ཤིག་བཅོ་ན་ཡོང་ཟེར་དེ། རྟམ་ཕོངས་ལ་བཏང་སྟེ་འཁྱེརས། དེ་ནས་ལྷ་ཅོས་ལམ་བསྟན་དེ་འཁྱེར་དེ། པ་ཆི་དཔལ་དོང་མཁར་ལ་དཔལ་ལེ་རྒོད་པོ་སྡུན་ལ་བསླེབ་སོང་། གཉན་མ་ཚང་མ་ཅིའི་ཕོ་ལ་མ་བསླེབ་ཟེར་ན། ལམ་རྫོག་པོ་ཚེར་ མང་གི་ཚོགས་ དང་ལྷུང་ མའི་ཚོགས་ མང་པོའི་ནང་ ནས་ཐར་ཅིས་མེད་རྫུག། དེ་ཚོགས་པོ་བཅད་དེ་ན་སོང་སྟེ། ཞག་རེ་རེ་ལ་ཐག་པ་གང་རི་མིན་པ་ལམ་མ་ཐིང་བར། དེ་ནུག་གིས་འགོར་སོང་། དཔལ་ལེ་རྒོད་པོ་ལྷ་ཅོ་དང་མཉམ་པོ་སོང་པ་དེ་ཙུ་བསླེབ། དེ་ཡུལ་གྱི་མཛུག་ལ་ཨ་ཕི་རྒད་མོ་ཞིག་ཡོད་རྫུག། ཁོ་དེ་ཙུ་བྲང་ས་ལ་འདུགས།།

No. 9.

དེ་ནས་ཞག་ཁ་ཅིག་སོང་སྟེ་ཁོས་ཨ་ཕི་ལ་ཁ་རྗོད་བཅད་ཏེ་འདྲིས་པ། ཨ་ཕི་ལེ། འདི་མཁར་གྱི་ནང་དུ་ནོར་བུ་ཅི་རི་ཡོད་ཟེརས་པ། ཨ་ཕིས་ལན་དུ་ལྷ་

བྲུ་ཚ། ངས་ཚོར་མཁན་ཚང་མ་ཁྲི་རང་ལ་བཤད་ཡིན་ཟེར་དེ་ཟེར་ས། གླིང་ཡུལ་ལ་ཕེབས་ཐོན་པ་དང་ཡུམ་སྟོན་མོ་ཟེར་མཁན་གཉིས་ལ་ཇོ་ཇོ་འབྲི་གུ་མ་ཟེར་མཁན་ཞིག་བལྟམ་ཆེན་ཟེར་འདུག། དེ་ནས་གླིང་མཁར་གྱི་སྟོད་ལ་ཨ་པོ་ཞིག་ཡོད་ཚོད། དེ་ཨ་པོ་མགར་བ་ཞིག་ཡིན་ཚོད་རག། ཁོ་ལ་བུ་མོ་གསུམ་སྐྱེ་ཆེན་ཟེར་འདུག། བུ་མོ་གཅིག་གི་མིང་ལ་དཀར་ཐིག་མོ་བདག་ཆེན་ལོ། བུ་མོ་གཅིག་ལ་ནག་ཐིག་མ་བདག་ཆེན་ལོ། བུ་མོ་གཅིག་ལ་མ་མོག་བཟང་ལྷ་མོ་བདག་ཆེན་ལོ། དེ་ནས་སྟང་ལྷ་ཡུལ་ལ་ལྷའི་དབང་པོ་རྒྱབ་བཞིན་ལ་བུ་ཚ་གསུམ་སྐྱེ་ཆེན་ལོ། བུ་ཚ་ཨ་ཇོའི་མིང་ལ་དོན་ལྡན་ཞུ་ཡིན་ལོ། བུ་བར་པ་ལ་དོན་ཡོད་ཞུ་ཡིན་ལོ། ཆུང་ངུན་པོ་ལ་དོན་གྲུབ་དཀར་པོ་ཞུ་ཆེན་ལོ། དེ་ཆུང་སྟགས་པོ་གླིང་མགོ་མེད་ལ་མགོ་ལ་འགྱུར་ཆེན་ལོ། དེ་བོ་ག་ཟུག་ལ་འགྱུར་ཡིན་ཟེར་ན། བུ་དོན་གྲུབ་དཀར་པོ་སྟང་ལྷ་ཡུལ་ནས་ཚོ་ཐོས་བདང་ཆེན་ཟེར་འདུག། ཚོ་ཐོས་པ་སང། དེ་མགར་ར་བཀྲ་ཤིས་ཀྱི་བུ་མོ་མ་མོག་བཟང་ལྷ་མོ་ལ་བལྟམ་ཆེན་ཟེར་འདུག། བྲུ་ཁྲ་ཡུག་རྒྱལ་པོ་ལ། བྲུ་འོང་ལྷོ་རི་སྐྱེ་ཆེན་ཟེར་འདུག། བྲུ་འོང་ལྷོ་རི་ལ། བྲུ་ཉི་མ་ཁྲུང་རུང་སྐྱེ་ཆེན་ཟེར་འདུག། བྲུ་ཉི་མ་ཁྲུང་རུང་གི་གཟུགས་པོའི་ཁ་ནོར་བུ་སྣ་དག་ཡོད་ལོ། བྲུ་དེ་སྨིན་པོའི་སྐྱེ་བ་ཡིན་ལོ། ཁོས་གླིང་ཀེ་སར་རྒྱལ་པོ་བདུལ་ཅེས་ཡིན་ཟེར་འདུག། ཀེ་སར་སྐྱེ་སྐྱེ་ཚུག་པ་ནམ་མཁའི་ཀླུ་བ་དང་ཉི་མའི་ཟུར་ལ་མཚམས་བཅད་བདང་སྟེ་འདུག་ཆེན་ལོ། ཁོའི་ནོ་དེ་བྲུ་སོ་མིག་དམར་ཟེར་མཁན་ཞིག་སྐྱེ་ཆེན་ལོ། ཁོ་བྲག་མཐོན་པོ་ཞིག་ལ་ཀེ་སར་སྐྱེ་མིན་གྱི་ཁ་བར་ཉན་ཅེས་ལ་བོར་ཆེན་ལོ། དེ་ཟུག་ཟེར་ཚར་དེ། ཨ་ཀུ་དཔལ་ལེས་ཡང་འདྲིས་པ། དེ་ཚང་མ་ར་ཚོར་བ། ཨ་ཕེ་ལེ། འདི་པ་ཆི་དཔལ་དོང་མཁར་ནང་དུ་ནོར་བུའི་

རིགས་ཅི་རེ་ཡོད་ཟེར་དུ་འདྲིས་པས། ཨ་ཕིས་ལན་ལ། ཆ་ལག་གི་ནོར་བུ་རིག་ཁ་དམར་དང་ཟངས་བུ་ཁ་ཡོད། ཕྱ་རི་བླ་བ་དཀར་པོ་ཡིན། ཐག་པ་རྒྱ་སྐུག་ཁྲ་བོ་ཡིན། སྐེ་མོ་དཀར་མོའི་སྔོང་ཞོང་ཡིན། རྟའི་འགོ་ན་རྒོད་མ་ཆ་ལངས་ཡིན། བ་གླང་གི་འགོ་ན་མཛོ་མོ་རྟ་ཡོན་ཡིན། ར་མའི་འགོ་ན་ར་དཀར་མོ་ཡིན། ལུག་གི་འགོ་ན་ལུག་རྡོ་མོ་ཡིན། བོང་བུའི་འགོ་ན་ནག་པོ་ཁ་དཀར་ཡིན། ཁྱིའི་འགོ་ན་ཁྱི་མོ་དཀར་མོ་ཡིན། བི་ལའི་འགོ་ན་བི་ལ་ནག་མོ་ཡིན། རྒ་པོ་ཁ་ལ་མེ་བར་ཡིན། ཕོ་ལད་རི་གཞུ་མོ་ཡིན། གསེར་རི་སྒྲིད་བུ་ཡིན། དངུལ་གྱི་སྒྲིད་བུ་ཡིན། དུང་ངེ་ལྗུ་གུ་ཡིན། ཟངས་ཀྱི་ཁྲི་གུ་ཡིན། རྩ་རྩའི་ལག་པ་ཡིན། མུ་ཏིག་གི་གྲུ་གུ་ཡིན། གཡུའི་རྩོག་བུ་ཡིན། དེ་ཚང་མ་ནོར་བུ་ཡིན་ཟེར་དུ་ཨ་ཕིས་བསླབས། དེ་ནས་དཔལ་ལེ་རྒོད་པོ་དེ་མཁར་ལ་སོང་སྟེ་ཨ་ཕིས་བསླབ་ཁན་ཚང་མ་ཁྲིར་དེ། ཁོ་གླིང་ཡུལ་ལ་སོང་སྟེ་གླིང་དཀར་གྱི་མཁར་ལ་གཏེར་མཛོད་བཅོ་སྟེ་བོར་ས། དེ་ནས་པ་ཆི་དཔལ་དོང་མཁར་ནས་དཔལ་ལེ་སོང་སྟེ་ཞག་བདུན་སོང་བ་དང་། སློན་ལ་སོང་མཁན་གྱི་དཔའ་བོ་ཚང་མ་དཔལ་དོང་མཁར་ལ་བསླེབ། ནོར་བུའི་རིགས་ཚང་མ་དཔལ་ལེས་འཁྱེར་དེ་མེད་པས། ཁོང་ཚང་གས་གསེར་རེ་དང་དངུལ་རེ་ཡང་ཟངས་ནོར་རེ་ཁུར་དེ་གླིང་ཡུལ་ལ་སོང་སྟེ། རང་རང་གི་ཁང་པ་རུ་སོང་། པ་ཆི་དཔལ་དོང་མཁར་ནོར་ཚང་མ་འཁྱེརས་པ་སང། བཞག་སོང་ནས། ཅི་ཡང་མ་ལུས་སོང།།

Prologue to the Kesar-saga.

Abstract of Contents.

1. In the land *Kalakol* there lived the fore-father *bKrashis shis* and his wife.*) They made a little field, borrowed some seed from another man and sowed it. There only grew a single plant, which they watered well, until it became a tree. From this tree (perhaps the later tree of the world) they received a rich harvest of wheat and barley, each grain being of the size of a pigeon. Then they built a barn and stored it up.

2. One day in spring, when the fore-father went to look after the grain, he found that all the grain had turned into worms. Then these worms ate up one another; until only one huge worm was left, who alone filled the barn. After seven days, when the fore-father went to see the worm, it had become a very beautiful child, so tender, that if placed in the sun, it would melt; if placed in the shade, it would freeze. It had golden locks falling from the fore-head down to the breast, and a silver pig-tail falling down to the waist.

3. The fore-father went to the teacher *r Tse dgu*, who lived in a hermitage in "the cold valley, to ask what name ought to be given to the child; and the teacher told him to call the child *Dong γsum mila sngonmo*.

4. The boy *Dong γsum mila sngonmo* loved to go a-hunting with two dogs. Once these dogs seized (arrested) an ogre with nine heads on the rock above the hermitage. The ogre implored the boy not to kill him and promised to be his helper in war and sport. The boy, who did not know what to do, went to ask the teacher about it.

5. The teacher told him that it was necessary to kill the ogre, and that out of his body the land *g Ling* would come into existence: Out of four of his heads the four walls of the *g Ling*-castle, out of four other ones the four corners (towers) of the *g Ling*-castle, out of one of the heads the floor of the castle, out of his legs the large beams, out of his arms the smaller beams; the fingers would become the sticks of the roof, the ribs the twigs of the roof, and the interior parts the earth of the roof. The lungs would become the golden gold-hill, and the heart

---

* This *bkrashis* is probably identical with the fore-father smith *bkrashis*, mentioned in No. 9.

the white silver-hill. The stomach would become the *Groma*-plain, the principal of all plains, and the bowels the *rGyuma*-gorge, the principal of all gorges. The little stomach would be turned into the hunting ground *Spotho nangma*, and the eyes into the spring *Thsangya;* out of his nose would arise the [place] *Skad snyan glingbu*, and out of the kidneys the rock *r Gyab rten.**

6. Before all this was finished seven days elapsed, and on the seventh day *Dong rsum mila sngonmo* and his dogs came back hungry to the fore-father and his wife. The latter had been fearing that the boy had stayed away for such a long time, because he was angry with them for not yet having given him a bride. For this reason the fore-father went to the teacher and asked him to cast lots and find out from which of the four directions the bride would come. The teacher advised him to call together eighteen girls from the street, and to see that all of them had been born in the sheep-year. On the occasion of the *Bangri*-festival, when many guests had assembled, all those girls of the sheep-year were placed in a separate room, and the boy was sent into the same room too.

7. As soon as the girls had seen the boy, they all were with child, and after nine months and ten days the first child was born. All were startled, because it had a goat's head instead of a human head, and *Dang rsum mila sngonmo* went to the teacher to ask what should be the name of the child. When he said that a child of very bad caste with a goat's head had been born, the teacher advised him

* This account of the creation of *gLing* out of the body of the ogre is what I have called "the creation of the world (earth)." After the opening of Tibet it will probably be possible to find all the places mentioned in the account, and thus to determine the geographical situation of the land *gLing* (perhaps the *Lik* of the Mongols). Although the land *gLing* would then appear to cover only a small portion of the surface of the globe, we must not forget, that in the minds of those early men of *gLing* it may have constituted the whole world known to them. Even at the present time the conceptions of the Tibetans with regard to the size of the earth are extremely narrow. The name *gLing mkhar* castle of *gLing* may have been originally the name of a high mountain with many peaks. Thus for instance the name of a hill not far from the *Saspola* bridge is *Kesarri mkhar*, castle of Kesar. If in future times it should be possible to fix the situation of *gLing*, the question will arise: Do we now actually know the home of the Kesar-saga? I do not believe that the question will be settled so soon. In other countries another version of the saga may mention quite different localities. Besides that not all of the names of the Kesar-saga appear to be of Tibetan origin, some of them have a distinctly non-Tibetan character, and others look like translations from another language. Finally, the question of the zodiac of the mythology of *gLing*, as represented in the Agus, will have to be considered before it will be possible to decide the question of the home of the saga.

not to speak of bad caste and to call the child *Pasang ldan ruskyes.* When he came back, another child was born which had a lizard's head. This also was considered to be of bad caste, but the teacher was of different opinion and said that this child's name was to be *Angar ltsangspa.* Then the teacher told the boy not to come again, and gave him a letter containing the names of sixteen more Agus, who were to be born.*

8. When all of the eighteen Agus were born they marched out in the order of their birth, built houses and took wives. Because they had no riches, they started in search of the castle *Pachi dpal dong,* to get them from there. The Agu *dPalle rgodpo,* whose mother was a smith's daughter and who was believed to be very stupid, started after the others had left. When crossing a brook, he found a fox who could not get out of the water and who asked to be allowed to jump on the Agu's horse. This he was invited to do and in return showed the way to the castle, where Agu *dPalle* arrived first of all. The other Agus had lost the way and become entangled in thorns.

9. After some time Agu *dPalle* asked the grand-mother, who was living in the castle, to tell him what treasures there were in the castle, and the grand-mother answered: "In the land *gLing* there will be born to father *Thonpa* and mother *sNgonmo* a daughter called *a' Briguma* (*a'Bruguma*). In the *gLing* castle to the fore-father, the smith *bKrashis,* there will be born three daughters, *dKar thigmo, Nag thigma* and *Gog bzang lhamo.* To the lord of heaven there will be born three sons, *Don ldan, Don yod* and *Don grub dkarpo.* The latter will die in heaven and be born to *Gog bzang lhamo,* to become the head of the land *gLing.* To the bird *Khu yug rgyalpo* will be born the bird *'Ong ldore,* and to this one the bird *Nyima khyung rung.* The latter will subdue Kesar, and will mark the frontier of sun and moon on the sky (the horizon), until Kesar will be reborn. His younger brother, the bird (bat)*So mig dmar* will then be born and remain on the high rock to hear the news, whether Kesar will be reborn or not." Then *dPalle* said: "But the treasures, what kinds of them are there here?" and the grand-mother answered: "There is a pot with a red mouth and a kettle with a crooked mouth; the white moon is the axe; there is the rope of several colours *rGya stag* and the white bag, "Hold-thousand"; the first of horses, the mare *Thsa langs;* the first of cattle, *mDzomo ru yon;* the first of goats, *Ra dkarmo;* the first of

* The names of these Agus will be found in the "Vocabulary and Comments." A list of the 18 Agus with their characteristic marks was also published in the "Indian Antiquary," December, Part II, 1901.

sheep, *Dromo;* the first of asses, *Nagpo kha dkar;* the first of dogs, the bitch *dKarmo;* the first of cats, *Nagmo;* there is the gelding with fire in his mouth; a bow; golden and silver hearth-stones; a pearl-white lamb and a copper [coloured] dog; pearls and a grinding-stone of turquoise." All these treasures Agu *dPalle* brought to the *gLing* castle and put them into a store-room. Seven days after he had left, the other Agus arrived and carried off some gold, silver and copper each. When nothing was left, the castle *Pachi dpal dong* went to pieces and nothing of it remained.*

GENEOLOGICAL TABLE.

bKrashis †

out of his field	from his wife
Dong ysum mila sngonmo	dKarthigmo Nagthigma Gogbzanglhamo
the 18 Agus	Kesar (son of Gogbzanglhamo)

dBangpo rgyab bzhin	Thonpa, Sngonmo	Khuyug rgyalpo
Don yod, Don ldan, Dongrub dkarpo reborn as Kesar.	'a Bruguma	'Ong ldore
		So mig dmar, Nyima Khyung rung

* In facing the danger of being ridiculed by experts on mythology, I cannot help proposing to interpret passages in No. 9 with the help of the course of the sun. This is suggested in the first place by the occurrence of the word *nyima* "sun" in the name of the supposed sun-bird. I hope that visitors to Ladakh will take the trouble of ascertaining that this is actually the case. The statement that the sun-hero will be killed by the sun-bird, fire by fire, reminds us of the story of the bird Phœnix, who is burnt and arises again alive and young out of the ashes. This story has, I think, always been explained with the fact that the setting sun disappears in the golden-coloured clouds of the evening sky. Then the prophecy, that the sun-bird will mark the frontier of sun and moon on the sky (the horizon) during the death of Kesar, seems to lend itself easily to the interpretation, that during winter the sun is near the horizon (especially in our mountains). The next prohecy, that the bird (bat) *So mig dmar* will remain on the high rock and wait for the news of Kesar's rebirth, may refer to a day-myth.

The bat *So mig dmar* may be the morning star which announces the rising of the sun. All the treasures of the castle down to the cat *Nagmo*, carried away by Agu *dPalle*, seem to be objects of nature; the rest seem to be ordinary treasures.

As regards the animals, there will be no difficulty. The first treasures I am inclined to interpret in this way: The pot with the red mouth is the sun, the kettle with the crooked mouth the moon, who mostly does not show her full circular shape; the moon axe may be the new-moon of sickle shape, the rope *rgya stag* of several colours the rain-bow, and the white bag "Hold thousand" the cloud.

† bKrashis in No. 1 and No. 9 are accepted to be identical.

VOCABULARY AND COMMENTS.

No 1.

ཀ་ལ་ཀོལ། Kalakol, name of the first country.

ཨ་པོ། Apo, great-grand-father, fore-father.

ཨ་བི།=ཨ་ཕྱི། grand-mother.

ཐོང་རོས། thongros, ploughed field.

རྨོ་ཐོ། rmotho, time for ploughing.

ལྡར་ཆུ། ldar chu, first irrigation of a field.

མེན་པ། menpa, = ma yinpa, besides.

ཟེརས་པ། Lower Ladakhi for ཟེར་པ། said.

ཟ་ན།=ཙ་ན། at the time of.

ཟམ། zam = tsam, so much.

དྲིམ། drim, trunk of any tree.

བུ་དྲ། budra, tree.

ཕོ་རོན། phoron = phugron, dove.

ཟོད། zod = thsod, measure, alike.

ཡུལ་ཐག། yul thag, threshing-floor.

ཇལ་ལ། jalla = zhalba, clay.

སྐྱ་སྟེ། skyaste, transporting; related to skyelba.

No. 2.

འབུ་རྩིག། 'abu rtsig, caterpillar.

འཁྱངས་ཅེས། 'akhyangsces, to freeze.

ཚུན་ཚུན། chun chun = chunpo, locks or fringes on the fore-head.

ཅོ་ཏི། coti = cuti, pig-tail.

No. 3.

དྲི་དོན། dridon, a cake used for offerings.

ཤོག་དོན། burnt-offering of the pencil-cedar.

གསན། γsan, not γson, listen, imperative tense. The respectful verbs do not change *a* to *o* in the imperative tense.

རྩེ་དགུ། rtse dgu, nine summits; was also explained as meaning rtsi dgu, counting up to nine in sorcery.

དོང་གསུམ་མི་ལ། Dongγsum mila, name of the boy of ḅkra shis; is said to mean "three pits to a man." I am, however, more inclined to spell it γdong γsum mila "three faces to [one] man," which explanation would perhaps point to some figure similar to Brahma. The latter part of the name we find perhaps again in the name Milaraspa.

No. 4.

རྗེས་པོ། rjespo = rjessu, after.

སྐར་ཅས། skarcas, to keep an animal in its place by surrounding it (when hunting).

ཀྱེ་མ། kyema, careful, carefully.

བཟངས་པོ། bzangspo = bzangpo, good.

No. 5.

དགོས་སུག། dgossug = dgos 'adug, must, pres. tense.

གྲུ་བཞི། gru bzhi, four corners; is said to refer to the towers of the castle.

ས་སྐང། sa skang, said to mean "floor."

མ་གདུང། ma γdung, "mother-beam," the thick beams in the roof of a house.

བུ་གདུང། bu γdung, "daughter beam," the thinner beams in the roof.

ཕྲན་མོ། phranmo, "the little ones,'' expression for "fingers."

ཐོག་ཀྲབ། thog krab, the branches which are placed on the sticks of the roof, before the earth is stamped on it.

ཚའི་ཕོ་བ། thsei phoba, is said to be "the little stomach."

སྤོ་མཐོ་ནང་མ། spo mtho nangma, name of a hunting ground.

ཚང་ཡ། thangya, name of springs of water; compare this word in Jäschke's dictionary.

ཕོ་ལོང། pholong=phabong, rock.

སྐད་སྙན་གླིང་བུ། skad snyan glingbu, "well-sounding flute," name of a place where probably the whistling of the wind can be heard.

རྒྱབ་རྟེན། rgyab rten, "lean backwards;" name of a rock; against this rock Agu Khromo was thrown.

No. 6.

མོ་དཔེ། mo dpe, the book for casting lots.

བང་རི། bang ri, the feast given to celebrate the birth of a child; it may, however, be given many years later, if the parents are poor.

བིང་ཅེས། bingces, to come out.

བཏགས། btags, from 'adegspa, to raise [a meal], = give a meal.

ལྟན་མོ། ltanmo, a spectacle.

ཁྱེ་རང། khye rang = khyed rang, you.

No. 7.

ཟླ་དགུ་དངོས་བཅུའི་ཞག་ལ། nine months, and then exactly on the tenth day.

སྔོན་ལ་རང་། sngonla rang, the first (first-born).

ལྟས་ངན། ltas ngan, here the same as rigs ngan, low caste.

ཡང་དུ་སྒྱུར་ཅས། yangdu sgyurcas, to change back. The meaning is here: you must take back your word that the child was of low caste.

ལྩངས་པ། ltsangspa = rtsangspa, lizard.

པ་སང་ལྡན་རུ་སྐྱེས Pasang ldan ru skyes, name of the first Agu; it means "possessing the Friday (Venus), horns growing."

ཨང་གར་ལྩངས་པ། Angar ltsangspa, name of the second Agu. The second part means "lizard;" the first part does not appear to be Tibetan.

མེ་མེ་སིས། memesis, by the grand-father; Lower Ladakhi form of the instrumental in *si*.

སྐྱེ་ཅེས་ཅན། skyececcan, is almost a participle of the future tense, "they who will be born."

བྲིས་ཡོད། bris yod, is written; a form of the perf. tense, which is hardly ever used in Ladakh proper.

ཁ་རྒན་དགའ་ནི། Kha rgan dga ni, name of the third Agu; the latter part of the name is perhaps *dga nyi;* then it would mean "Old month, day of joy," or *Gani* alone would mean 'coat of mail.'

ཁྲའི་མགོ་ཁྲའི་ཐུང་། Khrai mgo khrai thung, name of the fourth Agu; it means "falcon's head, short falcon."

སྐྱ་བ་རྒོད་པོ། Skyaba rgodpo, name of the fifth Agu; it means "wild soup-spoon."

ཟླ་བ་བཟང་པོ། Zlaba bzangpo, name of the sixth Agu; it means "good moon, or month."

མདའ་དཔོན་གོང་མ། mDa dpon gongma, name of the seventh Agu; it means "the high headman of bow-men."

ཨ་ལ་ཅོང་གོལ། Ala conggol, name of the eighth Agu; does not appear to be Tibetan; is said to mean "a boot's sole, the stupid one."

འབུ་དམར་ལམ་བསྟན། 'aBu dmar lam bstan, name of the ninth Agu; it means "red worm, way-leader."

ཤེལ་ལི་བུ་ཞུང། Shelli buzhung = buchung, name of the tenth Agu; it means "little boy of glass (or crystal)."

དགའ་ནི་གོང་བ། d Ga ni gongba, name of the eleventh Agu; it means "day (?) of joy, the collar," or "coat of mail, the collar."

ལག་ལག་རིངས། Lag lag rings, name of the twelfth Agu; it means "long hand."

རྐང་རྐང་རིངས། rKang rkang, rings, name of the thirteenth Agu; it means "long foot."

བོང་ནག་ལྡུམ་བུ། Bong nag ldumbu, name of the fourteenth Agu; the first part means "black ass"; ldumbu is said to be a plant.

བཀའ་བློན་ལྡན་པ། bKa blon ldanpa, name of the fifteenth Agu; it means "the state-minister, the possessor."

རངས། rangs, an ornament.

དཔལ་ལེ་རྒོད་པོ། dPalle rgodpo, name of the sixteenth Agu; it means "wild splendour, glory."

རྣ་གཡུ་རྣ་རྩལ། rNa jya rna rtsal, name of the seventeenth Agu; it means "ear-turquoise, skilful ear;" there was a misprint in my previous list of the Agus with regard to this name.

ཟླ་བ་དཀར་པོ། Zlaba dkarpo, name of the eighteenth Agu; it means "white moon, or month."

No. 8.

སྐྱེའི་ཚིར། skyei thsir, the order of their birth.

མགར་མོ། mgarmo, wife or daughter of a smith.

གྲིབ་ཕོག་སྟེ། grib phogste, got a black spot; used also in the sense of "being stupid."

པ་ཆི་དཔལ་དོང་། Pachi dpal dong, name of the castle of treasures; the first part I cannot explain; the second means "well or pit of splendour."

རྟམ་ཕོངས། rtam phongs = rta 'aphongs, sit (behind you) on a horse.

No. 9.

ཨ་ཕི། aphi = aphyi, grand-mother; in Central Ladakh the pronunciation of this word is *abi*.

ཁ་ཚོད་བཅད་ཅེས། Kha thsod bcadces, spy out, examine.

ཅི་རེ། cire, what each = what kinds?

ཡབས། yabs = yab, father.

ཡབས་ཐོན་པ། yabs thonpa, name of 'aBruguma's father, "the beautiful (fair) father."

ཡུམ་སྔོན་མོ། yum sngonmo, name of 'aBruguma's mother, "the blue mother;" in the Sheh-version we find the name *chorol*.

འབྲི་གུ་མ། 'aBriguma, name of Kesar's bride; here the MS. has 'aBriguma instead of 'aBruguma; it means "the young female Yak." Just as in India, in Tibet also beautiful women are compared to cows; see Wintermythus der Kesarsage, No. V, 25.

ཡིན་ཚོད། yin thsod, yodthsod, it is, are forms of the dubitative.

ཨ་ཅོ། aco, lower Ladakhi for ajo, elder brother.

ཚེ་ཕོས་བཏང་ཅེས། thse phos btangces, to die; compare *'aboba* for *phos.*

ནོ། no, younger brother.

མགར་བ་བཀྲ་ཤིས། mGarba bkrashis, name of the smith of gLing; it means "the smith good-fortune."

དཀར་ཐིག་མོ། dKar thigmo, name of the first daughter of the smith of *gLing;* it means probably "the white-spotted one."

ནག་ཐིག་མ། nag thigma, name of the second daughter of the smith of gLing; it means probably "the black-spotted one."

མ་གོག་བཟང་ལྷ་མོ། ma gog bzang lhamo, name of the third daughter of the smith of gLing; here we find even *bazang* for *za;* the form *tsa,* which I am told, occurs in the epic, has not yet been discovered in the oral tales; the name means "mother good-ashes, the goddess."

དབང་པོ་རྒྱབ་བཞིན། dBangpo rgyab bzhin, name of the Lord of the gods; I am still keeping to this form of the name, because I find it spelled thus in the MS.; but because also the Mongolian version has Indra, it is quite possible that, as Prof. Grünwedel and Dr. Laufer suggest, the name ought to be spelled *brgya sbyin* = śatakratu. But it must be remembered that the latter mode of spelling the word can account only for the pronunciation *rgya zhin,* not for *rgyab zhin.*

དོན་ལྡན། Don ldan, name of the first son of the gods; it means "having an aim."

དོན་ཡོད། Don yod, name of the second son of the gods; it means "having an aim."

དོན་གྲུབ་དཀར་པོ། Don grub dkarpo, name of the third son of the gods; it means "the white one, fulfiller of the aim." The epithet "white" in the form of *garbo* can also be found in the Mongolian version. It is not at all necessary to speak of Buddhist influences, because the name Dongrub corresponds to Siddhârta. As has been shown, the name of Siddhârta was in common use as a personal name in Pre-Buddhist times, just as the name of Dongrub is often met with in Ladakh at the present time. Both may go back to similar mythological conceptions.

བྱ་ཁུ་ཡུག་རྒྱལ་པོ། bya Khuyug rgyalpo, name of the grand-father of the sun-bird; it means "the king-bird Khuyug."

བྱ་འོང་ལྡོ་རེ། bya 'ong ldore, name of the father of the sun-bird; does not appear to be Tibetan.

བྱ་ཉི་མ་ཁྱུང་རུང་། bya nyima khyuug rung, name of the sun-bird; it means "the sun-bird khyung rung." Here we see the application of laws of sound No. 3 (Ladakhi Grammar) with regard to the name of the sun-bird, which is in full *khyung dkrung*. (Compare the Ladakhi Prebuddhist Marriage Ritual in the "Indian Antiquary," 1901, Introduction). A similar case we find in the name Lamayuru with regard to the svastika. The latter part of this name is spelt even now-a-days γYung dkrung. The modern pronunciation of this name being yuru, has not only lost the tenuis before *r*, (besides the prefixes), but also the final *ng*.

བྱ་སོ་མིག་དམར། bya so mig dmar, name of the younger brother of the sun-bird; it means "bat red-eye."

ཀེ་སར། kesar, name of the hero of the saga; the passage in No. 9 speaks very much in favour of the view, that the name of Kesar is to be derived from *skye γsar*, the reborn one (newly born).

དེག། deg, pot; an Urdu word.

ཁ་ཡོན། kha yon, a crooked mouth.

སྒེ་མོ། sgemo = sgyemo, bag.

སྟོང་ཤོང་། stongshong, holding one thousand (bushels).

རྟའི་འགོ་ན། rtai 'agona, in the origin of the horse, *i.e.*, the first horse.

ཚ་ལངས། thsa langs, name of the first mare; the name means "rising of envy;" for this idiom compare 'A Ladakhi Bonpo Hymnal,' song No. IV, Note on No. 9. "Indian Antiquary," Vol. XXX, p. 361. In my paper 'the spring-myth of the Kesar-saga' we find the name ཚ་ལྡང་། thsa ldang, which probably means the same and can be translated in two ways.

རུ་ཡོན། ru yon, "crooked horns," name of the mother of all cattle.

ར་དཀར་མོ། ra dkarmo, "white goat," name of the mother of all goats.

དྲོ་མོ། dromo, "heat," name of the mother of all sheep.

ནག་པོ་ཁ་དཀར། nagpo Kha dkar, "black, and white mouth," name of the mother of all donkeys.

ཁྱི་མོ་དཀར་མོ། khyimo dkarmo, the white bitch, name of the mother of all dogs; in my 'springmyth of the Kesar-saga' she is called *drumbu brang dkar*.

བི་ལ་ནག་མོ། bila nagmo, black cat; name of the mother of all cats.

ཁ་ལ་མེ་བར། Khala me bar, "fire burns in the mouth;" name of a famous gelding.

སྒིད་བུ། sgidbu = sgyidbu, hearth-stone.

ཅུ་རུ། curu, = byiru, coral; a branch of corals is called a "hand of corals."

ཚིག་བུ། thsigbu = thsigu, grinding stone.

༄༅། གླིང་རྒྱལ་ལྷམ་ཀ་ཤར་གྱི་སྐྱེ་རབས། སྐྱུངས་ཡིན།

No. 1.

༄༅། དེ་ནས་དཔལ་ལེ་རྒོད་པོ་གླིང་གི་ར་རྫི་གཙོ་འིན་ཞིག་འདུགས། ཞག་ཅིག་རི་ལ་ར་མ་འཁྲིད་དེ་སོང་པ་སང་། རི་དཀར་པོའི་ནང་ནས་བྱ་དཀར་པོ་ཞིག་ཡོངས། རི་ནག་པོའི་ནང་ནས་བྱ་ནག་པོ་ཞིག་ཡོངས། ཁོས་བལྟ་སྡེ་འདུགས་པ། དེ་གཉིས་ཀས་རྩོལ་གྱུག་བདངས་པས། ཁོས་ཞིབ་ཆ་བལྟ་སྡེ་འདུགས་པ། སྔ་མོའི་དུས་ལ་བྱ་ནག་པོ་དེ་རྒྱལ་འཐབས་སོང་། ཉི་མ་ཕྱེད་ཟམ་ལ་གཉིས་ཀ་འདྲ་འདྲ་སོང་། ཕྱི་ཐོག་བྱ་དཀར་པོ་དེ་རྒྱལ་ཆོད་སོང་། དེ་ནས་ཁོས་བྱ་དཀར་པོ་རྒྱལ་ཆོད་སོང་བསམ་སྡེ་འཐད་གྱིན་ཞིག། ར་མ་འཁྲིད་དེ་ཕྱིར་ལོག་སྡེ་ཁང་པ་རུ་ཡོངས།

ཐོ་རངས་ཁོས་ཡང་དེན་ནའི་ས་ཁྲོད་ལ་བལྟ་ཅེས་ཕེ་ལ་ར་མ་འཁྲིད་དེ་སོང་བས། ཡང་དེ་རི་དཀར་པོ་ནས་གཡག་དཀར་པོ་ཞིག་ཕིང་སྡེ་ཡོངས། རི་ནག་པོ་ནས་གཡག་ནག་པོ་ཞིག་ཕིང་སྡེ་ཡོངས། ཡང་ཁོང་གཉིས་ཀ་རྩོལ་བས། སྔ་མོའི་དུས་ལ་གཡག་དཀར་པོ་རྒྱལ། ཉི་མ་ཕྱེད་ལ་གཉིས་ཀ་འདྲ་འདྲ་སོང་། ཕི་ཐོག་ལ་གཡག་ནག་པོ་རྒྱལ་རྒྱལ་རིག་ཆའད་ཚུག་པས། ཁོས་བསམ། དེ་གཡག་ནག་པོ་བདུད་ཅིག་ཡིན་ཆོད་འདུག། དེ་ཀཡག་ནག་པོ་ངས་བསད་ཡིན་བསམ་སྡེ། རི་ཐོན་པོ་ཞིག་ལ་སོང་སྡེ་གླུ་འདི་ལྟར།།

རི་དཀར་པོའི་ནང་ནས་གཡག་དཀར་པོ་ཞིག་ཐིང་ལོ།

རི་ནག་པོའི་ནང་ནས་གཡག་ནག་པོ་ཞིག་ཐིང་ལོ།

གཡག་དཀར་པོ་ལ་བལྟ་ན་སྤྲུང་བའི་ལྷ་ཞིག་ཡིན་ནམ།

གཡག་ནག་པོ་ལ་བལྟ་ན་ཟ་བའི་འདྲེ་ཞིག་ཡིན་ནམ།

གཡག་ནག་པོ་དེ་ངས་བསད་སྐྱིང་རིག་རག་ལོ།

མི་མིའི་དུས་ལ་གཡོགས་མཁན་རིག་ཡིན་ལོ།

ཨ་བའི་དུས་ལ་ལྷས་མཁན་རིག་ཡིན་ལོ།

བུ་ཚང་རི་དུས་ལ་ཁུར་མཁན་རིག་ཡིན་ལོ།

ར་ཡུག་བོང་མཐིལ་ཁྲི་ལྡུག་གསུམ་ཡོད་ལོ།

རྗོ་བ་ཆེ་ཆེ་ཟམ་ནི་ཧ་གྲོད་ཟམ་བདང་ཡིན་ལོ།

རྗོ་བ་བར་པ་ཟམ་ནི་གཡག་གྲོད་ཟམ་ཞིག་བདང་ཡིན།

ཆུང་ཆུང་ཟམ་ནི་ར་གྲོད་ཟམ་ཞིག་བདང་ཡིན་ལོ།

དེ་སང་ཆུང་ཆུང་ནི་འཇུག་མ་འཇུག་རིང་ཞིག་བདང་ཡིན་ལོ།

གཡག་ནག་པོའི་རུ་ཅོ་གཡས་པའི་ནང་དུ་བདང་ཡིན་

རུ་ཅོ་གཡས་པ་ལ་ལྷུམ་པ་བཅོ་བརྒྱད་རིག་འཕྱུད་ཡིན་ལོ།

ལྷུམ་པ་གཅིག་ནི་ལྷའི་དབང་པོ་རྒྱ་ཞིན་ལ་འཕྱུལ་ཡིན་ལོ།

ལྷུམ་པ་གཅིག་ནི་བར་བཙན་གྱི་ཨ་མ་སྐྱབས་བདུན་ལ་འཕྱུལ་ཡིན་ལོ།

ལྷུམ་པ་གཅིག་ནི་འོག་ཀླུའི་ཀླུ་རྒྱལ་ལྡོགས་པོ་ལ་འཕྱུལ་ཡིན།

ལྷུམ་པ་གཅིག་ནི་ཕ་ལྷ་སྐྱེར་རྫོང་སྟན་པོ་ལ་འཕྱུལ་ཡིན།

ལྷུམ་པ་གཅིག་ནི་མ་ལྷ་བཀུར་དམན་རྒྱལ་མོ་ལ་འཕྱུལ་ཡིན།

ལྷུམ་པ་གཅིག་ནི་གླིང་གི་དཔའ་བོ་བཅོ་བརྒྱད་ལ་འཕྲུལ་ཡིན།
ལྷུམ་པ་གཅིག་ནི་གླིང་མཁར་རྩེ་དགུའི་མགོ་ལ་འཕྲུལ་ཡིན།
ལྷུམ་པ་གཅིག་ནི་གསེར་པོའི་གསེར་རི་ལ་འཕྲུལ་ཡིན།
ལྷུམ་པ་གཅིག་ནི་སྔོན་པོའི་གཡུ་རི་ལ་འཕྲུལ་ཡིན།
ལྷུམ་པ་གཅིག་ནི་ཆུ་མིག་ཚང་ཡ་ལ་འཕྲུལ་ཡིན།
ལྷུམ་པ་གཅིག་ནི་གྲོ་མ་ཐང་གི་ཐང་འགོ་ལ་འཕྲུལ་ཡིན།
ལྷུམ་པ་གཅིག་ནི་དཔལ་མའི་ཨ་སྟག་ལ་འཕྲུལ་ཡིན།
ལྷུམ་པ་གཅིག་ནི་སྤྲི་ཆུ་རབས་སི་རབས་འགོ་ལ་འཕྲུལ་ཡིན།
ལྷུམ་པ་གཅིག་ནི་སྤྲོ་ཐོ་ནང་མའི་ལིངས་ས་རུ་འཕྲུལ་ཡིན།
ལྷུམ་པ་གཅིག་ནི་ཡབས་ཁྲོན་པ་དང་ཡུམ་སྔོན་མོ་ལ་འཕྲུལ་ཡིན།
ལྷུམ་པ་གཅིག་ནི་ཞེལ་ལྷམ་འབྲུ་གུ་མ་ལ་འཕྲུལ་ཡིན།
ལྷུམ་པ་གཅིག་ནི་ལྷེམ་ལྷེམ་མི་ལྷེམ་མཁར་ལ་འཕྲུལ་ཡིན།
ལྷུམ་པ་གཅིག་ནི་དཔལ་ལེ་ང་རང་ལ་བོར་ཡིན།

དེ་ཟུག་ཟེར་རིན་ཞིག་དང་ཁོས་ དབྱུག་རྡོ་བཏང་སྟེ་ གཡག་ནག་པོ་དེ་ཤི་སོང་། གཡག་ནག་པོ་དེ་བདུད་ཙུ་ཙུ་ལུ་གུ་ཡིན་ཚུག། གཡག་དཀར་པོ་དེ་ལྷའི་དབང་པོ་རྒྱབ་ཞིན་ཡིན་ཚུག། དེ་ཞག་ལ་དཔལ་ལེ་རྒོད་པོས་གཡག་ནག་དེ་མ་བསད་ས་པིན་ན། བདུད་ཙུ་ཙུ་ལུ་གུ་དེ་རྒྱལ་ནས། ལྷའི་དབང་པོ་རྒྱབ་ཞིན་དེ་བསད་ཅེས་ཡོད་ཚུག། དེ་ནས་རི་དཀར་པོའི་ནང་ནས་སྦྲུ་གུ་ཁྲུ་གང་ཟམ་ཞིག་ཕིང་སྟེ་དཔལ་ལེ་རྒོད་པོའི་མདུན་ལ་ཡོང་སྟེ་ཟེར་ས་ཟ། དཔལ་ལེ་ཁྱོད་ང་ལ་དྲིན་ཅན་སོང་། འདི་རིང་ཉེ་རང་མེད་པིན་ན། ང་བདུད་ཀྱིས་བསད་ཅེས་ཡོད་པིན།

ཁྱེད་ལ་ངས་ཊན་པ་རྒྱལ་བ་ཞིག་བཏང་ཡིན། མཁར་བྱེད་བཏང་ཡིན། ཡུལ་གྱི་བྱེད་བཏང་ཡིན། ནོར་ཅི་དགོས་མཁན་བཏང་ཡིན། དེ་ནས་དཔལ་ལེ་རྒོད་པོས་ཟེར་སྐབས། ང་ལ་ཊན་པ་ཅིའང་མི་དགོས། རྟོན་པའི་ཡི་ལ་ངས་གཡག་ནག་པོ་མ་བསདས་པིན། ཉི་རང་ལྷའི་དབང་པོ་རྒྱབ་ཞིན་ཡིན་ན། ངས་མ་ཤེས། ཡིན་ན་རྒྱལ་ལ་སོང༌། ཉི་རང་ལ་བུ་ཚ་དོན་ཡོད་དོན་ལྡན་དོན་གྲུབ་གསུམ་ཡོད་ལོ། དེའི་ནང་ནས་ཕྲུ་གུ་གཅིག། ང་ཞ་གླིང་མགོ་མེད་ལ་མགོ་ལ་སྦུལ་ན། ང་འཐད་ཅེས་རག་ཟེརས། དེ་ནས་ལྷའི་དབང་པོ་རྒྱབ་ཞིན་གྱིས་ཟེརས་པ། ཕྲུ་གུ་གཅིག་ནི་བལྟ་བའི་མིག་གཡས་པ་ཡིན། གཅིག་ནི་མིག་གཡོན་པ་ཡིན། གཅིག་ནི་ཟསམ་པའི་སྙིང་ཡིན! ཡིན་སྐྱང་དཔལ་ལེ་ཁྱོད་ནིང་ངའི་སྒྲོ་སྒྲིག་ལ་སྐྱོབས་བཅོས་པ་སང༌། སེན་མི་ཟེར། ང་སོང་སྟེ་སྟེང་ལྷ་ཡུལ་ལ་ཕྲུ་གུ་ཀུན་ལ་འདྲི་སྟེ་ཞག་བདུན་ལ་བཟང་ངན་བཏང་ཡིན་ཟེར་དེ་ཁ་ཆད་བཅོས།།

No. 2.

དེ་ནས་ལྷའི་དབང་པོ་རྒྱབ་ཞིན་སྟེང་ལྷ་ཡུལ་ལ་སོང་བས། དཔལ་ལེ་རྒོད་པོས་ར་མ་འཁྲིད་དེ་རང་གི་ཡུལ་ལ་ཡོངས། ལྷའི་དབང་པོ་རྒྱབ་ཞིན་དེ་རང་གི་ མཁར་ ལ་ བསླེབ་ སྟེ་ ནང་ མིག་ ཅིག་ གི་ ནང་ དུ་ མགོ་བདུམ་ སྟེ་ གཉིད་ ལོག་ སྟེ་འདུགས། དེ་ནས་བུ་དོན་ལྡན་གྱིས་གསང་མ་དང་གསོལ་ཛ་ཁྱེར་སྟེ་ཞུས་པ། ཨ་བ་ལེ། གསོལ་ཛ་དང་གསང་མ་འདོན་ལེ། ཉི་རང་ལ་ཚེར་ཀ་ཅི་དྲག། དེ་ནས་ཨ་བས་ཟེརས་པ། འདི་རིང་བདུད་ཙུ་རྩུ་ཕྲུ་གུ་དང་ང་འཐམ་མོ་སོང་སྟེ། བདུད་རྒྱལ་དེ་ང་བསད་ཅེས་ཡོད་པ་ཡིན། དེ་ནས་གླིང་པའི་དཔལ་ལེ་རྒོད་པོ་ཡོང་སྟེ། བདུད་ཙུ་རྩུ་ཕྲུ་གུ་དེ་བསད་སོང༌། དེ་ནས་ངའི་སྒྲིག་ཐར་སོང༌། ཁོ་ལ་ཊན་པ་ཞིག་བཏང་ཡིན་ཟེརས་པ། ཁོས་ཅིའང་མི་དགོས། ཁྱེད་རང་ལ་བུ་ཚ

གསུམ་འདུག། དེའི་ནང་ནས་གླིང་མགོ་མེད་ལ་མགོ་བཙོ་ཅེས་ལ། ཕྲུ་གུ་གཅིག་རྡོང་ཟེར་འདུག། ཁྱེད་ཆ་ན་ངས་ཛ་དང་ཟ་ཅེས་ཟ་ཡིན། དེ་མིན་ན་མི་ཟ་ཟེརས་པ། དེ་ནས་ཕྲུ་གུ་དོན་ལྡན་གྱིས་ང་མི་ཆ། ལྷའི་ཕྲུ་གུ་མི་ཡི་ཡུལ་ལ་ག་རྒྱུག་ལ་ཆ་ཡིན། ཟ་ཅེས་ཟ་ན་ཟོ། མ་ཟ་ན་ངོར་ཟེར་དེ་ལོག་སྟེ་ཡོངས།

དེ་ནས་ཡང་ནོ་བར་པས་ཛ་དང་ཟ་ཅེས་འཁྲར་དེ་འཁྱེར་ནས་ཨ་བ་ལ་ཞུས་པ། ཨབ་རྒྱལ་པོ་ལེ། གསང་མ་དང་གསོལ་ཛ་འདོན་ལེ། ཉེ་རང་ལ་ཐུགས་སྐྱོ་ཅིའི་ཕི་ལ་བཞུགས་འདུག། ཡང་ཨ་བས་ཟེརས། ནོ་རང་གླིང་མགོ་མེད་ལ་མགོ་ལ་ཆ་ན་ངས་ཟ་ཅེས་ཟ་ཡིན། དེ་མིན་ན་མི་ཟ། དེ་བུ་ཚས་ཀྱང་ང་ལྷའི་ཕྲུ་གུ་མིའི་ཡུལ་ལ་ཕི་ཆ་ཟེརས། ཟ་ཅེས་ཟ་ན་ཟོ། མ་ཟ་ན་འདུག་ཟེར་དེ་ཡོངས།

དེ་ནས་ཆུང་ཧྲགས་དོན་གྲུབ་དཀར་པོ་ཡོང་སྟེ་ཞུས་པ། ཡབ་རྒྱལ་པོ་ལེ། འདི་རིང་ཉེ་རང་ལ་ཐུགས་སྐྱོ་ཅི་ལ་དྲག། གསང་མ་འདོན་གསོལ་ཛ་འདོན་ལེ་ཟེརས། ཨ་བས་འདི་རིང་བདུད་ཙུ་རྩུ་ལྔུ་གུས་ང་བསད་ཅེས་ཡོད་པིན་པ། མི་ཡུལ་ལི་ཨ་ག་དཔལ་ལེ་ཟེར་མཁན་པོ་ཡོང་སྟེ། བདུད་དེ་བསད་སོང་། ངའི་སྲོག་ཐར་སོང་། ཁོ་ལ་དྲིན་པ་ལ་ཕྲུ་གུ་གཅིག་གླིང་མགོ་མེད་ལ་མགོ་ལ་བཏང་ཆད་ཡིན། ཁྱེད་རང་ཆ་ན། ངས་ཟ་ཅེས་ཟ་ཡིན། དེ་མིན་ན་ངས་མི་ཟ་ཟེརས། དེ་ཕྲུ་གུས་ཞུས་པ། ཨ་བ྄་རང་གིས་ག་རྩ་བཏང་ནའང་ང་ཆེན། ཤི་ས་ལ་བཏང་ནའང་། སྡོར་ས་ལ་བཏང་ནའང་ང་ཆེན། ཨ་བ྄་རང་གིས་འདོན་ཐང་འདོན་ལེ་ཟེརས།

དེ་ནས་ཨ་བྲ་འཕྲད་དེ་ཟ་ཅེས་ཟེར།།

No. 3.

དེ་ནས་རྫིང་མ་ཞིག་ལ་རྒྱལ་པོས་བུ་ཚ་ཚང་ཀ་ལ་ཟེར་ས་པ། འདི་རིང་ཁྲིད་ཚང་ཀོའི་ནང་ན་སུ་རྒྱལ་པོག་བལྟ་ཡིན། མདའ་རྫོང་ཅོ་གང་རེ་ཁུར། དེ་ཝུ་ཚགས་མ་གང་རེ་ཁུར། ཧ་རྒྱལ་བ་རེ་རེ་ལ་ཞོན་དེ་ཐུར་ལ་ངང་བཏང་གིན་ཞིག། དེ་ཝུ་ཚགས་མ་གང་པོ་གཡོག་གིན་སོང་། གྲིན་ལ་བང་འཁྱིང་ཟ་ན། མདའ་རེ་རེ་ལ་དེ་ཝུ་སྐར་གྲིན་ཡོང་། འདྲ་འདྲ་ཆ་རྒྱུག། སྤུ་ཞིག་ལ་ཉན་ནའང་། འདིར་བོར་ཡིན། ཕམ་མཁན་པོ་གླིང་མགོ་མེད་ལ་མགོ་ལ་བཏང་ཡིན་ཟེར་དེ། མདའ་བསག་སྟག་གང་རེ་དང་། དེ་ཝུ་ཚགས་མ་གང་རེ་བཀལ་དེ། ཧ་རྒྱུགས་བཏང་རྒྱུགས། ཐུར་ལ་ཆ་ཟ་ན། དེ་ཝུ་གཡོག་གིན་ཞིག་སོང་། ལོག་ལམ་ལ་ཧའི་བང་གི་ནང་དུ་དེ་ཝུ་བསྐྱུ་འཇིན་ཞིག་མདའ་ལ་སྐར་རིན་ཞིག་ཡོངས་པ། ཨ་ཅོ་དང་ནར་པ་གཉིས་ཀ་ལ་ལྷ་དྲུག་རེ་མིན་བ་སྐར་མ་ཐུབ། ནོ་ཆུང་ཅུན་པོ་ལ་ཚང་མ་བསྐྱུ་སྟེ་མདའ་རེ་རེ་ལ་སྐར་ཚར་དེ་འདྲ་འདྲ་སོང་།

ཡང་རྫིང་མ་ཞིག་ལ་ཁོང་ལ་ཅུང་དཀར་བྲི་གང་རེ་བཀལ་དེ་ཟེར་ས། ཁྲིད་ཀུན་ཐུར་ལ་ཆ་ཟ་ན། ཅུང་དཀར་གཡོག་གིན་ཞིག་སོང་། ཁྲིན་ལ་བང་འཁྱིང་སྟེ་བང་གི་ནང་ན་ཅུང་དཀར་བསྐྱུ་འཇིན་ཞིག་འཁྱིང་སྟེ་བྲི་སྐང་དགོས་ཟེར་ས། ཁོང་ལ་ཧ་རེ་རེ་བཏང་སྟེ་རྒྱུག་རྒྱུགས། ཐུར་ལ་ཆ་ཟ་ནགཡོག་གིན་སོང་། གྲིན་ལ་ཡོང་ཟ་ན་ཅུང་དཀར་བསྐྱུ་འཇིན་ཞིག་ཡོངས་པ། ཨ་ཅོ་དང་ནར་པ་གཉིས་ཀ་ལ་ལྷ་དྲུག་རེ་མིན་བ་མ་ཐོབ། ནོ་ཆུང་ཅུན་པོ་ལ་ཚང་མ་བསྐྱུ་ཚར་དེ་བྲི་སྐང་སྟེ་ཁྱོངས།

དེ་ནས་ཨ་ཅོ་དང་ནར་པ་གཉིས་ཀ་ལ་སེམས་ངན་སོང་སྟེ་ཟེར་ས།

ང་དང་གཉིས་ཀ་ཅི་ཡང་མ་རྒྱལ་པ་སང༌། གླིང་མགོ་མེད་ལ་མགོ་ལ་བཏང་ཅེས་སོང༌། ནོ་རྩུང་ཙུན་རྒྱལ་པ་སང༌། འདིར་ལྷ་ཡུལ་ལ་འདུག་ཅེས་སོང་ཟེརས། དེ་ནས་ཡང་ཨ་བས་ཟེརས། ཁྲིད་དང་བུ་ཚ་ཚང་ཀ་རི་ལ་ཡིངས་ལ་སོང་ཞིག། སུ་ལ་སྐྱིན་དང་འབྲོང་མང་པོ་ཉན་ནདང། གླིང་ཡུལ་ལ་མི་བཏང། སུ་ལ་མ་ཉར་ན། གླིང་ཡུལ་ལ་བཏང་ཡིན་ཟེར་དེ། ཁོང་ཡིངས་ལ་བཏངས། དེ་ནས་ཁོང་ལུང་པ་རི་རིའི་ནང་ལ་སོང་སྟེ། ཨ་ཅི་དང་བར་པ་གཉིས་ཀ་ལ་སྤྲག་པ་གཅིག་ཡང་མ་ཉན། ནོ་རྩུང་ཙུན་པོ་ལ་སྐྱིན་དང་འབྲོང་མང་པོ་ཉན་དེ། ལུང་པ་ཞིག་གི་ནང་དུ་ཡོད་ཚུག། ཨ་ཅོ་གཉིས་ཀ་ལ་ཅི་ཡང་མི་ཉན་ཅེས་ཞེས་དེ་ཁོས་ཟེརས་པ། ལྷ་ཨ་ཅོ་གཉིས་ཀ། སྐྱིན་དང་འབྲོང་མང་པོ་ང་ལ་ཉན་དེ་ཡོད། ཁྲི་ཞ་གཉིས་ཀས་ཅི་བརྩལ་འདུག། འདིར་ཡོང་ཞིག་ཟེརས། དེ་ནས་ཁོང་གཉིས་ཀ་ཡང་དེ་རུ་སོང་སྟེ་བལྟས་པ། སྐྱིན་དང་འབྲོང་མང་པོ་བསད་དེ་ལུང་པ་ཚང་མ་བསྐང་སྟེ་ཡོད་ཚུག། དེ་ནས་ཁོང་ལ་ཐེབ་སེམས་ངན་སྐྱེ་སྟེ་ཟེརས་པ། དགས་ཁོ་ཟུམ་སྟེ། འདི་ཞིང་རྒྱལ་པོ་ལ་བདག་སྟེ་བོར་ཡིན་ཟེར་དེ། ཁོ་ཞིང་རྒྱལ་ཆེན་པོའི་རྩ་བཅིང་སྟེ་བོར་དེ། ཁོང་རང་གཉིས་ཀས་ཁོ་ལ་ཉན་མཁར་ནི་སྐྱིན་རེ་རེ་ཁུར་དེ། ཁང་པ་རུ་ཡོངས། ཡབ་རྒྱལ་པོས་ཡང་ཕྲུ་གུ་རྩུང་ཙུན་གར་ཡོད་མ་འདྲིས།

དེ་ནས་ཕྲུ་གུ་ཞིང་རྒྱལ་ལི་དྲིམ་པའི་རྩ་འདུགས་པ། དེ་རི་མཐོན་པོ་ཞིག་གི་མགོ་ནས་མི་ཡ་མཚན་ཞིག་བིང་ཅེས་མཐོངས། མིའི་སྟོད་དེ་དཀར་པོ། སྨད་པ་དམར་པོ་མཇུག་མ་ནག་པོ་ཡོད་ ཀཁན་ཞིག་གིས་ཁོ་ལ་གདམ་ལན་ལ་གླུ་འདི་ལྟར་བླང་སོ།

ཞིང་རྒྱལ་ལི་རྩ་ལ་ཡོད་པའི་མིས་དངོས་ལ་ཉེན་དང།

ཞིང་རྒྱལ་ལི་དྲིམ་ལ་བཅིངས་པའི་ཕྲུ་གུས་བདག་ཅིག་ལ་གསན།

ཁྱོད་ནི་ཕ་མ་ལ་ལན་ལོག་བཏང་མཁན་ཞིག་ཡིན་ནམ།
ཁྱེད་ནི་ཁྲི་བསད་མི་བསད་བཏང་མཁན་ཞིག་ཡིན་ནམ།
ཁྱེད་ནི་ཀུན་མ་མང་པོ་བཅོ་མཁན་ཞིག་ཡིན་ནམ།
ཁྱེད་ཀྱིས་ཅི་བཅོས་མཁན་ཞིག་ཡིན་ང་ལ་ཤོད་འདང་།

དེ་མིས་དེ་ཟླུག་ཟེརས་པ་སང། ཕྲུ་གུ་ལ་སྐྱོ་ཡོང་སྟེ། དེ་མི་ལ་ལན་དུ་གླུ་བཏངས།

ཁྱོད་སྟོད་དཀར་པོ་ཡོད་པའི་མིས་ངའི་དངོས་ལ་ཉེན།
སྨྱིད་པ་དམར་པོ་ཡོད་པའི་མིས་ཕྲུ་གུ་ངའི་བདག་ལ་གསན།
ཤམ་ནག་པོ་ཡོད་མཁན་གྱིས་ངའི་དངོས་ལ་ཉེན་དང་།
ཁྱོད་ཁྲ་སྤུག་ཡོད་པའི་མིས་ངའི་དོན་དག་ཅི་དགོས།
ང་ཕ་མ་ལ་ལན་ལོག་བཏང་མཁན་ཞིག་རང་ཡིན་ལོ།
ངས་ཁྲི་བསད་མི་བསད་བཏང་མཁན་ཞིག་ཡིན་ལོ།
ངས་ཀུན་མ་ཀུས་མཁན་ཞིག་ཡང་ཡིན་ལོ།
ཁྱོད་དེས་ང་ལ་སྐྱིབ་ཅིག་ལྟོས་ལོ།

དེ་ཟླུག་ཟེར་དེ། ཤིང་རྒྱལ་དེ་པ་དྲག་ནས་ཕྱུད་དེ་ཁྱེར་དེ། ཁང་པ་ལ་ཁྱོང་སྟེ། དེ་ཤིང་རྒྱལ་པོ་ཁང་པའི་སྒོ་ལ་ཁྱོངས་སྟེ། ངའི་ཕ་མ་གཉིས་ཀ་ལ་བསིལ་ཞིག་ལྷན་ཤིག་ཟེར་དེ། དེ་རུ་ཁོས་བཙུགས།

དེ་ནས་ཡང་ཞག་ཅིག་ཁོང་སང་ལུང་པ་ཞིག་གི་ནང་དུ་ཡིངས་ལ་བཏངས་པ། ཨ་ཙོ་དང་བར་པ་ལ་སང་ཅི་སང་མ་ཉན་པས། ནོ་དེ་ལ་སྐྱིན་ཤ་བ་སྣ་སོགས་མང་པོ་ཉན་སོང་། ཡང་དེ་ནོས་ཟེརས། ཕྲ་ཨ་ཙོ་གཉིས་ཀ། ང་ལ་མང་པོ་ཉན་དེ་ཡོད། ཁྲི་ཞ་གཉིས་ཀ་སང་འདེར་ཡོང་ཤིག་ཟེརས་པ།

དེ་ནས་ཁོང་གཉིས་ཀ་ཡང་ངེ་རུ་སོད་སྡེ་བལྟས་པ་སང༌། སྐྱིན་དང་ཤ་བ་འབྲོང་མང་པོ་བསད་དེ་ཡོད་ཚུག་པས། ཁོང་ལ་ཁྲེབ་སེམས་ཅན་སྐྱེས། ཁོང་གིས་ཟེརས། འདི་རིང་ཡང་ཁོ་རྒྱལ་སོང༌། ད་ཅི་བཅོ་དགོས། ཁོ་ནི་ཕ་མ་འི་རྩར་འདུག་ཅེས་སོང༌། ང་དང་གང་པོ་བདང་ནའང་གླིང་ཡུལ་ལ་བདང་ཅེས་སོང༌། ཁོ་ལ་ཅི་བཅོ་ཡིན། ཨ་མ་གཅིག་ལ་སྐྱེས་མཁན་ཡིན། བསད་ཅེས་པ་སང་ས་ཁྲང་ཞིག་གི་ནང་དུ་བདང་ཡིན་ཟེར་དེ། ཁོང་གཉིས་ཀས་ས་ཞིག་བྲུ་སྡེ་ས་མདོང་ཞིག་བཅོ་སྡེ། ཁོ་དེའི་ནང་དུ་བདང་སྡེ། ཁ་ལ་རྡོ་བ་ཆེན་མོ་ཞིག་ཁྱེར་སྡེ་ནན་དེ་བོརས། ཁོང་རང་གཉིས་ཀས་ཤ་རེ་ཁུར་ནས་ཁང་པ་ལ་ཡོངས། དེ་ས་དོང་གི་ཁ་ནས་བི་གང་ཚུང་ཙུན་ཞིག་ཞུས་དེ་ཡོད་ཚུག། དེ་བི་གང་པོའི་མདུན་ཡ་ཡངས་པ་ཞིག་བསླེབ་སོང༌། དེ་ཡངས་པ་ལ་དེ་བི་གང་པོའི་ནང་ན་མིའི་དྲི་མ་ཞིག་ཚོར་དེ་སྨྲུམས་པ། བི་གང་ནང་ནས་ས་འབུད་དེ་བྲུ་གུ་དེའི་མགོའི་ཁ་ཕོག། དེ་རྒྱུག་ཚོར་དེ་ཁོས་གླུ་འདི་ལྟར་སྨངས།།

འདི་དོང་གི་ནང་དུ་ས་བདང་མཁན་དེ་སུ་ཞིག་རང་ཡིན་ལོ།
ངའི་བཙོན་ཁང་ནང་དུ་ས་འཕང་མཁན་དེ་སུ་ཞིག་ཡིན་ལོ།
ང་ཉིག་ངའི་ཨ་ཅོ་གཉིས་ཀས་བཀག་སྡེ་རིག་ཡོད་ལོ།
ངའི་ཨ་ཅོ་གཉིས་ཀས་བཙོན་ལ་བདང་སྡེ་རིག་ཡོད་ལོ།
ང་མ་ཤེས་ན་ལྷའི་དབང་པོ་རྒྱབ་ཞིན་གྱི་བུ་ཞིག་རང་ཡིན་ལོ།
ང་མ་ཤེས་ན་བུ་དོན་གྲུབ་དཀར་པོ་ཞིག་རང་ཡིན་ལོ།
དེའི་ཁ་ཡོད་མཁན་པོ་ལྷ་ཞིག་ཡིན་ན་འདྲེ་ཞིག་ཡིན་ལོ།
ཁྱེ་ཞ་སུ་ཞིག་རང་ཡིན་ནའང༌། རང་གི་གནས་ལ་སོང་ཤིག།

ཁོས་ས་དོང་གི་ནང་ན་དེ་ཟུག་ཅིག་ཟེརས་པ།
ལྷངས་པས་ཡང་གླུ་འདི་ལྷར་སླངས༎
དོང་གི་མཐིལ་ན་ཡོད་པའི་མི་ཆུང་གིས་དངོས་ལ་ཉོན་དང།
སའི་ནང་ཡོད་པའི་ལྷ་ཕྲུག་གིས་འང་བདག་ལ་གསན་དང།
ཉི་རང་སའི་ནང་དུ་ཅི་ལ་བཏངས་སོ།
ཉི་རང་ཕ་མ་ལ་ལན་ལོག་བཏང་མཁན་ཞིག་ཡིན་ནམ།
ཉི་རང་ཁྲི་བསད་མི་བསད་བཏང་མཁན་ཞིག་ཡིན་ནམ།
ཉི་རང་ངས་ཕིང་ན་ཕིང་ཐབས་ཤིག་རང་མེད་ལོ།
ངའི་ཊི་མ་ལ་འཐམས་ན་ཟབ་ཟབ་རིག་ཡོད་ལོ།
དེ་བོ་རྩོག་པོ་རིག་མ་ཚོར་ན་དེ་ཊི་མ་ལ་འཐོམས་ལོ།
ངས་ནི་ཅམ་ཐུབ་གྱིན་ལ་འཐེན་ཡིན།

དེ་ལྩངས་པས་དེ་ཟུག་ཟེར་དེ་ཊི་མ་དེ་བི་གང་བོའི་ནང་ནས་ཐུར་ལ་བཏངས་པས། ཕྲུ་གུས་དེ་ཊ་མ་ལ་འཐམས་ཏེ་གྱེན་ལ་ཡོངས། དེ་བི་གང་པོ་ཆུང་ཙན་ཡོད་པས། ཕྲུ་གུ་དེའི་ཤ་དང་སྤགས་པ་ཚང་མ་རྗོ་བས་ཤུ་སྐྱེ་འཁྱིར་ཏེ་ཙམ་པ་མེན་ནེ་མ་ལུས། དེ་ནས་ཁོ་རང་ཕི་སྤུ་ལ་བིང་སྐྱེ་ཤ་ཚང་མ་ལ་ཐྲ་ཐྲུ་ཟེར་པ། ཤ་དང་སྤགས་པ་མལ་ལ་སོང་། ཤ་དེ་ཚང་མ་པོ་ཡད་ལ་གྱུར་སོང་། དེ་རྗོ་བ་གཉིས་ཀ་མགོའི་ཁ་འཁུར་ཏེ་ཁྱོང་སྐྱེ་ཁང་པའི་མདུན་ལ་འཁྱིར་ཏེ། ཤིང་རྒྱལ་ལི་ཡོག་ལ་བོར་ཏེ་ཁོས་སློན་ལམ་ཞིག་བཏབས། ཡ་དཀོན་མཆོག་མཁྱེན་མཁྱེན། འདི་རྗོ་བ་དེ་ཡབ་རྒྱལ་པོ་དང་ཡུམ་རྒྱལ་མོ་གཉིས་ཀ་ལ་ཞུ་པེན་ནི་ལྷངས་བུ་ལྷན་ཅིག། རྗོ་བའི་འོག་ན་བདུད་རྩིའི་ཆུ་མིག་བིང་ཤིག། མཐའ་

མ་རྫུན་དེ་ཨམ་བི་དི་ཕྲུ་ལུ་དང་འབྲས་བུ་མང་པོ་སྨིན་ཤིག་ཟེར་དེ། རྗོ་བ་དེ་རུ་བོརས། དེ་ནས་ཆུ་མིག་དང་ཤིང་འབྲས་བུ་སྣ་མི་སྣ་ཚང་སྐྱེས་སོང་། ཁོ་ནང་ལ་སོང་སྟེ་ཡབ་རྒྱལ་པོའི་པང་ངེ་ཁ་བསྐོ་སྟེ་དུ་ཡུ་ཟེརས་པས། ཡབ་རྒྱལ་པོས། འདི་རིང་ངལ་ལ་ཕྲ་བུ་ཚ་ཟེརས། བུ་ཚས་འདི་རིང་མང་པོ་ངལ་སོང་ལེ་ཟེ་རས།།

No. 4.

དེ་ནས་ དཔལ་ ལེ་གྲོད་ པོས་ ཞག་ བདུན་ ལ་ ལན་ བསླེབ་ ཅེས་ ཡིན་པ། ལན་ཅི་ཡང་མ་བསླེབ་བསམ། དེ་རིའི་ཁ་བསླེབ་སྟེ་མིན་བ། དཔལ་ལེ་གྲོད་པོ་ལ་ཡང་ཡིད་དུ་ཡོང་བ་མེད་ཙུག། དེ་ནས་ཁོས་ཡིད་དུ་ཡོང་ཅེས་སི་ཕི་ལ། ར་མ་དཀར་མོ་ཞིག་གི་སྣ་མཆོག་ལ་ཙ་རག་ཅིག་བདག་སྟེ་ཁྲིངས། ར་མ་སག་འཁྲིད་དེ་ཁང་པ་ལ་ཁྲིངས། དེ་ནས་དཔལ་ལེའི་ཨ་ནེ་དེ་ར་མའི་འོ་མ་བཙིར་ཅེས་ལ་སོང་སྟེ། ར་མ་དཀར་མོའི་སྣ་མཆོག་གི་ཙ་རག་རེ་ར་མའི་འགྲམ་པ་ལ་ཕོག་པ་སང་། དང་གི་པ་རི་བཙག་སྟེ་འོ་མ་ཚང་མ་པོས་བདངས། དེ་ནས་ཁོ་ལ་སྒྲོ་ཡོང་སྟེ་ཀ་ཅོ་ཆེན་པོ་བདང་གིན་ཞིག་ཡོངས་པ། དཔལ་ལེ་གྲོད་པོ་ལ་ཡིད་དུ་ཡོང་སྟེ། ཕྲོ་རི་སྤྲ་མོ་ཙུག་པོ་ལ་སྟེང་ལྷ་ཡུལ་ལ་སོང་། ཁོས་ལུང་མཁན་ཞིག་བཅོ་སྟེ་སོང་བ། རིམ་པ་བཞིན་དུ་སྟེང་ལྷ་ཡུལ་ལ་བསླེབ། དེ་ནས་ལྷའི་དབང་པོ་རྒྱབ་ཞིན་ཉི་མ་ཞིག་ལ་འདུག་སྟེ་ཡོད་ཙུག། དེ་ནས་དཔལ་ལེ་གྲོད་པོས་གླུ་ཞིག་འདི་ལྟར་བླངས།

ལྷའི་དབང་པོ་རྒྱབ་ཞིན་ཞུག་ཉིད་ལ་ཞུགས་ལོ།
ཀྱེད་ཀྱིན་ཀྱེད་ཀྱིན་ཕྱུག་གསུམ་རིག་ཕྱུལ་ཡིན།

ཀྱེ་མ་སྐྱུ་སྟེ་ཞུ་ཕྲུལ་རིག་ཡང་ཕྲུལ་ཡིན།

ཁ་བདག་དཀར་པོ་ཞིག་མཛལ་དར་ལ་ཕྲུལ་ཡིན།

ང་ལ་རྟ་ཞིག་བཙོང་ཅེས་མི་འདུག་ག་ལེ།

དཔལ་ལེ་རྒོད་པོས་དེ་ཐུག་ཞུས་པ།

ལྷའི་དབང་པོ་རྒྱབ་ཞིན་གྱིས་ལན་ལ་གླུ་འདི་ལྟར།

རྟ་ཞིག་འདིར་བཙོང་ཅེས་མེད་དཔལ་ལེ་ལེ།

རྟ་ཞིག་འདིར་བཙོང་ཅེས་མེད་རྒོད་པོ་ལེ།

གསེར་ཅ་ཞིག་ཉིད་ལ་ལམ་བཙུགས་ལ་བདང་ཡིན།

དེ་ཐུག་ཟེར་དེ། གསེར་ཅ་ཞིག་ལམ་བཙུགས་ལ་བདངས། དེ་ནས་གསེར་ཅ་དེ་ཁྲར་ནས་དཔལ་ལེ་ཕྱིར་ལོག་ཡོང་སྟེ། འོག་ཀླུ་ཡུལ་ལ་སོང་། དེ་རུ་ཀླུ་རྒྱལ་ལྡོགས་པོ་མཐོང་སྟེ་གླུ་འདི་ལྟར་བླངས།

ཀླུའི་ཀླུ་རྒྱལ་ལྡོག་པོ་དེ་ཞུག་ཉིད་ལ་ཞགས་ལོ།

ཀྱེད་ཀྱིན་ཀྱེད་ཀྱིན་ཕྲུག་གསུམ་རིག་ཕྲུལ་ཡིན།

ཀྱེ་མ་སྐྱུ་སྟེ་ཞུ་བ་གསུམ་ཕྲུལ་ཡིན།

ཁ་བདག་དཀར་པོ་ཞིག་མཛལ་དར་ལ་ཕྲུལ་ཡིན།

ང་ལ་རྟ་ཞིག་བཙོང་ཅེས་མེད་ད་ཀླུ་རྒྱལ་ལྡོག་པོ་ལེ།

དེ་ཐུག་ཞུ་བ་ཕྲུལ་པ་སང། ཀླུ་རྒྱལ་ལྡོག་པོས་ལན་དུ་གླུ་འདི་ལྟར་བླངས།

རྟ་ཞིག་བཙོང་ཅེས་ང་ལ་མེད་དཔལ་ལེ་ལྷ།

རྟ་ཞིག་བཙོང་རྒྱུ་ང་ལ་མེད་རྒོད་པོ་ལྷ།

གཡུའི་གཡུ་ཅ་ཞིག་ཁྲེད་ལ་ལམ་བཙུགས་ལ་བདང་ཡིན།

དེ་ཟུག་ཟེར་དེ་གཡུ་ཙ་ཞིག་བདངས་པ་སང༌། དཔལ་ལེས་དེ་ཁུར་དེ་ཕྱིར་ལོག་ཡོང་སྟེ་བར་བཙན་ཡུལ་ལ་སོང༌། དེ་རུ་བསླེབ་སྟེ་ཨ་མ་སྐྱབས་བདུན་མ་ལ་ཞུས། གླུ་འདི་ལྟར།

ཨ་མ་སྐྱབས་བདུན་མ་ཞུ་ག་ཉིད་ལ་ཞུགས་ལོ།
ཀྱེད་ཀྱིན་ཀྱེད་ཀྱིན་ཕྱུག་གསུམ་རིག་ཕྱུལ་ཡིན།
ཀྱེ་མ་སྐྲུ་སྟེ་ཞུ་བ་ཞིག་ཕྱུལ་ཡིན།
ཁ་བདག་དཀར་པོ་འི་མཛལ་དར་ཞིག་ཕྱུལ་ཡིན།
ང་ལ་ཧྲ་ཞིག་བཙོང་ཅེས་རིག་མེད་ད།

ཁོས་དེ་ཟུག་ཞུས་པ་སང༌། ཨ་མ་སྐྱབས་བདུན་གྱིས་ལན་ལ་གླུ་འདི་ལྟར་སླངས།

ཁྱེད་ལ་ཧྲ་ཞིག་དགོས་ན་བཙོང་ཅེས་ཡོད་དཔལ་ལེ་ལྷ།
ཧྲ་ཞིག་ཉོ་ན་བཙོང་ཅེས་ཞིག་ཡོད་ཆོད་པོ་ལྷ།
ཧྲའི་སྤུ་ཅག་རེ་ལ་རིན་ཆེ་གྲངས་རེ་ཟེར་ཅན།

ཨ་མ་སྐྱབས་བདུན་མས་དེ་ཟུག་ཟེརས་པ་སང༌། དཔལ་ལེས་ལན་དུ་གླུ་འདི་ལྟར་སླངས།།

ཨ་མ་སྐྱབས་བདུན་མས་ངའི་དངོས་ལ་ཉེན་དང༌།
ལོ་གསུམ་གླིང་པའི་ར་རྫེ་རིག་བཙོས་པིན།
ར་གཅིག་ལ་པེལ་དེ་ར་བརྒྱ་རིག་སོང་ལོ།
གཅིག་ཅིག་གིས་མེན་ནེ་སྟོང་ཁ་རིག་ཀེད་ལོ།
དེ་ཀུན་ཧྲའི་རྟ་རིན་ལ་ཕྱུལ་ཡིན་ལོ།
སྤོ་རོག་པོན་པོན་གྱི་ཧྲ་རིན་ལ་ཕྱུལ་ཡིན།

ལོ་གསུམ་གླིང་པའི་ལུག་རྫི་རིག་བཙོས་པིན།
ལུག་གཅིག་ལ་པེལ་དེ་ལུག་བརྒྱ་རིག་སོང་ལོ།
གཅིག་གིས་མེན་ནེ་སྐྱོང་ཁ་རིག་ཡོད་ལོ།
དེ་ཀུན་དུའི་དུ་རིན་ལ་སྦུལ་ཡིན་ལོ།
སྤོ་རོག་པོན་གྱི་དུ་རིན་ལ་སྦུལ་ཡིན།
ལོ་གསུམ་གླིང་པའི་རྟ་རྫི་རིག་བཙོས་པིན།
རྟ་གཅིག་ལ་པེལ་དེ་རྟ་བརྒྱ་རིག་སོང་ལོ།
གཅིག་གིས་མེན་ནེ་སྐྱོང་ཁ་རིག་ཡོད་ལོ།
དེ་ཀུན་དུའི་དུ་རིན་ལ་སྦུལ་ཡིན།
སྤོ་རོག་པོན་པོན་གྱི་རྟ་རིན་ལ་སྦུལ་ཡིན་ལོ།
ལོ་གསུམ་གླིང་པའི་གཡག་རྫི་རིག་བཙོས་པིན།
གཡག་གཅིག་ལ་པེལ་དེ་གཡག་བརྒྱ་རིག་སོང་ལོ།
གཅིག་གིས་མེན་ནེ་སྐྱོང་ཁ་རིག་སོང་ལོ།
དེ་ཀུན་དུའི་དུ་རིན་ལ་སྦུལ་ཡིན་ལེ།
སྤོ་རོག་པོན་པོན་གྱི་དུ་རིན་ལ་སྦུལ་ཡིན།
ལོ་གསུམ་གླིང་པའི་བ་རྫི་རིག་བཙོས་པིན།
བ་གཅིག་ལ་པེལ་ཏེ་བ་བརྒྱ་རིག་སོང་ལོ།
གཅིག་གིས་མེན་ནེ་སྐྱོང་ཁ་རིག་ཡོད་ལོ།
དེ་ཀུན་དུའི་དུ་རིན་ལ་སྦུལ་ཡིན་ལོ།
སྤོ་རོག་པོན་པོན་གྱི་དུ་རིན་ལ་སྦུལ་ཡིན།

དེ་ཚང་མ་སང་རིན་མ་འཁོར་ཟེར་ན།
དངུལ་ཞོ་གྲངས་ཙམ་ཟེར་ནའང་ཕུལ་ཡིན་ལོ།
ད་སྔོ་རིག་པོན་པོན་དེ་ང་ལ་སྐུལ་བ་དགོས་སྲུག་ལེ།

ཨ་ཀུ་དཔལ་ལེས་དེ་ཟུག་ཟེརས་པ་སང། ཨ་མ་སྐྱབས་བདུན་མས་ད་དེ་བདངས། དེ་ནས་དཔལ་ལེ་དེ་དའི་ཁ་ཞེན་དེ། རལ་གྲི་ཆག་པོ་ཞིག་ཁྱེར་དེ་ཁང་པ་ལ་མ་ཡོང་བ། སྟེང་ལྷ་ཡུལ་ལ་སོང། དེ་ཙ་ཀོ་སྟེང་ལྷ་ཡུལ་ལ་བསྐྱིབ་ཟ་ན། བུ་དོན་གྲུབ། དོན་ལྡན། དོན་ཡོད་གསུམ་གྱི་སྤྱིད་མོ་དེ། པོ་བྲང་གི་ཁ་ཐོག་ལ་ཡོད་ཅེས་མཐོང་སྟེ། དཔལ་ལེས་གླུ་འདི་ལྟར་བླངས།

དེའི་ཁ་ཐོག་ལ་ཡོད་པའི་ཇོ་ཇོས་དངོས་ལ་ཉན་ལེ།
ཁ་ཐོག་གི་ཟུར་ལ་ཡོད་པའི་ལྷ་མོས་བདག་ལ་གསན།
ལྷའི་དབང་པོའི་ཕོ་བྲང་ག་ཙ་ཡོད་ལོ།
དབང་པོ་བརྒྱ་བྱིན་གྱི་ཕོ་བྲང་ག་ཙ་ཡོད།

དཔལ་ལེ་གྲོད་པོས་དེ་ཟུག་འདྲིས་པ་སང། བུ་མོས་ལན་ལ་གླུ་འདི་ལྟར་བླངས་སོ།

ལྷ་ཡུལ་ལ་འདྲི་སྐད་ཕེང་མཁན་ཞིག་ཁྱོད་གྲུ་ནས་ཡོངས།
ལྷའི་དབང་པོ་བརྒྱ་བྱིན་དང་ཁྱོད་ལ་ཅི་བཅོ་ཡིན།
ལྷའི་དབང་པོའི་ཁང་པ་དང་ཁྱོད་ལ་ཅི་བཙོ་ཡིན།
གྲེན་ལ་ཆ་ན་ཁྱོད་རང་གྲེན་ལ་སོང་དང།
ཐུར་ལ་ཆ་ན་ཐུར་ལ་སོང་ལོ།
ཁྱོད་རང་གི་བུ་ལོན་ང་ལ་མེད་ལོ།

བུ་མོས་དེ་ཟླུག་ཅིག་ཟེརས་པ་སང། དཔལ་ལེ་རྒོད་པོ་ལ་སྨྲོ་ཆེན་པོ་ཡོང་སྤེ་སྤྱུ་འདི་ལྟར་བཏངས།

ལྷ་ཨ་མའི་བུ་མོ་དངོས་ཤིག་ལ་ཉོན་དང།
ལྷ་ཛེ་ཛེ་ཁྱོད་རིས་ངའི་བདག་ལ་གཟན་དང།
ཧ་མ་ཤེས་ན་སྤྲོ་རོག་པོན་པོན་ཡིན་ལོ།
མི་མ་ཤེས་ན་དཔལ་ལེ་རྒོད་པོ་རིག་ཡིན་ལོ།
གྲི་མ་ཤེས་ན་རྫོ་ཆོད་མ་རལ་གྲི་རིག་ཡིན་ལོ།
དེ་གྲི་ནི་ཆོན་ཆན་ཞིག་མེན་ལོ།
ལོ་གསུམ་གངས་ཀྱི་ཡོག་ལ་བོར་མཁན་ཞིག་ཡིན་ལོ།
གངས་ཀྱི་གངས་ངར་ཕོག་མཁན་ཞིག་ཡིན་ལོ།
ལོ་གསུམ་ཆུའི་མཐིལ་ལ་བོར་མཁན་ཞིག་ཡིན་ལོ།
ཆུའི་ཆུ་ངར་ཕོག་མཁན་ཞིག་རང་ཡིན་ལོ།
ལོ་གསུམ་སའི་མཐིལ་ལ་བོར་མཁན་ཞིག་ཡིན་ལོ།
སའི་ས་ངར་ཕོག་མཁན་ཞིག་རང་ཡིན་ལོ།
ཁྱོད་ཀྱིས་ལྷའི་དབང་པོའི་ཕོ་བྲང་བསྟན་ན་རྒྱལ་ལོ།
གལ་ཏེ་ཁྱོད་ཀྱིས་མི་བསྟན་རིག་ཟེར་ན།
ཁོག་སྟོད་བཅད་དེ་རྨ་ལ་ཕང་ཡིན་ལོ།
ཁོག་སྨད་བཅད་དེ་སའི་མཐིལ་ལ་བཏང་ཡིན་ལོ།

དཔལ་ལེ་རྒོད་པོས་དེ་ཟླུག་ཟེརས་པ་སང། བུ་མོ་དེ་འཛིགས་ཏེ། ཁ་ཐོག་ནས་བབ་སྤེ་ནང་ལ་སོང་བ། ལྷའི་དབང་པོ་རྒྱབ་ཞེན་གྱིས་བུ་མོ་ལ་

འདྲིས་པ། ལྷ་བུ་མོ། ཁྱོད་ཀྱིས་སྤུ་ལ་གདམ་ཞིག་ཟེརས། ཟེརས་པ། བུ་མོས། ཨ་བཱ་ལེ། ང་དང་གི་མཁར་རྩ་ལ་ཏ་ཞོན་མཁན་ནི་མི་ཞིག་ཡོང་སྟེ། ལྷའི་དབང་པོ་རྒྱབ་ཞིན་གྱི་ཁང་པ་གར་ཡོད་ཟེར་རག། ངས་ཁྱོད་ལ་ཁང་པ་དང་ཅི་བཅོ་ཡིན་ཟེརས་པ། ཁོ་ལ་སྒྲོ་ོང་སྟེ་བཤད་བཏང་ཡིན་ཟེར་རག། ང་འཛིགས་དེ་ནང་ལ་ཡོངས་པ་ཡིན་ཟེརས་པ། ལྷའི་དབང་པོ་རྒྱབ་ཞིན་གྱིས་བུ་མོ་ལ་ཁ་སྐྱེ་སྟེ་ཟེརས། གླིང་གི་དཔའ་བོ་ཡིན་པའི་ཚོད་རག། ཁྱོད་ཀྱིས་ཁོ་ལ་ལན་ཅི་ཕི་ལ་ཟེརས་ཟེར་དེ། ལྷའི་དབང་པོ་རྒྱབ་ཞིན་སྒོ་ལ་བེང་སྟེ་ཡོངས། དེ་ནས་ཁོང་གཉིས་ཀས་ལག་འཕྲད་རེ་བཏང་སྟེ་ན། མཁར་ནང་དུ་ཡོངས། དེ་རྩ་དཔལ་ལེ་རྒོད་པོས་ཞུས་པ། ཉི་རང་གིས་ཞལ་ཛུན་མང་པོ་བཏངས་ཞུས་པ། ལྷའི་དབང་པོ་རྒྱབ་ཞིན་གྱིས་ཟེརས་པ། མི་སྟོ། གླིང་གི་དཔའ་བོ་ལེ། ངའི་སྤྲུ་གུ་གཅིག་ག་ཟུག་གིས་ཡང་བཏང་ཅེས་ཡིན། དེ་ཟུག་ཟེར་དེ་ཞག་བདུན་ལ་བུ་དོན་ཀུབ་བཏང་ཅེས་བཅོ་སྟེ། དཔལ་ལེ་རྒོད་པོ་ཕྱིར་ལོག་ཡོངས ॥

No. 5.

དེ་ནས་ཞག་གསུམ་སོང་བ་དང་། བུ་དོན་ཀུབ་ཀྱིས་ཟེརས་པ། ཨ་བཱ་ལེ། ང་སྟོན་ལ་གླིང་ཡུལ་ལ་ལྷ་སྐོར་ལ་ཆ་ཡིན་ཟེར་དེ། བྱ་བདེ་མོ་ཞིག་ལ་ཛུ་སྟེ་སོང་སྟེ། སྟོན་ལ་རང་ཁྲའི་མགོ་ཁྲུ་ཐང་གི་ཁང་པའི་ཟུར་ལ་བབ་སྟེ་འདུགས་པ! ཁྲའི་མགོ་ཁྲུ་ཐང་ལ་བྱ་དེ་བདེ་མོ་མཐོང་སྟེ། རང་གི་ཨ་ནེ་ལ་ཟེརས། སྒྲུ་འདི་ལྷར་སྐྱངས།

དེ་རིང་ང་དང་གི་ཁ་ཐོག་ལ་བྱ་རིགས་ཅན་ཞིག་འདུག་ལོ།
དེ་བྱ་ནི་བདུད་བྱ་ཞིག་ཡིན་ཚོད་འདུག་ལོ།

ཇོ་ཇོ་རང་ལང་སྐྱེ་ཐབ་ལ་མེ་ཞིག་ཕྱུས་ལོ།
ཨེ་ཞིག་ཕྱུ་སྐྱེ་རྡོ་ལྕོག་ཅིག་ཀོལ་ལོ།
དེ་རིང་ང་དང་གིས་བྱ་ཤ་ཞིག་ཟེན་ལོ།
མདའ་ཁང་ལ་སོང་སྐྱེ་མདའ་ཞིག་ཡང་ཁྱེར་ལོ།
གཞུ་ཁང་ལ་སོང་སྐྱེ་གཞུ་མོ་དེ་ཡང་ཁྱེར་ལོ།
འདི་རིང་བྱའི་བྱ་སྐྱགས་ཤིག་རང་བཙོ་ཡིན།

ཁྲའི་མགོ་ཁྲུ་ཐུང་གིས་དེ་ཟུག་ཟེརས་པ་སང་། གཞིད་མད་དེ་ལང་སྐྱེ་མེ་ཕྱུས། རྡོ་ལྕོག་བཀལ་དེ། མདའ་ཁང་ནས་མདའ་ཁྱེངས། གཞུ་ཁང་ནས་གཞུ་ཁྱེང་སྐྱེ། ཁྲུ་ཐུང་གཾ་ལག་ལ་བདངས་པ་སང་། བྱ་དེས་བྱ་རྒྱུག་ཅིག་བདང་སྐྱེ་ན། ཕྱུར་སོང་། དེ་ནས་གླིང་གི་དཔའ་བོ་ཚང་མའི་ཁ་ཐོག་ལ་བབས་པ་སང་། དཔའ་བོ་ཚང་མ་འཐད་དེ་ལྷ་ཡུལ་ལི་བྱ་ཞིག་ཡིན་ཚོད་འདུག་ཟེར་དེ། དཔལ་ལེ་རྒོད་པོས་རང་གི་གཞིད་མད་པོ་ལ་གླུ་འདི་ལྟར་སླངས།

ངའི་ཇོ་ཇོས་འང་ངའི་དངོས་ལ་ཉོན་དང་ལོ།
འདི་རིང་ང་དང་གི་ཁ་ཐོག་ལ་བྱ་ཞིག་འདུག་ལོ།
ལྷ་ཡུལ་ལི་ལྷབ་བྱ་ཞིག་ཡིན་ཚོད་རིག་འདུག་ལོ།
ཀླུའི་ཀླུ་བྱ་རིག་ཡིན་ཚོད་རིག་འདུག་ལོ།
ཇོ་ཇོ་ཉེ་རང་བཞངས་དེ་དྲི་དོན་ཞིག་ཅོས་ལོ།
ཇོ་ཇོ་ཉེ་རང་བཟུངས་དེ་ཕོག་དོན་ཞིག་དེང་ལོ།
སྤྲུལ་མགོ་མ་ཆབ་རྒྱན་ལ་མཐོ་དགུ་ཀ་ལྟོར་ཞིག་རོན་ལོ།
དེ་ཟུག་ཟེར་དེ་ཕོག་ཀ་ལྟོར་ཁེར་དེ་ཁ་ཐོག་ལ་སོང་བ་དང་། བྱ་དེ་ཕྱུར་

དེ་སྟེང་ལྷ་ཡུལ་ལ་སོང་། དེ་ནས་སྟེང་ལྷ་ཡུལ་ལ་བསླེབ་སྟེ། ཨ་བས་བུ་ཚ་ལ་འཁྲིས་པ། ཕྲ་བུ་ཚ། གླིང་ཡུལ་ལི་མི་ཚང་མ་དང་ཡུལ་ཚང་མ་ག་ཐུག་རིག་འདུག་ཟེར་ས་པ་སང་། བུ་དོན་གྲུབ་ཀྱིས་ཨ་བཱ་ལ་ཞུས་པ། ཁྲའི་མགོ་ཁྲུ་ཐུང་ཟེར་མཁན་པོ་མི་རྩོག་པོ་རིག་ཡོད་ཚོད་འདུག། དེ་མེན་ནེ་ཚང་མ་རྒྱལ་ལ་ཡོད་ཅེས་འདུག་ལི་ཟེར་ས།

No. 6.

དེ་ནས་ཨ་བཱ་དང་ཨ་མ་ཨ་ཅོ་ནོ་སྲིང་མོ་ཚང་མ་ནང་མིག་གཅིག་གི་ནང་དུ་འཛོམ་སྡེ་འདུགས། དེ་རུ་ཨ་མས་བུ་དོན་གྲུབ་ལ་ངུ་འིན་ཞིག་ཟེར་ས། བུ་དོན་གྲུབ་དང་འདྲ་བའི་བུ་ཞིག་སུ་ཡང་མི་འདུག། དོན་གྲུབ་དཀར་པོ་དང་འདྲ་བའི་མི་ཞིག་སུ་ཡང་མི་འདུག། བུ་དོན་གྲུབ་ཁྱེ་རང་མི་ཡུལ་ལ་ཆ་དགོས། དམག་གི་དམག་རེས་ཡིན་ན། ངས་ནོར་བཏང་ཡིན་བ། བུ་ལོན་ཞིག་ཡོད་ན། ངས་འཇལ་ཡིན་བ། ཨ་བའི་ཁ་ཆད་པོ་སློག་པ་མི་ཉན། སྔོན་ལ་ཟེར་མཁན་གྱི་དཔེ་ར་ལ་བཅོ་ཐབས་མི་ཡོང་། ཨ་མས་དེ་ཐུག་ཟེར་ས་པ་སང་། བུ་དོན་གྲུབ་ཀྱིས་ཨ་བཱ་ལ་ཞུས་པས། གླུ་འདི་ལྟར་བླངས།

ངའི་ཨ་བས་འང་བུ་ཚ་ངའི་དངོས་ལ་ཉོན་ལོ།
དབང་པོ་རྒྱབ་ཞིན་གྱིས་དོན་གྲུབ་ཀྱི་བདག་ལ་གསན།
ང་ལ་མ་སྐལ་མེད་པ་མི་ཡུལ་ལ་ག་ཐུག་གིས་ཆ་ཡིན།
ང་ལ་མཁར་སྐལ་མེད་པ་མི་ཡུལ་ལ་པ་ཐུག་གིས་ཆ་ཡིན།
ང་ལ་རྟ་སྐལ་མེད་པ་མི་ཡུལ་ལ་ག་ཐུག་གིས་ཆ་ཡིན།
ང་ལ་ཨ་ཅོ་ཞིག་མེད་པ་མི་ཡུལ་ལ་ག་ཐུག་གིས་ཆ་ཡིན།

ང་ལ་མདའ་གཞུ་ལག་ཆ་མེད་པ་མི་ཡུལ་ལ་ག་ཐུག་གིས་ཆ་ཡིན།

ང་ལ་ཟངས་བུ་མེད་པ་མི་ཡུལ་ལ་ག་ཐུག་གིས་ཆ་ཡིན།

ང་ལ་ར་སྐལ་ཞིག་མེད་པ་མི་ཡུལ་ལ་ག་ཐུག་གིས་ཆ་ཡིན།

ང་ལ་སྐྱོ་གླང་མེད་པ་མི་ཡུལ་ལ་ག་ཐུག་གིས་ཆ་ཡིན།

ང་ལ་སྲུང་བའི་ལྷ་ཞིག་མེད་པ་མི་ཡུལ་ལ་ག་ཐུག་གིས་ཆ་ཡིན།

ང་ལ་མ་ལྷ་ཞིག་མེད་པ་མི་ཡུལ་ལ་ག་ཐུག་གིས་ཆ་ཡིན།

ང་ལ་གྲོགས་སྐལ་ཞིག་མེད་པ་མི་ཡུལ་ལ་ག་ཐུག་གིས་ཆ་ཡིན།

དེ་ཐུག་ཟེརས་པ་སང་། ཨ་བས་ལན་དུ་གླུ་འདི་ལྟར་བླངས།

བུ་དོན་གྲུབ་གླིང་ཡུལ་ལ་འགྲོ་དགོས་བྱུང་།

ཁྱེད་ལ་མ་སྐལ་གོག་བཟང་ལྷ་མོ་ཡིན་ལོ།

ཁྱེད་ལ་མཁར་སྐལ་གླིང་མཁར་རྩེ་དགུ་ཡིན།

ཁྱེད་ལ་རྟ་སྐལ་ལ་ཀྱུང་བྱུང་དབྱེར་པ་ཡིན།

ཁྱེད་ལ་ཨ་ཙོ་དེ་གསེར་སྦལ་གསེར་པོ་ཡིན།

ཁྱེད་ལ་ནོ་དེ་གཡུ་སྦལ་སྔོན་པོ་ཡིན་ལོ།

ཁྱེད་ལ་མདའ་མོ་ལྡོང་དཀར་མ་ཡིན་ལོ།

ཁྱེད་ལ་གཞུ་སྐལ་དེ་ཡོ་ལད་གྱད་གཞུ་ཡིན་ལོ།

ཁྱེད་ལ་ལག་ཆ་དེ་རྡོ་ཆོད་མ་རལ་གྲི་ཡིན་ལོ།

ཁྱེད་ལ་མདུང་སྐལ་དེ་མདུང་དཔལ་ཟམ་རིང་མོ་ཡིན།

ཁྱེད་ལ་ཟངས་བུ་དེ་ཟངས་བུ་ཁ་ཡོན་མ་ཡིན།

ཁྱེད་ལ་རིག་སྐལ་དེ་རིག་བུ་ཁ་དམར་ཡིན།

ཁྱེད་ལ་ར་སྐལ་དེ་ར་སྐྱེས་སྐྱེ་དམར་ཡིན།
ཁྱེད་ལ་རྨོ་གླང་དེ་མཛོ་ཕོ་རྐང་དཀར་ཡིན།
ཁྱེད་ལ་སྐྱུང་བའི་ཕ་ལྷ་ཀེར་རྫོང་སྟན་པོ་ཡིན།
ཁྱེད་ལ་སྐྱུང་བའི་མ་ལྷ་བཀུར་དམན་རྒྱལ་མོ་ཡིན།
ཁྱེད་ལ་གྲོགས་སྐལ་དེ་ཞིལ་ལྕམ་འབྲུག་མོ་ཡིན།

དེ་ཟླུག་ཟེར་དེ་ཨ་བས་ཚང་མ་བསླབ་སྟེ་བདངས་པ་སང། ཚང་མ་ལ་ངུ་ཅེས་རེ་ཡོངས། བུ་དོན་གྲུབ་ དོན་ལྡན་ དོན་ཡོད་གསུམ་ཀའི་སྐྲོག་དེ་འོ་མ་ཀོ་རེ་གང་རེ་ཡོད་ཙུག། འོ་མའི་ཀོ་རེ་ཚང་ཀ་ཨ་བའི་ལག་ཏུ་ཡོད་པས། ཨ་བས་བུ་མོ་ལ་ཟེརས་པ། ལྷ་བུ་མོ། ཁྱོ་རང་ཁང་ཆུང་ནང་དུ་སོང་སྟེ་ཀོ་རེ་ཆེ་ཆུང་གསུམ་གྱི་ནང་ལ་འོ་མ་བསྐང་སྟེ་ཡོད། དེ་ནང་ནས་ཀོ་རེ་ཆུང་ཅེ་དེ་ཁུར་དེ་ཁྱོང་ཟེརས་པ། བུ་མོ་སོང་སྟེ་དེ་ཀོ་རེ་ཆུང་ཅེ་བོ་ཁུར་དེ་ཁྱོངས། དེ་ནས་འོ་མ་ཕོ་སྟེ་ཀོ་རེ་དེ་ཁ་ཟླུབ་ལ་དོང་ཟེརས་པ། སྲིང་མོས་འོ་མ་ཕོ་སྟེ་ཀོ་རེ་ཁ་ཟླུབ་ལ་བདངས། དེ་ནས་བུ་དོན་གྲུབ་དཀར་པོ་རེན་ནམལ་ལ་གྲོངས་སོང།།

No. 7.

དེ་རུ་ནམ་འཁོར་ཆེན་པོ་སོང་སྟེ་རླུང་རག་དང་སེ་ར་རུ་མང་པོ་འབབས་ཀྱིན་ཞིག་གླིང་ཡུལ་ཕྱོགས་ལ་སོང། གླིང་ཡུལ་ལ་གཏང་ངེ་ཡུད་པའི་ཕུ་ལ་པ་སང་ལྡན་ར་སྐྱེས་ཀྱིས་ཐགས་འཐག་གིན་ཞིག་ཡོད་ཙུག! གོག་བཟང་ལྷ་མོས་ཕྲུ་རི་ཞིག་འཐུལ་གྱིན་ཡོད་ཙུག། ཁོང་གཉིས་ཀའི་ཀོ་རེ་ལ་ཛ་རི་སླག་སྟེ་ཡོད་པེན། དེ་ནས་མ་གོག་བཟང་ལྷ་མོའི་ཀོ་རེ་ནང་དུ་སེ་ར་རུ་ཆེན་པོ་ཞིག་འབུད་དེ་ཡོངས། གོག་བཟང་ལྷ་མོས་པ་སང་ལྡན་རུ་སྐྱེས་ལ་འདྲིས་པ། པ་སང་ལྡན་རུ་སྐྱེས་ལེ།

ངའི་ཀོ་རེ་ནང་ལ་སེ་ར་རྩ་ཆེན་པོ་ཞིག་འབུད་དེ་ཡོངས། དེ་འཕངས་བཏང་ང་ཟ་ཟེརས་པ། ཡ་སང་ལྷན་ར་སྐྱེས་ཀྱིས་ཀོ་རེ་ནང་དུ་འབུད་མཁན་དེ་དཀོན་མཆོག་གིས་ཁྱེད་ལ་ཟ་ཅེས་ལ་བཏངས་མཁན་ཡིན་ཚོད། འཕང་མ་འཕང་། ཟོས་དོང་། ཟེརས། དེ་ནས་ཁོས་ཆེན་མོ་ཡོད་པ་སང་། སེན་མོ་དང་བཅག་གིན་ཞིག་ཟོས་པས། མ་གོག་བཟང་ལྷ་མོ་ལ་གཟུགས་པོ་མ་བདེ་བ་འདུགས། དེ་ནས་ཟླ་བ་གཉིས་གསུམ་སོང་བ་དང་། མི་ཚང་མས་གོག་བཟང་ལྷ་མོ་ལ་རྒྱལ་པོ་ཀ་སར་སྐྱེ་ཆེན་ལོ་ཟེར་རེད་ཚུག། ཟླ་དགུ་ཞག་བཅུ་ངོ་ལ་ཁའི་ནོ་མོ་དཀར་ཐིག་མ་དང་ནག་ཐིག་མ་གཉིས་ཀ་ལ་སེམས་ཅན་ཞིག་སྐྱེས། དེ་ཅི་འདི་ཡི་ལ་ཡིན་ཟེར་ན། ཨ་ཅི་ལ་རྒྱལ་པོ་ཀ་སར་སྐྱེ་ཆེན་ལོ་ཟེརས་པའི་ཡི་ལ། དེ་ནས་དཀར་ཐིག་མ་དང་ནག་ཐིག་ན་གཉིས་ཀ། མ་གོག་བཟང་ལྷ་མོའི་སྨ་ཁྲུ་ཅེས་ལ་ཡོངས། ཁོང་གཉིས་ ཀ་ལ་སེམས་ཅན་སྐྱེས་ པ་ སང་ གཟབས་ བཅོ་སྡེ་ཐབ་ ཀྱི་ལྕུགས་ སྐྱིད་བུ་ལ་སྐའི་ལན་བུ་ཞིག་བདག་སྡེ་བོརས། ཐབ་ཀྱི་ཁ་འདི་མ་སྒོ་བ་ལ་བཀལ་དེ་ཡོད་ཚུག། ནོ་མོ་དེ་ཐི་སྤུ་རྩ་སོང་སྡེ་ར་མ་ཞིག་ཁྲིད་དེ་ནང་ལ་འཕུད་བཏངས་པ། འོ་མའི་མདུན་ལ་བསྙིབ་པ་སང་། ནོ་མོས། ཨ་ཆེ། ར་མ་ཡོངས། འོ་མ་ཟློག་ཡིན་ཟེརས་པ། ཨ་ཆེ་མགྲོས་པ་ལངས་དེ་ར་མ་རྒྱབ་པ་སོང་། ལྕུགས་སྐྱིད་ལ་བདགས་མཁན་འཕེན་བཏངས་པ། འོ་ན་ཚང་མ་ཐབ་ཀྱི་ནང་དུ་ལོག་སོང་། དེ་ནས་མ་གོག་བཟང་ལྷ་མོ་ལ་ཤུ་བ་མང་པོ་བྱིང་སོང་། ཕྲུ་གུ་སྐྱེ་ཅེས་ཀྱི་ཞག་བསྙིབ་པས། ཕྲུ་གུས་ཨ་མ་རི་གྲོད་པའི་ནང་ནས་དཔེ་ར་བཏང་སྡེ་ཟེརས། གླུ་འདི་ལྟར།

ཨ་མ་ལ་བུ་ཞིག་སྐྱེན་དོ་ཟླ།
གོག་བཟང་ལ་བུ་ཞིག་སྐྱེན་དོ་ཟླ།

ང་ནི་རི་གསུམ་གྱི་རྩེ་ལ་སྐྱིན་ལོ།

རི་གསུམ་གྱི་རྩེ་ལ་རྡོ་བ་གསུམ་གདུང་གསུམ་རྩིག་ལོ།

ཚུ་རུའི་གྲལ་ཚད་རིག་དོང་ལོ།

སྤུ་དིག་གི་སྤྲི་ལབ་རིག་དོང་ལོ།

ཕེ་མར་རི་ཐོགས་རིག་ནོན་ལོ།

དེ་ནས་ཁོས་དེ་ཐུག་ཟེར་ཅེས་ཆོར་པ་སང་། ཨ་མ་རི་ལ་སོང་སྟེ་རྡོ་བ་གསུམ་ཁྱེར་སྟེ། སྐྱོར་དེ་ཁྲམ་སྟེ་འདུགས། ཡང་ཕྲུ་གུས་ཟེརས། གླུ་འདི་ལྟར་སླངས།

ང་རི་གསུམ་གྱི་རྩེ་ལ་སྐྱེ་སྟེང་ཤ་ང་རིག་མེན།

ང་སྐྱིན་དོ་སྐྱིན་ལུང་གསུམ་གྱི་མདོ་རུ་སྐྱེར་ལོ།

ལུང་གསུམ་གྱི་མདོ་རུ་རྡོ་བ་གསུམ་གདུང་གསུམ་རྩིག་ལོ།

ཚུ་རུའི་གྲལ་ཚད་རིག་དོང་ལོ།

སྤུ་དིག་གི་ཐོག་གྲབ་རིག་དོང་ལོ།

ཕེ་མར་རི་ཐོགས་རིག་ནོན་ལོ།

དེ་ཐུག་ཟེརས་པ། ཨ་མ་ཡང་ཡངས་དེ་ལུང་གསུམ་གྱི་མདོ་རུ་ཡོང་སྟེ་རྡོ་བ་གསུམ་ཁྱེར་སྟེ་སྐྱོར་དེ་ཁྲམ་སྟེ་འདུགས་པ། ཡང་ཁོས་གླུ་འདི་ལྟར།

ང་ལུང་གསུམ་གྱི་མདོ་རུ་སྐྱེ་སྟེང་ལྷ་ཙེ་མེན་ལོ།

སྐྱིན་དོ་སྐྱིན་ང་ཆུ་ཆེན་མོའི་ཐུར་ལ་སྐྱིན་ལོ།

ཆུའི་ཐུར་ལ་རྡོ་བ་གསུམ་གདུང་གསུམ་རྩིག་ལོ།

ཚུ་རུའི་གྲལ་ཚད་རིག་དོང་ལོ།

སྦུ་དིག་གི་སྒོག་གླུབ་རིག་དོང་ལོ།

ཕེ་མར་རི་སྒྲོགས་རིག་ནོན་ལོ།

དེ་ནས་ཨ་མ་ལངས་དེ་རྩུའི་ཟུར་ལ་སོང་སྟེ་འདུགས། ཕྲུ་གུས་ཡང་གླུ་འདི་ལྟར་བླངས།

ང་རྩུ་ཟུར་ལ་སྐྱེ་སྟེ་ང་ཉ་མོ་རིག་མིན་ལོ།

སྐྱེན་དོ་ང་སྐྱེན་མ་ཞིང་གི་དཀྱིལ་ལ་ང་སྐྱེན་ལོ།

མ་ཞིང་གི་དཀྱིལ་ལ་རྡོ་བ་གསུམ་གདུང་གསུམ་རྩིག་ལོ།

ཙུ་རུའི་གྲལ་ཚད་རིག་དོང་ལོ།

སྦུ་དིག་གི་སྒོང་།་གླུབ་རིག་དོང་ལོ།

ཕེ་མར་རི་སྒྲོགས་རིག་ནོན་ལོ།

དེ་ནས་ཨ་མ་ལངས་དེ་ཡང་མ་ཞིང་གི་དཀྱིལ་ལ་སོང་སྟེ་འདུགས། ཕྲུ་གུས་ཡང་གླུ་འདི་ལྟར་བླངས།

ང་མ་ཞིང་གི་དཀྱིལ་ལ་སྐྱེ་སྟེ་ཞིང་གི་ཡ་མ་ང་མིན།

སྐྱེན་དོ་སྐྱེན་ང་མ་ཁང་གི་སྒོ་རྒྱབ་ལ་སྐྱེན་ལོ།

དེ་ནས་ཨ་མ་སྒོ་རྒྱབ་པོ་ལ་སོང་སྟེ་ཁྲུམ་སྟེ་འདུགས་པ། ཕྲུ་གུས་ཡང་གླུ་འདི་ལྟར།

སྒོ་རྒྱབ་ལ་སྐྱེ་སྟེ་ང་བི་ཕྲུག་ཅིག་མིན་ལོ།

སྐྱེན་དོ་ང་སྐྱེན་པད་མ་ཙན་དུག་དག་པ་ཁ་སྐྱེན།

དེ་ནས་ཨ་མ་ལངས་དེ་པ་དྨ་ཙན་དུག་པའི་ཁ་སོང་པ། ཁོས་ཡང་གླུ་འདི་ལྟར།

སྐྱེན་དོ་ང་སྐྱེན་མགོའི་དཀྱིལ་ན་སྐྱེན་ལོ།
མགོ་ཤ་ཁམ་གཅིག་འཁུར་རེ་སྐྱེན་ལོ།
སྐྱེན་དོ་ང་སྐྱེན་རྩིག་མའི་ཕྱོགས་ནས་ང་སྐྱེན་ལོ།
རྩིབ་ཤ་ཁམ་ཅིག་འཁུར་དེ་སྐྱེན་ལོ།
སྐྱེན་དོ་ང་སྐྱེན་རྐང་པའི་རྐང་མཐིལ་ན་སྐྱེན།
རྐང་ཤ་ཁམ་ཅིག་འཁུར་དེ་སྐྱེན་ལོ།

དེ་ཟུག་ཟེར་ས་པ་སང་། ཨ་མ་ལ་འཛིག་རི་མང་པོ་ཡོང་ས། རྗེང་ནས་སྤྲུ་གུས་བདེན་པ་བསླབས། ད་ལྟ་འདི་དོན་ཡོག་དོན་དོང་། ང་དང་མཉམ་པོ་ནོར་བུ་མང་པོ་སྐྱེ་ཆེན། དེ་ཚང་མ་ལ་ཉ་ར་བཙོ་དགོས་ཟེར་ས། དེ་ནས་ཉི་མ་དང་ཟླ་བ་གཉིས་ཀ་སྐྱེ་སྡེ་ནམ་སྟོད་ལ་སོང་། སྐྱིན་ཆེན་བ་རྒན་སྐྱེ་སྡེ་བྲག་སྟོད་ལ་སོང་། སེང་གེ་གཡུ་རལ་ཅན་སྐྱེ་སྡེ་གངས་སྟོད་ལ་སོང་། འབྲོང་ཆེན་ཁམ་པ་ཀུན་སྐྱེ་སྡེ་སྤང་སྟོད་ལ་སོང་། བྱ་རྒྱལ་རྒོད་པོ་སྐྱེ་སྡེ་རི་སྟོད་ལ་སོང་། ཉ་མོ་གསེར་མིག་སྐྱེ་སྡེ་མཚོམ་སྟོད་ལ་སོང་། བྱ་ཕྲན་ཤོག་གྲོག་སྐྱེ་སྡེ་ཤིང་ཐོག་ལ་སོང་། དེ་མ་འཚད། ལྷའི་དབང་པོ་རྒྱབ་ཞིན་གྱིས་བསླབས་མཁན་གྱི་ནོར་དང་ཕྱུགས་ཚང་མ། མ་གོག་བཟང་ལྷ་མོ་ལ་ཞག་གཅིག་གི་ནང་དུ་སྐྱེས་སོང་། དེ་ཚང་མའི་རྗེང་ནས། མགོ་ཆེན་མོ་ཞིག་སྐྱེ་ཁྲ་མོ་ཐ་ལ་ཅིག་མཚོགས་ཤིག་སྐྱེས་པས། ཨ་མས་ཁའི་ནང་དུ་བྲ་ཕེ་ཞིག་བཏང་སྟེ། ཚིག་གི་ཡོག་ལ་ནན་དེ་བོར་ས། དེ་ནས་ཨ་ནེ་བཀུར་དམན་མོ་ཡོང་སྡེ་གཟུག་མེད་རི་སྨྲ་ཐོས་དེ་ཟེར་ས། ཀླུ་གོག་བཟང་ལྷ་མོ། ཁྱོད་ལ་སྤྲུ་གུ་ག་ཟུག་ཅིག་སྐྱེས་ཟེར་ས་པ། གོག་བཟང་ལྷ་མོས་ཟེར་ས། ང་ལ་ཕན་ཐོག་ཅིས་ཅན་ཞིག་མ་སྐྱེས། སེམས་ཅན་མང་པོ་སྐྱེ་སྡེ་དཀར་ཁྲང་ནས་བིང་སྡེ་སོང་།

དེ་ཚང་མའི་རྫིང་ན་རྒལ་ཅིག་སྐྱེ་སྟེ་ཀོག་པའི་ཡོག་ལ་ནན་དེ་ཡོད་ཟེརས་པ། ཨ་ནེ་བཀུར་དམར་རྒྱལ་མོས་ཁ་སྐྱེ་འདིན་ཞིག་དང་ཀོག་པོ་འཐེན་བཏངས་པ། དེའི་ཡོག་པོ་ལ་གླིང་རྒྱ་ལྷམ་ཀེ་སར་ལ་གྱུར་དེ་ཡོད་ཚུག།།

No. 8.

དེ་སེ་ར་ཏུ་བབས་པའི་དུས་ལ། ཨ་གུ་དཔལ་ལེན། པ་ཆི་དཔལ་རྡོང་མཁར་ནང་ནས་ཁྲིངས་པའི་ནོར་བུའི་རིགས། སེམས་ཅན་ཚང་མ་ལ་སེ་ར་ཏུ་ཕོག་པ་སང། མ་གོག་བཟང་ལྷ་མོ་དང་མཉམ་པོ་དུས་གཅིག་ལ་སྐྱེ་ཅེས་ཅན་སོང། དེ་ནས་གོག་བཟང་ལྷ་མོ་ལ། ཀེ་སར་སྐྱེ་བའི་ཞག་ལ་དེ་སེམས་ཅན་ཚང་མ་ལ་ཕྲུ་གུ་རེ་རེ་སྐྱེས་པས།

དེག་བུ་ཁ་དམར་ལ།
དེག་བུ་སྐྱེ་རིངས་སྐྱེས།
ཟངས་བུ་ཁ་ཡོན་ལ།
ཟངས་བུ་ཁ་ཆོད་སྐྱེས།
སྟུ་རི་ཟླ་བ་དཀར་པོ་ལ།
ཕོ་ལད་དི་སྟེ་པོ་རང་ཆོད་སྐྱེས།
ཐག་པ་རྒྱ་སྟག་ཁྲ་བོ་ལ།
ཐག་བུ་ཁྲུ་གང་སྐྱེས།
སྐྱེ་མོ་དཀར་མོའི་སྟོང་ཤོང་ལ།
ཕད་ཁྲ་བོ་སྐྱེས།
རྟ་རྒོད་མ་ཚ་ལངས་ལ།

ཁྱུང་རྒོད་དཀྱིར་པ་སྐྱེས།
མཛོ་མོ་ཏུ་ཡོན་ལ།
མཛོ་ཕོ་ཀང་དཀར་སྐྱེས།
ར་མ་དཀར་མོ་ལ།
ར་སྐྱེས་སྐྱེ་དམར་སྐྱེས།
ལུག་དྲོ་མོ་ལ།
ལུག་ཕོར་ཟྲེ་སྐྱེས།
བོང་བུ་ནག་པོ་ཁ་དཀར་ལ།
བོང་བུ་ཁམ་པ་སྐྱེས།
ཁྱི་མོ་དཀར་མོ་ལ།
ཁྱི་ཕོ་གསེར་ལིངས་སྐྱེས།
བྱི་ལ་ནག་པོ་ལ།
བྱི་ལ་ཁྲ་སྤུག་སྐྱེས།

No. 9.

དེ་རྒྱལ་ཅིག་པོ་ལ་བདངས་པ་འི་བྲ་བོ་ཟམ་ཀྱི་བྲང་རྒྱས་ཤིག་བཞང་སྟེ་མདུན་ལ་བོར་དེ་ཡོད་ཚུག། ཨ་ནེ་སེམས་པང་གི་ཁ་ལེན་དེ་གླུ་འདི་ལྟར་སླངས།
སྟེང་ཕྱོགས་ལྷ་ཡུལ་ཀུན་ནོན་པའི་ཨ་མ་ལ་བྱ་ཞིག་བསྔམས།
བར་ཕྱོགས་བཙན་ཡུལ་ཀུན་ནོན་པའི་གོག་བཟང་ལ་སྤྲས་ཤིག་བསྔམས།
ཡོག་ཕྱོགས་ཀླུ་ཡུལ་ཀུན་ནོན་པའི་ཨ་མ་ལ་བྱུ་ཞིག་བསྔམས།
དེ་ཟུག་གི་ལྷ་སྤྲུག་ཀུན་བསྔམས་ཙ་ན་མི་ཡུལ་པོ་འོད་ཀྱིས་ཁྲངས།

རྒྱལ་ལྷམ་ཀེ་སར་ཀུན་བལྟམས་ཙ་ན་འཛམ་བུ་གླིང་འོད་ཀྱིས་ཁྱངས།
ཨ་ནེ་བའི་ཚོ་ཛེ་ཀུན་འཁྱུར་རེ་ན་ཨ་ལོ་ད་ལོ་ཞིག་སྐྱུག་ཡིན་ལོ།
བཀུར་དམན་གྱིས་ཀེ་སར་ཀུན་འཁྱུར་རེ་ན་ཨ་ལོ་ཞིག་སྐྱུག་ལོ།

དེ་ནས་ཡང་བྲ་བོའི་ཕེ་ལ་བཅོས་པའི། འབྲང་རྒྱས་དེ་ཨ་ནེ་བཀུར་དམན་མོས་ལེན་དེ་གསོལ་མཆོད་ཅིག་བཏངས། གླུ་འདི་ལྟར།

འོ་ན་གསོལ་ལོ་དང་མཆོད་དོ་རིག་སྟེང་ལྷ་ཡུལ་ལ་མཆོད་དོ།
གསོལ་ལོ་དང་མཆོད་དོ་རིག་དབང་པོ་རྒྱབ་ཞིན་ལ་མཆོད་དོ།
ངས་གསོལ་བའི་དུས་སུ་ཉེ་ཚམས་འདོན་པ་རིག་དགོས་སུག།
འདོམ་པའི་དུས་ལ་བུ་ལ་སྐྱུང་བ་རིག་མཛད་ལོ།
དཀགས་པོའི་དུས་ལ་ཀེ་སར་ལ་རོགས་རིག་མཛད།
འོ་ན་གསོལ་ལོ་དང་མཆོད་དོ་རིག་བར་བཙན་ཡུལ་ལ་མཆོད་དོ།
གསོལ་ལོ་དང་མཆོད་དོ་རིག་ཨ་མ་སྐྱབས་བདུན་ལ་མཆོད་དོ།
ངས་གསོལ་བའི་དུས་ལ་ཉེ་ཚམས་འདོན་བ་རིག་དགོས་སུག།
འདོམ་པའི་དུས་ལ་བུ་ལ་སྐྱུང་བ་རིག་མཛད་ལོ།
དཀགས་པོའི་དུས་སུ་ཀེ་སར་ལ་རོགས་རིག་མཛད་ལོ།
འོ་ན་གསོལ་ལོ་དང་མཆོད་དོ་རིག་འོག་ཀླུ་ཡུལ་དུ་མཆོད་དོ།
གསོལ་ལོ་དང་མཆོད་དོ་ཀླུ་རྒྱལ་ལྡོག་པོ་ལ་མཆོད་དོ།
ངས་གསོལ་བའི་དུས་མ་ཉེ་ཚམས་འདོན་བ་རིག་དགོས་སུག།
འདོམ་པའི་དུས་ལ་བུ་ལ་སྐྱུང་བ་རིག་མཛད་ལོ།
དཀགས་པོའི་དུས་ལ་ཀེ་སར་ལ་རོགས་རིག་མཛད་ལོ།

རེ་ཟླུག་ཟེར་དེ་གསོལ་མཆོད་བདང་སྟེ་ན། ཕྲུ་གུ་དེ་ཨ་མའི་ལག་ལ་བདང་སྟེ། ཨ་མ་ལ་ཟེར་ས། ལྷ་གོག་བཟང་ལྷ་མོ། འདི་རིང་ནས་ཕར་ལ་ཕྲུ་གུ་དེ་སྲུའི་ལག་དུ་མ་བདང༌། མི་སྲུ་ཞིག་ཡོང་སྟེ་དོང་ཟེར་ཆེན། སྲུའི་ལག་ལ་ཡང་མ་བདང་ཟེར་དེ། ཨ་ནེ་ནཀུར་དམན་མོ་ལོག་སྟེ་སོང༌། དེ་ནས་ཀེ་སར་སྐྱེ་སྟེ་ཡོད་ཅེས་དེ་བཀའ་བློན་ལྡན་པ་ལ་ཆོར་དེ། བཀའ་བློན་ལྡན་པ་དེ་བདུད་ལྷ་ཅེན་གྱི་བུ་ཚ་ཡིན་པས། ཁོའི་སྤྱོད་དེ་བདུད་ཀྱི་རིགས་ཡོད་པས། སྐད་དེ་གླིང་པའི་མི་མཆོགས་ཡོད་ཚུག། ཁོས་ཤར་གྱི་ཤ་རན་དྲེ་བ་རན་དྲེ་ཚང་ཀ་ལ་བསླབས། མ་གོག་བཟང་ལྷ་མོ་ལ་གླིང་ཀ་སར་རྒྱལ་པོ་སྐྱེ་ཚར་ལོ། ཁྲོ་ཞ་ཚང་ཀ་ཁོའི་སྐོ་ལ་སོང་སྟེ། ཐབས་བཅོས་ནས་ཕྲུ་གུ་དེ་ཁྲོངས་དེ་མི་ལ་སྲོག་སྟེ་བསད་དགོས། རྡིང་ནང་དང་ཚང་ས་ལ་གནོད་པ་སྐྱལ་ཆེན་ཟེར་དེ་བསླབ་སྟེ་ན། ཁོ་རང་ཀློ་ཕྱོགས་ལ་སོང་བས། ཤར་ཕྱོགས་ཀྱི་ཤར་རན་དྲེ་བ་རན་དྲེ་ཟེར་མཁན་གྱི་བདུད་གསུམ་བླ་མ་རེ་ལ་ཛུ་སྟེ། མ་གོག་བཟང་ལྷ་མོའི་ཁང་པའི་སྐོ་ལ་ཡོང་སྟེ་སྐད་བཙོལ་བདངས། གོག་བཟང་ལྷ་མོས་ཕེ་བདངས་པ། མ་དགོས། མར་བདངས་པ། མ་དགོས། དེ་ནས་ཏེ་ཞལ་ཅི་དགོས་ཡིན། ཡང་ནོར་མང་པོ་ཕུལ་ནང་ལ་མེད་ཟེར་ས། བླ་མ་ཀུན་ནས་ཟེར་ས། ཕེ་མི་དགོས། མར་མི་དགོས། ནོར་ཅི་ཡང་མི་དགོས། ཁྱོ་རང་གི་ཕྲུ་གུ་ལ་ང་ཙས་ཆོས་བསླབ་ཡིན། ཞག་བདུན་ལ་ཆོས་བསློབ་བཙུག་སྟེ་ལོག་སྟེ་ཁྱོང་ཕི་ན། ཕྲུ་གུ་དེ་དོང་ཟེར་ས་པ། གོག་བཟང་ལྷ་མོས་བསམ། ང་རང་གི་ཕྲུ་གུ་ལ་ཆོས་བསླབ་ན། རྒྱལ་བ་ཆེན། ཕྲུ་གུ་བདང་ཡིན་བསམས་སྟེ། ཕྲུ་གུ་བླ་མ་ཀུན་ལ་བདངས། ཁོང་གིས་ཕྲུ་གུ་ཁྲར་དེ་གླིང་ཡུལ་གྱི་མ་གོ་ལ་འཁྱེར་དེ་བླ་མ་ཀུན་གྱིས་བླུ་འདི་ལྟར།

གླིང་གི་ཤར་པ་ཚང་མས་ཚོར་ཁུར་བརྒྱ་ཙམ་ཁྱོང།
གླིང་གི་ན་ཆུང་ཚང་མས་མར་བྲི་བརྒྱ་ཙམ་ཁྱོང།
སྟུ་ལ་མི་བདུལ་བའི་སྤྲིན་བུ་ང་ཞ་ལ་བདུལ་ལོ།
སྟུ་ལ་མི་ཐོབ་པའི་བདུད་ཕྲུག་དེ་ང་ཞ་ལ་ཐོབ་ལོ།
གླིང་གི་མགར་བ་ཀུན་གྱིས་ལྕགས་ཟེར་རིག་ཁྱོང་ལོ།
འདི་རིང་ང་དང་གིས་བདུད་ཕྲུག་དེ་བདུལ་ཡིན།
འདི་རིང་ང་དང་གིས་སྤྲིན་བུ་དེ་བསད་ཡིན།
ལྕུག་གུ་ནམ་སྐྱིལ་ན་ཡལ་ག་སོང་སྟེ་མི་ཉན་ལོ།
ཆུང་དུན་ལ་མ་ཉན་ན་ཆེན་མོ་སོང་སྟེ་མི་ཉན་ལོ།
གླིང་གི་ཤར་པ་ཀུན་གཟིགས་མོ་ལ་སྐྱོད་ལོ།
གླིང་གི་ན་ཆུང་ཚང་མ་གཟིགས་མོ་ལ་སྐྱོད་ལོ།
བདུད་དེ་བདུད་ཕྲུག་གསོན་སྲིགས་ལ་བཏང་ཡིན།

དེ་ཟླུག་ཟེར་དེ་ཀུ་ཙོ་ཆེན་མོ་བཏངས་པ་སང་། གླིང་ཡུལ་ལི་ཤར་པ་ཚང་མས་ཚོར་ཁུར་རེ་འཁུར་དེ་ཡོངས། ན་ཆུང་ཚང་མས་མར་བྲི་གང་རེ་འཁུར་དེ་ཡོངས། དེ་ཟླུག་གི་ཚོར་མ་ཁུར་བརྒྱ་དང་མར་བྲི་བརྒྱ་ཟམ་བསྡེབ། མགར་བ་ཚང་མས་ལྕགས་ཟེར་ཡང་ཁྱོངས། དེ་ནས་ཕྱོགས་བཞི་ལ་ལྕགས་ཙེར་རྒྱབས། ཚོར་མའི་ཤིང་ཚང་མ་སྤུངས། དེའི་གཞུང་ལ་ཕྲུ་གུ་དེ་བཏངས། མར་ཚང་མ་དེ་ཁ་བླུགས། དེ་ནས་ཨ་ནེ་ཤ་ཀུར་དམན་མོ་ཨ་མ་ཆུང་ཙེ་དཀར་གྲིག་མ་ལ་རྫུ་སྟེ་མ་གོག་བཟང་ལྷ་མོའི་ཙར་སོང་སྟེ། ལྷ་གོག་བཟང་ལྷ་མོ། ཕྲུ་གུ་དེ་གར་ཡོད་ཟེརས་པ། ཨ་མས། ཕྲུ་གུ་དེ་ཐླམ་གསུམ་ཡོང་སྟེ་ཆོས་བསླབ་པ་འཁྱེརས།

ཕྱི་ཐོག་ལ་ལོག་སྟེ་འཁྱིང་ཆེན་ཟེརས། དེ་ནས་དཀར་ཐིག་མ་མགྱོགས་པ་ལྟ་ལ་སོང་པ་སང། ཕྲུ་གུ་དེ་མིའི་གཞུང་ལ་བདང་སྟེ་ཡོད་ཚུག། དཀར་ཐིག་མས་ཏུ་འདིན་ཞིག་ཟེརས།

མི་དང་ཀུན་ནི་ཁྲིམས་ལ་ལྷང་མཁན་ལ་ཡེ་བདང་ཅེན།
གོག་བཟང་ལྷ་མོས་ཡེའི་ཚབས་ལ་ཕྲུ་གུ་བདངས།
ཨ་མ་གོག་བཟང་ཕྲུ་གུ་ལ་སྨུན་ཏེ་བདུད་དེ་ལག་ལ་བདངས།
ངའི་ཕྲུ་གུ་ག་ཟུག་ལ་འཁྱིང་ཡིན།

དེ་ཟུག་ཟེར་ཏེ་ཏུས་པ་སང། ཕྲུ་གུས་ཨ་མ་ཡ་ཟེརས། གླུ་འདི་ལྟར།

བུ་ཚའི་ཨ་མ་ཆུང་བས་ངའི་དངོས་ལ་ཉེན་དང།
མ་དཀར་ཐིག་མས་བུ་ཚ་ངའི་བདག་ལ་གསན།

ནམ་སྟོད་མཐོན་པོ་ལ་བལྟས་པ།
ཉི་ཟླ་གཉིས་ཀ་ཁྲ་གསལ་ལེ་ཞུགས།
སྐར་ཚོགས་འཛོམ་མོ་གཞུང་ལ་སྨྲུང་སྟེ་འདུག།
ང་ལ་ཕ་མ་མེད་མཁན་སོང།
གངས་སྟོད་མཐོན་པོ་ལ་བལྟས་ཀྱང།
གངས་སེ་སེང་གེ་ཁྲ་གསལ་བ་འདུག !
སེང་ཕྲུག་ལེགས་མོ་མདུན་ལ་སྨྲུངས།
ང་ལ་ཕ་མ་མེད་མཁན་སོང།
བྲག་སྟོད་མཐོན་པོ་ལ་བལྟས་ཀྱང།

སྐྱིད་ཆེན་ཨ་ཕ་དྲིང་ན་འདུག།
ཨ་མ་དན་མོ་སྤྲན་ལ་འདུག།
ཤ་ཕྲུག་ལེགས་མོ་གཞུང་ལ་སྤྲུངས།
ང་ལ་ཕ་མ་མེད་མཁན་སོང།
མཚོམ་སྟོད་མཐོན་པོ་ལ་བསྐྱུས་ཀྱང།
ཉ་མོ་ཨ་མ་སྤྲོན་ལ་འདུག།
ཉ་ཕོ་ཨ་ཕ་དྲིང་ན་འདུག།
ཉ་ཕྲུག་ལེགས་མོ་གཞུང་ལ་སྤྲུངས།
ང་ལ་ཕ་མ་མེད་མཁན་སོང།
མི་དང་ཀུན་གྱིས་ལྕུང་མཁན་ལ་ཕེ་བདང་ཅེན་པ།
ངའི་ཨ་མས་ཕེ་ཚབ་ལ་ཕྲུ་གུ་བཏང་སོང།
མ་ཤུམས་ཨ་མ་གཟིགས་མོ་ལྟོས།
ཕྱོགས་བཞི་ལྷུགས་ཐག་བརྐྱང་བ་དེ།
གླིང་བཞི་ང་ལ་ནོན་པའི་རྟགས་ཤིག་ཡིན།
མ་ཤུམས་ཨ་མ་གཟིགས་མོ་གཟིགས།
ཚེར་ཁྲུར་བརྒྱ་དེ་ངའི་ལག་སྐྱོས་ཤིག་ཡིན།
མར་བྲེ་བརྒྱ་དེ་ངའི་ལག་སྐྱུད་ཅིག་ཡིན།
མ་ཤུམས་ཨ་མ་གཟིགས་མོ་གཟིགས།
གླིང་གི་ཤར་པ་ཚང་མས་གཟིགས་མོ་གཟིགས།
གླིང་གི་ན་ཆུང་ཚང་མས་གཟིགས་མོ་གཟིགས།

ཤར་རན་བྲི་བ་རན་བྲི་གསུམ་ཀ་མེ་ནང་དུ་ཕང་ཡིན།

བུ་ཚ་ང་རང་སིང་གི་མཆོགས་མཆོངས་ཡིན།

དེ་ཧྲུག་ཟེར་དེ་བུ་ཚ་དེ་མིའི་ནང་ནས་བིང་སྡེ། ཞྭགས་ཐག་དེ་བཅད་དེ་བིང་སྡེ་ཕར་མཆོངས་ཚུར་མཆོངས་བདང་ངེན་ཞིག། ཤར་རན་བྲི་བ་རན་བྲི་གསུམ་ཀ་ཧྲུམ་སྡེ་མིའི་དཀྱིལ་ལ་ཕང་སྡེ་བདངས་པ། དེ་མི་ཚོགས་ཚང་མ་འཇིགས་དེ་ཨ་མཚན་སོང་སྡེ་ཤོར་དེ་སོང་། དེ་ནས་མ་དཀར་ཁྲིག་མ་དང་ཕྲུ་གུ་གཉིས་ཀ་ཁང་པ་ལ་ཡོངས། དཀར་ཁྲིག་མས་མ་གོག་བཟང་ལྷ་མོ་ལ་ཟེརས། ཨ་གོག་བཟང་ལྷ་མོ། ཁྱོ་རང་གི་ཕྲུ་གུ་དེ་ཐམ་ཚང་ཀས་འཁྱེར་དེ་མིའི་གཞུང་ལ་སྦྱོགས་བཞི་ལ་ཞྭགས་ཐག་བདགས་དེ་འདུག། དགས་ཁོ་རང་བིང་སྡེ་ཡོངས། ད་ནས་ཕར་ལ་མི་སུ་ལ་ཡང་མ་བདང་ཟེར་དེ་དཀར་ཁྲིག་མ་ལོག་སྡེ་ཁང་པ་ལ་སོང་།།

No. 10.

ཨ་མ་གོག་བཟང་ལྷ་མོ་ལ་ཕྲུ་གུ་མ་སྐྱེ་བའི་སྔོན་ལ་མཛེ་ནད་ཕོག་སྡེ་ཡོད་ཚུག། ཞག་ཅིག་ཕྲུ་གུས་ཟེརས། ཨ་མ་རང་གིས་སྨྲ་འཕྲུ་སྡེ་ན། གཞན་མའི་ནང་ལ་མ་ཆ། ང་དང་ངེ་ནང་དུ་བུ་མོ་ཞིག་ཁྱོང་སྡེ་ལྷ་བཙུག། དེ་མེན་ནང་དང་གི་ནང་ལ་ཀུན་མ་ཞུགས་ཡིན། ང་ཤིང་ཞིག་འཁྱོང་བ་རི་ལ་ཆེན་ཟེར་དེ་ཐག་པ་ཞིག་དང་ལོག་པ་ཞིག་ཁུར་དེ། བུ་ཚ་ཤིང་ལ་སོང་། ཕྲུ་གུ་སོང་ཚར་ར་དང་། ཡ་མས་སྨྲ་ལྷ་ཅས་ལ་ཁྲིམ་མཆོས་པའི་རྩ་སོང་། ཕྲུ་གུ་ལ་དེ་ཧྲུག་མཐོང་སྡེ་ལོག་སྡེ་ཡོང་སྡེ། ནང་ན་ཅི་ཡོད་མཁན་ནི་ཆ་ལག་ཚང་མ་སྦྲས་དེ་མེད་མཁན་བཅོས། ཀག་ཆག་ཅིག་གི་ཀ་ས་ཅེ་ཞིག་བོར་དེ་ན། ཡང་རི་ལ་ལོག་སྡེ་སོང་། ཤིང་

ཁར་དེ་ཡོང་ཟེ་ན། ཨ་མ་ད་རུང་སྨྲ་ལྷ་མ་ཚར་བ། ཁྲིམ་མཆོས་པའི་རྩ་ཡོད་ཚུག ། ཕྲུ་གུས་བོས་དེ་གཉིས་ཀ་ནང་ལ་བསླེབ་སྡེ་བལྟ་ཟེ་ན། ཀུན་མས་འཁྲིར་དེ་ཆ་ལག་ཅི་ཡང་མེད་ཚུག ། ཕྲུ་གུས་ཨ་མ་ལ་ཟེར་ས། ཨ་མ་རང་ལ་ངས་སྔོན་ལ་ཟེར་ས། ཡ་མ་རང་མིའི་ཙོ་སོང་པ་རྨང། ཀུན་མ་ཡོངས། ང་ལྡོགས་ས་རག ། ཟ་ཅེས་ཞིག་དོང་ཟེར་ས་པ། ཨ་མས། ཟ་ཅེས་ཅི་བདང་ཡིན། ནང་དུ་ཅི་ཡང་མི་འདུག ། ཀག་ཆག་ཅིག་གི་ཁ་ས་ཅོ་ཞིག་འདུག་ཟེར་ས་པ། བུ་ཚས་དེ་ས་ཅོ་བོ་གཡོས་ཞིག་བཟོས་དེ་དོང་ཟེར་ས། ཨ་མས་གཡོས་བཟོས་པ་སང། ཡང་བོར་ཅས་སི་སྣོད་མེད་ཚུག ། ཕྲུ་གུས་ངའི་ལག་པའི་ཁ་དོང་ཟེར་ས་པ། ཨ་མས། ཁྱོ་རང་ཕྲུ་གུའི་ལག་པ་ཏ་ས་ཡོང་ཆེན། ངའི་ཀོན་ལག་སྐྲན་དེ་ཡོང་ཡིན་འགྲོ། ངའི་ལག་པའི་ཁ་དོང་ཟེར་ས། ཨ་མའི་ལག་པའི་ཁ་བདང་སྡེ་ས་ཚན་དང་གཡོས་ཚན་པོ་ཨ་མའི་ལག་པའི་ནང་ལ་བསྒམས་དེ་བོར་ས། ཨ་མ་ལ་ཚན་དེ་ཡོང་སྡེ་ཀུ་ཅོ་བདངས་པ། ཕྲུ་གུས། ངའི་ཨ་བཱ་གར་ཡོད་སྡོན། ང་ལ་ཨ་བཱ་མེད་པ། མི་ཚང་མས་ཁ་སྐྱེ་སྡེ་ནལ་ལུ་ཟེར་འདུག ། མི་ཚང་མ་ལ་ཨ་བཱ་འདུག ། ང་ཨ་བཱ་མེད་ཅེས་ཅི་ཡིན་ཟེར་ས། ཨ་མས་ཟེར་ས། ཁྱོ་རང་གི་ཨ་བཱ་དེ་སྲུ་ཡིན་ང་ལ་གྲུས་མེད། མེ་མེ་བསློབ་དཔོན་རྩེ་དགུ་ལ་འདྲི་བ་ལ་སོང། མི་མི་ལ་གྲུས་ཡོང་ཡིན་འགྲོ་ཟེར་ས་པ། ཡ་མའི་ལག་པ་འཕྲུད་བདངས་པ། ལག་པ་ཚང་མ་ཆོལ་སྐྱང་བིང་སྡེ་ཡོད་ཚུག ། དེ་ནས་ཕྲུ་གུས་ཏུ་ཏ་ཟེར་དེ་ལག་པ་དང་ཞད་པ། སྔོན་མེའི་མཆོགས་སོང། མཛེ་ནད་ཕོག་མཁན་ནི་གཟུགས་པོ་ཡང་ཕན་སོང༎

THE STORY OF KESAR'S BIRTH.

Abstract of Contents.

1.

One day, when Agu *dPalle rgodpo* was tending goats, there came a white bird out of a white hill, and a black bird out of a black hill, who fought with one another. In the morning the black bird was winning, at noon both were equal, and in the evening the white bird was winning.

The next day a white yak came out of a white hill, and a black yak out of a black hill. In the morning the white yak was winning, at noon both were equal, and in the evening the black yak was winning. Agu *dPalle* who believed the black yak to be a devil, decided to kill him with his sling and to break 18 pieces out of his right horn. Those will be dedicated: to *dBangpo rgyabzhin*, mother *sKyabs bdun*, nâga-king *lJogpo*, *sKyer rdong snyanpo*, *bKur dman rgyalmo*, the 18 Agus, the top of the *gLing*-castle, the golden hill, the turquoise hill, the spring *Thsangya*, the *Groma-plain*, to *dPalmai astag*, the ford *sBi chu*,[1] the hunting-ground *sProtho nangma*, to father *Thonpa*[2] and mother *sNgonmo*, to *'aBruguma*, to the store-house of his treasures, and the last piece to himself.

The white yak had been a transformation of *dBangpo rgyabzhin*, and the black yak of the devil *Curulugu*. Then out of the white hill there came a child, about a yard high (another transformation of *dBangpo rgyabzhin*), and offered all his treasures and half of his land and castle to the Agu in recognition of the services rendered to him. The Agu refused to accept anything, but demanded that one of the three sons of the king of heaven should be sent to the headless

[1] *dPalmai astag*, the glorious little village, and the ford *sBi chu*, are parts of the *gLing*-land, which were probably omitted in the history of the creation. Prologue to the Kesar-saga, No. 5. *dPalmai astag* is also the name of a female agu.

[2] Here 'aBruguma's father is called *Thonpa*; later on the name *br Tanpa* turns up again; he has two names apparently.

gLing-land as its head. The king of heaven promises to send word after seven days[1].

2.

dBangpo rgyabzhin returned to the upper land of the gods, and went to sleep with his head wrapped up. His eldest son *Don ldan* brought him his meal and tea and asked him about the reason of his sorrow. The father told him of his promise to send one of his sons to the *gLing*-land; if he would not like to go? *Don ldan* said: "How could a son of the gods go to the land of men? Eat the food, if you like; and leave it, if you do not like!"

The second son *Donyod* was asked the same questions, but he also refused to go.

When the third son *Don grub* was asked if he would go to the land of men, he said: "I shall go wherever my father may send me, even to a place where I shall have to die or get lost!" Then the father took the tea and the meal.

3.

The next day the King [of heaven] said to his three sons: "Take a quiver each and a sieve full of arrow-blades each. When riding downwards, scatter the arrow-blades about; when riding upward, gather the arrow-heads and put them on to the arrow-shafts. Who wins in the contest, will remain here; who loses, will have to go to the land of men!" The little son *Don grub* won and did not miss a single arrow-head.

The following day the king gave them a bushel filled with mustard-seeds each and told them to scatter them about, when riding downward, and to gather them, when riding upward. Again *Don grub* won, because he did not miss a single mustard-seed.

Then the elder brothers were full of wrath and said: "Well, we shall have to go as its head to the *gLing*-land, and *Don grub* is to

1 This version of the birth-story of Kesar will be usefully compared with the one published in the Indian Antiquary, and which I shall call the *Sheh*-version. (Spring Myth of the Kesar Saga, No. I-V). In the *Sheh*-version only a fight of two birds is mentioned. It is not at all necessary to believe, that the report of a double fight in the shape of birds and yaks is the original tale. Here the Lower Ladakhi version simply shows one of the characteristics of the oral versions of the Kesar Saga, *i.e.*, the tendency to take hold of other versions which are current in other villages, and to embody them into the original version of the village by telling one after the other, leaving the versions almost entirely untouched. Other instances we shall notice later on. This characteristic has been mentioned in the I. A.

remain here!" Again their father sent them a-hunting, saying: "Who of you will bring me many wild goats and wild yaks, will not be sent to the *gLing*-land!" It was *Don grub* who alone was successful. Therefore his wrathful elder brothers tied him to a high tree, and went home with his booty. Father did not even ask where *Don grub* remained.

Out of a hill came a man whose upper part was white, the middling part red, and the lower part black,[1] and said to *Don grub*: "Did you perhaps not obey father and mother, did you kill a man or a dog, or are you a thief, that you are tied to this tree?" *Don grub* replied: "Yes, I did all you say, but now look at me!" Saying this, he pulled out the tree and carried it home, where he planted it before the door of the house, to give shade to his father and mother.

Again the three brothers were sent a-hunting, and again the little one alone was successful. This time he was thrown into a pit by his elder brothers, and relieved by a lizard, whose tail he seized. Because the hole through which he was dragged, was very narrow, all his flesh and skin came off. He simply said '*thu thu*' and his flesh and skin was restored to him and turned into steel. The two stones [with which the hole had been covered], he carried home, and made two thrones out of

1 This figure represents in his person the three different colours of the world Whilst according to the Sheh-version *sTang lha* is white, *Bar btsan* red, and *Yog klu* blue; according to this Lower Ladakhi version *sTang lha* is white, *Bar btsan* red, and *Yog klu* black. This fact confirms my supposition that there is a certain connection between the black and blue colours in the Kesar Saga, and that the realm of the black devil, which often appears to be separated from the three realms of the world, originated out of that of the water-demons (*Yog klu*). In the Mongolian version of the Kesar Saga (I. J. Schmidt's translation) we find as respective colours white, yellow and black. This is another step further in the development of the colours. With regard to this I may add that, when conversing on *mchod rten* of white, red and blue colour with the Kardar of Lower Ladakh, this gentleman told me that the red colour was wrong, and that the *mchod rten* in the middle ought to show the yellow colour, as is actually the case in a group of three *mchod rten* at Saspola. This transition of the red colour into the yellow colour I am inclined to connect with the movement started by *Tsongkhapa*. Although this reformer only tried to replace the red colour of the lama's robes by the yellow one, the idea seems to have developed, that the red colour is not a holy colour at all, and ought to be exchanged for the yellow one. It is not only the system of colours, but a great many other instances, which speak in favor of a greater antiquity of the Tibetan version of the Saga. At the present time a number of Russian folklorists show a tendency to derive European folklore from that of the Mongolians. Perhaps they are right; but many Mongolian tales seem to have their prototypes in Tibetantales. That even in Tibet we are probably not yet at the fountain-head, I have mentioned already.

them for his parents. According to his prayer the well of nectar appeared underneath the thrones, surrounded by fruit-trees of all kinds.[1]

4.

Agu *dPalle* had tied a stone to the ear of one of his goats to be reminded of *dBangpa rgyabzhin's* promise. He forgot all the same; but when his wife was milking the goat, and the stone hit against the goat's cheek, so that the goat shied and spilt the milk, he knew again and started for the upper kingdom of the gods. The king of the gods was lying in the sunshine. After *dPalle* had saluted him with due respect and offered a white riband, he asked if not a horse could be sold to him. This was not the case, but he received a golden fish as a bakhshish.

Then he went to the lower kingdom of the Nâgas and found King *lJogpo* lying in the sunshine. To him also a white riband was offered, and *lJogpo* was asked if he could not sell a horse. This was not the case, but Agu *dPalle* received a turquoise fish as a bakhshish.

Now *dPalle* went to the firm place in the middle, offered a white riband to mother *sKyabs bdun*, and asked her if she could not sell him a horse. She said, yes, if he would pay 4 Rs. 8 Annas for each little hair of the horse. *dPalle* said that he had been a shepherd of goats, sheep, horses, yaks and oxen in *gLing*. Every one of those animals had become 100 through his care. All of these animals and as much silver as the mother would ask, he was ready to pay for the horse *sNgorog pon pon*. Then he received the horse.[2]

Then Agu *dPalle* mounted the horse, girded a broken sword on his

[1] Here again, in the two hunting-tales, we have two parallel tales, probably belonging to two different versions, both of which are intended to show the meanness of *Don grub's* elder brothers. I wish to draw attention to the fact that the Kesar myths (and other folklore also) are very fond of showing the parallelism of *three* members not only in verses of three lines, but also in tales of three occurrences. Because both of my Sheh-versions of the Kesar Saga speak of a threefold contest of the sons of the King of heaven, it is highly probable that this Lower Ladakhi version also had the story of a threefold instead of a fourfold contest originally. The fourth tale of the contest is, however, the most important, as it belongs to that group of tales which tell of the turning of the hero's skin into steel and similar substances. Compare I. A., list of additions, No. V.

[2] Does this version of the Agu's purchasing a horse go back to the same source as the report of *Don grub's* obtaining his horse from his red uncle? (because mother *sKyabs bdun* also represents the red colour); both these stories stand in nearly corresponding places in the saga. Compare I. A. Springmyth, tale No. III, 22-25.— Here also *dPalle's* relationship to silver and the white colour (his white ribands) can be noticed. Compare I. A. Springmyth, tale No. VIII, 17-20.

loins and rode back to the country of the gods. There he met with *Don yod*, *Don ldan* and *Don grub's* sister who was on the top of the roof. He asked her, where the house of the king was. She answered: "What do you want to do with him? Go wherever you like!" The Agu said: "Do you know, who I am? The horse is *sNgorog pon pon*, the man is *dPalle rgodpo*, the sword is the sword 'stone-cutter.' This sword was hardened by placing it for three years in ice, water and in the ground. If you will not show me the house, I shall throw your upper half into the sky, and your lower half into the centre of the earth!" Then the girl ran away and told her father, who knew at once that the stranger was Agu *dPalle.* He went out and shook hands with the Agu. *dPalle* blamed him for having told lies, but again they agreed on sending *Don grub* after seven days.

5.

Don grub wished to have a look at the *gLing*-land, before going there as King Kesar. He took the shape of a beautiful bird and descended to Agu *Khrai mgo khru thung's* house. This Agu told his wife to bring out his bow and to make hot water ready for the soup, they were going to cook from the bird. But the bird flew away, leaving some dung. The other Agus were kinder, and Agu *dPalle* brought an offering of food and pencil-cedars. When *Don grub* arrived back in heaven, his father asked his opinion on the *gLing*-land, and *Don grub* answered that everything was alright, only Agu *Khrai mgo khru thung* was a bad man.

6 and 7.

Then *Don grub* asked his father how he could go to the land of *gLing* without a mother, castle, horse, brother, bow and arrow, kettle, goat, plough-ox, protecting god and goddess, and without a wife. The father said: "Your mother will be *Gog bzang lhamo*, your castle the *gLing*-castle, your horse *rKyang byung dbyerpa*, your brothers *γSer sbal* and *γYu sbal*, your arrow *lTong dKar*, your bow *Gyad γzhu* of steel, your tool the 'Stone-cutter,' your spear *dPal jan*, your kettle *Zangsbu Kha yon*, your pot *Kha dmar*, your goat *Ra skyes skye dmar*, your plough-ox *rKang dkar*, your protecting goddess *bKur dman rgyalmo*, and your wife will be *'áBrugmo*.

The lives of the children of the king of heaven were bound to a cup of milk each. The king ordered his daughter to pour the milk out of *Don grub's* cup, and at that very moment *Don grub* died.[1]

[1] Here the tale of *Don grub's* death in heaven is entirely different from that of the Sheh-version. The belief that the lives of the ogres are bound to certain things

Then a great storm went over the earth. At that time Agu *Pasang ldan ra skyes*[1] was weaving, and *Gog bzang lhamo* was turning her spindle; each of them had a cup of tea before them. Into the lady's cup fell a hail-stone, which the Agu advised her to eat, because it was a gift from the gods apparently. After that she was with child. When people began to say that King Kesar would be born to *Gog bzang lhamo*, her two younger sisters became envious. They secrety tied one of her pigtails to one of the iron hearth-stones and sent a goat into the room. Then they shouted: "Sister, turn the goat out of the room!" *Gog bzang lhamo* rose to do so, tore the pigtail off her head, and upset the milk. After that she got many ulcers.

On the day of birth the child cried from inside the mother: "I shall be born on the top of three hills. Go there and put up three stones and three beams, take coral sticks and pearl-white twigs and cover [the house] with roof-earth of butter and flour!" This the mother did, and it said: "I am not the deer of the hills! Go to three valleys, and build a similar house!" Then she was told to build another house on the shore of the lake, another one in the middle of the field; after that she was sent behind the door of her house, then to the elevated place in her house. Then the child threatened her to come out of her head, carrying away some part of the head. Again the child threatened the mother to come out between the ribs, or out of the sole of the foot. Finally the child told the truth, saying: "Bring an offering of food and pencil-cedar, together with me many creatures will be born!"[2]

At first sun and moon were born and went up to the sky, then the wild goat, who went to the rock; the lioness with the turquoise mane, who went to the glacier; the wild yak, who went to the

outside their bodies, was applied here to the lives of the gods. Because it will be interesting to compare the report of *Don grub's* outfit for the *gLing*-land with that of the Sheh-version, I shall give the latter according to my fullest copy of the Sheh-version in the appendix.

[1] Agu *Pasang ldan ra skyes* in his relation to Kesar's mother is the germ of that extremely comic figure, into which he developed in the Mongolian version, where he is called *Sanglun*. I have made special enquires about him; but according to the views of *Ladakh*'s he has never been *Gog bzang lhamo's* husband although he was often teased to have had something to do with her.

[2] For comparison I give specimen verses from the Sheh-version, which refer to the same scene, in the appendix. That the Sheh-versions also have slightly different creatures, is shown in the I. A. list of additions, No. 3. In the I. A. I made a mistake, saying, that all the creatures were born at the place where the little house was built. They were born in *Gog bzang lhamo's* house, and went through the window to the places prepared by the mother.

meadows; the eagle, who went to the top of the hill; the fish golden-eye, who went to the lake; the little bird, who went upon a tree; and all the treasures and the cattle, which *dBangpo rgyabzhin* had prophecied. After all this also a large head with a small neck, like a lizard, was born. The mother put some buckwheat-flour in its mouth, and a large stone on it. Then *bKur dmanmo* came. When she heard a voice without seeing a body, she asked the mother: "What sort of a child was born to you?" *Gog bzang lhamo* said: "Many creatures were born to me, but went out through the window. After all of them a lizard was born to me, who is now underneath the stone!" *bKur dmanmo* scolded the mother and lifted the stone. Underneath it she saw the child which had taken the shape of the godly King Kesar.

8.

When the hail was falling, some hail-stones fell on the treasures and creatures, which Agu *dPalle* had brought from the castle *Paci dpal dong.* They all became pregnant together with mother *Gog bzang lhamo.* On the day of Kesar's birth also to these creatures children were born: To the pot with the red mouth—a pot with a long neck; to the kettle with the crooked mouth—a kettle with a broken mouth; to the white moon-axe—a steel-axe; to the many-coloured rope—a rope of a yard in length; to the white bag 'Hold thousand'—a bag of many colours, to the mare *Thsa langs—rKyang rgod dbyerpa*; to the *Dzo* with crooked horns—the *Dzo* 'White foot'; to the white goat—the goat 'Red neck;' to the sheep *Dromo*—the sheep *Porze*; to the ass 'Black with a white mouth'—a brown ass; to the white bitch—the yellow hound; to the black cat—a cat of many colours.[1]

9.

Then an offering was erected from the flour which had been given to the lizard, and *Ane bKur dmanmo* sang a lullaby and a hymn to the

[1] In the appendix two specimen verses, referring to the same scene in the Sheh-version, are given. That the list of creatures is not quite the same in both versions is proved by list of additions No. 2. (Indian Antiquary).

As we have seen, also the Lower Ladakhi version of the Kesar saga is in possession of two different tales regarding the population of the earth with animals, etc. Compare No. 7 and No. 8 above. According to No. 7 it is *Gog bzang lhamo* who produces everything; according to No. 8 it is the castle *Paci dpal dong*, which contained everything. Here we may either have two entirely different versions of the same tale; or one of them (perhaps No. 8) may belong to the ancient account of the first creation of the world, and the other (perhaps No. 7) may be the account of the re-creation and re-population of the world in spring every year.

land of the gods, the earth, and the land of the Nâgas.[1] Then she returned the child to the mother and advised her not to give the child into anybody's hands.

Agu *bKa blon ldanpa*, the son of the devil *lHa cin*, whose upper half was like a devil and whose lower half was like that of a man of *gLing*, said to all the *Sharrandre barandre* of the East that King Kesar of *gLing* was born to *Gog bzang lhamo* and that they must bring him at once and throw him into the fire, because later on Kesar would do them great harm. Then the bad Agu went to the South.

Those *Sharrandre barandre* took the shape of lamas and went to *Gog bzang lhamo's* house. They accepted neither flour nor butter, but, asked for the child to teach it religion. They promised to return it after seven days. When they had gone, they called together all the boys, girls and smiths of *gLing* and told them to bring thorns, butter (for burning) and nails. After everything had arrived, the nails were fastened in four directions [to hold the ropes with which the child was bound], the thorns were thrown on a heap, and the child was placed in the middle of it. Then *Ane bKur dmanmo*, taking the shape of *dKar thigma*, went to see what was being done with the child. When she saw the child in the middle of the fire, she cried and said: "It is the custom of all men to give flour to beggars; *Gog bzang lhamo* gave the child instead. How shall I get the child back?" The child answered, that, although the stars were well protected by sun and moon, the young lions by the ice-lion, the young deer by the old wild goat, the little fishes by their parents, he had lost father and mother. "But the four chains are a sign, that the four *gLing* will be subdued by me. The fire only warms my hands, the butter serves to anoint them. Now look, my mother, and all you boys and girls of *gLing*! I shall throw the three *Sharandre barrandre* into the fire. I shall jump like a lion!" This he did, and all people ran away from fear. Then he and *dKar thigmo* went home again.

Although it is quite in accordance with the general ideas of nature-mythology, that the sun, the moon, the rainbow and the cloud have children (because the sun of the second day may be called the child of the sun of the first day), the names of the children as given in No. 8: a pot with a long neck, a steel-axe, etc., look more like the names of practical instruments. This development from the parable to the practical implement which had been used for comparison, is not quite inconceivable, if we keep in mind that also Kesar probably was the personification of a power of nature, before he became humanized in the course of time.

[1] This very same hymn is sung at every wedding feast at Khalatse, when three pieces of the wedding cake are thrown towards the sky, over the earth and downwards.

10.

Before the child was born to *Gog bzang lhamo*, she was smitten with leprosy. One day the child said to her: "If you wish to get your hair washed, you must not go to the house of another woman, but tell another woman to come here. Otherwise a thief might come, whilst I shall go for some wood. But the mother went to some other woman; and the child ran home at once, hid everything and put some grain mixed with sand on a broken clay-pot. Then he went to the hills for wood. When he came home with a load, he called his mother and blamed her for having gone away, because a thief had plainly come. "But now let me have some food!" As there was nothing else left, he asked his mother to parch the grain mixed with sand on his hand, for there was no other vessel. The mother proposed to use her own hand instead of the child's, and when hers was filled with the red-hot grain, he seized it and did not allow her to open it until she would tell him who was his father. The mother said that she really did not know, and that he had better go to the teacher *rTse dgu*, to ask him about it. Then he let her hand go. It had become one great burning wound; but when the child said *huha* and caressed it, it healed at once, and her body became entirely free from leprosy.[1]

1 It strikes me that *Gog bzang lhamo* is suffering from leprosy before and after the birth of those many creatures, and that she is healed by means of heat. This looks like a parable for snow being removed by the sun. But the story, as we have it now, is a little too full to be original in all its parts. That it is winter before the birth of Kesar, is indicated also by the fact that *dBangpo rgya bzhin* and *lJogpo* are lying in the sunshine. Ladakhis do that only during winter.

APPEND TO ABSTRACT OF CONTENTS.

Specimen verses from the Sheh-version, which have not yet been quoted in full.

According to the fullest copy of the Sheh-version, *Don grub's* outfit for the *gLing*-land is the following :—

pha lha skyer rdzong snyanpo snams	Accept *sKyer rdzong snyanpo* as your paternal deity.
ma lha bkur dman rgyalmo snams	Accept *bKur dman rgyalmo* as your maternal deity.
thurru rkyang byung dbyerpa snams	Accept the foal *rKyang byung dbyerpa*,
log ngo shespai rta zhig yin	It is a horse that always knows the way back.
'aphurla mkhaspai rtä zhig yin	It is a horse that knows to fly.
sdigpai grigu sor γsum snams	Accept the knife 'three fingers long' for the sinful,
sdigpala btangbai gri zhig yin	It is a knife to stab the sinful.
sangs rgyas dunggi picag snams	Accept the shell-knife for Buddha,
sangs rgyasla btangbai gri zhig yin	It is a knife to stab Buddha. *
γzhu ni srin γzhu sngonmo snams	Accept the blue bow *Srin γzhu*,
mdā ni rang log thubpa yin	The bow, whose arrow flies back again.
srinpo thamscad btulzana	When subduing all the ogres,
srinmo thamscad grogsla 'agug	Call the female ogres to thy help.
bya Khyung krung nyima btulzana	When subduing the bird *Khyung krung*, the sun,
byamo dkarmo grogsla 'agug	Call the white bird (the moon) to thy help.
hor gur dkar rgyalpo btulzana	When subduing king *Gur dkar* of *Hor*,
mgar rtsa chos sgrol grogsla 'agug	Call the smith's lady *Chos sgrol* to thy help.
'adre lha btsan bog btulzana	When subduing *'aDre lha btsan bog*,

* For men, who do not wish to meet with a statement of adversity to Buddhism in the Ladakhi Kesar myths, it is most easy to say that such lines were simply invented by Mr. Francke. Here you have Buddha again. The above song was dictated by *Zarra*, daughter of *Natshab Ali*, of *Sheh*. She is still alive and young, and may be examined by everyone who takes an interest in the Kesarsaga.

dzemo 'abamza 'abum skyid grogsla 'agug	Call *Dzemo 'abamza 'abum skyid* to thy help.
Ron btsan khromo btulzana	When subduing *Ron btsan khromo*,
shel lcam 'aBrugmo grogsla 'agug.	Call the crystal wife *'aBrugmo* to thy help.

Specimen verses from the birth story according to the Sheh version, list of additions No. 3 :—

The child says from inside the mother; according to MS. I :—

Amala skyé skye ní	Being born to the mother,
nám stod mthóla skyé yin	I shall be born on the high zenith
námstodla skyéces ní	[Although] being born on the high zenith,
nyí zla γnyísko ní nga mán	Yet I am not sun and moon.

And so on through all the different creatures.

Or according to MS. II :—

Ngá 'adirú mi skyé	I shall not be born here,
rii mgóru skyé yin	I shall be born on the top of the hill.
ríi mgóla skyéste	[Although] being born on the hill-top,
sháva rídvags ní nga mán	Yet I am not a deer.

And so on through all the different creatures.

Specimen verses from the birth story according to the Sheh version, list of additions No. 2. When the hail came, Agu *dPalle* said :—

mi thsangmas kha shor rgyabs	All men ran away,
gogza lhamo shulla lus	*Gog za lhamo* remained back,
dPalle nga mi 'adug ltala chen	I, *dPalle*, am not [at home], I shall go to look [after her].
rta thsangmas kha shor rgyabs	All horses ran away,
rgodma thsalangs shulla lus	The mare *Thsa langs* remained back,
dPalle nga mi 'adug ltala chen.	I, *dPalle*, am not [at home], I shall go to look [after her].

And so on through all the different creatures.

VOCABULARY AND COMMENTS.

1.

རྣོལ། *rnol*, = *snol gyag*, a fight.

ཕེད། *phed*, = *phyed*, half.

ཕི་ཐོག། *phithog,* = *phyithog,* evening.

གཡོག་ཅས། *γyogcas,* to cover; here in the sense 'to spin,' cove the spindle stick.

ང་རི། *ngari,* = *ngaranggi,* my.

ར་ཡུག། *rayug* = *ra dbyug,* sling to throw stones at goats.

བོང་མཐིལ། *bong mthil,* sling to throw stones at donkeys.

ཁྱི་ལྗག། *khyi ljag,* sling to throw stones at dogs.

འཇུག་མ། *'ajugma,* or *'ajugring,* oblong.

ལྟུམ་པ། *ltumpa,* piece, fragment.

བར་བཙན། *bar btsan,* 'the firm place in the middle,' the earth.

ཨ་མ་སྐྱབས་བདུན་མ། *ama skyabs bdunma,* mother 'seven helps'; name of the goddess of the earth, instead of *bdunma, mdunma* also occurs.

ལྗོགས་པོ། *lJogspo,* is probably *lCogpo,* the 'lower one'; name of the king of the nâgas. An exactly parallel case is *ljam* instead of *lcam* for 'spouse.'

སྐྱེར་རྫོང་སྙན་པོ། *skyer rdzong snyanpo,* the 'well-sounding (speaking) companion of men'; a name of the father of the gods.

བཀུར་དམན་རྒྱལ་མོ། *bkur dman rgyalmo,* the 'respectable godly wife.' Name of the mother of the gods.

དཔལ་མའི་ཨ་སྟག། *dpalmai· astag,* 'the glorious village'; *astag* is probably the same as *asta,* a part of the village.

སྦི་ཆུ་རབས། *sbi chu rabs,* the ford *sBi;* name of the principal of fords; *sbi* is probably *spi* or *spyi,* principal. This ford and the village were probably forgotten in the account of the creation of *gLing,* see fasc. No. 1.

སྤྲོ་ཐོ། *spro tho;* here the name shows an *r* in addition, it seems to mean 'high joy.'

ཤེལ་ལྗམ་འབྲུ་གུ་མ། *shel ljam 'abruguma,* (*ljam* = *lcam*), the crystal wife *'aBruguma.* It is interesting, that here the name appears again in the form of *'aBruguma*, instead of *'aBriguma.* My translation of this name as 'little grain' or 'seed' is not so very improbable, if we consider, that *Dong γsum mila* also originated from the grains of the tree.

ལྡེམ་མཁར། *ldem mkhar*, is said to be the store-room of the castle, (where all the treasures brought from *dPal dong* castle were stored up).

ཅུ་རུ་ལུ་གུ། *curulugu,* name of the giant (devil) in the north.

2.

གསང་མ། *γsangma,* meal.

ཉེ་རང། *nyerang,* = *nyidrang,* you, respectful address.

འཐམ་མོ། *'athammo,* = 'athabmo, fight.

མེནྣ། menna, = *ma yinna,* if this be not [the case].

བཞངས། *bzhangs,* = *bzhengs,* rise.

ཡོད་པིན་བ། *yodpinba,* was; the termination *ba* is used here in a similar sense as the emphatic article.

བཏང་ཆད། *btang chad,* a promise to give.

དྲག། *drag,* Lower Ladakhi for *rag,* to feel, perceive.

3.

རྒྱལ་ལོག། *rgyallog,* win; another case of the present tense in *og.*

ཏོང་ཙེ། *tongtse,* = *dong,* quiver.

དིའུ། *diu,* arrow-blade.

སྐར་ཅས། *skarcas,* to put on; (the arrow-blade on the arrow-stick).

བསག་སྟག། *bsag stag*, = *bsag sdag*, quiver.

བསྡུ་ཅས། *bsducas*, = *sdudpa*, collect.

ཡོངས་པ། *yongspa*, came; the participle alone is used here to express the past, as has been the case in other sentences also.

ཉུང་དཀར། *nyung, dkar*, = *yungs dkar*, mustard.

སྲག་པ། *sragpa*, = *sregpa*, partridge.

ཁྱེ་ཞ། *khyezha*, = *khyed cag*, you.

རྩལ་ཅས། *rtsalcas*, seek; compare perfect tense of *'athsolba*. The *r* may be due to the *b* of the forms *btsol* and *btsal*.

དེ། འདི། *de*, *'adi*, that, this; these pronouns are always placed before the word to which they belong, contrary to the usage of Central Ladakh. They are often furnished with the termination of the genitive. The latter I have taken off again, because the spoken language does not confirm this usage of the genitive.

ཁྲ་སུག། *khrasug*, = *khrabo*, many-coloured.

དོན་ཏག། *don tag*, = *don*, meaning, business.

སྲིབ་ཅིག། *sribcig*, suddenly, a short time; *srib* means 'darkness,' originally. The above meaning of *sribcig* is to be explained in this way When the eye is covered by the eye-lid, it is dark for a moment. Thus it means literally, 'within the twinkling of the eye.'

བ་ཏྲག། *batrag*, = *bathag*, root.

སྣ་སོགས། *snasogs*, = *.na thsogs*, different.

བསད་ཅེས་པ་སང་། *bsaJces pasang*, 'better than killing'; this comparative in *pasang* seems to throw some light on the development of the comparative in *sang*. Here *'ang*, *also*, may have been added to the comparative in *pas*. Then the first part of the ending *pasang* was lost and *sang* only remained.

ཟག་ཟག། *zag zag*, rough, uneven, (like a rasp).

སྤགས་པ། *spagspa*, =pagspa, skin.

མེན་ནེ། *menne*, = *ma yinnas*, besides.

ཨུ་པེན། *upen*, a high mouarch.

ལྡངས་བུ། *ldangsbu*, throne; perhaps related to *γden*, throne.

ཟུན་ཅས། *zuncas*, surround.

ཨམ་བི་ཏི། *ambitī*, all sorts of fruit.

ཕྲུ་ལུ། *phrulu*, fruit.

སྣ་མི་སྣ་ཚང་། *sna mi sna thsang*, very different.

ཧུ་ཡུ། *huyu*, exclamation to express tiredness.

4.

ཅ་རག། *čarag*, a stone which is fastened to the ear of a goat or sheep, to remind you of a certain thing; like the knot in the handkerchief.

ལྩང་མཁན། *ltsangmkhan*, beggar.

རིམ་པ་བཞིན་དུ། *rimpa bzhindu*, slowly.

སྒུ་ཅེས། *sguces*, to bow.

ལམ་བཙུགས། *lam bcugs*, bakhshish; literally 'to put [you] on the way.'

ཉག། *nyag*, each single one.

ཞོ། *zho*, means 6 × 12 annas, *i.e.*, 4½ rupee, so I am told.

སྔོ་རོག་པོན་པོན། *sngo rog pon pon*, 'blue black with a curled-mane,' name of *dPalle's* horse.

ཆག་པོ། *chagpo*, broken ; adjective formed from *'achagpa.*

ཆོན་ཆན། *chon chan*, in vain.

གངས་ངར། *gangs ngar*,
ཆུ་ངར། *chu ngar*,
ས་ངར། *sa ngar*,
— the sudden placing of hot iron into ice, water or earth, to harden it.

ཁ་སྐྱེ་ཅེས། *kha skyeces*, = *kha kyeces*, to scold.

ལག་འཕྲད། *lag 'aphrad*, shake hands; this is not a Tibetan custom ; but is observed in Purig and Baltistan.

བཏང་སྟེན། *btangstena*, giving ; in Lower Ladakh we often meet with an additional *na* after a gerund.

5.

ལྟ་སྐོར། *lta skor*, go about to see something.

ཁྲུ་ཐུང། a short yard ; occurs in the name of the falcon ; it seems to indicate that the bird is not quite of the size of a yard.

As will have been noticed, the dialect of this version is not always pure. Lower Ladakhi forms which are at the base of the whole, are mixed with Central Ladakhi and classical forms. This was apparently done with a view to let its language appear a little more cultured.

རྡོ་ལྟོག། *rdo ltog*, a pot made of serpentine stone.

ཀོལ། *kol*, imperative tense of *bkalces*, to load.

གཞིད་མད། *γzhidmad*, = *γzhismad*, wife, family.

ཀ་ལྕོར། *kalcor*, the little pieces of butter which are smeared round the rim of a beer-pot, to honour a guest.

རོན། imperative tense of *'rances*, to smear, to direct ; perhaps related to *'adrenpa.*

6.

དཔལ་ཛན། *dpaljan,* = *dpalcan,* having glory.

ཀེར་ཟོང་། *Ker zong,* = *skyer rdzongs*; name of the father of the gods, who often officiates as a paternal deity only.

Do the different names of the same god develop into different gods?

ཁ་ཟུབ། *Kha zub,* or *kha sbub,* = *kha bub,* with the mouth turned downwards.

དེན་ན་མ་ལ། *denna mala,* in that very same moment.

7.

སེ་ར་རུ། *seraru,* = *serba,* hail.

ར་སྐྱེས། *ra skyes,* instead of *ru skyes*; *rva* has become divided into two words, *ra* and *ru*, both meaning the same.

པུ་རི་འཐུལ་ཅས། *puri 'athulcas,* to work with the shuttle.

ཁྲུ་ཅས། *khrucas,* = *'akhrudpa,* wash.

སྐྱེན། *skyen,* = *skye yin,* will be born.

ཏོ་ཝ། *towa,* or *to,* exclamation.

གྲལ་ཆད། *gral chad,* roof-laths.

སྦི་ལབ། *sbilab,* perhaps *spyilab,* twigs of the Tibetan roof.

སྐྱོར་ཅས། *skyorcas,* put up in a circle.

ཐོག་གྲབ། *thog grab,* twigs of the roof.

ཞིང་གི་ཨ་མ། *zhinggi ama,* 'mother of the field,' name of the lark.

རྟག་ཏག་པ། *rtagtagpa,* the elevated place in a room.

རྩིག་མ། *rtsigma, rtsibma,* rib; but in the next line there is *rtsib sha,* flesh near the ribs.

མཚོམ། *mthsom,* = *mthso,* lake.

སྐྱིན་ཆེན་བ་རྒན། *skyin chen ba rgan,* the 'big' wild goat, the old ox, name of the wild goat, born to *Gog bzang lhamo.*

སེང་གེ་གཡུ་རལ་ཅན། *sengge γyu ral can,* the 'lion with the turquoise locks'; name of the lion, born to *Gog bzang lhamo.*

འབྲོང་ཆེན་ཁམ་པ། *'abrong chen khamba,* the 'large and brown wild yak'; name of the yak, born to *Gog bzang lhamo.*

བྱ་རྒྱལ་རྒོད་པོ། *bya rgyal rgodpo,* the 'wild bird king'; name of the eagle, born to *Gog bzang lhamo.*

ཉ་མོ་གསེར་མིག། *nyamo γser mig,* the 'fish golden eye'; name of the fish, born to *Gog bzang lhamo.*

8.

མ་འཚད། *ma 'athsad,* the measure not being full; in classical language *ma zadde.*

ཚིག། *thsig,* air-brick.

སྐྱེ་རིངས། *skye rings,* 'long neck'; name of the pot, born to *Degbu kha dmar.*

ཁ་ཆོད། *kha chod,* 'broken mouth'; name of the kettle, born to *Zangsbu kha yon.*

སྟེ་པོ་རང་ཆོད། *stepo rang chod,* the 'axe cutting by itself'; name of the axe born to *stari zlaba dkarpo.*

ཐག་བུ་ཁྲུ་གང། *thagbu khru gang,* the 'rope one full yard [in length]'; name of the rope, born to *thagpa rgya stag.*

ཕད་ཁྲ་བོ། *phad khrabo,* the 'many-coloured bag'; name of the bag, born to *sGyemo dkarmoi stong shong.*

རྐྱང་རྒོད་དབྱེར་པ། *rkyang rgod dbyerpa,* ' the genuine wild kiang, name of Kesar's horse, born to *Thsa langs.*

མཛོ་ཕོ་རྐང་དཀར། *mdzo pho rkang dkar*, the 'white-footed Dzo name of the Dzo, born to m *Dzomo ru yon.*

ར་སྐྱེས་སྐྱེ་དམར། *ra skyes skye dmar*, the 'kid red-neck;' name of the kid, born to *Rama dkarmo.*

ལུག་པོར་ཟེ། *lug porze*, the 'sheep golden mouth;' name of the sheep, born to *Lug dromo.*

བོང་བུ་ཁམ་པ། *bongbu khamba*; the 'brown donkey'; name of the donkey, born to *Nagpo kha dkar.*

ཁྱི་ཕོ་གསེར་ལིངས། *khyi pho γser lings*, the 'golden-hound'; name of the dog, born to *Khyimo dkarmo.*

བི་ལ་ཁྲ་སུག། *bila khra sug*, the 'many-coloured cat'; name of the cat, born to *Bila nagpo.*

9.

ལྷ་ཕྲུག་ཀུན། *lha phrug kun*, the children of the gods; although only one child is born, the plural sign *kun* is used. Should this be a sign of respect?

ཚོ་ཇོ། *thso jo*, aristocratic offspring.

འཁུར་རེ་ན། *'akhurrena = 'akhurcesna*, in carrying [the child].

གསོལ་ལོ། མཆོད་དོ། *γsollo, mchoddo*, the addition of *o* in both words is due to the tune of the song.

འདོམ་པ། *'adompa*, dangerous.

In the MS. the gerund in *bai* is often used, which I have not yet observed in ordinary language. In some places I have changed it to *bas*, in others I have crossed it out.

ཤར་རན་དྲེ་བ་རན་དྲེ། sharrandre barandre, this is the Lower Ladakhi pronunciation of *sharri andhe bandhe.* In many cases a distinct *r* is sounded after dentals in Lower Ladakh in such words which do not suggest any *r* in Central Ladakh.—A *bandhe* is a lama who has not yet been to Lhassa.

བདུད་ལྷ་ཅིན། *bdud lha cin* (perhaps *γcin*); the 'devil, urine of the gods;' name of a devil, *bka blon ldanpa's* father.

སྙད་བཙོལ། *snyad btsol*, temptation, attempt.

ང་ཅ། *ngaca*, we , Lower Ladakhi for *ngacag*, *ngazha*.

སྐྱིལ་ཅེས། *skyilces*, to detain, hinder.

གཟིགས་མོ། *γzigsmo*, spectacle.

ཆེན། *chen*, will go; termination of the future tense; the MS. often has *cen* instead of *chen*. I am inclined to believe that these two terminations have to be differentiated, *chen* = *cha yin*, will go, is the termination of neuter verbs. *Cen* is probably contracted from *bco yin*, will do, and is the termination of active verbs.

སུན་ཅེས། *sunces*, to long after.

ལག་སྐུད། *lag skud*, smearing the hand [with oil.]

As regards the number of the *Andhe bandhe*, we find three as well as seven in the same version.

10.

འཁྲུ་སྟེ་ན། *'akhrustena*, when you will get your hair washed.

ལྷ་ཅས། *lhacas*, to plait; from *sleba*.

ལོག་པ། *logpa*, the goat-skin, worn by men and women.

ཀག་ཆག། *Kag chag*, potsherd.

ཧ་ས། *hasa*, tender.

ནལ་ལུ། *nallu*, = *nalbu*, = bastard.

ཆོལ་སྒང་། *chol sgang*, a wound caused by fire.

འགྲོ། *'agro*, = *dro* of the dubitative voice.

No. 1.

དེ་ནས་ཨ་མ་ལ་ཞིང་རི་དང་ཆུ་རི་ཁྱིང་སྟེ། ཕྲུ་གུ་དེ་མེ་མེ་ཀླྀ་དཔོན་རྩེ་དཀུ་ལ་ཨ་བ་འདྲི་བ་ལ་སོང་། མེ་མེ་ཀློ་དཔོན་རྩེ་དགུས་མི་མང་པོ་ལ་རིའི་རྩྭ་ཛ་བཅུག་གིན་ཞིག་ཡོད་ཚུག། དེ་མི་ཀུན་ལ་མེ་མེས་ཟེར་ས། འདི་རིང་འདི་ཙུ་མི་ཞིག་ཡོང་ཆེན། ཁོ་ལ་ཅང་མ་ཟེར་བ། ངའི་རྩ་ཡོང་བཅུག་ཟེར་དེ། མེ་མེ་མཚམས་ཁང་ལ་ལོག་སྟེ་སོང་བ་དང་། དེ་ཕྲུ་གུ་དེ་ཙུ་རྩྭ་ཛ་ས་ཙུ་བསླེབ་པ། མི་ཚང་མས་ཟ་ཅེས་ཟའད་ཚུག། མི་ཚང་མས་ཁོ་ལ་ཟ་ཅེས་ཁམ་བུ་རི་བཏངས་པ། ཁོས་ཟ་ཧྲོན་བཏང་ངོན་ཞིག་ཕུ་ཐུངས་ནང་དུ་སྦས་དེ་བོར་ས། ཕྲུ་གུས་གསེར་སྦྲང་ཞིག་ལ་སྐྱུད་པ་བཏགས་སེ། ཕུར་བཅུག་གིན་ཞིག་བོར་ས་པ། དེ་མི་ཞིག་གིས་ཟེར་ས། གསེར་སྦྲང་པོ་ངས་གཅིག་འཁོར་ཡིན་ཟེར་ས། ཕྲུ་གུས་སྦྲང་བུ་འབུད་དེ་ཆ་ན། ཁྱོ་རང་ལ་འདྲ་ཡིན། སྦྲང་བུ་སྟོར་ན། ངས་འདྲ་འཁོར་ཡིན་ཟེར་རེ། ཁོས་ཉེན་དེ་ཁྱིངས་པ། སྦྲང་བུ་སྟོར་སོང་། དེ་ནས་ཕྲུ་གུས་སྐྱིད་བདང་སྟེ་ཟེར་ས། གླུ་འདི་ལྟར།

ཁྱིང་ལྷ་ཁྱིང་ངའི་གསེར་སྦྲང་དེ་ཁྱིང་ལོ།
ཁྱིང་ལྷ་ཁྱིང་ངའི་གཡུ་སྦྲང་རེ་ཁྱིང་ཀོ།
ང་ཐང་ལ་ཆ་ན་རྒྱང་གོད་དབྱེར་པ་ཡིན་ལོ།
ང་སྐོམ་པ་རིག་ཆ་ན་ཨ་རག་བཏུད་རྩེ་ཡིན་ལོ།

ང་ལྟོགས་པ་རིག་ཆ་ན་ཞིམ་ཟག་མངར་ཆུ་ཡིན་ལོ།
ང་སྐྱུ་ན་པ་རིག་ཆན་སི་སྐྱན་གླིང་བྱ་རིག་ཡིན་ལོ།
ངའི་གསེར་སྒྲང་མ་ཁྲིང་ན་ང་ཁྲོ་རང་ངི་རྩ་ཤི་ཡིན་ལོ།
ངའི་གཡུ་སྒྲང་མ་ཁྲོང་ན་ངའི་སྲོག་ཁག་བཀལ་ཡིན།

དེ་ཟུག་ཟེར་དེ་མི་དེ་རྐོང་རྩ་འཐམ་སྟེ་འཛིང་མོ་བཏངས་པ། མི་ཚང་མས་ཟེརས། ཁྲོ་རང་ལ་ང་ཞུས་ཟ་ཅེས་མང་པོ་བཏངས་པ་ཡིན། དེ་ཚང་མ་ལོག་སྟེ་དོང་ཟེར་ས་པ། ཁོས་ཕྲུ་ཐུངས་སི་ནང་ནས་ཟ་ཅེས་ཕིང་སྟེ། ཚང་མ་ལ་རང་རང་གིས་བཏངས་མཁན་གྱི་ཁམ་བུ་རང་རང་ལ་ལོག་སྟེ་བཏངས། དེ་ནས་མི་ཚང་མ་ལ་ཟེར་ཐབས་ཅང་མ་ཡོངས་པ་སང་། ཕྲུ་གུ་དེ་ལ་ཚང་མས་ཧུ་ཟེར་དེ། ང་ཞ་ལ་མེ་མེ་སིས་ཆང་ཟ་མ་ཞིག་དང་ར་ཐོང་ཞིག་འཁྱེར་ཅེན། དེ་ཁྲོ་རང་ལ་བཏང་ཡིན་ཟེར་དེ་ཁ་ཆད་བཅོས། དེ་ནས་ཚ་བིག་འགོར་དེ་ན། མེ་མེ་སིས་ཆང་ཟ་མ་གཅིག་དང་ར་ཐོང་གཅིག་ཁྲིངས་པ་སང་། དེ་ཕྲུ་གུ་ལ་ཐོབ། མི་ཚང་མ་ལ་ཟ་ཅེས་ཉེ་ཙུན་སོང་སྟེ། རྩ་ཊ་མ་ཐབ་པ་ལུས་སོང་། དེ་ནས་ཕྲུ་གུས་རྩ་ལུས་ན། ཁོང་ལ་མེ་མེ་སི་ཁ་སྐྱེ་ཡིན། ཁོང་སྡིག་པ་བསམ་སྟེ། སློན་ལམ་བཏབས། རྩ་ཁྲོལ་ལི་ཁ་ཚང་མ་ཊ་སྟེ་ལྕང་པོ་ལ་སྐྱུ་བཅུག་སྟེ་མེ་མེ་ཁ་ཐོག་ལ་འདྲེན་དེ་བསྐྱིབ་བཅུག་ས། དེ་ནས་མི་ཚང་མ་ཡ་མཚན་སོང་སྟེ། མང་པོ་འཐད་སོང་། ཕྲུ་གུས་ཆང་དེ་མཐུངས། ར་ཐོང་དེ་ཁྲིད་དེ་མེ་མེ་མཚམས་ཁང་གི་དཀར་ཁང་མདུན་ལ་སོང་སྟེ། མེ་མེ་ལ་མཐོང་བཅུག་སྟེ། ར་མ་བསད་པ་གྱི་ཕིངས་པས། མེ་མེ་ལ་མཐོང་སྟེ་ཟེརས། ཡ་ཕྲུ་གུ། ཁྲོ་རང་གིས་ར་མ་བསད་ན། ངའི་མདུན་ལ་མ་བསད། ཕག་ཅིག་ལ་འཁྲིར་དེ་སོད་ཟེརས་པ།

ཕྲུ་གུ་དེས་ཟེརས། མེ་མེ་རང་གིས་ངའི་ཨ་བ་སྟོན། ངའི་ཨ་བ་མ་བསྟན་ན། ར་ཐོང་དེ་མེ་མེ་རང་གི་མདུན་ལ་བསད་ཡིན། ང་ལ་མི་ཚང་མས་ཨ་བ་མེད་མཁན་ནི་ནལ་བུ་ཟེར་འདུག་ཞུས་པ། མེ་མེས་ཟེརས། ཁྱོ་རང་གི་ཨ་བ་ངས་མི་ཤེས། ཐང་ཆེན་མོ་ཞིག་གི་ཁ་ཉེ་ཡོར་དཀར་ནག་དམར་གསུམ་ཡོད། ཁྱོ་རང་དེར་སོང་སྟེ་ཐེ་ཡོར་ལ་འདྲིས། དེ་ཐེ་ཡོར་གྱི་ནང་ནས་དབུགས་མེད་ཀྱི་སྒྲ་བྱུང་སྟེ་ཁྱོ་རང་ངེ་ཨ་བ་བསྟན་ཡིན་མོལ་པ། ཕྲུ་གུས་ར་མ་ཐུད་དེ། ཐང་ཆེན་མོ་ཡོད་ས་རུ་སོང་པ། དེ་རུ་མེ་མེ་སྐྱོན་ལ་སོང་ལྟེ། ཐེ་ཡོར་ཞིག་གི་ནང་དུ་ཞུག་སྟེ་འདུགས་པ། ཕྲུ་གུ་དེར་བསླེབ་སོང་། འདྲིས་པ། གླུ་འདི་ལྟར།

ཐང་གི་ཐང་སྟོད་ན་ཐེ་ཡོར་དཀར་པོ་ཁྱོད་ཉིད་དང་།
ཐང་གི་ཐང་དཀྱིལ་ལ་ཡོད་པའི་ཐེ་ཡོར་དམར་པོ་ཉིད་དང་།
ཐང་གི་ཐང་མཇུག་གི་ཐེ་ཡོར་ནག་པོས་ད་དངོས་ལ་ཉིད་དང་།
ང་ནི་ཕ་མེད་ཕྲུ་གུ་ཞིག་ཡིན་ལོ།
རིའི་ཤ་བ་ཀུན་ལ་ཡང་ཨ་བ་འདུག་ལོ།
ཨ་བ་མེད་པའི་ཕྲུ་གུ་ཞིག་གར་ཡང་མེད་ལོ།
ང་ལ་ཨ་བ་མེད་པའི་ཁས་དམན་ཆེན་པོ་འདུག་ལོ།
ངའི་ཨ་བ་གར་ཡོད་བསྟན་རོགས་མཛོད་ལོ།

ཁོས་དེ་ལྟག་ཟེརས་པ་སང་། ཐེ་ཡོར་གྱི་ནང་ནས་གདམ་ལན་དུ་གླུ་འདི་ལྟར།

ཁྱོད་ཕ་མེད་ཕྲུ་གུས་ངའི་དངོས་ལ་ཉིད་དང་།
ཁྱོད་ཕ་མེད་ཀེ་སར་གྱིས་ཐེ་ཡོར་ང་ལ་གསན་དང་།
ཁྱོ་རང་གི་ཨ་བ་གཡང་གི་ལུང་པའི་ཕུ་ཡ་ཡོད་ལོ།

པ་སང་ལྷན་ར྄་སྐྱེས་ཁྲོ་རང་གི་ཨ་བ་ཡིན་ལོ།
ཁྲོ་ར་ང་མགྲོགས་པ་གྲུང་གི་ལུང་པའི་ཕུ་ལ་སོང་ལོ།

ཀ་སར་ལ་ཨ་བ་མནན་ན་མེད་པས། དེ་ཟུག་གི་རྫོང་བཏངས་པ་སང་། དེ་གྲུང་གི་ལུང་པའི་རི་ལྡོགས་ཀྱི་རྩ྄་ཞིང་ནགས་ཚལ་ཚང་མ་ལ་སྲིབ་ཅིག་ལ་མི་བདུགས་དེ་སོང་སྟེ། ནག་པོ་གྱུར་སོང་། དེ་ནས་ཀ་སར་གྱིས་དེ་ནགས་ཁྲོད་ཚང་མ་ལ་སྡིག་པ་ཆོར་ཟེརས། འདི་རྩ྄་ཞིང་ནགས་ཚལ་ཚང་མ་སྔོན་མའི་མཆོགས་སོང་ཞིག་ཟེར་དེ་སྨོན་ལམ་ཞིག་བཏབས་པ། སྲིབ་ཅིག་ལ་ཁོལ་བཏང་སྟེ་སྔོན་པོ་སོང་། དེ་ནས་ཁོ་ལུང་པའི་ཕུ་ལ་སོང་པ་སང་། པ་སང་ལྷན་རྩ་སྐྱེས་དེ་ཉིད་ལོག་སྟེ་ཡོད་ཚུག། ཁོ་མདུན་ལ་སོང་སྟེ། ངའི་ཨ་བ་ཐུ་ལེ་ཟེརས་པ། པ་སང་ལྷན་རྩ་སྐྱེས་ཀྱིས་མིག་དེ་བཙུམ་སྟེ་ཟེརས། ང་ལ་ཨ་བ་ཟེར་མཁན་དེ་སུ་ཡིན། ད་ཚུག་པ་ང་ལ་བུ་ཚ་ཞིག་མེད་པ། ཁྱོད་ག་ནས་ཡོངས་ཟེརས་པ། དེ་ཟུག་ཟེར་ན་ཡང་། ཀྱེ་སར་གྱིས་པ་སང་ལྷན་རྩ་སྐྱེས་ལ་དབང་བཙོ་སྟེ། ཞིང་མང་པོ་ཞིག་བཀལ་དེ་སྣ་ལོ་གདག་སྟེ་ཁྲིད་དེ་ཁྱོང་སྟེ་ཁང་པ་ལ་བསླེབ་སོང་། དེ་ནས་ཨ་མ་ལ། ཨ་མ་ལེ་ངའི་ཨ་བ་ཁྲིབ་སོང་ཟེརས་པ། ཨ་མ་ཡང་འཐད་སོང་།།

No. 2.

དེ་ནས་བུ་ཚས་ཨ་བ་དང་ཨ་མ་གཉིས་ཀ་དྲི་མོ་དག་ཚོད་ཟེར་མཁན་གྱི་ལུང་པའི་ནང་ལ་འཁྱེར་དེ་ཨ་མ་ལ། ངའི་ཨ་མ་ལེ། ཨ་བ་དེ་ཞོར་དེ་ཆ་མ་བཙུག། ཟེར་དེ་ཁོ་རང་གླིང་ཡུལ་ལ་ལོག་སྟེ་ཡོངས་པ། གླིང་གི་དཔའ་བོ་ཚང་ཀ་གླིང་ཡུལ་ལི་མཁར་དང་ཡུལ་ལི་ཞིང་ཚང་མ་རང་རང་ལ་སྐྲོ་ཅེས་སི་ཕི་ལ་ལུང་པ་ཞིག་གི་ནང་དུ་འདུ་སྟེ་ཡོད་ཚུག། ཕྲུ་གུ་ལ་དེ་ཟུག་ཆོར་དེ། ཁོ་ཡང་དེ་

ལུང་པའི་ནང་ལྟ་ལ་སོང་བས། ཁོས་མི་ལ་མི་ཞིམ་ཅས་བཙོ་སྡེ། གྲུབ་པ་ཞིག་བཙོ་སྡེ་སོང་། ཨ་ཁུ་དཔལ་ལེ་དེ་ལམ་ན་དྲ་ཞིག་ལ་ཞོད་དེ་ཚའད་སྡུག། ཁོས་ཨ་ཁུ་ལ་ཟེརས། ཨ་ཁུ་ལེ། ཉི་རང་དྲ་ལ་ཞོན་དེ་འདུག། ང་འགྲུལ་དེ་ངལ་ཅེས་རུག་ཟེརས་པ། ཨ་ཁུས། ཁྱོ་རང་ངལ་ན། ངའི་རྒྱབ་ལ་དྲའི་ཁ་ཞོན་ཟེར་དེ་ཁོ་དྲམ་འཕོངས་ལ་བཏངས། དེ་ནས་སྤྲུ་གུ་དེས་ཞིག་ཁྲི་ཚོ་གཅིག་ཕེང་སྡེ། ཨ་ཁུའི་གཟུགས་པོའི་ཁ་བཏངས་པ། ཨ་ཁུ་དེ་ལ་ཞིག་གིས་ཟོས་དེ་སྨྱོན་པ་མཆོགས་སོང་སྡེ་ཟེརས། ལྷ་སྤྲུ་གུ། ཁྱོ་རང་ནུར་དགོས། ཞིག་མང་པོ་ཡོད་སྡུག། ང་ལ་མང་པོ་འབུར་སོང་ཟེརས་པ། བདེན་བདེན་ང་དཀྱུལ་བ་ཅན་ལ་ཞིག་ཡོང་ཡིན་ཟེར་དེ་ཁོ་འགྲུལ་དེ་སོང་། དེ་ཟུག་གིས་དཔའ་པོ་ཚང་མ་ཡོད་ས་རུ་བསླེབ་སོང་།།

དེར་བསླེབ་ཟ་ན། མཁར་ཞིང་ཚང་མ་སྐྱོའད་སྡུག། ཁོས་ཨ་ཁུ་ཀུན་ལ་ཞུས་པ། ཨ་ཁུ་ཀུན་མཁྱེན་ནོ། ང་ལ་ཡང་ས་ཁྲད་ཉུ་ཏུན་ཞིག་བསྐྱལ་དགོས་ཇུ་ཞུས་པ། ཨ་ཁུ་ཀུན་ནེས་གཟབས་བཙོ་སྡེ་ཁོ་ལ་ཟེརས། ཁྱོ་རང་ལ་རོ་འཁྱེར་ཅེས་སི་རོ་སྣ། བག་མ་འཁྱེར་ཅེས་སི་བག་སྣ། སྤྲི་ཆུ་རབས་སི་རབས་འགོ། གྲོ་མ་ཐང་གི་ཐང་འགོ་བཏང་ཡིན་ཟེརས་པ། སྤྲུ་གུ་དེ་འཐད་དེ་ང་ལ་དེ་ཟུག་བསྐྱལ་ན་གྲིག། ཨ་ཁུ་པ་ཇུ་ཟེརས། དེ་ནས་ཞག་ཅིག་མི་ཞིག་ཤི་བས། ཁོ་དེ་རུ་སོང་སྡེ་རོ་འཁྱེར་བའི་རོ་སྣང་ཡིན་ཟེར་དེ། གོན་ཅེས་སོ་མ་ཞིག་གོན་དེ་རོ་འི་སྔུན་ལ་སྒྲུ་བཏང་ངིན་ཞིག་སོང་། དེ་རུས་མི་ཚང་མས་ཟེརས། ལྷ་མོ་ངན་གྱི་སྐྱོང་སྤྲུག། ང་ཉ་ཚང་མ་ལ་མི་ཤི་སྡེ་ཆེར་ཀ་ཡོད། དེ་ཟུག་ཅིག་མ་ཟེར་ཟེརས་པ། ཁོས་སྒྲུ་མང་པོ་བཏངས། དེ་ནས་མི་ཤི་མཁན་ནི་བདག་

པོས་ཁྲོ་ལ་ནོར་མང་པོ་བཏངས་པ། ཁོ་རྒྱབ་བཅད་དེ་སོང་། ཡང་ཞག་ཅིག་བག་མ་ཞིག་འཁྱེར་རད་ཚུག། ཡང་ཁོ་དེ་རུ་སོང་སྟེ་བག་མའི་སྔོན་ལ་ཏུ་འདིན་ཞིག་ཀུ་ཅོ་བཏངས་པས། དེ་མི་ཚང་མས་ཟེརས། ལྦ་མོ་ངན་ནི་སྐྱོང་ཕྲུག། དེ་ཟུག་མ་ཟེར། བག་མ་ཞིག་འཁྲིང་ན། རྩེས་དང་གླུ་བཏང་ཅེན། ཏུ་མ་ཏུ་ཟེརས་པ། ཁོ་ཡང་ཐེབ་མང་པོ་ཏུས། དེ་ནས་ཡང་བག།མ་ཁྲིང་མཁན་ནི་བདག་པོས་ནོར་མང་པོ་བཏངས་པ། རྒྱབ་བཅད་དེ་འདུགས།

ཨ་ག་ཁྲའི་ཐུང་དེས་གླིང་གི་མགོ་བཅོ་སྟེ། ཛོ་ཛོ་འབྲུ་གུ་མ་དེ་ཁོ་ལ་བག་མ་ལ་འཁྲིང་ཅས་ལ་གླིང་གི་དཔའ་བོ་ཚང་མས་གྲབས་བཅོས། དེ་ཟུག་མོ་ངན་སྐྱོང་ཕྲུག་ལ་ཀོར་ཏེ། སྐྱོ་ཡོང་སྟེ། སྤྲི་རྒྱ་རབས་ལ་སོང་སྟེ་སྒྲུད་སྟེ་འདུགས་པ། ཞག་ཅིག་ཨ་ག་ཁྲའི་ཐུང་རྟ་ཞིག་ལ་ཞོན་ཏེ་ཡོང་ངད་ཚུག། ཨ་གུ་རྒྱའི་དཀྱིལ་ལ་བསླེབ་པ་དང་། ཁོ་མགྱོགས་པ་སོང་སྟེ་ཀོང་རྩ་ནས་ཟུམ་སྟེ། རྟ་ཐོག་ནས་ཕབ་སྟེ། རྒྱའི་དཀྱིལ་ལ་གནན་ཏེ་མང་པོ་རྡུངས། དེ་ནས་ཐམ་ལ་བིང་སྟེ། ངའི་ཨ་ག་ཁྲའི་ཐུང་ཡིན་ནོག། ང་ལ་མ་ཞེས་ཟེར་རིན་ཞིག་ཏུ་རྟོན་བཏངས། ཨ་གུས་ཟེརས། ཁྱོད་ལ་མ་ཞེས་ན་ཁག་མེད་ཟེར་ཏེ་སོང་།།

No. 3.

དེ་ནས་ཡང་ཁོ་གྲོ་མ་ཐང་ལ་སྤྱུང་བ་སོང་སྟེ་འདུགས། ཞག་ཅིག་ཛོ་ཛོ་འབྲུ་གུ་མ་དང་གཡོག་མོ་ཚང་མ་དེ་རུ་གྲོ་མ་འབྲུ་བ་ལ་ཡོངས། དེ་རུ་ཁོང་ཚང་མས་གྲོ་མ་བྲུས་པ། ཛོ་ཛོ་དང་གཡོག་མོ་ཀུན་ལ་ཞུ་ཏུན་རེ་ཐོབ་པ། མོ་ངན་ནི་སྐྱོང་ཕྲུག་ལ་གྲོ་མའི་ཏ་ཀྱི་ཞིག་བིང་སོང་། ཁོས་ཛོ་ཛོ་ལ་བསྟན་ཏེ། སོ་བཏབས་པ།

ཡང་གསོལ་བས་དེ་ཡོངས། གཡོག་མོ་ཞིག་གིས་ཟེར་ས། ལྷ་མོ་ངན་ནི་སྤྲིང་ཕྲུག། ང་ཞིའི་ཇོ་ཇོ་ལ་སོ་ཞིག་བདབ་བཙུག་ཟེར་ས་པ། མོ་ངན་ནི་སྤྲིང་ཕྲུག་གིས། ད་ཀི་ལ་སོ་རྫིས་ལུས་ན། དགྲ་བཀལ་ཡིན་ཟེར་ས་པ། གཡོག་མོས། ཁྱོད་མོ་ངན་ནི་སྤྲིང་ཕྲུག་ལ་སོ་རྫིས་ལུས་པ་མི་དུག། ང་ཞིའི་ཇོ་ཇོ་ལ་མང་ང་མི་ལུས་ཟེར་ས་པ། མོ་ངན་ནི་སྤྲིང་ཕྲུག་གིས། ཡ་ཇོ་ཇོ་ལི། འདོན་འང་ཟེར་དེ་བདངས་པ། ཇོ་ཇོས་སོ་བདབས་པ། མ་གསོལ་བས་པ་རྫིས་ལུས་སོང། དེ་ནས་མོ་ངན་ནི་སྤྲིང་ཕྲུག་གིས་ཟེར་ས། ཨ་ཧོ་ཧོ་ཇོ་ཇོ་ལི། ང་མོ་ངན་ནི་སྤྲིང་ཕྲུག་ཡིན་ནའང། ད་གསོལ་བས། ཉི་རང་རིགས་བཟང་ཇོ་ཇོ་ཡིན་ནའང། ད་ཀི་ལ་རྫིས་བིང། ཉི་རང་བས་སང་ང་རྒྱལ་ལ་སོང། ཨོ་ཧོ་ཧོ། ཁྱི་ཐུག་ཁྱི་ལ་བཤད་ཡིན། མི་ཐུག་མི་ལ་བཤད་ཡིན་ཟེར་ས།།

ཇོ་ཇོ་མང་པོ་ཁྲེལ་དེ་ཟེར་ས་པ། ལྷ་མོ་ངན་ནི་སྤྲིང་ཕྲུག། ཁྱོ་རང་གིས་དེ་ཟླུག་མ་ཟེར་ཧྲུ་ཧྲུ། ཐོ་རས་ལ་ང་ཞིའི་ཨི་སྨན་ཡོང་ཆེན། ཨི་སྨན་ལ་ཁྱེ་རང་ཡང་ཐེ་ཡིན་ཟེར་ས་པ། མོ་ངན་ནི་སྤྲིང་ཕྲུག་གིས་རྒྱལ་ཟེར་དེ་འདུགས། ཐོ་རེ་ཚུག་པོ་ཨི་སྨན་གྱི་འབྲང་ས་ཤེས་དེ། མོ་ངན་ནི་སྤྲིང་ཕྲུག་དེ་ཁང་པ་ལ་སོང་སྟེ། སྒོ་ལྕག་པོ་ལ་ཡིབ་སྟེ་འདུགས་པ་སང། ཇོ་ཇོ་དང་གཡོག་མོ་ཚང་མ་འཛོམ་སོང། ཇོ་ཇོ་འགྲུ་གུ་མས་ཟེར་ས་པ། ལྷ་ས་དོ་པ་ཀུན། ང་དང་ཚང་མ་འཛོམ་ན་སྒོ་སྣན་དེ་བཙུག། མོ་ངན་ནི་སྤྲིང་ཕྲུག་ཡོང་ཡིན། ཁོས་རྩེག་པོ་བཙོ་རྟུག་ཟེར་ས་པ། མོ་ངན་ནི་སྤྲིང་ཕྲུག་ལ་དེ་ཟླུག་ཟེར་ཅེས་ཤེས་དེ། ཇོ་ཇོ་ལི་ཧྲུ། ང་འདིར་ཡོང་སྡུ་ཡོད་ཟེར་ས་པ། ཇོ་ཇོ་ཡམ་ཚན་ཞིག་སོང་སྡུ་ཟེར་ས་པ། ཨོ་ཡོངས་ས། ང་ཞེས་མོ་ངན་ནི་སྤྲིང་ཕྲུག་ལ་བོས་པ། རྒྱལ

ཟེར་རྡང་པ། མོ་ངན་ནི་སྲོང་ཕྲུག་གིས། ཨོ་མོལ་ལ་རག་ཇོ་ཇོ་ལེ་ཧུ། ཉི་རང་ཕ་མ་བཟང་པོ་འི་བུ་མོ་ཡིན་པའི་མ་ཤང་པོ་ཞིག་འདུག་ཇོ་ཇོ་མཁྱེན་ཟེརས་པ།།

དེ་ནས་ཁོང་གཡངས་པ་བཅོ་འཇིན་ཞིག་འདུགས། ཚ་བིག་འགོར་དེ་ཇོ་ཇོ་མགོ་ལ་བདུག་སྟེ་ཚང་མ་ཆོར་ལ་གཉིད་ཡོགས་པ། མོ་ངན་ནི་སྲོང་ཕྲུག་ཕི་སྟུ་ལ་བིང་སྟེ་ཡོངས། ཁྲིམ་མཆོས་པ་ཞིག་ལ་བོང་བུ་ཞིག་ཡོད་ཚུག། དེ་བོང་བུ་ལ་ཀ་རུག་སྐྱེ་ཅེས་ཡོད་ཚུག། དེ་བོང་བུ་ལ་རྟོག་ཆེང་ཞིག་བདང་སྟེ། ཀ་རུག་འཕང་བརྒྱུག་སྟེ་བོང་ཀ་རུག་གི་མགོ་བཅད་དེ་ཁྲིང་སྟེ། ཁོ་ཇོ་ཇོ་ཡོད་པའི་ནང་ལ་སོང་སྟེ་ཚང་མའི་སང་མཇུག་ལ་ཡོད་ མཁན་ནི་ བུ་མོ་ཞིག་གི་མལ་ཅི་ནང་བོར་དེ་ཕི་སྟུ་ལ་ཡོང་སྟེ། ནང་གི་དཀར་ཁང་དང་སློ་བི་གང་ཚང་མ་མི་མཐོང་ཅེས་བཅོ་སྟེ་བཀག་སྟེ་བོརས། ཇོ་ཇོ་དང་བུ་མོ་ཚང་མས་ད་རུང་ནམ་མ་ལངས་བསམ་སྟེ་འདུགས། དེ་ཟུག་གིས་ཉི་མ་ཤར་སོང་། དེ་ནས་མོ་ངན་ནི་སྲོང་ཕྲུག་གིས་སློ་དཀར་ཁང་བི་གང་ཚང་མ་དུས་གཅིག་ལ་ཕྱེས་བདང་སྟེ། ཁོ་ནང་ལ་སོང་སྟེ་ཟེརས་པ། ལྷ་བསམ་པ་མེད་མཁན་ནི་ཇོ་ཇོ་ཚང་མ། ད་རུང་གཉིད་ལོག་སྟེ་ཡོད་ད། ཉི་མ་ཕེད་ཟམ་སོང་། ཉི་ཞ་ལ་ལས་མེད་མཁན་རེ་ཡིན་ན། ང་ལུང་མཁན་ཡིན་ནའང། གྲོང་ཚང་མ་ལ་སོང་སྟེ། ཕེ་ཁྲོང་སྟེ་ཟ་ཅེས་ཟ་ཚར་ཟེརས་པ། ཁོང་ཁྲིལ་ཁྲིལ་རིག་སོང་སྟེ། མཇུག་ནས་ཕར་ལ་ལངས་པ། མཇུག་གི་བུ་མོ་འི་མལ་ཅི་ནང་ན་བོང་བུ་ཀ་རུག་གི་མགོ་ཞིག་ཡོད་ཚུག། ཁོ་ཁྲིལ་དེ་ལྟུག་གི་བུ་མོ་འི་མལ་ཅི་ནང་དུ་བདངས། དེ་བུ་མོས་ཡང་ལྟུག་གི་བུ་མོ་འི་ནང་དུ་བདངས། དེ་ཟུག་བཅོ་འཇིན་ཞིག་ཇོ་ཇོ་ཚུག་པ་བསླེབ་པས། བུ་མོ་ཞིག་གིས་ཇོ་ཇོ་འི་གཡོག་གོར་གྱི་ནང་ལ་བོར་སོང་། ཁོང་ཚང་མ་ལངས་ཚར་ཚར་ཚུག་པ་མོ་ངན

ཉི་སྤྲོང་ཕྲུག་བལྟ་སྟེ་འདུགས། ཇོ་ཇོ་འབྲུ་ག་མ་ཡངས་ཙ་ན། གཡོག་གོར་རི་ནང་ནས་ཀ་ཙུག་གི་མགོ་བིང་སོང་། དེ་ནས་མོ་ངན་གྱི་སྤྲོང་ཕྲུག་གིས་ཀ་ཙོ་བཏང་སྟེ་ཟེར་ས། ཨོ་ཧོ་ཧོ། འདི་རིང་ཇོ་ཇོ་འབྲུ་ག་མ་ལ་བོང་བུའི་མགོ་ཞིག་སྐྱེས་དོག་ཟེར་ས།. མི་དང་ཐུག་ན་མི་ལ་བ་ཤད་ཡིན། ཁྱི་དང་ཐུག་ན་ཁྱི་ལ་བ་ཤད་ཡིན་ཟེར་ས་པ།།

ཇོ་ཇོ་ཁྲེལ་ལིན་ཞིག་ཟེར་ས་པ། ལྷ་མོ་ངན་ནི་སྤྲོང་ཕྲུག་ཧུ་ཧུ། དེ་ཟུག་མ་ཟེར། ཞག་བཟང་པོ་འི་ཞག་ལ་ངའི་གོགས་ཆང་ཞུ་ཙེན། དེ་ཞག་ལ་ཁྱོ་རང་ལ་འང་ཞུ་ཡིན་ཟེར་ས། དེ་ཟུག་གོགས་ཆང་ཞུ་ཙེས་བཙོ་སྟེ་འདུགས། མོ་ངན་ནི་སྤྲོང་ཕྲུག་གིས་ཀ་ཙུག་གི་རྣ་མཆོག་གཅིག་པོ་བཅད་དེ་ཁུར་ཏེ་འདུགས། དེ་ནས་ཞག་བཟང་པོ་བསླེབ་སྟེ་ན། ཡུལ་གྱི་མི་ཞིག་གིས་ཚང་མ་ལ་སྐད་བཏངས། འདི་རིང་ཇོ་ཇོ་འབྲུ་ག་མའི་གོགས་ཆང་ཞུ་ཙུག། གླིང་གི་དཔའ་བོ་ཚང་མ་ཁྲིམ་ལ་ཡོང་ཟེར་ས་པས། མི་ཚང་མ་འདུས། ཨ་ག་ཁྲའི་ཐང་ལ་གསེར་ཁྲི་བཏང་སྟེ་དེའི་ཁ་འདུགས། གཞན་མ་དཔའ་བོ་ཚང་མ་གཡུ་ཁྲི་དང་དུང་ཁྲི་ཁ་འདུགས། མོ་ངན་ནི་སྤྲོང་ཕྲུག་དེ་ལྕང་ མཁན་ཚང་མའི་ མགོ་ལ་ཤག་གི་ཁྲི་རྒྱབ་ སྟེ་འདུགས། དེ་ནས་ཇོ་ཇོ་འབྲུ་ག་ མས་ ནང་ན་སྤྲུལ་ མགོ་མ་ ཆབས་ རྐྱེན་ལ་ཆང་ བསྐངས་དེ། མཐོ་དགུ་མ་ཀ་ལྷོར་རོན་དེ། ཁར་དེ་དར་དཀར་ཞིག་རིང་དུ། དར་དམར་ཞིག་ཐང་དུ་གོན་ཏེ་ཁྲིམ་ལ་ཡོངས། དེ་ནས་ཨ་ག་ཁྲའི་ཐང་གི་མདུན་ལ་ཡོང་སྟེ་གླུ་འདི་ལྟར།།

འདི་རིང་གི་ཞག་བཟངས་ལ་ནོ་མོ་ང་རི་གོགས་ཆང་ཞུ་ཡིན།

འདི་རིང་གི་སྐར་བཟངས་ལ་ཇོ་ཇོ་འབྲུག་མོ་འི་གོགས་ཆང་ཞུས།

སྤྲུལ་མགོ་ཅན་རྒྱན་ལ་མཐོ་དགུ་ཀ་ལྷོར་རོན་ཡོད།

སྤྲུལ་མགོ་ཅན་རྒྱན་ནང་ཡང་དཀར་ནས་ཀྱི་གསུམ་ཆང།

ཡང་དཀར་ནས་ཀྱི་གསུམ་ཆང་དེ་མི་ཆེན་ཁྲོད་ལ་ཞུས།

ཕྱག་ནི་ཕྱག་སོར་བཅུ་པ་དང་མ་ལེན་པ།

ཞལ་ནི་པདྨ་འི་མེ་ཏོག་དང་ཐུག་མ་བཙུག་པ།

ལྕེ་མོ་དར་གྱི་མདུད་པ་དང་མ་སྦྱང་བ།

ཨོལ་ལྡིང་གསེར་གྱི་ཕྲུང་པ་དང་མ་རྨིད་པ།

སེམས་བྱང་ཆུབ་ཀྱི་སེམས་དང་ལེན་དེ་ས་ལ་ཕོབ།

ཆང་གང་དེ་དོན་དེ་ཇ་གང་དེ་མདུན་ལ་ཕོབ་ལོ།

དེ་ཟླུག་ཟེར་དེ་ཨ་གུ་ཁྲའི་ཐང་ལ་ཆང་དེ་ཞུས་པ། ཁྲའི་ཐང་གིས་ཆབ་རྒྱན་དེ་ལག་ལ་ལེན་དེ་ན། མོ་ངན་ནི་སྤྱོད་ཕྲུག་མཐོང་སྟེ། ཡམ་ཚན་སོང་སྟེ་ཆབ་རྒྱན་དེ་ལག་ནས་འབུད་སོང་། དེ་ནས་ཀ་ལྷོར་ཚང་མ་ཞིག་སོང་བས། ཇོ་ཇོ་འབྲུ་གུ་མ་མགྲོགས་པ་ཁང་པ་ཙ་སོང་སྟེ་ཡང་ཀ་ལྷོར་རོན་དེ་ཆང་བསྐང་སྟེ་ཁྲའི་ཐང་ལ་མ་ཞུས། གཡུ་ཁྲི་མདུན་ལ་སོང་སྟེ་ཆོད་པོའི་དཔལ་ལེ་ལ་ཞུས་པ། ཆོད་པོའི་དཔལ་ལེ་དང་ཡང་དཔའ་བོ་ཚང་མས་ཇོ་ཇོ་ལ་ཞུས་པ། ཇོ་ཇོ་ལེ། ཉེ་རང་གི་གྲོགས་ཆང་མཐུང་མཁན་ནི་མི་མེད་འགྲོ། ང་ཞིས་མཐུང་མི་ཐུབ་ཟེར་དེ། སུས་ཀྱང་མ་མཐུངས་པས། དེ་ཟླུག་གིས་མོ་ངན་ནི་སྤྱོད་ཕྲུག་གི་མདུན་ལ་བསྐྱེབ་པ། ཇོ་ཇོས་མ་མཐོང་ཧུན་རྒྱབ་སྟེ་སོང་བ། མོ་ངན་ནི་སྤྱོད་ཕྲུག ། ས་ཇོ་ཇོ་ལེ། འདིར་གཟིགས་འང་ཟེར་དེ། ཀ་ཙུག་གི་ཉ་མཆོག་དེ་བསྟནས་པ། ཇོ་ཇོ་ལོག་སྟེ་ཡོང་སྟེ་ཁོ་ལ་གྲོགས་ཆང་ཞུ་བ་ལ་ཡོང་སྟེ་གླུ་འདི་ལྟར།།

ཤག་གི་ཤག་ཁྲིའི་སྟེང་ན་པན་ཚུང་སྔོང་པོ་ཀུན་འདུག་ལོ།
བེར་ཀའི་བེར་ཁྲི་སྟེང་དུ་མོ་ངན་ཉི་སྔོང་ཕྲུག་ཀུན་འདུག་ལོ།
ལག་པ་སེ་ཡག་ཅན་དང་མ་ལེན་པ་མཐུང་ལོ།
ཁ་དེ་ཆག་ར་དང་མ་ཐུབ། པ་མཐུང་ལོ།
ལྷེ་སག་གདར་དང་མ་སྦུང་བ་མཐུང་ལོ།
ཨོལ་ལྡོང་རིང་མོ་ནས་ས་རྨིད་པ་མཐུང་ལོ།
དུག་སེམས་དེ་དང་ལེན་དེ་ས་ལ་ཕེབ་ལོ།
ཚང་གང་མཐུང་སྟེ་ཇ་གང་མདུན་ལ་ཕེབ་ལོ།
དེ་ཟུག་ཟེར་ དེ་སྤྲུལ་ མགོ་མ་ ཆབ་ ཀྱུན་མོ་ངན་ ཉི་སྔོང་ཕྲུག་ གི་ལག་ལ་
བཏངས། མོ་ངན་ཉི་སྔོང་ཕྲུག་གིས་གསོལ་མཆོད་ཅིག་འདི་ལྟར།

ཀླུ་ཉམ་པོ་སྐྱེས་པའི་ལྷ་དགུ་ལ་མཆོད།
འདི་རིང་ང་ལ་སྐྱུང་རོགས་མཛོད།
མཉམ་པོ་སྐྱེས་པའི་ཀླུ་དགུ་ལ་མཆོད།
འདི་རིང་ང་ལ་སྐྱུང་རོགས་མཛོད།
སྟེང་ལྷའི་དབང་པོ་རྒྱབ་ཞིན་ལ་མཆོད།
འདི་རིང་ང་ལ་སྐྱུང་རོགས་མཛོད།
བར་གྱི་ཨ་མ་སྐྱབ་བདུན་ལ་མཆོད།
འདི་རིང་ང་ལ་སྐྱུང་རོགས་མཛོད།
འོག་གི་ཀླུ་རྒྱལ་ལྡོགས་པོ་ལ་མཆོད།
འདི་རིང་ང་ལ་སྐྱུང་རོགས་མཛོད།

ཕས་ལྷ་ཀར་རྫོང་སྨན་པོ་ལ་མཆོད།

འདི་རིང་ང་ལ་སྐྱུང་རོགས་མཛོད།

མས་ལྷ་བཀར་དམན་རྒྱལ་མོ་ལ་མཆོད།

འདི་རིང་ང་ལ་སྐྱུང་རོགས་མཛོད།

དེ་ཟླུག་ཟེར་དེ་གསོལ་མཆོད་བཏངས། སྨོན་ལམ་བཏབ་སྟེ། ཆང་གཟ་དོན་དེ་ཇ་གང་མདུན་ལ་ཕོབ་ཟེར་དེ། ཁྲི་སོ་ཅན་བཞར་ཀ་ནང་གཅིག་བཏང་སྟེ་ནམ་མཁའ་ལ་ཕངས། ཆང་གང་མཐུང་སྟེ་ཇ་གང་པོ་མདུན་ལ་ཕབས། དེ་ནས་ལྕང་མཁན་ཚང་མས་ཀ་ཅོ་བཏངས། ཇོ་ཇོ་འབྲུག་མ་དེ་ང་ཞིའི་སློང་ཕྲུག་ལ་ཐོབ་སོང་ཟེར་དེ་ཧབ་ཆོད་བཏངས།།

No. 4.

ཡབས་གྲོན་པ་དང་ཡུམ་སྟོན་མོ་གཉིས་ཀས་གསེར་ཁྲི་རྒྱབ་སྟེ། དར་དཀར་གྱི་ཡོལ་ལ་བདང་སྟེ་ཡོད་ཙུག། མོ་ངན་ནི་སློང་ཕྲུག་ལ་ཇོ་ཇོ་ཐོབ་ཟེརས་པ་སང་། གསེར་ཁྲི་འཐེན་དེ་ཡོལ་བ་ཡང་འཐེན་དེ། ཆ་ལི་ནག་པོ་འི་ཡོལ་བ་ཞིག་བཏངས། སྨན་ཆད་པོ་ཞིག་ཕིར་ལོག་ལ་བཏིང་སྟེ་བོརས། དེ་ནས་མོ་ངན་གྱི་སློང་ཕྲུག་དེ་ལྕང་མཁན་ཚང་མས་ཤག་གི་ཁ་པལ་ཀྱི་ལ་ཁུར་དེ་ཡབ་བརྟན་པ་དང་ཡུམ་སྟོན་མོ་འི་ཁང་པར་ཁྲིརས། དེ་ནང་ལ་བསྐྱིབ་པ། སྨན་ཕིར་ལོག་ལ་ཡོད་པ་སང་། ཁོ་ཕིར་ལོག་ཁ་འདུགས། དེ་ནས་ཡབ་བརྟན་པ་དང་ཡུམ་སྟོན་མོས་ཟེརས། ཁྱོད་ལྕང་མཁན་ད་ཡིན་ནོག། སློང་པོ་ད་ཁྱོད་ཡིན་ནོག། ཕིར་ལོག་ལ་འདུག་དེ་ཟླུག་ཟེརས་པ། སློང་ཕྲུག་གིས། སྨན་ཁ་ཕིར་ལོག་ལ། འགྲོན་ཁ་ཕིར་ལོག་ལ་འདུག་དགོས་ཟེརས་པའི། དེ་ནས་སོ་བའི་ཕེའི་ཟན་ཞིག

གཡོ་སྟེ་ཁྲོ་འི་མདུན་ལ་བདང་སྟེ། ཨ་བས་མིག་ལོག་བལྟས། ཨ་མས་ས་མིག་བལྟས། ཇོ་ཇོས་ཐབ་བི་ནང་ནས་བྲུས། ཁྲིམ་ཤང་དེ་ལ་ཁྲི་སྦྲུག་གཅིག་ཡོད་ཚུག། མོ་ངན་ནི་སྐྱོང་སྦྲུག་གིས་ཁྲི་སྦྲུག་དེ་ལ་ཟེརས་གླུ་འདི་ལྟར།།

ཁྲིམ་ཤང་ལ་ཡོད་པའི་ཁྲི་སྦྲུག་ཁྱོད་ཉོན་དང༌།
ཁྲིམ་འཛུག་ལ་ཡོད་པའི་ཁྲི་ཆུང་དེས་དངོས་ལ་ཉོན།
སྔོན་ལ་བལྟ་ན་ཕིར་ལོག་ལ་འདུག།
མདུན་ལ་བལྟ་ན་སོ་བ་ཟན་ཞིག་འདུག།
གཡལ་མགོ་ལ་བལྟ་ན་ཨ་བས་མིག་ལོག་ལྟ་ཙུག།
འབང་ལ་བལྟ་ན་ཨ་མས་ས་མིག་ལྟ་ཙུག།
དཀྱིལ་ལ་བལྟ་ན་བུ་མོས་ཐབ་བྲུ་ཙུག།
ཁྱེད་ཁྲི་གུ་ལང་སྟེ་རྩེས་ཤིག་ཁྱོང་དང༌།
ཤར་ལ་ལྟ་སྟེ་གོམ་གསུམ་རྒྱོབ་དང༌།
ནུབ་ལ་ལྟ་སྟེ་གོམ་གསུམ་རྒྱོབ་དང༌།
ལྷོ་ལ་ལྟ་སྟེ་གོམ་གསུམ་རྒྱོབ་དང༌།
བྱང་ལ་ལྟ་སྟེ་གོམ་གསུམ་རྒྱོབ་དང༌།

ཞེ་ཟླུག་ཟེརས་པ་སང། ཁྲི་སྦྲུག་དེ་སྨྱོན་པ་མཆོགས་སོང་སྟེ། ཤར་ལྷོ་ནུབ་བྱང་ཚང་མ་ལ་གོམ་པ་གསུམ་གསུམ་བརྒྱབས་པ། ཁྲི་སྦྲུག་དེས་ཁྲི་ཀྲུག་དང་ཁྲི་སྨིན་དང་ནང་ཚང་མ་བསྐངས་བདངས། དེ་ཟླུག་བཙོས་པ་སང། མི་ཚང་མ་དང་ལྷུང་མཁན་ཚང་མ་ནང་ནས་ཕྱི་སྤུ་ཙུ་ཤོར་དེ་སོང།

དེ་ནས་མཚན་སོང་སྟེ་ཨ་བ་དང་ཨ་མས་ཁུ་མོ་ལ་ཟེརས། ཕྲ་བུ་མོ།

མོ་ངན་ནི་སྤྲོང་ཕྲུག་དེ་ཕྲུག་རགས་ལ་སྐྱལ་བ་ཁྲིར་ཟེར་ས་པ། ཇོ་ཇོས་ཤང་ཀོག་ཅིག་ཁྲིར་དེ། ཕྲུག་རགས་ལ་ཁྲིར་དེ་བོར་དེ་ལོག་སྡེ་ཡོང་ས། ཡབས་བརྟན་པ་དང་ཡུམ་སྒྲོན་མོ་འི་སྒོ་ཁྲི་ལ་སྡུག་གཟིག་དང་ གཙན་ཟན་མང་ པོ་ཡོད་ཚུག་པས། མོ་ངན་ནི་སྤྲོང་ཕྲུག་མཚན་ཕྱེད་ཟམ་ལ་ལང་སྡེ། ཤང་ལག་དེ་ཚང་མ་བཅད་དེ་རུས་པ་ཁ་ཅིག་དང་མཉམ་པོ་སྒོ་ལ་ཕང་སྡེ་ན། མོ་ངན་ནི་སྤྲོང་ཕྲུག་དེ་ཞོར་དེ་དྲི་མོ་དག་ཆོད་ཀྱི་ལུང་པའི་ནང་དུ་ཡོང་སྡེ་ཨེ་མའི་རྩ་བསྒྲིབ་སྡེ་འདུགས།།

དེ་ ནས་ གནམ་ ལང་ སྡེ་ལྷང་ མཁན་ ཚང་ མ་ ཡོང་ སྡེ་སྒོ་ ནས་ ཟེར་ས། ཀྲ་ཡབ་བརྟན་པ་དང་ཡུམ་སྒྲོན་མོ་ཇོ་ ཇོ་འཁྲུག་མོ། ང་ཞའི་མོ་ངན་ནི་སྤྲོང་ཕྲུག་ལ་སྐྱིབ་ཅིག་ལྟོས་ཟེར་འང་ཟེར་ས་པ། ཇོ་ ཇོ་དེ་ཕྲུག་རགས་ལ་ལྟ་ལ་སོང་བ་མེད་ཚུག། ཇོ་ ཇོ་མགྲོགས་པ་ལོག་སྡེ་ཨ་བ་དང་ཨ་མ་ལ། མོ་ངན་ནི་སྤྲོང་ཕྲུག་མི་འདུག་ཟེར་ས་པ། ཁོང་ཚང་ཀས་ཕྱི་ནང་ཚང་མ་ལ་བལྟས་པ་མེད་ཚུག། སྒོ་ལ་བལྟས་པ། ཤང་ལག་དེ་བཅད་དེ་ཕང་སྡེ་ཡོད་ཚུག། དེ་རུ་རུས་པ་རེ་ཡང་ཡོད་ཚུག། དེ་ནས་ཁོང་ཚང་ཀས། མོ་ངན་ནི་སྤྲོང་ཕྲུག་དེ་འདི་གཙན་ཟན་ཀུན་ཉིས་ཟོས་མཁན་ཡིན་ནོག་ཟེར་དེ་ཡམ་ཚན་སོང་། དེ་ནས་ལྷང་མཁན་ཚང་མས་ཡང་ཟེར་ས། ང་ཞའི་མོ་ངན་ནི་སྤྲོང་ཕྲུག་དེ་ཁྱི་ཞིས་བསད་མཁན་དངོ་དོག་ཡིན། མོ་ངན་ནི་སྤྲོང་ཕྲུག་གི་མི་ཤ་ཡིན་ཟེར་ས་པ། ལྷང་མཁན་ཀུན་ལ་ཕེ་དང་མར་མང་པོ་བདང་སྡེ་བོར་ས། ཇོ་ ཇོ་ དེ་གསེར་དུ་བུག་གང་ངེ་ཁ་གསུའི་ཚིག་བུ་བཀལ་དེ། ཨ་གུ་དགའ་ནི་རྩ་མོ་བདབ་པ་སོང་བས། ཨ་གུའི་སྐོ་ན་གླུ་འདི་ལྟར།།

ཨ་གུ་རང་མཁྱེན་ལོ་དགའ་ནི་རང་མཁྱེན་ལོ།
གསེར་རི་དུ་བུག་གང་པོ་འི་ཁ་གསུའི་ཚིག་བུ་རིག་ཡོད་ལོ།

ང་ལ་སྙིང་གི་པན་ཚུང་དེ་སྟོར་དེ་རིག་སོང་ལོ།
མོ་ངན་གྱི་སྤྲོང་ཕྲུག་སྟོར་དེ་རིག་སོང་ལོ།
མོ་དཔེ་བཏིང་སྟེ་མོ་ཞིག་རྟོབ་ལོ།
རྩིས་དཔེ་བཏིང་སྟེ་རྩིས་ཤིག་སྐོར་ལོ།
ཤི་སྟེ་འདུག་གསོན་དེ་འདུག་གཟིགས་ལོ།
ཤོར་དེ་སོང་ང་ཡིབ་སྟེ་འདུག་གཟིགས་ལོ།
ང་ལ་པན་ཚུང་སྤྲོང་པོ་འི་མི་ཤ་རིག་ཐོག་འདུག།
མོ་ངན་ནི་སྤྲོང་ཕྲུག་གི་སྐྲོ་ཁག་རིག་ཐོག་འདུག།

དེ་ཟླུག་ཟེརས་པ། ཨ་གུ་དགའ་ནི་ལ་དེ་ཟླུག་སྒྲོ་ཡོངས། སྟོན་ལ་
པན་ཚུང་ལ་ཡ་ཤ་མ་བཙོས་པའི་ཕྱི་ལ། ཨ་གུས་ལན་དུ།

ཡབས་བརྟན་པའི་བུ་མོ་ཁ་དམར་མོ་ཉེན་དང་།
ཡུམ་སྟོན་མོ་འི་བུ་མོ་ལྷེ་དམར་མོ་ཉེན་དང་།
ཞིམ་པོ་བཟོས་པའི་ཚོལ་སོགས་མོ་ཉེན་ལོ།
ལགས་མོ་གོནས་པའི་སྤྲང་ཁོར་མོ་ཉེན་ལོ།
ཁྲོད་ལྷས་ངན་ནི་བུ་མོ་ཞིག་ཡོད་ལོ།
པན་ཛུང་དེ་ནི་ཤི་མཁན་རིག་ཡིན་ནོག།
མོ་ངན་ནི་སྤྲང་ཕྲུག་དེ་ཤི་སྟེ་ཡོད་ལོ།
ཁོ་འི་མི་ཤ་ཁྲོད་ལ་ཐོག་ཡིན་ལོ།
ཁོ་འི་སྐྲོ་འདྲ་ཁྲོད་ལ་ཐོག་ཡིན་ལོ།
ང་ལ་མོ་དང་རྩིས་རིག་མི་ཤེས་ལོ

དེ་ཟླུག་སྒྲོ་བཤད་དེ་ཟེརས་པ་སང་། ཛོ་ཛོ་འབྲུ་གུ་མ་ཏྲུ་འིན་ཞིག་ལོག་སྟེ་ཡོངས། ཁང་པ་ལ་བསླེབ་སྟེ་ཨ་བ་དང་ཨ་མ་ལ། ཨ་གུས་ང་ལ་སྒྲོ་བཅོ་སྟེ་ཁ་མང་པོ་ཀྱིས་ཟེརས་པ། དེ་ནས་ཁིང་ཚང་ཀ་ཨམ་ཚན་སོང་སྟེ། ཡང་ཚ་རྒྱལ་ཟེར་དེ། གསེར་རི་ད་བག་ཅིག་གི་ཁ་རྒྱུ་དིག་བསྐངས་དེ་བཀལ་དེ་ཛོ་ཛོ་སོང་སྟེ། ཨ་གུའི་སྒྲོན་གླུ་འདི་ལྟར།

བྲུ་མོ་ངའི་ཨ་གུས་ཞང་དངོས་ལ་ཉེན་དང་།
ཨ་གུ་དགའ་ཉིས་ཞང་བྲུ་མོ་ལ་ཉེན་དང་།
གསེར་རི་ད་བག་གང་ལ་རྒྱུ་དིག་རིག་ཡོད་ལོ།
ཉེ་རང་གིས་མི་དཔེ་བཏིང་སེ་མོ་ཞིག་དེབ་ལོ།
རྩིས་དཔེ་བཏིང་སེ་རྩིས་ཤིག་སྐོར་ལོ།
ཁོ་ཤི་སྟེ་འདུག་གསོན་དེ་འདུག་གཟིགས་ལོ།
ཁོ་གསོན་དེ་ལ་ཡོད་ན་ང་བཙལ་བ་རིག་ཆེན་ལོ།
ཁོ་ཤི་སྟེ་རིག་ཡོད་ན་མི་ཤ་ཐག་ཆོད་རིག་ཐོག་ཡིན།

དེ་ཟླུག་ཟེར་རིན་ཞིག་མང་པོ་ཏྲུས་སོང་། དེ་ནས་ཁོ་ཏྲུ་ཅེས་མཐོང་སྟེ་སྡིག་པ་བསམ་སྟེ། ཨ་གུས་གླུ་འདི་ལྟར།

ཡབས་ཐྲིན་པའི་བྲུ་མོ་ངའི་དངོས་ལ་ཉེན་དང་།
ཡུམ་སྤྲིན་མོ་འི་བྲུ་མོ་དངོས་ཤིག་ལ་ཉེན་དང་།
སྤྲིན་ལ་ར་གན་གྱི་རི་ལ་འཛོགས་དགོས་ཡོང་ཡིན།
རྫིང་ན་གསེར་གྱི་རི་ལ་བསླེབ་ཅས་ཡོང་ཡིན།
སྤྲིན་ལ་རོ་ཉའི་རི་ལ་འཛོགས་དགོས་ཡོང་ཡིན།

རྫིང་ན་དངུལ་གྱི་རི་ལ་བསྐྱིབ་ཙམ་རིག་ཡོང་ཡིན།

སྔོན་ལ་བྲ་ཟན་དང་སྐོག་ཆུ་ཟ་དགོས་བྱུང་ཡིན།

རྫིང་ན་ཞིམ་ཟས་དང་དངར་ཆུ་ཐོབ་ཙམ་ཡོང་ཡིན།

གླིང་གི་པན་ཇུང་མ་སྟོར་བ་ཡོད་ལོ།

མོ་ངན་ནི་སྒྲོང་ཕྲུག་མ་ཤི་བ་ཡོད་ལོ།

དྲི་མོ་དགུ་ཚོད་ཀྱི་ལུང་པའི་ནང་དུ་ཡོད་ལོ།

ཇོ་ ཇོ་ཉེ་རང་དེ་རུ་ལྟ་ལ་སོང་ལོ།

དེ་ལུང་པའི་ནང་དུ་སྐྱང་གཅིག་རང་ཡོད་ལོ་།

དེ་སྐྱང་པོ་འི་ཁ་ཇོ་ ཇོ་ཉེ་རང་སོང་ལོ།

ཤི་ལང་གི་ཕག་ར་ཞིག་རང་ཚོས་ལོ།

ཕག་ར་དེའི་ནང་ན་ཡིབ་སྡེ་རིག་ལྟོས་ལོ།

སྒྲོང་ཕྲུག་ཁོ་དེ་ནས་ཁྲིད་ལ་ཐོབ་ཡིན།

དེ་ནས་ཇོ་ ཇོ་འབྲུ་གུ་མ་མང་པོ་འཐད་རིན་ཞིག་དང་ཁང་པ་ལ་ལོག་སྡེ་ཡོང་སྡེ། ཨ་བ་དང་ཨ་མ་གཉིས་ཀ་ལ་ཏྲུན་དེ་ཚང་མ་ཟེརས། དེ་ནས་ཇོ་ ཇོ་རང་དང་གཡོག་མོ་ཞིག་ཁྲིད་དེ། དྲི་མོ་དགུ་ཚོད་མའི་ནང་དུ་སོང་། དེ་རུ་སྐྱང་ཞིག་ཡོད་ཚུག། ཁོང་དེ་སྐྱང་མགོ་ལ་བསྐྱིབ་སྡེ་ཤི་ལང་གི་ཕག་ར་ཞིག་བཙོ་སྡེ། དེའི་ནང་ལ་ཡིབ་སྡེ་འདུགས། དེ་ནས་མོ་ངན་ནི་སྒྲོང་ཕྲུག་རེས་ཀ་སར་གྱི་ལུགས་ལ། སྟངས་དང་གྲོས་བསླབ་བིན་ཞིག་ཡོད་ཚུག་པས། ཧ་ཞིག་ལ་ཞེན་ད་དེ་ཨུ་ཚགས་མ་གང་ཧའི་ཁ་ནས་ཕང་གིན་ཞིག་བང་བཏང་ངེད་ཚུག། ཐུར་ལ་ཡོང་ཙ་ན། དི་ཨུ་ཚགས་མ་གང་པོ་བསྡུ་འིན་ཞིག་མདའ་ལ་སྐར་ཚར་རད་ཚུག།

ཡང་ཅུང་སྐར་བྲེ་གང་ཁྲུར་དེ་གྲེན་ལ་ཆ་ཟ་ན་གཡོག་གིན་སོང་། ཐུར་ལ་ཆ་ཟ་ན། བསྒྱུ་འིན་ཡོང་སྟེ་བྲེ་བསྐང་ངེད་ཚུག། དབྱུང་པ་གཡས་པའི་ཁ་ཉེ་མ་ཤར་བ་འདྲ་ཡོད་ཚུག། དབྱུང་པ་གཡོམ་མའི་ཁ་ཟླ་བ་ཤར་བ་འདྲ་ཡོད་ཚུག། ཛོ་ཛོ་དང་གཡོག་མོ་གཉིས་ཀ་དེ་ཟུག་མཐོང་སྟེ་ཧབ་རྒོད་བཏངས་པ། དེ་ནས་ར་རྩ་དྲག་པོ་ཡོང་སྟེ། ཁ་ཆར་རླུང་མང་པོ་ཞིག་ཡོང་སྟེ། མི་མཐོང་ཅེས་སོང་། དེའི་རྗེང་ན་ཆར་པ་ཆད་དེ་ན། སྔོན་མའི་མཆོགས་སེ་མོ་ངན་ནི་སྤྱང་ཕྲུག་བཅོ་སྟེ་གླུ་འདི་ལྟར།

ཀླུ་ཡབས་སྔོན་པའི་བུ་མོ་ཁ་དམར་མོ། ཁ་དམར་མོ།
ཡུམ་སྔོན་མོ་འི་བུ་མོ་ལྕེ་དམར་མོ། ལྕེ་དམར་མོ།
ཞིམ་པོ་ཟོས་པའི་ཚིལ་སོགས་མོ། ཚིལ་སོགས་མོ།
ལགས་མོ་གནས་པའི་སྤྲང་ཁོར་མོ། སྤྲང་ཁོད་མོ།
ཁྲོད་ངའི་ལུང་པའི་ནང་དུ་ཅི་ལ་ཡོངས། ཅི་ལ་ཡོངས།
ངས་གཡའ་དཀར་ནས་ཁྲོངས་པའི་རྫབ་དཀར་ཁྲོང། རྫབ་དཀར་ཁྲོང།
ངས་གཡའ་ནག་ནས་ཁྲོངས་པའི་རྫབ་ནག་ཁྲོང། རྫབ་ནག་ཁྲོང།
ངའི་ཟ་ཅེས་སི་འདོད་པོ་ཡང་དེ་བོ་ཡིན། དེ་བོ་ཡིན།
ངའི་མཐུང་ཅེས་སི་འདོད་པོ་ཡང་དེ་བོ་ཡིན། དེ་བོ་ཡིན།
ངའི་ཞོན་ཧ་ཟེར་ནའང་དེ་བོ་ཡིན། དེ་བོ་ཡིན།
ངའི་ནང་ནོར་ཟེར་ནའང་དེ་བོ་ཡིན། དེ་བོ་ཡིན།
ངའི་ཕི་ནོར་ཟེར་ནའང་དེ་བོ་ཡིན། དེ་བོ་ཡིན།

ངའི་རྫབ་ར་དཀར་པོ་ག་ནས་ཁྲོང་ནའང་ཁྲོང་། ཁྲོང་ནའང་ཁྲོང་།

ངའི་རྫབ་ར་ནག་པོ་ག་ནས་ཁྲོང་ནའང་ཁྲོང་། ཁྲོང་ནའང་ཁྲོང་།

དེ་ ཟུག་ ཟེར་ དེ་ཇོ་ ཇོ་དང་ གཡོག་ མོ་གཉིས་ ཀ་ལ་ སྐད་ མང་ པོ་ ཞིག་ བཏངས། དེ་ནས་ཇོ་ ཇོས་ཁོ་འི་ རྐང་པ་ལ་འཁམ་སྦེ་ཐུ་མང་པོ་བཙོ་སྦེ་ཟེརས། མོ་ངན་ནེ་སྐྱོང་སྤྲུག ཐུ་ཐུ་གྲུལ། ང་ལ་ཁྲོ་རང་གི་ལུང་མཁན་ཀུན་ནིས། མོ་ངན་ནེ་སྐྱོང་སྤྲུག་གི་མི་ཤ་ཁྲོང་ཟེར་དེ་སྐད་བཏང་འདུག། མོ་ངན་ནེ་སྐྱོང་སྤྲུག་གིས་ཟེརས། དེ་ནས་ང་ཆེན། ད་ལྟ་ང་ཞའི་ཁང་པ་ལ་སྐྱིབ་ཅིག་གྲུལ་ཟ་ཅས་རེ་ཟོས་དེ། དེ་ནས་ཆ་ཡིན་ཟེར་དེ་ཚང་ཀ་ཁང་པ་ལ་སོང་།

ཁང་པ་རུ་བསླེབ་སྦེ་མོ་ངན་ནེ་སྐྱོང་སྤྲུག་གིས། ཨལ་ཅོ་ཞིག་ཐབ་ཟི་ཁ་བཀལ་དེ་མེ་ཞིག་སྤ་སྦེ་ཤ་ཞིག་བཙོས། ཤ་དེ་སྐྱིན་གྱི་ཡིན་ན་ཡང་། ཇོ་ཇོས་རྫབ་ར་ཁ་ཅིག་བཙོ་བ་ལ་མཐོང་སོང་། ཤ་དེ་བཙོས་ས་དང་། མོ་ངན་ནེ་སྐྱོང་སྤྲུག་གིས་རྫབ་ར་ཞིག་ཟུམ་སྦེ་ཁྲོང་སྦེ་བསད་དེ་ཇོ་ཇོ་འི་ལོག་པའི་ཡོག་ལ་ཤེས་མ་བཙུག་པ་བཏང་སྦེ་བོརས། དེ་ནས་ཤ་འཚོ་སྦེ་པོག་སྦེ་ན། ཨལ་ཅོ་ནང་ནས་ཕིངས། ཤ་གཅིག་ཅིག་མ་ཚང་བས། མོ་ངན་ནེ་སྐྱོང་སྤྲུག་གིས་ཟེརས། ཤ་མ་ཚང་། སུས་ཟོས་ཟེརས་པ། ཨ་མས་ངས་མ་ཟོས་ཟེརས། ཇོ་ཇོའི་གཡོག་མོ་ལ་འདྲིས་པ། མ་ཟོས་ཟེརས། དེ་ནས་ཇོ་ཇོ་ཁོ་རང་ལ་འདྲིས་པ། ཇོ་ཇོ་ཡམ་ཚན་སོང་སྦེ་ཟེརས། ལྟ་མོ་ངན་ནེ་སྐྱོང་སྤྲུག། དགས་རྩུག་པ་ངས་རྒྱུ་མི་ཤེས། ཁྱོད་རིས་ཅི་ཟེར་དེ་ཡིན་ཟེར་རིན་ཞིག་ཀག་ལངས་པ་སང་། རྫབ་ར་དེ་ཙབ་བུད་དེ་ཡོངས་པ་སང་། མོ་ངན་ནེ་སྐྱོང་སྤྲུག་གིས། ཀུ་རོ་བཏང་སྦེ་ཟེརས། ཁྱོད་པ་མ་བཟང་པོ་འི་བུ་མོ། རྒྱན་མ་ཞིག་ཡོད་རྩུག།

ངས་མི་ཐུག་མི་ལ་ཤད་ཡིན།
ཁྲི་ཐུག་ཁྲི་ལ་ཤད་ཡིན།
ཟེར་དེ་ཇོ་ཇོ་ཁྲེལ་བཙུགས།

No. 5.

དེ་ནས་མོ་ངན་ནི་སྲོང་ཕྲུག་གིས་ཟེར་ས། ཇོ་ཇོ་རང་པ། སྔོན་ལ་གུལ་ཤིག། ངས་ཨ་མ་ལ་ཤིང་རེ་ཚུ་རེ་ཁྱེར་སྟེ་དེང་ན་ཡོང་ཡིན་ཟེར་ས་པ། ཇོ་ཇོ་དང་གཡོག་མོ་གཉིས་ཀ་སྔོན་ལ་འགྲུལ་བཙུགས། ཇོ་ཇོ་པ་ཟླ་ལམ་གྱིས་ཆ་ཆ། ཁོ་བྲེ་མའི་ལམ་གྱིས་སོང་སྟེ། གླིང་ཡུལ་ལ་ཁོ་སྔོན་ལ་བསླེབ་སོང་། དེ་ཡང་མཁན་ཚང་མ་སོང་སྟེ་མེད་ཚུག། ཡང་གླིང་གི་དཔའ་བོ་ཚང་མ་ལ་ཨི་ཟུག་ལྷན་ཞིག་བཏངས། བྲོང་ཆེན་རི་རི་བསད་དེ། བྲོང་སྤགས་དེ་ཁྱེར་སྟེ་གླིང་མཁར་ལ་བཏིང་སྟེ། མཁར་ཡུལ་ཚང་མ་ཁྲིད་དེ་འདོམ་དགུ་ལྷག་མ་ལུས་བཙུག་མཁན་ལ་ཇོ་ཇོ་འབྲུ་ག་མ་བག་མ་ལ་བཏང་ཡིན་ཟེར་དེ་སྐད་བཏངས། དེ་ནས་དཔའ་བོ་ཚང་མ་སྔོན་ལ་སོང་ཚར། མོ་ངན་ནི་སྲོང་ཕྲུག་ལུས་འདུག་པ། ཡབ་བརྟན་པ་དང་ཡུམ་སྔོན་མོ་གཉིས་ཀས་ཁོ་ལ་ཟེར་ས། ཁྱོ་རང་མོ་ངན་ནི་སྲོང་ཕྲུག་ཡང་བྲོང་བསད་པར་ཆ་དགོས། རྒྱགས་འཁུར་ཅེས་ལ་སྣོད་ཅིག་དོང་ཟེར་ས་པ། ཁོས་ཀྲ་ཕྲུས་སེའི་རྐྱལ་ལྷུ་ཞིག་བཏངས། དེ་ཀྲ་ཕྲུས་སེའི་རྐྱལ་ལྷུ་ཡི་ནང་དུ་ཕེ་ཁལ་བརྒྱ་བཏང་ནའང་། མ་གང་སོང་། དེ་ནས་ཁོས་ཟེར་ས་པ། ཇོ་ཇོ་འི་འདོན་ཕྲོ་ན་ཞིག་སྐུལ་ཟེར་ས་པ། དེ་ནང་ནས་ཉང་ཏུན་ཞིག་བཏངས་པ་གང་སོང་། ཡང་མར་ཁུར་སྣོད་ཅིག་ཁྱེར་ཟེར་ས་པ། སྟེར་གའི་ཁོམ་བུ་ཞིག་བཏངས་སོང་། དེའི་ནང་དུ་མར་བ་ཏྲི་བརྒྱ་བཏངས་པ་མ་གང་། ཡང་ཁོས་ཟེར་ས། ཇོ་ཇོ་འི་

འདོན་སྒྲོ་ན་ཞིག་སྨུ་ལ་ཨ་མ་ལེ་ཟེརས། དེ་ནས་ཡང་ཅུང་ཙུན་ཞིག་བདངས་པ། སྐྱིབ་ཅིག་ལ་གང་སོང་།།

དེ་ནས་དྲང་གེ་དང་དྲོང་གེ་གཉིས་ཀ་ཁོ་ལ་ཡ་དོ་ལ་བདངས་པས། དེ་ཡུལ་ཞིག་ལ་བསླེབ་སོང་། དཔའ་བོ་ཚང་མ་འཛོམ་སྡེ་འདུགས། མོ་ངན་ནི་སྲོང་ཕྲུག་དེ་སོ་སོར་འདུགས། དེ་ནས་དཔའ་བོ་ཚང་མས་ཟེརས། ཐོ་རི་ན། ཡུལ་ཡོད་ར་མེད། ཆུ་དང་ཞིང་ཡོད་ར་མེད། ང་དང་སྲུ་ལ་ཡང་རྒྱུས་མེད། མོ་ངན་གྱི་སྲོང་ཕྲུག་ལ་རྒྱུས་ཡོད་འགྲོ། ཁོས་ཅི་ཟེར་འདུག་ལྟ་ལ་ཆ་རྒྱལ་ཟེར་དེ། ཨ་ག་དཔལ་ལེ་བདངས། མོ་ངན་ནི་སྲོང་ཕྲུག་ལ་ཕག་ཅན་པ་ཡོང་ཅེས་ཞེས་དེ། དྲང་གེ་དང་དྲོང་གེ་གཉིས་ལ་ཟེརས། ལྷ་དྲང་གེ་དང་དྲོང་གེ། ཐྲོ་རི་ང་དྲང་ལ་ཞིང་སྨི་ཐོབ་ཞིང་འཁོར་ན་རྒྱལ་ཆུ་མང་པོ་ཡོད་ཟེརས། དེ་ནས་དཔལ་ལེ་ལ་དེ་ཐུག་ཟེར་ཅེས་ཚོར་དེ་ཡིད་ཆེས་དེ། དཔའ་བོ་ཚང་མ་ལ་ཞིང་བཀལ་དེ་ཁྲིམས། མོ་ངན་ནི་སྲོང་ཕྲུག་གིས་ཞིང་མ་འཁོར་ར། ཆུ་ཆང་རྒྱལ་གསུམ་བཀལ་དེ་ཁྲིམས། ཁོང་ཚང་མ་དེ་རུ་དགོངས་ལ་འཛོམ་ཅན། ཞིང་མང་པོ་ཡོད་ཚུག། ཆུ་མན་ན་མེད་ཚུག། དེའི་ཕྱི་ལ་དཔའ་བོ་ཀུན་ལ་ཆུ་མེད་དཀགས་པོ་སོང་སྟེ། མོ་ངན་ནི་སྲོང་ཕྲུག་ལ་རྫ་ཟེརས་པ། ཁོས་ཚང་མ་ལ་ཆུ་ཅུང་ཙུན་རེ་བདངས།།

དེ་ནས་ཡང་ཕྱི་དྲོ་ལ་དཔའ་བོ་ཚང་ཀས་ཟེརས། མདང་ཨ་གུ་དཔལ་ལེ་ལ་ཧམ་གོ་བ་ཡིན་ནོག། འདི་རིང་ཨང་གར་ལངས་པ་ཅན་པ་ལ་སོང་། མོ་ངན་ནི་སྲོང་ཕྲུག་གིས་ཞིང་འཁོར་འདུག་ག། ཆུ་འཁོར་འདུག་ཅན་པ་སོང་ཟེར་དེ་བདངས། མོ་ངན་ནི་སྲོང་ཕྲུག་ལ་ཕག་ཅན་བདང་བ་ཡོང་ཅེས་དེ་ཞེས་དེ། ཡང་ཁོས་ཕྱིར་ལོག་ཟེརས། ལྷ་དྲང་གེ་དང་དྲོང་གེ། ཐོ་རས་ལ་ཞིང་སྨ་མང་

པོ་ཡོད། ཆུ་དཀོན་མོ་ཡོད། ཆུ་ཁར་ཤིག་ཟེར་ས་པ། ཨང་གར་ལྕངས་པས་དེ་ཟུག་ཡིད་ཆེས་དེ། ལོག་སྐྱེ་སོང་སྐྱེ་དཔའ་བོ་ཀུན་ལ་ཟེར་ས། གྲོ་རས་ལ་ཤིང་ཡོད་ལོ། ཆུ་དཀོན་མོ་ཞིག་ཡོད་ལོ། ཆུ་ཁར་ཤིག་ཟེར་དེ་ཆུ་མང་པོ་འཁར་བཙུགས། མོ་ངན་གྱི་སྤྱོང་ཕྲུག་གིས་དྲང་གེ་དང་དྲོང་གེ་གཉིས་ཀ་ལ་ཤིང་ཁར་རེ་བཀལ་དེ་རྫིང་ན་སོང་བས།། ཡང་དེ་རུ་བསླེབ་ཙ་ན། ཆུ་ཡོད་ཚུག། ཤིང་མེད་པ། དཔའ་བོ་ཀུན་ལ་ས་དཀགས་བོ་སོང་སྐྱེ། ཡང་མོ་ངན་ནི་སྤྱོང་ཕྲུག་གི་མདུན་ལ་ཡོང་སྐྱེ་ཧུ་ཟེར་ས་པ། ཡང་ཤིང་ཅང་ཚུན་རེ་བཏངས།།

དེ་ནས་ཡང་དཔའ་བོ་ཀུན་གྱིས་ཟེར་ས། ཁྱོ་ཞ་གཉིས་ཀ་ལ་ཡང་ཏ་མ་གོ་པ་ཡིན་འགྲོ། འདི་རིང་ཨ་གུ་དགའ་ནི་རང་སོང་ཟེར་དེ་བཏངས་པ། མོ་ངན་ནི་སྤྱོང་ཕྲུག་ལ་པག་ཅུར་བཏང་ཅེས་ཤེས་དེ། ཡང་ཟེར་ས། ཕྲ་དྲང་གེ་དང་དྲོང་གེ། གྲོ་རས་ལ་ཡུལ་ཆེན་པོ་ཞིག་དང་གྲུག་ཆེན་གོན་ཅེས་སོ་མ་རེ་གོན་ཤིག། ཁྱོད་དཔའ་བོ་ཚང་མས་གོ་ཤེན་གོན་ཡིན་འགྲོ། ཟེར་ས་པ། ཨ་གུ་དགའ་ནི་ཡིད་ཆེས་དེ་ལོག་སྐྱེ་ཡོང་སྐྱེ། དཔའ་བོ་ཀུན་ལ་ཟེར་ས། གྲོ་རས་ལ་ཡུལ་ཞིག་དང་གྲུག་ཆེན་ལོ། གོན་ཅེས་སོ་མ་རེ་གོན་དེ་གྱུལ་ཟེར་འདུག། ང་དང་ཡང་ཟབ་ན་ཀྱལ་ཟེར་དེ་གོ་ཤེན་རེ་གོན་དེ་སོང་བ། ལམ་ཚང་མ་ལ་ཀོར་མའི་ཀོགས་ཆེན་པོ་ཞིག་ཡོད་ཚུག། ཁོང་གི་གོ་ཤེན་ཚང་མ་ཀོར་མང་གིས་བཅད་དེ་ཚར་དེ། ལམ་ཚང་མ་ལ་ཕང་གིན་སོང་བ། མོ་ངན་ནི་སྤྱོང་ཕྲུག་གིས་གོ་ཤེན་བུད་མཁན་ཚང་མ་སྨྱུ་འིན་ཞིག་སོང་པ། གོ་ཤེན་གྱི་གོན་ཅེས་གཅིག་སོང་། དེ་དཔའ་བོ་ཚང་མའི་གོ་ཤེན་ཆད་དེ། ཡུལ་ལ་བསླེབ་ཟ་ན་མེད་མཁན་སོང་། ཁོང་ལ་མི་སུས་ཀྱང་ཡ་ཤ་མ་བཅོས་པའི། མོ་ངན་ནི་སྤྱོང་ཕྲུག་དེས་བུད་མཁན་ནི་གོ་ཤེན

ལ་འཕྲད་དེ་གོན་དེ་སོང་པ་སང། དེའི་ཡུལ་པ་ཚང་མས་ཚོག་ཀ་སྐོར་ཁྲར་དེ་བསྐུས་དེ་ཡོངས། དེ་དཔའ་བོ་ཚང་མ་ལ་ཅང་རིན་མ་ཡོངས་པ་སང། དེན་ན་ཟ་ན་ལྦུང་པ་སོ་སོ་ཡི་ནང་དུ་འགྲོང་བཙལ་བ་སོང།།

མོ་ངན་ནི་སྤྲོང་ཕྲུག། དེ་ཡུལ་གྱི་མགོ་ལ་སྤང་ཞིག་ཡོད་ཚུག། དེ་རུ་སོང་སྟེ། ཕྱུ་ཐུངས་གཅིག་གི་ནང་དུ་མགོ་བདངས། གཅིག་གི་ནང་དུ་ཀང་པ་བདང་སྟེ་གཉིད་ལོག་སྟེ་འདུགས། དཔའ་བོ་ཚང་མས་རིའི་ཤ་བ་མང་པོ་བསད་དེ་ཤ་མང་པོ་ཟའད་ཚུག། དེ་ནས་དྲང་གེ་དང་དྲོང་གེ་གཉིས་ཀས་ཟེརས་པ། ཁྱང་དང་གཉིས་ཀ་མོ་ངན་ནི་སྤྲོང་ཕྲུག་ལ་ཡ་དོ་ལ་ཡོང་སྟེ་ཅང་མ་ཐན། དཔའ་བོ་ཚང་མ་དང་མཉམ་པོ་ཡོད་པིན་ན། ང་དང་ལ་ཡང་ཤ་ཐོབ་པིན། མོ་ངན་ནི་སྤྲོང་ཕྲུག་དེ་གཉིད་ལོག་སྟེ་འདུགས་པ་སང། ང་དང་ལ་ཅང་ན་ཐོབ་སོང་ཟེརས་པ། དེ་ཟླུག་ཟེར་ཅེས་མོ་ངན་ནི་སྤྲོང་ཕྲུག་ལ་གཉིད་དི་ནང་ལ་ཆོར་སོང། དེ་ནས་སྤྲོང་ཕྲུག་འདུག་སའི་ཁ་ཐོག་ལ་བྲག་ཅིག་གི་ཁ་རུ་སྤྲིན་ཅིག་ཡོད་ཚུག་པས།

དེ་ལ་མོ་ངན་ནི་སྤྲོང་ཕྲུག་གིས་སོག་ལྷི་ཞིག་བདངས་པ། སྤྲིན་དེ་ཤི་སྟེ་ཁོང་གི་མདུན་ལ་བསླེབ་སོང་བས། དྲང་གེ་དང་དྲོང་གེ་གཉིས་ལ་ཟེརས། ཁྱ་ཀུན་ནིག། འདི་སྤྲིན་པོ་དེ་གངས་ཀྱི་ཁ་ཁྲེར་དེ་ཤུས། གངས་ཀྱི་ཁ་ཁྲག་ཅ་བིག་འང་གོས་མ་ཐུག། ཅ་བིག་གོས་ན། ཁྱོ་ཞའི་སྐྱེ། ངའི་གྱི་ཡིན་ཟེརས། དེ་ནས་དྲང་གེ་དང་དྲོང་གེ་འཇིགས་སེན་ཞིག་ཁྲེར་དེ་གངས་ཀྱི་ཁ་བ་ཤུས། ཁྲག་ཅ་ཕིག་གོས་ན། ཁོང་གིས་ལྷུ་དང་བལྟག་སྟེ་མེད་མཁན་བཅོས་སོང། ཤ་ཁྲིང་སྟེ་ཟ་འིན་ཞིག་འདུགས་པ། ཡང་ཞག་གཅིག་སོང་སྟེ། དེ་བྲག་གི་ཁ་ཡང་གསེར་རི་རུ་ཅོ་ཡོད་མཁན་ནི་སྤྲིན་ཞིག། དངུལ་གྱི་རུ་ཅོ་ཡོད་མཁན་ཞིག།

དང་གི་རྩ་ཆེ་ཡོད་མཁན་ཞིག། སྨུ་དིག་གི་རྩ་ཆེ་ཡོད་མཁན་ཞིག། ཟངས་ཀྱི་རྩ་ཆེ་ཡོད་མཁན་ཞིག། གཡུའི་རྩ་ཆེ་ཡོད་མཁན་ཞིག། བྱུ་རུའི་རྩ་ཆེ་ཡོད་མཁན་ཞིག། དེ་ཟུག་བདུན་ཡོང་སྟེ་ཡོད་ཚུག། དེ་སྐྱིན་བདུན་གྱིས་མོ་ངན་ནི་སྤྱོང་ཕྲུག་ལ་གླུ་ཞིག་འདི་ལྟར།།

སྟེང་ལྷ་ཡུལ་ན་བདགས་པའི་དོན་གྲུབ་དཀར་པོ་གསེན་དང༑
གླིང་ཡུལ་གཞུང་ན་བདགས་པའི་མོ་ངན་ནི་སྤྱོང་ཕྲུག་ཉིན་དང།
ཤ་ཚོང་ཞས་བདགས་པའི་གླིང་རྒྱལ་ལྷམ་ཀ་སར་གསན་དང།
གླིང་གི་དཔའ་བོ་ཀུན་ཡོང་སྟེ་ང་ཞའི་ཤ་རབས་བཅད་འདུག།
གླིང་གི་དཔའ་བོ་ཚང་ཀ་ཡོང་སྟེ་ང་ཞའི་ས་བོན་བཅད་འདུག།
དེའི་ཕྱི་ལ་ཉིད་ཀྱིས་ཐུགས་རྗེ་རིག་གཟིགས་ལོ།
དེའི་ཕྱི་ལ་ཀ་སར་གྱིས་སྐྱོབས་རིག་མཛད་ལོ།
ཉེ་རང་གིས་སྐྱུང་བ་རིག་མ་མཛད་ན་ང་ཞ་མི་ལུས་ཐག་ཆོད་འདུག།

ཀ་སར་ལ་དེ་ཟུག་ཞུས་པ་སང། ཀ་སར་གྱིས་ལན་དུ་ཡང་གླུ་འདི་ལྟར་སླངས་སོ།

ཁྱེད་ལྷ་སྐྱིན་ཚང་ཀས་ངའི་དངོས་ལ་ཉོན།
ཁྱེད་ཀླུ་སྐྱིན་ཚང་མས་བདག་ལ་གསན་ལོ།
འབྲོང་ཆེན་རི་རིའི་འདུགས་ག་རུ་ཡོད་ལོ།
འབྲོང་ཆེན་ཁམས་བ་ལ་ག་རུ་འདུག་ས་རིག་ཡིན་ལོ།
འབྲོང་ཆེན་འདུག་ས་བསྟན་ན་ཁྱེད་ལ་རོགས་བཅོ་ཡིན།
འབྲོང་ཆེན་རི་རི་མ་བསྟན་ན་ཁྱེད་ལ་སྐྱུང་ཅེས་ཞིག་མེད་ལོ།
འབྲོང་ཆེན་ཁམས་བ་མ་བསྟན་ན་ཁྱེད་ཀུན་ལ་རོགས་མི་ཡོང།

དེ་ཐུག་གི་ལན་བཏངས་པ་སང། སྐྱིན་ཚང་ཀ་ཡམ་ཚན་སོང་སྤེ་ཟེརས། འབྲོང་དེ་བསྟན་ན། ང་དང་ལ་མཐའ་ཡོད། མ་བསྟན་ན། ང་དང་ཚང་མ་ཤི་ཅེས་སོང། ད་ཅི་བཅོ་ཡིན་ཟེརས་པ། སྐྱིན་གཅིག་གིས་ཟེརས། འབྲོང་ཆེན་ཁོ་རང་བསྟན་ན། ང་དང་ལ་མཐའ་ཡོང་ཡིན། དེ་བས་འབྲོང་དེ་ཡོད་པའི་རི་བསྟན་ཡིན་ཟེར་དེ་གླུ་འདི་ལྟར།

གླིང་གི་རྒྱལ་ལྷམ་ཆེན་མོ་ང་ཞའི་དངོས་ལ་ཉོན་དང།
རྒྱལ་ལྷམ་ཀེ་སར་ཉིད་ཀྱིས་དངོས་ཤིག་ལ་ཉོན་ལོ།
འབྲོང་ཆེན་བསྟན་པར་ང་ཞ་ལ་མཐའ་ཞིག་ཡོད་ལོ།
གཡས་པ་རི་ཕྱོགས་ལ་ཉེ་རང་སྐྱོད་ལོ།
དེ་རི་ཐུན་དེ་སྐྱོད་ན་འབྲོང་དེ་ཐོབ་ཡིན།

དེ་ཐུག་ཟེརས་པ་སང། མོ་ངན་ནི་སྤྲོང་ཕྲུག་འཐད་ནས་སློན་ལམ་ཞིག་བཏབས་པ། མཉམ་པོ་སྐྱེས་པའི་ལྷ་དགུ་མཆེད་ལོ། མཉམ་པོ་སྐྱེས་པའི་ཀླུ་དགུ་མཆེད་ནོ། དགས་རྩུག་པ་དུ་བག་ལ་སྐད་ཅིག་ཐིང་བ་མི་འདུག། སྐད་དེ་མ་ཐིང་པ་སང། སེམས་ཅན་མང་པོ་ཤི་རྡུག། དགས་དུ་བག་ལ་སྐད་ཆེན་པོ་ཞིག་ཐིང་ཤིག་ཟེརས་པ། དེ་ནས་ཕར་ལ་དུ་བག་ལ་སྐད་ཆེན་པོ་ཞིག་ཐོན་སོང་བས། དེ་ནས་ཕར་ལ་སེམས་ཅན་ཚང་མ་ལ་ཕན་ཐོགས་ཤིག་ཡོངས། ཅི་ཕན་ཟེར་ན། ནམ་དུ་བག་ཅིག་བཏང་ན། སེམས་ཅན་གཅིག་ལ་ཐོག་ན། གཞན་མ་ཚང་མ་ལ་སྐད་ཚོར་པ་སང། ཤོར་དེ་སྤྲོག་འབུད་འདུག། དེ་ནས་དེ་ལྷ་སྐྱིན་ཚང་ཀ་འཐད་དེན་ཞིག་ལོག་སྤེ་རི་ལ་སོང།།

མོ་ངན་ནི་སྤྲོང་ཕྲུག་དེ་རི་གཡས་པ་ཐུན་དེ་འཛོགས་དེ་སོང་པ་སང།

འཁྲོང་ཆེན་རི་རི་དེ་རི་ཞིག་གི་ཁ་མགོ་བཀལ་དེ། རི་ཞིག་གི་ཁ་རྐང་པ་བོར་དེ་གཉིད་ལོག་སྡེ་ཡོད་ཚུག། མོ་ངན་ནི་སྤྲོང་ཕྲུག་དེ་འཛིགས་དེ། ཕོ་ལོང་ཞིག་གི་ཡོག་ལ་ཡིབ་སྡེ་ན། གླུ་འདི་ལྟར།

ཨ་པ་འཁྲོང་ཆེན་ཉིད་རང་འཁྲོང་བརྒྱུའི་དཔོན་པོ་ཞིག་ཡིན་ལོ།
འཁྲོང་ཆེན་རི་རི་དེ་འཁྲོང་བརྒྱུའི་དཔོན་པོ་ཞིག་ཡིན་ལོ།
བུ་ཚ་ང་རང་ནི་མི་བརྒྱུའི་དཔོན་པོ་ཞིག་ཡིན་ལོ།
མི་རྒྱུང་ང་རང་དེ་མི་བརྒྱུའི་དཔོན་པོ་ཞིག་ཡིན་ལོ།
ང་དང་དཔོན་པོ་གཉིས་ཀ་དེ་མཛའ་པོ་ཞིག་ཟུམ་ཡིན།
མི་ཆེན་འཁྲོང་ཆེན་གཉིས་ཀ་མཛའ་པོ་ཞིག་བཙོ་ཡིན།

མོ་ངན་ནི་སྤྲོང་ཕྲུག་གིས་དེ་ཟུག་ཟེརས་པ། འཁྲོང་ཆེན་དེས་གཉིད་ཀྱི་ནང་ནས་མགོ་ཙོག་ཙོག་བཙོའད་ཚུག། དེ་ནས་མོ་ངན་ནི་སྤྲོང་ཕྲུག་ནས་བསམ། འཁྲོང་དེ་གཉིད་ལ་སོང་སྡེ་འདུག། ང་ཉེ་མོ་ཞིག་ལ་ཆ་ཡིན་ནསམ་སྡེ་སོང་སྡེ་ཡང་གླུ་འདི་ལྟར།

ཨ་བ་འཁྲོང་ཆེན་དེ་འཁྲོང་བརྒྱུའི་དཔོན་པོ་ཡིན་ལོ།
འཁྲོང་ཆེན་རི་རི་དེ་འཁྲོང་བརྒྱུའི་དཔོན་པོ་ཞིག་ཡིན་ལོ།
བུ་ཚ་ང་རང་ཞིང་མི་བརྒྱུའི་དཔོན་པོ་རིག་ཡིན་ལོ།
ངའི་རྟ་རྒྱུང་དེ་ནི་རྟ་བརྒྱུའི་དཔོན་པོ་ཞིག་ཡིན་ལོ།
ཀྱང་རྒོད་དབྱེར་པ་དེ་རྟ་བརྒྱུའི་དཔོན་པོ་ཞིག་ཡིན་ལོ།
ང་དང་ཚང་ཀ་མཛའ་པོ་ཞིག་མི་ཟུམ་མ།

དེ་ཟླུག་ཟེརས་པ། འབྲོང་དེས་མགོ་སྣུག་སྟེ། མགོ་ཅོག་ཅོག་བཅོས་པ། མོ་ངན་ནི་སྤྲོང་ཕྲུག་ལ་འབྲོང་གི་རྭ་ཅོ་མཐོང་སྟེ་མང་པོ་འཇིགས་ཏེ་ཟེརས།

ཨ་བ་འབྲོང་ཆེན་དེ་ངའི་དངོས་ལ་ཉེན་དང་།

འབྲོང་ཆེན་རི་རི་དེ་ངའི་གནམ་ལ་ཉེན་དང་།

ཨ་བ་ཉེ་རི་རྭ་ཅོ་ལ་ང་ལ་འཇིག་འཇིག་རིག་རག་ལོ།

འབྲོང་ཆེན་ཉེ་རི་རྭ་ཅོ་གཡས་པ་ཕུད་དེ་བཏང་ན་ལོ།

བུ་ཚ་ང་རི་མདའ་མགོ་གཡས་པ་བོ་ཕུད་དེ་བཏང་ཡིན།

དེ་ཟླུག་ཟེརས་པ་སང་། འབྲོང་དེ་བདེན་ཆེས་ཏེ་རྭ་ཅོ་གཡས་པ་ས་ལ་རྡེན་ནས་ཕུད་དེ་ཕངས་པས། ཡང་མོ་ངན་ནི་སྤྲོང་ཕྲུག་གིས་ཟེརས་པ།

ཨ་བ་འབྲོང་ཆེན་ལེ་ཉེ་རི་རྭ་ཅོ་གཡོན་པ་ལ་འཇིགས་ས་རག།

ཉེ་རང་གི་རྭ་ཅོ་གཡོན་པ་ཕུད་དེ་བཏང་ན།

བུ་ཚ་ང་རི་གཞུ་མགོ་གཡོན་པ་བོ་བཅག་ཡིན།

དེ་ཟླུག་ཟེརས་པ་སང་། རྭ་ཅོ་གཡོན་པ་ཡང་ཕུད་དེ་ཕངས་པས། དེ་ནས་མོ་ངན་ནི་སྤྲོང་ཕྲུག་དེ་མདུན་ལ་སོང་སྟེ་འབྲོང་དེ་ཕ་སྐལ་བཅོས། མོ་ངན་ནི་སྤྲོང་ཕྲུག་དེ་བུ་སྐལ་བཅོ་སྡེའུ་དགས། མཚན་ལ་གཉིད་ལོག་ཅ་ན། འབྲོང་གི་རྣ་མཆོག་ནང་དུ་འདུག་གད་ཚུག། ཞག་ཅིག་མོ་ངན་ནི་སྤྲོང་ཕྲུག་གིས་ཁ་རའི་ད་ཀྱི་ཞིག་ཟོས་དེ། ད་རུམ་དུ་རུམ་བཅོས་པ་སང་། འབྲོང་ཆེན་གྱིས་ཟེརས། ཨྱ་མོ་ངན་ནི་སྤྲོང་ཕྲུག་འདི་རིང་ཀྱོ་རང་གིས་ཅི་ཟའད་ཟེརས་པ། མོ་ངན་ནི་སྤྲོང་ཕྲུག་གིས། ཨ་བ་འབྲོང་ཆེན་ལེ། འདི་རིང་ངས་ང་རང་གི་མིག་གཡས་པ་ཕིང་སྟེ་ཟའད་པ། རྣ་ཞིམ་པོ་ཞིག་དྲག་ཟེརས་པ། འབྲོང་གིས་ཟེརས། ང་ལ་

ཙ་བིག་དོང་། ངས་སྲུང་ཡིན་ཟེར་ས་པ། མོ་ངན་ནི་སྤྲོང་ཕྲུག་གིས་ཁ་རའི་ད
ཀྱིར་ཞིག་བདངས། འབྲོང་གིས་དེ་བོ་ཟོས་དེ་མ་ཞིམ་པོ་ཞིག་ཚོར་དེ། ཕྲ་མོ་
ངན་ནི་སྤྲོང་ཕྲུག། ངའི་མིག་པོ་ཡང་ཕིང་སྟེ་དོང་ཟེར་ས་པ། མོ་ངན་ནི་སྤྲོང་
ཕྲུག་གིས། འབྲོང་དེའི་མིག་གཡས་པ་ཕིང་སྟེ་ཕང་སྟེ། ཚབས་ལ་ཁ་ར་ཞིག་
ཟ་ལ་བདངས། འབྲོང་ལ་མ་ཞིམ་པོ་ཚོར་དེ་ཡང་ཟེརས། ཕྲ་མོ་ངན་ནི་སྤྲོང་ཕྲུག།
འདི་བོ་མ་ཞིམ་པོ་ཞིག་རག། ཡང་མིག་གཡོ་མ་ཡང་ཕིང་སྟེ་དོང་ཟེར་ས་པ།
མོ་ངན་ནི་སྤྲོང་ཕྲུག་གིས་མིག་གཡོ་མ་ཡང་ཕིངས། དེ་ནས་འབྲོང་ཆེན་ལ་མི་
མཐོང་ཙམ་སོང་པ་སང་། མོ་ངན་ནི་སྤྲོང་ཕྲུག་གིས་ཞག་དང་ཞག་དུག་རྩ་དང་
དུག་ཆུ་རེ་བདང་གིན་ཞིག་བོར་ས་པ། འབྲོང་ཆེན་དེ་ཞག་དང་ཞག་གླེན་པ་ཞིག་
སོང་། དེ་ནས་མོ་ངན་ནི་སྤྲོང་ཕྲུག་གིས་ཟེར་ས་པ། ཨ་བ་འབྲོང་ཆེན་རི་རི།
ཉེ་རང་གླེན་གླེན་སོང་དོག་པ། ཅི་ཞིག་རག་ལེ། འབྲོང་གིས། ང་ཞག་དང་
ཞག་གླེན་པ་ཞིག་ཆ་རག་ཟེར་ས་པ། དེ་ནས་ཡང་མོ་ངན་ནི་སྤྲོང་ཕྲུག་གིས། ཨ་བ་
རང་ལ་གྲིབ་ཅིག་སོང་མཁན་ཡིན་ནོག། ངས་སངས་ཤིག་བདང་ཡིན་ཟེར་དེ།
ཤིང་དུམ་བུ་བརྒྱ་ཟམ་བཙོ་སྟེ། འབྲོང་དེ་ལང་བཙུག་སྟེ་གྲོད་པའི་ཨོག་ལ་བོར་
དེ་མེ་ཞིག་བདུག་སྟེ་ཁོས་ཀ་ཙོ་བདང་སྟེ་ཟེརས། སང་ངོ། སྟེང་ལྷ་ཡུལ། བར་
བཙན་ཡུལ། འོག་ཀླུ་ཡུལ། སང་ངོ་ཟེར་དེ། འབྲོང་གི་སྤྲུ་ཁ་ཚང་མ་མེ་ལ་
བདུག་སྟེ་མན་ན་མེད་མཁན་བཙོས། དེ་ནས་མོ་ངན་ནི་སྤྲོང་ཕྲུག་གིས་ས་དོང་ཆེན་
མོ་ཞིག་བཙོ་སྟེ། དེ་ལ་ཕྲག་སྐྱབ་མོ་ཞིག་བཙོ་སྟེ་བོརས་ནས་གླུ་འདི་ལྟར་རོ།།

ཨ་བ་འབྲོང་ཆེན་ཁྱོད་རིས་ད་ཉིན་དང་།
འབྲོང་ཆེན་རི་རིས་འང་བདག་ལ་གསན་དང་།

འདི་རིང་ང་དང་གིས་རྩེན་མོ་ཞིག་རྩེན་ལོ།

ཕ་བུ་གཉིས་ཀས་ཡངས་པ་ཞིག་རྩེན་ལོ།

བུ་ཚ་ང་རང་ཞོར་རྩོལ་ཞིག་བཙོ་ཡིན་ལོ།

ཨ་བ་ཉེ་རང་གིས་འདེད་རྩོལ་ཞིག་ཙམ་ལོ།

དེ་ཟུག་ཟེརས་པ། འགྲོང་དེ་ལ་སྒྲོ་ཡོང་སྟེ་ཟེརས། ཁྱོད་མི་ཡུལ་ལི་མི་དེ། ཁྲིམ་མེད་མཁན་འདུག་ཟེར་དེ། ཀུ་ཙོ་དྲག་པོ་ཞིག་བདང་གིན་ཞིག་རེད་བཏངས་པ། གོམ་པ་གསུམ་བཏང་སྟེ་ན། འགྲོང་ཆེན་རི་རི་དེ་ས་དོང་ནང་དུ་བུད་དེ་སོང་། དེ་ནས་མོ་ངན་ནི་སྦྲོང་ཕྲུག་མགྱོགས་པ་ཡོང་སྟེ། མདའ་དང་མདང་རྒྱབ་སྟེ་འགྲོང་ཆེན་དེ་ནང་དུ་བསད་བཏངས། ལྷགས་པ་དེ་ཤུ་ཅེས་པ་མགོ་ཟུག་པ། ཡང་ཤུས་པ། ཡང་གསོབ་སྟེ། མ་ཉན་བ། དེ་ནས་ནམ་མཁའ་ན་པོ་རོག་པོ་མོ་གཉིས་ཕུར་དེ་ཆའད་རྩུག། དེ་གཉིས་ཀས་དཔེ་ར་ཞིག་བཏངས། མོ་པོ་རོག་དེས་པོ་པོ་རོག་ལ་ཟེརས། ལྷ་པོ་པོ་རོག། དེ་མི་ཡུལ་ལི་མི་ལ་ལྟོས་འང། འགྲོང་དེ་བསད་པ་ཤེས། ཤུ་ཅེས་དེ་མ་ཤེས་པ་ཡིན་ནོག། པོ་པོ་རོག་གིས་ཟེརས། དེ་ནས་ག་ཟུག་ལ་ཤུ་ཅེན་ལྷ་ཟེརས་པ། མོ་པོ་རོག་གིས། དེ་ཟུག་ལ་ཤུ་ན། ཁོ་ལ་ཟླ་བ་གཅིག་ལ་ཤུ་མི་ཚར། ཙ་བིག་ཤུ་འཛིན་ཞིག་དང་གསེད་དེ་བུར་ཆ་ཞིག་རྒྱབ་ན། དེ་ནས་མགྱོགས་པ་ཤུ་ཚར་ཡིན་ཟེརས། དེ་ཟུག་མོ་ངན་ནི་སྦྲོང་ཕྲུག་ལ་བུ་སྐད་གོ་སྟེ་གསེད་དེ་བུར་ཆ་ཞིག་བཙོ་སྟེ། ཤུ་ཡི་ཚོར་དང་བུར་ཆ་རྒྱབས་པ། དེ་ནས་སླ་མོ་ཞིག་ལ་ཉན་སོང་། ཤ་ཚང་མ་བོར་དེ། ལྷགས་པ་དེ་རྒྱང་ཀོད་དབྱེར་པ་ལ་བཀལ་དེ་གླིང་ཡུལ་ལ་ཁྱོངས་པ། དེ་རུ་བསླེབ་སྟེ་མཁར་ལ་ཁྱེར་དེ་བདེངས་པ་སང་། གླིང་

མཁར་དང་ཡུལ་ཚང་མ་ཁྲིད་དེ། འདོམ་དགུ་ལྷག་མ་ལུས། དེ་ནས་ཡང་མོ་ངན་ནི་སྡོང་ཕྲུག་ལ་ཇོ་ཇོ་འབྲུ་གུ་མ་ཐོབ་ཟེར་དེ་ལྷུང་མཁན་ཚང་མས་ཀུ་ཅོ་བཏངས།།

No. 6.

དེ་ནས་ཡང་ཡབ་བཙན་པ་དང་ཡུམ་སྡོན་མོ་གཉིས་ཀྱིས་སྐྱོན་བཅོ་སྟེ་ཟེརས། དེ་ལ་མི་བདང། བྱ་ཏི་མ་ཁྱུང་རྡུང་གི་ཤོག་པ་ཞིག་ཤུས་ཁྲིང་ན། དེ་ལ་ངའི་བུ་མོ་བག་མ་ལ་བདང་ཡིན་ཟེརས་པ། ཡང་གླིང་གི་དཔའ་བོ་ཚང་མ་བྱ་ཏི་མ་ཁྱུང་རྡུང་གི་ཤོག་པ་འཁྲིང་བ་ལུང་པ་སོ་སོའི་ནང་དུ་སོང་བས། མོ་ངན་ནི་སྡོང་ཕྲུག་དེ་བྱ་ཚང་མའི་ཡུལ་ལ་སོང། དེ་ལམ་ཐོག་དུ་དུག་ཤ་བོ་ལོང་དེ་ཡོད་ཚུག། མི་ཚང་མ་དེ་ཤ་བོ་ལོང་ལ་འཁོར་དེ་མེད་བ་ཆ་ཉན་བ་མེད་ཚུག། འཁོར་དེ་ཆ་ན། ཟླ་བ་གཅིག་གི་རིང་ཡོད་ཚུག་པས། མོ་ངན་ནི་སྡོང་ཕྲུག་དེ་ལམ་དྲང་པོ་ཟུན་དེ་སོང་བས། དུག་ཤ་བོ་ལོང་གི་མདུན་ལ་བསླེབ་སྟེ། ཀྲུང་ཀོད་དབྱེར་པའི་ཁ་ཞོན་དེ། ཤ་ལོང་ངེ་ཁ་སོང་སྟེ། གླུ་ཞིག་བཏངས་སོ།

ཤ་དུག་ཤ་བོ་ལོང་ཁྲིད་ཉེན་དང་ལོ།
ཁྲོད་དུག་ཤ་བོ་ལོང་གིས་ཉེན་དང་ལོ།
ང་ལ་བདུད་ཙུ་རྩུ་ལུ་གུ་ཀུན་བདུལ་ན།
ཤར་ལ་ལྷ་སྟེ་གོམ་པ་བདུན་ཟམ་དོང།
ང་ཡ་གླིང་མཁར་རྩེ་དགུའི་མགོ་རི་ལྷན་ན།
ནུབ་ལ་ལྷ་སྟེ་གོམ་པ་བདུན་ཟམ་དོང!
ང་ལ་ཇོ་ཇོ་འབྲུག་མོ་གྲོགས་ལ་ཐོབ་ན།
བྱང་ལ་ལྷ་སྟེ་གོམ་པ་བདུན་ཟམ་དོང།

ང་ལ་བྱ་ཉི་མ་ཁྱུང་རྒྱུང་གི་ཤོག་པ་ཐོབ་ན།

སྒོ་ལ་ལྷ་སྟེ་གོམ་པ་བདུན་ཟམ་དོང།

དེ་ཟླུག་ཟེར་དེ་ཕོ་ལོང་ལ་སླ་ལོ་བདག་སྟེ། ཕོ་ལོང་གིས་ཤར་དང་སྒོ་ནུབ་བྱང། ཕྱོགས་བཞི་རྒྱ་གོམ་པ་བདུན་རེ་བཏངས། དེ་ནས་མི་དང་བྱ་རིགས། འགྲུལ་མཁན་ཚང་མ་ལ་གནོད་པ་མི་སྐྱུལ་ཅས་སི་ཕི་ལ་མནའ་བོར་དེ་ན། མོ་ངན་ནི་སྒྲོང་ཕྲུག་དེ་སོང་སྟེ། ཁོ་བྱ་ཡུལ་ལ་བསླེབ་སྟེ། བལྟ་ཟ་ན། མདའ་གང་ས་དང་མ་ཐུག་པ། མདའ་གང་གཉམ་དང་མ་ཐུག་པའི་ཁང་པ་ཞིག་ཡོད་རྒྱུག། དེ་ཁང་པ་ལ་སྒོ་དཀར་ཁང་མེད་རྒྱུག། ཕི་གང་རྒྱུང་རྡུན་ཞིག་ཡོད་རྒྱུག། དེ་འི་ནང་ན་བྱ་ཉི་མ་ཁྱུང་རྒྱུང་གི་གཞིར་དམར་དེ་ཡོད་རྒྱུག། མོ་ངན་ནི་སྒྲོང་ཕྲུག་གིས་ཁང་པའི་ཕི་གང་པོ་འི་མདུན་ན་གླུ་འདི་ལྟར།།

མདའ་གང་ས་དང་མ་ཐུག་པའི་ཁང་པའི་ནང་དུ་སུ་ཡོད་ལོ།

མདའ་གང་གཉམ་དང་མ་ཐུག་པའི་ཁང་པའི་ནང་ན་མི་ཆེན་སུ་ཡོད་ལོ།

འདི་རིང་བུ་ཚ་ང་ཐང་དེ་ལ་ལུས་དེ་ཡོད་ལ།

མོ་ངན་ནི་སྒྲོང་ཕྲུག་དེ་ཐང་སྟོང་ལ་ལུས་ལོ།

འདི་རིང་ང་ལ་བྲང་ས་ཞིག་ཅོས་འང་ལེ།

དེར་ཟ་བའི་འདྲེ་ཞིག་ཡོད་ད། སྲུང་བའི་ལྷ་ཞིག་ཡོད་ལོ།

དེ་ཟླུག་ཟེརས་པ། དེའི་ནང་ནས་ལན་དུ་བྱ་མོ་དཀར་མོས་གླུ་འདི་ལྟར།།

ཁྱོད་མི་ཡུལ་ལི་མི་ཆུང་གིས་ངའི་དངོས་ལ་ཉེར་དང།

ཁྱོད་མི་ཡུལ་ལི་ཕྲུ་གུས་བདག་ཅིག་ལ་གསན་ལོ།

གཉམ་ལྟར་རི་བྱ་ཡང་ཕྱིངས་ས་རིག་མེད་ལོ།

འོག་ལྷར་རི་མི་ཡང་ལྡིངས་ས་རིག་མེད་ལོ།
འདི་རིང་ཚུག་པ་མིའི་སྐད་ཅིག་མ་ཆོར་ལོ།
འདི་རིང་ཚུག་པ་བྱ་སྐད་ཅིག་ཀྱང་མ་ཆོར་ལོ།
ཁྲིད་མི་ཚུང་དེ་འདི་ཙ་ག་ཟུག་ལ་བསླེབ་ལོ།
ངས་བྲང་ས་བཙོ་བ་ལ་ཉན་ཅེས་རིག་མེད་ལོ།
ང་ལ་བིང་ཙམ་སི་སྐྲོ་ཞིག་མེད་ལོ།
ཁྲུ་རང་ཡོང་ཅེས་སི་ལམ་ཞིག་མེད་ལོ།
ཁྲོ་རང་ཡོང་ན་བྱ་ཚངས་མ་བ་ཤིག་པ་ཡོང་ལོ།
ཁྲོ་རང་ཡོང་བ་ཉན་ན་བྱ་སྒོང་མ་བཅག་པ་ཡོང་ལོ།
ཁྲིད་ལ་ཤོག་པ་ཡོད་ན་འཕུར་དེ་རིག་ཡོང་ལོ།

དེ་ཟུག་ཟེརས་པ་སང། མོ་ངན་ནི་སྦྲོང་ཕྲུག་དེ་ཕུ་རོན་ཞིག་ལ་ཧྲུ་སྤྱེ་ཕུར་དེ། དེ་བི་གང་ནང་ནས་ཞུག་སྤྱེ་སོང་སྤྱེ་ནང་དུ་བསླེབ་སོང། དེ་ནས་ཁོང་གཉིས་ཀས་ཡངས་པ་བཙོ་ཡིན་ཞིག་དང་ཟླ་བ་གཅིག་ཟམ་འདུགས།།

ཞག་ཅིག་མོ་ངན་ནི་སྦྲོང་ཕྲུག་གིས་མཁས་པ་བཙོ་སྤྱེ། བྱ་མོ་དཀར་མོ་ལ་འདྲིས་པ། ཕྱ་བྱ་མོ་དཀར་མོ་ལེ། བྱ་ཉི་མ་ཁྲུང་ཙུང་དེ་དག་ས་ག་ཙ་ཡོད་ཚུག་ཟེརས་པ། བྱ་མོ་དཀར་མོས། བྱ་ཉི་མ་ཁྲུང་ཙུང་དེ་ཟླ་དང་ཉི་མའི་བར་ལ་མཚམས་ལ་འདུག་སྤྱེ་ཡོད། ཁོའི་ནོ་བྱ་སོ་མིག་དམར་དེ་བྲག་སྟོད་ཅིག་ལ་ལམ་སྐྱུང་ང་ལ་བོར་དེ་ཡོད། བྱ་ཉི་མ་ཁྲུང་ཙུང་ལ་མཚམས་ཀྱི་ཞག་འཚང་བ་དང། མི་ཡུལ་ཚང་མ་བ་ཤིག་པ་ཡོང་ཅེན། ཁོའི་ཤ་ཚང་མ་ཕོ་ལད་ལ་འགྱུར་ཅེན། ཁོའི་གྲོད་པའི་ནང་དུ་ནུར་བུ་རིན་པོ་ཆེ། གསེར་ དངུལ་

ཟངས་ ལྕུགས་ དུང་ལ་སོགས་པ་ཡོང་ཆེན། རྫིང་ན་ཁོ་སྲུ་ལ་ཡང་བསད་པ་མི་ཉན་ཅེས་ཡིན་ཟེར་ས་པ། མོ་ངན་ནི་སྤྲོང་ཕྲུག་གིས་ཡང་འདྲིས། ཁོའི་མཚམས་ཀྱི་ཞག་ནམ་གང་ཡིན་ཟེར་ས། བྱ་མོ་དཀར་མོས། ཞག་ཉི་ཤུ་རྩ་གཉིས་ན་མཚམས་ཀྱི་ཞག་འཚང་བྱས་ཡིན། དེ་ཚུག་པ་ཁྲོ་རང་སོང་། སྔོན་ལ་བྱ་སོ་མིག་དམར་བསད་དགོས། དེའི་རྫིང་ན་བྱ་ཉི་མ་ཁྲུང་རྩུང་བསད་ཐབ་ཡིན་ཟེར་ས་པ། དེ་ནས་མོ་ངན་ནི་སྤྲོང་ཕྲུག་དེ་སོང་བས། ཞག་བདུན་འགྱུལ་དེ། བྱ་སོ་མིག་དམར་ཡོད་ས་ཡི་བྲག་གི་དེ་རྩ་བསླེབ། དེ་རྩ་བྲག་གི་བ་ཧོ་ཞིག་གི་ནང་དུ་ཡིབ་སྡེ་འདུགས་པ། དེ་མཚན་ལ་བྱ་སོ་མིག་དམར་ལ་སྨི་ལམ་མང་པོ་ཞིག་མཐོང་པས། གནམ་མ་ལངས་པ། བྱ་སྐད་དང་པོ་བཏང་ངེན་ཞིག། བྱ་སོ་མིག་དམར་གྲིས་གླུ་འདི་ལྟར།།

འདི་རིང་མཚན་ནི་སྨི་ལམ་ངན་པ་ཞིག་མཐོང་ལོ།
མཚན་ངན་ཉིད་དེ་སྨི་ལམ་ངན་པ་ཐག་ཆོད་རིག་མཐོང་ལོ།
ཨ་ཡི་བྲག་གི་ནང་ན་ཧ་མི་གཉིས་ཡོང་བ་རིག་མཐོང་ལོ།
བྱ་སོ་མིག་དམར་ང་རང་ཤི་བ་རིག་མཐོང་ལོ།
རྫིང་ན་བྱ་ཉི་མ་ཁྲུང་རྩུང་ཤི་བ་རིག་མཐོང་ལོ།
བྱ་ཉི་མ་ཁྲུང་རྩུང་གི་ཤོག་པ་དེ་གླིང་ཡུལ་ལ་བསླེབ་པ་མཐོང་ལོ།
འདི་རིང་གི་མཚན་པོ་ངན་པ་ཞིག་རག་ཀྱི་ཀྱི།
འདི་རིང་གི་སྨི་ལམ་རྩོག་པོ་ཞིག་རག་ཀུང་ཀུང།

དེ་ཟུག་ཟེར་ས་པ། མོ་ངན་ནི་སྤྲོང་ཕྲུག་གིས་བསམ། འོ་མི་སྡོ། ཁོ་ཤི་ཅེས་སོང་བསམ་སྡེ་མང་པོ་འཐད་སོང་། དེ་ནས་གནམ་ལངས་ས་དང་།

བྱ་སོ་མིག་དམར་བྲག་ཅིག་གི་ཁ་ཕིང་བ་སང་། མོ་ངན་ནི་སྲོང་ཕྲུག་གིས་མདའ་རྒྱབ་སྟེ་བྱ་དེ་བསད་བཏངས།།

ཁོ་གྲེན་ལ་སོང་སྟེ་བལྟས་པ། ནམ་མཁའི་ལྟོངས་ན་གར་མཆོགས་ཤིག་མཐོང་ངད་ཚུག། དེའི་ནང་ན་བྱ་ཉི་མ་ཁྱུང་རྭུང་ཡོད་ཚུག། མོ་ངན་ནི་སྲོང་ཕྲུག་ལ་དེ་བོ་ཐྲག་རིངས་ལ་ཡོད་ཅེས་ཞེས་དེ། ནང་ང་ཆེར་དེ། ཁོ་ང་ལ་ནམ་ཐུབ་ཡིན་བསམ་སྟེ་ཡི་སྨུག་སྟེ། ཕྱུ་ཐུངས་གཅིག་གི་ནང་དུ་མགོ་བཏངས། གཅིག་གི་ནང་དུ་ཀང་པ་བཏང་སྟེ་གཉིད་ལོག་སྟེ་འདུགས། ཞག་བདུན་ཟམ་སོང་སྟེ། ཨ་ནེ་བཀར་དམན་མོ་ཡོང་སྟེ། དབུགས་མེད་དི་སྐྲ་ཐོས་ནས་གླུ་ཞིག་འདི་ལྟར།

མདའ་ཁྱོད་དཀར་པོས་ལམ་བསྟན་འགྲོ་དགོས་འབྱུང་།
བྱ་ཉི་མ་ཁྱུང་རྭུང་བསད་ཅེས་ལ།
མདའ་ནག་པོས་སྲོག་བཅད་འགྲོ་དགོས་འབྱུང་།
མདའ་དམར་པོས་ཁྲག་ལྷགས་འགྲོ་དགོས་འབྱུང་།
བྱ་ཉི་མ་ཁྱུང་རྭུང་བདུལ་ཅེས་ལ།
ཁྱོད་ཚང་ཀས་བྱ་དེ་བསད་རོགས་མཛོད།
ཁྱེད་ཚང་ཀས་ཉི་མ་ཁྱུང་རྭུང་བདུལ་རོགས་མཛོད།

ཨ་ནེ་སིས་དེ་ཟུག་ཟེརས་པ་སང་། མདའ་ཚང་ཀ་བསག་སྒྲག་ནང་ནས་ཕིང་སྟེ་ན། ནམ་མཁའི་ལྟོངས་ལ་སྐྲ་ཕིང་གིན་ཞིག་སོང་སྟེ། བྱ་ཉི་མ་ཁྱུང་རྭུང་དེ་དུས་གཅིག་ལ་བསད་དེ། ས་སྟེང་དུ་བྱུད་དེ་ཡོངས། དེ་ནས་ཨ་ནེ་བཀར་དམན་རྒྱལ་མོས་མོ་ངན་ནི་སྲོང་ཕྲུག་ལ་གཉིད་བཅདས་པས། དེ་དེ་ཚུག་

པ་ས་ལ་བྱུང་ཚར་དེ། མོ་ངན་ནི་སྤྲིང་ཕྲུག་དེ་གཉིད་ཐེ་རལ་ལ་ཡམ་ཚན་སོང་སྟེ། ཕོ་ལད་དཀར་པོ་འི་སྤུ་རི་དང་རྫུངས་པ། གྲོད་པ་དེ་ཆད་སོང་། དེའི་ནང་ན་ནུར་བུ་མང་པོ་ཡོད་ཚུག། དེ་ནོར་བུ་ཚང་མ་ཁྲུལ་ལི་ཁོ་མགས་ནང་དུ་རྒྱུང་སྟེ། ཤོག་པ་ཡང་ཁྲུར་དེ། སྤྲིང་མཁར་ཕྱོགས་ལ་ཡོངས།།

No. 7.

སྤྲིང་གི་དཔའ་བོ་དང་ཕྱུལ་མི་ཚང་མ་ལ། མོ་ངན་ནི་སྤྲིང་ཕྲུག་གིས་དེ་ཚང་མ་འཁྲུར་དེ་ཡོང་ཅེས་ཀྱི་ཧྲུན་ཚོར་དེ་གསུང་གྲོས་བཙོ་སྟེ། ཁོ་ལ་སྲུས་མི་བདང་བ་རྒྱལ་ཟེར་དེ་ཨ་གུ་དཔལ་ལེ་བདངས། དེ་ནས་ལམ་དུ་མོ་ངན་ནི་སྤྲིང་ཕྲུག་དང་ཐུག། ཨ་གུ་དཔལ་ལེས་མོ་ངན་ནི་སྤྲིང་ཕྲུག་གིའི་ཀང་པ་ཐམ་སྟེ་ཞུས་པ། འདི་རིང་ནས་ཕར་ལ་ཉེ་རང་སྤྲིང་གི་མགོ་རི་ཡིན། སྤྲིང་རྒྱལ་ལྷམ་ཀེ་སར་ཡིན། ཛོ་ཛོ་འབྲི་གུ་མ་གྲོགས་སྐལ་ཡིན། ཛོ་ཛོ་ལ་དངོས་བསྟུན་ན་མཛོད་ཞུས་པ། མོ་ངན་ནི་སྤྲིང་ཕྲུག་གིས་རྒྱལ་མོལ་དེ་ཡོངས། སྤྲིང་ཕྱུལ་ལ་ཙ་བིག་མ་བསྐྱིབ་པ། རྒྱལ་ལྷུང་ལྷུང་གི་ལྷུང་སྟོད་ཟེར་བའི་ས་ཁྲིད་ཅིག་ཡོད་ཚུག། དེ་རུ་སྤྲིང་གི་དཔའ་བོ་ཚང་མ་དང་ཕྱུལ་མི་དང་། ཛོ་ཛོ་འབྲུ་གུ་མ་ཟབ་སྟེ། དར་དཀར་ཞིག་རིང་དུ། དར་དམར་ཞིག་ཐུང་དུ་བདང་སྟེ། གཡས་ལ་ཛ། གཡོན་ལ་ཆང་ཁྲུར་དེ་ཐོག་ཀ་ལྷོར་མང་པོ་དང་། ཛོ་ཛོ་ལ་ཞབ་ཤི་ལ་དར་ལྷ་གི་ཆོད་མོ་ཁྲིད་དེ། བུ་མོ་བརྒྱ་ཟམ་དེ་རུ་བསྐྱིབ་སོང་། དེ་ནས་ཛོ་ཛོ་འབྲུ་གུ་མས་གླུ་ཞིག་བླངས།།

རྒྱལ་ལྷུང་ལྷུང་གི་ལྷུང་སྟོད་ན་ལྷ་སྐད་ཅིག་ཚོར།
དེ་བོ་རྒྱལ་ལྷམ་ཆེན་མོ་འི་གསུངས་སྐད་རིག་ཡིན་ལོ།

རྒྱལ་ལྷུང་ལྷུང་གི་ལྷུང་སྟོད་ན་ཞབས་སྐད་ཅིག་ཆོར།
དེ་བོ་རྐྱང་རྒོད་དབྱེར་པའི་ཞབས་སྐད་ཅིག་ཡིན་ལོ།
རྒྱལ་ལྷམ་ཆེན་མོས་དབུ་རྨོག་ཀུན་བསྣམས་ཅན།
གནམ་སྟོད་མཐོན་པོ་ལ་ཉི་དྭངས་ཐོག་པ་འདྲ།
གླིང་ཀེ་སར་རྒྱལ་པོས་ནམ་ཟ་བསྣམས་ཟ་ན།
མི་ཡུལ་འོད་དེས་ཁྱངས་པ་དང་འདྲ།
རྒྱ་ལྷམ་ཆེན་མོས་སྐུ་སྐྱེ་རགས་བསྣམས་ཟ་ན།
རི་སྟོད་ལ་ཉི་ཟེ་ཐོག་པ་དང་འདྲ།
རྒྱ་ལྷམ་ཀེ་སར་གྱིས་ནམ་ཙར་བསྣམས་ཟ་ན།
བྲག་སྟོད་ལ་ཆུ་ཆར་ཐག་པ་དང་འདྲ།
སྔོན་ལ་ང་ཟངས་ཀྱི་རི་ནང་ཐུག་སོང་།
དག་ས་ང་གསེར་གྱི་རི་ནང་ཐུག།
སྔོན་ལ་ང་རོ་ཉའི་རི་ནང་ཐུག་སོང་།
དག་ས་ང་དངུལ་གྱི་རི་ནང་ཐུག།

དེ་ཟུག་ཟེར་རིན་ཞིག་ཇོ་ཇོས་ཀ་ལྷོར་བླུགས་པ། ཀེ་སར་གྱིས་ཅང་མ་ཟེར་བ། གླིང་སྟོད་ལ་དེ་བང་བང་ཟེར་བའི་རི་ཞིག་ཡོད་ཚུག། དེ་ཏུ་སྐྱོད། དེ་ཚུག་པ། མོ་ངན་ནི་སྤྲིང་ཕྲག་བཅོ་སྦེ་སྐྱོད་སོང་། དེ་རི་ལ་བསྒྲིབ་སྦེ་ན། མོ་ངན་ནི་སྤྲིང་ཕྲུག་གིས་བླུ་འདི་ལྟར།

གླིང་གི་ཁྲོག་ཐོང་ཚང་མ་འདེར་འདུས་ཤིག།
ཁྱེད་ཁྲོག་ཐོང་ཚང་མ་ལ་དངུལ་གྱི་འགྱེད་བཏང་ཡིན།

གླིང་གི་ན་ཆུང་ཚང་མ་འདིར་ཡོང་ཞིག།
ཁྱེད་ན་ཆུང་ཚང་མ་ལ་གཡུའི་འགྱེད་བདང་ཡིན།
གླིང་གི་རྒན་པོ་ཚང་མ་འདིར་ཡོང་ཞིག།
ཁྱེད་རྒན་པོ་ཚང་མ་ལ་དུང་གྱི་འགྱེད་བདང་ཡིན།
གླིང་གྱི་ཨ་མ་ཚང་མ་འདིར་ཡོང་ཞིག།
ཁྱེད་ཨ་མ་ཚང་མ་ལ་མུ་ཏིག་གི་འགྱེད་བདང་ཡིན།
གླིང་གི་བླ་མ་ཚང་མ་འདིར་ཡོང་ཞིག།
ཁྱེད་བླ་མ་ཚང་མ་ལ་གུར་གུམ་གྱི་འགྱེད་བདང་ཡིན།
གླིང་གྱི་མོན་ཚང་མ་འདིར་ཡོང་ཞིག།
ཁྱེད་མོན་ཚང་མ་ལ་དྲམ་བུའི་འགྱེད་བདང་ཡིན།
གླིང་གི་གསེར་མགར་ཚང་མ་འདིར་འདུས་ཞིག།
ཁྱེད་གསེར་མཁར་ཚང་མ་ལ་གསེར་གྱི་འགྱེད་བདང་ཡིན།
གླིང་གི་མགར་བ་ཚང་མ་འདིར་འདུས་ཞིག།
ཁྱེད་མགར་བ་ཚང་མ་ལ་ལྕགས་ཀྱི་འགྱེད་བདང་ཡིན།

དེ་ཟླུག་མོལ་ཡིན་ཞིག་དང་། མི་ཚང་མ་ལ་ནུར་བུའི་རིགས་ཚང་མ་འགྱེད་བདང་ཚར་དེ། མོ་ངན་ནི་སྨོང་ཕྲུག་དེ་མེད་པ། གླིང་རྒྱལ་ལྷམ་ཀ་སར་ལ་གྲུར་དེ། མིའི་ཡུལ་ཚང་མ་འོད་ཀྱིས་ཁྱངས་སོང་། དེ་ནས་དྲ་མན་ཏ་རིབ་ཟླ་གྲོལ་མོ་བདང་ངེན་ཞིག་གླིང་གི་མཁར་ལ་སྐྱོད་དེ། ཛོ་ཛོ་འབྲུ་གུ་མ་སྒྲོགས་ལ་བོར་ས། དེ་ནས་སྐྱིད་པོ་བཅོ་སྟེ་ཞག་བདུན་མཁར་ལ་འདུག་སྟེ་ན། བག་

སྟོན་ཆེན་མོ་ཞིག་སྐྱགས། ཁྲོམ་ཆེན་མོ་ལ་འདུས་ནས། བ་ལུ་དུང་དུང་གིས་གྲལ་རིག་གིན་ཞིག་གླུ་འདི་ལྟར།

ཡབས་ཕྱོན་པ་ཨ་བའི་བག་སྟོན་ཞིག་རིག་ལོ།
ཡུམ་སྤྱོན་མོ་ཨ་མའི་བག་སྟོན་ཞིག་རིག་ལོ།
ཡབས་ཕྱོན་པ་ཨ་བཱ་གསེར་ཁྲི་ཁ་ཞུགས་འདང།
ཡུམ་སྤྱོན་མོ་ཨ་མ་གཡུ་ཁྲི་ཁ་ཞུགས་འདང།
ཕ་སྤྲུན་བཞི་བཅུ་ཞ་ལྷོ་གཡས་གྲལ་ལ་ཞུགས་འདང།
མ་སྤྲུན་བཞི་བཅུ་ཞ་ལྷོ་གཡོན་གྲལ་ལ་ཞུགས་འདང།
ཐང་དཀར་བབས་པའི་ཆད་པོ་གཞུང་གྲལ་ལ་ཞུགས་འདང།
གྲོ་ཡོས་ཡས་པའི་ན་ཆུང་སྐོར་མོ་གྲལ་ལ་ཞུགས་འདང།
སྟག་སོ་སྡིགས་པའི་ཁྲུག་ཐོང་སྐྱུ་རྩེས་ལ་ཞངས་འདང།
བ་ལུ་དུང་དུང་ང་རང་དུང་ཁྲིའི་ཁ་འདུག་ཡིན་ལོ།

དེ་ཟླུག་ཟེར་དེ་གྲལ་བདེ་མོ་རིགས། དེ་ནས་ཁྲོམ་སྐྱིད་པོ་ཞིག་བཅོས། ཁྲོམ་བ་ཤོལ་དེ། ཡུལ་པ་ཚང་མ་རང་རང་གི་ཁང་པ་རུ་སོང་ངོ། རྒྱལ་ལྷམ་ཀི་སར་དང་ཇོ་ཇོ་འབྲུ་གུ་མ་དང་ཞབ་ཤི་ཚང་མ་མཁར་ལ་སོང་སྟེ་སྐྱིད་པོའི་ནང་དུ་འདུགས་སོ།

ABSTRACT OF CONTENTS.

THE STORY OF 'ABRUGUMA'S MARRIAGE TO KESAR.

No. 1.

The child (Kesar) went to the teacher *r Tse dgu*, to ask him, who was his father. The teacher, knowing that he would come, had ordered his servants who were cutting grass, to send the child to him. The servants gave the child some food, which he pretended to eat, whilst hiding it in his sleeve. Then the child fastened a golden fly to a string and played with it. One of the servants asked to play with the fly. Because he lost it, Kesar asked for a compensation. The servants said, that he had received a compensation already, having got so much food. Now Kesar opened his sleeve and returned to every one what had been given to him. Then the servants acknowledged themselves to be in Kesar's debt and brought some beer and a goat to please him. After that he did them a special favor and cut the grass for them in a miraculous way.

Kesar took the goat before the window of the hermitage and made preparations to kill it. The teacher asked him not to do so, and Kesar promised not to kill it, if the teacher would tell him, who was his father. *r Tse dgu* advised the boy to go to the plain, 'with the three stone-pyramids of black, white and red colour' because there he would be told. The teacher had arrived there secretly before the boy, and was now hidden in one of the pyramids. When the child asked his question, the hermit answered from inside the pyramid, that Agu *Pasang ldan ru skyes* was Kesar's father. Because this was a lie, all the grass and the trees of the 'cold valley' faded at once and became black. Kesar restored the trees and the grass to life again and went to the innermost part of the valley, where he found *Pasang ldan ru skyes*. This Agu was astonished to be called 'father' by Kesar. He was loaded with wood and, being furnished with a nose-ring, was led to *Gog bzang lhamo*, where he was introduced as Kesar's father.

No. 2.

The boy (Kesar) heard, that the Agus had decided to distribute the land *gLing* among them. He went to the place of meeting, dressed like a monk. On the way there he met with Agu *dPalle*, who invited him to take a seat on the horse behind him. He did so and caused a host of lice to attack the Agu, so that the Agu almost lost his temper.

The boy asked the Agus to let him have a part of the land of *gLing*, but the Agus gave him only the privilege of being present at every wedding and at every burial and besides that the ford *s Byichu* and the *Groma*-plain. The boy made use of his privilege, but sang comic songs at burials and solemn songs at weddings. To keep him silent, the parties had to give him much money (*nor*).*

* Compare Spring-myth of the Kesar Saga, (Sheh-version) No. V. 37.

Agu *Khrai thung* was made chief of the *gLing* land, and to him *'aBruguma* was to be given as his wife. The boy went to the ford *sByichu*, and when he saw *Khrai thung* crossing it, he tore him down from his horse and almost drowned him. Then he excused his rough behaviour, saying that he had not known, that the rider was Agu *Khraï thung.**

No. 3.

Then Kesar went to the *Groma*-plain to gather *Groma*-roots. Maiden *'aBruguma* went there for the same purpose together with her servant. She was not successful, and her hand-maid asked the street-child (Kesar) to give some *Groma*-bread to the lady. He gave his bread under the condition that every bit which was eaten, would grow again, as was the case when he ate. Because, however, nothing was brought back again, he teased the maiden, saying: 'When I meet a dog, the dog shall hear of it; when I meet a man, the man shall hear of it.' †

To please the street-child, *'aBruguma* invited him to a festival next morning. The boy went to her house earlier than anybody else and hid himself behind the upper door beam. When all the girls were assembled, *'a Bruguma* told them to shut the door and to keep the street-child away, because he would make everything dirty (*rtsogpo*). Then the boy made his appearance on the upper door-beam.‡

He touched the heads of the girls, and all of them fell asleep. A neighbour had a she-ass that was with child. He kicked her, and a foal was born. He cut off the foal's head and placed it on the bed of the girl who was nearest to the door. Then he opend the windows and called up the girls. She who was nearest to the door, put the foal's head on her neighbour's bed, and so on, until the last of the girls placed it in *'aBruguma's* goat-skin. When she rose, it fell to the ground. Then the street-child, making much noise, cried: 'A donkey's head was born to maiden *'a Bruguma!* When I meet a dog, the dog shall hear of it; when I meet a man, the man shall hear of it.' §

The girl invited the street-child to an engagement-feast (*grogs chang*), and the boy went there, carrying one ear, cut from the donkey's head. Agu *Khrai thung* was seated on a golden throne, and all the other agus were seated on turquoise thrones. The street-child sat on a wooden chair at the head of all beggars. Maiden *'aBruquma* went before Agu *Khrai thung* with a pot of beer and said: 'Not touching the pot with your ten fingers, not touching your lotus-mouth, not

* Compare Spring-myth of the Kesar-Saga No. V, 26-36. It is interesting to see, that Agu *Khromo* of the Sheh-version is represented by two different Agns in this Lower Ladakhi version, here by Agu *Khrai mgo khra thung*, and in fasc. No. II, by Agu *bKa blon ldanpa.*

† As regards this tale and the following, they may be compared to Spring-myth of the Kesar Saga, No. VI-IX. This tale in particular to No. VI, 1-9. The quotation 'when I meet a dog, etc.' seems to have its origin in the belief of the Ladakhis that the dog is the most perfect creature next to man; it is believed to be a higher creature than woman. The Ladakhi lamas will say, that the spirit of the gods may dwell in a dog, but never in a woman.

‡ Compare Spring-myth, No. VI, 10-16.

§ Compare Spring-myth (Sheh-version), additions No. 10.

tasting with the silken knot of your tongue, not swallowing it with the golden vessel of your throat; take the beer and tea with your soul, and place it again on the ground!' The agu took the pot with his hands, but when he saw the street-child, he became quite confused, and the pot fell to the ground. Then Agu *d Palle* and all the other agus were asked to drink, but none of them could do as required.

When the maiden came before the street-child, he said. 'Look here, lady!' and showed her the donkey's ear. Then she addressed the boy as a 'beggar on a wooden chair, with dirty hands, with a mouth like a privy, with a tongue like a rasp, and a long throat.' Before drinking, the street-child rendered a prayer to the nine *lha* and *klu* who were born with him, to *dBangpo rgyabzhin*, mother *sKyabs ldun*, *l Jogpo*, and to his paternal and maternal deity. Then with his stick studded with dog's teeth he threw the pot towards the sky, drank all the beer and placed the tea-pot filled on the ground. Now all the beggars made a noise, saying: 'Our street-child has received maiden *'aBruguma'* [as his bride].*

No. 4.

'aBruguma's parents had prepared a golden throne and a curtain of white silk for the bridegroom. But because a street-child had become the bridegroom, they exchanged the silken curtain for one of black goat's hair, and the golden throne for a ragged carpet, which was spread on the floor the wrong way. When the boy arrived on a litter carried by beggars, he sat down wrong way about on the carpet (with his face towards the wall). For his food he received some flour with chaff. Father *Thonpa* was looking away, mother *sNgonmo* was looking at the floor, and *'aBruguma* was poking the fire. Then the street-child taught the little dog to jump three times in each of the four directions. This he did and left so much dung, that everybody had to leave the room on account of the bad smell.†

At night the boy received an old hide and was taken to the straw-barn. *'a Bruguma's* parents had tigers, leopards and other beasts to watch the door. The boy cut the hide into many pieces, and left it before the door, together with some bones. Then he ran away to the valley *Drimo dgu chod*.‡

Next morning the beggars came to see the boy, and as he could not be found, *'aBruguma* was afraid of the vengeance of the beggars. She went to Agu *d Gāni*, and asked him to cast the lot and to tell her what had happened to the street-boy. He said: 'Oh thou girl with a red mouth, with a red tongue, who art fat in consequence of eating good food, who art walking about in the streets with a beautiful dress! The vengeance of the beggars will overtake you! I do not know the science of casting lots.' The girl went home crying, but was sent to Agu *d Gāni* once more with a golden plate, filled with pearls. Now the agu told her, that she would have to go first to the copper-hill and to the gold-hill, then to the lead-hill and to the silver-hill, and that

* Compare Spring-myth, No. VI, 17-69.
† Compare Spring-myth, No. VIII, 1-3.
‡ Compare Spring-myth, No. VIII, 4-6.

she would have to eat buck-wheat and leek-water, later on cakes and sweet water. 'In the valley *Drimo dgu chod* there is a little elevation. On that you must build a wall of dung; then you will see him.!'

'aBruguma went home and came back with her servant. In the valley *Drimo dgu chod* she found the street-child who had taken the beautiful shape (Kesar's body) and was doing some exercise. (This kind of exercise was described in 'Birth-story of Kesar, fasc. No. II, 3). It was as if on his right shoulder the sun was rising and on his left shoulder the moon. The girls laughed when they saw him. Suddenly a storm came with snow and hail, and Kesar disappeared entirely. When the rain was gone, he was again the street-child which he had been before. After he had teased the girls, *'aBruguma* entreated him to go home with her; otherwise the beggars would avenge him on her.*

Having arrived at *'aBruguma's* house, the boy took an earthen pot and cooked some game in it; but in the eyes of the girls the meat appeared to be that of mice (according to Kesar's sorcery). Then he killed a real mouse and put it secretly into the goat-skin of *'aBruguma*. When the meat was cooked, he said: 'One piece is missing! Who is the thief?' All present assured him that no one had stolen anything, but when *'aBruguma* rose, the mouse came falling out of her goat-skin. Again the street-child made a noise and teased her.†

No. 5.

They went to the land of *gLing*. Although the ladies had started before the street-child, the latter arrived before them. The agus were told, 'Lady *'a Bruguma* will be given to him who will bring the hide of the wild yak *Riri*, and who can spread it over the whole land and castle of *gLing* in such a way, that a remnant of nine *'adom* will remain.' *'aBruguma's* mother provided the boy with food, and his bag of the skin of a mouse as well as his nut-shell held an immense amount of food, whilst *'a Bruguma's* bag was filled at once.

Kesar started with his servants *Drangge* and *Drongge*, and in the evening had his halting-place a short distance from that of the agus. The agus who did not know the country through which they were travelling, wished to find out whether there would be wood or water in the next station. Therefore they sent Agu *dPalle* to find out, what kind of preparations the street-child was making for the next day. Kesar, knowing that *dPalle* was listening in a hidden place, told his servants to gather much wood and to take it along to the next station. Meanwhile Kesar ordered his servants to fill the hides with water, and to carry them to the next station. When the agus arrived there laden with wood, on the second day, they discovered that there was much wood in that place, but no water. All the wood had been carried in

* Compare Spring-myth, No. VIII, F. 26. It is evident that this Lower Ladakhi version contains a great deal more of nature-mythology than the Sheh-version. This passage shows plainly, that Kesar's beautiful shape is connected with sunshine, and his ugly shape with rain and storm.

† Compare Spring-smyth, No. VIII, 33-41.

vain, and they were obliged to ask the street-child to let them have some water. Each of them received a few drops.

This time they sent Agu *Anggar l Tsangspo* to the boy's camp to listen. Again they were deceived, because when they had carried much water to the next station (according to what the agu had found out), they discovered that there was plenty of water, but no wood.

Now they sent Agu *dGāni* to the camp of the street-child, and he heard Kesar ordering his servants to open the boxes with the finest clothes, because to-morrow they would arrive in a town. All the agus put on their finest dress, whilst Kesar was using his ordinary dress. There were many thorns on the way, and all the agus arrived in rags in the town and were despised. Only Kesar was honoured with pencil-cedars and beer-pots, adorned with pieces of butter.*

Whilst the agus were killing much game, Kesar was sleeping. His servants said they were hungry. Kesar killed a wild goat for them but forbade them to spill any of its blood. What they could not help spilling, they licked up at once. On the next day there appeared seven wild goats, with horns of gold, of silver, of shell, of copper, pearl, of turquoise and of coral. They entreated Kesar to protect them, otherwise the agus would annihilate their kind. Kesar promised to help them, if they would show him the place of the yak *Riri*. The wild goats said, that they were under a vow not to show that place. All the same they advised him to go in the direction of the hill to the right. Kesar was pleased to hear that, and in recognition of their services he prayed to the gods and nâgas, who were born with him: 'Up to the present day the weapon for hunting was noiseless (the bow); now the weapon may produce a loud noise (the rifle)!' All animals can hear it, when one of them is killed and will run away. This will be their advantage. Formerly they were not warned in such a way.†

Kesar soon found the yak *Riri* and flattered him much. He called him his father and said that he, his son, was frightened by his large horns. The yak readily threw off both his horns, and Kesar went near him.

One day Kesar ate some sugar-bread, and when the yak *Riri* asked him what he was eating, he said: 'I took out my right eye, and I am eating it. It is very sweet.' The yak wished to taste it, and Kesar gave him some sugar-bread instead. The yak now desired to eat his own right eye, which Kesar took out and quickly gave him some sugar-bread instead. In the same manner the yak also lost his left eye. When he was blind, Kesar gave him only poisonous grass and water, until the yak became quite dizzy. To be cured, the yak wished to bring an offering of the pencil-cedar, which Kesar lit under his belly, so that all the yak's skin came off.

* There is a similar tale to that in the Mongolian version of the saga. (Compare I. J. Schmidt's translation, pp. 74-76). But it looks as if the Mongolian tale was a somewhat misunderstood version of the Tibetan tale.

† It is remarkable that Kesar is said to be the introducer of fire-arms. This is quite in accordance with the belief that he wields the sword of lightning. Compare Ind. Ant. Lad. Songs. No. XXIX.

Then Kesar dug a pit which was covered with a thin roof, and told the yak to try to catch him. The yak made only three steps and fell into the pit. There he was killed with arrows and a spear. When Kesar tried to take off the skin, he did not succeed, because it went back again to the yak's body. Then he heard two crows speaking with one another. They said: 'If that man goes on skinning like that he will not come to an end within a month. He ought to fasten to the ground with pegs of Lonicera, whatever little piece is taken off!' Kesar did according to the advice and succeeded. He carried the skin to the *gLing* land, and when he spread it over the land and castle, a remnant of nine *'adom* remained. Again the beggars made a noise and said: 'The street-child has received lady' *aBruguma.**

No. 6.

'aBruguma's parents did not wish to give her daughter to the street-child, and said: 'Our daughter will be given to him, who will bring a wing of the bird *Nyima Khyung rung.* The agus went to different valleys, but the street-child went to the land of the birds. Mid-way there was the rock *Dug sha* (poison-flesh). All ordinary people had to spend a full month in going round it. But the boy went to its top and said: 'If I shall be victorious over the devil *Ourulugu,* and if I shall gain the *gLing*-castle, *'aBruguma* and a wing of the bird *Nyima Khyung rung,* will you, please, make seven steps towards east, west, north and south.' Then he fastened a nose-ring to the rock, and the rock jumped about as required. Kesar admonished the rock not to do harm to any creature and went to the land of the birds.

There he saw a house which did not touch the earth nor the sky by an arrow's length. It had neither doors nor windows, but a small hole. In that house there lived the family of the bird *Nyima Khyung rung.*†

Kesar asked to be taken in, and *Byamo dkarmo* (probably the moon) answered: 'He may come in, if he is able to fly, but he must take care not to destroy neither nest nor egg'! Therefore Kesar took the shape of a dove and entered the house. About a month he stayed there, enjoying the company of *Byamo dkarmo.* Then he enquired about *Nyima-khyung rung's* abode, and *Byamo dkarmo* said: 'Now he is living in a hermitage between sun and moon, and the bird *So mig dmar* is watching the road to it. When his days of confinement are finished, he will come to destroy the land of men.'‡

In his stomach there are many treasures: gold, silver, copper, iron, shell, etc. His body will become steel, and then nobody will be able to

* Although it would not be advisable to explain every incident of this tale on the ground of nature-mythology, it does not look unlikely, that the yak *Riri* was the personification of a cloud in the original version.—Here again two versions are apparently told one after the other. According to the first version the skin is taken off by fire, and according to the second by regular skinning.

† Does not this house of the birds look almost like the empty space between the earth and the stars?

‡ That the supposed sun-bird will come to destroy the land of men, is an idea which was probably introduced from India.

conquer him. He will sit in the hermitage for twenty-two more days. Until then you must kill the bird *So mig dmar;* after him you will be able to kill the bird *Nyima khyung rung*.'

After seven days' walking Kesar arrived before *So mig dmar's* cave. He heard the bird sing, that he had dreamed, how he died himself, and how the bird *Nyima khyung rung* was killed. Then, when he left his hole, Kesar killed him at once with an arrow.

Kesar saw something like a tent in the height of the sky. This was *Nyima khyung rung's* dwelling-place. Because he did not know how to get there, he went to sleep in sorrow. *Ane bkur dmanmo* said with a voice without breath to Kesar's arrows of white, black and red colour: 'Go and kill the bird.' Therefore the arrows flew off with a great noise, killed the bird, and just when the street-child woke up, the bird fell to the ground. Kesar was still a little drowsy, but opened the bird's stomach with his axe of white steel. All the treasures he put into his egg-pocket, took one of the wings and started for the *gLing*-land.*

No. 7.

When the agus and the men of *gLing* heard that Kesar was coming, they held a council and sent Agu *dPalle* to meet him. Agu *dPalle* said: 'From this time henceforth thou art the highest hill of *gLing*, the godly King Kesar, and *'aBruguma* is thy bride! Please show thy true self to that lady!' Kesar said 'Alright!' and went. At a place called 'top of the king-willow' (the tree of the world) he met with *'aBruguma* and many other people who came to greet him. *'aBruguma* sang: 'There was a noise like that of many feet, it was caused by *rKyang byung dbyerpa's* feet. When thou [O king], didst put on thy helmet, it was as if the light of the sun was touching the high sky; when thou didst put on thy garment, it was as if the land of men was filled with light; 'when thou didst put on thy girdle, it was as if the morning sun was touching the summits; when thou didst put on thy shawl, it was as if the rain was wetting the rocks. First I went to the copper-hill; now I am near the gold-hill. First I went to the lead-hill; now I am near the silver hill!' Kesar again took the shape of the street-child and went to the hill *Ti bangbang*. Here he distributed his treasures (which he had found in *khyung rung's* stomach). The young men received the silver—the young ladies the turquoises—the old men the shells—the mothers the pearls—the lamas orange flowers—the mons some reeds—the gold-smiths some gold—the black-smiths some iron.

* This tale of the conquest of the sun by Kesar is possibly to be understood in this way: although the men of *gLing* could see the sun on the sky during winter, they noticed that he did not do anything profitable to the earth. They did not know that the power of the sun depends on the angle of his rays. But they saw that several months later the earth was blessed by the sun. Therefore they concluded that there must exist a power superior to that of the sun (Kesar in his nature of a spring-god or god of the seasons), which compelled the sun to yield his treasures. The killing of the sun-bird as well as that of the giants is not to be taken seriously. They all come to life again, their death seems to express the idea that the conquest is a complete one.

Then again he took the shape of Kesar, and the whole land of men was filled with light. They went with music to the *gLing* castle, where he received *'aBruguma* as his wife, and they remained together for seven days.

Then the little dwarfs came and arranged the feast in this way: Father *Thonpa* was placed on a golden throne, and mother *sNgonmo* on a turquoise throne, 45 *phaspun* (male relatives) sat on the right side, and 45 *maspun* (female relatives) on the left side, the old men, beautiful like white eagles, sat in the middle, the girls, beautiful like fresh parched grain, formed a circle; the young men, with their beautiful teeth, rose for a dance, and the little dwarfs sat on thrones of shell.

When the feast was over, all went to their homes, but Kesar and *'aBruguma* went to the *gLing*-castle and lived there in peace.

Vocabulary and Notes.

No. 1.

ཁམ་བུ། *khambu*, a bite (of bread).

ཕུ་ཐུངས། *phuthungs*, =*phu dung*, sleeve.

ངས་གཅིག་འཁུར་ཡིན། I shall carry [it] a little; *γcig* = a little.

འདྲ་ཅས། *'adracas*, compensate.

འདྲ། *'adra*, compensation.

ཟེར་རེ། *zerre*, =*zerte*, saying.

སི་སྙན། *si snyan*, said to be the same as *γsung snyan*, well-sounding.

སྲོག་ཁག། *srog khag*, responsibility for [somebody's] life.

རྒོང་། *rgong*, =*gongba*, collar.

ཟེར་ཐབས། *zer thabs*, argument.

ཟ་མ། *zama*, =*rdzama*, pot.

ཐེ་ཡོར། *theyor*, a stone-pyramid, erected on hill tops in honour of the gods.

ཁས་དམན། *khas dman*, shame, contempt.

རོགས། *rogs*, = *sgrogs*, help.

མེ་བཏུག་ཅེས། *me btugces*, to light a fire, the same as *bdugces*.

ཁོལ། *khol*, bud; eye of a tree.

དྲི་མོ་དགུ་ཆོད། *drimo dgu chod*, said to mean 'smell of dung;' name of a valley.

No. 2.

སྒོ་ཅེས། *sgoces*, = *bgodpa*, distribute.

རོ་སྣ། བག་སྣ། *ro sna bag sna*, a man who is present at burials and weddings, and who receives some food in recognition of his presence.

གྲིག། *grig*, good; enough.

གོན་ཅེས། *gonces*, clothes.

ཁྲའི་ཐུང་། *khrai thung*, the abridged name of Agu *Khrai mgo khra* thung.

ཐ་མ། *thama*, shore; the 'end' of the water.

No. 3.

ཏ་གི། *tagi*, bread; the original spelling is probably *takyir*; it became *tagir* and *tagi* in Central Ladakh, when the *y* was lost. Compare *kyirmo* = *girmo*, Rupee.

མང་ང་མི་ལུས། *mangnga mi lus*, it will remain the less.

ཡ། *ya*, exclamation, meaning about 'yes'; it does not express much respect for the addressed person.

ཨོ་ཧོ་ཧོ། *ohoho*, exclamation, expressing contempt.

ཁྲེལ་ཅས། *khrelcas*, to feel shame.

ཐོ་རས། *thoras*, = thore, to-morrow.

ཨི་སྨུན། *isun*, a feast with beer; compare *i* in Jäschke's dictionary.

ཨོ། *o*, exclamation, expressing astonishment.

ཟེར་རད་པ། *zerradpa*, said; abridged for *zerradpin*.

ཤང་པོ། *shangpo*, clever.

གཡངས་པ། *γyangspa*, pleasure, games.

རྡོག་ཆོང། *rdog chong*, a kick with the foot.

མལ་ཙེ། *maltse*, bed.

གཡོག་གོར། *γyog gor*, = *γyog khor*, or *γyog skor*, the sheep-skin worn by ladies.

ཤག་གི་ཁྲི། *shaggi khri*, a throne made of willow-branches.

མཐོ་དགུ་མ། *mtho dguma*, 'ninefold on the top,' *i.e.*, there were nine pieces of butter (*kalcor*) on the top of the beer-pot.

བཟངས། *bzangs*, = *bzang*, good.

དཀར་ནས། *dkar nas*, white barley; the best kind of barley.

གསུམ་ཆང། *γ sum chang*, 'the third beer;' when a girl is to be given to a husband, there are at least three feasts given to the suitors; each about one month after the preceding one. Here two feasts have been given already; this is the third.

བུང་པ། *bungpa*, = *pungpa*, vessel.

རྨིད་པ། *rmidpa*, = *midpa*, to swallow.

པན་ཆུང། *pan chung*, a little lama of no rank; compare *panpon*.

སྲོང་པོ། *srongpo*, or *srungpo*, beggar.

སྲོང་ཕྲུག་ཀུན། *srong phrug kun*, 'you street-child and you other low-caste people!'

སེ་ཡག་ཅན། *seyagcan*, rough.

ཆག་ར། *chagra*, the privy.

རིང་མ་ནས། *ringmanas*, with the long [throat]. The ablative is used here instead of the instrumental.

སྤུང་རོགས། *spung rogs* (*sgrogs*), assistance.

ཕས་ལྷ། མས་ལྷ། *phas lha mas lha ;* in these words the spelling is incorrect; the actual pronunciation, according to Mr. Ribbach's researches in Sheh and Leh, and my own researches in Khalatse, is *pha zla* and *ma zla*. The forms *pha zla* and *ma zla* are used alternatively with *pha hla* and *ma hla*. (This is the actual pronunciation of *lha*). It is quite possible that in the compounds *pha zla* and *ma zla* the original form of the name of the gods (*lha*) was preserved; *zla* was pronounced *hla*, when all consonants before *l* became *h ; hla* was wrongly written *lha*, perhaps for graphic reasons.

ནང། *nang*, = *dang*, with.

No. 4.

ཡབས། *yabs*, = *yab*, father.

ཡོལ་ལ། *yolla*, = *yolba*, curtain.

ཕིར་ལོག་ལ། *phirlogla*, = *phyilogla*, perverse in the wrong way.

ཤག་གི་ཁ། *shaggi kha*, on broken branches.

པལ་ཀྱི། *palkyi*, dandy, palanquin ; Urdu ; *palkyila*, like a palki.

བརྟན་པ། *brtanpa*, this is the other name of *'aBruguma's* father.

ཁྱིམ་ཤང། *khyim shang*, the principal part of the room in a house.

འབང། *'abang*, place of the women (in a house).

གྲལ་མགོ། *gral mgo*, place for men (in a house).

This is the plan of the principal room of a Lower Ladakhi house :

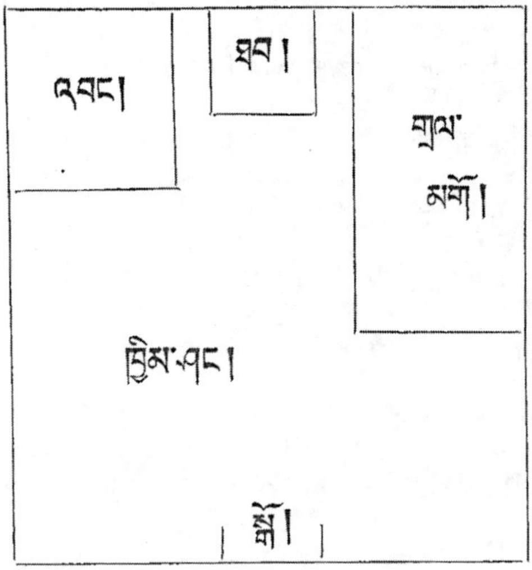

ལྕིན། *lcin*, = *lci*, dung, urine.

ཕུག་རགས། *phug rags*, barn for broken straw (phub.)

སྙལ་བ། *snyalba*, put down ; causative of *nyalba*.

ཤང་ཀོག། *shang kog*, a skin, used for clothing.

དོང་ཏོག། *dong tog*, really.

པན་ཇུང། *pan jung*, = *pan chung*, little lama.

སྒོ་ཁག། or སྒོ་འདྲ། *sgo khag*, *sgo 'adra*, responsibility for somebody's life.

ལགས་མོ། *lagsmo*, = *legsmo*, good, beautiful.

སྲང་ཁོར་མོ། *srang khormo*, idler in the streets, is also used for public woman.'

འཛག་ཅས། *'adzagcas*, = *adzegpa*, climb.

ཤི་ལང། *shi lang,*=*lci·lang,* dung.

གཡོམ་མ། *γyomma,*=*γyonma,* left.

ར་རུ། *raru,* wind.

གཡའ། *γyā,* heap of stones; (slate ?)

རྫབ། or རྫབ་ར། *rdzab, rdzabra,* kind of a mouse.

ནང་ནོར། *nang nor,* riches in the house, (*nang*).

བཙོ་ཅས། *btsocas,*=*'athsodpa,* to cook.

པོག་ཅས། *pogcas,* take away (from the stove).

འཚང་ཅས། *'athsangcas,* to be complete.

ཟེར་ཏེ་ཡིན། *zerte yin,*=*zerpa yin,* said.

ཀག། *kag* and ཅབ། *cab,* suddenly.

No. 5.

ཇོ་ཇོ་པ། *jojopa,* or *jojorangpa,* the ladies as a body (of walkers).

རྫ་ལམ། *rdza lam* a stony (not a clayey) road.

རི་རི། *Riri,* name of a wild yak.

འཁྱེད་ཅས། *'akhyedcas,* overshadow, (not only 'distribute').

ཀྲ་ཕུས་སེ། *kraphusse,* rat.

འདོན་ཕྲོ་ན། *'adon phrona,* portion of food.

དྲང་གེ། དྲོང་གེ། *Drangge, Drongge,* names of Kesar's servants; till now-a-days very simple people are called by those names.

ཆང་རྐྱལ། *chang rkyal,* hides for beer.

ཟབ་ན། *zabna*, if [we] put on silk (or another beautiful dress).

དེན་ན་ཟ་ན། *denna zana*, at the very same time.

སོག་ལྡི། *sog ldi*, elastic piece of wood to throw stones with.

གོས་ཙས། *goscas*, to spill.

ཟུན་ཏེ། *zunte*, entering, traversing.

ཏུ་བག། *tubag*, = *tupag*, gun, rifle.

ཏེ། སྟེ། *te* or *ste*; as regards my system of differentiating between the *te* and *ste* of the gerundive: besides those cases where only *te* is possible, *te* is also used, if the present tense of the verb shows an *s* already.

Thus I write འཛིགས་ཏེ། but བཏང་སྟེ། I write ཤེས་ཏེ། but ཟུམ་སྟེ།

མགོ་ཅོག་ཅོག། *mgo cog cog*, nod with the head; instead of saying 'yes.'

སྟག་སྟེ། *stagste*, = *btagste*, lifting.

གཞུམ་མགོ། *γzhum mgo*, = *γzhu mgo*, bow-head.

ཕ་སྐལ་བཅོ་ཙས། *pha skal bcocas*, honour [a man] like a father.

ཏུ་རུམ་། *turum*, imitates the sound of chewing.

སངས། *sangs*, offering of pencil-cedar.

ཏུམ་བུ། *tumbu*, probably the original form of *dumbu*, a certain quantity; see Lad. Grammar, introduction, tenuis.

སང་ངོ། *sangngo*, = *sangs lo*, hallo, an offering!

རྩེན་མོ། *rtsenmo*, a spectacle.

རྩེན་ལོ། *rtsen lo,* = *rtse yin lo,* [we] will play.

ཡངས་པ། *yangspa,* = *γyangspa,* spectacle; perhaps related to *dbyangs.*

མགོ་ཟུག་ཅས། *mgo zugces,* = *mgo 'adzugpa,* begin.

བུར་ཆ། *burcha,* = *bur,* bolt, peg.

No. 6.

བྱ་ཉི་མ་ཁྱུང་རུང་། *bya nyima khyung rung,* the bird, the sun *khyung rung,* name of the sun-bird; compare *khyung dkrung.*

དུག། *dug,* poison, is invariably written *tug* in my MS. Also the Ladakhi pronunciation of this word is *tug.* I suppose that *tug* is the original form, and that the tenuis without a protection became a media. Lad. Grammar, introduction.

ལྡིངས་ས། *ldingssa,* = *ldingspa,* a flying one.

ཚངས། *thsangs,* = *thsang,* nest.

བ་ཧོ། *baho,* cave.

སྙི་ལམ། *snyilam,* = *rmilam,* dream. Dr. Stein's Endere-relics have the form rmyilam.

ཀྱི་ཀྱི། ཀུང་ཀུང་། *kyi kyi, kung kung,* imitates the voice of *Bya so mig dmar.*

གཉིད་ཐེ་རལ། *γnyid the ral,* sleepy, drowsy; compare Jâschke, *the rel.*

ནུར་བུ། *nurbu,* = *norbu,* jewel.—I have been collecting words, showing the change from long or short *o* to *u,* or *u* to *o.* This is a list of them:—

norbu	becomes	*nurbu*
srungpo	becomes	*srongpo*
ombu	becomes	*umbu*
dondrub	becomes	*dundrub*
bumo	becomes	*bomo*
numo	becomes	*nomo*
nubo	becomes	*no* (= *nobo*).

In all these cases the vowel of the first syllable is influenced by the vowel of the second syllable; it becomes the same which we find in the second syllable. There seems to exist in Tibetan a law of sound which is closely related to Professor J. Schmidt's law of assimilation, as proved for Greek. If this Tibetan law of sound should turn out to be correct, it would follow that the name of *'aBrugmo* could easily become *'aBrogmo;* but *'aBrogmo* could not become *'aBrugmo; i.e.*, the word *'aBrogmo* cannot be accepted as the original form for *'aBrugmo.*

ཁོ་མགས། *kho mags,=kho ma*, knapsack, bag.

རྐྱང་ཅས། *rkyangcas*, fill; probably a causative form of *khyangcas;* both are secondary forms of *gangba, skangba.*

No. 7.

སུས་མི། *sus mi*, a man who is sent to meet a person.

རྒྱལ་ལྕང་ལྕང་། *rgyal lcang lcang*, or *rgya lcang lcang*, the 'chief willow,' or the 'broad willow;' the willow of the world, compare Lad. Songs, No. XXI.

ཞབ་ཤི། *zhabshi,=zhabs phyi*, servant, service.

དར་ལྷ་གོ་ཆོད་མ། *dar lha go chodma*, name of *'aBruguma's* servant-girl, compare Spring-myth.

ནམ་ཟ། *nam za,=na bzā*, clothing.

ཉི་རྩེ། *nyi rtse*, literally 'sun-hill-top'; *i.e.*, the first rays of the sun on high snow-hills.

ནམ་ཙར། *nam tsar*, the shawl which is placed over the shoulders when dancing.

ཏི་བང་བང་། *Ti bang bang*, name of a mountain in *gLing;* seems to mean 'drenched with water' (*bangcas, sbongba*).

དྲམ་བུ། *drambu,='adambu*, reed.

དྲ་མན། *draman*, = *daman*, drum.

ཧ་རིབ། *harib*, clarionet.

གྲོལ་མོ། *grolmo*, or *rolmo*, musical instrument.

སྡགས། *sdags*, causative of *'adegspa*, prepare.

བ་ལུ། *balu*, dwarf.

ཏུང་ཏུང། *tung tung*, white.

General Note on the Vocabulary :—When writing fascicle No. I and II, I entered only those words in my vocabulary which could not be found in Jäschke's dictionary. Meanwhile Sarat Chandra 'Das' dictionary was published, and as I believed that all the material contained in Jäschke's dictionary, besides new matter, could be found in Sarat Chandra Das' dictionary, I decided to enter only those words which were not contained in Sarat Chandra Das' dictionary. However, accidentally I discovered that many West-Tibetan words of Jäschke's dictionary cannot be found in S. Ch. Das' dictionary. Probably they were considered superfluous. Therefore I resumed my old practice and noted only those words which are not given by Jäschke. It is evident that Jäschke's dictionary cannot yet be treated as a matter of the past.

No. 1.

རྒྱལ་ལྷམ་ཀ་སར་ལ་རྒྱལ་ཁག་བདུན་བདུལ་དེ་ན། རི་དཀར་པོ་ནག་པོ་དམར་པོ་གསུམ་གྱི་རྩ་རུ་མཚམས་ལ་འདུགས་པས། ལོ་གསུམ་གྱི་བར་དུ་འདུག་ཅེས་བཙོས་པ། དེ་ཅི་ལ་ཡིན་ཟེར་ན། རྒྱ་ནག་གི་ལམ་མ་ཐོབ་པ་སང། ཀ་སར་གྱིས་བསམ། ང་ལོ་གསུམ་མཚམས་ལ་འདུག་ཡིན། དེ་ནས་རྒྱ་ནག་རྒྱལ་པོ་ལ་མཐུ་བཏང་ཡིན། རྒྱལ་ཁག་འཁྲུགས་ན་ང་ལ་ལམ་ཐྲོབ་ཡིན་བསམ་སྟེ། མཚམས་ཡོག་ལ་ར་མ་ཀ་བུ་ལུ་ཟེར་བ་ཞིག་བོར་ནས་མཚམས་ལ་འདུགས། དེ་ནས་ལོ་ཕྱེད་འང་གཉིས་སོང་བ་དང། རྒྱལ་ལྷམ་ཀ་སར་ནས་རྒྱ་ནག་རྒྱལ་པོ་ལ་མཐུ་བཏངས། མཐུ་དེས་རྒྱ་ནག་རྒྱལ་པོའི་མཁར་གྱི་ཕྱོགས་གཅིག་ཞིག་ནས། རྒྱལ་པོ་ལ་ཐོག་པས། རྒྱ་ནག་རྒྱལ་པོ་ལ་སྐྱིང་གཟུགས་ཆེ་བ་ཡོངས་ནས། ཟན་ཅི་ཡང་ཟ་མ་བཙུགས་པ། ནང་མིག་ནང་ནས་ཁྲི་སྦྲ་རུ་བིང་མ་ཐུབ། དེ་ནས་མོ་པ་བཀྲ་ཁྲོངས། རྩིས་པ་བཀྲ་ཁྲོངས། དབོན་པ་ཚང་མ་ཁྲོང་སྟེ། མོ་བཏབ་བཙུགས་པས། མོའི་ནང་ནས་འདི་ཟུག་ཅིག་བིང་སོང། ཟུར་མོ་དེ་གླིང་རྒྱལ་ལྷམ་ཀ་སར་གྱི་སྐྱོན་འདུག། ཀ་སར་རྒྱལ་པོ་ཁོ་རང་འདིར་སྐྱོད་དེ་མིན་བ། ཟུར་མོ་དེ་པན་ཅེས་མི་འདུག་ཟེརས་པ།།

དེ་ནས་རྒྱལ་པོ་དང་སྒྲ་དྲག་མང་པོ་འདུས་དེ་གྲབས་བཅོ་སྟེ། རྒྱལ་པོ་ཀ་སར་ལ་ཞུ་ཤོག་ཅིག་སྤུལ་ཅེས་ལ་ཁ་འཆམས་ནས། ཞུ་ཤོག་དེ་མི་ཡིས་

འཁྱེར་ན། ཀ་སར་གྱིས་བསད་ཡིན་བསམ་སྟེ། བྱ་མོ་ལྷོར་རེ་ཟེར་མཁན་ཞིག་དང་བཀལ་བས། བྱ་རིས་ཡི་གེ་འཁྱེར་ཏེ་ཀ་སར་རི་མཚམས་ཁང་གི་དཀར་ཁང་ནང་དུ་ཕངས། དེ་ནས་རྒྱལ་པོ་ཀ་སར་གྱིས་ཡི་གེ་གསིལ་པ། ཡི་གེ་ནང་དུ་འདི་ཟུག་བྲིས་ཡོད་ཚུག། ཁྱེ་རང་ལ་ཟན་དགོས་ནའང་། ནོར་དགོས་ནའང་། གསེར་སྨུལ་ནོར་བུ་ཅི་དགོས་ཕུལ་ཡིན། ཁྱེ་རང་མ་སྐྱོད་ན། རྒྱ་ནག་རྒྱལ་པོ་མི་ཕབ་ཅེས་འདུག་ཟེར་ཏེ་འདུག་པ། དེ་ནས་ཀ་སར་གྱིས་བསམ། མི་ཞིག་མ་ཡོང་ན། ང་མི་ཆ། ལམ་ཡང་མི་ཤེས་བསམ་སྟེ་མ་སྐྱོད།།

རྒྱ་ནག་རྒྱལ་པོ་ལ་ཐེབ་ཟུར་མོ་མང་པོ་ཡོངས། དེ་ནས་རྒྱ་ནག་རྒྱལ་པོས་རང་གི་ལག་པ་བཅད་དེ་ཁྲག་ཕིང་སྟེ། ས་ཞིག་རྩ་སྟེ་མི་བཅོ་སྟེ། དེ་བོ་ལ་དབུགས་བཙུག་སྟེ་ཡང་ཡི་གེ་ཞིག་བཀལ། དེ་མིས་ཡི་གེ་དེ་འཁྱེར་ཏེ། ཀ་སར་གྱི་མདུན་ལ་ཕང་སྟེ་ན། མི་དེ་སྟོར་སོང་། ཀ་སར་གྱིས་ཡི་གེ་ལ་བལྟ་སྟེ་བསམ་བློ་བཏངས་པ། ང་རང་ཆ་ན་མཚམས་ལ་འདུག་ཅེས་ཀྱི་ལོ་མ་ཚང་། དེ་ཚུག་པ་ཨ་གུ་ཁྲའི་ཐུང་བཏང་ཡིན་བསམ་སྟེ། ཁྲའི་མགོ་ཁྲའི་ཐུང་བཏངས། དེ་ནས་ཁྲའི་ཐུང་རང་གི་རྟ་ལ་ཞོན་ནས་སོང་བས། ཁྲའི་ཐུང་ལ་ལམ་མ་ཤེས་པ། སྨུན་འཁོར་ཡོང་གིན་ཞིག་ལུས་སོང་། དེ་ནས་རྒྱལ་པོ་ཀ་སར་ལ་ལོ་གསུམ་སོང་བ་དང་། ང་རང་ཆ་དགོས་ཡིན་བསམ་སྟེ། མཚམས་གཡོག་ལ་ཡོད་པའི་ར་མ་ཀ་བུ་ལུ་བསད་དེ། བྱ་ཞིན་ལ་བཏང་སྟེ་ན། ཀ་སར་ཡབ་བསྟན་པ་དང་ཡུམ་སྒྲོན་མོ་གཉིས་ཀྱི་མདུན་ལ་སོང་སྟེ་གླུ་འདི་ལྟར་བཏངས།

རི་ལུངས་ཆུད་པའི་ཕྲུག་ཅེམ་རིག་ཡོད་ན།
ཨ་ཕྲ་རང་ཕྲུག་པོ་ཡིན་ཡབས་ཐོན་པ་ཕྲུག་པོ་ཡིན།

ཁྲེ་ཐང་ཆུད་པའི་ཀྱུལ་བྲུ་རིག་ཡོད་ན།

ཨ་བཱ་རང་ཕྱུག་པོ་ཡིན་ཡབས་ཕྲོན་པ་ཕྱུག་པོ་ཡིན།

ལྕངས་པོ་ཆུད་པའི་བུང་པ་རིག་ཡོད་ན།

ཨ་བཱ་རང་ཕྱུག་པོ་ཡིན་ཡབས་ཕྲོན་པ་ཕྱུག་པོ་ཡིན།

ཤིག་གི་གྱུས་པ་ཆུན་ཅིག་ཡོད་ན།

ཨ་བཱ་རང་ཕྱུག་པོ་ཡིན་ཡབས་ཕྲོན་པ་ཕྱུག་པོ་ཡིན།

སྤྲུར་པ་དམར་པོ་འི་ཁོང་ཁྲག་རིག་ཡོད་ན།

ཨ་བཱ་རང་ཕྱུག་པོ་ཡིན་ཡབ་ཕྲོན་པ་ཕྱུག་པོ་ཡིན།

གསེར་གྱི་གསེར་པེ་ཁལ་ཅིག་ཡོད་ན།

ཨ་བཱ་རང་ཕྱུག་པོ་ཡིན་ཡབ་ཕྲོན་པ་ཕྱུག་པོ་ཡིན།

སྲིན་མོ་རོ་ནེ་མོའི་འགྲམ་མཚལ་ཡོད་ན།

ཨ་བཱ་རང་ཕྱུག་པོ་ཡིན་ཡབ་ཕྲོན་པ་ཕྱུག་པོ་ཡིན།

སྲིན་པོ་རག་ཤའི་ལག་པ་ཡོད་ན།

ཨ་བཱ་རང་ཕྱུག་པོ་ཡིན་ཡབ་ཕྲོན་པ་ཕྱུག་པོ་ཡིན།

ཉི་མའི་ཉི་གཟེར་ལག་པ་གང་ཡོད་ན།

ཨ་བཱ་རང་ཕྱུག་པོ་ཡིན་ཡབ་ཕྲོན་པ་ཕྱུག་པོ་ཡིན།

ཟླ་བའི་ཟླ་གཟེར་ལག་པ་གང་ཡོད་ན།

ཨ་བཱ་རང་ཕྱུག་པོ་ཡིན་ཡབ་ཕྲོན་པ་ཕྱུག་པོ་ཡིན།

དར་གྱི་ཐལ་བ་བྲེ་གང་ཡོད་ན།

ཨ་བཱ་རང་ཕྱུག་པོ་ཡིན་ཡབ་ཕྲོན་པ་ཕྱུག་པོ་ཡིན།

ཀེ་སར་གྱིས་དེ་རྟག་འདྲིས་པ་སང། ཡབ་བློན་པས་ལན་དུ་གླུ་འདི་ལྷར་བཏངས།།

གླིང་གི་རྒྱལ་ལྷམ་གྱིས་ངའི་དངོས་ལ་ཉོན།
རྒྱལ་ལྷམ་ཀེ་སར་གྱིས་ངའི་བདག་ལ་གསན།
རི་ལུང་ཆུང་བའི་ཕྲུག་ཚོལ་དེ་ང་ལ་ཡོད།
ཁྲི་ཐང་ཆུང་བའི་རྒྱལ་བུ་དེ་ང་ལ་ཡོད།
ལྕངས་པོ་ཆུང་བའི་བྱང་པ་དེ་ང་ལ་ཡོད།
ཤིག་གི་རྒྱུས་པ་ཆུན་ཅིག་དེ་ང་ལ་ཡོད།
སྤྲུར་པ་དམར་པོ་འི་ཁོང་ཁྲག་དེ་ང་ལ་ཡོད།
གསེར་པེ་ཁལ་གཅིག་དེ་ང་ལ་ཡོད།
དར་གྱི་ཐལ་བ་བྲི་གང་དེ་ང་ལ་ཡོད།
ཉི་མའི་ཉི་གཟེར་ལག་པ་གང་ང་ལ་ཡོད།
ཟླ་བའི་ཟླ་གཟེར་ལག་པ་གང་ང་ལ་ཡོད།
སྐར་མའི་སྐར་ཚོགས་ལག་པ་གང་ང་ལ་ཡོད།
སྲིན་མོ་རོ་ནེ་མོ་འི་འགྲམ་བ་ང་ལ་མེད།
སྲིན་པོ་རག་ཤའི་ལག་པ་ང་ལ་མེད།
དེ་གཉིས་ཀྱི་ཕྱི་ལ་གྲང་གི་ལུང་པའི་ཕྲུ་ལ་སོང།
དེ་རུ་ངའི་ཨ་ཞང་གཅིག་མཚམས་ལ་ཡོང།
དེ་མི་མི་ལ་སྲིན་པོ་འི་ལག་པ་ཐོབ་ཡིན།
མི་མི་མཚམས་པ་ལ་སྲིན་མོ་འི་འགྲམ་པ་ཐོབ་ཡིན།

ཡབ་ཕྲོན་པས་དེ་ཟུག་ཟེར་པ། རྒྱལ་པོ་ཀེ་སར་ལྕུང་པའི་ནང་སོང་སྟེ། མཚམས་ཁང་གི་མདུན་ནས་མེ་མེ་ལ་གླུ་འདི་ལྟར་བླངས།།

ངའི་མེ་མེས་འང་ངའི་དངོས་ལ་ཉོན་དང་།
མེ་མེ་མཚམས་པས་བདག་ལ་གསན་དང་།
ངའི་ཨ་བ་ཕྲོན་པས་ལོན་ཅིག་བཀལ་དེ་ཡོད།
ཡབ་ཕྲོན་པས་ལོན་ཅིག་བཀལ་དེ་ཡོད།
སྲིན་མོ་རོ་ནེ་མོ་འི་འགྲམ་བ་ཉེ་རང་ངེ་ལག་ལ་ཡོད་ལོ།
སྲིན་པོ་རག་ཤའི་ལག་པ་ཉེ་རང་གི་ལག་དུ་ཡོད་ལོ།
དེ་གཉིས་ཀ་ཡོད་ན་མེད། ཁ་བར་རིག་ཤོད་ལོ།

མེ་མེས་ལན་ལ་གླུ་འདི་ལྟར་བཏངས།

ངའི་ཚ་བོས་འང་དངོས་ལ་ཉོན་དང་།
ཀེ་སར་རྒྱལ་པོས་འང་བདག་ལ་གསན་དང་།
སྲིན་མོ་འི་འགྲམ་བ་ངའི་ལག་དུ་མེད་ལོ།
སྲིན་པོ་འི་ལག་པ་ངའི་ལག་དུ་མེད་ལོ།
དེ་གཉིས་བཙལ་བ་ངའི་ཁྲིའུ་བཏང་ཡིན།
ཉེ་རང་ཞག་བདུན་སྲིང་དགོས།

དེ་ཟུག་ཟེར་དེ། མེ་མེ་མཚམས་པ་ལ་ཟངས་ཀྱི་ཁྲིའུ་གཉིས་ཀ། སྲིན་མོ་རོ་ནེ་དང་། སྲིན་པོ་རག་ཤ་གཉིས་ཀ་འཁྲོང་བ་ལ་བཏངས་པ། དེ་ཚུག་པ་ཀེ་སར་དང་མེ་མེ་གཉིས་ཀས་ས་རྡོང་ཞིག་བྲུ་སྟེ། རྒྱལ་པོ་ཀེ་སར་མདའ་དང་གཞུ་ཁུར་ནས། དེ་ས་རྡོང་ནང་དུ། དཀར་ཁང་ཆུང་ཙུན་ཞིག་བཅོ་སྟེ་ཡིབ་སྟེ་

འདུགས་པ། ཞག་བདུན་སོང་བ་དང༌། ཟངས་ཀྱི་ཁྲིའུ་གཉིས་ཀས་སྲིན་པོ་དང་སྲིན་མོ་གཉིས་ཀ་རིའི་ཤ་བ་འཁྲོང་བ་ལྟར་བཀག་སྟེ་ཁྲོངས་པ། ཀེ་སར་རྒྱལ་པོ་ནས། མགྲོགས་པ་མདའ་དང་གཞུ་ཕེང་སྟེ། ས་དོང་གི་དཀར་ཁང་ནང་ནས་མདའ་བརྡངས་པ། སྲིན་པོའི་ལག་པ་དང༌། སྲིན་མོའི་འགྲམ་བ་སྲིབ་ཅིག་ལ་ཐོབ་སོང༌། སྲིན་པོའི་ལག་པ་དང༌། སྲིན་མོའི་འགྲམ་བ་བོར་ཏེ། སྲིན་པོ་དང་སྲིན་མོ་ཤོར་ཏེ་སོང༌། དེ་ནས་ཀེ་སར་གྱིས་སྲིན་པོའི་ལག་པ་དང༌། སྲིན་མོའི་འགྲམ་བ་ཁར་ཏེ་གླིང་ཡུལ་ལ་ཡོང་སྟེ་རང་གི་རྟ་རྐྱང་བུང་དཀྱེར་པ་ཁྲིད་དེ་ཇོ་ཇོ་འབྲི་གུ་མ་ལ་ཡང་མ་ཟེར་བ། མདའ་དང་གཞུ་ཁར་ཏེ་རྒྱ་ནག་ཕྱོགས་ལ་སོང་།།

No. 2.

དེ་ནས་ཞག་གསུམ་སོང་བ་དང༌། རི་མཐོན་པོ་ཞིག་ལ་བསླེབ་པས། རེ་རྟུ་ཨ་གུ་ཁྲའི་ཐུང་ལ་ལམ་ཨ་ཐོབ་པར་ཡོད་ཚུག། ཀེ་སར་རྒྱལ་པོ་ཁམ་བ་ཞིག་བཙོ་སྟེ་སོང་ནས། ཨ་གུ་ལ་གཏམ་ལན་ལ་གླུ་འདི་ལྟར་བླངས།།

ཁྱེད་རྟ་གཅིག་གི་མི་གཅིག་ཁྱོད་དངོས་ལ་ཇོན།
ཡུལ་མེད་པའི་ཐང་དུ་ཁྱེད་ག་ནས་ཡོངས།
ཁྱེད་འགྲོ་བ་དེ་ནི་གང་དུ་འགོ་ཆེན།
ཁྱེད་ཡོང་བ་དེ་ནི་གང་ནས་ཡོངས།

དེ་ནས་ཨ་གུ་ཁྲའི་ཐུང་གིས་ཀེ་སར་རྒྱལ་པོ་ཨ་ཤེས་པ་གླུ་འདི་ལྟར་བླངས།།

ཨ་གུ་ཁམ་པ་ངའི་དངོས་ལ་ཇོན།
ཡོང་ནི་ང་གླིང་མཁར་སྟོད་ནས་ཡོངས།
འགྲོ་བ་དེ་ནི་རྒྱ་ནག་ཁྲི་སྐོར་གསུམ་དུ་འགྲོ།

གླིང་རྒྱལ་ལྷམ་ཀེ་སར་རི་ཕྲུག་འབྲིས་ཡོད།
རྒྱ་ནག་རྒྱལ་པོ་ལ་ཞུ་ཡིག་ཅིག་འཁྱེར་ཡོད།
འགྲོ་བའི་འགྲོ་ལམ་ཞིག་ང་ལ་མ་ཐོབ་པས།
ཐང་སྟོང་པ་འདི་རུ་ལུས་དེ་འདུགས།
ཁ་ལ་ཟ་རྒྱུ་མེད་པ་ཡོད།
ལུས་ལ་གོན་རྒྱུ་མེད་པ་ཡོད།
ང་ལོག་སྡེ་ཆ་ན་ཀེ་སར་གྱི་བཀའ་སྐྱོན་ཡོང་།
ཉིད་གླིང་ཡུལ་ལ་ཆ་མཁན་ཞིག་མེན་ན།
ངས་རྒྱལ་ལྷམ་ཀེ་སར་ལ་ལོན་ཅིག་ཕྲུལ་ཡིན།

ཨ་ཀུ་ཁྲའི་ཐུང་གིས་དེ་ཟུག་ཟེརས་པ། ཀེ་སར་རྒྱལ་པོས་ལན་དུ་གླུ་འདི་ལྟར།།

ཁྱེད་གླིང་གི་དཔའ་བོ་དངོས་ལ་ཉེན་དང་།
ཁྲའི་མགོ་ཁྲ་ཐུང་བདག་ལ་གསན་དང་།
ཁྱེད་སྔོན་ལ་གླིང་གི་ཁག་འཁྱེར་ཅི་ལ་བཅོས།
ཁྱེད་ཀྱིས་དཔའ་བོ་ཚང་མའི་ཁག་དེ་ཅི་ལ་བཅོས།
ཁྱེད་གླིང་ཡུལ་ལ་འདུག་ཟ་ན་རང་སྟོད་བཏང་མཁན་ཡིན།

དེ་ཟུག་ཟེར་དེ། ཀེ་སར་ནས་ཁ་མང་པོ་སྐྱེས་དེ། ད་ཁྱོད་རང་ལོག་སྡེ་སོང་ཟེར་ནས། ཁྲའི་ཐུང་གླིང་ཡུལ་ལ་ལོག་སྡེ་བཏངས། ཀེ་སར་རྒྱལ་པོ་སོང་བའི་ཞག་བདུན་སོང་བ་དང་། རི་ཆེན་པོ་བྲག་ཆེན་པོ། དེ་གཉིས་ཀྱི་བར་ལ་

མཚོ་ཆེན་པོ་ཡོད་པའི་ས་ཁྲུད་ཅིག་ལ་བསླེབ་པ། ལམ་མ་ཤེས་པས། ཞག་ཁ་ཤས་འཁོར་ནའང་ལམ་མ་ཐོབ། དེ་ནས་རི་ལུང་ཆུད་པའི་ཕྲུག་ཅོལ་དང་། རྒྱ་མཚོ་ཆུད་པའི་བྱུང་པ་གཉིས་ཀ་འཕངས་བཏངས་པས། རི་དང་མཚོ་ཚང་མ་མེད་མཁན་སོང་། དེ་ནས་ཀ་སར་འཐད་ཀྱིན་ཞིག་སོང་བ། ཡང་ཞག་གསུམ་སོང་བ་དང་། བྱེ་མ་མང་པོ་ཡོད་པའི་ས་ཁྲུད་ཅིག་ལ་བསླེབ་པ། དེ་རྡུ་རྣ་མི་གཉིས་ཀ་འགྲུལ་མ་ཐུབ། ནག་མང་པོ་མཐོང་བས། དེ་ལ་ཡང་བྱེ་མ་ཆུད་པའི་རྐྱལ་ལུ་འཕངས་པ། བྱེ་མ་མེད་མཁན་སོང་། དེ་ནས་ཡང་ཞག་གསུམ་འགྲུལ་ནས། ཤིག་མང་པོ་འི་མདུན་ལ་བསླེབ་པས། དེ་ཤིག་ཚང་མ་ལ་རྒྱུས་པ་མེད་ཚུག། ཤིག་ཚང་མས་ཀ་སར་གྱི་ཤ་ཚང་མ་ཟོས་དེ་བཀགས་པོ་བཅོས་པས། དེ་ཤིག་ཚང་མ་ལ་རྒྱུས་པ་བསྒུག་སྒོ་བཏངས་པ། ཀ་སར་དེ་ནས་ཡང་ཐར་སོང་། ཡང་ཞག་གསུམ་འགྲུལ་དེ་ན! སྤྲུར་པ་དམར་པོ་མང་པོ་ཡོད་པའི་མདུན་ལ་བསླེབ་པས། དེ་སྤྲུར་པ་ཚང་མ་ལ་ཁྲག་མེད་ཚུག། ཀ་སར་གྱིས་དེ་ཚང་མ་ལ་ཁྲག་བཏངས་པ། གནོད་པ་མ་སྐྱུལ་བ་ཐར། ཡང་ཞག་གསུམ་འགྲུལ་དེ་སོང་བས། དེ་ཞག་ལ་མཚན་སོང་ནས་གནམ་མ་ལངས་པར། ཞག་བཅུ་སྲུན་འཁོར་ཡོང་གིན་ཞིག་འདུགས་པ། མི་ལ་ཟན་མ་ཐོབ། རྟ་ལ་རྩྭ་མ་ཐོབ། དེ་ཟླུག་ནག་མང་པོ་མཐོང་སྟེ། ཀ་སར་ནས་ངུ་འིན་ཞིག་ཨ་ནེ་བཀུར་དམན་མོ་ལ་སླུ་འདི་ལྟར།།

ངའི་ཨ་ནེས་འང་དངོས་ཤིག་ས་ཉོན་དང་།
བཀུར་དམན་རྒྱལ་མོས་འང་ངའི་བདག་ལ་གསན།
བྱ་ཆ་ང་རང་ལ་ཉི་མ་མ་མཐོང་བ་ཞག་བཅུ་སོང་།

ཧ་མི་གཉིས་ཀ་ལ་ཉི་འོད་མ་མཐོང་བ་ཞག་བཅུ་སོང་།
ཨ་ནེ་རང་གིས་ང་ལ་རོགས་ཤིག་མཛོད་ལེ།
དེ་ཟླུག་ཟེར་སླ་པ། ཨ་ནེ་བཀུར་དམན་མོས་ལན་དུ་སླུ་འདི་ལྟར།
ངའི་ཚ་བོས་འང་དངོས་ཡ་ཉིན་དང་།
རྒྱལ་ལྷམ་ཀེ་སར་གྱིས་བདག་ལ་གསན།
ཉི་གཟེར་ཟླ་གཟེར་སྐར་འོད་གསུམ།
འདི་རིང་མ་ཕན་ན་ཅི་བཅོ་ཡིན།

ཨ་ནེ་བཀུར་དམན་མོས་དེ་ཟླུག་ཟེར་ས་པ། དེ་ནས་ཀེ་སར་རྒྱལ་པོ་ལ་བསམས་བློ་ཡོང་སྟེ། ཉི་གཟེར་ཟླ་གཟེར་སྐར་འོད་ཚང་ཀ་ཕིངས་པ། ཉི་མ་ཤར། ཟླ་བ་ཤར་དེ། འོད་ཅན་སོང་པ་སང་ཀེ་སར་མང་པོ་འཐད་སོང་། མཚན་ལ་ལམ་ཨོར་མཁན་གྱི་རྗེས་པོ་མཐོང་སྟེ་ཡམ་མཚན་སོང་།།

དེ་ནས་ཡང་ཞག་གསུམ་འགྲུལ་དེ། སྲིན་པོ་ལམ་སྲུངས་པ་མང་པོ་ཡོད་ཚུག། དེ་སྲིན་པོ་འི་ཁྲོ་ལ་སྡོད་ལ་ལག་པ་བཀོག་མཁན་ནི་སྲིན་པོ་ཡོད་ཚུག། དེ་སྲིན་པོ་ལ་ཀེ་སར་གྱིས་ཟེར། ལྷ་སྲིན་པོ་ང་ཕུད་བདང་ན། ཁྱེད་རང་གི་ལག་པ་ངས་བཅོ་ཡིན་ཟེར་ས་པ། སྲིན་པོས། ངའི་ལག་པ་བཅོན་ཕུད་བདང་ཡིན་ཟེར། དེ་ནས་ཀེ་སར་གྱིས་སྲིན་པོ་འི་ལག་པ་ཕིང་སྟེ་བཅོས་པ། སྲིན་པོ་འཐད་ནས། ལམ་གྱི་ཕྱོགས། བསྟན་དེ་བཏངས། ཡང་ཞག་གསུམ་སོང་བ་དང་སྲིན་མོ་འི་ལམ་པ་དང་ཐུག། དེ་རྩ་ཡང་སྡོད་ལ་འགྲམ་བ་བཀོག་མཁན་ནི་སྲིན་མོ་ཡོད་ཚུག་ཀེ་སར་གྱིས་ཡང་དེ་སྲིན་མོ་ལ་ཟེར། ལྷ་སྲིན་མོ། ང་ཕུད་བདང་ན། ཁྱེ་རང་གི་འགྲམ་བ་ངས་བཅོ་ཡིན་ཟེར་པ། སྲིན་མོས་ཟེར།

ངའི་འགྲམ་བ་བཙོན། ཁྲིད་ཕུད་བཏང་ཡིན་ཟེརས་པ། ཀ་སར་གྱིས་སྲིན་མོའི་འགྲམ་བ་བཙུགས་པས། ཀ་སར་ཕུད་བཏངས།།

ཡང་ཞག་གསུམ་སོང་བ་དང་། གངས་ཀྱི་ལ་མཐོན་པོ་ཞིག་ལ་བསླེབ་པས། དེ་ལ་དར་གྱི་ཐལ་བ་གཡོག་གིན་ཞིག་མཛེགས་པ། མ་བཀགས་པོ་སོང་སྟེ་མ་ཐར། དེ་གངས་ལ་ལོག་སྟེ་སོང་བ། མི་དམུལ་བ་ཅན་ལྕུང་མཁན་གསུམ་དང་ཐུག། དེ་མི་ཀུན་ལ་གསེར་རེ་བཏངས་པ་ཁོང་གིས་ལམ་བསྟན་ཏེ་འཁྲིདས། དེ་ཐུག་གིས་སོང་པ་སང་། གླིང་རྒྱལ་ལྷམ་ཀ་སར་སྐྱོད་ཅེས་ཚོར་ཏེ། རྒྱ་ནག་རྒྱལ་པོས་རྟ་དང་མི་མང་པོ་བསུ་སྟེ་བཀལ་ཏེ་བསླེབ་སོང་། དེ་རྒྱ་ནག་རྒྱལ་པོའི་མཁར་དེ་མཚོའི་དཀྱིལ་དུ་ཡོད་ཚུག། དེ་ནས་རིམ་པ་བཞིན་དུ་ཀ་སར་རྒྱ་ནག་རྒྱལ་པོའི་མདུན་ལ་བསླེབ་པས། རྒྱ་ནག་བྲུལ་པོའི་ཐུར་མོ་དེ། རྒྱལ་ལྷམ་ཀ་སར་བསླེབ་མ་ཐག་ཏུ་ཕན་སོང་།།

No. 3.

དེ་ནས་ཨ་ག་ཁྲའི་ཐང་ཕྱིར་ལོག་སྟེ་ཡོང་སྐབས་སུ་འདི་ཐུག་བསམ། རྒྱལ་ལྷམ་ཀ་སར་ལ་ལམ་མ་ཐོབ་པར་ཤི་ཡིན། མཁར་ནང་དུ་ང་རང་ཆེན། ཇོ་ཇོ་འབྲུ་ག་མ་ཕིངས་བཏང་ཡིན་བསམ་སྟེ། ཁྲའི་ཐང་གླིང་མཁར་ལ་སོང་སྟེ་ཇོ་ཇོ་འབྲུ་ག་མ་ལ་ཟེརས། ཨ་ཇོ་ཇོ། ཁྱོད་རང་འདི་མཁར་ནང་དུ་མ་འདུག། མཁར་དེ་ང་ལ་ཐོབ་ཆེན་ཟེར་ཏེ་ཇོ་ཇོ་ལ་ཟ་ཅེས་ཤིག་དང་རེ་བོ་ནག་པོ་ཞིག་བཏང་སྟེ། ཡུལ་གྱི་མཇུག་ལ་ཕིངས་པས། དེ་ཙ་རེ་བོ་ནག་པོ་སླབ་སྟེ་ཇོ་ཇོ་འདུགས། ཁྲའི་མགོ་ཁྲའི་ཐང་མཁར་ལ་འདུག་སྟེ་རྒྱལ་པོ་བཙོ་སྟེ་འདུགས། དི་པི་གསུམ་རྟག་སྟེ་གོནས། རྟ་ལ་འོབ་ཆེན་གསུམ་བདགས།

ཁྲི་ལ་ཁྱོག་དམར་གསུམ་བཏགས། མི་ཚང་མ་ལ་ཧུ་ཀུམ་དྲག་པོ་བཏང་གིན་ཞིག་འདུགས། རྒྱལ་བློམ་ཀ་སར་རྒྱ་ནག་རྒྱལ་པོ་འི་མཁར་ལ་ཞག་ཉི་ཤུ་ཟམ་ལུས། རྒྱ་ནག་རྒྱལ་པོ་ལ་བུ་མོ་གཡུའི་དཀོན་མཆོག་མོ་ཟེར་མཁན་ཞིག་ཡོད་ཚུག། དེ་བུ་མོས་ང་ཀ་སར་དང་མཉམ་པོ་ཆེན་ཟེར་དེ་དབང་བཙོས་པས། ཞག་ཅིག་ལ་ཀ་སར་གྱིས་ང་ཆེན་ཟེར་དེ། རྒྱ་ནག་རྒྱལ་པོ་ལ་དགོངས་པ་ཞུས། ཀ་སར་ཆེན་ཟེརས་པ། བུ་མོ་གཡུའི་དཀོན་མཆོག་མོ་ཡང་ཀ་སར་དང་མཉམ་པོ་ཆེན་ཟེར་དེ་སོང་། དེ་དང་མཉམ་པོ་ནོར་བུ་ཚང་མ་འབྲང་སེ་སོང་། དེ་ནས་དྲག་རིགས་ཚང་མ་དང་ཡུལ་པ་ཚང་མ་འདུས་དེ་གྲབས་བཙོས་པས། ཀ་སར་དང་མཉམ་པོ་ཇོ་ཇོ་དང་ནུར་བུ་ཚང་མ་སོང་། ཀ་སར་ཆ་མ་བཙུག་པ། འབྲུ་ཁང་དུ་བཏང་སྟེ་ཤི་བཙུག་ཡིན་ཇེར་དེ། སློན་པོ་དེ་ཀ་སར་ལ་ཧྲས་དེ་སོང་སྟེ་ཟེརས་པ། ལྷ་རྒྱལ་པོ་ཀ་སར་ཉེ་རང་གླིང་ཡུལ་ལ་སྐྱོད་འདུག། ང་ཞའི་འབྲུ་ཁང་པོ་མ་མཐོང་བ་ཆ་ཡིན་ན། གླིང་ཡུལ་ལི་མི་ཚང་མས་འདྲི་ན། འབྲུ་ཁང་མཐོང་ང་མ་མཐོང་ཟེར་ཡིན་ཞུས་པ། ཀ་སར་ནས་བསམ། འབྲུ་ཁང་པོ་ག་ཟུག་ཅིག་འདུག་སྟེན་བསམ་སྟེ་ཕྱིར་ལོག་སོང་། དེ་ནས་རྒྱ་ནག་གི་སྐུ་དྲག་ཚང་མས་འབྲུ་ཁང་གི་སྒོ་ཕྱེ་སྟེ། ཀ་སར་ལ་ལྟ་བཙུགས་པ། ཀ་སར་ནས་མགོ་ཐུར་ལ་བཏང་སྟེ་ལྟས་པ་སང་། མི་ཚང་མས་ཀ་སར་ཕངས་བཏངས། དེ་འབྲུ་ཁང་ནང་དུ་འབྲུ་དཀར་ལྷམ་བུ། འབྲུ་ནག་ལྷམ་བུ། འབྲུ་གསེར་ལྷམ་བུ་གསུམ་ཡོད་ཚུག་པས། ཀ་སར་དེའི་ནང་དུ་བསླིབ་པ། འབྲུ་དཀར་ལྷམ་བུ་བསད་དེ་སྟན་ལ་བཏིངས། འབྲུ་ནག་ལྷམ་བུ་བཤད་དེ་སྐས་ལ་བཙུགས། འབྲུ་གསེར་ལྷམ་བུ་བསད་དེ་གོས་ལ་གོནས། དེ་ནས་ཀ་སར་ནས་ས་དོང་ནང་ནས་གླུ་འདི་ལྟར་བླངས།།

འབྲུ་དཀར་ལྷུམ་བུ་བསད་དེ་སྟོན་ལ་བཙུགས་ཡོད།
འབྲུ་དཀར་ལྷུམ་བུ་བ་སང་དྲོན་མོ་མི་ཡུལ་ལ་མེད་ལོ།
འབྲུ་ཤ་མཚོགས་སེ་ཞིམ་པོ་མི་ཡུལ་ལ་མི་འདུག།
འབྲུ་ནག་ལྷུམ་བུ་བསད་དེ་སྐྱས་ལ་བཙུགས་དེ་ཡོད།
འབྲུ་ནག་ལྷུམ་བུ་སང་དྲོན་མོ་མིའི་ཡུལ་ལ་མེད།
འབྲུ་ཤ་མཚོགས་སེ་བྲོད་ཅན་མི་ཡུལ་འཁོར་ནང་མེད་ལོ།
འབྲུ་གསེར་ལྷུམ་བུ་བསད་དེ་གོས་ལ་གོན་ཡོད།
འབྲུ་གསེར་ལྷུམ་བུ་བ་སང་དྲོན་མོ་མི་ཡུལ་ལ་མེད།
འབྲུ་ཤ་མཚོགས་སེ་ཞིམ་པོ་མི་ཡུལ་འཁོར་ནང་མེད་ལོ།
དེ་ཐུག་སྐྱིད་པོ་ཞིག་གླིང་ཡུལ་ལ་ཡང་མེད་ལ།།

ཀ་སར་ནས་དེ་ཐུག་གླུ་བཏངས་པ། མི་ཚང་མ་ཡམ་ཚན་སོང་སྟེ་ཟེརས་པ། ཀ་སར་མ་ཤི་བ། གླུ་བཏང་ངེན་ཞིག་རག། ད་ཁོ་ག་ཐུག་ལ་བསད་ཡིན་ཟེར་ཏེ་གྲབས་བཅོས། དེ་ནས་ཀ་སར་ལ་རྫོང་གི་ནང་དུ་རྡོ་བ་རྩུབ་ལ་བཏང་ཙེས་ལ་ཁ་བཙམས་པས། ཨ་ནེ་བཀུར་དམར་མོ་ལ་དེ་ཐུག་ཟེར་ཙེས་ཚོར་དེ། ཀ་སར་ལ་ཟེརས་པ། ལྷ་བསམ་མེད་ཀྱི་ཀ་སར། འདི་རིང་ཁྱེ་རང་རྡོ་རྩུབ་ལ་བཏང་སྟེ་བསད་ཅན། ཁྱེ་རང་གསེར་སྤྲང་ཞིག་ལ་རྫུ་སྟེ། རྡོ་བ་གཅིག་བཏང་བ། ཁ་ཐོག་ལ་ཕིང༑ གཉིས་བཏང་བ། ཁ་ཐོག་ལ་ཐིང༑ དེ་ཐུག་བཙོ་འཛིན་ཞིག་ཕི་སྟུ་རྩུ་ཕིང་སྟེ་ཡོང་ཟེར་ཏེ་བསླབས་པ། དེ་ནས་རྒྱ་ནག་པའི་མི་མང་པོ་འདུ་སྟེ། རྡོ་བ་མང་པོ་རྒྱབ་སྟེ་ས་རྡོང་པོ་གང་སོང༑ ཀ་སར་གྱིས་ཨ་ནེ་བཀུར་དམན་མོས་ཟེར་མཁན་ནང་ལྟར་བཙོ་སྟེ་ཁ་དོག་ལ་ཕིང་ཐབ་པས།

མི་སྲུ་ལ་ཡང་མཐོང་མ་བཙུག་པར། ཀེ་སར་གླང་གི་ལྗུང་པའི་ཕྲུ་ལ་སོང་སྟེ། ངན་ཆོས་བཙོ་སྟེ་རྒྱ་ནག་པའི་ཡུལ་ལ་མཛོ་ནད་ཕོག་སྟེ་བཀགས་པོ་སོང༎

No. 4.

དེ་ནས་རྒྱ་ནག་པས་ཡང་མོ་པ་བརྒྱ་བསྡུ་སྟེ་མོ་རྒྱབས། ཅིས་པ་བརྒྱ་ཁྲིངས་དེ་ཅིས་སྐོརས་པ། རྒྱལ་པོ་ཀེ་སར་གྱི་སྐྱོན་འདུག ཁོ་ལ་བག་སྲིས་བཙོ་སྟེ་མེན་པ། ཟུར་མོ་ཕན་ཅེས་མི་འདུག་ཟེརས་པ། མི་ཚང་མ་ཡམ་མཚན་སོང་སྟེ་ཀེ་སར་རྡོ་བ་རྩུབ་ལ་བཏང་སྟེ་ཤི་ཅེས་ཡོད་ཟེརས་པ། མོ་པ་ཅིས་པ་ཚང་མས་ཀེ་སར་གླང་གི་ལྗུང་པའི་ཕྲུ་རུ་འདུག་ཟེརས། དེ་ནས་རྒྱལ་པོ་དང་སྐུ་དྲག་ཚང་མ་ལྟ་ལ་སོང། ཀེ་སར་དེ་རུ་མཚམས་ལ་ཡོད་ཚུག་པས། ཁོང་གིས་ཀེ་སར་ལ་ཞུས་པ། ཀེ་སར་ལེ། ཉེ་རང་ལ་ནར་བུ་ཅི་དགོས་མཁན་ཚང་མ་བཏང་ཡིན། རྒྱལ་མོ་གཡུའི་དཀོན་མཆོག་མོ་ཉེ་རང་ལ་ཕུལ་ཡིན་ཞུས་པ། དེ་ནས་རྒྱལ་པོ་ཀེ་སར་ཡང་མཚམས་ནང་ནས་ཐོན་སྟེ། རྒྱ་ནག་ཡུལ་ལ་སྐྱོད་པ། མཛོ་ནད་ཚང་མ་ཕན་སོང། ཞག་བཅུ་ཟམ་འདུག་སྟེ་ན། ཀེ་སར་གྱིས་ཆེན་ཟེར་དེ་ནར་བུ་རེ་དང་ རྒྱལ་མོ་གཡུའི་དཀོན་མཆོག་མོ་ཁྲིད་དེ་གླིང་ཡུལ་ལ་སྐྱོད། གླིང་ཡུལ་ལ་ཞག་གཅིག་གིས་མ་བསླེབ་པ། ལྗུག་ནག་པོ་བཙོ་སྟེ་སྟན་ནག་པོ་ཞིག་བསྟད་དེ། ཁམ་བ་ཞིག་བཙོ་སྟེ་མི་ལ་མི་ཤེས་ཅེས་བཅོས། ཛོ་ཛོ་གཡུའི་དཀོན་མཆོག་མོ་དང་ནར་བུ་ཅི་ཡོད་མཁན་ཚང་མ་ཅན་དྲའི་ནང་དུ་ཁུར་དེ་སློང་མོ་པ་བཙོ་སྟེ་སོང། དེ་ནས་ཀེ་སར་ཡུལ་གྱི་མཇུག་ལ་བསླེབ་པ། རེ་བོ་ནག་པོ་ཞིག་གི་ནང་དུ་ཛོ་ཛོ་འབྲུག་མ་ཡོད་ཚུག། ཀེ་སར་མཁར་ལ་ལྟ་ལ་སོང་པ། ཨ་གུ་ཁྲའི་ཐུང་གིས་རྟ་ལ་འོབ་ཆེན་གསུམ་བདག་སྟེ་ཡོད་ཚུག།

ཁྲི་ལ་ཁྲོག་དམར་གསུམ། ཁོ་རང་ལ་དྲི་བ་གསུམ་གཏོང་དེ་ཡོད་ཚུག། ཀ་སར་ནས་གླུབ་པ་བཅོ་སྡེ། ཁྲིའི་ཐུང་ལ་འདྲིས་པ། ལྷ་རྒྱལ་པོ་ལེ། རྒྱལ་པོ་ཚང་མས་དྲི་བ་གཅིག་མེན་ནེ་གཏོང་ན་མི་འདུག། ཉེ་རང་གིས་དྲི་བ་གསུམ་གཏོང་ཅེས་དེ་ཅི་ཡིན། རྟ་ལ་འོབ་ཆེན་གསུམ་བདག་ཅེས་དེ་ཅི་ཡིན། ཁྲི་ལ་ཁྲོག་དམར་གསུམ་བདག་ཅེས་དེ་ཅི་ཡིན་ཟེརས་པ། ཁྲིའི་ཐུང་གིས་ཟེརས་པ།།

དྲི་བ་གཅིག་ནི་ཀ་སར་རྒྱལ་པོ་ཞི་བའི་རྟགས་ཡིན།
གཅིག་ནི་གླིང་མཁར་ང་རང་ལ་ཐོབ་པའི་རྟགས་ཡིན།
གཅིག་ནི་ང་རང་ལ་ཐོབ་འོས་པའི་དྲི་བ་ཡིན།
རྟ་ལ་འོབ་ཆེན་གཅིག་ནི་ཀ་སར་ཞི་བའི་རྟགས་ཡིན།
གཅིག་ནི་གླིང་མཁར་ང་རང་ལ་ཐོབ་པའི་རྟགས་ཡིན།
གཅིག་ནི་རྟ་ཁོ་རང་ལ་ཐོབ་འོས་པ་ཡིན།
ཁྲི་ལ་ཁྲོག་དམར་གཅིག་ནི་ཀ་སར་ཞི་བའི་རྟགས་ཡིན།
གཅིག་ནི་ང་རང་ལ་གླིང་ཡུལ་ཐོབ་པའི་རྟགས་ཡིན།
གཅིག་ནི་ཁྲི་ཁོ་རང་ལ་ཐོབ་འོས་པ་ཡིན།

དེ་ནུབ་ཟེརས་པ། ཀ་སར་ཕྱིར་ལོག་སྡེ་ཡོངས་ནས། ཡུལ་མཇུག་ལ་འབྲུ་གུ་ཡོད་ས་རུ་ཡོང་སྡེ། བེ་ཞིག་དོང་ཟེརས་པ། ཛོ་ཛོས་བེ་ཞིག་བདང་སྡེ་ན་ཁ་བར་འདྲིས་པ། མེ་མེ་གླུབ་པ་ལེ། ཉེ་རང་ག་ནས་ཡོངས་པ་ཡིན། མེ་མེ་གླུབ་པ་དེས་ཟེརས་པ། ང་རྒྱ་ནག་ཡུལ་ནས་ཡོངས། དེ་ནས་ཛོ་ཛོ་འབྲུ་གུ་མས་འདྲིས་པ། མེ་མེ་ལེ། ཀ་སར་རྒྱལ་པོ་ཟེར་མཁན་ཞིག་ཡོད་པ། དེ་དང་མ་ཐུག་ག། གླུབ་པ་དེས་ཟེརས་པ། གླིང་ཀ་སར་རྒྱལ་པོ་ཟེར་མཁན་

ཞིག་རྒྱ་ནག་ཡུལ་ལ་ཕྱི་སོང་། རྒྱ་ནག་རྒྱལ་པོས་ཟན་དང་ཆེན་པོ་ཞིག་བཏངས། བླ་མ་ཆེན་པོ་ཀུན་ལ་སྟོང་ཚར་རེ་ཕུལས། བླ་མ་ཆུང་བ་ཀུན་ལ་བརྒྱ་ཚར་རེ་ཕུལས། གྲུབ་བ་ང་རང་ལ་ཡང་ལུག་ནག་གཅིག་དང་སྣུན་གཅིག་བཏངས་ཟེརས་པ། ཇོ་ཇོ་འབྲུ་གུ་མ་མང་པོ་ཏུ་སྐྱེ་སྤུན་སོང་། དེ་ནས་ཀེ་སར་ནས་ཇོ་ཇོ་ཏུ་ཙེས་དང་སྤུན་ཙེས་མཐོང་སྟེ། ཀེ་སར་གྱིས་དངོས་བསྟན་དེ་ཀེ་སར་ང་ཡིན་ཟེརས་པ། ཇོ་ཇོ་མང་པོ་འཐད། ཀེ་སར་ལ་སྤྲོ་ཡོང་སྟེ། རྟ་ལ་ཞོན་དེ་ཁྲའི་ཐང་ལ་རྟབ་རེད་བཏང་སྟེ་ཁྲའི་ཐང་ལ་མདུང་རྒྱབ་སྟེ་བསད་སོང་། དེ་ནས་ཀེ་སར་རྒྱལ་པོ་ཇོ་ཇོ་འབྲུ་གུ་མ། རྒྱལ་མོ་གཡུའི་དཀོན་མཆོག་མོ་ཚང་མ་མཁར་ལ་སོང་སྟེ་སྐྱིད་པོ་བཅོ་སྟེ་འདུགས། གླིང་གི་དཔའ་བོ་ཚང་མ་ཡང་མང་པོ་འཐད་སོང་།།

KESAR'S JOURNEY TO CHINA AND MARRIAGE TO gYUI dKON mCHOGMO.

Abstract of Contents.

1.

After seven kingdoms had been subdued by Kesar, he went to the hermitage near the white, black and red hill. He went there, because he could not find the road to China, and because he thought he would be able to show his [magic] power to the King of China, after having been in the hermitage for three years. Underneath the hermitage he had placed the goat *Kabulu*, and when 2½ years had elapsed, he showed his magic power to the King of China. In consequence of this, the King of China's castle went to pieces on one side, and the King himself began to suffer from heart-ache. The lot-casters and astrologers who were consulted, knew at once that the misfortune had been caused by Kesar. "Kesar must come here himself, there is no other means of curing the King!" thus they said.

The Chinese were afraid to send a man to Kesar, because he might be killed. Therefore they sent the bird *lDorre* with a letter. Although the Chinese promised to present Kesar with everything he should like to possess, he refused to go, until they would ask him through a human messenger.

Then the King of China cut his hand and mixed its blood with some earth. He formed a man and made him alive by putting in breath and sent him to Kesar. There this new creature threw the letter before Kesar and disappeared.

Because Kesar's time of sitting in the hermitage had not yet elapsed, he sent Agu *Khrai mgo Khrai thung* meanwhile. The Agu did not know the way, and when a dark fog came, he lingered somewhere on the road.

After the three years were fulfilled, Kesar killed the goat *Kabulu* and gave her flesh to the birds of prey. Then he went to father *bsTanpa* and mother *sNgonmo* and asked them to give him the following things: A basket which will hold the valleys and hills; a leather bag which will hold the deserts; a pot which holds the waters of the rivers; a bundle of sinews from lice; the blood of red beetles; one bushel of gold-dust; the red cheek of the ogress *Ronemo;* the hand of the ogre *Ragsha;* a handful of sunbeams, a handful of moonbeams, and one bushel of ashes of [burnt] silk.

Father *Thonpa* answered that he could give him all the articles required, with the exception of the cheek of the ogress and the hand of the ogre. To get these, it would be necessary to go to the cold valley and ask the hermit about them. The hermit could not give them either, but lent his copper (coloured) dogs. Whilst these dogs were away searching for the ogres, Kesar and the hermit made a pit with a window. Just when they had finished, the dogs came back, driving the ogres before them. Kesar shot his arrows out of the window and cut off the cheek and the hand of the two ogres who fled away. Then Kesar started for China.

2.

After three days Kesar arrived at a high hill, and there he found Agu *Khrai thung.* He took the shape of a traveller and asked the Agu how he had got there. The Agu answered that he was a messenger of King Kesar on his way to China, and that he had lost the way and was near starving. Kesar blamed him for having undertaken what he was unable to perform, and for having been conceited. Then he sent him back to the land of *gLing.*

After having travelled for seven more days, he arrived before a high hill and a rock, with a lake between. Although he went about for several days, he could not find the way. Then he threw off the basket which held the valleys and hills, and the pot which held the sea and the hills, and the waters disappeared.

After another three days they (Kesar and his horse) came to a sandy desert, where neither man nor horse could go, and both experienced much misery. This obstacle was removed by the bag which held the deserts.

Again after three days they came to a country with a host of lice which had no sinews. After they had eaten all the flesh of Kesar, he gave them some sinews, and then he escaped.

After three more days they came to many beetles which were without blood. When Kesar gave them some blood, he could pass without experiencing any harm.

Then, after three days, it became perfectly dark for ten days; there was a dark fog, the man was without food, and the horse without grass. Kesar cried and complained to *Ane bkur dmarmo,* that for ten days he had not seen the sun. *Ane bkur dmanmo* reminded him of his handfuls of sunbeams and moonbeams. He took them out, and the sun as well as the moon rose. When he saw the tracks of the road where he had strayed about during night, he felt astonished.

Having travelled for another three days, they discovered that the road was barred by ogres. Kesar saw the ogre whose hand he had robbed. He promised to restore the hand, if the ogre would let him pass. The ogre was pleased to receive his hand back, and showed Kesar the way. In a similar way Kesar had a free passage through the land of the ogresses, three days later, when he restored the cheek to the ogress who had none.

After three days they arrived on a glacier-pass, where icy dust was scattered over them.[1] They had great difficulties, and were obliged to go back. Then they met three poor men. Kesar gave them some gold, and they showed him the way.

When the King of China, who lived in a castle in the middle of a lake, heard that Kesar was approaching, he sent many of his men to meet him. As Kesar was gradually drawing near, the King of China's pain became less.

3.

Agu *Khrai thung*, when coming back to the land of *gLing* sent *'a Bruguma* out of the castle and gave her a black tent. He himself became king and tyrannized over the country. He wore three hats, piled one on the other, his horse had three stirrups, and his dog three red collars.

The King of China had a daughter called *γYui dkon mchogmo*. This girl wished by all means to run away with Kesar and asked leave of her father. When both went, all the riches followed after them.

The nobility did not like this, and to bring Kesar back, they pursued him and asked him how he could go away without having seen the pit of the dragons. Kesar went back, and when he was looking into the pit, the Chinese noblemen pushed him in. There were three dragons of white, black and yellow colour. Kesar killed them. The white one he used as a carpet, the black one as a pillow, and the yellow one as a dress. He ate their flesh, sang a song and was happy.

Then the Chinese tried to kill Kesar with stones, but *Ane bkur dmanmo* advised him to take the shape of a golden fly and escape. He did that and escaped, although the Chinese filled the pit with stones. Kesar went to the cold valley and practised sorcery, in consequence of which all China was smitten with leprosy.

---

[1] The Tibetan word for silk and ice is the same (*dar.*) According to the Tibetan text it looks almost as if Kesar himself was scattering the dust about.

4.

The Chinese found out, with the help of their magicians, that Kesar was the source of the illness and that he was sitting in the cold valley. They sent an embassy to him and offered him all their treasures and the queen *γYui dkon mchogmo.* Therefore Kesar left the hermitage and went to China. This stopped the leprosy; but he did not stay for longer than ten days and returned to the *gLing* land together with many treasures and *γYui dkon mchogmo.*

One day before arriving at *gLing* he made a black sheep, put on a black carpet, took the disguise of a vagabond and put the queen and all his treasures in his pocket. He found *'a Bruguma* in a black tent and Agu *Khrai thung* on the throne with his three hats, etc. He asked him what was the meaning of his three hats, three stirrups and three collars for the dog. *Khrai thung* said that always the first of the three articles was a sign that Kesar had died; the second a sign that the castle of *gLing* had come into the Agu's possession; and the third was for ordinary use.

Kesar went back to *a'Bruguma* in his disguise; and *a'Bruguma* who took him for a travelling monk from China, asked him if he could not give her some news of Kesar. He answered that Kesar had died in China, and that the King of China on the occasion of his death had given presents to the lamas: 1000 (Rs.?) to the great monks, 100 (Rs.?) to the little monks, and a black sheep and a carpet to him. *a'Bruguma* cried and fainted. Now Kesar showed his true self to the lady. Then he pursued Agu *Khrai thung* and killed him with a spear. Kesar went with his two wives to the *gLing* castle and lived there in happiness. Also the Agus were greatly pleased.

NOTES.

In my first brief sketch of Kesar's journey to China (*rGya Nag*), in Mémoires de la Société Finno-Ougrienne, No. XV, 2, p. II, III, I made the remark that this episode of the Kesar Saga was probably a winter myth. Looking at the version as contained in the preceding pages, I cannot help believing that there are a great number of passages in the Saga which allow themselves of being explained as parables of the winter. If a number of passages cannot be explained with the help of the seasons, all the same, we must not forget that the Kesar Saga, as we have it now, is not the original Kesar Saga, as it was shaped by the ancient men of *gLing*; but that we possess it in the form into which it has grown in the course of many centuries, nay, thousands of years. I wish to draw attention to the following passages, which according to my view speak in favor of a winter myth, forming the basis of the Saga :—

(*a*) The baskets and bags which hold the waters and hills (probably heaps of snow and ice and the melting snow). People might have explained in this way the disappearance of ice and snow at the approach of the spring-god.

(*b*) The bloodless beetles and the lice without sinews might be the snowflakes and hail-stones. They are changed into ordinary beetles and lice by Kesar in spring (he gives them blood and sinews). The unpleasant perception of the extreme cold in winter reminded the men of *gLing* of the sting of lice during summer.

(*c*) The red cheek of the ogress which is stolen may be explained in this way: The ogress is the personification of a mountain, the top of which glows like red fire in the rays of the sun during summer. During winter the morning and evening sun may never touch it, and thus the red cheek is stolen. But as the giants are chased about, it would perhaps be easier still to take them for personifications of clouds.

(*d*) Kesar's crooked way to China (*rGya nag* = the black extent) may have been suggested by the spiral-like downward course of the sun during winter. That the ornament is probably an illustration of Kesar's route, is suggested by the Ladakhi name of the ornament, *rgya srang*, which is understood to mean 'Chinese street,' not 'broad street' or 'Indian street,' which are other possible translations.

(*e*) The fact that Kesar has not seen the sun for ten days occurs here in many places during winter. There are many valleys, to the bottom of which the rays of the sun do not attain at all for even a longer period.

(*f*) It is also remarkable that the whole of China is smitten with leprosy, which illness is removed by Kesar's advance towards China. This may point to snow.

The story of Kesar's marriage to *γYui dkon mchogmo*, shows in particular the close relationship between Kesar and *Srong btsan sgampo.* That Kesar's two wives are representatives of the two colours, white and blue (or green), as is also the case with *Srong btsan sgampo's* wives, is shown in the first case by the name *γYui dkon mchogmo*, which means 'the turquoise goddess.' She stands for the blue and green colours. *'aBruguma* stands for the white colour as is shown by *gLing glu* of *Phyang*, No. IV. It may be added that the Mongolian version of Kesar's journey to China has not much in common with the Lower Ladakhi version.

VOCABULARY AND COMMENTS.

1.

ཀ་བུ་ལུ། *kabulu*, perhaps more correctly *khabulu* [animals] with a black and white mouth.

ཕྱེད་འང་གཉིས། *phyed 'ang γnyis*, one and half; how is the *'ang* to be explained in these cases?

མིན་པ། *minba*, = *ma yinpar*, besides; unless.

བྱ་མོ་ལྡོར་རེ། *byamo ldorre*, name of a bird.

མུལ། *mul*=*dngul*, silver.

འདངས་ཅས། *'adangscas*, recover.

རུ་ཅས། *rucas*, knead.

མུན་འཁོར། *mun 'akhor*, mist; dark fog.

ལུངས། *lungs*, = *lung*, valley; cultivated district.

ཕུག་ཙེལ། *phug tsel*, basked.

ལྩངས་པོ། *ltsangspo*, = *γtsangpo*, river.

གསེར་ཕེ། *γser phe*, gold dust (literally gold flour).

རོ་ནེ་མོ། *ronemo*, name of an ogress; is said to mean 'corpse-eater.'

རག་ཤ། *ragsha*, name of an ogre; this is probably the Indian रचस।

བྱ་ཞིན། *bya zhin*, offering, gift to birds; the original form is *bya sbyin*. It means that Kesar gave the flesh of the goat to birds of prey.

In Mémoires de la Société Finno-Ougrienne, No. XV, 2, p. 66, I said that Laws of Sound No. 1. (see Sketch of Ladakhi Grammar, J.A.S.B., Vol. LXX, Part I, Extra No. 2, p. 5) ought to have been given in full, in this form: s + c = sh, s + j = zh, s + ts = s, s + dz = z. It must be added that the *s* may always be replaced by *r* or *l*, even by the prefixes *b*, *γ*, *d*, if they are pronounced as *r* or *s*. Starting with *bya sbyin* = *bya sjin* = *bya zhin*, which illustrates the formula s + j = zh, I shall now give those examples, illustrative of the rule, which have occurred to me during the edition of the Kesar Saga :—

s (or *l*, *r*, etc.,) + *j* = zh.

ljogs becomes *zhogs* or *γzhogs* ; *'ajogpa* has *bzhag* as its perfect stem, and *'ajugpa—zhugs* ; in both cases the *b* prefix of the perfect stem seems to have caused the change of *j* to *zh* (although it is no more written in *zhugs*). Here also *sbyin* = *sjin* = *zhin*, *sbyar* = *sjar* = *zhar* and similar cases must be mentioned.

s (or *l*, *r*, etc.,) + ts = s.

rtsogpo becomes *sogpo* ; *rtsab bzang* becomes *sab bzang* ; the classical words *γnyid sad* and *nyams sad* have their ancient prototypes in the Lower Ladakhi forms *γnyid* (*b*) *tsad* and *nyams* (*b*) *tsad*. Thus the *s* of *sad* is the result of the work of a prefix on *ts*.

s (or *l*, *r*, etc.,) + dz = z.

rdzing becomes *zing* ; *skyer rdzong* becomes *ker zong* ; *rdzama* becomes *zama* ; in *mgo zugcas* instead of *mgo 'adzugcas* we may suspect the influence of a prefix on the original *dz*, which in this case did not become *ts*, as a secondary form has it. There are several parallel cases to this.

འགྲམ་མཚལ། *'agram mthsal*, red cheek.

ཡབས་ཐོན་པ། *yabs thonpa*, is often spelled *yabs stonpa* ; probably the concluding *s* of the first syllable was pronounced with the second, and instead of the impossible *sthonpa*, *stonpa* was written.

2.

ཁ་བར། *khabar*, news ; it is the Urdu khabar.

ཁམ་པ། *khampa* = *khamspa*, man of Khams ; is used for every traveller, even a vagabond.

བཀའ་སྐྱོན། *bkā skyon*=*bkā bkyon*, rebuke.

ཁྲུ་ཐུང། *khru thung* instead of *Khra thung*; this may be a case of assimilation to the last syllable.

ནག། *nag*, misery, great strain; *nag mthongba*, to suffer much.

སྐྱལ་བ། *skyalba*=*skyelba*, cause [harm].

རྗེས་པོ། *rjespo*, track.

ཁྲོ་ལ། *khrola*=*khrodla*, among, in the crowd.

ལམ་པ། *lampa*, guard (of a road); sentinel.

རིམ་པ་བཞིན་དུ། *rimpa bzhindu*, here in the sense of 'by and by.'

3.

རེ་བོ། *rebo*=*regur*, tent of yak's hair. This kind of tent shows that this version of the Saga may belong to a tribe in the east of Ladakh, because the Ladakhis do not make use of such tents.

སྤུབ་ཅས། *spubcas*, to put up [a tent]; literally 'turn over'; perhaps because the tent has to be turned about in many directions before the work is finished.

ཏི་བི། *tibi*, hat.

རྩག་ཅས། *rtsagcas*, to pile up; probably causative of *'adzegpa*, to climb.

འོབ་ཆེན། *'obchen*=*yob chen*, stirrup.

ཁྲོག་དམར། *khrog dmar*, red collar; *khrog* seems to mean 'throat' originally.

ཧུ་ཀུམ། *hukum*, order, commandment; it is the Urdu *hukm*.

དགོངས་པ་ཞུ་ཅས། *dgongspa zhucas*, ask for leave.

གཡུའི་དཀོན་མཆོག་མོ། *gyui dkon mchogmo*, turquoise goddess; name of the King of China's daughter.

རྡ་སྟེ། *rdaste*, prosecuting; probably the same as *bdaste*, chasing.

སྐུ་དྲག། *sku drag*, nobility.

ལྡུམ་བུ། *ldumbu*, occurs in the names of the three dragons (*'abu*) as well as in that of an Agu; what it means in this connection I have not yet found out.

སྙས། *snyas, sngas*, = pillow.

བྲོད་ཅན། *brodcan*, savoury.

4.

ཅན་དྲ། *candra*, pocket.

ནང་དུ། *nangdu*, in, inside; this form is used here in many places, where the colloquial has *nangna*; simply to imitate the classical, or, more correctly, the Central Tibetan language.

གྲུབ་པ། *grubpa*, fulfiller [of the law]; title of monks.

མེན་ནེ། *menne* = *mannas*, besides.

ཟན་ཏང། *zan tang*, perhaps more correctly *zan btang*, a meal in honour of a dead person.

ཚར། *thsar* = *thser*, once, one turn; *stong thsar re* means: he gave 1000 [Rs.] each turn to each (of the lamas).

མུན་ཅས། *muncas*, to faint.

རྡབ་དེད། *rdab ded*, prosecution on horseback. This compound makes it probable that the perfect tense of *'adedpa*, prosecute, had a *b* prefix originally.

No. 1.

༄༅།། དེ་ནས་ལོ་གཅིག་གཉིས་སོང་སྟེ་ན། ཀེ་སར་གླང་གི་ཁྱུང་པའི་ནང་དུ་མཚམས་ལ་བཞུགས། ལོ་གཅིག་སོང་སྟེ་ན། ཨ་ནེ་བཀུར་དམན་རྒྱལ་མོ་མཚམས་ཁང་གི་སྒོ་ལ་སོང་སྟེ། གླུ་འདི་ལྟར།།

འོ་ན་ཨ་ནེ་བའི་ཚ་བོས་ཨ་ནེའི་དངོས་ལ་ཉེན་དང།
གླིང་ཀེ་སར་རྒྱལ་པོས་ཨ་ནེའི་བདག་ལ་གསན་དང།
ད་ལོ་འི་ལོ་ལ་ཚ་བོ་མཚམས་ལ་འདུག་པ་མི་ཉན་ལོ།
འདིའི་ལོ་ལ་ཀེ་སར་མཚམས་ལ་འདུག་པ་མི་ཉན་ལོ།
ད་ལོ་བདུད་ཀྱི་ལོ་ཁམས་མི་ལ་ཡོད་ལོ།
ཁྲུབ་པ་ལག་རིངས་ཀྱི་ལོ་ཁམས་མི་ལ་ཡོད།
ཚ་བོ་ཉི་རི་ལོ་ཁམས་ཀླུ་ཁམས་རིག་ཡིན་ལོ།
ལྷའི་བུ་ཀེ་སར་གྱི་ལོ་ཁམས་ཀླུ་ཁམས་རིག་ཡིན།
མི་ལ་ཀླུ་ཞིག་ཕྲུག་ན་ཤི་ཅེས་ཤིག་ཡིན་ལོ།
མི་སྒྲ་ཀླུ་ཡིས་བསད་པ་ཉན་ཅེས་ཤིག་ཡིན་ལོ།
ནང་མོ་བདུད་ཀྱི་ལོ་ཁམས་ཀླུ་ལ་ཡོད་ལོ།
རྫིང་མ་ལོ་ལ་བདུད་ཀྱི་ལོ་ཁམས་ཀླུ་ལ་ཡིན་ལོ།
ཚ་བོ་ཉི་རི་ལོ་ཁམས་མི་ལ་ཨོད་ལོ།
ལྷའི་བུ་ཀེ་སར་གྱི་ལོ་ཁམས་མི་ཁམས་ལ་ཡིན།

ད་ལོ་བདུད་མ་བདུལ་ན་བཙོ་ཐབས་རིག་མེད་ལོ།
ད་ལོ་བདུད་མ་ཞི་ན་ནང་མོ་ཚ་བོ་ཉེ་རང་ཞི་ཡིན་ལོ།
ཚ་བོ་མཚམས་ལ་མ་ཞུགས་བདུད་བདུལ་བ་ལ་ཐིང་སྟེ་སྐྱོད་ལོ།

དེ་ཟུག་ཟེར་ས་པ་སང་ཀ་སར་གྱིས་བསམ། ང་མཚམས་ལ་འདུག་ཙེས་ལ་ཨ་ནེ་བཀུར་དམན་མོ་མ་འཐད་པ་ཡིན་ནོག། ང་སི་ཆ་བསམ་སྟེ་མཚམས་ཁང་ནས་མ་ཐིང་བ་འདུགས་པས། ཞག་བདུན་སོང་སྟེ། ཨ་ནེ་བཀུར་དམན་མོ་ཡང་མཚམས་སྒོ་ཏུ་ཡོང་སྟེ་གླུ་འདི་ལྟར།།

བླ་ཨ་ནེ་སི་ཚ་བོ་བསམ་མེད་ཁྱོད་ཨ་ནེའི་དངོས་ལ་ཉེན་དང་།
བླ་ལྷའི་བུ་ཀ་སར་གྱིས་བཀུར་དམན་མོ་འི་བདག་ལ་གསན་ལོ།
ཁྱོད་མཚམས་ལ་འདུག་སྟེ་གླིང་གི་མགོ་རི་ཞིག་མི་ལྡན་ལོ།
ཁྱོད་མཚམས་བཅད་བཏངས་སྟེ་གླིང་བཞི་གྱ་བརྒྱད་ག་ཟུག་ལ་དོན་ཡིན།
ད་ལོ་བདུད་མ་བསད་ན་ནང་མོ་ཁྱོ་རང་ཞི་ཙེས་རིག་ཡིན་ལོ།
ཁྱོ་རང་མཚམས་ལ་མ་འདུག་ཐིང་སྟེ་རིག་ཡོང་ལོ།

ཨ་ནེས་དེ་ཟུག་ཟེར་དེ་ཁ་སླེས་པ་སང་། ཀ་སར་གྱིས་ཨ་ནེ་བདེན་བསམ་སྟེ། མཚམས་ཁང་ནས་ཐིང་སྟེ་གླིང་མཁར་དུ་སྐྱོད། དེར་སྐྱོད་དེ་ཛོ་ཛོ་འབྲུག་མ་ལ་དེ་ཚང་མའི་གནས་ཚུལ་ཞིབ་ཆ་བཤད་དེ་ཀ་སར་གྱིས་གླུ་ཞིག་སླངས་སོ།

ངའི་ཛོ་ཛོ་ས་དངོས་ཞིག་ལ་གསན་དང་།
ཛོ་ཛོ་འབྲུག་མས་བདག་ཙིག་ལ་གསན་ལོ།

ད་ལོ་ང་བདུད་ཡུལ་ལ་ཆ་དགོས་བྱུང་ལོ།
བདུད་ཁྲ་བ་ལག་རིངས་བདུལ་བ་ཞིག་ཆེན་ལོ།
ད་ལོ་བདུད་ཀྱི་ལོ་ཁམས་མི་ཁམས་རིག་ཡིན་ལོ།
བྱུ་ཚ་ང་རི་ལོ་ཁམས་ནི་རྒྱ་ཁམས་ལ་ཡོད་ལོ།
མི་ལ་རྒྱ་ཞིག་ཐྲུག་པ་ཞིག་ཆེན་ལོ།

མི་ལ་རྒྱ་ཞིག་བཏང་ན་ཤི་ཅེས་རིག་ཡིན།
ནང་མོ་བདུད་ཀྱི་ལོ་ཁམས་རྒྱ་ཁམས་ཡིན་ལོ།
ངའི་ལོ་ཁམས་མི་ཁམས་རིག་ཡིན་ལོ།
ནང་མོ་བདུད་ཀྱིས་མི་ལ་རྒྱ་ཞིག་ཐྲུག་ཡིན་འགྲོ།
ད་ལོ་བདུད་མ་བསད་ན་ནང་མོ་བདུད་ཀྱིས་ང་བསད་ཡིན།

སྒྲ་དང་སྒྲ་རྒྱུང་སྒྲོ་དེ་ཙུ་ཕིང་ལོ།
སྒྲོ་ལ་ཕིང་སྟེ་ལན་གསུམ་རིག་སྐྱུག་ལོ།
མཚོ་མོ་འི་མཐིལ་ན་རྒྱ་སྐྱུག་རིག་དོང་ལོ།
ཙན་དན་དམར་པོ་འི་བསངས་ཤུག་རིག་བདུག་ལོ།

ཙུ་ཙུ་བཟང་པོ་འི་སྒྲིད་དེ་སྒྲོ་ལ་ཕིང་ལོ།
སྒྲོ་ལ་ཕིང་སྟེ་ལན་གསུམ་རིག་སྐྱུག་ལོ།
མཚོ་མོའི་མཐིལ་ན་རྒྱ་སྐྱུག་རིག་དོང་ལོ།
ཙན་དན་དམར་པོའི་བསངས་ཤུག་རིག་བདུག་ལོ།

སྤུ་རིག་བཟང་པོའི་མགོ་ཐུར་སྒོ་ལ་ཕྱིང་ལོ།
སྒོ་ལ་ཕྱིང་སྐྱེ་ལན་གསུམ་རིག་སྒྲུག་ལོ།
མཆོ་མོ འི་མཐིལ་ན་རྒྱ་སྒྲུག་རིག་རྡོང་ལོ།
ཙན་དན་དམར་པོའི་བསངས་ཤུག་བདུག་ལོ།

གསེར་རང་བརྡུངས་ཀྱི་འོབ་ཆེན་སྒོ་ལ་ཕྱིང་ལོ།
སྒོ་ལ་ཕྱིང་སྐྱེ་ལན་གསུམ་རིག་སྒྲུག་ལོ།
མཆོ་མོའི་མཐིལ་ན་རྒྱ་སྒྲུག་རིག་རྡོང་ལོ།
ཙན་དན་དམར་པོའི་བསངས་ཤུག་བདུག་ལོ།

པད་མ་ཅན་དོ་སྒོམ་སྒོ་དེ་རུ་ཕྱིང་ལོ།
སྒོ་དེ་ལ་ཕྱིང་སྐྱེ་ལན་གསུམ་རིག་སྒྲུག་ལོ།
མཆོ་མོའི་མཐིལ་ན་རྒྱ་སྒྲུག་རིག་རྡོང་ལོ།
ཙན་དན་དམར་པོའི་བསངས་ཤུག་བདུག་ལོ།

བརྒྱ་དང་བརྒྱད་བཅུ་བཏངས་པའི་ཞུར་ལེ་དེ་སྒོ་ལ་ཕྱིང་ལོ།
སྒོ་ལ་ཕྱིང་སྐྱེ་ལན་གསུམ་རིག་སྒྲུག་ལོ།
མཆོ་མོའི་མཐིལ་ན་རྒྱ་སྒྲུག་རིག་རྡོང་ལོ།
ཙན་དན་དམར་པོའི་བསངས་ཤུག་བདུག་ལོ།

དངུལ་རང་བཅོས་པའི་ཁ་སྦབས་སྒོ་ལ་ཕྱིང་ལོ།
སྒོ་ལ་ཕྱིང་སྐྱེ་ལན་གསུམ་སྒྲུག་ལོ།

མཚོ་མོའི་མཐིལ་ན་ཆུ་སྐྱུག་རིག་དོང་ལོ།
ཙན་དན་དམར་པོའི་བསངས་ཤུག་བདུག་ལོ།

མག་མལ་ལི་རྦུ་ཞྭ་སྒོ་ལ་ཕྱིང་ལོ།
སྒོ་ལ་ཕྱིང་སྤེ་ལན་གསུམ་སྐྱུག་ལོ།
མཚོ་མོའི་མཐིལ་ན་ཆུ་སྐྱུག་རིག་དོང་ལོ།
ཙན་དན་དམར་པོའི་བསངས་ཤུག་བདུག་ལོ།

གོས་ཆེན་དར་ཡུག་སྒོ་ལ་ཕྱིང་ལོ།
སྒོ་ལ་ཕྱིང་སྤེ་ལན་གསུམ་སྐྱུག་ལོ།
མཚོ་མོའི་མཐིལ་ན་ཆུ་སྐྱུག་རིག་དོང་ལོ།
ཙན་དན་དམར་པོའི་བསངས་ཤུག་བདུག་ལོ།

པད་ཀའི་སྐྱི་རགས་སྒོ་ལ་ཕྱིང་ལོ།
སྒོ་ལ་ཕྱིང་སྤེ་ལན་གསུམ་རིག་སྐྱུག་ལོ།
མཚོ་མོའི་མཐིལ་ན་ཆུ་སྐྱུག་རིག་དོང་ལོ།
ཙན་དན་དམར་པོའི་བསངས་ཤུག་བདུག་ལོ།

འབན་དུམ་ཙ་དར་སྒོ་ལ་ཕྱིང་ལོ།
སྒོ་ལ་ཕྱིང་སྤེ་ལན་གསུམ་རིག་སྐྱུག་ལོ།
མཚོ་མོའི་མཐིལ་ན་ཆུ་སྐྱུག་རིག་དོང་ལོ།
ཙན་དན་དམར་པོའི་བསངས་ཤུག་བདུག་ལོ།

དུང་ཡོ་བ་ཡི་ཅག་སྒོ་ལ་ཕིང་ལོ།

སྒོ་ལ་ཕིང་སྤེ་ལན་གསུམ་རིག་སྐྱུག་ལོ།

མཚོ་མོའི་མཐིལ་ན་ཆུ་སྐྱུག་དིང་ལོ།

ཅན་དན་དམར་པོའི་བསང་ཤུག་བདུག་ལོ།

མཁའ་བཟོ་མ་ཀ་གུ་སྒོ་དེ་ལ་ཕིང་ལོ།

སྒོ་ལ་ཕིང་སྤེ་ཡན་གསུམ་རིག་སྐྱུག་ལོ།

མཚོ་མོའི་མཐིལ་ན་ཆུ་སྐྱུག་རིག་དིང་ལོ།

ཅན་དན་དམར་པོའི་བསངས་ཤུག་བདུག་ལོ།

རྗེ་བ་ཆོད་མ་རལ་གྲི་སྒོ་དེ་ལ་ཕིང་ལོ།

སྒོ་ལ་ཕིང་སྤེ་ལན་གསུམ་རིག་སྐྱུག་ལོ།

མཚོ་མོའི་མཐིལ་ན་ཆུ་སྐྱུག་རིག་དིང་ལོ།

ཅན་དན་དམར་པོའི་བསངས་ཤུག་བདུག་ལོ།

གནམ་འཁྲིད་མ་ཕ་ལི་སྒོ་ལ་ཕིང་ལོ།

སྒོ་ལ་ཕིང་སྤེ་ལན་གསུམ་སྐྱུག་ལོ།

མཚོ་མོའི་མཐིལ་ན་ཆུ་སྐྱུག་རིག་དིང་ལོ།

ཅན་དན་དམར་པོའི་བསངས་ཤུག་བདུག་ལོ།

དེ་ཞི་ལི་ཙ་མག་སྒོ་དེ་ལ་ཕིང་ལོ།

སྒོ་དེ་ལ་ཕིང་སྤེ་ལན་གསུམ་རིག་སྐྱུག་ལོ།

མཚོ་མོའི་མཐིལ་ན་ཆུ་སྐྲུག་རིག་དོང་ལོ།
ཙན་དན་དམར་པོའི་བསངས་ཤུག་བདུག་ལོ།

པོར་གར་རི་སྨན་རྩམ་སྒོ་དེ་ལ་ཕེང་ལོ།
སྒོ་དེ་ལ་ཕེང་སྤྱི་ལན་གསུམ་རིག་སྐྲུག་ལོ།
མཚོ་མོའི་མཐིལ་ན་ཆུ་སྐྲུག་རིག་དོང་ལོ།
ཙན་དན་དམར་པོའི་བསངས་ཤུག་བདུག་ལོ།

རོང་ཡུལ་ལི་དུ་བག་སྒོ་དེ་ལ་ཕེང་ལོ།
སྒོ་དེ་ལ་ཕེང་སྤྱི་ལན་གསུམ་རིག་སྐྲུག་ལོ།
མཚོ་མོའི་མཐིལ་ན་ཆུ་སྐྲུག་རིག་དོང་ལོ།
ཙན་དན་དམར་པོའི་བསངས་ཤུག་བདུག་ལོ།

མི་ཁར་བཅོ་བརྒྱད་ཀྱི་སག་སྟག་སྒོ་ལ་ཕེང་ལོ།
སྒོ་ལ་ཕེང་སྤྱི་ལན་གསུམ་རིག་སྐྲུག་ལོ།
མཚོ་མོའི་མཐིལ་ན་ཆུ་སྐྲུག་རིག་གདོང་ལོ།
ཙན་དན་དམར་པོའི་བསངས་ཤུག་བདུག་ལོ།

དེ་ཟུག་ཟེརས་པ། ཇོ་ཇོས་ཆོར་ལ་ཕེངས་པ། ཞག་བདུན་ལ་མེན་ནེ་ཕེང་མ་ཚར། དེ་ཚང་མ་ཕེང་ཚར་ར་དང་། སརྗོ་བ་རི་རབས་ཚང་མ་འགལ་ཅེས་མཐོང་སོང་། དེ་ནས་ཇོ་ཇོ་ལ་ཆོར་ཀ་མང་པོ་ཨོང་སྤྱི་ཀ་སར་ལ་གླུ་འདི་ལྟར།།

གླིང་རྒྱལ་ལྷམ་ཆེན་མོས་དངོས་ཤིག་ལ་གསན་དང་།
ལྷའི་བུ་ཀ་སར་གྱིས་བདག་ཅིག་ལ་གསན་དང་།

གནམ་སྟོད་མཐོན་པོ་ཀུན་མ་བཞུགས་བྱུང་དེ་ལ་སྐྱོད་ན།
ཉི་ཟླ་གཉིས་ཀྱི་གློ་གདང་སུ་ཞིག་ལ་ཡིན་ལོ།

གངས་སྟོད་མཐོན་པོ་མ་བཞུགས་བྱུང་དེ་ལ་སྐྱོད་ན།
སེང་གེ་གཡུ་རལ་གྱི་གློ་གདང་སུ་ཞིག་ལ་ཡིན་ལོ།

བྲག་སྟོད་མཐོན་པོ་མ་བཞུགས་བྱུང་དེ་ལ་སྐྱོད་ན།
སྤྲིན་ཆེན་པ་ཤན་གྱི་གློ་གདང་སུ་ཞིག་ལ་ཡིན་ལོ།

སྤང་སྟོད་མཐོན་པོ་ཀུན་མ་བཞུགས་བྱུང་དེ་ལ་སྐྱོད་ན།
འབྲོང་ཆེན་ཁམས་པའི་གློ་གདང་སུ་ཞིག་ལ་ཡིན་ལོ།

མཚོམ་སྟོད་མཐོན་པོ་ཀུན་མ་བཞུགས་བྱུང་དེ་ལ་སྐྱོད་ན།
ཉ་མོ་གསེར་མིག་གི་གློ་གདང་སུ་ཞིག་ལ་ཡིན་ལོ།

ཐང་སྟོད་མཐོན་པོ་ཀུན་མ་བཞུགས་བྱུང་དེ་ལ་སྐྱོད་ན།
ཤང་ཀུ་མཐུག་ཧུམ་གྱི་གློ་གདང་སུ་ཞིག་ལ་ཡིན་ལོ།

ལུང་པ་ཆེན་མོ་མ་བཞུགས་བྱུང་དེ་ལ་སྐྱོད་ན།
ལྷ་མོ་འབྲུལ་ལི་ཡི་གློ་གདང་སུ་ཞིག་ལ་ཡིན་ལོ།

རྩ་ཤིང་ནགས་ཚལ་མ་བཞུགས་བྱུང་དེ་ལ་སྐྱོད་ན།
བྱ་དང་བྱིའུ་ཡི་གློ་གདང་སུ་ཞིག་ལ་ཡིན་ལོ།

རྒྱལ་ལྷམ་ཀེ་སར་མ་བཞུགས་བྱུང་དེ་ལ་སྐྱོད་ན།
ཇོ་ཇོ་འབྲུ་གུ་མའི་གློ་གདག་སུ་ཞིག་ལ་ཡིན་ལོ།

གླིང་མཁར་རྩེ་དགུ་མ་བཞུགས་བྱུང་དེ་ལ་སྐྱོད་ན།
ལྷེམ་ལྷེམ་གྱི་ལྷེམ་མཁར་གྱི་གློ་གདང་སྒུ་ཞིག་ལ་ཡིན་ལོ།

ཀྱང་གོད་དབྱེར་པ་ཀུན་མ་བཞུགས་བྱུང་དེ་ཙ་སྐྱོད་ན།
གོད་མ་ཚ་ལངས་ཀྱི་གློ་གདང་སྒུ་ཞིག་ལ་ཡིན་ལོ།

མཛོ་པོ་ཀང་དཀར་ཀུན་མ་བཞུགས་བྱུང་དེ་ཙ་སྐྱོད་ན།
མཛོ་མོ་ཙ་ཡོན་གྱི་གློ་གདང་སྒུ་ཞིག་ལ་ཡིན་ལོ།

རྒྱ་བོང་ཁ་དཀར་ཀུན་མ་བཞུགས་བྱུང་དེ་ཙ་སྐྱོད་ན།
བོང་མོ་ཁམ་པའི་གློ་གདང་སྒུ་ཞིག་ལ་ཡིན་ལོ།

རྩེད་བུ་སྐྱེ་དམར་ཀུན་མ་བཞུགས་བྱུང་དེ་ཙ་སྐྱོད་ན།
ར་མ་དཀར་མོའི་གློ་གདང་སྒུ་ཞིག་ལ་ཡིན་ལོ།

པོ་ལགས་མགོ་གསེར་མ་བཞུགས་བྱུང་དེ་ལ་སྐྱོད་ན།
མ་མོ་ཁམ་པའི་གློ་གདང་སྒུ་ཞིག་ལ་ཡིན་ལོ།

ཁྲི་པོ་གསེར་ལིང་མ་བཞུགས་བྱུང་དེ་ཙ་སྐྱོད་ན།
ཁྲི་མོ་ལྗོམ་དཀར་གྱི་གློ་གདང་སྒུ་ཞིག་ལ་ཡིན་ལོ།

བི་ལ་ནག་ཆུང་ཀུན་མ་བཞུགས་བྱུང་དེ་ཙ་སྐྱོད་ན།
བི་མོ་ཁྲ་སུག་གི་གློ་གདང་སྒུ་ཞིག་ལ་ཡིན་ལོ།

ཇོ་ཇོས་དེ་ཟླུག་ཞུས་པ། ཀ་སར་གྲིས་ལན་དུ་གླུ་འདི་ལྟར་བཏངས་སོ།

ངའི་ཇོ་ཇོ་ཁྲོད་དངོས་ཤིག་ལ་ཉོན་དང་།

ཇོ་ཇོ་འབྲུ་གུ་མས་ངའི་བདག་ལ་གསན་དང་།

གནམ་སྟོད་མཐོན་པོ་ཀུན་མ་བཞུགས་བྱུང་དེ་ཙུ་སྐྱོད་ན།

སྤྲིན་དོ་གོམ་ཟམ་ཞིག་ཞུགས་ཉིད་ལ་བཞུགས།

ཉི་ཟླ་གཉིས་ཀྱི་གློ་གདང་ཁོ་དེ་ལ་ཡིན་ལོ།

གངས་སྟོད་མཐོན་པོ་མ་བཞུགས་བྱུང་དེ་ལ་སྐྱོད་ན།

གངས་སེ་ལོང་ཟམ་ཞིག་ཞུགས་ཉིད་ལ་བཞུགས།

སེང་གེ་གཡུ་རལ་གྱི་གློ་གདང་ཁ་དེ་ལ་ཡིན་ལོ།

བྲག་སྟོད་མཐོན་པོ་མ་བཞུགས་བྱུང་དེ་ལ་སྐྱོད་ན།

བྲག་པར་ཕུར་ཟམ་ཞིག་ཞུགས་ཉིད་ལ་བཞུགས།

སྐྱིན་ཆེན་བ་ཤན་གྱི་གློ་གདང་ཁ་དེ་ལ་ཡིན་ལོ།

སྤྱང་སྟོད་མཐོན་པོ་མ་བཞུགས་བྱུང་དེ་ཙུ་སྐྱོད་ན།

སྤྱང་དོ་གོམ་ཟམ་ཞིག་ཞུགས་ཉིད་ལ་བཞུགས་ལོ།

འབྲོང་ཆེན་ཁམ་པའི་གློ་གདང་ཁོ་ཀུན་ལ་ཡིན་ལོ།

མཚོམ་སྟོད་མཐོན་པོ་ཀུན་མ་བཞུགས་བྱུང་དེ་ལ་སྐྱོད་ན།

ཆུ་མིག་ཀྱུལ་ཀྱིལ་ཟམ་ཞིག་ཞུགས་ཉིད་ལ་བཞུགས།

ཉ་མོ་གསེར་མིག་གི་གློ་གདང་ཁོ་ཀུན་ལ་ཡིན་ལོ།

ཐང་སྟོད་མཐོན་པོ་ཀུན་མ་བཞུགས་བྱུང་དེ་ལ་སྐྱིད་ན།
ཐང་བྲུ་ཀྲུར་ཀྱིར་ཟམ་ཞིག་ཞུགས་ཉིད་ལ་བཞུགས།
ཤང་ཀུ་མཛུག་རྩུམ་གྱི་གློ་གདང་ཁ་ཀུན་ལ་ཡིན་ལོ།

ཡུང་པ་ཆེན་མོ་ཀུན་མ་བཞུགས་བྱུང་དེ་རྩ་སྐྱིད་ན།
ཡུང་པ་སྣ་ཁྲུང་ཟམ་ཞིག་ཞུགས་ཉིད་ལ་བཞུགས་ལོ།
ཡྲ་ཙེ་འགྲོལ་མོ་འི་གློ་གདང་ཁ་ཀུན་ལ་ཡིན་ལོ།

ཙྭ་ཤིང་ནགས་ཚལ་མ་བཞུགས་བྱུང་དེ་ལ་སྐྱིད་ན།
ཚོར་མ་པར་ཕྲུར་ཟམ་ཞིག་ཞུག་ཉིད་ལ་བཞུགས་ལོ།
བྱ་ཤོག་ཐོག་གི་གློ་གདང་ཁ་ཀུན་ལ་ཡིན་ལོ།

རྒྱལ་ལྷམ་ཀེ་སར་མ་བཞུགས་བྱུང་དེ་ལ་སྐྱིད་ན།
འབུ་དམར་ལམ་བསྟན་ཐེ་ཕོང་ཟམ་བཞུགས་ལོ།
ཛོ་ཛོ་འབྲུ་གུ་མའི་གློ་གདང་ཁ་ལ་ཡིན་ལོ།

ཐུ་རྩ་ཀྱུང་གོད་མ་བཞུགས་བྱུང་དེ་ལ་སྐྱིད་ན།
ཐུ་རྩ་ཀེར་ཟེ་ཟམ་ཞིག་ཞུགས་ཉིད་ལ་བཞུགས།
གོད་མ་ཚ་ལངས་ཀྱི་གློ་གདང་ཁ་ལ་ཡིན་ལོ།

མཛོ་ཕོ་རྐང་དཀར་མ་བཞུགས་བྱུང་དེ་ལ་སྐྱིད་ན།
མཛོ་ཕྲུག་ར་མ་ཟམ་ཞིག་ཞུགས་ཉིད་ལ་བཞུགས།
མཛོ་མོ་རྩ་ཡོན་གྱི་གློ་གདང་ཁ་ལ་ཡིན་ལོ།

རྒྱ་བོང་ཁ་དཀར་ཀུན་མ་བཞུགས་བྱུང་དེ་ཙ་སྐྱོད་ན།
ཀ་ཙུག་བི་ལ་ཟམ་ཞིག་ཞུགས་ཉིད་ལ་བཞུགས་ལོ།
བོང་མོ་ཁམ་པའི་གློ་གདན་ཁོ་དེ་ལ་ཡིན་ལོ།

ཅིད་བུ་སྐྱེ་དམར་ཀུན་མ་བཞུགས་བྱུང་དེ་ཙ་སྐྱོད་ན།
རི་གུ་ཁ་སྔོན་དེ་ཞུགས་ཉིད་ལ་བཞུགས་ལོ།
ར་མ་དཀར་མོའི་གློ་གདན་ཁོ་ལ་ཡིན་ལོ།

ཕོ་ལགས་མགོ་གསེར་མ་བཞུགས་བྱུང་དེ་ལ་སྐྱོད་ན།
ཞུག་གུ་ཏྲི་མོ་ཞུགས་ཉིད་ལ་བཞུགས་ལོ།
མ་མོ་ཁམ་པའི་གློ་གདན་ཁོ་ལ་ཡིན་ལོ།

ཁྲི་ཕོ་གསེར་ལིང་མ་བཞུགས་བྱུང་དེ་ལ་སྐྱོད་ན།
ཁྲི་གུ་ཁྲ་ཚུང་ཞུགས་ཉིད་ལ་བཞུགས་ལོ།
ཁྲི་མོ་སྨོམ་དཀར་མོའི་གློ་གདན་དེ་ཁོ་ལ་ཡིན་ལོ།

བི་ལ་ནག་ཚུང་མ་བཞུགས་བྱུང་དེ་ལ་སྐྱོད་ན།
གཡའ་ནང་གི་ལ་དེར་ར་ཞུགས་ཉིད་ལ་བཞུགས་ལོ།
བི་མོ་ཁྲ་སྡུག་གི་གློ་གདན་ཁོ་ལ་ཡིན་ལོ།
ལྷེམ་ལྷེམ་གྱི་ལྷེམ་མཁར་གྱི་གློ་གདན་དེ་ཨ་གུ་དཔལ་ལེ་ཡིན་ལོ།།

No. 2.

དེ་ཟླུག་ཟེར་དེ་ཧ་རྒྱུང་ཆོད་དབྱེར་པ་ལ་སྨ་བསྟུད་དེ། ཀེ་སར་ནང་ལ་སོང་སྟེ། དྲི་དོན་བཏངས། ཕོག་དོན་བཏངས། ལྷ་གསོལ་བཏང་སྟེ། ཛེ་ཛེ་

འབྲུ་ག་མ་ལ་ཀལ་ཅོར་བཀལ་དེ། གླིང་མཁར་གྱི་སྒོ་ལ་བསླེབ་སྟེ་ནས། ཡམ་ཚམ་སོང་སྟེ་ཛོ་ཛོ་ངུས། ཀེ་སར་གྱིས་ཛོ་ཛོ་ལ་གླུ་ཞིག་བླངས ;།

མ་ཤུམས་འང་ཛོ་ཛོ་ལེ་མ་ཤུམས་འང།
ཛོ་ཛོ་འི་སྤྱན་མིག་ལགས་མོ་ལ་གནོད་ཅས་ཡིན།
མ་ཤུམས་འབྲུག་མོ་མ་ཤུམས་འང།
འབྲུག་མོའི་ཤ་མདོག་ལགས་མོ་ལ་གནོད་ཅས་ཡིན།
ང་སྐྱོང་ར་ཁར་ཁོར་ནང་སོང་སྟེ་སྒྲ་དཀར་ཐར་ཐོར་ནང་བསླེབ་ཡིན།
སྒྲ་དཀར་ཐར་ཐོར་ནང་སོང་སྟེ་སྨ་ར་སྨུ་རི་ནང་བསླེབ་ཡིན།
སྨ་ར་སྨུ་རི་ནང་སོང་སྟེ་དགུ་སྐོར་ནོན་དེ་ང་བསླེབ་ཡིན།
ཛོ་ཛོ་མ་ཤུམས་འང་ལེ་འབྲུག་མོ་མ་ཤུམས་ལེ།

དེ་ཙུག་ཟེརས་པ། ཛོ་ཛོ་ཐེབ་མང་པོ་ངུས་སོང་། དེ་ཙུག་བཅོ་འིན་ཞིག་དང། ཞག་བདུན་སོང་བས། ཨ་ནེ་བཀུར་དཀྲན་མོས་ཀེ་སར་ལ་ཟེརས། ལྷ་ཤེས་ཅན་ནི་ཤེས་མེད། ལྷའི་བུ་ཀེ་སར། ཁྱོ་རང་གིས་བུ་མོའི་གདམ་ལ་ཉན་དེ། ག་ཙུག་ལ་བདུད་བདུལ་ཡིན་ཟེརས་པ། དེ་ནས་ཀེ་སར་གྱིས་ཐྲ་ཙུ་ཀྱང་ཁོད་དབྱེར་པའི་ཁ་ཞོན་དེ་སོང། ཛོ་ཛོ་ཡང་ཁོད་མ་ཚ་ལངས་ལ་སྨ་བསྟད་དེ; ཀེ་སར་གྱི་རྟིང་རང་ནས་བྲང་སྟེ་སོང། ཡང་ལམ་གསུམ་འཛོམ་ཅིག་ལ་ཀེ་སར་ཐུག་སོང། དེ་ཙུ་ཀེ་སར་གྱིས་ཛོ་ཛོ་ལ་གླུ་ཞིག་བཏངས།།

ངའི་ཛོ་ཛོས་དངོས་ཤིག་ལ་ཉོན་དང།
ཛོ་ཛོ་འབྲུ་ག་མས་བདག་ཅིག་ལ་གསན་ལོ།

ཨ་ཡི་རི་དཀར་པོ་སྨུའི་སྲུང་རི་ཞིག་ཡིན་ལོ།
དེ་བོ་ང་ཤོད་ན་ཇོ་ཇོ་འགྲོ་བ་ལ་ཐག་ཆོད་སོང་ལོ།

ཨ་ཡི་རི་དམར་པོ་དེ་སྨུའི་སྲུང་རི་ཞིག་ཡིན་ལོ།
དེ་བོ་བ་ཤོད་ན་ཇོ་ཇོ་འགྲོ་བ་ལ་ཐག་ཆོད་སོང་ལོ།

ཨ་ཡི་རི་ནག་པོ་དེ་སྨུའི་སྲུང་རི་ཞིག་ཡིན་ལོ།
དེ་བོ་བ་ཤོད་ན་ཇོ་ཇོ་འགྲོ་བ་ལ་ཐག་ཆོད་སོང་ལོ།

ཨ་ཡི་རི་ལྗང་ཁུ་དེ་སྨུའི་སྲུང་རི་ཞིག་ཡིན་ལོ།
དེ་བོ་བ་ཤོད་ན་ཇོ་ཇོ་འགྲོ་བ་ལ་ཐག་ཆོད་སོང་ལོ།

ཨ་ཡི་རི་སྔོན་པོ་དེ་སྨུའི་སྲུང་རི་ཞིག་ཡིན་ལོ།
དེ་བོ་བ་ཤོད་ན་ཇོ་ཇོ་འགྲོ་བ་ལ་ཐག་ཆོད་སོང་ལོ།
དེ་ཀུན་མ་བ་ཤོད་ན་ཇོ་ཇོ་མི་འཁྱེར་ཐག་ཆོད་ཡིན།

དེ་ནས་ཇོ་ཇོས་ལན་དུ་གླུ་ཞིག་བཏངས་སོ།

ཨ་ཡི་རི་དཀར་པོ་དེ་ལྷའི་དབང་པོ་རྒྱབ་བྱིན་གྱི་སྲུང་རི་ཡིན།
ཨ་ཡི་རི་དམར་པོ་དེ་ཨ་མ་སྐྱབས་བདུན་གྱི་སྲུང་རི་ཡིན།

ཨ་ཡི་རི་ནག་པོ་དེ་ཀླུ་རྒྱལ་ལྡོགས་པོའི་སྲུང་རི་ཡིན།
ཨ་ཡི་རི་ལྗང་ཁུ་དེ་རྒྱལ་ལྷམ་ཀི་སར་གྱི་སྲུང་རི་ཡིན།
ཨ་ཡི་རི་སྔོན་པོ་དེ་ཇོ་ཇོ་ང་རང་གི་སྲུང་རི་ཡིན་ལོ།

དེ་ཟུག་ཟེརས་པ། ཇོ་ཇོ་མཉམ་པོ་ཆ་ཅེས་སོང་། དེ་ནས་ཁྲོང་གཉིས་ཀ་སོང་སྟེ། མཚོ་ཆེན་པོ་ཞིག་གི་མདུན་ལ་བསླེབ་སོང་། དེ་རུ་ཇོ་ཇོས་འདོན་དང་ཞིག་བཅོས། ཀེ་སར་གཉིད་ཅིག་ལོག་སྡེ་འདུགས་པ། ཉིད་དེ་ནང་དུ་ཨ་ནེ་བཀར་དམན་མོའི་སྐད་ཅིག་གླུ་འདི་ལྟར་ཞིག་ཚོར་རོ།

ཕྲ་ཤེས་ཅན་ནི་ཤེས་མེད་ཀེ་སར་རྒྱལ་པོ་ཉིན་དང་།
ཕྲ་གྲོས་ཅན་ནི་གྲོས་མེད་ལྷའི་བུ་ཀེ་སར་གསན་དང་།
ཁྱེད་ཀྱིས་བུ་མོ་འཁྲིད་དེ་བདུད་ག་ཟུག་ལ་བདུལ་ཡིན།
ཁྱེད་ཀྱིས་ཇོ་ཇོ་འཁྲིད་དེ་བདུད་ཡུལ་ལ་ག་ཟུག་ལ་ཆེན།
ཁྱེད་ཀྱིས་ཇོ་ཇོ་སློག་པ་མ་ཉན་ན་བདུད་བསད་པ་མི་ཉན་ལོ།
ཁྱེད་ཀྱིས་ཐབས་ཤིག་བཅོ་སྟེ་ཇོ་ཇོ་ལོག་སྟེ་དོང་ལོ།

གཉིད་ཀྱི་ནང་དུ་དེ་ཟུག་ཚོར་ཏེ། ཀེ་སར་མགྱོགས་པ་ལངས་ཏེ་ཇོ་ཇོ་ལ་ཅང་མ་ཟེར་བ། ཉ་ཞིག་ལ་བརྫུ་སྟེ་མཚོའི་ནང་དུ་སོང་། མཚོའི་དཀྱིལ་ལ་བུ་ཊ་ཆེན་པོ་ཞིག་ཡོད་ཚུག། དེ་བུ་ཊའི་ཁ་སོང་སྟེ་གྲུབ་པ་ཞིག་ལ་བརྫུ་སྟེ་མགོ་བཏུམ་སྟེ་བཞུགས་སོང་། ཇོ་ཇོ་ལ་འདོན་དང་འཐོན་དེ་བལྟ་ཟ་ན། ཀེ་སར་མེད་ཚུག། དེ་ནས་ཇོ་ཇོ་ངུ་འིན་ཞིག་ཏ་རྫེས་བཙདས། མི་རྫེས་བཙདས་པ་མ་ཤེས་པས། ཕར་ལྟ་ཚུར་ལྟ་བཅོས་པ། མཚོའི་དཀྱིལ་ལ་གྲུབ་པ་ཞིག་མཐོང་སྟེ། གསེར་དང་དངུལ་གྱི་མཐལ་ནལ་ཞིག་ཕྱུལ་ཏེ། ཇོ་ཇོ་ལོག་སྟེ་ཡོང་ཅེས་ལ་འཆམས། དེ་ནས་ཨ་ནེ་བཀར་དམན་མོ་སྐྱིད་དེ་ཐུམ་འཕྲུལ་ཡི་ཁ་ལྷ་མོ་མང་པོ་ཁྲིད་སྟེ། ཇོ་ཇོ་སྲུན་མ་བཙུག་པར། གླིང་མཁར་དུ་ཁྲིརས། ཀེ་སར་མཚོའི་ནང་ནས

ཕྱི་ང་སྤྱི། བདུད་ཡུལ་ཕྱོགས་ལ་སྐྱོད་པས། ཞག་ཁ་ཅིག་འགྲུལ་དེ་ན། ས་རོག་མོ་ལྐུང་པ་གསུང་འཛོམས་ཤིག་ནས་པར་ལ་ས་ཁྲང་གི་མཐིལ་ན་འགྲུལ་ཅེས་ཤིག་ཡོད་ཚུག། དེ་བོ་མཐོང་སྤྱི་སྤྱང་ང་སྐྱོས་དེ། དཱ་ཙ་ཞིག་ཕིང་སྤྱི་སྤྲུག་གིན་ཞིག་དང་སྤྲུ་འདི་ལྟར།།

ལྷ་འཁོར་གསུམ་བརྒྱ་དྲུག་བཅུ་མཁྱེན་ནོ།
འདི་རིང་ང་ལ་དཔུང་རོགས་མཛོད།

ཀླུ་འཁོར་གསུམ་བརྒྱ་དྲུག་བཅུ་མཁྱེན་ནོ།
འདི་རིང་ང་ལ་དཔུང་རོགས་མཛོད།

མཉམ་པོ་སྐྱེས་པའི་ལྷ་དགུ་མཁྱེན།
འདི་རིང་ང་ལ་དཔུང་རོགས་མཛོད།

མཉམ་པོ་སྐྱེས་པའི་ཀླུ་དགུ་མཁྱེན།
འདི་རིང་ང་ལ་དཔུང་རོགས་མཛོད།

ཕས་ལྷ་ཀིར་རྫོང་སྐམ་པོ་མཁྱེན།
འདི་རིང་ང་ལ་དཔུང་རོགས་མཛོད།

མས་ལྷ་བཀུར་དམན་རྒྱལ་མོ་མཁྱེན།
འདི་རིང་ང་ལ་དཔུང་རོགས་མཛོད།

ལྷའི་དབང་པོ་རྒྱབ་ཞེན་མཁྱེན།
འདི་རིང་ང་ལ་དཔུང་རོགས་མཛོད།

བར་གྱི་ཨ་མ་སྐྱབ་བདུན་མཁྱེན།

འདི་རིང་ང་ལ་དཔུང་རོགས་མཛོད།

འོག་གི་ཀླུ་རྒྱལ་ལྷོགས་པོ་མཁྱེན།

འདི་རིང་ང་ལ་དཔུང་རོགས་མཛོད།

དེ་ཟླུག་ཟེར་རིན་ཞིག། མགར་མ་ཞིག་བཏངས་པ། ཁོ་ལ་འོད་རྒྱལ་པ་ཞིག་མཐོང་སྟེ་ལམ་གསལ་པོ་མཐོང་སོང་། དེ་ནས་བིང་སྟེ་ཞག་བདུན་སོང་སྟེ་ན། བདུད་ཀྱི་ས་སྣ་བ་ལ་བསླེབ་ནས། ར་ཛི་དང་ཐུག་སོང་། ར་ཛི་སྲུ་སྲུ་སྡོན་ལ་ཉོར་གྱིས་གླིང་པའི་མི་ཟླུམ་སྟེ་ཁྱེར་མཁན་ཡོད་ཚུག། སྲུ་སྲུ་བདུད་ཀྱི་མི་རེ་ཡོད་ཚུག། ཁོང་གི་མདུན་ལ་གཟུབ་པ་ཞིག་བཙོ་སྟེ་སོང་བས། དེ་ར་ཛི་ཀུན་གྱིས་ཟེརས་པ། ཕྲ་གཟུབ་པ་ཁྱོད་འདིར་ཅི་ལ་ཡོངས། འདིར་བདུད་ཡུལ་ཡིན་ཟེརས་པ། ཟེར་ནའང་། ཁོ་དེ་ཙ་འདུགས། ཁོས་འཕྲུལ་བཙོ་སྟེ། བདུད་ཀྱི་ར་མ་རྒྱགས་པ་ཚང་མ་ལ་ཤ་དང་ཆོལ་ཚང་མ་ཤུར་རིན་ཟ་འདིན་ཞིག་འདུགས། དེ་ནས་ར་ཛི་ཀུན་གྱིས་ཟེརས་པ། ཁྱེ་རང་གཟུབ་པའི་ཕ་ཡུལ་ག་ན་ཡིན་ཟེརས་པ། གཟུབ་པ་དེས་ང་གླིང་ཡུལ་ནས་ཡོངས། ངའི་ཡུལ་ང་ལ་ཡང་མི་ཤེས་ཟེརས་པ། ར་ཛི་ཀུན་གྱིས་འདྲིས་པ། གླིང་རྒྱལ་ལྷམ་ཀེ་སར་བདུད་བདུལ་བ་ཡོང་ཆེན་ཟེར་འདུག་པ། ནམ་ཡོང་ཅེས་འདུག། གཟུབ་པ་ཁྱོད་ལ་ཁ་བར་མེད་ད་ཟེརས་པ། གཟུབ་པས་ཟེརས། ཀེ་སར་ཨང་མགྱོགས་པ་ཡོང་ཅེས་འདུག་ཟེརས། དེ་ནས་གླིང་པའི་མི། ར་ཛི་ལ་ཨང་ཡོད་པའི་མི་ཀུན་ལ་ཀེ་སར་གྱི་དངོས་བསྟན་དེ་ཟེར་པ། ང་གླིང་རྒྱལ་ལྷམ་ཀེ་སར་ཡིན། ང་བདུད་བདུལ་

བ་ལ་ཡོངས་པ་ཡིན། བདུད་ཀྱི་མཁར་ནང་དུ་སྲུ་ཡོད། མཁར་གྱི་ལམ་སྐྱུངས་ལ་སྲུ་ཡོད་འདྲིས་པ། དེ་ནས་གླིང་གི་མི་ཀུན་འཐད་དེ། དེའི་གནས་ཚུལ་ཚང་མ་ཞུས་པ། བདུད་ཀྱི་མཁར་ནང་དུ་ཇོ་མོ་བམ་ཟ་བྲུམ་སྐྱིད་ཡོད། མཁར་གྱི་སྒོ་སྐྱུངས་ལ་སྟག་གཟིག་གི་ལམ་སྐྱུངས་ཡོད། དེ་ཚང་མ་གསོན་དུ་མེད། སོབ་རྒྱུངས་དེ་བོར་དེ་ཡིན། ཉི་རང་མ་འཛིགས་ལེ་ཟེརས་པ། དེ་ནས་ཀ་སར་འཐད་ཀྱིན་ཞིག་སོང་སྟེ། མཁར་གྱི་མདུན་ལ་ཅ་ཞིག་མ་བསླེབ་པ་གླུ་ཞིག་བཏངས།།

མདའ་གང་གནམ་དང་མ་ཐུག་པའི་མཁར་དེ་སྲུའི་ཡིན་ལོ།
མདའ་གང་ས་དང་མ་ཐུག་པའི་ནང་དུ་སྲུ་ཞིག་ཡོད།

དེ་སྐུ་མཁར་པོའི་ནང་མི་ཆེན་སྲུ་ཞིག་བཞུགས་ལོ།
ཟ་མཁན་ནི་འདྲེ་ཞིག་ཡོད་ད་སྐྱུང་བའི་ལྷ་ཞིག་ཡོད་ལོ།

ང་ཁ་ལ་ཟས་མེན་པ་ཟླ་དགུ་རིག་སོང་ལོ།
ལུས་ལ་གོས་རིག་མེད་པ་ལོ་དགུ་རིག་སོང་ལོ།

ང་ལ་ཟས་ཞིག་སྐྱུལ་རོགས་རིག་མཛོད་ལོ།
ལུས་ལ་འགོན་སྙིང་རི་སྐྱུལ་བར་མཛོད་ལོ།

ཁ་ལ་ཟས་ཞིག་སྐྱུལ་དེ་ནང་བསད་ནའང་ཕྱིག་ལོ།
ལུས་ལ་གོས་ཞིག་སྐྱུལ་དེ་ནང་བསད་ནའང་ཆོག་ལོ།།

ཀ་སར་གྱིས་དེ་ཟུག་ཟེ་རས་པ་སང། མཁར་གྱི་ནང་ན་ཇོ་མོ་བམ་ཟ་བྲུམ་སྐྱིད་ཀྱིས་དཀར་ཁང་ནང་ནས་མགོ་ཕིང་སྟེ་བལྟས་པ། དེ་རུ་པན་ཧྲུང་སྤྲོང་སྤྲུག་ཅིག་ཡོད་ཚུག་པས། ཇོ་མོ་ལ་སྒྲོ་སྒྲིབ་ཅིག་ཡོང་སྟེ་གླུ་འདི་ལྟར།།

ལྷ་ཁྲོད་མི་ཡུལ་ལིཾ་སྨིན་བྲ་ཞིག་ག་ནས་ཡོངས་ལོ།
ཁྲོད་མི་ཡུལ་ལི་ལང་ཕྲུག་དེ་གང་ནས་ཡོངས་ལོ།
ཚ
ཁྲོད་དེ་སྒྲིག་ལ་ཕངས་པ་ཚོར་ར་མི་རག་ག།
ཁྲོད་རང་སྒྲིག་འཁྱུར་རེ་རང་ཡུལ་ལ་སོང་ལོ།

འདི་བདུད་ཡུལ་ཡིན་པ་མ་ཤེས་ས།
འདི་བདུད་མཁར་ཡིན་པ་མ་ཤེས་ས།

ཁྲེད་ལ་ལང་ཕེ་ཞིག་དགོས་ན་མཁར་གྱི་སྒོ་ལ་ཡོང་།
ཚ
ཁྲེད་དབང་ཅན་རིག་ཡིན་ན་བ་ཤིག་པ་རིག་ཡོང་ལོ།

དེ་ཟླུག་ཟེར་ས་པ། ཀེ་སར་གྱིས་ལན་དུ།

ཤར་རི་སྒོ་ལ་རྟ་དཀར་ལ་ཞོན་པའི་མི་དཀར་འདུག།
དེ་བོ་ལ་ང་ག་ཟླུག་ལ་ཡོང་ཡིན་ལོ།

ལྷོ་འི་སྒོ་ལ་རྟ་སྔོན་ལ་ཞོན་པའི་མི་སྔོན་ཅིག་འདུག།
དེ་བོ་ལ་ང་ག་ཟླུག་ལ་ཡོང་ཡིན་ལོ།

ནུབ་ཀྱི་སྒོ་ལ་རྟ་ནག་ལ་ཞོན་པའི་མི་ནག་ཅིག་འདུག།
དེ་བོ་ལ་ང་ག་ཟླུག་ལ་ཡོང་ཡིན་ལོ།

བྱང་གི་སྒོ་ལ་རྟ་གསེར་ལ་ཞོན་པའི་མི་གསེར་འདུག།
དེ་ལ་ང་ག་ཟླུག་ལ་ཡོང་ཡིན་ལོ།

དེ་ཟླུག་ཟེརས་པ་སང། ཛོ་མོ་བམ་ཟ་བུམ་སྐྱིད་ཀྱིས་ལན་དུ།།

མི་ཡུལ་ལི་སྨིན་བུ་དངོས་ལ་ཉེན་དང།
མི་ཡུལ་ལི་སྨོང་ཕྲུག་བདག་ལ་གསན་ལོ།

ཤར་གྱི་སྒོ་སྲུངས་དེ་ངའི་མིང་བོ་ཡིན་ལོ།
ལྷོ་འི་སྒོ་སྲུངས་དེ་ངའི་ཨ་ཞང་ཡིན་ལོ།

ནུབ་ཀྱི་སྒོ་སྲུངས་དེ་ངའི་ཨ་བ་ཡིན་ལོ།
བྱང་གི་སྒོ་སྲུངས་དེ་ངའི་བུ་ཚ་ཡིན་ལོ།

དེ་རྣམས་ཀྱིས་གནོད་པ་མི་སྐྱལ་ལོ།
དེ་ཚང་མ་ལ་ངས་ཟེར་ཡིན་ལོ།

དེ་ཟླུག་ཟེརས་པ། ཀི་སར་མཁར་གྱི་སྒོ་མདུན་ལ་སོང་བ། རྟ་སྒོ་སྲུན་དུ་བཙུག་སྡེ་ཡོད་ཚུག། དེ་ནས་ཀི་སར་གྱིས་གླུ་ཞིག་བཏངས་སོ།།

ཁྲིད་བདུད་ཀྱི་ཛོ་ཛོས་དངོས་ལ་ཉེན་དང།
ཛོ་མོ་བམ་ཟ་བུམ་སྐྱིད་བདག་ལ་གསན་ལོ།

དཀར་ཞིག་རང་དཀར་ན་ཛོ་ཛོ་འི་སོ་དང་སེན་མོ་དཀར་ལོ།
དེ་ཟླུག་གི་ཛོ་ཛོ་བོར་དེ་ཛོ་ཛོ་ཉེ་རི་མིང་འདྲི་སྡེ་ཡོངས་ཡིན།

དཀར་ཞིག་རང་དཀར་ན་འབྲུ་གུ་མའི་སོ་དང་སེན་མོ་ཀུན་དཀར་ལོ།
དེ་ཟླུག་གི་འབྲུ་གུ་མ་བོར་དེ་ཛོ་མོ་འི་མིང་འདྲི་སྡེ་ཡོངས་ཡིན།

ནག་ཅིག་རང་ནག་ན་ཇོ་ ཇོའི་སྐྲ་དང་མིག་སྨ་ནག་ལོ།
ནག་ཅིག་རང་ནག་ན་འབྲུ་གུ་མའི་སྐྲ་དང་མིག་སྨ་ནག་ལོ།

དེ་ཟུག་གི་ཇོ་ ཇོ་བོར་དེ་ཇོ་ ཇོ་ཉེ་རང་གི་ཕི་ལ་ཡོངས་པིན།
དེ་ཟུག་གི་འབྲུ་གུ་མ་འཕང་སྤོ་ཇོ་མོ་བམ་ཟ་བུམ་སྐྱིད་བཙལ་དེ་ཡོངས་པིན།

ང་མཁར་གྱི་ནང་དུ་ཡོང་ཚུག་ག་མཛོད་ཇོ་ ཇོ་མཁྱེན་ལོ།
ང་ལ་ཧ་སྒོ་ཕྱེ་རོགས་རིག་མཛོད་འང་ཇོ་མོ་མཁྱེན་ནོ།

དེ་ཟུག་ཟེརས་པ་སང། ཇོ་མོ་མང་པོ་འཐད་སྒོ་ཕྱེ་སྤེ་མཁར་གྱི་ནང་དུ་སོང་སྟེ། ཁྱོཾང་གཉིས་ཀ་སྐྱིད་པོའི་ནང་དུ་གནས་སོང༎

No. 3.

དེ་ནས་ཞག་ཙོ་ལྔ་ཟམ་སོང་སྟེ་ན། ནམ་མཁའི་འབྲུག་སྒྲ་ལྟར་སྐད་ཆེན་པོ་འབོད་ནས། ས་དང་གནམ་ཚང་ན་ཆིག་ཆིག་གུལ་ཅེས་ཡོངས་པས། ཀ་སར་གྱིས་ཇོ་མོ་ལ་འདྲིས་པ། ཇོ་མོ་ལེ། འདི་སྐད་ཆེན་པོ་དེ་ཅི་ཡིན་ཟེརས་པ། ཇོ་མོས་ཟེརས། འོ་རྒྱལ་པོ་ལེ། ད་བདུད་ཁྲབ་པ་ལག་རིངས་ཡོང་ཅེས་ལ་ཁ་གྲུར་དེ་ཡིན་ནོག་ཟེརས་པ། དེ་ནས་ཡང་ཞག་བཅུ་སོང་སྟེ་ན། ཡང་སྔོན་མའི་སང་ཐེབ་སྐད་ཆེན་པོ་ཞིག་བཏངས། ཡང་ཀ་སར་གྱིས་འདྲིས་པ། ད་འདི་སྐད་དེ་ཅི་ཡིན་ཇོ་མོ་ལེ། ཇོ་མོས་ཟེརས། ད་ཞག་བཅོ་ལྔའི་ལམ་ལ་བསླེབ་སྟེ་ཡིན་ཟེརས། དེ་ནས་ཡང་ཐེབ་སྐད་དྲག་པོ་ཞིག་བཏངས་པ། ཀ་སར་གྱིས་ཡང་འདྲིས། ཇོ་མོ་ལེ་ད་ཅི་ཡིན་ཟེརས་པ། ཇོ་མོས་ཟེརས། ད་བདུད་ཞག

ལྷའི་ལམ་ལ་བསླེབ་ཚར་ཟེརས་པ། ཀི་སར་མང་པོ་འཛིགས་དེ་ཟེརས། ད་ང་སློས་ཇོ་མོ་ལེ་ཟེརས་པ། ཇོ་མོས་སྨྲ་བའི་ས་ཁྲད་ཅིག་མེད། ས་དོང་ཅིག་འབྲུ་སྡེ། དེའི་ནང་དུ་འདུག་ན་ཉན་ཡིན། ང་དང་ལ་མི་ག་ནས་ཁྱོང་ཡིན། ཀི་སར་གྱིས་ཟེརས་པ། མི་ང་རང་གིས་ཁྱོང་ཡིན་ཟེར་དེ། ཀང་པའི་མི་ཚུ་བཅུ། ལག་པའི་མི་ཚུ་བཅུ་འཕུད་དེ། མི་བཅོ་སྡེ་ཁོ་རང་དང་བཅུ་གཅིག ཇོ་མོ་དང་བཅུ་གཉིས་བཅོ་སྡེ། མཁར་གྱི་ནང་ས་དོང་ཆེན་པོ་ཞིག་འབྲུ་སྡེ། དེའི་ནང་དུ་སྡེན་སྐམས་བོལ་མོ་བཅོ་སྡེ། ཀི་སར་དེའི་ནང་དུ་བོར་དེ། ཟླ་བ་གཅིག་གི་ཟ་ཅེས་ཞིམ་པོ་ཞིག་ཡང་མཉམ་པོ་བོརས། མགོ་འི་ཁ་བྲུ་རིགས་ཚང་མའི་ཤོག་པ་སྣ་སོགས་བདངས། ས་དོང་ལ་སྒོག་སྤྲུབ་སྡེ། དེའི་ཁ་ས་མོ་ཆེ་ངདངས། དེའི་ཁ་ལུད་མོ་ཆེ་བདངས། དེའི་ཁ་སྒྲིད་མོ་ཆེ་བཙུགས། དེའི་ཁ་ཟངས་མོ་ཆེ་བཀལ་དེ། ཚུ་སྐང་སྡེ། དེའི་ཡོག་ལ་མེ་ཆེན་པོ་ཞིག་སྦུ་སྡེ་བོརས། དེའི་ནང་དུ་བདུད་ལ་ཟ་ཅེས་བཅོ་སྡེ་བོརས།།

དེ་ནས་བདུད་ཁྲབ་པ་ལག་རིངས་བསླེབ་སོང་བས། ཇོ་མོས་ཟ་ཅེས་ཚང་མ་བདང་སྡེ་ན། བདུད་ཀྱིས་ཇོ་མོ་ལ་ཟེརས། ཇོ་མོ་ལེ་མི་དྲི་ཞིག་རག་པ། ཅི་ཡིན། ཇོ་མོས་ཟེརས་པ། རྒྱལ་པོ་ལེ་མི་དྲི་ཞིག་ག་ནས་ཡོང་ཡིན། ཏ་རོ་བརྒྱ་དང་མི་རོ་བརྒྱ་དེ་ཉེ་རང་གིས་འཁྱེར་དེ་འདུག། ང་ལ་ཏ་རོ་དང་མི་རོ་ཞིག་ག་ནས་ཡོད། བདུད་ཀྱིས་མེན་མེན་ཇོ་མོ། ནང་ནས་ངའི་དཔེ་ཆ་དེ་ཁྱོང་། ངས་མོ་ཞིག་བདབ་ཡིན། དཔེ་ཆ་དེ་ལ་ཡོག་མ་བདང་བ། ལག་པ་གཡོན་པ་ལ་མ་འཁྱེར་བ། ལག་པ་གཡས་པ་ལ་འཁྱེར་དེ་ཁྱོང་ཟེརས་པ། ཇོ་མོ་ནང་ལ་སོང་སྡེ། དཔེ་ཆ་ཀང་པའི་ཡོག་ལ་བདངས་དེ། ལག་པ་གཡོན་པ་ལ་

འཁོར་དེ་ཁྲོང་སྤྲེ་བདངས་པ། ཁེ་ནས་བདུད་ཀྱིས་མོ་བདབས་པ། མོ་འི་ནང་ནས་འདི་ཟུག་བིང་། ས་རྫོང་གི་མཐིལ་ན་གླིང་ཀ་སར་ཡོད། མགོའི་ཁ་བྲ་སྣ་ཚང་གི་ཤོག་པ་ཡོད། དེའི་ཁ་ས་མོ་ཆེ་ཡོད། དེའི་ཁ་ལུད་མོ་ཆེ་ཡོད། དེའ་ཁ་སྐྲིད་མོ་ཆེ་ཡོད། དེའི་ཁ་ཟངས་མོ་ཆེ་བཀལ་དེ། ཟ་ཅེས་སྐོལ་གྱིན་ཡོད་ཟེརས་དེ་བིང་། དེ་ནས་བདུད་ཡམ་ཚན་ཞིག་སོང་སྟེ་ཇོ་མོ་ལ་ཟེརས་པ། ཇོ་མོ་ལེ། ངའི་མོ་དཔེའི་ནང་ནས་འདི་ཟུག་ཅིག་བིང་སོང་། དེ་བདེན་བ་མེན་འགྲོ་ཟེར་དེ། ཚང་མ་མེ་ལ་བདབས་བདངས་པ། ཇོ་མོས་མེའི་ནང་ནས་ཕིང་རྫུན་བདང་གིན་ཞིག། མེའི་མཐིལ་ལ་ཐིབ་བདང་སྟེ། ཉུ་ངུན་ཞིག་མེན་བ་ལུས་མ་བཙུགས། ཡང་བདུད་ཀྱིས་ཇོ་མོ་ལ་ཟེརས་པ། ཇོ་མོ་ལེ་ང་སྤྲོལ་གཉིད་ཁམ་པ་ལོག་ག། བྲ་གཉིད་དམ་དུམ་ལོག་འདྲིས་པས། ཇོ་མོས་ཟེརས། རྒྱལ་པོ་ལེ། དགའ་ས་རང་གི་ཁང་པ་ཡིན་ནོག། སྤྲོལ་གཉིད་ཁམ་བ་ལོག་ལེ། བྲ་གཉིད་དམ་དུམ་དེ་བེས་ལ་ལོག་ཆོག། བདུད་ཀྱིས་བདེན་བདེན་ཟེར་དེ། སྤྲོལ་གཉིད་ཁམ་པ་ལོག་ཡིན་ཟེར་དེ་ལོགས། དེ་ནས་ཉིད་དི་རྐྱིལ་ལ་སོང་སྟེ། དབུགས་ནང་དུ་འཐེན་ཟ་ན། ས་རྡོ་བ་ཅི་ཡོད་མཁན་ཚང་མ་སྣ་ཁྲང་ནང་ལ་འཁྱེར་རད་ཚུག། དབུགས་ཕི་སྤྲ་ལ་ཕིང་ཅ་ན། ཡང་ཚང་མ་ཕིང་སྤྲེ་ཁྲོང་ངད་ཚུག།

ཇོ་མོས་གཉིད་ལ་སོང་སྟེ་ཡིན་ནོག་བསམ་སྟེ། ཐོ་བ་གཡས་རྫེས་མ་རྫེས་བདང་སྟེ་ཟངས་པོགས། སྐྱིད་བུ་འཐེན་དེ། ས་མོ་ཆེ་ལུད་མོ་ཆེ་བྲུ་སྟེ། ས་རྫོང་གི་ནང་ནས། གླིང་ཀ་སར་རྒྱལ་པོ་ཕིང་སྤྲེ་ཁྲོངས། ཀ་སར་ལ་བདུད་མཐོང་སྟེ་འཛིགས་དེ་འདར་རད་ཚུག་པ། ཇོ་མོས་ཀ་སར་འཛིགས་ཅེས་ཤེས་དེ། ཀ་སར་རི་ཐུར་རྟུ་ལ་ཞོན་དེ། བདུད་ཀྱི་གཟུགས་པོའི་ཁ་བིང་སྟེ། གྱེན་ལ་བང་

གཅིག་ཐུར་ལ་བང་གཅིག་བཏངས་པ། དེ་ནས་ཀ་སར་ལ་དམ་པ་སྐྱེ་སྟེ། ཀ་སར་ཡང་ཐུར་ཏུ་རྒྱང་ཐོད་དབྱེར་པ་ལ་ཞོན་དེ་བང་གཅིག་བཏངས་པ། བདུད་ཀྱིས་ཨ་ཚ་ཚ། ཤིག་གིས་ཟེ་རག་ཟེར་རིན་འདུགས། དེ་ནས་ཀ་སར་གྱིས་བདུད་ཀྱི་གོང་རྩ་ནས་ཟུམ་སྟེ་ཟེརས་པ། ལྷ་བདུད་ངན། དཁྱོ་རང་ངས་བསད་ཡིན་ཟེར་དེ། རྟག་པ་ཅན་གྲི་གུ་ལག་ལ་འཁུར་དེ་ཡོད་ཚུག་པ། བདུད་ཀྱིས་ཟེརས་པ། ལྷ་ཁྱོད་སུ་ཡིན། དེ་ནས་ཀ་སར་གྱིས་ཟེརས། ང་ལྷའི་དབང་པོ་རྒྱབ་བཞིན་ཡིན་ཟེརས་པ། འོ་ཁོའི་ལག་ལ་ང་ཤི་ཅིས་མེན། ཀ་སར་གྱིས་ཡང་ཟེརས་པ། ང་བར་བཙན་གྱི་ཨ་མ་སྐྱབས་བདུན་ཡིན་ཟེརས། བདུད་ཀྱིས་འོ་ཁོའི་ལག་ལ་ཡང་ང་མི་ཤི་ཟེརས། ཡང་ཀ་སར་གྱིས། ང་ཀླུ་རྒྱལ་ལྡོགས་པོ་ཡིན་ཟེརས། འོ་ཁོའི་ལག་ལ་ཡང་མི་ཤི་ཟེརས། དེ་ནས་ཀ་སར་གྱིས། ང་གླིང་རྒྱལ་ལྷམ་ཀ་སར་ཡིན་ཟེརས། བདུད་ཀྱིས་འོ་ཀ་སར་ཡིན་ན། ཁྱོ་རང་ངེ་ལག་ལ་ང་ཤི་ཐག་ཆོད་ཡིན། ངའི་ལོ་ཁམས་མི་ལ་ཡོད། ཁྱེད་ཀྱི་ལོ་ཁམས་རྒྱ་ལ་ཡོད། མི་ལ་རྒྱུ་ཞིག་སླུག་ན་ཤི་བ་ཡིན། ང་མ་བསད་ཀ་སར་མཁྱེན། ང་ཉེ་རང་གི་གཡོག་པོ་བཅོ་ཡིན། གླིང་ཡུལ་དགྲུར་ས་བཅོ་བ་མཛད། བདུད་ཡུལ་དགུན་ས་ཚོས་ལེ། ང་ཉེ་རང་གི་ཁྲི་ཛྷི་བཅོ་སྟེ་འདུག་ཡིན་ཀ་སར་མཁྱེན་ཟེརས་པ། ཀ་སར་ལ་སྙིང་རྗེ་ཆོར་དེ་ཐེ་ཚོམས་སྐྱེས་པ། དེ་ནས་ཨ་ནེ་བཀུར་དམ་ཀ་མོ་སྐྱོད་དེ་ཟེརས། ལྷ་བསམ་བ་མེད་མཁན་ནི་ཀ་སར་རྒྱལ་པོ། བདུད་མ་བསད་ན། ཉིད་ལ་གནོད་པ་མེན་བ་ཕན་ཐོགས་མི་ཡོང་། རྟག་པ་ཅན་གྲི་གུ་དང་མགྱོགས་པ་སྙིང་ཤག་དགོས་ཟེརས་པ། དེ་ནས་ཀ་སར་གྱིས་བདེན་བསམ་སྟེ། རྟག་པ་ཅན་གྲི་གུ་ཕིང་སྟེ་བདུད་ཀྱི་སྙིང་ཁ་ཤགས། དེ་ནས་བདུད་ཤི། རོ་ལ་ཁོག་སྟོད་

ཁོག་སླད་ཡེ་སྦེ། ཁོགི་སྤྱོད་པོ་མེ་ལ་སྲེག་སྦེ་རོམ་ཁང་བཙོ་སྦེ་བོརས། ཁོག་སླད་
དེ་ས་བྲུ་སྦེ་དེའི་ནང་དུ་བཀབ་སྦེ་ཡང་གར་ཞིག་བཙོ་སྦེ་བོརས། ཞག་ཁ་ཅིག་
སོང་སྦེ་སྐོ་སྲུང་མཁན་ནི་སྟག་གཟིག་ཚང་མ་མི་ལ་བདུགས། དེ་ནས་ཀེ་སར་དང་
ཇོ་མོ་གཉིས་ཀས་ཚོ་ལོ་རྩེ་འདིན་ཞིག་འདུགས། ཇོ་མོས་ཀེ་སར་གླིང་ཡུལ་ལ་
ཆེན་བསམ་སྦེ། རྗེད་ཟན་དང་རྗེད་ཚུ་བདང་གིན་ཞིག་བོརས། ཐུ་ཙུ་ཀྲུང་གོད་
དབྱེར་པ་ལ་རི་ནས་ཤིང་ཁུར་བཀྱུ་ཁྲོང་བཙུགས། ནང་ནས་ཐལ་ཁུར་བཀྱུ་རེ་
ཡིང་བཙུགས། ཡི་སྟུ་ལ་ཆ་ཟ་ན་རྟོག་ཚོང་རི་བདང་གིན་འགྱུལས། ནང་ལ་ཆ་
ཟ་ན་སྲུལ་ཁྲུག་བདང་གིན་འགྱུལས། ཐུ་ཙུ་རི་བཀལ་པ། དཙུང་རྒྱུགས་འདུག་
ཟེརས། དེ་ཟླུག་བཙོ་འདིན་ཞིག་འདུགས་པ། ཀེ་སར་དང་ཇོ་མོ་གཉིས་ཀྱི་བར་
ལ་བུ་མོ་ཞིག་སྐྱེས་པས། ཀེ་སར་ལ་གླིང་ཡུལ་རྗེད་དེ་འདུགས།།

KESAR'S VICTORY OVER THE GIANT OF THE NORTH.

ABSTRACT OF CONTENTS.

1.

After two or three years Kesar went to the cold valley to live there in a hermitage. He had been there for one year only, when the queen *Ane bkur dmanmo* arrived there and told him not to sit in the hermitage any longer, but to go and fight the devil of the north. "This year," she said, "is a favourable year for Kesar, because Kesar's portion will be the element of water, and the devil's portion the element of fire; and water, will be able to quench the fire.[1]" After seven days, *Ane bkur dmanmo* came again to the door of the hermitage, and advised Kesar to go soon. "If you do not go, you will not remain in possession of the high hills of *gLing;* if you go, with what success will you be able to subdue (press) the four continents with their eight corners!" Now Kesar arose, went to *'aBruguma* and said: "Take the following articles out of the house, brush them three times, wash them three times in the depth of the sea, and bring an offering of sandalwood for each of them[2]: The saddle; the crupper studded with corals; the halter studded with pearls; the stirrups of pure gold; the saddle-cloth with a lotus-pattern; the cloth to cover the hind part of the horse, for which 180 (cows, rupees?) were paid; the bridle-bit of pure silver; the velvet cap; the silk suit; the red girdle-cloth; the beautiful shawl; the knife with a shell handle; the talisman shaped like kidneys; the sword 'stone-cutter'; the shield 'sky-coverer'; the steel tinderbox; the powder-bag of Russian leather; the rifle from *Rong;* the quiver of such weight that eighteen men have to carry it.—*'aBruguma* had to work hard for eight days before she had carried everything out of doors; and when she had finished, there was an earthquake.

---

1 It is remarkable that according to the Sheh-version (Mémoirs de la Société Finno-ougrienne, No. XV-2, p. 3.) *Ane bkur dmanmo* comes to warn Kesar not to go; and that he goes in spite of her warnings, trusting in the efficacy of his religious merits.

2 In Ladhakh, the wood of the pencil-cedar is often called sandal-wood.

Then *'aBruguma* sings a song of sorrow, in which she mentions all the articles and creatures, who either themselves or the glory of them will go to the north. She asks who will act the part of comforter for those who have to stay behind.

List of the creatures and other articles who either themselves or whose glory will go.

(1) γnam stod mthonpo, the high sky.
(2) gangs stod mthonpo, the high glacier.
(3) brag stod mthonpo, the high rock.
(4) spang stod mthonpo, the high meadows.
(5) mthsom stod mthonpo, the high lake.
(6) thang stod mthonpo, the high plain.
(7) lungpa chenmo, the great valley.
(8) rtsva shing nags thsal, the grass and forests.
(9) rgyal lham Kesar, the godly King Kesar.
(10) gling mkhar rtse dgu, the gLing castle with nine turrets.
(11) rkyang rgod dbyerpa, the genuine wild kiang.
(12) mdzo pho rkang dkar, the white-footed male Dzo.
(13) rgya bong kha dkar, the white-mouthed chief ass.
(14) rtsidbu skye dmar, the red-necked he-goat.
(15) pho lags mgo γser, the yellow-headed ram.
(16) khyi pho γser ling, the yellow hound.
(17) bila nag chung, the little black cat.

List of the creatures and other articles, who will wail on account of the other's departure.

(1) nyi zla γnyis, sun and moon.
(2) sengge γyu ralcan, the lioness with the turquoise mane.
(3) skyin chen ba rgan, the big ibex, the old ox.
(4) 'abrong chen khampa, the big brown wild yak.
(5) nyamo γser mig, the female fish 'golden eye.'
(6) shangku mjug rdum, the bushy-tailed wolf.
(7) wamo 'ajolli, the vixen clever in hiding.
(8) bya dang byiu, fowls and little birds.
(9) jojo 'aBruguma, lady 'aBruguma.
(11) rgodma thsalangs, the much-coveted mare.
(12) mdzomo ruyon, the female Dzo with crooked horns.
(13) bongmo khampa, the brown she-ass.
(14) rama dkarmo, the white she-goat.

(15) mamo khampa, the brown ewe.
(16) khyimo ltom dkar, the bitch with a white belly.
(17) bimo khrasug, the many-coloured she-cat.[1]

Kesar said in reply to *'aBruguma's* song, that there would be little, ones to be a comfort to the wailing animals. This is a list of them :—

(1) spriu togom zam zhig, a cloud of the size of a saddle-cloth.
(2) gangs melong zam zhig, ice of the size of a mirror.
(3) brag parpur, some little rock.
(4) spang togom zam zhig, a meadow of the size of a saddle-cloth.
(5) chu mig kyal kyil, some wells here and there.
(6) thangbu kyar kyir, a little plain.
(7) lungpa sna khung zam zhig, a valley of the size of nostrils.
(8) thserma par pur, a few thorns.
(9) 'abu dmar lam bstan thepong, Agu 'Redworm, way-leader thumb.'
(10) agu dpalle, Agu JPalle, the 'glorious one.'
(11) thurru kerze zam zhig, a little foal of the size of a lentil.
(12) mdzo phrug rama zam zhig, a Dzo-calf of the size of a goat.
(13) kurug bila zam zhig, a little donkey of the size of a cat.
(14) rigu kha sngon, the blue-mouthed kid.
(15) luggu dromo, the lamb called 'heat.'
(16) khyigu khra chung, the little particoloured dog.
(17) latirra, a weasel.[2]

---

1 The song consists of two parts: the first part comprises Nos. 1-8 of the lists, the second part comprises Nos. 9-17. The principal idea of the first part is, that (in winter probably) the glory of certain places will come to an end, and that in consequence of this the creatures living there will have a sad time. Even sun and moon are considered as creatures feeding on the sky. The principal idea of the second part of the song is that all male creatures will leave their female fellow-creatures (winter is not a suitable time for breeding on the whole), and that for this reason the female creatures will be wailing. In the Sheh-version the first part only of this song occurs. According to it the creatures complain, not because the places will lose their glory, but (which is practically the same) because Kesar will leave the places. In the next fascicle it will be interesting to meet with a song, according to which, together with *rKyang rgod dbyerpa's* return to *gLing*, the animal life altogether wakes up again.

2 It is not impossible that there existed answers only for the second part of the song (9-17) originally; 9-17 may have been quite a separate song, and its principal idea may have been this: when the male animals leave the female ones, the latter have the comfort of new offspring in different stages of development. Later on, when the first part of the song was united with the second part, it was considered necessary to invent little ones for the different places.

2.

'*aBruguma* cried, and Kesar told her that he would have to stay away for 108 years: his beard would grow, his hair would turn white, and his back would become crooked! Being admonished once more by *Ane bkur dmanmo*, Kesar rode off towards the north and met again with '*aBruguma*, who had travelled by a different road. He allowed her to go with him, on the condition that she should guess this riddle: Whose watchhills are: the white hill, the red hill, the black hill, the green hill, and the blue hill? '*aBruguma* answered at once, that the white hill was *dBangpo rgyabzhin's;* the red hill, *Ama sKyabs bdun's;* the black hill, *Klu rgyal l Jogpo's*, the green hill, *rGyallham Kesar's;* and the blue hill, her own watchhill. Thus she was allowed to go with Kesar; but again *Ane bkur dman rgyalmo* appeared to him in a dream and ordered him to send *a'Bruguma* back; otherwise he would not be able to subdue the devil of the north. Therefore Kesar took the shape of a fish and swam to the middle of a lake, where there was a tree. He then took the shape of a monk, ascended the tree and sat there with his face wrapped up. '*aBruguma*, who could not find her husband anywhere, decided to go back. She was taken home quickly by *Ane bkur dmanmo* and a host of other goddesses.

Kesar came to a place where three valleys meet, and where he had to go through a tunnel. As he was afraid, he performed on a ritual drum and prayed to the 360 gods; the 360 water-spirits; the nine gods and water-spirits who were born together with him; the father-god *Ker zong snyanpo;* the mother-god *bkur dman rgyalmo; dBangpo rgyabzhin; Ama skyabs bdun;* and to King lJogpo. Therefore he received a bright light and came safely to the end of the tunnel.

After seven days, he came to the frontier of the devil's realm and met with the devil's herdsmen, some of whom had been carried away from *gLing* by the devil. He killed some of the fattest goats and sheep, and ate their meat and grease. The shepherds said, they had heard that King Kesar would come soon to fight the devil; could he not give them some news? He said that Kesar would certainly come soon, and showed his real self to the captives from *gLing.* They were pleased to see their King and told him, that at present *Bamzubumskyid* was alone in the castle, and that the tigers and leopards, placed before the gates,[1] were not alive, but stuffed with straw.

Ariving before the castle, Kesar asked, "Who lives in this castle,

[1] Does this refer to the ice of the north, which often shows the figures of all kinds of animals?

which by an arrow's length touches neither earth nor sky?" [1] Then he said that he was a wanderer who for nine months had not received any food, and no new clothes for nine years. *Bamzabumskyid* told him to come to the gate, where he would receive some flour. He replied that he was afraid of the watchmen before the four gates of white (east), blue (south), black (west), and yellow (north) colour.[2] *Bamzabumskyid* said, she would speak to the watchmen, who were her brother, uncle, father and son. However, when Kesar went near, the gates were still locked up. He then sang a song saying, "If there is anything in the world which deserves to be called white, it is *a Bruguma's* teeth and nails; and if there is anything which deserves to be called black, it is *'aBruguma's* hair and eyebrows. Such a beautiful lady I left in order to make the acquaintance of lady *Bamzabumskyid.* I am King Kesar himself." When the *Dzemo* heard this, she was greatly pleased, opened the door, and both lived in the castle in happiness.

3.

After some time they heard a terrible noise, which was ever increasing. It was caused by the devil, who was approaching the castle. The *Dzemo* proposed to hide Kesar in a pit, but did not know how to dig it. Kesar produced ten hand-bones and ten foot-bones, formed ten men out of them, and they all digged a deep hole in the ground.[3] When it was completed, Kesar descended into it and received food, blankets and provisions to keep him alive for a month. Then a roof was built, and a pot placed on it, in which some food was cooked for the devil.

The devil arrived, and smelt at once that a man had come. The *Dzemo* said that such a thing was impossible, and that he was smelling the corpses of 100 men and horses, which he was carrying on his shoulders. He wished to hear what the magic book would tell him, and ordered the *Dzemo* to bring it, not treading on it, carrying it in her right hand. She did exactly the opposite. Out of the book a voice was heard, saying that Kesar had arrived and was sitting in a pit with a roof of feathers, manure and earth above him, and a kettle

---

[1] This description of the castle is probably borrowed from the description of the castle of sun, moon and stars (*bya rigs*). Compare fasc. No III.

[2] This system of colours was apparently suggested by that of the Lokapâlas. Compare Grünwedel, Mythologie des Buddhismus, S. 181. For the west, a wrong colour is given here; instead of 'black' there ought to be 'red.'

[3] According to the Sheh-version it is the *Dzemo*, who produces the workmen to dig the pit.

with boiling food on the top. The devil thought that all this could not be possible, and threw the book into the fire. The *Dzemo*, feigning to take it out again, pushed it in even further. Then the devil asked whether he had better sleep lightly or soundly, and the *Dzemo* advised him to sleep fast, because he was in his own house. He went to sleep at once. When taking in the breath, all the stones and earth round about came flying into his nostrils; when blowing out his breath, they were turned out again.

When the devil was fast asleep, Kesar left the pit. Seeing the devil he trembled from fear, but the *Dzemo*, to encourage him, rode about on the devil's body. Then Kesar, mounting *rKyang rgod dbyerpa*, rode about on him also, and the devil complained of the many lice, which were bothering him, as he believed. Now Kesar advanced to kill the devil with the poisoned knife. He pretended to be *dBangpo rgyabzhin*, mother *sKyabs bdun* and *lJogpo*.[1] The devil did not mind them all, and awoke only when he was told that King Kesar had arrived to kill him. He implored Kesar to spare his life. "I shall be your servant and will give you my warm land wherein you may live in winter." Kesar felt inclined to spare his life, but was admonished to kill the devil by *Ane bkur dmanmo.* He was then killed with the poisoned knife,[2] and cut into halves. The upper half was placed in an ordinary grave, the lower half in a Musulman grave.

Bamzabumskyid gave Kesar the food and drink of forgetfulness, and both remained in the castle, playing at dice; Kesar's horse was treated badly, and had to do hard work. To Kesar and the *Dzemo* a little girl was born. Kesar forgot the *gLing* land entirely.

---

1 According to the Sheh-version, Kesar pretends to be several of the Agus.

2 According to the Sheh-version, the nine lives of the devil have to be killed separately.

Vocabulary and Comments.

1.

འདི་ཅིག་གི་ལོ། *'adi ciggi lo*, or *dalo*, this year.

ལོ་ཁམས། *lo khams*, the omens of a year.

ཁྱབ་པ་ལག་རིངས། *khyabpa lagrings*, 'coverer, long-hand,' name of the devil *Curulugu*. In the original MS. *khyaba* is written, but explained to mean khyabpa.

ནང་མོ། *nangmo*, next year.

མཚམས་བཅད་བཏང་ཅས། *mthsams bcad btangcas*, the same as *mthsams γcodpa*, sit in a hermitage.

ཞིབ་ཆ། *zhibcha*, = zhibtu, accurate, minutely.

ང་རི། *ngari*, = ngarangngi, my.

སངས་ཤུག། *sangs shug*, offering of pencil-cedar, instead of sandal-wood.

མགོ་ཐུར། *mgo thur*, halter, respectful term; the ordinary word for 'halter' is *thur mgo*.

ཏོ་སྒོམ། *to sgom*, or *togom*, a felt which is placed between the wooden saddle and the back of the horse, a saddlecloth.

ཞུར་ལེ། *zhurle*, a cloth to cover a horse from the shoulders to the tail.

ཁ་སྲབས། *kha srabs*, *srab*, bridle (head-harness) of a horse.

མག་མལ། *magmal*, velvet; Urdu maḳhmal.

དར་ཡུག། *dar yug*, in Ladakh the name of a silk dress, worn for instance by the *nyopa*.

པད་ཀ། *padka*, red linen.

འབན་དུམ། *'abandum*, probably *bandum*; said to mean 'beautiful.'

ཙ་དར། *tsadar*, a shawl, worn over the shoulders when dancing.

ཡོ་བ། *yoba*, handle [of a knife].

པི་ཅག། *picag*, knife.

ཀ་གུ། *kagu*, amulet; perhaps *bkāgu*, a 'little word.'

འཁྱེད་མ། *'akhyedma*, comprising.

ཏི་ཤི་ལི། *tishili*, a good kind of steel.

ཅ་མག། *camag*, fire-steel.

བོར་གར། *borgar*, or *bolgar*, or *bulhar*, Russian leather.

སྨན་རྩས། *sman rcas*, = *sman chas*, powder-bag.

རོང་ཡུལ། *rong yut*, Upper Ladakh; the rifles of this district used to be famous.

མཚོམ་སྟོད། *mthsom stod*, = *mthso stod*, the high lake, the centre of the lake.

ཝ་མོ་འབྱོལ་ལི། *wamo 'abyolli*, the vixen who is clever in 'hiding'; *'abyolli* is probably related to *'abyolla*.

ལྡེམ་ལྡེམ་གྱི་ལྡེམ་མཁར། *ldem ldemgyi ldem mkhar*, seems to mean 'the shaky castle.' The stores of *gLing* are kept in it.

ཕོ་ལགས། *pholags*, a ram.

ལྟོམ་དཀར། *ltom dkar,*=*ltoba dkarpo,* white stomach, white belly.

ཏོ་གོམ། *togom,* see *to sgom.*

ཞུགས་ཉིད་ལ། *zhugs nyidla,* its very place, instead of.

བྱ་ཤོག་ཐོག། *bya shog thog,* birds 'with wings on the top'; name of all birds.

ཐེ་ཕོང། *the phong,*=*the pho,* thumb.

ཀེར་ཟེ། *kerze,* lentil.

ལ་ཏིར་ར། *latirra,* weasel, the same as *sremo.*

2.

སྨང་ར། *smang ra,*=*smang skra,* Lexicon *sma ra,* beard.

ཁར་ཁོར། *khar khor,* a little [beard].

ཐར་ཐོར། *thar thor,* a little; in this connection: there will be a little white in my hair.

སྒ་ར་སྒུ་རེ། *sgara sgure,* bent down by age.

སྐོར། *skor,* the cycle of the twelve years; *dgu skor*=9×12=108 years.

ནོན་ཏེ། *nonte,* pressing; here in the sense of 'exceeding,' exceeding 108 years.

འདོན་ཏང། *'adontang,* perhaps *'adon btang,* meal.

བུ་དྲ། *budra,* tree.

འཐོན་ཅས། *'athoncas,* here in the sense of 'being ready'; when the food leaves the kettle, it is ready cooked.

རྗེས་བཅད་ཅས། *rjes bcadcas,* search by looking after the tracks.

མན་ཏལ། *mantal,* = मण्डल circle of offerings.

རྫུམ་འཕྲུལ། *rdzum 'aphrul,* = *rdzu 'aphrul,* magical illusion.

སྣང་ང། *snangnga,* = *myangan* (?); *snangnga skyocas,* be sad.

དཱ་རུ། *dāru,* a small drum, used for expelling demons.

ས་སྣམ། *sa snam,* frontier.

རྒྱངས་ཅས། *rgyangscas,* to fill; probably a causative form of *khyangcas,* be full.

སྲོག་ལ་ཕངས་པ་ཚོར་ཅས། *srogla phangspa thsorcas,* be sorry for losing his own life.

འཁུར་རེ། *'akhurre,* = *'akhurte,* carrying.

བཤིག་པ་རིག་ཡོང་། *bshigpa rig yong,* come as a destroyer.

ཆིག་ཆིག། *chig chig,* a little; (shaking a little).

ཁ་གྱུར་ཅས། *kha gyurcas,* turn the mouth, *i.e.,* return.

མི་ཅུ། *micu,* the bones of the hands, fingers, toes and feet.

སྣ་སོགས། *sna sogs,* = *sna thsogs,* different.

སྤུབ་ཅས། *spubcas,* causative of *'abubspa,* put on a roof.

ས་མོ་ཆེ། *samoche,* much earth; *ludmo che,* much dung, etc.

ཡོག་བཏང་ཅས། *yog btangcas,* put underneath.

སྲོལ་གཉིད་ཁམ་པ། *srol γnyid khampa,* healthy sleep in ordinary fashion. Instead of *srol,* the Sheh-version has *sro; srol* is probably the original form. Lad. Grammar, Laws of Sound, No. 4.

ཏམ་ཏུམ། *tam tum,* a little [sleep]; Sheh-version has *tum tum.*

བེས་ལ། *besla*, =*byesla*, on the journey.

ཐོ་བ། *thoba*, skirt [of a garment].

གཡས་རྫེས་མ་རྫེས་བཏང་ཅས། *γyas rdzes ma rdzes btangcas*, to gird up [a coat].

པོག་ཅས། *pogcas*, take off (a pot from the fire).

རྡུག་པ་ཅན། *rdugpacan*, poisonous. That the word, *dug*, poison, presupposes a prefix in Lower Ladakh, is made probable not only by this form, but also by the other form *tug*; the change of the *d* to *t* presupposes the work of a prefix.

ཤི་བ་ཡིན། *shiba yin*, here in the sense of *shicas yin*, I am to die.

ཐེ་ཚོམས། *the thsoms*, =*the thsom*, doubt.

ཤག་ཅས། *shagcas*, =*bcagcas*, cut, break.

ལང་གར། *langgar*, tomb (of Mohamedan Tibetans).

བཏུག་ཅས། *btugcas*=*bdugcas*, see ante.

རྡོག་ཆོང་། *rdog chong*, kick with the foot.

མུལ་ཁྲུག། *mul khrug*, beat with the fist, box; the Sheb-version has *mul thug*.

No. 1.

དེ་ནས་ཧོར་ཡུལ་ལ་ཧོར་པ་དཔལ་ལྷེ་རྒྱལ་པོ་ལ་མདུན་མ་མེད་པ། ཡུལ་ཚང་མ་ལ་མེད་པ། ཨང་ག་ཡུལ་ལ་འདུག་ལྷ་ཅེས་ལ་ཕོ་རོག་འབྲུང་ཤེས་གཉིས་ཀ་བདང་སྟེ། ལོ་མང་པོ་སོང་སྟེ་ཡོད་ཚུག། དེ་ནས་ཀེ་སར་གླིང་ཡུལ་ལ་མེད་ཅེས་ཚོར་དེ། ཧོར་གྱིས་ཇོ་ཇོ་འབྲུ་གུ་མ་འཁྱོང་ཅེས་ལ་དམག་འཁྱེར་ཡིན་ཟེར་དེ། གྲབས་བཅོ་སྟེ་ཁྱོངས། གླིང་ཡུལ་ལ་དཔའ་བོ་ཚང་མ་གྲུང་གི་ལུང་པའི་ནང་དུ་ཡིངས་བཏང་གིན་ཞིག། གཡངས་པ་ལ་སོང་སྟེ་མེད་ཚུག། ཨ་གུ་ཁྲའི་མགོ་ཁྲའི་ཐུང་ལྷེམ་ལྷེམ་མི་ལྷེམ་མཁར་ནང་ཡོད་ཚུག། ཁྲའི་ཐུང་གིས་དེ་ཕི་གཉིས་གོན་དེ། ཁྱི་ལ་ཁྲོག་དམར་གཉིས་བདག་སྟེ་ཡོད་ཚུག། དེ་ཙེ་ཡིན་ཟེར་ན། ཀེ་སར་བདུད་ཡུལ་ལ་སྟོར་དེ་མེད་པ་སང་། གླིང་ཡུལ་ལི་དཔོན་པོ་ང་རང་ཡིན་བསམ་སྟེ་ཡིན་ནོག། དེ་ནས་ཞག་ཅིག་ལ་ཇོ་ཇོ་འབྲུ་གུ་མ་ལ་སྐྱི་ལམ་ངན་པ་ཁ་རྒྱུང་མཐོང་བས། ཨ་བི་མོན་ཁར་མོ་ཁྱོང་སྟེ། ཨ་བིའི་མདུན་ལ་ཇོ་ཇོས་སྐྱི་ལམ་བཤད་དེ་ཀླུ་འདི་ལྟར།།

ངའི་ཨ་ཕིས་དངོས་ཞིག་ལ་ཉོན་ལོ།

ཨ་ཕི་ལོན་ཁན་མོས་བདག་ལ་གསན་ལོ།

འདི་རིང་ཞག་ངན་གྱི་སྐྱི་ལམ་པོ་ངན་པ་རིག་མཐོང་ལོ།

འདི་རིང་མཚན་ངན་གྱི་སྐྱི་ལམ་པོ་རྨོག་པོ་རིག་མཐོང་ལོ།

གླིང་གི་གླིང་སྟོད་ན་ཆུ་ཆེན་ཞིག་ཁྲུག་པ་རང་མཐོང་ལོ།

ཆུའི་ཆུ་སྣ་ལ་ཇོ་ཇོ་ང་རང་ཁྱེར་བ་རིག་མཐོང་ལོ།

ཆུའི་ཆུ་དཀྱིལ་ལ་འབྲུ་དམར་ལམ་བསྟན་མཆོངས་པ་རིག་མཐོང་ལོ།

ཆུའི་ཆུ་ཞུལ་ལ་རྒྱལ་ལྷམ་ཀེ་སར་བསླིབ་པ་མཐོང་ལོ།

གླིང་གི་གླིང་སྟོད་ལ་མེ་ཆེན་ཞིག་འབར་བ་མཐོང་ལོ།

མེའི་མེ་སྣ་ལ་ཇོ་ཇོ་ང་རང་འདུགས་པ་མཐོང་ལོ།

མེའི་མེ་དཀྱིལ་ལ་འབྲུ་དམར་ལམ་བསྟན་མཆོངས་པ་རིག་མཐོང་ལོ།

མེའི་མེ་ཞུལ་ལ་ཀེ་སར་རྒྱལ་པོ་བསླིབ་པ་མཐོང་ལོ།

གླིང་མཁར་རྩེ་དགུ་ཞལ་མ་ལ་འགྱུར་བ་མཐོང་ལོ།

ཇོ་ཇོ་ང་རང་ཧོར་གྱིས་ཁྱེར་བ་ཞིག་མཐོང་ལོ།

འབྲུ་དམར་ལམ་བསྟན་ཧོར་གྱིས་བསད་པ་མཐོང་ལོ།

གླིང་གི་ཞ་སྐྱིང་ཧོར་གྱིས་ཟ་ལ་མཐོང་ལོ།

གླིང་གི་མར་སྐྱིང་ཚང་མ་ཧོར་གྱིས་ཟ་ལ་མཐོང་ལོ།

ཨ་ཕི་ཉེ་རང་གིས་མོ་ཞིག་དོབ་ལོ།

ཨ་ཕི་མོན་ཁན་མོས་མོ་ཞིག་དོབ་ལོ།

ཀུན་ནི་མོ་སྟན་ལ་ཕད་ཅེ་ཡོང་ཆེན་ལོ།

ངའི་མོ་སྟོན་ལ་གོ་ཞེན་དར་ཡུག་བཏང་ཡིན།
ཀུན་ནི་མོ་རྡི་ལ་རྡི་དཀར་རྡི་ནག་ཡོང་ཆེན་ལོ།
ངའི་མོ་རྡི་ལ་སྨུ་ཏིག་དང་གཡུའི་མོ་རྡི་བཏང་ཡིན་ལོ།
མོ་བཟང་པོ་བཏབ་ན་ཧྲན་པ་ཅི་དགོས་བཏང་ཡིན་ལོ།
མོ་ངན་པ་བཏབ་ན་རིན་ཅན་སྒྲོག་ལ་ཆད་པ་ཡིན་ནོ།

དེ་ནས་ཨ་ཕིས་མོ་བཏབས་པ། ཇོ་ཇོའི་སྐྱི་ལམ་ཅི་མཐོང་མཁན་ནང་ལྷར་མོའི་ནང་ནས་ཕིང་སོང་བས། ཨ་ཕིས་ཇོ་ཇོ་ལ་ཟེརས། ཇོ་ཇོ་ལེ། མོའི་ནང་ན་མཱ་བཟང་པོ་ཡང་མེད། མཱ་ངན་པ་ཡང་མི་འདུག། འབར་ཆོད་ཅིག་ཕིང་འདུག་ཟེརས། ཨ་ཕི་ཁོ་རང་གི་ཁང་པ་ལ་སོང།

No. 2.

དེ་ནས་རྒྱ་འཕྲུན་མོ་རྒྱ་ལ་སོང་བས། རྒྱ་འཕྲུན་མ་རྒྱའི་མཐའ་མ་ལ་བསླེབ་སོང། རྒྱའི་ཕར་ཁ་ལ་ཧོར་གྱི་དམག་སྣ་ལ་ཤན་ཀྲ་སི་ཧུ་ཟེར་མཁན་དེ་བསླེབ་སྡེ་ཡོད་ཚུག། དེ་ནས་ཤན་ཀྲ་སི་ཧུས་རྒྱ་འཕྲུམ་མ་ལ་གཏམ་ལབ་ལ་གླུ་ཞིག།།

རྒྱའི་ཕར་ཁ་ཧུ་ཡོད་པའི་ཨ་ཆེ་རྒྱ་འཕྲུམ་མས་དངོས་ལ་ཉོན་དང།
རྒྱམ་མཚོའི་ཕར་ཁ་ལ་ཡོད་པའི་རྒྱ་འཕྲུམ་མས་བདག་ལ་གསན།
མཁར་བཙན་པོའི་མིང་ལ་ཅི་ཞིག་ཟེ་ར་ཅན་ལོ།
མི་དཔའ་བོའི་མིང་ལ་ཅི་ཞིག་ཟེར་ཅན་ལོ།
རྟ་མགྱོགས་པའི་མིང་ལ་ཅི་ཞིག་ཟེར་ཅན་ལོ།

ཁྲི་ཙན་དེའི་མིང་ལ་ཅི་ཞིག་ཟེར་ཅན་ལོ།

ཇོ་ཇོ་མཛངས་མའི་མིང་ལ་ཅི་ཞིག་ཟེར་ཅན་ལོ།

ཕས་ལྷའི་མིང་ལ་ཅི་ཞིག་ཟེར་ཅན་ལོ།

མས་ལྷའི་མིང་ལ་ཅི་ཞིག་ཟེར་ཅན་ལོ།

རལ་གྲི་རྣོན་པོའི་མིང་ལ་ཅི་ཟེར་ཅན་ལོ།

མདའ་མགྱོགས་པའི་མིང་ལ་ཅི་ཟེར་ཅན་ལོ།

མདུང་རིང་མོའི་མིང་ལ་ཅི་ཟེར་ཅན་ལོ།

དེ་ཟྭག་ཟེརས་པ་སང་། ཆུ་འཕྲུམ་མས་ཅང་མ་ཟེར་བ། ཆུ་འཁྱེར་དེ་མཁར་ལ་སོང་བ། མཁར་ལ་བསང་ཆུ་འཁོར་དེ། ཇོ་ཇོས་ཁོ་ལ་ཁ་སྐྱེ་སྡེ་ཟེརས། ཁྱོ་རང་གིས་ཆུ་འགོར་བཅུགས། གནམ་གསུམ་ཟེར་མི་བཅུག། གོམ་གསུམ་སྐྱུབ་མི་བཅུག་ཟེརས་པ། ཆུ་འཕྲུམ་མས། ཇོ་ཇོ་ལེ། གོམ་གསུམ་མི་རྒྱུབ་ལེ། གནམ་གསུམ་ཞུ་བཅུག་ཟེརས་པ། ཇོ་ཇོས་གནམ་གསུམ་ཟེར་ན་ཡང་འགྲིག་ཟེརས། དེ་ནས་ཆུ་འཕྲུམ་མས་ཞུས། ང་ཆུའི་མཐའ་མ་ལ་བསླེབ། དེའི་ཕར་ཁ་ལ་མི་ཞིག་ཡོང་སྡེ་འདུག། ཁོས་མཁར་གྱི་མིང་དང་མིའི་མིང་ཚང་མ་འདྲི་ཟུག་པ། དེའི་གནམ་ལ་ཉན་དེ་ཙ་བིག་འགོར་སོང་ཞུས་པ། དེ་ནས་ཇོ་ཇོས་ཆུ་འཕྲུམ་མའི་གོས་ཚང་མ་གོན་དེ། ཆུ་གར་འཁྱེར་དེ་ལྷ་ལ་སོང་བས། དེ་མི་དེ་ཙ་ཡོད་ཚུག། ཡང་ཁོས་ཆུ་འཕྲུམ་མ་ལ་གནམ་ལན་ལ་གླུ་ཞིག་བཏང་ས།།

ཀྲ་ཆུའི་མཐའ་མའི་ཆུ་འཕྲུམ་མས་ཉོན་དང་།

གླིང་མཁར་གྱི་ཆུ་འཕྲུམ་མས་གསན་དང་།

ཁྱོད་ཀྱི་མཁར་བཙན་པོ་འི་མིང་ལ་ཅི་ཟེར་ཅེན།
ཁྱོད་ཀྱི་མི་དཔའ་བོ་འི་མིང་ལ་ཅི་ཟེར་ཅེན།
ཁྱོད་ཀྱི་རྟ་མགྱོགས་པའི་མིང་ལ་ཅི་ཟེར་ཅེན།
ཁྱོད་ཀྱི་ཁྱི་ཚན་དྲེའི་མིང་ལ་ཅི་ཞིག་ཟེར་ཅེན།
ཁྱོད་ཀྱི་ཇོ་ཇོ་མཛངས་མའི་མིང་ལ་ཅི་ཟེར་ཅེན།
ཁྱོད་ཀྱི་ཕས་ལྷའི་མིང་ལ་ཅི་ཞིག་ཟེར་ཅེན།
ཁྱོད་ཀྱི་མས་ལྷའི་ཤིང་ལ་ཅི་ཞིག་ཟེར་ཅེན།
རལ་གྲི་རྣོན་པོ་འི་མིང་ལ་ཅི་ཟེར་ཅེན།
མདའ་མགྱོགས་པའི་མིང་ལ་ཅི་ཟེར་ཅེན།
མདུང་རིང་མོ་འི་མིང་ལ་ཅི་ཟེར་ཅེན།

དེ་ཟུག་ཟེརས་པ་སྣང། ཇོ་ཇོས་ཁོ་ལ་གདམ་ལན་དུ་སྨྲ་ཞིག།

རྒྱའི་ཕར་ཁའི་མི་དེས་དངོས་ལ་ཉོན་དང།
རྒྱམ་ཚོའི་ཕར་ཁའི་མི་ཁྱོད་དངོས་ལ་ཉོན།
མཁར་བཙན་པའི་དོན་དེ་ཁྱོད་ལ་ཅི་ཞིག་དགོས།
མི་དཔའ་བོ་འི་དོན་དེ་ཁྱོད་ལ་ཅི་ཞིག་དགོས།
ཇོ་ཇོ་མཛངས་པའི་དོན་ཁེད་ལ་ཅི་ཞིག་དགོས།
རྟ་མགྱོགས་པའི་དོན་དེ་ཁྱོད་ལ་ཅི་ཞིག་དགོས།
ཁྱི་ཚན་དྲེའི་དོན་དེ་ཁྱོད་ལ་ཅི་ཞིག་དགོས།
ཕས་ལྷའི་དོན་དེ་ཁྱོད་ལ་ཅི་ཞིག་དགོས།
མས་ལྷའི་དོན་དེ་ཁྱོད་ལ་ཅི་ཞིག་དགོས།

རལ་གྲི་རྣོན་པོ་འི་དོན་ཁྲིད་ལ་ཅི་ཞིག་དགོས།

མདའ་མགྱོགས་པའི་དོན་ཁྲིད་ལ་ཅི་ཞིག་དགོས།

མདུང་རིང་མོ་འི་དོན་དེ་ཁྲིད་ལ་ཅི་ཞིག་དགོས།

དེ་རྣམས་ཁྲིད་ལ་དགོས་ན་ངས་བཤད་ཀྱི་ཡིན།

སྔོན་མ་མཁར་བརྩན་པའི་མིང་ལ་གླིང་མཁར་རྩེ་དགུ་ཟེར་ཅེན།

དག་ས་མཁར་བརྩན་པའི་མིང་ལ་ལྕེམ་ལྕེམ་མི་ལྕེམ་མཁར་ཟེར་ཅེན།

སྔོན་མ་མི་དཔའ་བོ་འི་མིང་ལ་རྒྱལ་ལྷམ་ཀ་སར་ཟེར་ཅེན།

དག་སའི་མི་དཔའ་བོ་འི་མིང་ལ་འབྲུ་དམར་ལམ་བསྟན་ཟེར་ཅེན།

སྔོན་མ་རྟ་མགྱོགས་པའི་མིང་ལ་རྐྱང་རྒོད་དབྱེར་པ་ཟེར་ཅེན།

དག་ས་རྟ་མགྱོགས་པའི་མིང་ལ་སྤྱི་རོག་པོན་པོན་ཟེར་ཅེན།

སྔོན་མ་ཁྲི་ཚན་དེའི་མིང་ལ་ཁྲི་པོ་གསེར་གླིང་ཟེར་ཅེན།

དག་སའི་ཁྲི་ཚན་དེའི་མིང་ལ་ཁྲི་མོ་ལྟོམ་དཀར་མོ་ཟེར་ཅེན།

སྔོན་མ་ཇོ་ཇོ་མཛངས་མའི་མིང་ལ་ཇོ་ཇོ་འབྲུ་གུ་མ་ཟེར་ཅེན།

དག་སའི་ཇོ་ཇོ་མཛངས་མའི་མིང་ལ་དཔལ་མའི་ཨ་སྟག་ཟེར་ཅེན།

སྔོན་མ་པས་ལྷའི་མིང་ལ་ཀེར་ཟོང་སྣན་པོ་ཞུ་ཅེན།

དག་སའི་པས་ལྷའི་མིང་ལ་པས་ལྷ་རབ་ལྷ་ཞུ་ཅེན།

སྔོན་མ་མས་ལྷའི་མིང་ལ་བཀུར་དམན་རྒྱལ་མོ་ཞུ་ཅེན།

དག་སའི་མས་ལྷའི་མིང་ལ་དྲག་ལྷ་རྒྱལ་མོ་ཞུ་ཅེན།

སྔོན་མ་རལ་གྲི་རྣོན་པོ་འི་མིང་ལ་རྟ་བ་ཚོད་མ་ཟེར་ཅེན།

དག་ས་རལ་གྲི་རྣོན་པོ་འི་མིང་ལ་མིག་སི་རི་རལ་གྲི་ཟེར་ཅེན།

སྔོན་མ་མདའ་མཀྲིགས་པོའི་མིང་ལ་མདའ་མོ་གསེར་མདའ་མཐུག་རིངས། དགུ་ས་མདའ་མགྲོགས་པ་ཊེ་མིང་ལ་མདའ་དཀར་པོའི་ལམ་བསྟན།

དེ་ཟུག་ཟེར་དེ་ན། ཪོ་ཪོ་མཁར་ལ་ལོག་སྟེ་ཡོངས། ཏོར་གྱི་ཤན་ཀྲ་མི་ཊུ་ལོག་སྟེ་ཏོར་གྱི་དམག་རང་ལ་སོང་།།

དེ་ནས་གླིང་གི་དཔའ་བོ་ཚང་ཀ་ལ་ཏོར་གྱིས་དམག་འཁྲོང་ཅེས་ཆོར་དེ། གླབས་ཞིག་བཅོས་པས། དཔའ་བོ་ཚང་མས་རང་གིས་མི་རི་ཕྲུ་སྟེ་རྟགས་བཅོ་སྟེ་ཟེརས། ང་དང་ཚང་མ་ཏོར་གྱི་དམག་ལ་ལྟ་སྐོར་ལ་ཆེན། ང་དང་སྲུ་ཞིན། འདིའི་སེ་ཡང་ཞི་ཡིན། སྲུ་གསོན་དེ་ལུས་ན། འདིའི་མི་ཡང་མ་ཞི་བ་ལུས་ཡིན་ཟེར་དེ། ཁོང་ཚང་མ་སོང་། དེ་ནས་ཁོང་ཏོར་གྱི་དམག་ཐང་དང་ཉེ་མོ་ལ་བསླེབ་སྟེ་བལྟས་པ། ཏོར་གྱི་རྟ་ཚང་མ་རྒྱལ་བ་མཐོང་སྟེ། མཚན་ལ་ཁོང་རྟ་ཀུ་བ་ལ་སོང་སྟེ། ཏོར་ཁྱི་རྟ་ཚང་མ་ཀུས་དེ་ཁྲོངས། འབུ་དམར་ལམ་བསྟན་ཕྲུ་གུ་ཡོད་པའི་ཕྱི་ལ། དཔའ་བོ་ཚང་མ་ལ་མ་ནོན་བ། ཉིང་ན་ཏོར་གྱི་ཐང་ས་ཊུ་བསླེབ། རྟ་ཚང་མ་འཁྱེར་ཚར་དེ་མེད་ཚུག། དེ་ཊུ་རྟ་ཁང་གསུམ་གཅིག་ཡོད་ཚུག། ཁོས་བསམ། འདི་བོ་འཁྱེར་ན། ཞ་བོ་ཞིག་འདུག་བསམ་མིན་ཞིག་འདུག་ཤ་པ། དེ་ཚུག་པ་གནམ་ལངས་སོང་། དེ་ནས་ཁོས་རིབ་ཞིང་ཞིག་མགོ་ལ་གཏོན་དེ་འདུགས་པ། གནམ་ལངས་པ་དང་། ཏོར་ཚང་མ་ལ་རྟ་མེད་པས། ཏེ་ལིང་སོང་། དེ་ནས་ཁོས་བལྟ་སྟེ་འདུགས་པ། སྔོན་ལ་གུར་དཀར་རྒྱལ་པོ་ལ་མདུན་མ་གར་འདུག་ལྟ་ཅེས་ལ་ཕོ་རོག་འབྲུང་ཞིས་གཉིས་ཀ་དེ་ཊུ་བསླེབ་སྟེ། གུར་དཀར་གྱི་གུར་གྱི་མགོ་ལ་བིང་སྟེ་སྨྲ་ཞིག་བཏང་ངོ་།།

ཕོ་རོག་ང་སྙིང་ཕྱོགས་ལྷ་ཡུལ་ལ་བསླེབ་ལོ།

ལྷའི་དབང་པོ་རྒྱབ་ཞིན་ལ་བུ་མོ་གསུམ་འདུག་ལོ།

བུ་མོ་གཅིག་ནི་ཧན་དྲང་ཞིག་འདུག་ལོ།

བུ་མོ་གཅིག་ནི་ཞར་བ་འདུག་ལོ།

བུ་མོ་གཅིག་ནི་ཀུད་ཅིག་འདུག་ལོ།

རྟ་ལ་ཟ་བའི་རྩྭ་ཡང་མི་འདུག་ལོ།

མི་ལ་ཟ་བའི་ཟན་ཡང་མི་འདུག་ལོ།

ལམ་འཕྲང་ཆུ་གསུམ་རྫོག་པོ་རང་འདུག་ལོ།

ཞ་ཟེས་ཀྱི་ཧུས་པ་ཕོ་རོག་ང་ལ་ཡང་མ་ཐོབ།

ཆང་འཐུངས་ཀྱི་སྦང་མ་ཕོ་རོག་ང་ལ་ཡང་མ་ཐོབ་ལོ།

ཕོ་རོག་ང་འོག་ཕྱོགས་ཀླུ་ཡུལ་ལ་ཡང་བསླེབ་ལོ།

ཀླུ་རྒྱལ་ལྡོགས་པོ་ལ་བུ་མོ་གསུམ་འདུག་ལོ།

བུ་མོ་གཅིག་ནི་ཀང་ཞ་རིག་འདུག་ལོ།

བུ་མོ་གཅིག་ནི་ལག་ཞ་རིག་འདུག་ལོ།

བུ་མོ་གཅིག་ནི་གྲོད་པ་ཆེན་མོ་ཞིག་འདུག་ལོ།

རྟ་ལ་ཟ་བའི་རྩྭ་ཡང་མི་འདུག་ལོ།

མི་ལ་ཟ་བའི་ཟན་ཡང་མི་འདུག་ལོ།

ལམ་འཕྲང་ཆུ་གསུམ་རྫོག་པོ་རིག་འདུག།

ཞ་ཟེས་ཀྱི་ཧུས་པ་ཕོ་རོག་ང་ལ་ཡང་མ་ཐོབ།

ཆང་འཐུངས་ཀྱི་སྦང་མ་ཕོ་རོག་ང་ལ་ཡང་མ་ཐོབ།

ཕོ་རོག་ང་ཞར་བཙན་ཡུལ་ལ་བསླེབ་སོང་།

ཨ་མ་སྐྱབ་བདུན་མ་ལ་བུ་མོ་གསུམ་ཟམ་འདུག་ལོ།

བུ་མོ་གཅིག་ནི་སྣ་ཡོན་ཞིག་འདུག་ལོ།

བུ་མོ་གཅིག་ནི་སྣ་མེད་ཅིག་འདུག་ལོ།

བུ་མོ་གཅིག་ནི་འཇིང་རིངས་ཤིག་འདུག་ལོ།

ལམ་འཕྲང་ཆུ་གསུམ་དེ་ཙོག་པོ་ཞིག་འདུག་ལོ།

ཧ་ལ་ཟ་བའི་རྩྭ་ཡང་མི་འདུག་ལོ།

མི་ལ་ཟ་བའི་ཟན་ཡང་མི་འདུག་ལོ།

ཤ་ཟོས་ཀྱི་རུས་པ་ཕོ་རོག་ང་ལ་ཡང་མ་ཐོབ།

ཆང་འཐུངས་ཀྱི་སྐྱང་མ་ཕོ་རོག་ང་ལ་ཡང་མ་ཐོབ།

ཕོ་རོག་ང་གླིང་མཁར་སྟོད་ལ་ཡང་བསླེབ་ལོ།

ཇོ་ཇོ་འབྲུ་ག་མ་གསེར་ཁྲིའི་ཁ་འདུག་ལོ།

ཁོག་སྟོད་གསེར་ལ་ཞངས་མཁན་ཞིག་འདུག་ལོ།

ཁོག་སྨད་གཡུ་ལ་ཞངས་མཁན་ཞིག་འདུག་ལོ།

དབུ་སྐྲ་གཉེར་ལ་ཡོད་མཁན་ཞིག་འདུག་ལོ།

ཉིད་ལ་མཛེས་པའི་ཇོ་ཇོ་དེ་ན་འདུག་ལོ།

གུར་དཀར་ལ་མཛེས་པའི་མདུན་མ་ཞིག་འདུག་ལོ།

རྒྱལ་ལྷམ་ཀེ་སར་བདུད་ཡུལ་ལ་སྟོར་ཏེ་མ་བསླེབ་མོ།

འབུ་དམར་ལམ་བསྟན་དེ་བྲུ་གུ་ལ་འདུག་ལོ།

དཔལ་ལེ་རྒོད་པོ་ཆས་དེ་ཞིག་འདུག་ལོ།

དཔའ་བོ་ཚང་མ་གྲང་གི་ལྷུང་པའི་ནང་དུ་འདུག་ལོ།
ལམ་ཁ་ཕྲང་ཆུ་གསུམ་བདེ་མོ་ནང་འདུག་ལོ།
རྟ་ལ་ཟ་བའི་རྩྭ་ཡང་འདུག་ལོ།
མི་ལ་ཟ་བའི་ཟན་ཡང་འདུག་ལོ།
ཤ་ཟོས་ཀྱི་ཙུས་པ་ཕོ་རོག་ང་ལ་ཡང་ཐོབ་ལོ།
ཚང་འཕྲུངས་ཀྱི་སྤྲང་མ་ཕོ་རོག་ང་ལ་ཡང་ཐྲོབ་ལོ།

དེ་ཟུག་ཟེར་ས་པ། འབྲུ་དམར་ལམ་བསྟན་ལ་སྒྲོ་ཡོང་སྟེ། སོག་ལྷི་ཞིག་བཏངས་པ། ཕོ་རོག་གཉིས་ཀ་སའི་ཁ་བུད་དེ་ཤི་སོང་། དེ་ནས་ཧོར་པ་ཧལ་ལྷེ་རྒྱལ་པོ་ཡམ་ཚན་ཞིག་སོང་སྟེ་ཟེར། ཡུ་ནས་མཁར་སྟོང་པ་ནས་ཅི་བུད་དེ་ཡོངས། ཕོ་རོག་གཉིས་ཀ་ལ་ཅི་ཕོག་ཟེར་རིན་ཞིག། ལེན་དེ་བཟླ་ཟ་ན་པོ་རོག་གཉིས་ཀ་ཤི་སྟེ་མེད་ཚུག། དེ་ནས་ཕོ་རོག་གཉིས་ཀ་ལས་ཞིག་བྲུ་སྟེ། དེའི་ནང་དུ་བཀབ་སྟེ་རོམ་ཁང་ཞིག་བཅོ་སྟེ་བོརས། འབྲུ་དམར་ལམ་བསྟན་གྱིས་དེ་མཚན་ལ་ཧོར་གྱི་རྟ་ཀང་གསུམ་དེ་ཀུ་སྟེ་ཁྲིད་དེ་ཁྱོང་སྟེ། གླིང་གི་དཔའ་བོ་ཚང་མའི་མདུན་ལ་བསླེབ་སོང་བ་སང་། ཁོ་མདུན་ལ་ཡོང་མ་བཙུགས། ཁྱོ་རང་ཚ་རྟ་ཀང་གསུམ་ཞ་བོ་ཞིག་ཐོབ་སྟེ་འདུག། རྟ་དེ་སྤུ་ལ་དགོས་ཡིན། ང་ཞའི་ཁྲིན་རྟའི་སློས་སྐལ་མི་བཏང་ཟེར་དེ་ཁོ་ལ་སྒྲོ་བཅོས་པ་སང་། འབྲུ་དམར་ལམ་བསྟན་ལ་སྒྲོ་ཡོང་སྟེ། ང་ལ་ཡང་མི་དཀོ་ཟེར་དེ། རྟ་དེ་འཕུད་བཏངས་པས། རྟ་ཀང་གསུམ་དེ་ལོག་སྟེ་ཧོར་གྱི་དམག་འབྲང་ལ་སོང་། དེ་ནས་ཧོར་གྱི་འཁྲུལ་རྟ་ཀང་གསུམ་ལ་ཞོན་དེ། ཧོར་གྱི་ཤན་ཀྲ་མི་ཙུ་དེ་རྟའི་ལྷ་སྐོར་ལ་ཡོངས། ཁོས་རྟ་རྫེས་

བཙན་དེ་ཨོངས་པ། གླིང་པའི་དཔའ་བོ་ཀུན་ཡོད་ས་རྩ་བསླེབ་པས། ཨ་གུ་དཔལ་ལེ་གུར་གྱི་མདུན་ལ་སོང་སྟེ་གླུ་ཞིག།

གུར་ཤིང་གཅིག་གནམ་ལ་སླང་སྟེ་འདུག་ལོ།
གུར་ཐག་གཅིག་ས་ལ་ལྷ་སྟེ་འདུག་ལོ།
དེ་གུར་ནང་དུ་མི་ཆེན་སྐུ་ཞིག་བཞུགས་ལོ།
དེ་གུར་ནང་དུ་དཔའ་བོ་སྐུ་ཞིག་བཞུགས་ལོ།
ཧོར་པ་ཧལ་ལྷེ་རྒྱལ་པོའི་རྟ་ཞིག་སྟོར་ལོ།
ང་རྟའི་ལྷ་སྐོར་ལ་ཡོངས་མཁན་ཞིག་ཡིན་ལོ།
ང་ཞའི་རྟ་དེ་འདིར་བསླེབ་སྟེ་རང་འདུག་ལོ།
ང་ཞའི་རྟ་དེ་སློག་སྟེ་སྟུལ་རིགས་རིག་མཛད་ལོ།
ཐོབ་མ་ལྷགས་ཤིག་ཀུས་པ་ཞིག་ཡིན་ལོ།
ཀུས་ལྷགས་ཤིག་ཐོབ་མཁན་ཞིག་ཡིན་ལོ།

ཧོར་གྱིས་དེ་ཟླུག་ཅིག་ཟེརས་པ། ཨ་གུ་དཔལ་ལེས་ལན་དུ་ཡང་ཟེརས།

གནམ་སྟོད་མཐོན་པོ་ན་ཕོ་རོན་གསུམ་ཨར་འདུག་ལོ།
ཕོ་རོན་སྔོན་མ་དེ་སྔོན་ལ་འཕུད་དེ་བཏང་ཡིན་ལོ།
ཕོ་རོན་ཧྲིང་མ་དེ་ཧྲིང་ན་བོར་ཡིན་ལོ།
ཕོ་རོན་དཀྱིལ་མ་དེ་ངས་ས་ལ་འཕབ་ཡིན་ལོ།
བྱ་སྤྲུ་གཅིག་གནམ་ལ་ཡན་མི་བཙུག, ལོ།
བྱ་ཁྲིག་ཅིག་ས་ལ་འབུད་མི་བཙུག་ལོ།
ཧོར་ངན་སོག་པོའི་སྐའི་མདུན་གྱི་ཁ་ཐེབ་ལོ།

དེ་རྒྱུག་ཟེར་དེ། དཔལ་ཡེས་མདའ་ཞིག་བདངས་པ། ཕོ་རོན་དཀྱིལ་མ་དེ་སྤྱིབ་ཅིག་ལ་ཧོར་གྱི་སྐྲའི་མདུན་གུའི་ཁ་ཕབས་པས། ཧོར་གྱིས་འཇིག་སྟེ། ཅང་མ་ཟེར་བ། ཡང་འབྲུ་དམར་ལམ་བསྟན་གྱི་གུར་གྱི་མདུན་ལ་སོང་སྟེ་གླུ་ཞིག་བཏངས།།

གུར་ཤིང་ཞིག་གནམ་ལ་སླང་སྟེ་འདུག་ལོ།
གུར་ཐག་ཅིག་ས་ལ་ལྷ་སྟེ་འདུག་ལོ།
དེའི་ནང་ལ་མི་ཆེན་སུ་ཞིག་བཞུགས་ལོ།
དེའི་ནང་ན་དཔའ་བོ་སུ་ཞིག་རང་བཞུགས་ལོ།
ཧོར་གུར་དཀར་རྒྱལ་པོ་འི་རྟ་ཞིག་སྟོར་ལོ།
གུར་དཀར་རྒྱལ་པོ་འི་རྟ་དེ་འདིར་འདུག་ལོ།
ང་ཞའི་རྟ་དེ་འདིར་བསྐྱེབ་སྟེ་རང་འདུག་ལོ།
ང་ཞའི་རྟ་དེ་ལོག་སྟེ་དེང་ལོ།
ཐོབ་མ་ལྷགས་ཤིག་ཀུས་པ་ཞིག་ཡིན་ལོ།
ཀུས་ལྷགས་ཤིག་ཐོབ་པ་ཞིག་ཡིན་ལོ།

དེ་རྒྱུག་ཟེརས་བ། འབྲུ་དམར་ལམ་བསྟན་ལ་སྒྲོ་ཡོང་སྟེ་ལན་ལ་གླུ་ཞིག།

ལྷ་ཧོར་ཁྲིད་ཀྱིས་དངོས་ལ་ཅིན་དང་།
ཁྲོད་རྟ་གཅིག་གི་མི་གཙུག་དངོས་ལ་ཅིན་དང་།
ང་ཞའི་ཁྲིམས་ལ་ཆོས་བཅུ་བཅོ་ལྔ་ཡིན་ལོ།
ཁྱོ་ཞའི་ཁྲིམས་ལ་ཤུ་ཀུར་ཤིང་ཤེར་ཡིན་ལོ།

སྟེང་གི་མི་ལ་བདང་ན་སྡིག་པ་རིག་འདུག་ལོ།
འོག་གི་རྟ་ལ་བདང་ན་སྡིག་པ་རིག་འདུག་ལོ།
གཞུང་གི་སྣ་ལ་མདའ་མོ་ཞིག་བདང་ཡིན་ལོ།

དེ་ཟུག་ཟེར་དེ་མདའ་ཞིག་བདངས་པ། ཧོར་གྱི་སྐའི་མདུན་གྲུ་ལ་ཕོག་སྟེ་མེད་མཁན་བཅོས་བདངས་པ། ཧོར་ཤན་ཀྲ་སི་ཏུ་འཛིགས་དེ། འཁྲུལ་རྟ་ཀང་གསུམ་དེ་ལ་སྐད་ཅིག་བདང་སྟེ་ན། བང་དྲག་པོ་ཞིག་ཁྲེངས་པ། རྟ་དེ་ཚང་མ་སྲིབ་གཅིག་ལ་མཉམ་པོ་སོང་། དེ་ནས་ཤན་ཀྲ་སི་ཏུ་ཧོར་གྱི་དམག་འཐང་ལ་རྟ་ཚང་མ་འཁྲིད་དེ་བསླིབ་སོང་།།

ཤན་ཀྲ་སི་ཏུས་གུར་དཀར་རྒྱལ་པོ་ལ་ཟེརས། ང་དང་གི་རྟ་ཚང་མ་གླིང་པའི་དཔའ་བོ་ཀུན་གྱིས་ཁྲེར་དེ་འདུག། གླིང་པའི་དཔའ་བོ་ཚང་མ་ལྟུང་པའི་ཕྲུ་ཞིག་ལ་སོང་སྟེ་འདུག། མཁར་དེའི་ནང་དུ་ཇོ་ཇོ་འབྲུ་གུམ་གཅིག་པོ་ཡོད་ཆོད་འདུག་ཟེརས་པ། དེ་ནས་གུར་དཀར་རྒྱལ་པོས་ཆེན་ཟེར་དེ། དམག་དང་ཚང་མ་གླིང་མཁར་ལ་སོང་། ལྷིམ་ལྷིམ་མི་ལྷིམ་མཁར་ལ་སོང་བས། དེ་ནས་ཨ་གུ་འཁྲིའི་ཐང་ཁ་ཐོག་ལ་བིང་སྟེ། ཧོར་ལ་གདམ་ལན་ལ་གླུ་ཞིག་བདངས།།

ཁྱེད་རྟ་མངས་ཀྱི་མི་མངས་དངོས་ལ་ཉོན་དང་།
ཁྱོད་ཧོར་གྱི་དམག་དེས་བདག་ལ་གསན་ལོ།
ཁྱེད་ཀུན་མདའ་རྩེས་ལ་དགའ་ན་འདིར་ཡོང་ལོ།
ཁྱེད་ཀུན་མདུང་རྩེས་ལ་དགའ་ན་འདིར་ཡོང་ལོ།
མདའ་རྩེས་བདང་ན་ང་དང་གིས་བདང་ཡིན་ལོ།

མདུང་རྩེས་བཏང་ན་ང་ཏང་གིས་བཏང་ཡིད་ལོ།

ཤ་སྐྱིད་ལ་དགའ་ན་གླིང་མཁར་ལ་སོང་ལོ།

མར་སྐྱིད་ལ་དགའ་ན་གླིང་མཁར་ལ་སོང་ལོ།

ཇོ་ཇོ་འབྲུ་གུ་མ་ལ་དགའ་ན་གླིང་མཁར་ལ་སོང་ལོ།

དེ་ལྟར་ཟེརས་པ། ཧོར་གྱིས། ང་ཞ་མདའ་རྩེས་དང་མདུང་རྩེས་ལ་མི་འཐད། ཤ་སྐྱིད་དང་མར་སྐྱིད་དང༌། ཇོ་ཇོ་ལ་འཐད་ཡིན་ཟེར་དེ། ཕྱིར་ལོག་སྟེ་གླིང་ཡུལ་ལ་སོང༌།།

No. 3.

དེ་ནས་ཇོ་ཇོ་འབྲུ་གུ་མ་ལ་ཧོར་གྱི་དམག་ཡོང་ཙམ་མཐོང་སྟེ། གཡུ་ཚང་མ་འཕྱུད་དེ་སྤྲ་ལ་པ་ལོ་རྒྱབ་སྟེ་ཁྲབ་རྨོག་གོན་ཏེ། མདའ་དང་རལ་གྲི་འཁུར་ཏེ་སྨོན་ལམ་ཞིག་བཏབས་སོ།།

མཉམ་པོ་སྐྱེས་པའི་ལྷ་དགུ་མཁྱེན་ནོ།

མཉམ་པོ་སྐྱེས་པའི་ཀླུ་དགུ་མཁྱེན་ནོ།

ཕས་ལྷ་ཀེར་ཟེང་སྐྱོན་པོ་མཁྱེན་ལོ།

མས་ལྷ་བཀུར་དམན་རྒྱལ་མོ་མཁྱེན་ནོ།

འདི་རིང་ང་ལ་དཔུང་རོགས་མཛད་ལོ།

དེ་ལྟག་ཟེར་དེ། ཧོར་གྱི་དམག་ཁྲོ་ལ་སོང་སྟེ། ཧོར་གྱི་དམག་མང་པོ་བསད་སོང༌། དེ་ནས་ཧོར་གྱི་ཤན་ཀྲ་མི་ཐུས་ཟེརས་པ། འདི་པོ་བུ་ཚ་ཞིག་མེད། བུ་མོ་ཞིག་ཡིན་ཚོད་འདུག ཚང་མས་ཀུ་ཅོ་དེང་ཟེརས་པ། ཧོར་གྱི

དམག་ཚང་མས་ཀུ་ཅོ་བཏངས་པ། ཇོ་ཇོ་ཡམ་ཙན་སོང་སྟེ་མཁར་གྱི་ནང་ལ་ལོག་སྟེ་སོང་། དེ་ནས་ཧོར་གྱི་དམག་ཚང་མས་དབང་བཙོ་རྡེ་མཁར་གྱི་ནང་དུ་སོང་བས། ཇོ་ཇོ་ལ་བཅོ་ཐབས་ཅི་ཡང་མེད་པ། ཧོར་གུར་དཀར་གྱི་གཉིད་མད་བཅོ་སྟེ། མཁར་གྱི་ཤ་སྐྱིང་མར་སྐྱིང་ཚང་མ་ཟ་འདིན་ཞིག་འདུགས། ཞག་ཁ་ཤས་ཤིག་སོང་སྟེ་ན་ཧོར་གུར་དཀར་གྱིས་ཟེརས། ད་ཧོར་ཡུལ་ལ་ཆ་ཡིན་འགྲུལ་ཇོ་ ཇོ་ལེ་ཟེརས་པ། ཇོ་ཇོས་ཤ་སྐྱིང་ཟ་ཚར་དེ་མེད་ནས་མི་ཆ་ཟེརས། ཤ་སྐྱིང་ཟ་ལ་ལོ་དགུ་སོང་། དེ་ནས་ཡང་འགྲུལ་ཟེརས་པ། ཡང་ཇོ་ཇོས་མར་སྐྱིང་ཟ་ཚར་དེ་མེད་ནས་མི་ཆ་ཟེར་དེ་འདུགས་པ། མར་སྐྱིང་ཟ་ལ་ལོ་དགུ་སོང་།།

དེ་ནས་ཡང་ཇོ་ཇོ་ལ་འགྲུལ་ཟེརས་པ། ཇོ་ཇོས། མདའ་གང་ས་ནང་མ་ཐུག་པ། མདའ་གང་གནམ་ནང་མ་ཐུག་པ་རིལ་མང་གི་མཁར་ཞིག་ཅོས། དེ་ནས་ང་ཆེན་ཟེརས་པ། ཧོར་གྱི་དམག་ཚང་མས་རིལ་མང་བསྒྱུས་དེ། མཁར་རྫིགས་པ། ལོ་དགུ་སོང་། དེ་ཟམ་གླིངས་པ། ཀ་སར་མ་བསླེབ་སོང་།

དེ་ནས་ཡང་ཧོར་གྱིས་འགྲུལ་ཇོ་ ཇོ་ཟེརས་པ། ཇོ་ཇོ་ལ་ཡང་ཅང་ཐབས་མེད་མཁན་སོང་། གླིང་མཁར་རི་ནང་དུ་ཅི་ཡང་མེད་མཁན་སོང་། ཇོ་ཇོས་ཆེན་ཟེརས། དེ་ནས་ཇོ་ ཇོའི་གཡོན་ཅེས་ཚང་མ་དང་། བདག་སྐྱེ་ཚང་མ་གཡོག་མོ་ལ་སྔོན་ཏེ་ན། ཇོ་ ཇོ་ཁོ་རང་ཆིབས་རའི་ནང་དུ་ལྷུད་བྲུ་སྟེ། དེའི་ནང་དུ་ཟངས་ཆེན་མོ་ཞིག་ཁ་ཐུབ་ལ་བཏང་སྟེ་ཤིབ་སྟེ་འདུགས། ཧོར་གྱིས་གཡོག་མོ་དེ་ཇོ་ ཇོ་ཡིན་ནོག་བསམ་སྟེ། མཁར་ནང་ནས་ཕེང་ཕྱེ་འཁྲིད་དེ་འཁྱེར་རད་ཚུག་པ། གླིང་ཡུལ་ལི་མཇུག་ལ་ཨ་བི་ནད་མོ་ཞིག་ཡོད་ཚུག། དེ་ཡོང་སྟེ་ཧོར་ལ་ཟེརས། གུར་དཀར་རྒྱལ་པོ་ལེ། གླིང་གི་ཤ་སྐྱིང་ཟ་ཚར། མར་སྐྱིང་ཟ་ཚར། ཇོ་ཇོ་

འབྲུ་གུ་ཡང་ཉེ་རང་ལ་ཐོབ། གླིང་རྒྱལ་ལྷམ་ཀེ་སར་རི་ཆིབས་རའི་ནང་དུ་རྟ་རྒྱུགས་ཤིག་མ་བཏང་བ། སྐྱོད་ཡིན་ན་ཟེརས་པ། ཇོར་གྱི་ཤན་ཀྲ་མི་རྩས་རེ་བོ་བདེན་ཟེར་དེ། ཇོར་རྟ་ཞིག་ལ་ཞོན་དེ་ཆིབ་རའི་ནང་དུ་བང་གཅིག་བཏངས་པ། དེའི་ནང་ན་ཛོ་ཛོ་འི་སྦྲ་ཞིག་རྟའི་རྐང་པ་ལ་འཁྲིལ་དེ; ཛོ་ཛོ་དེའི་ནང་ནས་ཕིང་སྦེ་ཡོངས། དེ་ནས་ཛོ་ཛོ་ཇོར་གྱིས་འཁྲིད་དེ་ཁྲིརས། ལྷེམ་མཁར་གྱི་ཁ་ཐོག་ལ་ཨ་གུ་ཁྲའི་ཐུང་གིས་བལྟ་སྦེ་ཡོད་ཚུག་པ། ཛོ་ཛོས་གླུ་ཞིག།།

གླིང་རྒྱལ་ལྷམ་ཆེན་མོ་དེ་བདུད་ཡུལ་ལ་སྟོར་སོང་།
གླིང་གི་ཤ་སྙིང་ཟ་ལ་ལོ་དགུ་སོང་།
གླིང་གི་སར་སྙིང་ཟ་ལ་ལོ་དགུ་སོང་།
རིལ་མང་གི་མཁར་རྩིག་པ་ལོ་དགུ་སོང་།
དེ་ཟམ་ཚུག་པ་ཀེ་སར་མ་བསླེབ་ལོ།
སྔོན་ལ་ཀེ་སར་ལ་ཞབ་ཤི་མང་པོ་ཞིག་ཡོད་པིན།
དག་ས་ཞབ་ཤི་གཅིག་ཀྱང་མི་འདུག་ལོ།
ཛོ་ཛོ་ང་རང་ཇོར་གྱིས་འཁྲིར་འདུག་ལོ།
ཀེ་སར་རྒྱལ་པོ་ཡོད་པའི་དུས་ལ་དཔའ་བོ་མང་ཟམ་ཡོད་པིན།
དག་ས་ཇོར་གྱི་དམག་ཡོང་ཟ་ན་དཔའ་བོ་གཅིག་ཀྱང་མི་འདུག།

ཛོ་ཛོས་དེ་ལྟུག་ཟེརར་པ། ཨ་གུ་ཁྲའི་ཐུང་ལ་སྒྲོ་ཡོང་སྟེ། མགྱོགས་པ་དམག་ཆས་བཏང་སྟེ། ཇོར་གྱི་རྩར་སོང་སྟེ་བརྒྱ་ཟམ་ཞིག་བསད་བཏངས། དེ་ནས་ཇོར་གྱི་ཤན་ཀྲ་མི་རྩས་ཀུ་ཙོ་རྡོང་ཟེརས་པ། ཇོར་གྱི་དམག་ཚང་མས་ཀུ

ཙོ་དྲུག་པོ་བཏངས་པ། ཨ་གུ་ཁྲའི་ཐྲུང་འཛིགས་དེ་ཕྱིར་ལོག་སྟེ་ལྡེམ་ལྡེམ་མི་ལྡེམ་མཁར་ནང་དུ་སོང་བས། ཛོ་ཛོ་རྡོར་གྱིས་འཁྲིད་དེ་འཁྱེར་ས། ཐང་ཞིག་གི་ཁ་བསྒྲིབ་པ། དེ་རུ་ཨང་གར་ལུངས་པ་དང་ཐུག་སོང་པ། རྡོར་གྱིས་རྒྱམ་སྟེ་བཙོན་ལ་བཅུག་པ་འཁྱེར་ས། དེ་ནས་གྲོང་གི་ལུང་པའི་ནང་དུ་དཔའ་བོ་ཚང་མ་ལ་ཚོར། གླིང་མཁར་གྱི་ཞ་སྐྱིང་རྡོར་གྱིས་ཟོས། མར་སྐྱིང་རྡོར་གྱིས་ཟོས། གླིང་མཁར་བཞིག་སྟེ་ཞལ་མ་ལ་སྒྲུངས། ཛོ་ཛོ་འབྲུ་གུ་མ་གུར་དཀར་གྱིས་འདུན་མ་ལ་ཁྱེརས།།

No. 4.

ང་དང་ལྷ་ལ་ཆ་ཡིན་ཟེར་དེ། འབྲུ་དམར་ལམ་བསྟན་ལྷ་ལ་ཡོངས་པ། གླིང་མཁར་སྟོད་དེ་ཙང་མེད་མཁན་བཙོ་སྟེ་རྡོར་གྱིས་འཁྱེར་དེ་མེད་ཚུག། དེ་ནས་འབྲུ་དམར་ལམ་བསྟན་ཨམ་ཚན་སོང་སྟེ། ཨ་གུ་དཔལ་ལེ་མདུན་ལ་སོང་སྟེ་གླུ་ཞིག་བཏངས་སོ།།

ངའི་ཨ་གུས་འང་དངོས་ཞིག་ལ་ཉོན་དང།
དཔལ་ལེ་རྒོད་པོས་འང་བདག་ལ་གསན་ལོ།
གླིང་མཁར་སྟོད་ལ་དམག་ཆེན་ཞིག་བསྒྲིབ་དགོ།
གླིང་མཁར་ལ་རྡོར་གྱི་དམག་ཆེན་ཞིག་ཡོངས་དགོ།
གླིང་གི་ཞ་སྐྱིང་ཚང་མ་རྡོར་གྱིས་ཟོས་དགོ།
གླིང་གི་མར་སྐྱིང་ཚང་མ་རྡོར་གྱིས་ཟོས་དགོ།
ཛོ་ཛོ་འབྲུ་གུ་མ་རྡོར་གྱིས་འཁྲིད་དེ་འཁྱེརས་ལོ།
དང་གི་སྒྲིད་བུ་ཡང་འཁྱེར་དེ་མི་འདུག་ལོ།

གསེར་ཉ་ཟླུངས་གཅིག་ཡང་འཁྱེར་དེ་སི་འདུག།
གཡུ་ཉ་ཟླུངས་གཅིག་ཡང་འཁྱེར་དེ་མི་འདུག།
ཧ་ཡོ་ཁ་ལ་མེ་འབར་ཡང་འཁྱེར་དེ་མི་འདུག།
ཡོ་ལད་རི་གྲུད་གཞུ་ཡང་འཁྱེར་དེ་མི་འདུག་ལོ།
དེའི་ཕི་ལ་ང་བདས་དེ་རང་ཆེན་ལོ།
ཧ་དེ་ཧ་གསར་རྒྱལ་ལ་ཧ་ཀན་རིག་རྒྱལ་ལོ།
གཞུ་དེ་གཞུ་གསར་རྒྱལ་ལ་གཞུ་ཀན་རིག་རྒྱལ་ལོ།
མདུང་དེ་མདུང་གསར་རྒྱལ་ལ་མདུང་ཀན་རིག་རྒྱལ་ལོ།
མདའ་དེ་མདའ་གསར་རྒྱལ་ལ་མདའ་ཀན་ཀྱིལ་ལོ།
གྲི་དེ་གྲི་གསར་རྒྱལ་ལ་གྲི་ཀན་རིག་རྒྱལ་ལོ།
ཁྲབ་དེ་ཁྲབ་གསར་རྒྱལ་ལ་ཁྲབ་ཀན་རྒྱལ་ལོ།
རྨོག་དེ་རྨོག་གསར་རྒྱལ་ལ་རྨོག་ཀན་རྒྱལ་ལོ།

དེ་ཟླུག་ཨ་ཀུ་དཔལ་ལེ་ལ་འདྲིས་པ། ཨ་ཀུས་ལན་དུ་སླུ་ཞིག།

ཨ་ཀུའི་ཚ་བོས་དངོས་ཤིག་ལ་སྙན་དང་།
དཔལ་ལེ་འི་ཚ་བོས་བདག་ཅིག་ལ་གསན་དང་།
ཨ་ཀུའི་ཚ་བོ་ལ་ཞལ་ལྟ་བདང་དགོས་ཡང་མེད་ལོ།
འབྲུ་དམར་ལམ་བསྟུང་། ཡ་བསླབ་བྱ་བདང་དགོས་རང་མེད་ལོ།
ཁྱེད་ཀྱིས་ཧ་གསར་མ་ཁྱེར་ཧ་ཀན་རིག་ཁྱེད་ལོ།
ཁྱེད་ཀྱིས་གཞུ་གསར་མ་ཁྱེར་གཞུ་ཀན་རིག་ཁྱེར་ལོ།

ཁྱེད་ཀྱིས་མདུང་གསར་མ་ཁྱེར་མདུང་རྒན་རིག་ཁྱེར་ལོ།
ཁྱེད་ཀྱིས་མདའ་གསར་མ་ཁྱེར་མདའ་རྒན་རིག་ཁྱེར་ལོ།
ཁྱེད་ཀྱིས་གྲི་གསར་མ་ཁྱེར་གྲི་རྒན་རིག་ཁྱེད་ལོ།
ཁྱེད་ཀྱིས་ཁྲབ་གསར་མ་ཁྱེར་ཁྲབ་རྒན་རིག་ཁྱེར་ལོ།
ཁྱེད་ཀྱིས་རྨོག་གསར་མ་ཁྱེར་རྨོག་རྒན་རིག་ཁྱེར་ལོ།
གྱེན་གྱེན་གྱེན་ལ་སེང་གེ་མཆོང་ལུགས་ཅོས།
ཐུར་ཐུར་ཐུར་ལ་ལྷ་མོ་འཁྱོལ་འཁྲོས་ཅོས།
འདབས་འདབས་འདབས་ལ་ཕོ་རོག་ཟུར་མཆོངས་དོང་།
རལ་གྲི་པ་བརྒྱ་བའི་གཡོན་ལ་མ་འདུག།
དུ་བག་པ་བརྒྱའི་གཡས་ཕྱོགས་ལ་མ་ཆ།
ཨ་གུའི་ཚ་བོ་ལ་བསླབ་བྱ་བཏང་དགོས་རིག་མེད་ལོ།
འབྲུ་དམར་ལམ་བསྟན་ལ་ཞལ་ལྟ་ངདང་དགོས་མེད་ལོ།

ཨ་གུས་དེ་ཟུག་ཟེརས་པ། འབྲུ་དམར་ལམ་བསྟན་གྱིས། ཨ་གུས་ཟེར་མཁན་ནང་ལྟར་ཚང་མ་འཁུར་དེ་དོར་ལ་བདས་དེ་སོང་། ཨ་གུ་དཔལ་ལེས་གནམ་གཅིག་བསླབ་པར་བརྗེད་སོང་། ག་ས་ཁྱེད་ཅིག་ལ་སྐོམས་ན་བུབ་རྒྱུ་མ་མཐུང། གནའ་ནི་རོགས་བུ་མ་གྲོལ་ཟེར་ཅེས་བརྗེད་སོང་། དེ་ནས་འབྲུ་དམར་ལམ་བསྟན་མགྱོགས་པ་སོང་སྟེ། དོར་ལ་ཉེ་ཞ་སོང་བས། གྱེན་ལ་སེང་གེ་མཆོངས་ལུགས་བཅོས། ཐུར་ལ་ལྷ་མོ་འཁྱོལ་འཁྲོས་བཅོ་འིན་ཞིག་དང་། དོར་གྱི་དམག་ཕྱེད་ཟམ་བསད་དེ་ན། ཇོ་ཇོ་འབྲུ་གུ་མ་ཐའི་ཁ་སྤྲུབ་སྟེ་ཕྱིར་ལོག་

སྦེ་ཁྲོངས་པ། འབྲུ་དམར་ལམ་བསྟན་ངལ་དེ། རྫའི་ཁ་གཉིད་ཡོང་གིན་ཞིག་ཡོངས་པ། རྗོར་གྱི་ཤན་ཀྲ་མི་ཙ་རྫིང་རང་ནས་ཡོང་སྦེ། འབྲུ་དམར་ལམ་བསྟན་ལ་ཚོར་མ་བཙུག་པ་ཇོ་ཇོ་ལ་ཟེརས། ཇོ་ཇོ་ལེ་ཧོར་གུར་དཀར་རྒྱལ་པོ་དང་མཉམ་པོ་འདུག་སྦེ་ལོ་འདི་ཟམ་སོང། ད་གུར་དཀར་རྒྱལ་པོ་མ་འཕང་ཟེརས་པ། ཇོ་ཇོས་ད་བཙོ་ཐབས་མི་ཡོང་ཡིན། འབྲུ་དམར་ལམ་བསྟན་གྱི་གཟུགས་པོ་ ཚང་མ་ཕོ་ལད་ལ་ཡོད། ཚང་གཡོག་གི་ནང་ལ་ཤ་མེ་ལོང་ཟམ་ཞིག་མན་ནས་མེད། ཅང་བཙོ་མི་ཉན་ཟེརས་པ། ཤན་ཀྲ་མི་ཙས། ཇོ་ཇོ་རང་གིས་ཅི་ཐབས་བཙོ་ནའང་ཅོས་ཟེརས་པ། དེ་ནས་ཇོ་ཇོས་ཤན་ཀྲ་མི་ཙ་ལ་བསླབ་སྦེ་ཟེརས། ཁྲོ་རང་སྤུན་ལ་སོང་སྦེ། ཨ་ཙ་རན་འཐག་ཅིག་ཡོད། དེ་རན་འཐག་གི་གཡོག་ཁང་ནང་དུ་སོང་སྦེ་འདུག། ངས་འབྲུ་དམར་ལམ་བསྟན་ནི་གན་ནི་རོགས་བྱ་འགྲོལ་དེ། རན་འཐག་གི་ལྷ་མགོ་ན་ཆུ་ཞིག་འཐུང་བཙུག་ཡིན། ཁྲེ་རང་གིས་ལྷའི་ནང་ནས་མདའ་དེ་ཚང་གཡོག་ལ་བལྟ་སྦེ་དོང། དེ་ནས་ཁོ་ཤི་ཡིན་ཟེརས་པ། ཤན་ཀྲ་མི་ཙ་སྔོན་ལ་སོང་སྦེ་རན་འཐག་གི་ནང་དུ་ཞུག་སྦེ་འདུགས། དེ་ནས་ཇོ་ཇོ་དང་འབྲུ་དམར་ལམ་བསྟན་གཉིས་ཀ་རན་འཐག་གི་མདུན་ལ་བསླེབ་སོང། ཇོ་ཇོས་ཟེརས་པ། ནོ་འབྲུ་དམར་ལམ་བསྟན་ལེ། ནོ་རང་ལ་དགས་གཉིད་ཡོང་འདུག། འདི་ཙ་ཅ་ཞིག་འདུག་ཡིན། གན་ནི་རོགས་བྱ་གྲོལ། རན་འཐག་གི་ལྷ་མགོ་ན་ཆུ་ཞིག་འཐུང། ཧོར་གྱི་ཁ་རྒྱལ་དེ་ང་འཁྲིད་དེ་ཁྲོངས་པ་སྣང། མང་པོ་འཐད་འདུག་ཟེརས་པ། འབྲུ་དམར་ལམ་བསྟན་གྱིས་རྒྱལ་ཇོ་ཇོ་ལེ་ཟེར་དེ། རྫའི་ཁ་ནས་བབ་སྦེ་གན་ནི་རོགས་བྱ་འགྲོལ་དེ། རན་

འཐག་གི་ལྷ་མགོ་ན་བུབ་ཙུ་ཞིག་འཐུངས་པ་སང། དེ་ཚུག་པ་ཤན་ཀྲ་མི་ཙུས་རན་འཐག་གི་ནང་ནས་འདའ་རྒྱབས་པ་སང། མདའ་དེ་འབྲུ་དམར་ལམ་བསྟན་གྱི་ཆང་གཡོག་ལ་ཕོག་སོང། དེ་ནས་ཇོ་ཇོས་འབྲུ་དམར་ལམ་བསྟན་ལ་དབང་བྱས་ཏེ། ཁོར་གྱི་ཤན་ཀྲ་མི་ཙུ་དང་མཉམ་པོ་སོང་བའི། འབྲུ་དམར་ལམ་བསྟན་ལ་མདའ་ཕོག་སྟེ་དེ་ཙུ་ལུས་འདུགས།།

དེ་ནས་དེ་ཙུ་དཔལ་ལེ་རྐོད་པོ་བསླེབ་པས། འབྲུ་དམར་ལམ་བསྟན་ལ་མདའ་ཕོག་སྟེ་ཡོད་ཅེས་མཐོང་སྟེ། ཡམ་ཚན་སོང་སྟེ་ཟེརས། སྔོན་ལ་ངས་གཏམ་གཅིག་བསླབ་པ་བརྗེད་སོང་འབྲུ་དམར་ལེ་ཟེརས་པ། འབྲུ་དམར་གྱིས་ཟེརས། ང་ཤི་ཡིན་ན་གསོན་ཡིན་ཨ་ག་ལེ། དཔལ་ལེས་ཟེརས། ཕན་ད་ཕན་ཡིན་བ། སྔོན་ལ་ང་ཁོར་ལ་བདས་ཏེ་ཆེན། འབྲུ་དམར་གྱིས་ཟེརས། དགས་ང་ཕན་བཙུག་ཨ་ག་ལེ། རྙིང་ན་ང་སོང་སྟེ་ཁོར་གྱི་རིགས་ལུས་མི་བཙུག། དེ་རྫུག་ཟེར་ནའང། ཨ་ག་དཔལ་ལེས་དབང་བཙོ་སྟེ་ཁོར་ལ་བདས་ཏེ་སོང་བ། ཤན་ཀྲ་མི་ཙུ་དེ་རྙིང་ན་ཡོད་ཚུག། རྩའི་ཕར་ཁ་ན་ཆ་ཅེས་མཐོང་སྟེ་ཟེརས། ལྷ་ཁོར་ངན། ཁྱེ་རང་གིས་ང་ཞའི་ཕྲུ་གུ་ཞིག་དང་གྲུད་འགྲན་བཏངས་སོག་པ། དགས་ང་དང་གྲུད་ཅིག་མོ་འགྲན་ན་ཟེརས་པ། ཤན་ཀྲ་མི་ཙུས་རྒྱལ་ཟེརས། དེ་ནས་མདའ་དེ་གང་པོས་སྔོན་ལ་བཏང་ཡིན་ཟེརས་པ། ཤན་ཀྲ་མི་ཙུས་ངས་བཏང་ཡིན་ཟེརས། དེ་ནས་དཔལ་ལེས་ཁོར་ལ་འདྲི་སྟེ། ཁྱོ་དང་གི་མདའ་གཙུ་ཕོག་ཅེས་ཡིན་ཟེརས་པ། ཁོར་གྱིས་དྲང་པོ་ཟེརས། ངའི་མདའ་དེ་མིག་ལ་རྒྱབ་ན། སྙིང་ལ་ཕོག་ཅས་ཡིན་ཟེརས་པ། དཔལ་ལེས།

ཨར་མཆོངས་འདིར་མཆོངས་མ་བཏང་ན་ཁྱོད་སྒོ་རོག་གི་པོན་པོན་མིན་ལོ།

དྲར་ཆད་དྲུར་ཆད་མ་བཏང་ན་ཁྱོད་རྗེ་ཆོད་མ་རལ་གྲི་མིན་ལོ།

རལ་གྲི་བཏང་སྟེ་མ་ཕོག་ན་དཔལ་ལེ་རྒོད་པོ་ང་ལ་མ་ཟེར་ལོ།

དེ་ཟུག་ཟེར་རིན་ཞིག་དང་། དཔལ་ལེ་ཡོང་སྟེ་རྗེ་བ་ཆོད་མ་རལ་གྲི་དང་རྒྱབ་སྟེ། ཤན་ཀྲ་མི་ཏྲ་ཁག་པོ་གཉིས་བཅས་བཏང་སྟེ། ཁོ་སྲིབ་ཅིག་ལ་ཤི་སོང་། དེ་ནས་ཁོ་འི་ལྤགས་པ་ཤུ་སྟེ། ས་ཞིབ་མོ་ཞིག་སྐང་སྟེ། ཁོ་རང་གི་རྟའི་ཁ་བཀལ་དེ། ལྤགས་པ་ལ་བི་གང་མང་པོ་ཕིང་སྟེ་ན། རྟ་འཕུད་བཏངས་པ། ཕང་དྲག་པོ་བཏང་གིན་ཞིག་ཧོར་དམག་གི་མདུན་ལ་སོང་པ། ལྤགས་པའི་བི་གང་ཚང་མའི་ནང་ནས་ས་ཕིང་སྟེ། ཐལ་སྤུབ་ཕིང་ཅེས་མཐོང་སྟེ། ཧོར་གྱི་དམག་ཚང་མ་འཛིགས། དེ་ནས་གུར་དཀར་གྱིས་ཛོ་ཛོ་ལ་འདྲིས་པ། ཛོ་ཛོ་ལེ་གླིང་ཡུལ་ཕྱོགས་ནས་རྟ་པ་དྲག་པོ་ཞིག་ཡོང་འདུག། དེ་སུ་ཡིན་ཟེར་ས་པ། ཛོ་ཛོས། དེ་རྟ་པ་ཀེ་སར་རྒྱལ་པོ་ཡིན་ཆོད་འདུག་ཁོ་ལ་ཅི་བཅོ་ནའང་། མི་ཉན་ཟེར་ས་པ། ཧོར་གྱི་དམག་དེ་ཚང་མ་འཛིག་སྟེ་སུ་ཆུའི་ནང་ལྷུབས། སུས་རང་དང་རང་གྱི་བཏང་སྟེ་ཤི་སོང་། རྟིང་ན་བལྟ་ཟ་ན། ཤན་ཀྲ་མི་ཏྲའི་ལྤགས་པ་དང་ཁོ་འི་རྟ་ཨིན་ནོག། དེ་ནས་གུར་དཀར་དང་དམག་དང་ཛོ་ཛོ་ཚང་མ་ཡམ་ཚན་སོང་སྟེ། ཧོར་ཡུལ་ལ་སོང་།།

དཔལ་ལེ་ལོག་སྟེ་བསླེབ་བསླེབ་ལ། འབྲུ་དམར་ལམ་བསྟན་གྱི་མདུན་ལ། ཁྲའི་ཕུང་བསླེབ་སྟེ། ཁོས་ཧོར་ངན་གྱི་མདའ་འཁུར་དེ། ཅི་ལ་འདུག ཨིན་ཟེར་དེ་འཕུད་བཏངས་པ། འབྲུ་དམར་ལམ་བསྟན་གྱི་སྙིང་དེ་མདའི་རྡེའུ་ལ་འཁད་དེ་ཕིང་སྟེ་ཁྱོང་སྟེ། དཔལ་ལེ་བསླེབ་ཟ་ན། བཅོ་ཐབས་མེད་མཁན་སོང་

སྟེ་ཤི་ཅན་ལ་ཁ་ཐུག་སོང་སྟེ། འབྲུ་དམར་གྱིས་ཨ་ཀུ་དཔལ་ལེ་ལ་ཁ་ཆེམས་
ཞིག་བོརས།།

ངའི་ཨ་ཀུས་འང་དངོས་ལ་ཉོན་ལོ།
དཔལ་ལེ་ཀློད་པོས་བདག་ལ་གསན་ལོ།
དེ་རིང་བྲུ་ཚང་ཤི་ཅེས་རིག་རག་ལོ།
འབྲུ་དམར་ལམ་བསྟན་ཤི་ཅེས་ལ་ཐུག་ལོ།
ཤར་ལ་བལྟས་པའི་ལུང་པའི་ནང་ན།
ཧ་མང་པོ་འི་ཁྲུ་ཞིག་རང་ཡོད་ལོ།
དེ་ལ་ཁག་པོ་གསུམ་ཟས་ཅོས་ལོ།
ཁག་གཅིག་གླིང་མཁར་ལ་ཞིག་སོབ་ཅེས།
ཁག་གཅིག་བྲུ་ཚང་རང་གི་དོན་ཞིག་ཅེས།
ཁག་གཅིག་གླིང་རྫོང་ཀི་སར་ལ་བོར།
ཀློ་རྒྱུ་བལྟས་པའི་ལུང་པའི་ནང་ན།
ར་མ་མང་པོ་འི་ཁྲུ་ཞིག་ཡོད་ལོ།
དེ་ལ་ཁག་པོ་གསུམ་ཟས་ཅོས་ལོ།
ཁག་གཅིག་གླིང་མཁར་ལ་ཞིག་སོབ་ཅེས།
ཁག་གཅིག་བྲུ་ཚང་རང་གི་དོན་ཞིག་ཅེས།
ཁག་གཅིག་གླིང་རྫོང་ཀི་སར་ལ་བོར་ལོ།
ནུབ་ལ་བལྟས་པའི་ལུང་པའི་ནང་ན།
ཡག་འབྲི་མང་པོ་འི་ཁྲུ་ཞིག་ཡོད་ལོ།

དེ་ལ་ཁག་པོ་གསུམ་ཟམ་ཅོས་ལོ།

ཁག་གཅིག་གླིང་མཁར་ལ་ཞིག་སོབ་ཅོས།

ཁག་གཅིག་བྲུ་ཚ་ང་རང་གི་དོན་ཅོས་ལོ།

ཁག་གཅིག་གླིང་རྗེད་ཀེ་སར་ལ་བོར།

བྱང་དུ་བལྟས་པའི་ལུང་པའི་ནང་ན།

ལུག་དང་ལུག་གུའི་ཁྲུ་ཞིག་ཡོད་ལོ།

དེ་ལ་ཁག་པོ་གསུམ་ཟམ་ཅོས་ལོ།

ཁག་གཅིག་གླིང་མཁར་ལ་ཞིག་སོབ་ཅོས།

ཁག་གཅིག་བྲུ་ཚ་ང་རང་གི་དོན་ཅོས་ལོ།

ཁག་གཅིག་གླིང་རྗེད་ཀེ་སར་ལ་བོར།

ཤར་ལ་གཟིགས་པའི་རབ་སལ་པོ་འི་ནང་ན།

གསེར་གྱི་རན་འཐག་རང་འཁོར་ཡོད།

ལྷོ་ལ་གཟིགས་པའི་རབ་སལ་པའི་ནང་ན།

སྤུ་རིག་གི་ཀྲུ་གུ་ཡོད་ལོ།

ནུབ་ལ་གཟིགས་པའི་རབ་སལ་པོ་འི་ནང་ན།

ཟངས་ཀྱི་ཁྲི་གུ་སྤུག་ཤེས་ཡོད་ལོ།

བྱང་ལ་གཟིགས་པའི་རབ་སལ་པོ་འི་ནང་ན།

དུང་གི་ལུག་གུ་འབྲུག་ ཤེས་ནང་ཡོད་ལོ།

དེ་ཚང་མ་ལ་ཁག་གསུམ་ཅོས་ལོ།

ཁག་གཅིག་གླིང་མཁར་གྱི་ཞིག་སོབ་ཅོས།

ཁག་གཅིག་བྱ་ཚ་ང་རང་གི་དོན་ཞིག་ཅོས།
ཁག་གཅིག་གླིང་རྫེད་ཀི་སར་ལ་བོར་ལོ།
གལ་དེ་ཀི་སར་བདུད་ཡུལ་ནས་བསླེབ་ཟེར་ན།
ཁ་དམར་མོ་འབྲུ་གུ་ཡང་ཁྱོང་ཡིན་འགྲོ།
ལོ་གསུམ་མགོ་འི་ཁ་འོལ་དོབ་ཟེར།
ལོ་གསུམ་ར་མའི་ར་རྫི་ལ་བོར་ཟེར།
ལོ་གསུམ་ལུག་གི་ལུག་རྫི་ལ་བོར་ཟེར།
ལོ་གསུམ་བ་གླང་གི་བ་རྫི་ལ་བོར་ཟེར།
ལོ་གསུམ་ཡུམ་པའི་མཐོང་ཀོལ་ལ་དོང་ཟེར།
ལོ་གསུམ་མཁར་གྱི་རྩུ་མ་ལ་བོར་ཟེར།

དེ་ཟུག་བསླབ་བྱ་ཚང་མ་ཟེར་དེ། འབྲུ་དམར་ལམ་བསྟན་གྲོངས་སོང་། དེ་ནས་ཨ་ག་དཔལ་ལེ་ཡིས་སྤྱུར་དེ་རི་མཐོན་པོ་ཞིག་ལ་འཁྱེར་དེ། མི་ལ་བསྒྲིག་ནས་སྤྱུར་ཁང་ཞིག་བཅོ་སྟེ་བོར་ནས། ཨ་ག་དཔལ་ལེ་གླིང་ཡུལ་ལ་ཡོང་སྟེ། ཞག་རེ་ལ་པེ་ཐུར་མངས་གང་རེ་འགས་མིན་ཞིག་སྦྱ་ངན་ལ་འདུགས། རྒྱལ་ལྷམ་ཀི་སར་དེ་བཏུད་ཡུལ་ལ་སྟོར།

འབྲུ་དམར་ལམ་བསྟན་རྗོར་གྱིས་བསདས།
གླིང་མཁར་རྩེ་དགུ་ཤལ་མ་ལ་སྒྱུར།
ཇོ་ཇོ་འབྲུ་གུ་མ་དོར་གྱིས་འཁྱེརས།
བསམ་སྡེ་སྨུག་བཅོ་སྡེ་འདུགས།།

No. 5.

དེ་ནས་ཞག་ཅིག་ལ་ཡུལ་མཇུག་གི་ཨ་བི་དཔལ་ལེའི་མདུན་ལ་ཡོང་སྟེ་ཟེརས། ལྷ་དཔལ་ལེ་རྒོད་པོ་ཁྲིད་སྡུག་བཅོ་སྟེ་མ་འདུག། ཀེ་སར་ཤི་ཅས་དང་སྟོར་ཅས་མི་ཡོང། བྲུ་ཁྲུང་ཁྲུང་དཀར་མོ་ཀུན་ལྷ་ལ་བདང་ན་ཐོབ་ཡིན་ཟེརས་པ། དཔལ་ལེས་སྒྲོ་བཅོ་སྟེ་ཅང་མ་ཟེརས། དེ་ནས་ཞག་ཅིག་ལ་ཨ་བི་ཡང་ཡོང་སྟེ་ཟེརས་པ། དཔལ་ལེ་ཡིད་ཆེས་དེ་བྲུ་ཀུན་ཁྱོངས་པ། བྲུ་ཀུན་ལ་ཟ་ཅེས་བདང་མཁན་མེད་པ་སང། ཤེད་མེད་མཁན་སོང་སྟེ་ཡོད་ཚུག། ཨ་གུ་དཔལ་ལེས་ཞག་དང་འཁྲུ་འིན་ཞིག། ཟ་ཅེས་རྒྱལ་ལ་བདང་ངེན་ཞིག་བོརས། དེ་ནས་ཞག་ཅིག་ཚོད་བལྟས་པ། གླིང་མཁར་ལ་ལན་ཅིག་ཀྱང་འཁོར་མ་ཐུབ་སོང། ཡང་ཞག་བདུན་བོར་དེ་བལྟས་པ། གླིང་མཁར་ལ་ལན་ཅིག་ཁོར། ཡང་ཞག་བདུན་སོང་སྟེ་ལན་གསུམ་ཁོར། དེ་ཟླུག་གི་ལན་དགུ་འཁོར་འཁོར་ཚུག་པ་གསོལ་བདང་གིན་ཞིག་བོརས་པ། ཞག་ཅིག་ལན་དགུ་ཁོར་སོང། དེ་ནས་དཔལ་ལེས་ཀེ་སར་ལ་ཡི་གེ་ཞིག་བྲིས། ལྷ་བསམ་མེད་ཀེ་སར། ལྷ་གླིང་རྗེད་ཀེ་སར་གར་ཡོད། འདིར་གླིང་ཡུལ་ལ་ཧོར་གྱི་དམག་ཡོང་སྟེ་བཅོ་ཐབས་མེད་མཁན་སོང། ཤ་སྐྱིང་ཟ་ཡ་ལོ་དགུ་འབུད། མར་སྐྱིང་ཟ་ལ་ལོ་དགུ་འབུད། ཟན་སྐྱིང་ཟ་ལ་ལོ་དགུ་འབུད། རིལ་མང་གྱི་མཁར་བརྩིག་པ་ལོ་དགུ་འབུད། དེ་ཚག་པ་ཀེ་སར་བསླེབ་མ་བསླེབ། གླིང་མཁར་རྩེ་དགུ་ཤལ་མ་ལ་གྱུར། ཛོ་ཛོ་འབྲུག་མ་ཧོར་གྱིས་འཁྲེརས། བུ་དམར་ལམ་བསྟན་ཧོར་གྱིས་བསདས། གླིང་མཁར་གྱི་ནུར་བུ་ཚང་མ་ཧོར་གྱིས་འཁྲེརས། ཨང་གར་ལྕངས་པ་ཧོར་གྱིས་བཙོན་ལ་བདང་བ་འཁྲེརས། དང་གི་རྒྱུད་བུ་དང་གསེར་ཉ། དུང་ཉ། ཕོ་ལད་གྱུད་གཞུ། རྟ་པོ་ཁ་

ལ་མི་འབར་ཚང་མ་འཁྱེརས། ཁྱོད་བསམ་བ་མེད་མཁན་གར་ཡོད། དཔལ་ལེ་ང་རང་སྨུག་གི་ནང་དུ་ཡོད། དེ་ཟུག་ཟེར་དེ། ཡི་གེ་གཉིས་བྲི་སྟེ། བྲུ་གཉིས་ཀ་ལ་རེ་རེ་བཀལ་དེ་བཏངས།

བྲུ་དེ་གཉིས་ཀས་ཡི་གེ་རེ་རེ་འཁྱེར་དེ། སྨོན་ལ་སྟེང་ལྷ་ཡུལ་ལ་སོང་བས། ཁོང་ཤིང་རྒྱལ་ཞིག་གི་ཁ་དགོངས་ལ་ལུས། ཤིང་རྒྱལ་དེའི་གཡོག་ལ་སྨིན་མོ་མ་བུ་གཉིས་ཡང་བསླེབ་སོང་། དེ་ནས་གཉིད་ལོག་སྟེ་འདུགས་པ་སང་། གནམ་མ་ལངས་པ་རིག་ལ། སྨིན་མོའི་བུ་མོས་ཨ་མ་ལ་ཟེརས། ཨ་ཨ་མ། གླིང་ཀེ་སར་རྒྱལ་པོ་དག་ས་གར་ཡོད་ཚུག་ཟེརས་པ། ཨ་མས་ཟེརས། ཨ་བུ་མོ། གླིང་ཀེ་སར་མེད་པ། ང་དང་ལ་ཟ་ཅིས་ལ་ཏྟ་རོ་ཟ་ནའང་། མི་རོ་ཟ་ནའང་ཐོབ་སྟེ་ཡིན་ནོག། ཀེ་སར་ཡོད་པིན་ན། ང་དང་བསད་དེ་གནན་ལུས་ཡིན། གླིང་པའི་མི་ཉན་དེ་ཡོང་ཆེན་ཚུབ་ཅན་དེ་འདུག་ཟེརས་པ། དེ་ནས་བུ་མོ་དེ་ཕི་སྟ་རྟ་བལྟས་པ། སུ་ཡང་མེད་ཚུག། བུ་མོས་ཟེརས། མི་སུ་ཡང་མིན་འདུག། ཟེར་འང་ཨ་མ་ཟེརས་པ། ཨ་མས། ཀེ་སར་བདུད་ཡུལ་ལ་སོང་སྟེ། རྗེ་མོ་བམ་ཟ་བྲུམ་སྐྱིད་དང་གཉིས་ཀས་ཚོ་ལོ་བཏང་གིན་ཞིག། གླིང་མཁར་དང་ཟན་ནོར་ཅི་ཡོད་མཁན་ཚང་མ་ཚོ་ལོ་ལ་བཙུག་སྟེ་བམ་ཟ་བྲུམ་སྐྱིད་ལ་ཐོབ་ཚར། དགས་ཁོང་རང་གཉིས་ཀའི་རྩི་བི་དིང་ཀུན་བཙུག་སྟེ་ཚོ་ལོ་རྩེའད། རྩི་བི་དིང་ཡང་བམ་ཟ་བྲུམ་སྐྱིད་ལ་ཐོབ་ན་ཀེ་སར་ཡང་ཤི་མིན་འགྲོ་ཟེརས་པ། བྲུ་གཉིས་ཀ་ལ་དེ་ཟུག་ཚོར་དེ། ཀུང་ཀུང་ཟེར་དེ། འཕུར་དེ་སོང་། དེ་ནས་ཨ་མ་ལ་སྤྲོ་ཡོང་སྟེ་བུ་མོ་ལ་རྗེ་བ་ཆེན་མོ་ཞིག་རྒྱབ་སྟེ། བུ་མོ་དེ་སྤྲིབ་གཅིག་ལ་ཤི་སོང་། རྗེ་བ་དེ་ཕར་ཕོག་ལ་ཡོང་སྟེ། ཨ་མ་ཁོ་རང་ལ་ཕོག་སྟེ་དེང་ན་ཨ་མ་ཡང་ཤི་སོང་།།

དེ་ནས་བྱ་གཉིས་ཀ་བདུད་ཡུལ་ལ་བལྟས་དེ་སོང་བས། བྱ་གཉིས་ཀ་བདུད་ཡུལ་ལ་བསླེབ་སྟེ། མཁར་གྱི་མདུན་ལ་བསླེབ་སྟེ་བལྟས་པ། ཀ་སར་དང་བམ་ཟ་བུམ་སྐྱིད་གཉིས་ཀ་ཆོ་ལོ་བཏང་གིན་ཞིག། ཨ་ར་ར་ཝུ་ཧུ་ཧུ་ཟེར་རིན་ཞིག་ཡོད་ཚུག། བྱ་གཉིས་ཀས་སྐད་ཅིག་བཏངས། དེ་ནས་ཀ་སར་ལ་སྐད་དེ་ཚོར་དེ་ཟེརས་པ། ཉིན་ཇོ་མོ། ངའི་གླིང་མཁར་གྱི་བྱ་ཀུན་གྱི་སྐད་ཅིག་རག་ཟེརས་པ། བམ་ཟ་བུམ་སྐྱིད་ཀྱིས་ཁྱེད་ཀྱི་བྱ་དེ་ག་ནས་ཡོད་ཟེར་དེ་ཐེབ་ཀུ་ཅོ་བཏངས། དེ་ནས་བྱ་ཀུན་གྱིས་ཞེད་དང་སྐད་ཅིག་བཏངས་པ། ཀ་སར་ལ་གསལ་པོ་ཚོར་སོང་། ཀ་སར་ཁ་ཕྲོག་ལ་ཐིང་སྟེ་བལྟས་པ། བདེན་པ། བྱ་དེ་ནམ་མཁའ་ན་ཡོད་ཚུག། དེ་ནས་ཀ་སར་གྱིས་ཐིང་དཀར་ཞིག་བཏིང་སྟེ། དེའི་ཁ་གསོན་ཤ་ཞིག་བོརས། ཐིང་ནག་ཅིག་བཏིང་སྟེ། དེའི་ཁ་ཤི་ཤ་ཞིག་བོརས། དེ་ནས་ཀ་སར་གྱིས་གླུ་ཞིག་བཏངས།།

ངའི་བྱ་མོ་གཉིས་ཀས་དངོས་ཤིག་ལ་ཉོན་དང།
བྱ་དེ་ཁྲུང་ཁྲུང་དཀར་མོ་ཀུན་བདག་ལ་གསན།
གླིང་མཁར་བདེ་མོ་ཞིག་ཡོད་ཟེར་ན།
ཐིང་དཀར་ལ་རེ་སྟེ་གསོན་ཤ་དེ་ཟོ་ལོ།
གླིང་མཁར་བདེ་མོ་ཞིག་མེད་ཟེར་ན།
ཐིང་ནག་ལ་རེ་སྟེ་ཤི་ཤ་དེ་ཟོ་ལོ།

དེ་ལྟག་ཟེརས་པ་སང། བྱ་ཀུན་གྱིས་ཐིང་ནག་ལ་རེ་སྟེ་ཤི་ཤ་དེ་ཟོས། དེ་ལྟག་ཤེས་དེ། ཀ་སར་སྙུན་དེ་ས་ལ་འགྱེལ་སོང་བ། བྱ་ཀུན་གྱིས་ཀ་སར་རི་

ཁའི་ནང་དུ་བྱ་ཀྱུག་རི་བཏང་ས་པ། ཀ་སར་གྱིས་མྱུན་སང་སྟེ། ལྷ་བྱ་ཁམ་ལོག་ཀུན། ངའི་ཁའི་ནང་བྱ་ཀྱུག་བཏང་ས་ཟེར་དེ། ཀ་སར་མང་པོ་སྐྱུགས་སོང་། དེ་སྐྱུགས་མཁན་ཚང་མ་དེ་རྫོ་མོས་བཏང་ མཁན་ནི་ ཟས་ངན་ཡིན་པས། ས་དོ་གོམས་ཤིག་གནམ་ལ་སོང་། གནམ་དོ་གོམས་ཤིག་ས་ལ་བབས་སོང་། དེ་ནས་ཀ་སར་གྱིས་ཡང་སྨྲ་འདི་ལྟར།།

ངའི་བྱ་ཀུན་གྱིས་དངོས་ལ་ཉོན་དང་།
བྱ་ཁྲུང་ཁྲུང་དཀར་མོས་བདག་ལ་གསན།
གླིང་གི་ཤ་སྙིང་མར་སྙིང་བདེ་མོ་ཡོད་ད།
ཕིང་དཀར་ལ་རི་སྟེ་གསོན་ཤ་དེ་ཟོ།
དེ་ཀུན་བདེ་མོ་ལ་མེད་ཟེར་ན།
ཕིང་ནག་ལ་རི་སྟེ་ཤི་ཤ་དེ་ཟོ་ལོ།

དེ་ཟུག་ཟེར་ས་པ། བྱ་ཀུན་ཡང་ཕིང་ནག་ལ་རི་སྟེ་ཤི་ཤ་དེ་ཟོས། དེ་ནས་ཀ་སར་ཡང་མྱུན་དེ་ས་ལ་འགྲེལ་སོང་། བྱ་གཉིས་ཀས་ཡང་ཁའི་ནང་བྱ་ཀྱུག་རི་བཏང་ས། ཡང་ཁམ་ལོག་ཚོར་དེ་ཀ་སར་སྐྱུགས་པ། ཡང་ཟས་ངན་སྐྱུག་སྟེ། ས་དོ་གོམ་ཞིག་གནམ་ལ་ཁྱེར་ས། གནམ་དོ་གོམ་ཞིག་ས་ལ་ཕབས་སོང་། དེ་ནས་ཡང་ཀ་སར་གྱིས་སྨྲ་ཞིག་བཏང་ས།།

ངའི་བྱ་རིས་དངོས་ཤིག་ལ་ཉོན་དང་།
བྱ་ཁྲུང་ཁྲུང་དཀར་མོས་བདག་ལ་གསན།
ངའི་ཛོ་ཛོ་འབྲུ་ག་མ་བདེ་མོ་ལ་ཡོད་ཟེར་ན།

ཕྱིང་དཀར་ལ་རེ་སྟེ་གསོན་ཤ་དེ་ཟེ།
ཛོ་ཛོ་བདེ་མོ་ལ་མེད་ཟེར་ན།
ཕྱིང་ནག་ལ་རེ་སྟེ་ཤི་ཤ་དེ་ཟེ་ལོ

དེ་ཟླུག་ཟེརས་པ། བྲ་གཉིས་ཀས་ཕྱིང་ནག་ལ་རེ་སྟེ་ཤི་ཤ་དེ་ཟེརས་པ། ཀེ་སར་ཡང་སྨུན་སོང་བས། བྲ་གཉིས་ཀས་ཡང་ཀེ་སར་རི་ཁའི་ནང་བྲ་རྒྱུག་རེ་བཏངས་སོང་། ཡང་ཟས་ངན་ཚང་མ་སྐྱུགས་པས། ས་དོ་གོམ་ཞིག་གནམ་ལ་སོང་། གནམ་དོ་གོམ་ཟམ་ཞིག་ས་ལ་པབས་སོང་། ཡང་ཀེ་སར་ཀྱིས་བླུ་ཞིག་བཏངས།།

ངའི་བྲ་གཉིས་ཀ་དངོས་ལ་ཉེན་ལོ།
བྲ་ཁྲུང་ཁྲུང་དཀར་མོས་བདག་ལ་གསན།
འབྲུ་དམར་ལམ་བལྟུན་བདེ་མོ་ཡོད་ན།
ཕྱིང་དཀར་ལ་རེ་སྟེ་གསོན་ཤ་དེ་ཟེ་ལོ།
འབྲུ་དམར་ལམ་བསྟུན་བདེ་མོ་མེད་ན།
ཕྱིང་ནག་ལ་རེ་སྟེ་ཤི་ཤ་དེ་ཟེ་ལོ།

དེ་ཟླུག་ཟེརས་པ། བྲ་གཉིས་ཀས་ཕྱིང་ནག་ལ་རེ་སྟེ་ཤི་ཤ་དེ་ཟེརས་པ། ཀེ་སར་ཡང་སྨུན་སོང་། ཡང་ཁའི་ནང་དུ་བྲ་རྒྱུག་རེ་བཏངས་སོང་། དེ་ནས་ཡང་ཟས་ངན་ཚང་མ་སྐྱུགས་པ། ས་དོ་གོམ་ཟམ་ཞིག་གནམ་ལ་སོང་། གནམ་དོ་གོམ་ཟམ་ཞིག་ས་ལ་བབས་སོང་། དེ་ཟླུག་གིས་ཟས་ངན་ཚང་མ་ཕྱིང་ཚར་དེ་ན། བྲ་ཀུན་གྱིས་ཡི་གེ་དེ་ཕྱིང་སྟེ་ཀེ་སར་ལ་བཏངས། དེ་ནས་ཀེ་སར་གྱིས་ཡི་གེ་དེ་

གསོལ་དེ། ཚང་མ་ཧ་གོ་སྟེ་ཇོ་མོ་ལ་ཟེརས་པ། ཇོ་མོ་ངའི་ཧ་དེ་གར་ཡོད་ཟེརས། ཇོ་མོས་ཅི་ཤེ། ཁྱོ་རང་ངི་ཧ་རྫོག་པོ་འདུག། ང་ལ་ཕྲ་བཏངས། སོ་བཏབས། དེ་ནས་རི་ལ་རྒྱབས་བཏངས་པིན་ཟེརས།།

No. 6.

ཀ་སར་ཕྲུ་ཧུ་བཙལ་བ་རི་ལ་སོང་བས། ཀ་སར་རི་མཐོན་པོ་ཞིག་ལ་བསླེབ་སྟེ་བལྟས་པ་སང། ལོ་གཅིག་སོང་མཁན་ནི་ཤི་ལང་ཞིག་དང་ཕྲུག་སོང། དེ་ནས་ཡང་སོང་བ་སང། ཟླ་བ་དགུ་སོང་མཁན་ནི་ཤི་ལང་ཞིག་དང་ཕྲུག་སོང། ཡང་སོང་བ། ཟླ་གཉིས་སོང་མཁན་ནི་ཤི་ལང་དང་ཕྲུག། དེ་ཟུག་ལ་ལྷ་འདིན་ཞིག་སོང་བ། ཕྲུ་ཧུ་གངས་དང་གཡའི་མཚམས་ལ་བསླེབ་སྟེ་ཡོད་ཚུག། ཚོག་མིག་རེ་ལ་སླལ་མིག་རེ་བིང་སྟེ་ཡོད་ཚུག། དེ་ནས་ཀ་སར་ལ་ཕྲུ་ཧུ་མཐོང་སྟེ་འཕད་དེ་གླུ་ཞིག་བཏངས་སོ།།

ངའི་ཕྲུ་ཧུས་ངའི་དངོས་ལ་ཉོན་དང།
རྒྱང་རྒོད་དབྱིད་པས་བདག་ལ་གསན།
འདི་རིང་ང་ལ་འདོམ་པ་རིག་ཡོད་ལོ།
གླིང་ཡུལ་གཞུང་ལ་རྟེར་དམག་རིག་ཡོངས་དོག།
གླིང་གི་ཤ་སྐྱིང་རྟེར་གྱིས་ཟློས་དོག།
གླིང་གི་མར་སྐྱིང་རྟེར་གྱིས་ཟློས་དོག།
གླིང་གི་ཟན་སྐྱིང་ཚང་མ་རྟེར་གྱིས་ཟློས།
ཨ་མ་འབྲུག་མ་རྟེར་གར་དཀར་གྱིས་ཁྱེར་དོག།

དུང་གི་སྤྲིད་བུ་དེ་རྡོར་གྱིས་ཁྲེར་དོག།
གསེར་ཉ་དུང་ཉ་ཚང་མ་ཡང་ཁྲེརས་ལོ།
རྟ་ཕོ་ཁ་ལ་མི་འབར་ཡང་རྡོར་གྱིས་ཁྲེརས་ལོ།
ཕོ་ལད་ཀྱི་གྲུད་གཉུ་དེ་ཡང་རྡོར་གྱིས་ཁྲེརས།
འབུ་དམར་ལམ་བསྟུན་རྡོར་གྱིས་མདའ་མཉམ་བསད་དོག།
ཨང་གར་ལྷུངས་པ་དེ་བཙོན་ལ་ཁྲེར་དོག།
གླིང་མཁར་ཚང་མ་ཞལ་མ་གྱུར་དོག།
ང་དང་གཉིས་ཀ་རྡོར་ལ་ཀ་ལེ་ལ་ཆེན་ལོ།
རྟ་མི་གཉིས་ཀ་གུར་དཀར་ལ་ཀ་ལེ་ལ་ཆེན་ལོ།
འཁྲུད་ན་རྡོར་ལ་ཀ་ལེ་སློག་ཡིན་ལོ།
མ་འཁྲུད་ན་གླིང་པའི་གཡོག་པོ་ཞིག་བཙོ་ཡིན་ལོ།

དེ་ཐུག་ཟེརས་པ་སང། ཐ་རྩུ་ལ་སྒྲོ་ཡོང་སྟེ་ལན་དུ་ཡང་གླུ་ཞིག་བཏངས།།

ཁྱོད་གླིང་རྫོང་ཀེ་སར་གྱིས་དངོས་ལ་ཉོན་དང།
ཟ་མཆོག་མེད་པའི་བོང་བུས་བདག་ལ་གསན་ལོ།
རྩ་བ་མེད་པའི་གླང་ཅུས་ང་ལ་ཉོན་དང།
གླིང་མཁར་ཞལ་མ་སྒྱུར་བ་ཁྱོད་ལ་དགས་ཆོར་ར།
ཞ་སླིང་མར་སླིང་ཚར་བ་ཁྱོད་ལ་ད་ཆོར་འདུག་ག།
དུང་གི་སྤྲིད་བུ་འཁྲེར་བ་ཁྱོད་ལ་ད་ཞེས་འདུག་ག།
གསེར་ཉ་དུང་ཉ་འཁེར་ཅེས་དེ་དགས་ཆོར་འདུག་ག།

ཛོ་ཛེ་འབྲུ་གུ་མཛོར་གྱིས་འཕྱིར་བ་ཁྱོད་ལ་ད་ཞེས་འདུག་ག།

རྟ་ཡོ་ཁ་ལ་མི་འབར་འཕྱིར་བ་ད་ཁྱོད་ལ་ཞེས་འདུག་ག།

འབྲུ་དམར་ལམ་བསྟུན་བསད་ཅེས་ད་ཞེས་འདུག་ག།

ཨང་གར་ལངས་པ་བཙོན་ལ་འཕྲིར་ཅེས་ད་ཞེས་འདུག་ག།
ཙ

ཐུ་རུ་ངའི་ཡིད་དུ་ད་ཡོང་འདུག་ག།

རྒྱང་རྒོད་ངའི་ཁ་བར་ད་ཁྱོད་ལ་ཡོང་འདུག་ག།

ཁྱོད་ཀྱི་ཛེ་མོས་ང་ནང་ལ་ཆ་ན་ཞིང་ཁུར་བརྒྱ་བཀལས།

ང་ཡི་སྟ་ལ་ཕིང་ན་ཐལ་ཁུར་བརྒྱ་བཀལས།

ང་ནང་དུ་ཆ་ན་སྨུལ་ཁྲུག་བརྒྱ་ཟམ་བདངས།

ང་ཡི་སྟ་ལ་ཡོང་ཟ་ན་རྫོང་ཆོང་བརྒྱ་ཟམ་བདངས།

ཚིག་མིག་རེ་ལ་སྐལ་མིག་རེ་འབུད་སོང་།

རང་སྒྲིག་འཁུར་དེ་ང་འདིར་ཞོར་དེ་ཡོངས་པིན།

ང་གླིང་ཡུལ་ལ་འགྲོ་བ་དེ་ཉན་ཅེས་མེད་ལོ།

ངའི་ཁ་ཁྱེད་རང་ཞོན་པ་ཉན་ཅེས་མེད་ལོ།

ཁྱེད་གླིང་ཡུལ་ལ་ཆ་ནའང་སོང་ལོ།

ཁྱེད་ཧོར་ཡུལ་ལ་ཆ་ནའང་སོང་ལོ།

ཐ་རུས་དེ་རྒྱུག་ཟེརས་པ། ཀི་སར་ཡམ་ཚན་ཞིག་སོང་སྟེ། ཡང་ཁ་འཛམ་པོ་ཀོལ་དེ་ཐུ་རུ་ལ་ཟེརས།།

ངའི་བྲ་ཙུས་དངོས་ལ་ཉོན་དང༌།
ཀླུ་ཧ་རྒྱང་རྒོད་ཀྱིས་བདག་ལ་གསན།
བདེན་ད་བྲ་ཙ་རྒྱང་རྒོད་བདེན་ལོ།
འདི་རིང་ང་ལ་འདོམས་པ་ཞིག་ཡོད།
ཧ་མི་གཉིས་ཀ་བྲེས་ལ་ཆེན་ལོ།
ང་དང་གཉིས་ཀ་རང་ཡུལ་ལ་ཆེན།
བྲ་ཙ་འབབ་སྤེ་སྤྱོད་འང་བྲ་ཙ་ལེ།
ཀླུ་ཧ་འབབ་སྤེ་སྤྱོད་འང་རྒྱང་རྒོད་ལེ།

དེ་ཟུག་ཟེརས་པ། བྲ་ཙུས་སྙིང་རྗེ་ཚོར་དེ། བབ་སྤེ་ཡོང་སྤེ། ཀེ་སར་ཀྱི་མདུན་ལ་བསྙེབ་སྤེ་བལྟས་པ། བྲ་ཙུའི་ཚིག་མིག་རེ་ལ་སྐལ་མིག་རེ་བྱིང་སྤེ། ཁྲག་དང་ཆུ་གསེར་བིང་ངེན་ཞིག་ཡོད་ཚུག། དེ་ནས་ཀེ་སར་དང་བྲ་ཙ་གཉིས་ཀ་མང་པོ་ཐུས་པས། བྲ་ཙུས། ཀེ་སར་ལེ། ང་དང་གཉིས་ཀ་ཐུ་འིན་ཞིག་འདུག་སྤེ་གླིང་ཡུལ་ལ་མི་བསྙེབ། ཧོར་ཡུལ་ལ་ཡང་མི་བསྙེབ། ང་གླིང་ཡུལ་ནས་ཡོང་ཟན། ངའི་ཨ་མ་འབྲུ་གུ་མས་བཀལ་མཁན་ནི་སྐལ་སྨན་ཇ་མཆོག་གཡས་པའི་ནང་ཡོད། གསེར་དང་དངུལ་གྱི་ཙ་གུ་དེ་ཇ་མཆོག་གཡོན་པའི་ནང་དུ་ཡོད། དེ་ཕིང་སྤེ་ཙ་གུ་དང་ངའི་ཤུལ་པ་དྲོས། སྨན་དེ་དོབ་ཟེར་དེ་བསྐྱབས་པ། ཀེ་སར་ཀྱིས་ཇ་མཆོག་ལ་བལྟས་པ་སང༌། སྨན་དང་ཙ་གུ་ཡོད་ཚུག། དེ་ཕིང་སྤེ་སྐལ་པ་ཚང་མ་ཙ་གུ་དང་དྲས་བཏངས། སྨན་བཏབས་པ། བྲ་ཙ་སྔོན་མའི་སང་རྒྱལ་ང་སོང༌། དེ་ནས་ཁོང་གཉིས་ཀ་མང་པོ་འཐད་ཀྱིན་ཞིག་གླབས་བཙོ་སྤེ་བྲ་ཙུས་ཟེརས། རྒྱལ་པོ་ལེ། ང་དང་རྗེ་མོའི་ཇ་བསྙེབ་པ་སང༌། རྗེ་སོས་ངའི་ཕྱི་ལ་

མར་ཟན་ཞིག་གཡོ་སྟེ་འཁྱོང་ཡིན། དེའི་ནང་དུ་བདུག་ཅིག་བདབ་སྟེ་ཡོང་ཡིན། དེ་བོ་ལ་ངས་ལག་མཐོ་བཏང་སྟེ། བཙག་ཡིན། ཁོས་ང་ལ་རྡུང་ཡིན། ཉེ་རང་གིས་རྡུང་མ་བཅུག་ལེ་ཟེར་དེ། ཁོང་ཇ་མི་གཉིས་ཀ་ཁང་པ་ལ་སོངས་པ། ཁོང་ཁང་པ་ལ་བསླེབ་མ་ཐག་ཏུ། ཇོ་མོས་ཕྲུ་གུ་ལ་མར་ཟན་གཡོ་སྟེ་ཁྱོངས། ཕྲུ་གུས་ལག་མཐོ་བཏང་སྟེ་ལྷུ་གུ་བཙག་སྟེ་བཏངས། མར་ཟན་ས་ལ་འབོ་སྟེ་སོང་བ། ས་ཚང་མ་གནམ་ལ་འཁོར་དེ་ཁྱེརས། ཇོ་མོའི་བསམ་པའི་ནང་དུ་འདི་ཟླུག་ཡོད་པ། ཕྲུ་གུ་ལ་བདུག་ཅིག་བཏང་སྟེ་ཤི་བཅུག་ཡིན། ཕྲུ་གུ་ཤི་ན་ཀེ་སར་གླིང་ཡུལ་ལ་ཆ་མི་ཐུབ་བསམ་པས། མར་ཟན་དེ་འཕོས་བཏངས་པ། ཇོ་མོ་ལ་སྒྲོ་ཡོང་སྟེ། ཕྲུ་གུ་ལ་རྡུང་བ་གདུང་མ་ཞིག་འཁོར་དེ་ཡོངས་པ། ཀེ་སར་གྱིས་ཟུམ་སྟེ་རྡུང་མ་བཅུགས།།

དེ་ནས་ཀེ་སར་གླིང་ཡུལ་ལ་ཆ་ཅེས་སོང་བས། ཇོ་མོ་དང་བུ་མོ་གཉིས་ཀས་ང་ཞ་ཡང་མཉམ་པོ་ཆ་ཡིན་ཟེར་དེ་འབྲངས། ཇོ་མོས་ཀེ་སར་ལ། བུ་མོ་དེ་རྨས་ཕོངས་ལ་དོང་ཟེརས་པ། ཀེ་སར་གྱིས་ངའི་རྟའི་ཁ་བུ་མོ་སྲུ་ཡང་ཞོན་ཆ་མིན་ཟེརས་པ། དེ་ནས་ཀེ་སར་སྔོན་ལ་སོང་པ། ཇོ་མོ་དང་བུ་མོ་གཉིས་ཀ་འབྲང་སྟེ་སོང་། རྒྱ་རབས་ཆེན་པོ་ཞིག་གི་མདུན་ལ་བསླེབ་པས། ཀེ་སར་གྱིས། ཇོ་མོ་རང་དང་བུ་མོ་གཉིས་ཀས་རྟའི་ཇ་མ་ལ་འཐམ་སྟེ་ཡོང་ཟེརས་པ། ཇོ་མོ་ཡིད་ཆེས་དེ་རྟའི་ཇ་མ་ལ་འཐམས། བུ་མོས་ཨ་མ་ལ་འཐམ་སྟེ་སོང་། དེ་ནས་རྒྱའི་ནང་ལ་བསླེབ་པ་སང་། ཕྲུ་གུས་ཕྲ་ཞིག་ཕྲང་སྟེ་ན། རྒྱའི་རྫོང་ཀ་ལ་ཐང་སྟེ་བཏངས། ཀེ་སར་དང་ཕྲུ་གུ་ཕར་ཀ་ལ་བསླེབ་སོང་། དེ་ནས་ཇོ་མོ་ལ་ཁྲོ་རླུང་ཆེན་མོ་ཡོང་སྟེ། རང་གི་བུ་མོ་ལེན་དེ་ཁག་པོ་གཉིས་བཙོ་སྟེ་ན་ཟེརས།

ཁྲིད་ཨ་བ་ཡིན་པ་སང་སྟོད་པོ་ཟེ། ང་ཨ་མ་ཡིན་པ་སང་སྨད་དེ་ཟའི་ན་ཟེར་དེ། བུ་མོའི་སྟོད་པོ་ཕར་ཀ་ལ་ཀེ་སར་ལ་བཏངས། སྨད་དེ་ཁོ་རང་གིས་ཟེས། དེ་ནས་ཀེ་སར་གྱིས་སྟོད་པོ་མེ་ལ་བསྲེག་སྟེ་མཆོད་རྟེན་ཞིག་བཙོས་པ། ཇོ་མོས་ང་རང་མི་འཁྱེར་ཅེས་ཡིན་ནོག་བསམ་སྟེ་ཀུ་ཅོ་ཞིག་བཏངས་པ། མི་ཡུལ་ལི་ཀེ་སར་ལ་ཁྲེལ་ཅེས་མི་འདུག། ལྷ་བདུད་ཁྲ་བ་ལག་རིངས་ཟེར་དེ། བདུད་ཀྱི་རོམ་ཁང་གི་ནང་ན་ཀུ་ཅོ་བཏང་སྟེ་ས་འགུལ་ཡོང་བ་མཆོགས་ཀྱི་སྐད་ཆེན་པོ་ཞིག་བཏངས། དེ་ནས་ཀེ་སར་གྱིས་བསམ། དེ་བདུད་པོ་ལངས་དེ་ཡོང་ཡིན་འགྲོ་བསམ་སྟེ། ཇོ་མོ་ལ་མཐོང་མ་བཅུག་པར། རྟ་མི་གཉིས་ཀ་རིབ་ཤིང་གོན་དེ་ལོག་སྟེ་ཡོང་སྟེ་བདུད་ཀྱི་རོམ་ཁང་ལ་སྦུགས་བརྒྱབ་སྟེ། སྟེང་ན་བེང་མི་ཉན་ཅེས་བཅོ་སྟེ་ན། ཁོང་རྟ་མི་གཉིས་ཀ་གླིང་ཡུལ་ལ་སོང་།།

No. 7.

དེ་ནས་གླིང་ཡུལ་དང་ཧོར་ཡུལ་གཉིས་ཀའི་ལམ་འབྲེ་རྩ་བསླེབ་སོང་། ཀེ་སར་གྱིས་ཐུ་རྩ་ལ་གླུ་ཞིག་བཏངས།།

ངའི་ཁྲ་རྩུས་འང་དངོས་ལ་ཉེན་ལོ།
ཀྱང་རྒོད་དབྱེར་པས་བདག་ལ་གསན།
ཐུ་རྩུ་ཉི་རང་གླིང་ཡུལ་ལ་སྐྱོད་ལོ།
བུ་ཚང་རང་ཧོར་ཡུལ་ལ་ཆ་ཡིན་ལོ།
ཐུ་རྩུ་ཉི་རང་ག་མ་སྟོད་མཐོན་པོས་མ་ཆ་ལོ།
གནམ་སྟོད་མཐོན་པོས་ཆ་ན་ཉི་མའི་ཉི་གཟེར་འཐོག་ཆེན།

ཐུ་རུ་ཉེ་རང་གངས་སྟོད་མཐོན་པོས་མ་ཆ།
གངས་སྟོད་ཀྱིས་ཆ་ན་སེང་གེའི་སོ་གཟུག་ཡིན།
ཐུ་རུ་ཉེ་རང་བྲག་སྟོད་མཐོན་པོས་མ་ཆ།
བྲག་སྟོད་མཐོན་པོས་ཆ་ན་སྐྱིན་ཆེན་གྱི་རུ་ཅོ་འཐོག་ཡིན།
ཐུ་རུ་ཉེ་རང་ཐང་སྟོད་ཀྱིས་མ་ཆ་ལོ།
ཐང་སྟོད་ཀྱིས་ཆ་ན་སྤྱང་ཁུའི་སོ་གཟུག་ཡིན།
ཐུ་རུ་མཆོམ་སྟོད་མཐོན་པོས་མ་ཆ་ལོ།
མཆོམ་སྟོད་ཀྱིས་ཆ་ན་ཉ་མོ་འི་ཤོག་པ་འཐོག་ཡིན།
ཁྲི་གཅིག་མི་གཅིག་དང་མ་ཐུག་པ་དུང་གི་བྲིས་ལ་སོང་།
མཚན་ཐུན་གཅིག་ལ་ཉེ་རང་སླེབ་པ་སོང་ལོ།

དེ་ཟུག་ཟེར་དེ་བསླབ་སྟེ་བདངས་པ། ཐུ་རུས་བསླབས་མཁན་ནང་ལྷར་ལ་ཡོངས། ཐུ་རུ་གླིང་མཁར་ལ་བསླེབ་སྟེ་དུང་གི་བྲིས་སི་རྒ་ན་གནམ་མ་ལངས་པ་སྐད་ཅིག་བདངས། གླིང་མཁར་སྤྱང་མཁན་ནི་ཨ་བི་ཞིག་དང་ཚ་བོ་ཞིག་ཡོད་ཚུག་པས། ཁོང་གཉིས་ཀ་ཧྲ་སྐད་ཆོར་མ་ཐག་ཏུ། དཔལ་ལེའི་རྒ་སོང་སྟེ། ཤེད་དང་ཀུ་ཅོ་བདང་སྟེ་སྐྱུ་ཞིག་བདངས།།

ལྷ་གླིང་གི་དཔལ་ལེ་དངོས་ལ་ཉོན་ལོ།
དཔལ་ལེ་རྒོད་པོས་བདག་ལ་གསན་ལོ།
འདི་རིང་གླིང་ཀེ་སར་གྱི་ཧྲ་སྐད་ཅིག་ཆོར་ལོ།
ཀུང་རྒོད་དབྱེར་པའི་སྐད་ཅིག་རང་ཆོར་ལོ།

མི་དེ་མ་བསླེབ་ཧ་དེ་བསླེབ་སོང་།
ཀེ་སར་མ་བསླེབ་ཐུ་ཙུ་བསླེབ་སོང་།
འདི་རིང་ཉི་མ་སྤྱུན་བདུན་ཤར་ཡིན།
གངས་སྟོད་མཐོན་པོ་ན་སེང་གེ་འགྱུལ་ཡིན།
བྲག་སྟོད་ན་སྐྱིན་ཆེན་འགྱུལ་ཡིན་ལོ།
སྤང་སྟོད་མཐོན་པོ་ན་འབྲོང་ཆེན་འགྱུལ་ཡིན་ལོ།
ཐང་སྟོད་ན་སྤྲང་ཁྲ་དུ་བ་ལ་ཆོར་ལོ།
ལུང་པའི་མདོ་ན་ལྷ་མོ་དུ་བ་ལ་ཆོར་ལོ།
མཚོམ་སྟོད་ན་ཉ་མོ་འགྱུལ་བ་ཞིག་མཐོང་ལོ།
ལུང་སྟན་ན་རྒྱ་སྟན་འགྱུལ་བ་ཞིག་མཐོང་ལོ།
བྲུ་སྟན་གྱི་སྐད་བྲེ་བ་ཞིག་ཆོར་ལོ།
རི་རྩྭ་མེད་ལ་རྩྭ་ཞིག་སྐྱེ་བ་ལ་མཐོང་ལོ།
ཤིང་ཐོག་སྐམ་པོ་ལ་ཁོལ་སྐྱེ་བ་རིག་མཐོང་ལོ།
རྒྱལ་ལྷམ་ཀེ་སར་གྱི་ཕྱུག་བྲིས་བསླེབ་པ་མཐོང་།
དཔལ་ལེ་ཉི་རང་སྤྱུག་ལ་མ་འདུག་བིང་སྟེ་ཡོང་ལོ།

དེ་ཐུག་ཐེརས་པ། དཔལ་ལེ་ནང་ནས་མགྱོགས་པ་བིང་སྟེ་ཡོང་སྟེ་བལྟས་པ། དུང་གི་བྲིས་ལ་ཐུ་ཙུ་བསླེབ་སྟེ་ཡོད་ཚུག། དེ་ནས་དཔལ་ལེས་དུང་གི་བྲིས་བསྒྱུ་སྟེ་བདེ་མོ་བཅོས། གླིང་པའི་མི་ཚང་མ་མང་པོ་འཐད་གྱིན་ཞིག་ཐུ་ཙུའི་སྤུ་ཚང་མ་སྤྱིན་རླབས་ལ་མགོ་འི་ཁ་བདག་སྟེ་བོརས། དེ་ནས་ཐུ་ཙུའི་སྐའི་མདུན་གུའི་ཁ་ཡི་གི་བྲིས་དེ་ཡོད་ཚུག། དེ་ཡི་གི་ཀླུ་མོ་དར་གྱི་གོ་ཆོད་མ་མེན་བ།

གསོལ་ཅེས་སྨྲ་ལ་ཡང་མི་ཤེས་པས། ཨ་ཀུ་དཔལ་ལེ་ཀླུ་མོ་ལ་བོས་པ།
མོ་ཚོ་མོའི་འགྲམ་ལ་སོང་སྟེ་གླུ་ཞིག་བཏངས།།

མཚོའི་དཀྱིལ་ན་ཀླུ་མོས་དངོས་ལ་ཉོན་དང་།
ཀླུ་མོ་དར་གྱི་གོ་ཆོད་མས་བདག་ལ་གསན་ལོ།
འདི་རིང་གི་ཞག་ལ་སྐད་བཟངས་ཤིག་ཚོར།
གླིང་ཀེ་སར་རྒྱལ་པོའི་ཁ་བར་ཞིག་ཚོར་ལོ།
ཐ་ཙ་རྐྱང་རྒོད་དབྱེར་པ་གླིང་ཡུལ་ལ་བསླེབ་ལོ།
ཐ་ཙའི་མདུན་གཟུའི་ཁ་ཀེ་སར་གྱི་ཡི་གེ་ཞིག་འདུག
དེ་ཡི་གེ་གསོལ་མཁན་མི་འདུག་ལོ།
དེ་ཡི་གེ་གསོལ་བ་སྐྱིད་རོགས་མཛོད་ལོ།
འོབ་རྒྱལ་མེད་པ་སྐྱིད་ཀླུ་མོ་མཁྱེན་ནོ།

དེ་ནུག་ཟེརས་པ། ཀླུ་མོ་ལ་ཡིད་མ་ཆེས་པར། སྲོ་བཙོ་སྟེ་ལན་དུ་གླུ་ཞིག་བཏངས།།

གླིང་གི་དཔའ་བོས་འང་དངོས་ལ་ཉོན་དང་།
དཔལ་ལེ་རྒོད་པོས་བདག་ཅིག་ལ་གསན་ལོ།
ཀེ་སར་རྒྱལ་པོ་བདུད་ཡུལ་ལ་སྐྱིད་དེ་ལོ་མང་པོ་སོང་།
རྐྱང་རྒོད་དབྱེར་པ་བདུད་ཡུལ་ལ་སྟོར་ཏེ་ལོ་འདི་ཙམ་སོང་།
ཀེ་སར་རྒྱལ་པོ་ཁྲིད་ལ་ག་ན་འདུག་ལོ།
རྐྱང་རྒོད་དབྱེར་པ་ཁྲིད་ལ་ག་ན་འདུག་ལོ།

ཁྱོད་གཉིད་མ་ལོག་པའི་སླབ་ལོ་མེན་ན།

ཁྱོད་ཆང་མ་འཐུངས་པའི་ར་རོས་ཤིག་མེན་ན།

དེ་ནུབ་ཟེརས་པ་སང། དཔལ་ལེ་ལ་ཡང་སྒྲོ་ཡོང་སྟེ། ཇུ་ཙོ་ཞིག་གི་ནང་དུ་བདུག་སྣན་མང་པོ་རྒྱང་སྟེ། མཚོའི་ནང་བདབས་པ། མཚོ་ཚང་མ་དྲག་པོ་འགུལ་ཏེ། ཀླུ་མོ་འི་ཁང་པ་ཞིག་ཅེས་ལ་ཐུག་སོང། དེ་ནས་ཀླུ་མོ་འཇིགས་ཏེ་མཚོའི་ནང་ནས་ཕི་སྤུ་ཇུ་བེང་སྟེ་ཡོང་སྟེ། དཔལ་ལེ་འཁྲིད་དེ་མཚོའི་ནང་ཁང་པ་ལ་འཁྱེར་ཏེ། ཟ་ཅེས་ཞིམ་པོ་བཏང་སྟེ་ཟེརས་པ། དཔལ་ལེ་ལེ། ཉི་རང་སྡོད་ལ་འགྲུལ། ང་ཡང་མགྲོགས་པ་ཡོང་ཡིན་ཟེརས་པ། དཔལ་ལེས་ཀྱིལ་ཟེར་དེ་སྡོད་ལ་ཡོངས། ཞག་གཅིག་གི་རྗེང་ན་ཀླུ་མོ་ཡང་ཡོངས། དེ་ནས་ཀླུ་མོས་སྐའི་ཡི་གེ་འཁར་ཏེ། དེས་སྲུ་ཇུ་ཟེར་བའི་རི་མཐོན་པོ་ཞིག་ཡོད་ཚུག། དེ་རིའི་ཁ་ན། སྟེང་ལྷ་ཡུལ། བར་བཙན་ཡུལ། འོག་ཀླུ་ཡུལ། ཚང་མ་མཐོང་ངད་ཚུག། དེའི་ཁ་ཡི་གེ་དེ་འཁྱེར་ཏེ། ཀླུ་མོས་ཤེད་དང་སྐད་ཆེན་པོ་བཏོན་ནས། ཡི་གེ་གསིལ་གྱིན་ཀླུ་ཞིག་བདངས།།

སྟེང་ལྷ་ཡུལ་གྱི་ལྷ་དམག་དེ་དམག་ལ་སྐྱོད་ལོ།

ལྷ་དམག་གི་དམག་མགོ་ལ་དབང་པོ་རྒྱབ་ཞིན་སྐྱོད་ལོ།

བར་བཙན་ཡུལ་གྱི་བཙན་དམག་དེ་དམག་ལ་སྐྱོད་ལོ།

བཙན་དམག་གི་དམག་མགོ་ལ་ཨ་མ་རྐྱབ་བདུན་སྐྱོད་ལོ།

འོག་ཀླུའི་ཀླུ་དམག་དེ་དམག་ལ་སྐྱོད་ལོ།

ཀླུ་དམག་གི་དམག་མགོ་ལ་ཀླུ་རྒྱལ་ལྡོགས་པོ་སྐྱོད་ལོ།

གླིང་དཔའ་བོ་འི་དམག་མགོ་ལ་དཔལ་ལེ་རྒོད་པོ་སྐྱིད་ལོ།
གླིང་གི་བུ་མོ་འི་དམག་མགོ་ལ་དཔལ་མའི་ཨ་སྟག་སྐྱིད་ལོ།
གླིང་གི་བླ་མའི་དམག་མགོ་ལ་སློབ་དཔོན་རྩེ་དགུ་སྐྱིད་ལོ།
གླིང་གི་མོན་དམག་གི་དམག་མགོ་ལ་པེ་ནག་སྐྱིད་ལོ།
གླིང་གི་མགར་བའི་དམག་མགོ་ལ་ཀ་རོག་ཡང་འཛིན་སྐྱིད་ལོ།
གླིང་གི་བེ་དའི་དམག་མགོ་ལ་བེ་ད་ཀོང་རིངས་སྐྱིད་ལོ།
བུ་ཚ་དགྲུག་རྗེ་བ་སྐོར་ཁྲུད་དམག་ལ་སྐྱིད་ལོ།
བུ་མོ་འཐང་འཁོར་ཁྲུད་དམག་ལ་སྐྱིད་ལོ།
རང་རྒྱུགས་ཡོད་མཁན་གྱིས་རང་རྒྱུགས་འཁོར་དེ་ཡོང་།
རང་རྒྱུགས་མེད་ན་གླིང་མཁར་ནས་འཁོར་དེ་ཁྱོང་།
རང་རྟ་ཡོད་མཁན་ཕྱིས་རང་རྟ་ལ་ཞོན་དེ་ཡོང་།
རང་རྟ་མེད་མཁན་གྱིས་མཁར་གྱི་རྟ་ལ་ཞོན་དེ་ཡོང་།
ཁྱེད་ཚང་མ་རྗེར་ཡུལ་ལ་ཡོང་ལོ།
ང་རྗེར་ཡུལ་ལ་སྡོར་ལ་ཆེན་ལོ།

དེ་ཟུག་ཟེར་དེ། ཡི་གེ་གསིལ་དེ་ཚང་མ་ལ་ཏ་གོ་བཙུགས་ནས། ཀླུ་མོ་ལོག་སྟེ་མཚོའི་ནང་དུ་སོང་། ཐ་རུ་ཡང་ལོག་སྟེ་ཀ་སར་གྱི་རྩར་སོང་། དེ་ནས་སྟེང་ལྷ་ཡུལ། བར་བཙན་ཡུལ། འོག་ཀླུ་ཡུལ། གླིང་ཡུལ་ཚང་མ་ལ་དམག་བསྐུལ་བཏང་སྟེ། སྟོང་ཕྲག་མང་པོ་འཛོམས་སྟེ་རྗེར་ཡུལ་ལ་སོང་།

ཞག་བདུན་འགྱུལ་དེ་ན། ཨ་ནེ་བཀུར་དམན་མོས་ཀ་སར་ལ་ཟེརས།

ལྷ་བསམ་མེད་ཀཱ་སར་འདི་ཟམ་དམག་མང་པོ་འཁྲིར་དེ་རྫོར་བསད་པ་མི་ཉན། དམག་ཚང་མ་སློག་སྟེ་དོང༌། ཁྲིད་རང་གཅིག་པོས་ཐབས་བཅོ་སྟེ་སོང་སྟེ་རྫོར་སོད་ཟེརས་པ། ཀཱ་སར་གྱིས་དམག་ཚང་མ་ལོག་སྟེ་བདངས། ཨ་གུ་ཁྲའི་ཐུང་ལ་རྒྱུགས་འཁོར་བ་འགྲུལ་ཟེརས། ཨ་གུ་ཁྲའི་ཐུང་གིས་གླིང་མཁར་ལ་རྒྱལ་ལ་མ་བལྟས་པས། འབྲུ་དམར་ལམ་བསྟན་ལ་རྫོར་གྱི་མདའ་འཕོག་ཟ་ན། ཐབས་མ་བཅོ་བ་ཞིད་དང་འཕྲུད་བདངས་པའི་ཕོ་ལ། འབྲུ་དམར་ལམ་ངསྟན་ཤི་བཙུགས། ཁོ་རང་གིས་དེ་པི་གསུམ་གོནས། ཁྲི་ལ་ཁྲོག་དམར་གསུམ་བདགས། རྟ་ལ་རྡིབ་ཤིལ་གསུམ་བདགས། དེ་ཚང་མ་ཅིའི་ཕི་ཡ་བདགས་ཟེར་ན། གཅིག་ནི་རང་གི་ཐོབ་ཡིན། གཅིག་ནི་ལྡེམ་ལྡེམ་མི་ལྡེམ་མཁར་ཐོབ་པའི་བཀྲ་ཤིས་ལ་ཡིན། གཅིག་ནི་ཀཱ་སར་བདུད་ཡུལ་ལ་སྟོར་བའི་བཀྲ་ཤིས་ཡིན་ཟེརས་པ། ཀཱ་སར་ལ་སྤྲོ་ཡོང་སྟེ། དེའི་ཕོ་ལ་རྒྱུགས་ཁལ་བཅོ་བརྒྱད་བཀལ་དེ་ཁྲིརས། དེ་ནས་ཀཱ་སར་གྱིས། ཁོ་ངལ་ཅེས་སི་ཕོ་ལ་བྲོ་མའི་ལམ་ནས་འགྲུལ་བཙུགས། ཞག་བདུན་འགྲུལ་དེ་ན། ཁྲའི་ཐུང་གིས་སྐྱོན་བཅོ་སྟེ་ཟེརས། ཀཱ་སར་ལེ། ངའི་གྲོད་པ་ལ་ལྟུར་མོ་ཡོང་ང་རག་ཟེརས་པ། ཀཱ་སར་གྱིས་གྲི་ཆེན་མོ་ཞིག་ལ་སྟར་བདངས། ཁྲའི་ཐུང་གིས། དེ་གྲི་ལ་སྟར་བདང་སྟེ་ཅི་བཅོ་ཡིན་ཚ་བོ་ཟེརས། ཀཱ་སར་གྱིས། ཨ་གུ་རང་གི་གྲོད་པ་ལ་ལྟུར་མོ་ཡོང་ན་སྟར་ཁ་བདང་ཡིན་ཟེརས་པ། ཁྲའི་ཐུང་ལ་གྲི་ཆེན་མོ་མཐོང་སྟེ་འཛེམས་དེ། ངའི་ལྟུར་མོ་ཕན་ཚར་ཚ་བོ་ལེ་ཟེརས། དེ་ནས་ཡང་སོང་བ། ལ་མཐོན་པོ་ཞིག་གི་མདུན་ལ་བསླེབ་སོང་བས། ཡང་ཁྲའི་ཐུང་གིས་སྐྱོན་བཅོ་སྟེ་ཟེརས། ངའི་མགོ་ལ་ལྟུར་མོ་ཡོང་ང་རག་ཚ་བོ་ཟེརས་པ། ཀཱ་སར་གྱིས་དཔའ་ཞུལ་ཟེད་ཅིག

བཙོ་སྤེ་ཁྱོངས། ཁྲའི་ཕྲུང་གིས་ཟེརས། དེ་དཔའ་དང་ཅི་བཙོ་ཡིན་ཚ་བོ་ཟེརས། ཀ་སར་གྱིས། ཨ་གུ་རང་གི་མགོ་ལ་ཟུར་མོ་ཡོང་ན། མགོའི་ཁ་མི་ཞིག་བདང་ཡིན་ཟེརས་པ། ཡང་ཁྲའི་ཕྲུང་འཇིགས་ཏེ་ད་ཟུར་མོ་ཕན་ཏེ་མི་རག་ཚ་བོ་ལེ་ཟེརས། དེ་ཟུག་གི་ནགས་མང་པོ་བསྡུནས་པ་སང། ཨ་ནེ་བཀུར་དམན་མོ་ལ་སྡིག་པ་ཚོར་ཏེ་ཀ་སར་ལ་ཟེརས་པ། ལྷ་ཀ་སར་རྒྱལ་པོ། ཁོ་ལ་ནགས་བསྡུན་ཏེ་ཕན་ཐོགས་ཅི་ཨང་མི་ཡོང། ཁྲའི་ཕྲུང་ཀྱིར་སློག་ཏོང་ཟེརས་པ། དེ་ནས་ཀ་སར་གྱིས་ཁྲའི་ཕྲུང་གི་རྣ་མཆོག་ལ་འཐམ་སྟེ་ན། གླིང་ཡུལ་ལ་སླེབས་ཤིག་ཟེར་ཏེ་འཕངས་བཏངས་པ། ཁྲའི་ཕྲུང་སྐྱིབ་ཅིག་ལ་གླིང་ཡུལ་ལ་བསླེབ་སོང༎

CAPTURE OF 'aBRUGUMA BY THE KING OF HOR.

ABSTRACT OF CONTENTS.

1.

The King of Hor had no wife, and therefore sent two wise ravens to all countries to find him a wife. He heard that king Kesar had left the land of *gLing* and decided to steal *'aBruguma*. All the Agus had gone to the 'cold valley' for sport. Only Agu *Khrai mgo khrai thung* was in the castle *lDem ldemmi ldem*. He was wearing two hats, and his dog had two red collars.[1] The reason for this was that, according to his belief, Kesar had got lost, and he himself had become the lord of *gLing*. Lady *'aBruguma* had a terrifying dream, in which she saw herself carried away by water and fire, and Agu *'aBu dmar lam bstan* killed by the king of Hor. When she asked the lot-casting witch about the meaning of this dream, the witch said that the dream was neither very good nor very bad, and went to her own house.

2.

'aBruguma's maid-servant went to fetch water, and, on the other shore of the lake, she saw *Shankramiru*, who was at the head of the army of Hor. *Shankramiru* asked the servant to tell him the names of the strong castle, the hero, the quick horse, the fierce dog, the wise lady, the paternal deity, the maternal deity, the sword, the arrow, and the spear.

The servant was frightened and ran away without making any reply. *'aBruguma* scolded her for being late, and said she would not allow her to walk three steps further, nor to say three words (of excuse). However, she allowed her to say three words, and the servant reported what she had seen. Now *'aBruguma* took the servant's dress and went away to find out herself. *Shankramiru* asked her the same questions, and *'aBruguma* said: Formerly the strong castle was *gLing mkhar*,

---

1 In Kesar's journey to China this Agu is wearing three hats, and the dog has three collars. I am informed that Kesar's journey to China ought to be told after the defeat of the king of Hor.

now it is *lDem ldemmi ldem mkhar;* formerly the hero's name was Kesar, now it is *'aBu dmar lam bstan;* formerly the quick horse's name was *rkyang rgod dbyerpa*, now it is *sNgorog pon pon;* formerly the name of the fierce dog was *γSer ling*, now it is the bitch *lTom dkar;* formerly the name of the wise lady was *'aBruguma*, now it is *dPalmai astag;* formerly the paternal deity's name was *Kerzong snyanpo*, now it is *Rab lha;* formerly the maternal deity's name was *bkur dman rgyalmo*, now it is *Drag lha rgyalmo;* formerly the name of the sharp sword was *rDoba chodma*, now it is *Mig siri ral gri;* formerly the name of the swift arrow was *γser mdā mjug rings*, now it is *mdā dkarpoi lam bstan.* Then the lady went back to the castle, and *Shankramiru* to the army of Hor.

The Agus who had come back from the 'cold valley,' decided in a counsel that they should go in turns to spy. They lighted fires for each of them, and said that the fire of him who was to be killed would expire. At night they all went to the encampment of Hor and stole all the horses of the enemy.[1] *'a Bu dmar lam bstan*, being a child, was not able to follow the other Agus, and nothing was left for him but a three-legged horse. When the light of the next morning appeared, he covered his head with the *ribshing* (the invisible cap, Nebelkappe, of German mythology) and became invisible.

Meanwhile the two ravens, which had been sent by the king of Hor to find him a wife, came back and reported: They had gone to Lhayul; *dBangpo rgyabzhin* had three daughters; one of them was dumb, the other blind, and the third deaf. There was neither food for man nor horse, and the road bad. Then they had gone to *Klu yul;* also *lYogspo* had three daughters, one limping, the other had stiff hands, and the third a big belly. Then they had gone to *Bar btsan;* mother *Skyabs bdun* had three daughters, the first had a crooked nose, the second a bald head, and the third a long neck. Finally they had gone to *gLing. 'aBruguma* was beautiful, her upper half golden, the lower half turquoise, and her hair golden.[2] Because also supplies for men and horses could be obtained in the *gLing* land, and the road was good, *'aBruguma* would be a suitable wife for the king of Hor. Kesar was lost in the devil's land, Agu *dPalle* had grown old, and the other Agus had gone to the 'cold valley.' The ravens had even found a bone and some beer-yeast for their food in the land of *gLing.*

When *'aBu dmar* heard the speech of the ravens, he killed them,

---

[1] This is the only incident of horse-stealing in the Tibetan version. The Mongolian version has numerous stories of this kind; they may be national history of the Mongolians.

[2] According to tale No. V, *'a Bruguma's* hair is black.

using his stick as a sling. The king of Hor, who could not see the Agu, was astonished to see his ravens fall down from the empty sky. He buried them, and Agu *'aBu dmar lam bstan* lead his three-legged steed before the Agus. Here he was ridiculed so much that he allowed his three-legged horse, which in reality was the magic horse of the king of Hor, to run back to the encampment of Hor.

Shankramiru mounted the magic horse and rode before the tents of Agu *dPalle* and Agu *'aBu dmar lam bstan.* Both Agus frightened him through their ability in shooting. The first shot the middle one of three flying pigeons so that it fell on *Shankramiru's* crupper; the other destroyed *Shankramiru's* crupper with an arrow; because on a day, which happened to be a Musulman as well as a Tibetan holy day, he was not willing to fight. Therefore *Shankramiru* uttered a certain sound, which made all the stolen horses run after the magic horse, and in this way the horses of Hor were recovered.

Because all the Agus were [again] in the 'cold valley,' the army of Hor went first to the *gLing* castle, and then to the castle *lDem ldemmi ldem.* Only lady *'aBruguma* and Agu *Khrai thung* were left. The latter invited the army to a tournament and to enjoy the stores of meat and butter and lady *'aBruguma.* Then the army of Hor went again to *gLing.* (The castle *lDem ldemmi ldem* is apparently outside the land of *gLing.*)

3.

'aBruguma took up arms and tried to fight the army of Hor; but she was frightened by the war-cry of the enemies who suspected her of being a woman. She had to submit and become the wife of the king of Hor, but refused to leave her home until the stores of meat and the stores of butter were exhausted, and a castle, which by an arrow's length neither touched the sky nor the earth, was built of sheep-dung. In this way she gained twenty-seven years.[1]

When all the conditions were fulfilled, *'aBruguma* gave her dress to her servant, and the king of Hor went off with the servant, believing her to be *'aBruguma.* *'aBruguma* remained in the house-stable of *gLing,* hidden beneath horse-dung and a copper-kettle. The king of Hor was advised by an old woman to go back once more to the land of *gLing* and have a horse-race in the stable. At this occasion *'aBruguma's* hair became entangled with the feet of a horse, and she was discovered and carried away. Now Agu *Khrai thung* made a feeble attempt to fight the army

---

1 According to the Sheh-version, the king of Hor has to procure a kiang, a wild yak, and a wolf, and in this way three years are gained.

of Hor. He killed one hundred men, but was frightened away by the war-cry, raised by the army. Agu *Anggar ltsangspa* was carried away and put into prison.

4.

'aBu dmar lam bstan, before setting out to fight the army of Hor, asked Agu *dPalle's* advice, in particular, whether it would be better to use old arms or new ones. Agu *dPalle* advised him to use old arms, and to imitate the lion, the fox, and the crow in fighting; never to go to the left of a sword-man, nor to the right of a rifle-man. One important advice he had forgotten to give: never to drink water direct with his mouth, and never to take off his coat of mail; for although the body of *'aBu dmar* was of steel, there was a spot of the size of a mirror under his shoulder which was of flesh. *'aBu dmar* killed half the army of Hor and re-took *'a Bruguma.* When taking her back on his horse, he was overpowered with sleep, and *Shankramiru*, who followed them, could secretly speak to *'aBruguma*, and ask about *'aBu dmar's* vulnerable spot. *'a Bruguma's* heart was inclined in love to the king of Hor, and she advised *Shankramiru* to ride on in front of them, and hide himself in the lower room of a water-mill. When *'aBruguma* arrived there with *'aBu dmar*, she persuaded the boy to have a rest, take off his coat of mail and drink some water. The boy who did not suspect evil, did according to her advice, and, when drinking, was shot in the fleshy spot by *Shankramiru.* Now *'aBruguma* and *Shankramiru* overpowered him and left him there.[1]

Soon after Agu *dPalle* arrived at the mill and resolved to avenge *'a Bu dmar lam bstan.* Although the boy implored him to heal him first, Agu *dPalle* went off and killed *Shankramiru.* He filled *Shankramiru's* skin with sand, placed the skin on *Shankramiru's* horse and sent it off in the direction of the army of Hor. There this spectacle caused a great consternation, but the king of Hor and *'aBruguma* arrived safely in the Hor land.

Meanwhile Agu *Khrai' thung* had arrived before *'aBu dmar* and torn out the arrow. Because the point of the arrow was barbed, the heart was torn out too. When Agu *dPalle* came back, there was no hope left of saving *'a Bu dmar's* life; but before dying, *'aBu dmar* said the following: In the valleys towards east, south, west and north, there are

---

1 The story of *'a Bu dmar lam bstan* is extremely similar to that of Siegfried in German mythology. The corresponding points are the following: Both use a cap to make themselves invisible; both have a vulnerable spot underneath the shoulder; both are killed when drinking water and when tired out; in both cases it is a woman who reveals the vulnerable spot to the enemy, although from different motives.

herds of horses, goats, yak-cows, and sheep respectively. In the balconies towards east, south, west, and north, there are a golden mill, a bundle of pearls, a copper-dog, and a pearl-white lamb, respectively. Make three portions of all these articles: one for the restoration of the *gLing* castle, one for me (*'aBu dmar's* burial ?), and one for king Kesar. Kesar will come back and re-take *'aBruguma.* This shall be her punishment: For three years lucerne is to be sown on her head [1]; for three years she is to tend goats; for three years sheep; for three years cattle; for three years she is to be everybody's servant; and for three years water-carrier.

Then *'aBu dmar lam bstan* died, and Agu *dPalle* burnt him on a high hill. During the time of mourning *dPalle* would not eat more than a spoonful of flour a day.

5.

Agu *dpalle* was called up by the grand-mother of the end of the village, who told him to send two storks with a message to Kesar. After the storks had been fed and washed well, and practised until they could fly nine times round the castle of *gLing*, they were sent off with a letter each. The night they spent on the top of a high tree, at the bottom of which two ogresses, mother and daughter, had their night-quarters. Towards morning the daughter was sent about to see if anybody was near. As nobody could be seen, the mother told the daughter some secrets about Kesar. Kesar was playing at dice with *Bamza bumskyid.* He had lost everything and would soon lose his life in the game; then nobody would be left to hinder the ogres from eating horse-flesh and human-flesh. Suddenly the storks said *Kung kung.* The mother who knew that the birds had listened, was so angry with the daughter, that she hurled a huge stone at her head. But the stone rebounded back and hit also the mother. Thus both died.

When Kesar, who was playing at dice, heard the voice of the storks, he ran away from the game and said to the birds: If you are the bringers of good news from the *gLing* castle, the stores of *gLing*, lady *'aBruguma* and *'aBu dmar lam bstan*, roll about on the white carpet and eat fresh meat! If not, roll about on the black carpet and eat the flesh of carcases! In answer to all questions, the birds went to the black carpet and ate the flesh of carcases. Kesar fainted each time, but the birds went on his mouth and dropped their excrements

[1] This is probably one of the few recollections from the time when *'a Bruguma* was still a personification of the earth.

in it. Kesar woke up at once and vomited. The advantage of this treatment was, that all the poison which *Bamza bumskyid* had given him, came out, and full memory was restored to him. The poison caused a plot of ground of the size of a saddle-cloth to fly up to the sky, and a similar plot of sky to fall to the earth. Kesar asked where his horse was, and the *Dzemo* said that it had been sent to the hills on account of his bad behaviour.

6.

Kesar went to seek his horse and found him near the ice and slate. He expressed his wish to start at once, but the horse refused on account of his sore back which was due to the cruel treatment by *Bamza bumskyid.* The horse advised Kesar to make use of the medicines and lancet put in his ears by mother *'aBruguma.* When they were applied, the horse became stronger than ever before.

Because the horse knew before-hand that *Bamza bumskyid* would offer him butter with poison, he knocked the basin out of her hand, and Kesar hindered the lady when she wished to beat the horse with a huge beam.[a]

Now they rode off; but *Bamza bumskyid* with her daughter, whom she had born to Kesar, ran behind. When riding through a deep water, *Bamza bumskyid* seized the horse's tail and followed. The horse suddenly kicked and threw her and the daughter back to the shore. *Bamza bumskyid* was so angry that she killed her daughter, and offered the upper half to Kesar for food. The lower part she devoured herself. Kesar built a stûpa for the upper half.

Bamza bumskyid ran to *Khyaba lagrings* (the devil's) grave, and howled into it. In consequence of this there was an earthquake. Kesar, making himself invisible, hurried to the grave, and recited strong magic spells, until it was impossible for the devil to leave his grave.

7.

When Kesar and the horse arrived at the frontier between *gLing* and Hor, Kesar sent the horse to *gLing*, urging it to hasten on, and not to travel by the sky, nor by the glaciers, nor by high rocks, nor by the high plain, nor by the lake, to escape from harm which might be caused by the creatures living there. When the horse was discovered in *gLing*, neighing before his shell-manger, the grand-mother and her grand-daughter cried for Agu *dPalle*, saying: To-day Kesar's horse arrived, to-day the sun will rise, on the glacier the lion will walk about, on the rock the big ibex and on the meadow the big yak; the wolves were heard howling on the plain, and the foxes in the valley; in the lake the fishes were seen moving, in the side-valleys water was seen flowing, the voice of the little birds was heard; on the bare hill grass was seen growing, buds were seen on the dry fruit-trees; a letter from king Kesar has arrived. Oh *d Palle*, do not remain in sadness![1]

dPalle came and cleaned the manger for the horse; all people gathered some hair of the horse and adorned their heads with it, as a means of acquiring a blessing.

A letter was found on the fore-part of the saddle, but only the Nâgî *Dargyi gochodma* was able to read it. When *d Palle* told her the joyful news, she would not believe it. *dPalle* had to throw poison into the lake and with difficulties persuaded her to come out and read the letter publicly. The Nâgî went to the top of the hill *Tissuru*, from whence *lHa yul*, *Bar btsan yul* and *Klu yul* could be seen. This letter contained the general call to arms.[2] The following were called:—

The armies of *lHa yul*, *Bar btsan yul* and *Klu yul* with their respective kings; the Agus of *gLing* with *dPalle* at their head; the lamas of *gLing* with *rTse dgu* at their head; the Mons (caste of carpenters) of *gLing* with *Penag* at their head; the smiths of *gLing* with *Karog yang 'adzin* at their head; the Bhedas (caste of musicians) of *gLing* with *rKang rings* (long-leg) at their head; the boys skilled in using the sling; and the girls skilful in the use of the spindle. Whoever had provisions and a horse, was to use them; who had none, was to receive them at the *gLing* castle.

This army had marched after Kesar for seven days, when suddenly *Ane bkur dmanmo* arrived, and told him to dismiss the host, and to fight the king of Hor alone. All went back; only Agu *Khrai thung* was loaded with 18 bushels of provisions as a punishment for his misdeeds, and had to carry them for Kesar. When he was tired, Kesar would sharpen a knife or light a fire, to cure him in a rude way. But *Ane bkur dmanmo* did not like the sport and ordered Kesar to send the Agu home too. Kesar seized him by his ears and threw him back, so that he arrived in the *gLing*-land in a moment.

---

1 If this song does not refer to the arrival of spring, I do not know to what else. Perhaps I shall be charged with having forged this song, or certain lines in it. But I hope that somebody will take the trouble and ascertain that this song is actually known to the people of Lower Ladakh.

2 This song is of a special interest, as it appears to contain the actual ancient Tibetan call to arms.

Vocabulary and Comments.

1.

པ་ཧལ་ལྡེ། *pahallde*, name of the king of Hor.

འབྱང་ཤེས། *'abyangshes*, possessing pure wisdom.

སྙི་ལམ། *snyi lam*, = *rmi lam*, dream.

མོན་ཁན་མོ། *mon khanmo*, = *mo mkhanmo*, a woman who casts lots.

ཆུ་སྣ། མེ་སྣ། *chu sna, me sna*, 'the nose of water and fire'; *i.e.*, the foremost part of them.

ཕད་ཙེ། *phad tse* or *phad tsa*, coarse sackcloth.

དར་ཡུག། *dar yug;* not 'narrow strips,' but a large piece of silk without seam.

མོ་རྡི། *mo rdi*, dice for casting lots.

འབྱི་དགོས། *'abyi dgos*, = *'abyin dgos*, what is proper to be offered.

2.

ཆུ་འཐུན་མོ། *chu 'athunmo*, or—'athummo ; or—'athumma, the maid-servant who fetches water.

བསང་ཆུ། *bsang chu*, respectful for 'water.'

ཆུ་ཀར། *chu kar*, pail.

དཔལ་མའི་ཨ་སྟག། *dpalmai astag*, name of a wise woman of *gLing ;* she is the female Agu.

རབ་ལྷ། *rab lha*, name of the intermediate paternal deity.

དྲག་ལྷ་རྒྱལ་མོ། *drag lha rgyalmo,* name of the intermediate maternal deity.

མིག་སི་རི། *migsiri,* name of a famous sword.

མདའ་མོ་གསེར་མདའ་མཇུག་རིངས། *mdāmo γser mdā mjug rings,* 'golden arrow, long tail,' name of an arrow.

མདའ་དཀར་པོའི་ལམ་བསྟན། *mdā dkarpoi lam bstan,* 'white way-leader,' name of an arrow.

ཤན་ཀྲ་མི་རུ། *shankramiru,* name of the captain of the army of Hor.

དམག་རང། *dmag rang,* = *dmag brang,* encampment; compare Lad. Grammar, Laws of Sound, No. 3.

མ་ནོན་པ། *ma nonba,* not being able to follow (*lit.* press on the people before him).

རིབ་ཤིང། *rib shing,* in full *grib sking* (Laws of Sound, No. 3), the invisible cap (Nebelkappe) of Tibet. Who puts it on his head becomes invisible.

ཧི་ལིང། *hiling,* astonished, surprised.

ཧན་དྲང། *handrang,* = *han ldang,* dumb.

ཞར་བ། *zharba,* blind, in West Tibet.

རྒུད། *rgud,* deaf.

སྦང་མ། *sbangma,* grains of barley that remain in beer.

སོག་ལྡི། *sog ldi,* stick to throw stones with.

ཨུར་ཅེས། *urces,* to fly.

མདུན་གྲུ། *mdun gru,* fore-part of the saddle.

ཤུ་ཀུར་ཤིང་ཤེར། *shukur shing sher,* name of a Mussulman festival.

མངས། *mangs,* = *mang,* much, many.

3.

པ་ལོ། *palo*, all the hair tied into a single knot.

གཞིད་མད། *γ zhid mad*, or *γzhis mad*, wife.

ཁ་ཤས། *kha shas*, several.

བཏག་སྐྱེ། *btag skye*, neck-bracelet.

ཁ་ཟུབ་ལ། *kha zubla*, or *kha sbubla*, turned upside down.

ཟུངས། *zungs*, = *zung*, a pair.

ཏུ་བག། *tubag*, = *tupag*, rifle.

4.

བུབ་ཆུ་འཐུང་ཙས། *bub chu 'athungcas*, drink water out of a brook, by bending down to it.

གན་ནི་རོགས་བུ། *ganni rogsbu*, a thick coat of mail, made of iron, chains.

སྤུབ་སྟེ། *spubste*, putting on the hind-part of the horse.

ཆང་གཡོག། *chang γyog*, below the shoulder.

རན་འཐག། *ran 'athag*, = *rang 'athag*, mill.

ཕན་ཙས། *phancas*, to heal, become well.

སྔོ་རོག་གི་པོན་པོན། *sngoroggi pon pon*, 'black-blue with tassels,' name of *dPalle's* horse.

དྲར་ཆད་དྲུར་ཆད། *drar chad drur chad*, cutting quite through.

ཞིབ་མོ། *zhibmo*, sandy, of fine sand.

ཐལ་སུབ། *thal sub*, or *thal thsub*, dust.

ལྕེབས་ཙས། *lcebscas*, jump (especially on a horse).

ཞིག་སོབ། *zhig sob*, healing from destruction, restoration.

རབ་སལ། *rab sal*, balcony.

ཀྲུ་གུ། *kruqu*, ball of yarn.

མུག་ཤེས། *mug shes*, knowing how to bark (of a dog).

འབྲག་ཤེས། *'abrag shes*, knowing how to shear (a sheep).

མཐོང་ཀོལ། *mthong kol*, slave of the whole community; *i.e.*, whosoever sees her may take her for his work.

ཐུར་མངས། *thur mangs*, =*thurma*, spoon.

5.

ཁྲུང་ཁྲུང་དཀར་མོ། *khrung khrung dkarmo*, stork; thus it is apparent that also in the Sheh-version, the birds coming from the south are not birds of prey but storks. They will fit much better in a myth of the seasons.

ཅུབ་ཅད་དེ། *cub cadde*, silent.

རྩི་བི་ཏིང་། *rtsibiting*, risk of neck or life.

ཀུང་ཀུང་། *kung kung*, voice of the storks.

ཨ་ར་ར་ཨུ་རུ་རུ། *arara ururu*, rattling of dice.

རེ་ཅས། *recas*, roll about.

མུན་སང་ཅས། *mun sangcas*, awake from fainting.

ཅི་ཤེ། *ci she*, =*ci shes*, who (what) knows?

ཕྲ་བཏང་ཅས། *phra btangcas*, to kick.

6.

ཤི་ལང་། *shi lang*, horse-dung.

ཚིག་མིག། *thsig mig*, the depressions between the elevations of the spine.

ཀ་ལེ། *kale*, revenge.

བཀོལ་ཏེ། *bkolte*, speaking [soft language].

གཡོ་ཅས། *γyocas*, cook.

ལག་མཐོ་བཏང་ཅས། *lag mtho btangcas*, to rear up (of horses).

ལྡུ་རུ། *lduru*, perhaps the same as *rdullu*, little stone-pot.

འཕོ་ཅས། *'aphocas* pour out; causative of *'aboba.*

ཁྲག་རླུང་། *khrag rlung*, anger (*lit.* blood-wind).

རོམ་ཁང་། *rom khang*, or *ro khang*, grave.

7.

མཚན་ཐུན། *mthsan thun*, perhaps the same as *thun mthsams*, at daybreak.

ཉི་མ་སྤུན་བདུན། *nyima spun bdun*, 'the sun, the seven brothers,' the seven Haritas.

ཤིང་ཐོག། *shing thog*, here in the sense of 'fruit-tree.'

ཁོལ། *khol*, bud of leaves.

ཀྱེ་སར། *Kyesar;* it is remarkable that here the form of *Kyesar* actually occurs, instead of Kesar. Many people in Lower Ladakh pronounce the hero's name in this way.

དར་གྱི་གོ་ཆོད་མ། *dargyi go chodma*, name of a *klumo;* in the Sheh-version the name of *'aBruguma's* handmaid is *Dar lha go chodma.*

སླབ་ལོ། *slab lo*, speaking as if in a dream.

རྒྱང་ཅས། *rgyangcas*, to fill.

ཏིས་སུ་རུ། *tissuru*, name of a hill.

པེ་ནག། *penag*, name of the captain of the Mon-army.

ཀ་རོག་ཡང་འཛིན། *Karog yang 'adzin,* name of the captain of the army of smiths.

རྐང་རིངས། *rkang rings,* 'long-leg'; name of the captain of the Bheda-army.

སྡར་བཏང་ཅས། *sdar btangcas,* sharpen [a knife].

སྟར་ཁ་བཏང་ཅས། *starkha btangcas,* to open [a vein].

དཔའ། *dpā,* tinder.

ཞུལ། *zhul,* a ball of food (to be thrown into the mouth).

ཀ་སར་གྱིས་ཧོར་པ་ནམ་ལྷེ་བདུལ་ཙམ་ཀྱི་སྒྲུངས་ཉིང་།

No. 1.

༄༅། དེ་ནས་ཀ་སར་གཅིག་པོ་ཙེ་ཧོར་ཡུལ་ལ་སོང་། ཀ་སར་ཆོར་མང་གི་ཚོགས་མང་པོ་ཡོད་པའི་ས་ཁྲུད་ཅིག་ལ་བསླེབ་པ། ལམ་མ་ཐོབ་པ་བཀགས་པོ་སོང་ནས། སྨོན་ལམ་ཞིག་བདབ་སྟེ་ཟེརས། མགར་བ་ཀ་རོག་ཡང་འཛོན་དང་ཡང་མགར་བ་ཚང་མ་སོལ་བའི་ཕི་ལ་སླེབ་ཤིག་ཟེརས་པ། མགར་བ་ཚང་མ་ཡོང་སྟེ་སྲིབ་ཅིག་ལ་སོལ་བ་བསད་དེ་ཁྲིརས་པས་ལམ་ཐོབ་སྟེ་སོང་། དེ་ནས་ཡང་གསེད་ཀྱི་ཚོགས་ཆེན་མོ་ཞིག་དང་ཐུག། དེ་རུ་ཡང་སྨོན་ལམ་ཞིག་བདབ་སྟེ་ཟེརས། ཛོ་ཛོ་འབྲུ་གུ་མའི་འཁོར་ཡོག་ཚང་མའི་ཕང་ཤིང་ལ་གྱུར་ཅིག་ཟེརས་པ། སྲིབ་ཅིག་ལ་བྲུ་མོ་མང་པོ་ཡོང་སྟེ་ཕང་ཤིང་ལ་ཁྲིར་དེ་མེད་མཁན་བཅོས། དེ་ནས་ཡང་སོང་པ་སང་། མ་ལྷུང་གི་ཚོགས་ཆེན་མོ་ཞིག་གི་མདུན་ལ་བསླེབ་སོང་། ཡང་སྨོན་ལམ་ཞིག་བདབ་སྟེ་ཟེརས། འདི་མ་ལྷུང་ཚང་མ་གླིང་གི་དཔའ་བོ་ཚང་མའི་མདའ་ཤིང་ལ་གྱུར་ཅིག་ཟེརས་པ། དེ་མཚོགས་ཚང་མ་ཡང་མེད་མཁན་སོང་། དེ་ནས་ཡང་སོང་བ། ཁུམ་བུའི་ཚོགས་ཆེན་མོ་ཞིག་གི་མདུན་ལ་བསླེབ་སོང་བས། ཡང་སྨོན་ལམ་བདབ་སྟེ་ཟེརས། འདི་ཁུམ་བུ་ཚང་མ་དཔལ་མོ་འི་ཨ་སྟག་གི་མདུང་གི་ཡུ་བ་ལྡན་ཅིག་ཟེརས་པ། སྲིབ་ཅིག་ལ་མེད་མཁན་སོང་། དེ་ཧྣག་གིས་ལམ་ཐོབ་སོང་།།

དེ་ནས་སྲར་གྱི་ལའི་མདུན་ལ་བསླེབ་སོང་། སྤྲང་དོ་གོམ་ཟམ་ཞིག་ཡོད་ཚུག། ཐ་རུ་དེའི་ཁ་བདག་སྟེ། ཀ་སར་རང་སྦྲ་ཐངས་གཅིག་ནང་མགོ

བོརས། ཕྱུ་ཕྲུངས་གཅིག་ནང་། ཁང་པ་བོར་དེ། གཉིད་ལོག་སྡེ་འདུག་ས། སྐར་གའི་ཁྲེམ་ཕྲུ་གང་གི་འོ་མ་ཡོད་ཚུག་པ། དེ་ངས་འཕྲུང་སྡེ་ཅི་འགྲངས་ཡིན་བསམ་སྡེ་མ་འཕྲུང་བ་འདུག་ས། ཕྲ་རུས་དེ་སྤྲང་པོ་མཆན་ཚེ་རེ་ཙུ་རུམ་ཙུ་རུམ་བཙོ་འི་ན་ཞིག་འདུག་ས། དེ་ནས་ཨ་ནེ་བཀར་དམན་མོས་ཀ་སར་སྙིང་ཅན་འདུག་ག་མི་འདུག་ཚོད་བལྟ་སྡེ། སྤྲུང་ཁ་དུ་བཙུགས། ལུང་མཇུག་ན་ཕྲ་ཙོ་བརྒྱལ་བཙུགས། གཡའ་མངས་ཚང་མ་ལ་ཤོག་སྐྲ་བིང་བཙུགས། རིལ་སྨང་ཚང་མ་ལ་ཁང་ར་ཕིང་བཙུགས། ཡང་སྐད་སྣ་གསུམ་བརྒྱ་དྲུག་བཙུ་ཕིངས། སྤྲོན་ལ་ཀ་སར་མང་པོ་འཛིགས་སོང་། རྫིང་ན་འོ། ཨ་ནེ་བཀར་དམན་མོས་མཛོད་མཁན་ཞིག་ཡིན་འགྲོ་བསམ། ཨ་ནེ་ལ་གླུ་ཞིག་བཏངས།།

ཨ་ནེ་བཀར་དམན་མོ་འི་ཚུལ་ནང་མི་ངན་ཞིག་འདུག་ལོ།
བཀར་དམན་གྱུལ་མོ་འི་ཚུལ་ནང་མི་ངན་ཞིག་འདུག་ལོ།
ལུང་སྟོད་ན་སྤྲུང་ཁ་ཞིག་དུ་བཙུགས་ལོ།
ལུང་མདོ་ན་ཕྲ་ཙ་ཞིག་བརྒྱལ་བཙུགས་ལོ།
རིལ་མང་ཁང་མེད་ཀྱི་ཁང་ར་ཞིག་ཚོར་ལོ།
གཡའ་མངས་ཤོག་མེད་ཀྱི་ཤོག་སྐྲ་ཞིག་ཚོར་ལོ།
ཨ་ནེ་བའི་ཚུལ་ནང་བདུད་སྐད་ཅིག་རག་ལོ།
བཀར་དམན་མོ་འི་ཚུལ་ནང་འདྲེ་སྐད་ཅིག་རག་ལོ།

དེ་ཟླུག་ཟེར་རིན་ཞིག་མགོ་ཕིང་སྡེ། བལྟས་པ་སང་། ཕྲ་རུས་དེ་སྤྲང་དོ་གོམ་ཟེད་པོ་ཟེ་སྡེ། འགྲང་སྡེ་ཡོད་ཚུག། ཀ་སར་གྲིས་ཀྱང་སྐར་གའི་ཁེམ་ཕྲུ་གང་གི་འོ་མ་དེ་འཕྲུངས་པ། འགྲངས་དེ་ཡང་དེན་ན་ཟེད་ཅིག་ལུས།

དེ་ནས་གནམ་ཡངས་དེ་བལྟས་པ། བྱ་རྫིས་མི་རྫིས་ཅི་ཡང་མེད་ཚུག། སྤྲར་གྱི་ལ་དེ་སྲ་མགྲོན་པོ་ཞིག་ཡོད་པས། ཀེ་སར་གྱིས་ཨ་ནེ་བཀུར་དམན་མོ་ལ་སྐོད་སྐྱུ་ཞིག་བཏངས།།

ངའི་ཨ་ནེས་འང་དངོས་ཤིག་ལ་ཉེན་དང་།
བཀུར་དམན་རྒྱལ་མོས་འང་བདག་ལ་གསན་ལོ།
ངརི་ཨ་ནེ་བའི་ཕྱུག་ལ་མི་ཉན་ཅེས་ཡང་མེད་ལོ།
བཀུར་དམན་མོ་འི་ཕྱུག་ལ་མི་གྲུབ་ཅེས་ཡང་མེད་ལོ།
སྤྲར་གྱི་ལའི་ཁ་ཙུ་སྤྱང་ཁུ་མཇུག་རྫུམ་ཆད་དེ་ལུས་དེ་འདུག།
ཨ་ནེ་བཀུར་དམན་མོས་རོགས་ཤིག་རང་མཛད་ལོ།
སྤྲར་གྱི་ལའི་སྤྱིང་དུ་པོ་རོག་ནག་ཆུང་ཆད་དེ་ལུས་དེ་འདུག།
བཀུར་དམན་རྒྱལ་མོས་ཁོ་ལ་རོགས་ཤིག་རང་མཛད་ལོ།
སྤྲར་གྱི་ལའི་ཁ་ན་ཟུང་ཁ་ཁ་དམར་མོ་ཆད་དེ་ལུས་དེ་འདུག།
ཨ་ནེ་བཀུར་དམན་མོས་ཁོ་ལ་རོགས་ཤིག་མཛད་ལོ།
སྤྲར་གྱི་ལའི་མཇུག་ན་ལྷ་མོ་འཛོལ་ལི་ལུས་དེ་འདུག།
བཀུར་དམན་རྒྱལ་མོས་ཁོ་ལ་རོགས་ཤིག་མཛད་ལོ།

དེ་ནུག་ཟེརས་པ། ཀེ་སར་གྱི་མདུན་པོ་ལ་ལྷ་ཅི་ཞིག་ཡོང་སྐྱེ་ཡོད་ཚུག། ཀེ་སར་གྱིས་ལྷ་ཅོ་ལ་འདེད་དེ་ཁྲིངས་པ་སང། ལྷ་ཅི་འཁོར་རིན་ཞིག་སོང་བ། ཀེ་སར་ཡང་རྫིང་རང་ཞུགས་དེ་སོང་བ་ལ་དེ་མགྱོགས་པ་འཁྲིལ་སོང་།

དེ་ནས་ཡང་ཞག་བདུན་འགྲུལ་དེ་སོང་བ། སྤྲམ་ལུའི་ལམ་སྣུངས་ཡོད་ཚུག། དེ་ཙ་སྤྲལ་ལུ་གསུམ་གྱིས་ཆེ་ལོ་རྩེ་འདིན་ཞིག་ཡོད་ཚུག། མི་སྲུ་

ཡོང་ན་ལྷ་ཅེས་སི་ཕི་ལ། ཏི་པི་ཞིག་བེར་ཀའི་མགོ་ལ་བོར་ཏེ་ཡོད་ཚུག། ཀ་སར་གྱིས་རིབ་ཤིང་གོ་ཏ་ཏེ་སོང་བ། ཏི་པི་དེ་ལ་ཀ་སར་ཡོང་ཅེས་མཐོང་སྟེ་འཁོར་རད་ཚུག། སྤྲལ་ལུ་ཀུན་ལ་མ་མཐོང་བ། ཀ་སར་ཉེ་མོ་རིག་ལ་བསླེབ་པ་སང་། ཏི་པི་ཐེབ་མང་པོ་འཁོར་བས། སྤྲལ་ལུས་བལྟས་པ། མི་སྲུ་ཡང་ཡོང་ཅེས་མ་མཐོང་བས། སྤྲལ་ལུ་གཅིག་ལ་སྨྲོ་ཡོང་སྟེ། ང་ཞེས་ཆོ་ལོ་རྩེ་ཅེས་ལ་ཁྲོ་རང་མ་འཐད་མཁན་ཡིན་ནོག་ཟེར་ཏེ། ཏི་པི་ཁྲོང་སྟེ་སྟན་ལ་བཏིང་སྟེ་བོརས། དེ་ནས་སྤྲལ་ལུའི་མདུན་ལ་ཀ་སར་བསླེབ་ཚར། དེ་སྤྲལ་ལུ་ཀུན་ཟུམས། སྤྲལ་ལུ་ཚང་ཀ་འཛོམས་ཏེ་ཀ་སར་ལ་སེམས་ཁུ་བཅོས་སྟེ་གླུ་ཞིག་བཏངས།།

གྱི་ལྷམ་ཀ་སར་དང་ཐུག་པ་དེ་ཀྱི་མ་ལན་ཅིག་ཡིན་ལོ།
སྤུལ་ཀྱུ་ཞིག་མེད་པ་གདུང་གདུང་རིག་རག་ལོ།
ཀ་སར་ཀྱལ་པོ་དང་མཛལ་བ་མང་པོ་འཐད་ལོ།
སྤུལ་ཀྱུ་མེད་པ་ནི་སེམས་ཆོར་རིག་རག་ལོ།

དེ་ཟུག་ཟེརས་པ་ཀ་སར་ཡང་འཐད་དེ་ཟེརས། ང་དང་ཚང་ཀས་ཆོ་ལོ་རྩེ་ཡིན་ཟེར་ཏེ་བརྩེས་པས། སྤྲལ་མོ་ཁྲོལ་འཛོམ་མོ་ཆོ་ལོ་འི་མིག་ནང་དུ་ཞུགས་ནས། ཀ་སར་ལ་ཆོ་ལོ་མ་ཡོངས་པས། སྤྲལ་ལུ་ལ་ཆོ་ལོ་ཡོང་སྟེ། ཀ་སར་གྱི་ཟན་ནོར་ཚང་མ་སྤྲལ་ལུས་ཁྲེརས། དེ་ནས་ཀ་སར་གྱིས་གླིང་མཁར་བཙུགས། སྤྲལ་ལུས་སྤྲལ་ཁང་ཀུ་བཞི་བཙུག་སྟེ་བཏངས་པ། གླིང་མཁར་ཡང་སྤྲལ་ལུ་ལ་ཐོབ་སོང་། ཡང་ཀ་སར་གྱིས་ཁུང་ཀོད་དབྱེར་པ་བཙུགས། སྤྲལ་ལུས་ཡང་རྟ་ཞིག་བཙུག་སྟེ་བཏངས་པ། ཁུང་ཀོད་དབྱེར་པ་ཡང་སྤྲམ་ཟུ་ལ་ཐོབ།

དེ་རིང་ནི་ཀ་སར་གྱིས་ཛོ་ཛོ་འབྲུ་གུ་མ་བཙུགས། སྤྲུལ་ལུས་སྤྲུལ་མོ་ཁྲོལ་ལོ་མོ་བཙུགས། ཛོ་ཛོ་ཡང་སྤྲུལ་ལུ་ལ་ཐོབ། དེ་རྒྱུག་ཀ་སར་གྱི་ནོར་ཚང་མ་ནོར་བུ་རིགས་ཚང་མ་སྤྲུལ་ལུ་ལ་ཐོབ་སོང་། དེ་ནས་ཅི་འདང་མ་ལུས་པ་སང་། རང་གི་རྩེ་བ་དེ་རིང་བཙུག་སྟེ་རྩེ་ཡིན་ཟེར་དེ་བརྩེས། དེ་ནས་ཨ་ནེ་བཀར་དམན་མོས་གསེར་སྒྲོང་གཅིག་ལ་ཛུ་སྟེ། ཀ་སར་གྱི་རྟ་མཆོག་གི་ནང་དུ་སོང་སྟེ་ཟེརས་པ། ལྷ་སྟོངས་ཅན་ནི་སྟོངས་མེད། ཀ་སར་རྒྱལ་པོ། གྲོས་ཅན་ནི་གྲོས་མེད་ལྷའི་བུ་ཀ་སར། གོང་བའི་ཁབ་པོ་འཕྲུད་དེ་རང་གི་ཚེ་ལོ་འི་མིག་དེ་བྲུས། སྤྲུལ་ལུའི་ཚེ་ལོ་བོར་དེ་ཉེ་རང་གི་དུང་ཚོལ་དེ་རྩེས་ཟེརས། ཀ་སར་གྱིས་རང་གི་དུང་ཚོལ་དེ་ཕིང་སྟེ། གོང་བ་ནས་ཁབ་ཕིང་སྟེ་ཚེ་ལོ་འི་མིག་དེ་བྲུས་པ་སང་། སྤྲུལ་མོ་ཁྲོལ་འཛོམ་དེ་ཚེ་ལོ་འི་མིག་ནང་ནས་བིང་སྟེ། ཨོ་ཧོ་ཧོ། ངས་ཞེས་ཨིན་ན་མི་ཞེས་ཚོད་བལྟས་པ་ཡིན་ཟེར་རིན་ཞིག་བིང་སྟེ་ཡོངས། དེ་ནས་རྩེ་བ་དེ་རིང་བཙུག་སྟེ་ཀ་སར་གྱི་དུང་ཚོལ་དེ་བརྩེས་པས། རྩེ་བ་དེ་རིང་དེ་ཀ་སར་ལ་ཐོབ་སོང་། དེ་ནས་སྤྲུལ་ལུ་ཀུན་ལ་བེར་ཀ་ཆོས་ཤིང་ཁྲ་སྨུག་ཅིག་ཡོད་ཚུག། སྤྲུལ་ལུ་ཀུན་གྱིས་ཀ་སར་ལ་མགྲོན་ཞིག་བདང་ཡིན་ཟེར་དེ། དེ་ཆོས་ཤིང་པོ་ལ་གླུ་ཞིག་བདངས།།

སྤྲུལ་ལུ་ངའི་ཆོས་ཤིང་ཁྲིད་དངོས་ལ་ཉེན་དང་།
ཆོས་ཤིང་ཁྲ་སྨུག་གིས་བདག་ལ་གསན་དང་།
དེ་རིང་ཀ་སར་ལ་མགྲོན་ཞིག་རང་ཕུལ་ཡིན།
གླིང་རྒྱལ་ལྷམ་ཆེན་མོ་ལ་སྐུ་མགྲོན་ཞིག་ཕུལ་ཡིན།
ཁྱེད་ཆོས་ཤིང་ཁྲ་སྨུག་དེ་རྒྱ་ནག་ཡུལ་ལ་སོང་ལོ།
རྒྱ་ནག་ཡུལ་ནས་གོ་ཞིན་འབྲུག་འབྲིས་མ་ཁྱེང་ཤོ།

ཚོམ་ཤིང་ཁྲིད་དབུས་གཙང་གཞུང་ལ་སོང་ལོ།
དབུས་གཙང་གཞུང་ནས་ཛ་ལགས་མོ་ཞིག་ཁྲིད་ལོ།
ཚོམ་ཤིང་ཁྲིད་རང་ཡར་ཁྲིན་གཞུང་ལ་སོང་ལོ།
ཡར་ཁྲིན་གཞུང་ནས་ཧོར་ཧྲ་གྲོང་གྲོང་ཞིག་ཁྲིད་ལོ།
ཚོམ་ཤིང་ཁྲི་རང་ལ་དྭགས་གཞུང་ལ་སོང་ལོ།
ལ་དྭགས་གཞུང་ནས་ནོར་བུ་སྣ་ཚོགས་ཁྲིད་ལོ།
ཚོམ་ཤིང་ཁྲི་རང་སྤྲལ་དྲི་ཡུལ་ལ་སོང་ལོ།
སྤྲལ་དྲི་ཡུལ་ནས་ཧལ་མན་པ་དིང་ཁྲིད་ལོ།
ཚོམ་ཤིང་ཁྲི་རང་བྲུ་རིག་ཡུལ་ལ་སོང་ལོ།
བྲུ་རིག་ཡུལ་ནས་གྲོ་དཀར་མེན་ཟེ་ཞིག་ཁྲིད་ལོ།
ཚོམ་ཤིང་ཁྲི་རང་ཁ་ཚུལ་གཞུང་ལ་སོང་ལོ།
ཁ་ཚུལ་གཞུང་ནས་འབྲས་དཀར་ཨོལ་ལོ་ཁྲིད་ལོ།
དེ་ཚང་མ་ཁྲིད་སྟེ་རྒྱལ་པོ་ལ་མགྲོན་བཙོ་ཡིན་ལོ།
དེ་ཚང་མ་སྤུས་དེ་ཀ་སར་ལ་མགྲོན་ཞིག་བཏང་ཡིན།

དེ་ཟླུག་ཟེར་པ་སང་ཚོམ་ཤིང་རེས། ཟེར་མ་ཐག་དེ་ཚང་མ་དུས་གཅིག་ལ་ཁྲིངས་པས། དེ་ནས་དེ་ཟླུག་མང་པོ་ཡོད་ཅེས་ཤེས་དེ། ཀ་སར་གྱིས་གསོལ་མཆོད་གཅིག་བཏང་སྟེ་སྐྱ་འདི་ལྟར།།

མཉམ་པོ་སྐྱེས་པའི་ལྷ་རྣམས་ལ་མཆོད་དོ།
མཉམ་པོ་སྐྱེས་པའི་ཀླུ་རྣམས་ལ་མཆོད་དོ།

ཤ་ལྷ་ཀྱེར་རྫོང་སྨན་པོ་ལ་མཆོད་དོ།

མ་ལྷ་བཀུར་དམན་རྒྱལ་མོ་ལ་མཆོད་དོ།

སྟེང་ལྷའི་དབང་པོ་རྒྱབ་ཞིན་ལ་མཆོད་དོ།

བར་བཙན་གྱི་ཨ་མ་སྐྱབ་མདུན་མ་ལ་མཆོད་དོ།

འོག་ཀླུའི་ཀླུ་རྒྱལ་ལྫོག་པོ་ལ་མཆོད་དོ།

དེ་ཐུག་གསོལ་མཆོད་བཏངས་པ་སང་། དེ་ཚང་མ་མིད་མཁན་སོང་། དེ་ནས་སྤྲལ་མོ་ཁྲོལ་ལི་མོས་ཀ་སར་ལ་ཀླུ་ཞིག་བཏངས།།

གླིང་ཀ་སར་རྒྱལ་པོས་དངོས་ལ་ཉོན།

ཁྱེད་སྤྲུལ་པའི་རྒྱལ་པོས་བདག་ལ་གསན།

གླིང་གི་གླིང་མཁར་འཁོར་དེ་ཉིད་ལ་བག་སྲིས་བཅོ་ཡིན།

ཐུ་རྩ་ཁྱུང་གོད་འཁོར་དེ་ཀ་སར་ལ་བག་སྲིས་ཐུམ་ཡིན།

ཇོ་ཇོའ་བྲུ་གུ་མ་འཁོར་དེ་ཉིད་ལ་བག་སྲིས་ཐུམ་ཡིན།

ལྷེམ་ལྷེམ་མི་ལྷེམ་མཁར་འཁོར་དེ་བག་སྲིས་ཤིག་ཐུམ་ཡིན།

གླིང་གི་ནོར་བུ་ཚང་མ་འཁོར་དེ་ཀ་སར་ལ་བག་སྲིས་ཐུམ་ཡིན།

གླིང་མཁར་རྩེ་དགུ་བསིལ་མོ་ཞིག་ཡིན། ཉིད་ཀྱིས་དབྱར་ས་ཅོས།

སྤྲལ་ཁང་གྱ་བཞི་གྲོན་མོ་ཡིན། ཉིད་ཀྱིས་དགུན་ས་ཅོས་ལོ།

སྤྲལ་ལུ་དུང་དང་ཉིད་ཀྱི་གཡོག་པོ་དེ་ཅོས་ལོ།

དེ་ཐུག་ཟེར་པ་སང་། ཀ་སར་གྱིས་ལན་དུ་གླུ་འདི་ལྟར་བཏངས་སོ།

གླིང་མཁར་རྩེ་དགུ་དེ་མི་དགོས་ཁྱེད་ཀྱིས་ཁྱེར་ལོ།

ཀྱུང་གོད་དཀྱེར་པ་དེ་མི་དགོས་ཁྱེད་ཀྱིས་ཁྱེར་ལོ།

ཇོ་ ཇོ་འབྲུག་བུ་མ་དེ་མི་དགོས་ཁྱེད་ཀྱིས་ཁྱེར་ལོ།
ལྷེམ་ལྷེམ་མི་ལྷེམ་མཁར་མི་དགོས་ཁྱེད་ཀྱིས་ཁྱེར་ལོ།
གླིང་གི་ནོར་བུ་ཚང་མ་མི་དགོས་ཁྱེད་ཀྱིས་ཁྱེར་ལོ།
དེ་ཚང་མ་ཁྱེད་ལ་ཐོབ་མཁན་གྱི་ནོར་ཡིན།
ང་ལ་ཐོབ་པའི་ནོར་དེ་ཁྱེད་ཀྱི་རྩེ་བི་དིང་དེ་ཡིན།
ང་རང་ལ་ཐོབ་མཁན་ནི་རྩེ་བི་དིང་ཕིང་ཡིན།

དེ་ཟླུག་ཟེར་ས་པ། སྤྲལ་ལྡུ་མང་པོ་འཛིགས། སྤྲལ་ལྡུས་ཡང་ལན་དུ་གླུ་ཞིག་བཏངས་སོ།

གླིང་རྒྱལ་ལྷམ་ཆེན་མོས་དངོས་ཞིག་ལ་ཉོན་དང་།
ཁྱེད་སྤྲུལ་པའི་རྒྱལ་པོས་བདག་ལ་གསན་ལོ།
སྤྲལ་ལྡུ་ང་མ་བསད་སྤྲལ་ལྡུ་ང་བོར་ན་གྲོལ་ལོ།
དུང་དུང་ང་མ་བསད་དུང་དུང་བཀོལ་ན་རྒྱལ་ལོ།
ཀ་སར་ཉིད་ལ་ཕན་ཐོགས་ཞིག་ཡོང་ཡིན་མོ།
བྲག་ཚ་བུ་དུང་དུང་ལ་སྤྲལ་ལྡུ་མེད་ན་མི་ཉན་ལོ།
རྡོ་བ་ས་ཕར་ནམ་ཕར་ལ་སྤྲལ་ལྡུ་ང་མེད་ན་མི་ཉན་ལོ།
ང་མ་བསད་ཉིད་ཀྱི་ཞབ་ཞི་ཞིག་བཅོ་ཡིན།

དེ་ཟླུག་ཟེར་ས་པ། ཀ་སར་ཡང་འཕྲད་སོང་སྟེ། སྤྲལ་ལྡུ་དང་གཉིས་ཀས་གཏམ་ཆད་བཅོ་སྟེ། སྤྲལ་ལྡུ་ཀ་སར་དང་མཉམ་པོ་སོང་།།

No. 2.

དེ་ནས་ཁོང་གཉིས་ཀ་བྲག་ཚ་ཝུ་དང་དུང་ལ་བསླེབ་སོང་བ། བྲག་དེ་ལ་ཏ་སྒོ་ཡོད་རྩུག། ཏ་སྒོ་དེ་རྩུག་སྟེ་མ་ཕྱེས་པས། སྤྲེལ་ལུས་ཟེརས་པ། ཕྲ་བྲག་སྒོ། སྤྲེལ་ལུ་ང་ཡོང་རྩུག། བྲག་སྒོ་དེ་ཕྱེ་སྟེ་བོར་ཟེརས་པ། བྲག་སྒོ་དེ་ཕྱེས་པས། ཀེ་སར་གྱིས་རྐྱང་གོད་དབྱེར་པ་ལ་ཞོན་དེ་མགྱོགས་པ་སྒོ་འི་ནང་ནས་སོང་བ་སང་། བྲག་སྒོ་དེ་ལ་ཀེ་སར་ཡིན་བ་ཤེས་དེ་མགྱོགས་པ་ཞུག་སྟེ་ཡོངས་ནས། ཕྲུ་ཙུའི་ཛ་མ་བྲག་བར་ནང་དུ་འཁད་སོང་བས། དེ་ནས་རྡོར་གྱི་ཕྲུ་གུ་གསེ་རལ་ཅར་དང་གཡུ་རལ་ཅན་གཉིས་ཀའི་མགོ་དེ་ཁྲོང་ཆད་བཅོས་པ་རྟའི་ཛ་མ་དེ་ཞུད་བཏངས།།

དེ་ནས་ཁོང་གཉིས་ཀ་སོང་པ་སང་། རྡོ་བ་ས་ཕར་ནམ་ཕར་དུ་བསླེབ་སོང་། དེ་རུ་བསླེབ་པ་རྡོ་བ་ཚང་མ་ཕར་གྱིན་སུ་གནམ་ལ་ཆའད་རྩུག། སུ་ས་ལ་འབུད་ཀྱིན་ཡོད་རྩུག། དེ་རུ་ཡང་སྤྲེལ་ལུས་ཟེརས། ཕྲ་རྡོ་བ་ཚང་མ་སྤྲེལ་ལུ་ང་ཡོང་རྩུག་ཟེརས་པ་སང་། རྡོ་བ་ཚང་མ་མལ་མལ་ལ་འདུགས།།

དེ་ནས་ཡང་ཁོང་གཉིས་ཀ་སོང་བས། ཁོང་འགྲོང་ཀ་ར་ཁམ་པའི་རྩར་བསླེབ། དེ་འགྲོང་ཡང་རྡོར་གྱི་ལམ་པ་ཡིན། དེ་རུ་སྤྲེལ་ལུ་སྔོན་ལ་སོང་སྟེ་འགྲོང་ལ་ཟེརས་པ། ཕྲ་འགྲོང་ཀ་ར་ཁམ་པ། ང་ལ་ཀེ་སར་གྱིས་ནག་བསྟུན་འདུག་ཟེར་དེ་ན། སྤྲེལ་ལུ་ཤོར་སོང་། འགྲོང་ལ་དེ་ཟུག་ཚོར་དེ་མགྱོགས་པ་ཡོང་སྟེ། ཀེ་སར་དང་ཕྲུ་རུ་གཉིས་ཀ་གསོན་དེ་ཡ་མིད་བཏངས། ཀེ་སར་རྣམི་གཉིས་ཀ་འགྲོང་གི་གྲོད་པའི་ནང་དུ་ཞག་ཁ་ཅིག་ལུས་དེ་འདུགས། དེ་ནས་ཨ་ནེ་བཀུར་དམན་མོས་ཀེ་སར་ལ་ཟེརས་པ། ཕྲ་བསམ་པ་མེད་མཁན་ནི་ཀེ་སར་

རྒྱལ་པོ། ཁོ་རང་འབྲོང་གི་གྲོད་པའི་ནང་དུ་ནམ་ཚུགས་པ་འདུག་ཆེན། ཁྱོ་རང་ལ་དུག་པ་ཅན་གྲི་གུ་མེད་ན། ཕོ་ལད་དཀར་པོའི་སྟེབ་ཆུང་མེད་ན། ཕོ་ལད་དཀར་པོའི་སྟེབ་ཆུང་དང་སྟུབ། དུག་པ་ཅན་གྲི་གུ་དང་ཅེད། རྩིབ་ལོག་སྒྲོགས་ནས་ཐེང་སྟེ་ཡོང་། འབྲོང་གི་སྙིང་དེ་བཅད་དེ་འཁུར་དེ་ཡོང་། དེ་ཟླུག་ཟེར་ས་པ། ཀེ་སར་གྱིས་གྲོད་པའི་ནང་ནས་གླུ་ཞིག་བཏངས།།

ལྷ་འབྲོང་ཆེན་ཀ་ར་ཁམ་པས་དངོས་ལ་ཉེན་ལོ།
འབྲོང་གྲོད་སང་གྲོན་མོ་མི་རག་ལོ།
འབྲོང་ཤ་བས་སང་ཞིམ་པོ་མི་རག་ལོ།
འདི་རིང་སྐྱིད་སྐྱིད་ཅིག་སྐྱིད་མི་ཤེས་ལོ།
འདི་རིང་མཆོགས་སེ་སྟན་བོལ་མོ་ཐྲབ་མི་ཤེས།
འདི་རིང་མཆོགས་སེ་སྐྱས་བོལ་མོ་ཞིག་མ་ཐོབ།

དེ་ཟླུག་ཟེར་རིན་ཞིག་འབྲོང་གི་ནང་ཆ་ཚང་མ་བཅད་ཀྱིན་ཞིག་དང་འདུགས་པ་འབྲོང་དེ་ཤི་སོང་བས། ཀེ་སར་གྱིས་རྩིབ་མའི་ནང་ནས་དཀར་ཁྲང་ཞིག་ཕིང་སྟེ་ཧ་མི་གཉིས་ཀ་ཕི་སྟ་རུ་ཐིང་སོང་། དེ་ནས་ཀེ་སར་གྱིས་སྤྲུལ་ལུ་དེ་བཙལ་དེ་ཁྲིད་སྟེ་ཟེར་ས། ལྷ་སྤྲུལ་ལུ། ཁྱོ་རང་གིས་ང་ཞ་ཧ་མི་གཉིས་ཀ་འབྲོང་ལ་ཟ་བཅུགས། ཁྱོད་ལ་ངས་སྣ་ལོ་ཤུད་དེ། ཁྱོ་རང་ངེ་ཁང་ཞོན་དེ་ཆེན་ཟེར་ས། སྤྲུལ་ལུས་ཀེ་སར་གྱི་ཞབས་ལ་འཐམ་སྟེ་ཧྲུ་ཟེར་ས། ད་འདི་ནས་པར་ལ་རྟོར་ཡུལ་ལ་བསླེབ་བསླེབ་ཚུགས་པ་ལམ་རྟོག་པོ་མེད། ཟམ་པ་དགུ་ཐུད་ཅིག་ཡོད་པ། དེ་ལ་འཇིགས་མོ་མེད་ཟེར་ས་པ། དེ་ནས་ཀེ་སར་གྱིས་ཡིད་ཆེས་དེ་སྤྲུལ་ལུ་སློག་སྟེ་བཏངས།།

ཀེ་སར་རང་དང་ཐུ་རུ་གཉིས་ཀ་སོང་སྟེ། ཟམ་པ་དགུ་ཐུད་ལ་བསླེབ་པ། དེ་རུ་ལམ་སྲུངས་རྡོར་གྱི་སྲོག་དགུ་པ་ཀློན་པོ་འི་བུ་ཚ་དང་དམག་མི་བརྒྱ་ཟམ་ཡོད་ཚུག། དེ་ནས་ཀེ་སར་གྱིས་མགྲོགས་པ་པན་ཧུང་སྐྱོང་པོ་བཙོ་སྟེ། ཁྲི་སོ་ཙན་བེར་ཀ་འཁུར་དེ་རིལ་མང་གི་འཕྲེང་བ་ཞིག་འཁུར་དེ་ཁམ་ལོག་ཅིག་བཙོ་སྟེ་སོང་བས། དེ་དམག་ཚང་མས་ཟེརས། ལྷ་སྐྱོང་པོ་ཁྲོ་རང་གནས་ཡོངས་ཟེར་པས། པན་ཧུང་གིས། ང་ཡང་མཁན་ཞིག་ཡིན་ཟེརས། དེ་ཞག་པོ་ལ་ཀེ་སར་གྱིས་ནམ་ནས་ཆར་པ་མང་པོ་ཞིག་པབ་སྟེ། དེ་དམག་ཚང་མ་ལ་འདུགས་མེད་པར་དཀགས་པོ་སོང་བས། པན་ཧུང་གིས་གན་དྲི་ཞིག་གོན་དེ་འདུགས་པ་ཆར་པ་ཙ་ཡིག་ཡང་མ་ཕོག། དེ་དམག་ཚང་མ་ཁོ་འི་མདུན་ལ་ཡོང་སྟེ་འདུགས། ཁོས་ཟེརས་པ། ཉེ་ཞ་ཚང་མ་མི་འདི་ཟམ་ཅིག་འདུག། ཁང་པ་ཞིག་མེད་པ་ག་ཐུག་ལ་འདུག་ཆེན། ཉེ་ཞ་རང་གིས་རྗོ་བ་ཁྲོང་། ངས་རྩིག་ཡིན་ཟེརས། དེ་ནས་ཁོང་ཚང་མས་རྗོ་བ་ཁྲོངས་པ། པན་ཧུང་གིས་བརྩིགས། དེ་ནས་མགྲོགས་པ་གྲུབ་སོང་། གདུང་མའི་མགོ་ཚང་མ་ཀ་གཅིག་ཅིག་གི་ཁ་བདང་སྟེ་བོརས། དེ་ནས་ཁང་པ་དེ་གྲུབ་སྟེ་ན། ཡང་ཆར་པ་མང་པོ་ཞིག་ཡོང་བཙུགས། དེ་དམག་ཚང་མ་ཁང་པའི་ནང་སོང་སྟེ་ཟེརས་པ། ལྷ་པན་ཧུང་ཁྲོ་རང་ཡང་ནང་ལ་ཡོང་ཟེརས་པ། པན་ཧུང་གིས། ང་ལ་ནང་ཞག་དང་གནས་ཐོབ་ཡིན། འདི་རིང་ཉེ་ཞ་རང་གིས་ནང་ལ་བོར་ཡིན་བ། ཐོ་རངས་ལ་ང་ཁང་པ་ཞིག་གནས་ཐོབ་ཡིན། ང་ཡི་སྟ་འདུག་ན་འཚང་གྲིག་ཟེརས་པ། ཁོ་ཡི་སྟ་འདུགས། དེ་ནས་མཚན་ཕྱེད་ཟམ་སོང་སྟེ། ཀེ་སར་གྱིས་ཀ་དེ་ལ་སི་ཀྲིམ་ཐག་པ་ཞིག་བདག་སྟེ་འཐེན་བདངས་པ། ཐོག་དེ་ཚང་མ་སྒྲིབ་ཅིག་ལ་རྡིབ་སྟེ་ཡོངས། དེ་དམག་ཚང་མ་ཤི

སོང་། དེ་ནས་གནམ་ལང་སྐྱེ་ན། དེ་རོ་ཚང་མ་ཟམ་པའི་ཁ་ནས། རྒྱལ་པངས། ཁང་པའི་གདུང་མ་ཚང་མ་མེ་ལ་དུག་ནས། རྗེས་མེད་ཤུལ་མེད་བཅོ་སྐྱེ་ན། ནོར་ཡུལ་ལ་སོང་།

དེ་ནས་ཨ་སམ་སལ་གྱི་གོང་ཀ་རུ་བསླེབ་སོང་། དེ་རུ་ རྟ་བརྒྱ་སྤྲོད་ལ་བདངས། རྟ་བརྒྱ་ཉིང་ན་བདངས། ཀེ་སར་རྟ་མི་གཉིས་ཀ་དཀྱིལ་ལ་འདུག་སྐྱེ་སོང་། དེ་ནས་ཨང་ཨ་ལོང་ཐང་གི་ཐང་སྟོད་ལ་བསླེབ་སོང་། དེ་རུ་རྟ་གཅིག་སྤྲོད་ལ་བདངས། རྟ་གཅིག་ཉིང་ན་བོརས། ཀེ་སར་རང་དཀྱིལ་ལ་འདུག་སྐྱེ་སོང་། དེ་རུ་ཁྲག་པ་ལན་གསུམ་བཛེས། ནོར་གྱི་གསེར་པོའི་གསེར་མཁར་ལན་གསུམ་འགལ་སོང་། དེ་ནས་སོང་པ་སང་། ནོར་གྱི་ར་ཛེ་ཀུན་དང་ཐུག་སོང་། དེ་རུ་ར་ཛེ་ཁ་ཅིག་གླིང་ཡུལ་ན་ཟུམ་སྐྱེ་ཁྲིར་མཁན་ནི་མི་ཡོད་ཚུག། ཁ་ཅིག་ནོར་ཡུལ་པ་ཡིན་པས། དེ་ཀུན་གྱིས་འདྲིས་པ། ཡྰ་སྟོང་ཐྲུག། ཁྲིད་ག་ནས་ཡོངས། གླིང་ཀེ་སར་རྒྱལ་པོ་ཡོང་བ་མི་འདུག་ག། གླིང་པའི་དམག་འཁྲོང་བ་མི་འདུག་ག་ཟེརས་པ། སྟོང་ཐྲུག་གིས་ལན་ལ་གླུ་འདི་ལྟར་བཏབས།།

གླིང་ཡུལ་གྱི་དམག་འཁྲོང་བ་མི་འདུག་ལོ།
གླིང་ཀེ་སར་རྒྱལ་པོ་བདུད་ཡུལ་ལ་ཤི་ཟེར་འདུག།
ཁོ་འི་ཕི་ལ་གདུང་རྟེན་ཞིག་བཞང་འདུག།
ཟླ་མ་ཚེ་ཚེ་ཀུན་ལ་རྟ་འགྲེད་རེ་ཐུལ་འདུག།
བར་པ་རྣམས་ལ་གཡག་འགྲེད་རིག་བདང་འདུག།
ཆུང་ཆུང་རྣམས་ལ་ར་ལུག་རེ་ཟདང་འདུག།
སྟོང་པོ་ང་ཡིན་ཀྱང་ལུ་ག་ཞིག་ཐོབ་ལོ།

ལུ་གུ་དེ་ལམ་གྱི་ཟ་ཅེས་ཞིག་སོང་ལོ།
ཡབ་སྟོན་པ་ཨ་པ་ཐང་ཞིག་གི་ཁ་ཞི་སྟེ་འདུག།
མིག་ཀུན་ཁ་དས་ཚོམ་གིན་ཞིག་འདུག་ལོ།
ཕུམ་སྦྲིར་མོ་ཨ་མ་རན་འཐག་ཚང་མ་ལ་ལང་འདུག།
ལང་པོ་སྐྱུང་ཅེས་མེད་པ་སྐྱི་གུ་ཞིག་ངས་བདངས་པ་ཡིན།

དེ་རྟག་ཟེརས་པ་སང་། གླིང་པའི་མི་ཀུན་ཏུ་ཅེས་ཡོངས། རྫོར་གྱི་ཨི་ཀུན་མང་པོ་འཐད་སོང་། དེ་ནས་གླིང་པའི་མི་ཀུན་ཏུ་ཅེས་མཐོང་སྟེ་སྨིག་པ་བསམ་སྟེ། ཀེ་སར་གྱིས་དངོས་བསྟན་དེ་ཟེརས། ཀེ་སར་ང་ཡིན་ཁྲི་ཞ་རང་རིངས་མ་རིངས་ཟེརས་པ་ཁོང་འཐད་སོང་།

No. 3.

དེ་ནས་ཡང་ཀེ་སར་སྤྱང་པོ་བཅོ་སྟེ་རྫོར་ཡུལ་ལ་སོང་། རྫོར་གུར་དཀར་གྱི་མཁར་གྱི་རྩ་རུ་བསླེབ་སོང་། དེ་རུ་རྒྱ་རྡོང་བཞི་ཡོད་ཚུག། གཅིག་ནི་གུར་དཀར་གྱི་ཡིན། གཅིག་ནི་གུར་རྒྱག་སླ་མའི་ཡིན། གཅིག་ནི་ཛེ་ཛེ་འབྲུ་གུ་མོའི་ཡིན། རྒྱ་རྡོང་གཅིག་ནི་མགར་ར་ཏེ་མིས་སི་ཡིན་ཚུག། གུར་དཀར་གྱི་རྒྱ་རྡོང་དེ་གསེར་གྱི་ཡོད་ཚུག། གུར་རྒྱག་སླ་མའི་ཟངས་ཀྱི་ཡོད་ཚུག། ཛེ་ཛེ་འབྲུ་གུ་མའི་གཡུ་ནི་ཡོད་ཚུག། མགར་ར་ཏེ་མིས་སི་ལྕགས་ཀྱི་ཡོད་ཚུག། དེ་རྒྱ་རྡོང་ཚང་མའི་ནང་དུ་སྲུའི་ནང་ཀོ་རེ། སྲུའི་ནང་ཀྲད་པ། སྲུའི་ནང་རྒྱུན་སྤྲང་སྟེ་བོརས། ཁོ་རང་ལམ་གག་ཅིག་གི་ཁ་གྱེལ་དེ་འདུགས། དེ་ནས་གུར་དཀར་གྱི་རྒྱ་མ་ཡོང་སྟེ་བལྟས་པ་སང་། རྒྱ་མདོང་ཚང་མའི་ནང་དུ་ཀྲད་ཀྱི་སྤྲང་

སྨེ་ཡོད་ཚུག། ཆུ་མས་ཟེར་ས་པ། ལྤ་སྤོང་པོ་ཁམ་ལོག་ང་ཞའི་གུར་དཀར་གྱི་ཆུ་དོང་པོ་འི་ནང་དུ་རྩོག་པོ་ཅི་ཕི་ལ་སྤྲངས་ཟེར་དེ། ཀུད་ཀྱི་ཕངས་ནས་ཆུ་ཁུར་དེ་ཡོངས་པ། སྤོང་པོ་ལམ་མི་ཁམ་ནུར་སོང་། ལྤ་སྤོང་པོ། ང་ཆ་ཐུག་ནུར་འང་ཟེར་ས་པ། སྤོང་པོས། ཁྲོ་རང་རིངས་ན་གོམ་སྨེ་སོང་། མ་རིངས་ན་འཁོར་དེ་སོང་ཟེར་ས་པ། ཆུ་མ་གོམ་སྨེ་ན་སོང་།

དེ་ནས་ཨང་ཇོ་ཇོ་འི་ཆུ་མ་དེ་ཡོངས་པ། ཡང་བལྷས་པ་ཆུའི་ནང་དུ་ཀུད་ཀྱི་སྤྲང་སྨེ་ཡོད་ཚུག་པ། ཆུ་མས་ཟེར་ས། ལྤ་སྤོང་པོ་ཁྲོད་ག་ནས་ཡོངས། ང་ཞའི་ཆུ་དོང་ཚང་མ་རྩོག་པོ་ཅི་ལ་བཅོས། ཨ་ངོས་ལ་ནུར་འང་ཟེར་ས། སྤོང་པོས་ཟེར་ས། ཨོ་ནོ་མོ་ལི། ཉི་རང་རིངས་ན་གོམ་སྨེ་སོང་། མ་རིངས་ན་འཁོར་དེ་སོང་། ང་ཐག་རིངས་ནས་ཡོང་མཁན་ཞིག་ཡིན། ངལ་དེ་རག་ཟེར་ས་པ། ཆུ་མས་ཀུད་པ་ཕིང་སྨེ་ཆུ་འཁུར་དེ་ཆ་ཟ་ན། སྤོང་པོས་གསེར་གདུབ་པོ་ཆུའི་ནང་དུ་ཕངས་བཏངས། ཆུ་མས་ཆུ་འཁུར་དེ་མཁར་ལ་སོང་། དེ་ཚུག་པ་མཁར་ལ་ཇོ་ཇོ་ལ་ཆུ་དཀོན་མོ་སོང་སྨེ། ཁོ་བསླེབ་པ་དང་། ཇོ་ཇོས་ཁོ་ལ་ཁ་སྐྱེས་དེ། ཁྲོ་རང་ཅི་ལ་འགོར་ང་ལ་ཆུ་དཀོན་མོ་སོང་ཟེར་ས་པ། ཆུ་མས་ཇོ་ཇོ་ལ་ཞུས་པ། ཇོ་ཇོ་ལེ། ང་དང་གི་ཆུ་དོང་པོ་འི་མདུན་ལ་སྤོང་པོ་ཞིག་ཡོང་སྨེ། ཆུའི་ནང་དུ་ཀུད་ཀྱི་རི་སྤྲང་སྨེ། ཀོ་རི་སྤྲང་སྨེ། ཁོ་རང་ལམ་མི་ཁ་གྱེལ་དེ་གཉིད་ལོག་སྨེ་འདུག། ངས་ཆུ་དོང་ནང་ནས་ཀུད་པ་དང་ཀོ་རི་ཕིང་སྨེ་ཡང་འཁྲུ་སྨེ་ཆུ་ཁུར་དེ་ཁྲོངས་པ། ཁོ་ལམ་མི་ཁ་ནམ་མ་ནུར་བ་འདུག། ངས་ནུར་ཟེར་ས་པ། ཁོས་ཁྲེ་རང་རིངས་ན་གོམ་སྨེ་སོང་། མ་རིངས་ན་འཁོར་དེ་སོང་། ང་ཐག་རིངས་

ནས་ཡོངས་མཁན་ཞིག་ཡིན་ཟེར་འདུག། དེའི་ཕྱི་ལ་ང་ཆུ་འགོར་སོང་བསམ་སྟེ། ང་གོམ་སྟེ་ཡོངས་པ་ཡིན་ཟེརས་པ། ཇོ་ཇོས་ཁོ་མིའི་ལུས་རི་ཉ་པོ་ཆེ་ཐོབ་མཁན་ཞིག་གི་ཁ་ཏི་ལ་གོམས་ཟེརས། དེ་ནས་ཇོ་ཇོས་ང་ལ་ཆུ་ཞིག་ཀླུག་ཟེརས་པ། གཡོག་མོས་ལག་ཆུ་ཀླུགས། དེ་ནས་ཇོ་ཇོའི་མཛུ་གུ་ལ་གསེར་གདུབ་དེ་རན་སོང་བ་ཇོ་ཇོས་བསམ། ཀེ་སར་བསླེབ་སྟེ་ཡིན་ནམ་བསམ་སྟེ་ནང་ལ་སོང་སྟེ་མར་ཟན་ཞིག་གཡོས། ཇོ་ཇོ་རང་གཟབ་སྟེ་གླིང་ཡུལ་ལི་གོས་གོན་དེ་མར་ཟན་དེ་ཁུར་ཏེ། དེ་མི་ལ་ལྟ་ལ་ཡོངས། དེ་མི་ད་རུང་ལམ་མི་ཁ་གྲོལ་དེ་ཡོད་ཆུག། དེ་ནས་ཇོ་ཇོས་དེ་མི་ལ་གླིང་ཡུལ་གྱི་ཁ་བར་འདྲིས་ནས་གླུ་འདི་ལྟར་བཏངས།།

ལྷ་པན་ཧུང་སྐྱོང་པོ་ཁྱོད་ག་ནས་ཡོངས་ལོ།
ཁྱོད་གླིང་ཡུལ་ལ་བསླེབ་མཁན་ཞིག་མིན་ན།
གླིང་རྒྱལ་ལྷམ་ཀེ་སར་དེ་བདུད་ཡུལ་ནས་བསླེབ་བ་མ་བསླེབ།
ཡབས་སྟོན་པ་ཨ་བཱ་ཁམས་བཟང་འདུག་ག།
ཡུམ་སྨོན་མོ་ཨ་མ་ཁམས་བཟང་འདུག་ག།
གླིང་གི་དཔའ་བོ་ཚང་མ་ཁམས་བཟང་འདུག་ག།
གླིང་གི་དཔལ་ལེ་ཀྲོད་པོ་མ་རྐྱས་པ་འདུག་ག།
ནོ་འབྲུ་དམར་ལམ་བསྟན་གྱི་ཟུར་མོ་ཕན་ན།
གླིང་མཁར་རྟེ་དགུ་ལ་ཞིག་གསོབ་ང་ཚོས་ས་མ་བཙོས།
ཁ་བར་བཟང་པོ་བཤད་ན་ཟ་ཙེས་ཏི་ཞིམ་གང་ཞིམ་བཏང་ཨིན།
ཁ་བར་ངན་པ་བཤད་ན་སྲ་ཟན་དང་སྐོག་ཆུ་བཏང་ཨིན།

དེ་ཟུག་ཟེརས་པ།   སྒྲོང་པོ་དེས་ལན་དུ་གླུ་འདི་ལྟར་བཏངས།

ཚོར་གྱི་ཇོ་ ཇོ་སོ་མས་དངོས་ལ་ཉོན་དང་།
ཇོ་ ཇོ་འབྲུག་མས་བདག་ལ་གསན་ལོ།
ང་གླིང་ཡུལ་ནས་ཡོང་སྟེ་ལོ་མང་པོ་ཞིག་སོང་ལོ།
གླིང་ཀེ་སར་རྒྱལ་པོ་བདུད་ཡུལ་ལ་ཤི་ལོ།

ཁོའི་དོན་ལ་གདུང་རྟེན་ཞིག་བཞང་འདུག།
གདུང་རྟེན་གྱི་ཞབས་རྣ་པོ་ཡང་ལ་བཙོ་རྒྱུག།
གདུང་རྟེན་གྱི་གཟུ་གཅིག་གསེར་ལ་བཙོ་རྒྱུག།
གདུང་རྟེན་གྱི་གཟུ་གཅིག་དངུལ་ལ་བཙོ་རྒྱུག།
གདུང་རྟེན་གྱི་གཟུ་གཅིག་ཟངས་ལ་བཙོ་རྒྱུག།

གདུང་རྟེན་གྱི་གཟུ་གཅིག་དུང་ལ་བཙོ་རྒྱུག།
གདུང་རྟེན་གྱི་ཕུང་པ་དེ་སྨུ་དིག་ལ་བཙོ་རྒྱུག།
སྒྲོག་ཤིང་དེ་ཙན་དན་ལ་འདུག་ལོ།
སྐྱན་དར་ལ་བཀྲ་ཤིས་ཁ་བཏགས་ཤིག་འདུག་ལོ།

དེ་ཀུན་གཟུབ་སྟེ་འབུལ་ཡ་ཞིག་འབུལ་འདུག།
ཟླ་མ་ཆེ་ཆེ་ཟམ་ལ་རྟ་དང་ཐྲ་རྒྱུ་རེ་ཕུལ་འདུག།
བར་པ་ཚང་མ་ལ་གཡག་དང་གཡག་གུ་རེ་ཕུལ་འདུག།
ཆུ་ཙུན་ཚང་མ་ལ་བ་གླང་རེ་དང་བེ་ཐོ་རེ་ཕུལ་འདུག།

སྤྲང་པོ་ང་ཡིན་ཀྱང་ལྷུག་དང་རི་གུ་ཞིག་ཐོབ་ལོ།
ལྷུག་དེ་ང་ལ་ལམ་ལ་ཟ་ཅེས་རིག་སོང་ལོ།

ཡབས་སྟོན་པ་ཨ་བྲ་ཤི་སྟེ་མི་འདུག་ལོ།
རོ་དེ་ཐང་ཆེན་མོ་ཞིག་གི་ཁ་འདུག་ལོ།
ཡུམ་སྤྲོན་མོ་ཨ་མ་དེ་རན་འཐག་ལ་ལྷུང་འདུག།
ལྷུང་སྐྱིག་མེད་པ་ངས་སྐྱི་གུ་ཞིག་བཏངས་པ་ཡིན།
འབྲུ་དམར་ལམ་བསྟན་ལ་རྡོར་གྱི་མ་དའ་ཐོག་སྟེ་ཤི་ལོ།
ཨ་གུ་དཔལ་ལེ་དེ་ཀྲས་དེ་འདུག་ལོ།
གླིང་གི་དཔའ་བོ་ཚང་མ་ཁམས་བཟང་འདུག་ལོ།
གླིང་མཁར་ལ་ཞིག་གསོབ་མ་བཅོས་དོག།
རྫིང་ན་བཙོ་ཅེན་ཟེར་འདུག།

དེ་ཟུག་ཟེར་ས་པ། ཇོ་ཇོ་ལ་ཚོར་ཀ་ཡོངས། དེ་ནས་ཇོ་ཇོས་མར་ཟན་དེ་པོ་སྟེ་ན། ལོག་སྟེ་མཁར་ལ་ཡོངས། དེ་ནས་མཁར་ལ་བསླེབ་སྟེ་ཇོ་ཇོས་བསམ། ཀེ་སར་ཡིན་ནོག་ཟེར་ན། མེན་ན་ཟེར་ན། ཡིན་ན་བསམ་མིན་ཞིག་འདུགས།

དེ་ནས་མགར་ར་ཧི་མིས་སི་རྒྱ་མ་རྒྱ་ལེན་པ་ཡོངས་པ། ཁོ་འི་རྒྱུ་དོང་ལ་ཀ་ལིག་བཅུག་སྟེ་ཡོད་ཚུག་པས། ཀ་ལིཕ་དེ་བཅག་སྟེ་དེ་ནང་དུ་ཀོ་རེ་སྦང་སྟེ་ཡོད་ཚུག། རྒྱ་མས་ཟེརས། ལྷ་སྤྲང་པོ་ཁྲུམ་པོ། ང་ཞའི་རྒྱུ་དོང་ནང་དུ་རྩོག་པོ་ཅི་ལ་བཅོས། ཁྱོད་ཨ་ངོས། ལ་སྐོང་ཟེརས་པ། སྤྲང་པོས་ཟེརས།

འོ་ནོ་མོ་ལེ་ནོ་མོ་རང་རིངས་ན་གོམ་སྟེ་སོང་། མ་རིངས་ན་འཁོར་དེ་སོང་། ང་ཐག་རིངས་ནས་ཡོངས་མཁན་ནི་སྤྱང་པོ་ཞིག་ཡིན་ཟེརས་པས། རྐུ་མས་ཟེརས་པ། ཁྱོ་རང་ཡང་མིའི་ལུས་ལ་སྐྱེས་མཁན་ཡིན། ང་གོམ་སྟེ་མི་ཚ་ཟེར་དེ། ཁ་འཁོར་དེ་སོང་བ། ཡང་སྤྱང་པོ་དེ་ཙ་པིག་རེ་དང་སོང་སྟེ། རྐུ་མ་དེ་རྐུའི་རྩ་བསྒྲིབ་མ་བཅུགས། དེ་ནས་བུ་མོ་ལ་སྒྲོ་ཡོང་སྟེ་ཟེརས། ཁྱོད་རང་སྤྱང་པོ་ཞིག་མིན། སྤྱང་རྫུས་ཤིག་ཡིན་ནོག། ཁྱོད་པན་རྡུང་མེན་། པན་རྫུས་ཤིག་ཡིན་ནོག། ཨ་སལ་སལ་གྱི་གོང་ཀ་ནས་ཡོང་ཙ་ན། རྟ་པ་བརྒྱ་སྡོན་ལ། རྟ་པ་བརྒྱ་རྡིང་ན། ཁྱོ་རང་དཀྱིལ་ལ་འདུག་སྟེ་མ་ཡོངས་ས། ཨ་ལོང་ཐང་གི་ཐང་སྟོད་ནས་ཡོང་ཙ་ན། རྟ་པ་གཅིག་སྡོན་ལ། རྟ་པ་གཅིག་རྡིང་ན། ཁྱོ་རང་དཀྱིལ་ལ་མ་ཡོངས་ས། ཨ་ལོང་ཐང་གི་ཐང་མཇུག་ན་ཁྱོད་ཀྱིས་ཁྲག་པ་ལན་གསུམ་མ་རྫེས་ས། གསེར་པོའི་གསེར་མཁར་ལན་གསུམ་འགུལ་མ་བཅུགས་ས། ཟེརས་པ། སྤྱང་ཕྲུག་གིས་ཟེརས་པ། འོ་ནོ་མོ་ལེ། ནོ་མོ་རང་ཞེས་མཁན་ཞིག་འདུག། ཨ་སལ་སལ་གྱི་གོང་ཀ་ནས་ཡོང་ཙ་ན། ཞིག་དཀར་བརྒྱ་སྡོན་ལ་ཡོད་པ་ཡིན། ཞིག་ནག་བརྒྱ་རྡིང་ན་ཡོད་པ་ཡིན། དེ་ནས་ཡུལ་ཞིག་འདུག་བསམ་སྟེ་ཁྲག་པ་ལན་གསུམ་སྐྱུགས་པ་ཡིན། དེ་བོ་ཨ་ཙི་ཏི་རང་ལ་གསལ་པོ་མཐོང་པིན། ངའི་ཨ་བ་མགར་ར་རྫི་མིས་ཡོད་ད། ང་ཨ་བའི་རྩ་ཡོངས་པིན། དེ་ནས་མགར་མོ་ལྷུམ་གྱིས་རྐུ་འཁྲུར་དེ་ཁྲིངས་པ། ཁང་པ་ལ་རྐུ་དགོན་མོ་སོང་བས། ཨ་བ་ལ་སྒྲོ་ཡོང་སྟེ། ཐོ་བ་ཆེན་མོ་དང་སྐམ་པ་ཆེན་མོ་འཁྲུར་དེ། བུ་མོ་ལ་རྡུང་བ་ཡོང་སྟེ། བུ་མོ་དང་ཐག་པ། བུ་མོས་ཟེརས། ཨ་བ་ལེ། ང་དང་གི་རྐུ་དོང་པོའི་ནང་དུ་ཀུ་ལིག་བཅག་སྟེ། སྤྱང་པོ་ཞིག་གིས་ཀྲད་པ་དང་ཀོ་རེ་སྦྲང་སྟེ་འདུག། ཁོ་རང་ལམ་

མི་ཁ་གྱེལ་དེ་འདུག། ཁྱོས་ང་ལ་ལམ་མ་བཏང་བ། ཆུ་འགོར་སོང་། དེ་མི་བོ་ཨ་བ་རང་གི་བུ་ཚ་ཡིན་ཟེར་འདུག། དེ་ཟུག་ཟེརས་པ། ཨ་བས་ང་ལ་ཕྲུ་གུ་ཞིག་མེད་ཟེར་དེ་འདུགས།

No. 4.

དེ་ནས་སྲོང་ཕྲུག་དེ། མགར་ར་ཧྲི་མིས་སི་སྨན་མའི་ཞིང་ཞིག་ཡོད་ཚུག། དེ་ནང་དུ་སོང་སྟེ་ཚང་མ་ཛ་སྟེ་ཕང་སྟེ་ཟོས་སྐྱུག་སྟེ། སྨན་མ་རྩོག་པོ་བཙོ་སྟེ་ཡོད་ཚུག། བུ་མོ་ཞིང་ལ་ལྟ་ལ་སོང་བ། ཞིང་ཚང་མ་གསེད་དེ་ཡོད་ཅེས་མཐོང་སྟེ། སྲོང་པོ་ལ་ཁ་སྐྱེས་དེ་ཟེརས། ཁྱོད་ཇམ་པོ། ང་ཞའི་ཞིང་ཚང་མ་དང་སྨན་མ་ཚང་མ་རྩོག་པོ་ཅི་ལ་བཙོས་ཟེརས་པ། སྲོང་པོས། ང་རང་གི་ཨ་བའི་ཞིང་ཡིན། ཁྱོ་རང་ལ་ཅི་རྣོགས་དགོས་ཟེརས་པ། བུ་མོ་མགྱོགས་པ་ཁང་པ་ལ་ལོག་སྟེ་སོང་། ཨ་བ་མགར་ར་ཧྲི་མིས་ལ་ཁར་སང་གི་སྲོང་པོ་དེས། ང་ཉང་གི་ཞིང་ཚང་མ་ཛ་སྟེ་རྩོག་པོ་བཙོ་སྟེ་འདུག་ཟེརས་པ། ཨ་བ་ལ་སྤྲོ་ཡོང་སྟེ་སྐམ་པ་དང་ཐོ་བ་དེ་འཁུར་དེ་ལྟ་ལ་སོང་བས། སྲོང་པོ་ལ་ཨ་བ་ཡོང་ཅེས་ཤེས་དེ། ཞིང་ཚང་མ་སྨིན་མའི་སང་རྒྱལ་བ་བཙོ་སྟེ། ཞིང་གི་མཐའ་མ་ལ་འདུག་སྟེ་ཡོད་ཚུག། མགར་ར་ཧྲི་མིས་དེར་བསླེབ་སྟེ་ཟེརས། ཡྭ་སྲོང་པོ་བུ་ཚ་ཁྱོ་རང་གིས་ང་ཞ་ལ་གནོད་པ་བཙོ་རུག་ག། སྨིན་ལ་ཆུ་དོང་རྩོག་པོ་བཙོས། དགས་ཞིང་ཚང་མ་ལ་ཅི་བཙོས་པིན་ཟེརས་པ། སྲོང་པོས་རྩོག་པོ་ཅི་ལ་བཙོ་ཡིན། ང་ཨ་བ་རང་གི་བུ་ཚ་ཡིན། ཞག་དང་ངས་ཞིང་སྲུང་ངད། ཨ་བ་རང་གིས་སྨོས་འང་ཟེརས། ཨ་བས་བལྟ་ཟ་ན་ཞིང་ཚང་མ་སྨིན་མའི་མཆོགས་ཡོད་

ཚུག། སྤྲང་པོ་དང་ཨ་བྭ་གཉིས་ཀ་ཁང་པ་ལ་ཡོང་སྟེ། བུ་མོ་ལ་ཟེར་ས། ལྷ་བུ་མོ་ཁྲོ་རང་གིས་རྫུན་བཤད་སྟེ་ཡིན་ནོག་ཟེར་དེ། སྐམ་པ་དང་འགྲམ་པ་འཐེན་ས། ཐོ་བ་དང་རྡུངས།

དེ་ནས་ཨ་བས་སྤྲང་པོ་ལ་འདྲིས་པ། ལྷ་བུ་ཚ་ཁྲོ་རང་ངའི་བུ་ཚ་ཡིན་ན། ངའི་ཆ་ལག་ཚང་མ་ཕྱིས་དེ་དོང་། སྤྲང་པོས་ངས་ཐོ་རས་ལ་ཕྱེ་ཡིན་ཟེར་ས། དེ་ནས་སྤྲང་པོས་ཨ་ནེ་བཀུར་དམན་མོ་ལ་ཞུ་བ་ཕུལ་ས་པ། ཨ་ནེ་སྐྱོད་དེ་བུ་ཚ་ལ་བསླབས་པ། ཐོ་རས་ལ་ང་གསེར་སྤྲང་ཞིག་ལ་རྫུ་སྟེ་ཡོང་ཡིན། ཆ་ལག་ཚང་མའི་ཁ་ང་འབབས་ཡིན། དེ་ཚང་མ་ང་རང་གི་ཡིན་ཟེར་དེ་ཞེས། དེའི་རྗེང་ན་ཐོ་བ་ཆེན་མོ་དང་སྐམ་པ་ཆེན་མོ་མི་འདུག་ཟེར། དེ་རྒྱུག་བསླབ་སྟེ་པོརས། ཐོ་རེ་ཚུག་པོ་ལ་མགར་ར་ཧྲི་མིས་ཀྱིས། མགར་ར་བརྒྱུའི་ཆ་ལག་ནང་དུ་ཁོ་རང་གི་ཆ་ལག་སླེ་སྟེ་པོར་ནས་སྤྲང་ཕྲུག་ལ་ཕེ་བཙུགས། དེ་ནས་ཁོས་བལྟས་པ་གསེར་སྤྲང་གཅིག་ཡོང་སྟེ། ཆ་ལག་ཚང་མའི་ཁ་འབབས་པ། ཁོས་དེ་ཚང་མ་ཕེས། དེ་ཚང་མ་ཕེ་ཚར་དེ་ན། ཐོ་བ་ཆེན་མོ་དང་སྐམ་པ་ཆེན་མོ་མི་འདུག་ཨ་བྭ་ཟེར་ས་པ། ཨ་བས་ཐོ་བ་དང་སྐམ་པ་ཆེན་མོ་དེ་གླིང་ཡུལ་ལ་ལུས་དེ་ཡོངས་པ་ཡིན། ངའི་བུ་ཁྲིད་ངོ་དོག་ཡིན་ནོག་ཟེར་དེ། ཁོ་ཁང་པ་ལ་བུ་ཚ་བཙོ་སྟེ་པོརས།

ཞག་ཅིག་མཁར་ན་རྫོ་རྫོ་འབྲུ་གུ་མ་ལ་གསེར་གྱི་ཅེ་མ་འབུམ་བཙོ་བ་ལ་གཡོག་མོ་ཞིག་ལ་གསེར་བཀལ་དེ། རྫོ་རྫོ་ཁོ་རང་པལ་ཀྱི་ལ་བཞུག་སྟེ། མགར་ར་ཧྲི་མིས་སི་རྩ་ཡོང་ངད་ཚུག། མགར་ཕྲུག་དེ་དེ་ཡི་འཕྲུད་དེ་པལ་ཀྱིའི་སྤྱོན་ལ་ཡོང་ངད་ཚུག། དེ་ནས་མགར་ར་ཧྲི་མིས་སོང་སྟེ་ཕྲུ་གུ་ཟུམ་སྟེ་ཟེར་ས།

ཨ་ཕུ་ངན་ཅི་བཅོ་ཙུག། ཧོར་གུར་དཀར་གྱི་ཇོ་ཇོ་ཡིན་དེ་ཟུག་མ་བཅོ་ཟེར་ས་པས། བུ་ཚས་ང་ཞའི་གླིང་ཡུལ་ལ་དེ་ཟུག་བཙོན་མགོ་རས་ཁྲབ་ཆེན་ཟེར་རིན་ཞིག་ལོག་སྡེ་ཡོངས། དེ་ནས་ཁོང་གིས་ཟེར་ས། ཇོ་ཇོ་ལེ། འདི་རིང་སོལ་བ་མེད། ཐོ་རངས་ལ་བཅོ་ཡིན་ཟེར་དེ། ཇོ་ཇོ་ལོག་སྡེ་བཏང་སོང་། ཐོ་རེ་ཚུག་སློ་ལ་མཁར་ར་རྡེ་མིས་སིས་བོང་བུ་བཅུ་ཟམ་ཞིག་བཙལ་དེ། མགར་ཕྲུག་ཐང་རྟེད་དང་། སྲིང་མོ་ལྷུམ་གཉིས་ཀ་སོལ་བ་ལ་བཀལ་དེ་བཏང་ས་པས། ཨ་ནས་བསླབ་སྡེ་ཟེར་ས་པ། གཡས་པའི་ལྗུང་པའི་ཚོགས་ཚང་མ་གུར་དཀར་རྒྱལ་པོ་འི་ལྷབ་ཚས་ཡིན། དེ་ལ་མི་ན་བདུག། གཡོན་པའི་ནང་དུ་སོང་སྡེ། སོལ་བ་བསད་དེ་ཁྱིང་ཟེར་ས་པས། ཁོང་གཉིས་ཀ་བུང་བུ་འཁྱིད་དེ་སོང་བས། མགར་ཕྲུག་ཐང་རྟེད་ཀྱིས་ཟེར་ས། ཨ་ཆེ་རང་གུ་ལེ་ལ་ཡོང་ཟེར་དེ་ན། ཁོ་རང་སྔོན་ལ་སོང་སྡེ་གཡས་པའི་ལྗུང་བའི་ནང་དུ་སོང་སྡེ། ཁོས་ཟེར་ས། ལྷ་གསུམ་བརྒྱ་དྲུག་བཅུ་ལྷ་ཡུལ་ལ་སོང་། ཀླུ་གསུམ་བརྒྱ་དྲུག་བཅུ་ཀླུ་ཡུལ་ལ་སོང་ཤིག། གླིང་ཡུལ་ལི་ལྷ་ཡོད་ན་གླིང་ཡུལ་ལ་སྐྱོད། ཧོར་ཡུལ་ལི་ལྷ་ཡོད་ན། མགོ་ལ་བལ་ཐོད་གོན་དེ་རྒྱལ་ཁམས་ལ་ཁྲམ་སྡེ་སོང་ཟེར་དེ་སྔ་རི་བརྒྱབས། དེ་ཚུག་པ་མགར་མོ་ལྷུམ་བསླབ་སྡེ་ཟེར་ས། ཨ་ཕུ་ཚ་དེ་ཚོགས་པོ་གུར་དཀར་གྱི་ལྷབ་ཚས་ཡིན། ན་བཅད་ཟེར་ས་པ། ཕྲུ་གུ་དབང་བཅོ་སྡེ། སོལ་བ་པད་བཅུ་ཟམ་ཞིག་བསད་བཏང་ས། དེ་ནས་བུང་བུ་ལ་བཀལ་དེ་ཁྱིངས། དེ་ནས་ཆུ་ཆེན་མོ་ཞིག་དང་ཐུག་སོང་།། དེ་ཙ་ཁོང་རང་གི་པ་སྤུ་སྤུད་དེ། བུང་བུ་སག་གི་པ་སྤུ་འབངས་ཡིན་ཟེར་དེ། རྗོ་བ་ཞིག་དང་ར་གོ་ཚང་མ་སྤུད་བཏང་ས། དེ་ནས་མགར་མོ་ལྷུམ་གྱིས་ཟེར་ས། ཨ་ཁྱོད་སྐྱོན་པ་ཞིག་མེད་ན། གུར་དཀར་གྱི་ལྷབ་ཚས་དེ་ཡང་མི་

ལ་འདུགས། དགས་བུང་བུའི་ར་གོ་ཚང་མ་ཕུད་བཏངས། ང་ཨ་བ་ལ་ཟེར་པ་ཆེན་ཟེར་དེ་སྔོན་ལ་ཡོངས། དེ་ནས་ཨ་བའི་མདུན་ལ་བསླེབ་སྟེ་ཟེར་ས། ཨ་བཱ་ལེ། ཨ་བཱ་རང་ལ་བུ་ཚ་རྒྱལ་པ་ཞིག་ཐོབས་དོག། གུར་དཀར་གྱི་ལྷབ་ཚས་ཡང་མི་ལ་བདུགས། རྩ་ཆེན་མོ་ཞིག་གི་མདུན་ལ་བསླེབ་པ། བུང་བུ་ཚང་མའི་ར་གོ་དེ་རྟོ་བ་དང་རྟུང་སྟེ་ཕུད་བཏངས། བུང་བུ་སག་རྒྱས་ཁྲིངས་ཟེར་སི། ཨ་བཱ་ལ་སློ་ཡོང་སྟེ། ཐོ་བ་ཞིག་དང་སྐམ་པ་ཞིག་འཁུར་དེ་ཁོ་ལ་རྟུང་བ་སོང་། དེ་ནས་བུ་ཚ་དང་ཐུག་པ། ཁོས་བུང་བུ་ཚང་མ་ལ་སོལ་བ་བཀལ་དེ་ཁྲིང་ངད་རྩུག། ཨ་བས་ཟེརས། ལྷ་བུ་ཚ་ཁྱོ་རང་གིས་གུར་དཀར་རྒྱལ་པོའི་ལྷབ་ཚས་དེ་ལ་མི་བདུགས་ལོ། བུང་བུ་ཚང་མའི་རྐང་པ་རྟོ་བ་དང་རྟུང་ས་ལོ། ཅི་བཅོས་པ་ཡིན་ཟེརས་པས། དེ་ནས་བུ་ཚས་ཟེརས་པ། ཨ་བཱ་ལེ། ཨ་བཱ་རང་ལ་བུ་ཚ་ཞིག་འབྱོར་པ་སང་། ཨ་ཆེ་མ་དགའ་ཡིན་ནོག། ཡང་བུང་བུ་རྒྱབ་ཅིས་ལ་མ་ལམ་པ་སང་། དེ་རྫུག་ཟེར་དེ་ཡིན་ནོག། གུར་དཀར་གྱི་ལྷབ་ཚས་ལ་མི་བདུག་ན་ཨ་བཱ་རང་གིས་ལྟོས་འང་། བུང་བུའི་ར་གོ་ཕུད་ན། ཨ་བཱ་རང་གིས་ལྟོས་ཟེརས་པ། ཨ་བས་བལྟས་པ། གུར་དཀར་གྱི་ལྷབ་ཚས་དེ་བདེ་མོ་ཡོད་རྩུག། བུང་བུའི་ར་གོ་ཡང་བདེ་མོ་ཡོད་རྩུག། དེ་ནས་ཨ་བཱ་དེ་བུ་ཚས་ཟེར་མཁན་ལ་བདེན་ཆེས་དེ་ཡོངས་པ། ཁང་པ་རུ་བསླེབ་སྟེ་བུ་མོ་ལ་སློ་བཅོ་སྟེ་སྐམ་པ་དང་བུ་མོའི་འགྲམ་པ་འབྲེནས། ཐོ་བ་དང་རྟུངས།

དེ་ནས་རྟིང་མ་ཞག་ལ་ཡང་ཇོ་ཇོ་གསེར་འཁུར་དེ་ཡོངས། བུ་ཚ་ལ་སྤྲད་པ་ཕུ་བཅུགས། གསེར་གྱི་ཅི་མ་འབུམ་དེ་ཕིང་སྟེ་བཟོ་རྟོ་འི་ཁ་རྟུངས་པ། བཟོ་རྟོ་འི་ཁ་ནས་པར་སོང་། དེ་ནས་མགར་ཐྲག་ཐང་རྟེད་གྱིས་གླུ་ཞིག་བཏངས།

ང་ཞིའི་གླིང་ཡུལ་ལ་སྤྲུད་པ་དེ་རླུངས་པོ་འདྲ་བ་ཞིག་ཡོད་ལོ།
ཨ་བཱ་མགར་ར་ཧི་མིས་སི་སྤྲུད་པ་ལ་ཡད་ཅིག་མི་འདུག།
ང་ཞིའི་གླིང་ཡུལ་ལི་སྐམ་པ་དེ་གཙན་གྱིས་ཟུམ་བ་མཚོགས་ཡོད།
ཨ་བཱ་མགར་ར་ཧི་མིས་སི་སྐམ་པ་ལ་ཡད་ཅིག་རང་མི་འདུག།
ང་ཞིའི་གླིང་ཡུལ་ལི་གྲོ་བ་དེ་འབྲུག་ཆེན་ལྡིར་བ་འདྲ་ཡོད།
ཨ་བཱ་མགར་ར་ཧི་མིས་སི་གྲོ་བ་ལ་ཡད་ཅིག་རང་མི་འདུག།
ང་ཞིའི་གླིང་ཡུལ་ལི་མགར་བ་དེ་བི་ལ་འདྲ་བ་འཇབ་འཇབ་འཇབ་བད།
ཨ་བཱ་མགར་ར་ཧི་མིས་ལ་ཡད་ཅིག་རང་མི་འདུག།

དེ་ཟུག་ཟེར་ས། དེ་ནས་གསེར་གྱི་ཅེ་མ་འབུམ་དེ་སྤོར་སོང་། མི་ཚང་མ་ནས་ལྫོངས་པ། གསེར་གྱི་ཅེ་མ་འབུམ་དེ་ཛོ་ཛའི་ཡོག་ན་ཡོད་ཚུག། དེ་ནས་མགར་ཕྲུག་གིས་ཟེར་ས། འོ་ཧོ་ཧོ། ཨ་བཱ་ནོ་རོའི་བུ་མོ། ཨ་མ་ནོ་རོའི་བུ་མོ། ཧོར་གུར་དཀར་རྒྱལ་པོའི་ཛོ་ཛོ་སོ་མ་ཡིན་ལོ། དེ་ཟུག་ཀུ་རུག་ཟེར་ས་པ། ཛོ་ཛའི་གཡོག་མོ་དེ་ལང་སྟེ། ཕྲུ་གུ་དེ་ལ་མགོ་ལྟུད་ཅིག་བཏངས་པ། ཕྲུ་གུའི་ཧི་པི་འབུད་སོང་བ། མགོའི་དཀྱིལ་ལ་རྨི་བ་ཞིག་ཡོད་ཚུག་པ། དེ་ཛོ་ཛོ་ལ་མཐོང་སོང་། ཛོ་ཛོས་བསམ་འདི་མི་བོ་ངོ་ཧོག་གླིང་ཀེ་སར་རྒྱལ་པོ་ཡིན་བསམ་སོང་། ཕྲུ་གུས་གཡོག་མོ་ལ་ཟེར་ས་པ། མི་སྟོ། ལྦྲ་གཡོག་མོ། ཁྱོ་རང་ལ་ངས་ལན་ཞིག་བཏང་ཐུབ་ཡིན་ཟེར་ས། དེ་ནས་གསེར་གྱི་ཅེ་མ་འབུམ་དེ་ངས་བཅོ་ཡིན་ཨ་བཱ་ཟེར་ས། དེ་ཁྱོང་སྟེ་གསེར་དེ་བཟོ་ཛོའི་ཡོག་ལ་བོར་ཏེ་ཁོས་གླུ་ཞིག་བཏངས།

གསེར་གྱི་ཅེ་མ་འབུམ་དེ་སྟེང་ལྷ་ཡུལ་ལ་སོང་ལོ།
སྟེང་ལྷ་ཡུལ་ནས་ལྷ་འབྲིས་ཞིག་ཁྲོང་ལོ།
གསེར་གྱི་ཅེ་མ་འབུམ་དེ་བར་བཙན་ཡུལ་ལ་སོང་ལོ།
ཨ་མ་སྐྱབས་འདུན་མའི་བཙན་འབྲིས་ཞིག་ཁྲོང་ལོ།
གསེར་གྱི་ཅེ་མ་འབུམ་དེ་འོག་ཕྱོགས་ཀླུ་ཡུལ་ལ་སོང་ལོ།
ཀླུ་རྒྱལ་ལྡོགས་པོ་ནས་ཀླུ་འབྲིས་ཞིག་ཁྲོང་ལོ།
མཉམ་པོ་སྐྱེས་པའི་ལྷ་དགུ་མཁྲེན་ནོ།
གསེར་གྱི་ཅེ་མ་འབུམ་ལ་བཟོ་ ཞིག་དྲོར།
མཉམ་པོ་སྐྱེས་པའི་ཀླུ་དགུ་མཁྲེན་ནོ།
གསེར་གྱི་ཅེ་མ འབུམ་ལ་བཟོ་ ཞིག་དྲོན།

དེ་ཐུག་ཟེར་ཚར་དེ་ན། བཟོ་རྗེ་འི་ལོག་ནས་ཕེབས་པ་མང་། གསེར་གྱི་ཅེ་མ་འབུམ་དེ་མེ་ཏོག་མཆོགས་བཅོ་སྟེ་ཡོད་ཚུག། དེ་ནས་ཇོ་ཇོས་བསམ། གསེར་གྱི་ཅེ་མ་འབུམ་དེ་ཀེ་སར་ལ་མིན་པ་བཅོ་མི་ཉན་བསམ་སྟེ། མཁར་ལ་སོང་སྟེ་གུར་དཀར་ལ་ཟེརས། རྒྱལ་པོ་ལེ། དེ་སྔོང་ཕྲུག་པོ་ཀེ་སར་ཡིན་ཚོད་རེག་འདུག། དམག་ཡོད་ན་དམག་སྐྱུང་། མཁར་མེད་ན་མཁར་རྩིག་ཟེརས།

No. 5.

དེ་ནས་ཇོ་ཇོ་དང་གུར་དཀར་གྱིས་གླབས་བཅོ་སྟེ་ཟེརས་པ། ང་དང་ཧོར་ཡུལ་གྱི་དཔའ་པོ་དང་། སྒྲོག་དགུ་པ་ཀློན་པོ་དང་ཚང་མ་ལ། ཕོ་ལད་ཀྱི་གྱད་གཉུ་འཐེན་བཅུག་ཡིན། ཁོ་ཀེ་སར་ཡིན་ན་ཕོ་ལད་ཀྱི་གྱད་གཉུ་འཐེན་

ཁྲབ་ཡིན་ཟེརས། རྡིང་མ་ཞིག་ལ་དམག་སྐད་ཅིག་བཏང་སྟེ་ཟེརས། འདི་རིང་
ཕོ་ལད་དི་གྱུད་གཞུ་སྲུ་ལ་འཐེན་ཁྲབ་ན། མཁར་ན་ཡི་ནུམ་མང་པོ་བཏང་འདུག།
དེ་ཕི་ལ་མི་ཚང་མ་ཡོང་ཤིག་ཟེརས། དེ་ནས་མི་ཚང་མ་དང་སྒྲོག་དགུ་པ་བློན་
པོ་ཡོངས། མགར་ར་ཧི་མིས་ཀྱིས་བུ་ཚ་ལ་ཟེརས། ཨྲ་བུ་ཚ། ང་དམག་
ཁྲོ་ལ་ཆ་ཡིན་ཟེར་དེ། འདིཨུ་ཚགས་མ་གང་དྲུད་པ་ལ་ཕིང་སྟེ་ན། ཁོ་རང་སོང་
བས། བུ་ཚ་དེས་འདིཨུ་སྦྱིབ་ཅིག་ལ་དྲུད་དེ་ཁུར་དེ། དམག་ཁྲོལ་སོང་སྟེ་
བལྟས་པ། སྲུ་ལ་ཡང་འཐེན་མ་ཐུབ་སོང་། དེ་ནས་སྒྲོག་དགུ་པ་བློན་པོས་
འཐེནས་པ། ནས་གང་མིན་པ་ཁོ་ལ་ཡང་མ་ཐུབ་སོང་། དེ་ནས་མགར་ཕྲུག་
ཐང་རྐྱེད་ཀྱིས་ཨ་བ་ལ་ཟེརས་པ། ཨ་བ་ལེ། དེ་ཨུམ་བུའི་དྲང་ཁང་པོ་ངས་ཙ་
ཕིག་འཐེན་ཡིན་བ་ཟེརས་པ། དེ་ཟླུག་ཟེར་ཅས་གུར་དཀར་རྒྱལ་པོ་ལ་ཀོར་དེ་
ཟེརས་པ། ཨྲ་ཁྲོ་རང་གི་བུ་ཚས་ཅི་ཟེར་འདུག་ཟེརས་པ། མགར་ར་ཧི་མིས་
ཀྱིས་ཁོས་འདི་ཨུམ་བུའི་དྲང་ཁང་པོ་སྐྱིལ་ཡིན་ཟེར་འདུག་ལེ་ཟེརས། གུར་
དཀར་རྒྱལ་པོས་ཟེརས། ཁྱོ་རང་གི་ཕྲུ་གུ་ལ་སྐྱིལ་ཆུག་ཟེརས་པས། མགར་
ཕྲུག་སོང་སྟེ་གཞུ་དེ་ཕྱིར་ལོག་ལ་ཁྱེརས། མི་ཚང་མ་ཧབ་གོད་བཏངས། དེ་ནས་
ཨ་བ་སོང་སྟེ་བཅོ་སྟེ་བཏངས་པ། ཕྲུ་གུས་ཟེརས། འདི་དྲང་ཁང་པོ་བཅག་
སྟེ་མི་སྲུ་ལ་ཐོག་ན། དགྲ་མེད་ད་ཟེརས་པ། གཞུ་རྒྱུད་དེ་མི་སུའི་སྐྱེ་ལ་ཁྲིལ་ན་
དགྲ་མེད་ད་ཟེརས། གུར་དཀར་གྱིས་དགྲ་མེད་ཟེརས་པ། དེ་ནས་ཁོས་གཞུ་
ཁུར་དེ་ན། སྐྱིང་གི་ཐིལ་ནས་སྨོན་ལམ་བཏབ་སྟེ། ཕོ་ལད་གྱུད་གཞུ་ཁྱེར་སྐྱིང་
ཡུལ་ལ་སོང་། ང་རང་གི་ལག་པའི་ནང་དུ་ཡང་གཞུ་ཞིག་སླེབ་ཤིག། གཞུ་དེ་
འཆག་སྟེ་ཧོར་གྱི་དཔའ་བོ་ཚང་མ་ལ་ཕོག་སྟེ་ཤི་ཤིག། གཞུ་རྒྱུད་དེ་ཧོར་གུར་

དཀར་རྒྱལ་པོ་འི་སྐྱེ་ལ་འཁྲིམ་དེ། ཕྱི་དབུགས་འཆད་དེ་ནང་དབུགས་ལ་ཁད་ཅིག། དེ་ང་རང་ལ་མེད་པ་བཀྲོལ་མ་ཅན་ཅིག་ཟེར་དེ། གཞུ་དེ་བསྐྱིལས་པ། གཞུ་དེ་ཆག་སྟེ་ཧོར་གྱི་དཔའ་བོ་ཚང་མའི་མིག་ལ་ཡོག་སྟེ་ཤི་སོང་། གཞུ་རྒྱུད་དེ་གུར་དཀར་རྒྱལ་པོ་འི་སྐྱེ་ལ་འཁྲིལ་དེ། ཕྱི་དབུགས་ཆད་དེ་ནང་དབུགས་ལ་ཁད་སོང་། དེ་ནས་གུར་དཀར་ཤི་ཅེས་ལ་ཐུག་སོང་། མགར་ཕྲུག་དེ་སོང་སྟེ་བཀྲོལས་པ་སང་། དེ་གྲོལ་སོང་། ཧོར་གུར་དཀར་མགར་ཕྲུག་ལ་མང་པོ་འཐད་སོང་ནས། མིང་ལ་མགར་ཕྲུག་སེང་གེ་དོན་ལྡན་བཏགས།

ཡང་རྙིང་མ་ཞིག་ལ་མི་ཚང་མ་འཐམས་ཅེས་ལ་བསྐྱུས་པས། དེ་ཞིག་ལ་མགར་བ་ཧི་མིས་སིས། མགར་ཕྲུག་ལ་ཁབ་ཚགས་མ་གང་དྲུད་པ་ལ་བོར་དེ་ན། ཁོ་རང་དམག་ཁྲི་ལ་སོང་བས། ཕྲུ་གུས་ཁབ་ཚང་མ་སྦྲིབ་ཅིག་ལ་དྲུད་དེ་ཁུར་དེ་སོང་བ། ཨ་བས་ཟེརས་པ། ལྷ་ཕྲུ་གུ་ཁྱོད་ཅི་ལ་ཡོངས་ཁབ་དེ་མ་དྲུད་པ་ཟེརས། ཕྲུ་གུས་ཁབ་ཚང་མ་དྲུད་དེ་ཁུར་དེ་ཡོད། ཨ་བུ་རང་ལ་དགོས་ཡིན་བསམ་སྟེ་ཁྱོངས་པ་ཡིན་ཟེརས། དེ་ནས་ཁོས་བལྟས་པ། སྒྲོག་དཀྲུ་པ་ཀློན་པོ་དཀྱིལ་ལ་ཡང་སྟེ་ང་དང་གཉན་མཁན་ཡོད་ན་ཡོང་ཟེར་རིན་ཞིག་ཡོད་ཚུག། དེ་ནས་ཕྲུ་གུས་ཨ་བུ་ལ་ཤུབ་སྟེ་ཟེརས། ཨ་བུ་ལེ། དེ་ཕྲུ་གུ་དང་ང་འཐམས་ཡིན་བ་ཟེརས། ཁྱེ་། བུ་ངན་གྱིས་ཅི་ཟེར་འདུག། མི་ཚང་མ་ལ་མ་ཁྲབ། ཁྱེད་ལ་ག་ཟུག་ལ་ཁྲབ་ཡིན་ཟེརས་པ། ཡང་གུར་དཀར་ལ་ཚོར་དེ་འདྲིས་པ། ལྷ་མགར་ར་ཧི་མིས་ཁྱེད་ཀྱི་བུ་ཚས་ཅི་ཟེར་འདུག། མགར་རས་ཁོ་བུ་ངན་གྱིས་སྒྲོག་དཀྲུ་པ་ཀློན་པོ་དང་འཐམས་ཡིན་ཟེར་འདུག་ལེ་ཟེརས།

གུར་དཀར་གྱིས་ས་རྒྱལ་ལ་ཆ་ཡིན། འཐམས་ཆུག་ཟེར་ས། དེ་ནས་མགར་ཕྲུག་ཡངས་དེ་གླུ་འདི་ལྟར་བཏངས།

སྟེང་ལྷའི་དབང་པོ་རྒྱ་ཞིན་ལ་སྨོག་གཅིག་ཡིན་ལོ།

བར་བཙན་གྱི་ཨ་མ་སྐྱབ་མདུན་མ་ལ་སྨོག་གཅིག་ཡིན་ལོ།

འོག་ཀླུའི་ཀླུ་རྒྱལ་ལྡོག་པོ་ལ་སྨོག་གཅིག་ཡིན་ལོ།

ཕ་ལྷ་ཀེར་ཟེང་སྐྱན་པོ་ལ་སྨོག་གཅིག་ཡིན་ལོ།

མས་ལྷ་བཀར་དམན་རྒྱལ་མོ་ལ་སྨོག་གཅིག་ཡིན་ལོ།

མཉམ་པོ་སྐྱེས་པའི་ལྷ་དགུ་ལ་སྨོག་གཅིག་ཡིན་ལོ།

མཉམ་པོ་སྐྱེས་པའི་ཀླུ་དགུ་ལ་སྨོག་གཅིག་ཡིན་ལོ།

གླིང་གི་ཕ་སྤུན་བཅོ་བརྒྱད་ལ་སྨོག་གཅིག་ཡིན་ལོ།

གླིང་གི་མ་སྤུན་བཅོ་བརྒྱད་ལ་སྨོག་གཅིག་ཡིན་ལོ།

དེ་རིང་ང་ལ་སྤྲུང་རོགས་ཤིག་མཛོད་ལོ།

དེ་ཟླུག་ཟེར་དེ་ན། སྨོག་དགུ་པ་སྔོན་པོ་དང་འཐམས་པ་སང་། སྨོག་དགུ་པ་སྔོན་པོ་ས་ལ་གྱེལ་དེ་ཤི་སོང་། དེ་མི་ཚང་མས་ཕབ་གྲོད་བཏང་སོང་། སྨོག་དགུ་པ་སྔོན་པོ་འི་གཉེན་ཚང་མ་ཡོང་སྟེ་རོ་དེ་ཁུར་དེ་ཁྱེར་ས། མི་ཚང་མ་ཡང་ཞོལ་སོང་།

དེ་རྗེང་མ་ཞག་ལ་ཧ་ཕོ་ཁ་ལ་མི་འབར་རི་ཁ་ལ་སྤུ་ཞོན་ཅན་ཡིན་ཚོད་ལྟ་ཡིན་ཟེར་དེ། མི་ཚང་མ་བསྡུས་པས། དེ་ཞག་ལ་མགར་ར་དེ་མིས་ཀྱིས་ཕྲུག་ཁང་པ་སྤྱུང་ཅེས་ལ་བོར་དེ་ཁོ་རང་སོང་། དེ་ནས་མི་ཚང་མ་འདུས་དེ།

རྟ་ཡོ་ཁ་ལ་མེ་འབར་ལ་སྐྲ་སྤྲར་བསྟད་དེ་འོབ་ཆེན་དགུ་ཡོད་ཚུག། དེ་ནས་ཡང
མགར་ཕྲུག་དེས་ཁང་པ་ཚང་མ་ཁྲུར་དེ་མིའི་ཁྲི་ལ་ལྷ་ལ་ཡོངས། ཨ་བས་ཁ་
སྐྱེས་དེ་ཟེརས་པ། ལྷ་བུ་ཚ། ཁང་པ་མ་སྲུང་བ་ཅི་ལ་ཡོངས་ཟེརས་པ། ཕྲུ་གུས་
ཟེརས། ཨ་བ༹་ལེ། ཁང་པ་དེ་ང་དང་ཚང་མ་ལ་མཐོང་ས་རུ་ཁྱོང་སྡེ་ཡོད་
ཟེརས་པ། ཨ་བ༹་ལ་ཅང་ཟེར་མ་ཉན་པས། དེ་ནས་མི་ཚང་མ་རྟའི་ཁ་ཞོན་ནད་
ཚུག་པ། མི་སྲུ་རི༹་འོབ་ཆེན་གཉིས་སི་ཁ་བསྐྱེབ། མི་སྲུ་རི་འོབ་ཆེན་གསུམ་མི་
བ་བསྐྱེབ། སྲུ་གཅིག་གི་ཁ་བསྐྱེབ། མགར་ཕྲུག་གིས་ཡང་ཨ་བ༹་ལ་ཟེརས།
ཨ་བ་ལེ། དེ་གྲུང་བུའི་ཁ་ང་ཞོན་ཡིན་བ་ཟེརས། དེ་ཐུག་གུར་དཀ༹ར་ལ་ཚོར་
དེ་འཇི༹གས་པ། ལྷ་མགར་ར་ཧེ་མིས། ཁྱོ་རང་གི་བུ་ཚོས་ཅི་ཟེར་འདུག་ཟེརས།
ཨ་བ༹་དེས་ཟེརས་པ། ཁོས་དེ་བོང་བུའི་ཁ་ཞོན་ཡིན་ཟེར་འདུག་ལེ་ཟེརས།
གུར་དཀར་གྱིས་མ༹་རྒྱལ་ལ་ཆེན་ཞོན་ཚུག་ཟེརས་པ། ཁོ་སོང་སྡེ་རྒྱབ་ན་ཞོན་
ནད་ཚུག་པ། མི༹་ཚང་མས་རབ་རྐྱེད་བཏངས། དེ་ནས་ཁོ་མདུན་ལ་སོང་སྡེ།
རྣམ་ཚོག་ལ་འཐམ་སྡེ་ཞོན་ནད་ཚུག། དེ་ནས་ཨ་བ༹་སོང་སྡེ། ཁྱོད་བུ་ངན་ཁྱོ་རང
ང་ཚུག་པ་རྟ་ལ་ཞོན་མི་ཤེས་མཁན་ཞིག་ཡིན་ན། འདི་ཕྱོགས་ན་ཞོན་ཟེར་དེ་
བསླབས་པ། དེ་ནས་ཁོ་སྤྲིབ་ཅིག་ལ་ཞོན་དེ། ནམ་མཁའ་ལ་སོང་ནས་གླིང་ཡུལ་
ལ་བསྐྱེབ་སྡེ། རྟ་ཡོ་ཁ་ལ་མེ་འབར་དེ་གླིང་ཡུལ་ལ་བོར་དེ། ཡང་རྟ་ཞིག་ལ་
ཞོན་དེ་ནམ་མཁའ་ནས་བུད་དེ་ཡོངས། དེ་ནས་རྟ་དེ་ཤི་སོང་། མགར་ཕྲུག་དེ་
གསོན་དེ་ལུས། དེ་ནས་མི་ཚང་མ་ཡམ་ཚན་སོང་། མགར་ཕྲུག་དེ་གུར་དཀར
གྱི་རིན་ཅན་སོང་། ཞག་ཁ་ཅིག་སོང་སྡེ་ན། གུར་སྐྱུག་བླ་མ་དེ་ལ་མཚན་ལ་སྐྱི་ཡམ་
ཡམ་ཚན་མང་པོ་མཐོང་སྡེ། གུར་དཀར་རྒྱལ་པོ་ལ་སླུ་ཞིག་འདི་ལྟར་བཏངས།

ཁྱེད་ཧོར་གྱི་རྒྱལ་པོས་བླ་མ་ངའི་དངོས་ལ་ཉོན་དང་།

ཁྱེད་ཕ་གུར་དཀར་རྒྱལ་པོས་གུར་སྐྱུག་ངའི་བདག་ལ་གསན་དང་།

དེ་རིང་མཚན་ནི་སྐྱི་ལམ་དེ་ངན་པ་ཞིག་མཐོང་ལོ།

དེ་རིང་གི་སྐྱི་ལམ་དེ་ལྟས་ངན་ཞིག་མཐོང་ལོ།

གླིང་གི་ལྷ་ཚང་མས་གསེར་ཐོད་གོན་པ་ཞིག་མཐོང་ལོ།

ཧོར་གྱི་ལྷ་ཚང་མས་བལ་ཐོད་གོན་དེ་དུ་བ་ཞིག་མཐོང་ལོ།

གླིང་གི་དམག་ཚང་མ་ཧོར་ཡུལ་ལ་བསྐྱིབ་པ་མཐོང་ལོ།

ཧོར་ཡུལ་གཞུང་ལ་མེ་ཆེན་ཞིག་འབར་ར་མཐོང་ལོ།

མེ་ཆེན་དེ་ལ་ཆུ་ཆེན་ཞིག་བླུག་པ་མཐོང་ལོ།

ཇོ་ཇོ་འབྲུ་གུ་མ་གླིང་ཡུལ་ལ་འཁྱེར་བ་རིག་མཐོང་ལོ།

གུར་དཀར་རྒྱལ་པོ་ཉི་རང་བསད་པ་ཞིག་མཐོང་ལོ།

གསེར་རལ་ཅན་དང་གཡུ་རལ་ཅན་གཉིས་ཀའི་མགོ་བྲག་ཚའུ་དུང་
དུང་ལ་ཐྲུམ་བ་མཐོང་ལོ།

ཁྱེད་ལ་དམག་ཡོད་ན་སྐྱུས་ལོ།

ཁྱེད་ལ་མཁར་མེད་ན་རྩིག་ལོ།

གསམ་གློ་སྔོན་ལ་མ་བཏང་ན་འགྱོད་པ་རྗེང་ན་ཡོང་ཡིན།

དེ་ཧྲུག་ཟེརས་པ་སང་། གུར་དཀར་དང་ཇོ་ཇོ་གཉིས་ཀྱིས་གྲབས་བཅོ་བཅོ་ཚུག་པ། གླིང་ཡུལ་ནས་དམག་བཏང་ཕྱིར་དུ་དཔའ་བོ་ཚང་མ་སྤྲར་གྱི་ལའི་རྩ་རུ་བསྐྱེབ་སྡེ་ཡོད་ཚུག། དཔལ་ལེ་རྒོད་པོས་གླུ་ཞིག་བཏངས།

ངའི་མདའ་མོ་ཁྱོད་ཧོར་ཡུལ་ལ་འགྲོ་དགོས་ལོ།
མདའ་མོ་དཀར་པོ་འི་ལམ་བསྟན་དེ་ཧོར་ཡུལ་ལ་སོང་ལོ།
ཧོར་གྱི་བྲུའི་ཀ་ལ་འཕོག་པ་རིག་དགོས་སུག།
གུར་དཀར་རྒྱལ་པོ་ལ་ཟུར་མོ་དྲག་པོ་ ཞིག་ཡོང་ཤིག།
གླིང་ཀེ་སར་ལ་མེད་ནེ་མདའ་འཕུད་པ་མ་ཉན་ཤིག།
མགར་ར་བརྒྱའི་མེ་བཙད་མ་ཕོག་ཤིག།
ཤིང་མཁན་བརྒྱའི་སྟེབ་བཙད་མ་ཕོག་ཤིག།
མི་ཤེད་ཅན་སུ་ལ་ཡང་འཕུད་པ་མ་ཉན་ཤིག།

དེ་ཟུག་ཟེར་དེ་མདའ་དཀར་པོ་འི་ལམ་བསྟན་དེ་བཏངས་པས། མདའ་དེ་ཧོར་གྱི་འབྲུས་སི་ཀ་བ་ལ་ཕོག་སོང་། དེ་ནས་གུར་དཀར་རྒྱལ་པོ་ལ་ཟུར་མོ་དྲག་པོ་ཡོངས་པས། ཡུལ་གྱི་ཤིང་མཁན་ཚང་མ་བསྡུ་སྟེ། མདའ་དེ་བཙདས་པ་ཙ་ཕིག་འང་མ་ཉན་སོང་།

དེ་ནས་མགར་ར་ཚང་མ་ཁྱོང་སྟེ་མེ་བཙད་བཏངས་པ་མ་ཉན། དེ་ནས་ཅི་ཡང་བཅོ་ཐབས་མ་ཡོངས་པས། མགར་ཁྲུག་སེང་གེ་དོན་ལྡན་ལ་བོས་པ། རྒྱལ་ཟེར་དེ་གཡོག་མོ་བལ་ཁྲོལ་མ་དེ་བོས་པ་བཏངས། ཁོ་སོང་སྟེ་ནགར་ཁྲུག་ལ་ཟེརས་པ། ལྷ་མགར་ཁྲུག། ཧོར་གུར་དཀར་རྒྱལ་པོ་ལ་ཟུར་མོ་དྲག་པོ་ཡོད། འབྲུས་སི་ཀ་ལ་གླིང་པའི་མདའ་ཞིག་ཕོག། སྐམ་ཆེན་ཁྲུར་དེ་ཡོང་། ཐོ་བ་ཆེན་མོ་ཁྲུར་དེ་ཡོང་ཟེརས་པ། མགར་ཁྲུག་གིས་སྐམ་ཆེན་ཁྲུར་དེ་ཨ་བ་ལང་བ་སོང་། ཐོ་བ་ཆེན་མོ་ཁྲུར་དེ་ཨ་མ་ལང་བ་སོང་། ང་ཐོ་རས་ལ་འཁྲུར་དེ་ཡོང་ཡིན་ཟེརས་པ། གཡོག་མོ་དེ་ལོག་སྟེ་སོང་། ཐོ་རེ་རྩུག་པོ་ལ་ཡང་བལ་

ཁོལ་མ་བོས་པ་ཡོངས་པ། མགར་ཕྲུག་སེང་གེ་དོན་ལྡན་མཁར་ལ་སོང་། དེ་ནས་བལྟས་པ། ཨ་གུ་དཔལ་ལེའི་མདའ་ཡིན་བ་ཤེས་དེ། ཇོ་ཇོ་འབྲུ་གུ་མ་ལ་ཟེརས། ཇོ་ཇོ་ལེ། ཉེ་རང་གིས་འདི་རིང་གླིང་ཡུལ་ལ་བཞུགས་པ་མཆོག སེ་གོན་ཅེས་གོན། ཕོག་ཅིག་དོང་། ཀལ་ཅེར་རོན། ཏུ་འིན་ཞིག་དེ་ཟུག་ཟེར།

གསེར་པོའི་གསེར་མཁར་མ་ལྡན་ཅིག།
གླིང་མཁར་རྩེ་དགུ་རང་མཁར་ལྡན་ཅིག།
རྗེར་གུར་དཀར་གྲོགས་སྐལ་མ་ལྡན་ཅིག།
གླིང་ཀེ་སར་གྲོགས་སྐལ་ལྡན་ཅིག།
གསེར་རལ་ཅན་དང་གཡུ་རལ་ཅན་བུ་སྐལ་མ་ལྡན་ཅིག།

དེ་ཟུག་ཟེར་ན་མདའ་དེ་འབུད་ཡིན་ཟེརས་པ། ཇོ་ཇོས་ཁོས་བསླབས་མཁན་ནང་ལྟར་ཏུ་འིན་ཞིག་དེ་ཟུག་ཟེརས་པ་མདའ་དེ་འབུད་དེ་ཡོངས། དེ་ནས་མདའ་སྟོང་ནང་དུ་མར་གྱི་ཡལ་ཅིག་བདང་སྟེ། གུར་དཀར་གྱི་མདའ་དོང་ནང་དུ་ཁྱེར་དེ་བོར་ཟེརས་པ། མདའ་དེ་མདའ་དོང་ནང་དུ་ཁྱེར་དེ་བོརས། དེ་ནས་གུར་དཀར་ཡང་ཕན་སོང་། མདའ་དེས་རྗེར་གྱི་མདའ་ཚང་མ་བཅག་སྟེ་མེད་མཁན་བཅོ་སྟེ་ན། མདའ་དེ་ལོག་སྟེ་དཔལ་ལེ་རྒར་སོང་།

No. 6.

རྗེར་གྱིས་གླིང་ཡུལ་གྱི་དམག་ངོ་ དོག་འཁྱོང་ཅེས་ཡིན་འགྲོ། ལྷ་མཁན་མི་ཞིག་བདང་ན་སུ་བདང་ཡིན་ཟེར་དེ་གྲབས་བཅོས་པ། མགར་ཕྲུག་སེང་གེ་དོན་ལྡན་བདང་ཅེས་ལ་ཁ་ཆམས། དེ་ནས་དེ་ཟུག་ཚོར་དེ་མགར་ཕྲུག་ཁང་ཕ་ལ་ཡོང་

སྟེ། ཨ་ཕཱ་དང་སྲིང་མོ་ལ་ཟེརས། ང་གླིང་པའི་དམག་ལ་ལྷ་སོ་ལ་སོང་ཟེར་འདུག་ཟེརས་པ། སྲིང་མོ་གར་ཆ་ཆེ་རིན་མོ་གུར་དཀར་རྒྱལ་པོ་ལ་ཞུ་ཕྱུལ་ལ་སོང་། གསེར་ཐ་ལི་གང་སྣང་སྟེ་ཁུར་དེ་སོང་སྟེ་གུར་དཀར་རྒྱལ་པོའི་རྟར་སོང་སྟེ་གླུ་འདི་ལྟར་གླངས།

ཧོར་གྱི་རྒྱལ་པོ་མཁྱེན་ནོ་དངོས་ལ་ཉོན།
གུར་དཀར་རྒྱལ་པོ་མཁྱེན་ནོ་བདག་ལ་གསན།
ངའི་མིང་པོ་དམག་ལ་ལྷ་མ་བཏང་ལོ།
ངའི་མིང་པོ་ལ་སྟངས་ཤིག་མེད་ལོ།
ངའི་མིང་པོ་ལ་གྲོས་ཤིག་ཙང་མེད་ལོ།
ཡང་ན་ཁོ་ལ་ཞོན་རྟ་ཞིག་མེད་ལོ།
ཡང་ན་ཁོ་ལ་མདའ་གཞུ་ཞིག་མེད་ལོ།
ཡང་ན་ཁོ་ལ་དཔུང་གཏད་ཅིག་མེད་ལོ།
ཡང་ན་ཁོ་ལ་ཁར་ཟ་ཡང་ཁུར་རྒྱུ་མེད་ལོ།

དེ་ནུག་ཟེརས་པ། གུར་དཀར་རྒྱལ་པོ་ལ་སྒྲོ་ཡོངསྟེ་གླུ་ཞིག་འདི་ལྟར་བཏངས།

མགར་མོ་ཁྲོད་ཚུར་མ་ཡོང་ཕར་ལ་སོང་།
ཁོ་ལ་ལམ་རྒྱུས་མེད་ན་གླིང་ཡུལ་ནས་འདིར་ག་ནུག་ལ་བསླེབ།
ཁོ་ལ་སྟངས་མེད་ན་ཆོ་ལད་གྱད་གཞུ་ཅགས་ས།
ཁོ་ལ་གྲོས་མེད་ན་སྒྲོག་དགུ་པ་བློན་པོ་བསདས་ས།

ཁོ་ལ་སྟངས་མེད་ན་ཧ་ཝོ་ཁ་ལ་མི་འབར་བཏུལ་ལ།
ཁྲིད་ཚུར་མ་ཡོང་ཕར་ལ་སོང་།

དེ་ཐུག་ཟེར་དེ་དབང་ཅོ་སྟེ། ཧོར་གྱི་དམག་རྒྱས་དང་ལག་ཆ་ཚང་མ་བཀལ་ཏེ། ཧ་རྒྱལ་བ་ཞིག་བཏང་སྟེ། ཧོར་གྱི་དཔའ་བོ་བཞི་བཅུ་མཉམ་པོ་བཏངས། དེ་ནས་སྤྱིང་མོ་མགར་ཆ་ཆེ་རོན་མོས། མགར་ཕྲུག་སེང་གེ་དོན་ལྡན་ལ་བསམ་བྱ་བཏང་སྟེ་གླུ་འདི་ལྟར།

ཨ་ཅེ་བའི་ནོ་ནོས་དངོས་ལ་ཉོན་ལོ།
མགར་ཕྲུག་སེང་གེ་དོན་ལྡན་བདག་ལ་གསན།
ཞག་གསུམ་སོང་སྟེ་ལམ་རྟོག་པོ་ཞིག་ཡོད།
དེ་ལམ་ལ་ཀར་དར་བཙོ་སྟེ་སོང་ལོ།
དེ་ནས་ལྷ་ཐོ་དཀར་པོ་ཞིག་ཡོད་ལོ།
སྟེང་ལྷ་ཡུལ་ལི་ལྷ་ཡིན་དེ་ཤིག་སྟེ་སོང་།
དེ་ནས་ལྷ་ཐོ་དམར་པོ་ཞིག་ཡོད།
དེ་བར་བཙན་གྱི་ལྷ་ཐོ་ཞིག་ཡིན་དེ་ཡང་ཤིག།
དེ་ནས་ལྷ་ཐོ་ནག་པོ་ཞིག་ཡོད།
དེ་འོག་ཀླུ་ཡུལ་ལི་ཡིན་དེ་ཡང་ཤིག་རྡེ་སོང་།
དེ་ནས་ལྷ་ཐོ་སྨུག་པོ་ཞིག་ཡོད།
དེ་ཧོར་གུར་དཀར་གྱི་ལྷ་ཐོ་ཡིན།
ར་སྐྱེས་སྨུག་པོ་ཞིག་བསད་དེ་གསོལ་དེ་སོང་།

དེ་ནས་སྤྲར་གྱི་ལའི་ཁ་སླེབ་ཆེན།
དེ་རུ་གླིང་པའི་དམག་བསླེབ་སྟེ་ཡོད་ན།
རྟ་མ་བསྡད་རྟ་མཆོག་སྔོན།
མདའ་མ་བསྡད་མདའ་ལྕོང་སྔོན།
བཞུ་མ་བསྡད་གཞུ་མགོ་སྔོན།
མི་མ་བསྡད་དི་པི་སྔོན།
གླིང་པའི་དམག་ངོ་དོག་ལ་ཡོད་ན།
རིའི་སེམས་ཅན་ཚང་མ་འགྲུལ་བ་མཐོང་ཡིན།

དེ་ཐུག་བསླབ་བྱ་བཏང་སྟེ་ན། མགར་ཕྲུག་སེང་གེ་དོན་ལྡན་དང་། ཧོར་གྱི་དཔའ་བོ་བཞི་བཅུ་མཉམ་པོ་སོང་། ཞག་གསུམ་འགྲུལ་དེ་ན། དེ་ལམ་རྩེ་གོ་པོའི་རྩ་རུ་བསླེབ་པ། ཁ་སྔོན་ལ་སོང་སྟེ་ལམ་ཕྲ་མོ་ཞིག་གི་རྩ་རི་བ་ཤིང་ཞིག་གོན་དེ་འདུག་སྟེ། ཧོར་གྱི་དཔའ་བོ་ཚང་མ་ཚེར་ལ་རྒྱའི་ནང་དུ་འཐུལ་དེ་བཏང་སྟེ། གཅིག་ཀྱང་མེད་མཁན་བཅོས་བཏངས། དེ་ནས་ཁོ་རང་གཅིག་པོ་སོང་། ལྷ་མཐོ་དཀར་པོ་དམར་པོ་ནག་པོ་ཚང་མ་དང་ཕྲུག་པ། ཁོས་གསོལ་གྱིན་མཆོད་ཀྱིན་ཞིག་སོང་བས། དེ་ནས་ལྷ་མཐོ་སྨུག་པོ་དང་ཕྲུག། དེ་ཧོར་གྱི་ཡིན་པ་སང་། ཤིག་སྟེ་མེད་མཁན་བཅོ་སྟེ་སོང་། དེ་ནས་ཨ་སྤྲར་སྤྲར་གྱི་ལ་མགོ་ལ་བསླེབ་སྟེ་བལྟས་པ། ཨ་རོས་ལ་རྩ་ལ་གླིང་པའི་དམག་བསླེབ་སྟེ་ཡོད་ཚུག། ཀྱང་གོད་དབྱེར་པ་ལ་སྔ་བསྡད་དེ་འོབ་ཆེན་དེ་བལྟབ་སྟེ་ཐེ་ཚེ་བཏང་སྟེ་ན། གླིང་པའི་དམག་འཐུང་ལ་འཐུད་བཏངས། ཁོ་རང་ལ་མགོ་ན་དབྱིབ་སྟེ་མགོ་ཕེང་སྟེ་འདུགས།

མདའ་ལྟོང་ཐིང་སྟེ་བོརས། གཞུའི་མགོ་དེ་ཐིང་སྟེ་བོརས་པ། གླིང་པའི་ལྟ་བ་མིག་གི་རབ་ལ་དེ་ལ་ལའི་མགོ་ན་མཐོང་སྟེ་གླུ་ཞིག་འདི་ལྟར་བཏངས།

ཀྱེ་མ་གསན་དང་ཨ་གུ་ལེ།
ཤེ་མ་གསན་དང་དཔལ་ལེ་ལེ།
སྨར་གྱི་ལ་ན་རྡོར་གྱི་སོ་པ་འདུག།
རྟ་ནི་མ་མཐོང་རྨ་ཆོག་ཟམ་མཐོང་འདུག།
མི་དེ་མ་མཐོང་དེ་པི་ཟམ་མཐོང་འདུག།
མདའ་དེ་མ་མཐོང་མདའ་ལྟོང་ཟམ་མཐོང་འདུག།
གཞུ་ནི་མ་མཐོང་གཞུ་མགོ་ཟམ་མཐོང་འདུག།
ང་དང་དཔའ་བོ་འི་ལྷག་རེས་སུ་ཞིག་ཡིན།
རྡོར་གྱི་སོ་པ་ལ་ལྟ་ལ་ཆ་དགོས་སུག།

དེ་ཟུག་ཟེརས་པ། ཨ་གུ་དཔལ་ལེས་ཞིབ་ཆ་བལྟས་པ། ཅི་ཡང་མ་མཐོང་བས། ལན་དུ་གླུ་འདི་ལྟར་བཏངས།

ཁྱེད་ལྟ་བ་མིག་གི་རབ་ལ་དངོས་ལ་ཉེན་ལོ།
མིའི་ཁྲིམས་ལ་མཚན་འདྲེ་མཐོང་ཅེན་ལོ།
ཁྱེད་ཀྱི་ཁྲིམས་ལ་ཉེན་འཾ་དྲེ་མཐོང་འདུག།
ང་ཞ་ཚང་མ་མཐོང་བ་མིན་འདུག་ལོ།
རྡོར་གྱི་སོ་པ་ག་ན་འདུག་ལོ།

དེ་ཟླུག་ཟེརས་པ། ལྷ་བ་མིག་གི་རབ་ལ་སྒྲོ་ཡོང་སྟེ། ཕྱུ་ཕྲུངས་གཅིག་ནང་དུ་མགོ་བཏངས། ཕྱུ་ཕྲུངས་གཅིག་ནང་ཀང་པ་བཏང་སྟེ་གཉིད་ལོག་སྟེ་འདུགས། དེ་ནས་ཨ་གུ་དཔལ་ལེས་ལྷ་འདིན་ཞིག་འདུགས་པ་སང་། ཁོ་ལ་ཡང་སྤྲིབ་ཅིག་མཐོང་སོང་བས། དཔལ་ལེས་གོང་མ་བྲུ་ཚ་ལྗོག་རིས་ལ་བསྐོས་པས། ཧ་དེ་དུང་གི་རར་དཀར་བཏང་སྟེ་ཁོ་སོང་། ཁོ་དེ་ལ་མགོ་ལ་བསླིབ་ཙ་ན། མགར་སྒྲུག་དེ་པོ་རོན་ཅིག་ལ་ཇུ་སྟེ་ནམ་མཁའ་རུ་ཕྱིར་སོང་། གོང་མ་བྲུ་ཚ་ཁྲ་ལ་ཇུ་སྟེ་ཇས་པ། ནོན་ཀྱིས་ཚ་འདིན་ཞིག་དང་། ས་བི་རྩེ་ཞིག་ལ་ཇུ་སྟེ། གཡའ་གསེབས་ཤིག་གི་ནང་ཏུ་ཕྱིར་བ། གོང་མ་བྲུ་ཚ་ལ་དེ་ར་ཞིག་ལ་ཇུ་སྟེ་ཇས། དེ་ཟླུག་མང་པོ་བཙོས་པ་སང་། གོང་མ་བྲུ་ཚ་ངལ་དེ་ལོག་སྟེ་ཡོང་སྟེ་དམག་འབྲང་ལ་བསླིབ་སོང་། ཨ་གུ་དཔལ་ལེ་ལ་ཟེརས། ངའི་ཧ་ཡང་ངལ་སོང་། ང་རང་ཡང་ངལ། ཡང་ཞིག་སྲུ་བཏང་ན་འང་དོང་ཟེརས།

ཡང་ལྗོག་རིས་དེ་དཔལ་མོའི་ཨ་སྟག་ཡིན་ཚུག་པས། དཔལ་མོའི་ཨ་སྟག་ལ་ཧ་ནག་ཁྲ་གློ་རིངས་བཏང་སྟེ། ཁོ་ཞོན་དེ་མདུང་སྐོར་ཁྲུང་ངེན་ཞིག་སོང་། ཁ་ན་མེ་འབར་རིན་ཞིག་དེ་ས་ཁྲུད་ལ་བསླིབ་པ་སང་། མགར་སྒྲུག་དེ་རིའི་ཤ་བ་ཞིག་ལ་ཇུ་སྟེ་ཕྱིར་སོང་། དཔལ་མོའི་ཨ་སྟག་ཁྲི་ཞིག་ལ་ཇུ་སྟེ་ཇས་པ། ཆུའི་ཉ་ཞིག་ལ་ཇུ་སྟེ་ཕྱིར་སོང་། དཔལ་མོའི་ཨ་སྟག་ཆུ་སྲམ་ལ་ཇུ་སྟེ་ཇས་པ། ཡང་ར་མ་ཞིག་ལ་ཇུ་སྟེ་ཕྱིར་བ། སྤྱང་ཀུ་ལ་ཇུ་སྟེ་ཇས། དེ་ཟླུག་མང་པོ་བཙོས་པ། ཧ་ནག་ཁྲ་གློ་རིངས་དེ་ངལ་དེ་ཆད་སོང་བ་སང་། ཧ་ལ་མང་པོ་ཇུང་སྟེ་དེར་པང་སྟེ། དམག་བྲང་ལ་ཡོང་སྟེ། ཀྱུང་ཀོད་དབྱེར་པ་ལ་ཞེན་ཅེས་བཙོས་པ། དཔལ་ལེས་ཟེརས། པ་དཔལ་མོའི་ཨ་སྟག། ཁྲོ་རང་སྐྱེན་པ་ཞིག་མིན་ན།

ད་ལྟ་ཚུག་པ་ཀྱུང་གོད་དབྱེར་པའི་ཁ་མི་སུས་ཀྱང་ལག་པ་མ་བཏངས། ཧ་དེ་གླིང་ཀ་སར་རྒྱལ་པོའི་ཡིན། ཁྱོད་ག་ཟུག་ལ་ཞོན་ཡིན་ཟེར་ས་པ། དཔལ་མོའི་ཨ་སྟག་ལ་སྒྲོ་ཆེན་མོ་ཡོང་སྟེ་ཟེར་ས། ཁྱོད་ཁྱི་གཞན་གྱིས་དེ་ཟུག་ཟེར་དེ་གླིང་གི་ཤ་སྐྱིང་མར་སྐྱིང་ཟན་སྐྱིང་ཚང་མ་ཚར་བཅུགས། ད་ལྟ་རྟོར་གྱི་སོ་པ་ནག་ཚང་འབུད་དེ་ཆེན་ཟེར་དེ་དབང་བཅོ་སྟེ། ཀྱུང་གོད་དབྱེར་པ་ལ་ཞོན་དེ་སོང་བས། ཀྱུང་གོད་དབྱེར་པ་ལ་ཀ་སར་ཡིན་བ་ཤེས་དེ་ཡང་རི་ཞིག་ལ་ཁུར་དེ་ཁྱེར་ས་པ། དེ་ནས་ཡང་ལོག་སྟེ་ཁྱོངས་པ། མགར་ཕྲུག་གིས་ཀ་སར་རི་དངོས་བསྟན་ས་པ། དཔལ་མོ་འི་ཨ་སྟག་ལ་སྒྲོ་ཡོང་སྟེ་ཟེར་ས། ཁྱེད་བསམ་བ་མེད་མཁན་ནི་ཀ་སར་རྒྱལ་པོ། ཁྱོད་དངོས་མ་བསྟན་བ། ང་ལ་ནགས་མང་པོ་མཐོང་། ཁྱེད་ཀྱིས་དེ་ཟུག་བཅོས་པ་གླིང་མཁར་ཤལ་མ་ལ་གྱུར་སོང་། ཇོ་ཇོ་འབྲུ་གུ་མ་རྟོར་གྱིས་ཁྱེར་ས། གླིང་གི་ཤ་སྐྱིང་ཚར། མར་སྐྱིང་ཟན་སྐྱིང་ཚང་མ་ཚར་སོང་། ད་རུང་ཡང་ཡངས་པ་བཅོ་རུག་ག་ཟེར་ས།།

No. 7.

དེ་ནས་ཀ་སར་དང་དཔལ་མོའི་ཨ་སྟག་གཉིས་ཀ་གླིང་པའི་དམག་འབྲང་ལ་སོང་། དེ་རུ་ཚང་མ་འཛོམས་སྟེ་ཀ་སར་གྱིས་ཟེར་ས། ང་སྔོན་ལ་ཆེན། ཁྱི་ཞ་དཔའ་བོ་བདུན་རྫིང་ན་ཡོང་ཟེར་དེ། ཀ་སར་སོང་ནས་རྟོར་ཡུལ་ལ་བསླེབ་སྟེ། གར་དཀར་ལ་ཟེར་ས་པ། རྒྱལ་པོ་ལེ། དམ་གཅིག་ཡོད་ན་སྨུས། མཁར་རྩིག་ན་རྩིག། གླིང་པའི་དམག་མང་པོ་ཡོང་འདུག། ང་དང་མཉམ་པོ་སོང་མཁན་ནི་དཔའ་བོ་ཚང་མ་གླིང་པའི་དམག་གིས་བསད་ཚར། ང་རང་གཅིག་པོ་འབུད་སོང་། གླིང་པའི་དམག་རྩལ་པ་འདུག་ཟེར་དེ་ན། ཁོ་མགར་བའི་ཁང་པ་ལ་

སོང་། དེ་ནས་མགར་ར་ཏི་མིས་ཡང་བྱ་ཆ་བསླེབ་ཟེར་ཏེ་མང་པོ་འཐད་སོང་། སྲིང་མོ་ཡང་འཕྲད་དེ་ཀལ་ཅེར་བླུགས། ཞག་བདུན་སོང་སྟེ་ན། གླིང་པའི་དཔའ་བོ་། ཨ་གུ་ག་ཉི། གོང་མ་བྱ་ཆ། ལྷ་བ་མིག་གི་རབ་ལ། ཉ་གཡུ་ཉ་ཙལ། མདའ་དཔོན་གོང་མ། དཔལ་མོ་འི་ཨ་སྟག། ཁྲོང་ཚང་ཀ་ཏྲ་རེ་ལ་ཞོན་ཏེ་ཏྲ་རེ་ཁྲིད་དེ་ཁྲོངས་པ། གུར་དཀར་རྒྱལ་པོ་ལ་མཐོང་སྟེ་ཛེ་ཛེ་ལ་གླུ་ཞིག་བཏངས་སོང་།

ཛེ་ཛེ་སོ་མས་དངོས་ལ་ཉོན་ལོ།
ཛེ་ཛེ་འབྲུ་གུ་མས་བདག་ལ་གསན་དང་།
ངའི་ཨ་བའི་དུས་ལ་ཏྲ་ཚོངས་པ་མ་བསླེབ་ལོ།
ངའི་མེ་མེའི་དུས་ལ་ཡང་ཏྲ་ཚོངས་པ་མ་བསླེབ་ལོ།
ཏྲ་རེ་ཚང་ཀ་ཁྲོང་སྟེ་བྱ་ལ་ཞོན་ཏྲ་ཞིག་བཅོ་ཡིན།
མི་དེ་སྔོན་མ་ཁྲོང་སྟེ་བྱ་ལ་གཟིམ་དཔོན་བཅོ་ཡིན།
དེ་སང་ཉིང་མ་ཁྲོང་སྟེ་བྱ་ལ་གསོལ་དཔོན་བཅོ་ཡིན།
དེ་སང་ཉིང་མ་ཁྲོང་སྟེ་བྱ་ལ་ཞིབ་དཔོན་བཅོ་ཡིན།
དེ་སང་ཉིང་མ་ཁྲོང་སྟེ་བྱ་ལ་ཆུ་དཔོན་བཅོ་ཡིན།
དེ་སང་ཉིང་མ་ཁྲོང་སྟེ་བྱ་ལ་ཞིང་དཔོན་བཅོ་ཡིན།
དེ་སང་ཉིང་མ་ཁྲོང་སྟེ་བྱ་ལ་སྒོ་སྲུངས་བཅོ་ཡིན།
དེ་སང་ཉིང་མ་ཁྲོང་སྟེ་བྱ་ལ་ཁྲི་ཛོ་བཅོ་ཡིན།

དེ་ཟུག་ཟེརས་པ། ལན་དུ་ཛེ་ཛེས་གླུ་འདི་ལྟར་བཏངས།

ཁྲིད་ཏོར་ངན་རྩོག་པོས་དངོས་ལ་ཉོན་ལོ།
ཁྲིད་ཟ་མེད་བོང་བུས་བདག་ལ་གསན་ལོ།

ཁྱེད་རྩ་བ་མེད་པའི་གླང་དུ་ཉེན་དང་།

དེ་ཧ་མི་ཚང་མ་གླིང་གི་དཔའ་བོ་ཡིན་ལོ།

གླིང་གི་དཔའ་བོ་རྒྱལ་བ་ཚང་ཀ་ཡིན་ལོ།

དེ་ཧ་མི་ཚང་མ་ཁྱེད་ལ་མི་ཐོབ་ཅས་ཡིན་ལོ།

དེ་ཟླུག་ཟེརས་པ། ཧོར་གུར་དཀར་རྒྱལ་པོ་ཡིད་མ་ཆེས་པས། ཨང་གར་ལྕངས་པ་བཙོན་ཁང་ནས་ཕྱིང་སྤྱི་འདྲིས་པ། ཨང་གར་ལྕངས་པས་ལན་དུ་གླུ་འདི་ལྟར་བཏངས།

ཁྱེད་བསམ་བ་མེད་པའི་ཧོར་ངན་དངོས་ལ་ཉེན།

དེ་ཧ་པ་ཚང་མ་གླིང་པའི་དཔའ་བོ་ཡིན།

གླིང་པའི་དཔའ་བོ་ཚང་ཀ་དེ་ཀུན་ཡིན་ལོ།

ཁྱེད་ཀྱིས་གླིང་ཡུལ་ལ་དཔའ་བོ་མེད་བསམ་མ།

སྔོན་ལ་ཧོར་ཡུལ་ལ་མེ་ཞིག་སྦྲ་ཡིན་ལོ།

ཉིང་ན་ཧོར་ཡུལ་ལ་ཆུ་ཞིག་ཆླུག་ཡིན་ལོ།

མེ་རེ་ཆུ་ཡིས་བསད་པ་ཞིག་བཙོ་ཡིན་ལོ།

ཁྱེད་ལ་དམག་ཅིག་ཡོད་ན་སློས་ལོ།

ཁྱེད་ལ་མཁར་ཞིག་མེད་ན་རྩིག་ལོ།

ཁྱེད་ལ་གདམ་གསུམ་ཟེར་བའི་ཟེར་ལོང་མི་ཡོང་།

ཁྱེད་ལ་གོམ་གསུམ་རྒྱབ་ལོང་མི་ཡོང་།

དེ་ཟླུག་ཟེརས་པ་ཇོར་གུར་དཀུར་ལ་སྤྲོ་ཡོང་སྟེ། ཡང་གར་ལྷུངས་པ་དེ་ལྷུགས་ཀྱི་ཏྭ་མིག་ནང་དུ་རྒྱུང་སྟེ། མཁར་གྱི་མགོ་ནས་ཆར་ལ་བཏངསྟེ་བོརས། དེ་ནས་མདའ་དཔོན་གོང་མ་ལྷ་ལ་སོང་བ་སང་། ཡང་གར་ལྷུངས་པ་ཆར་ལ་ཡོད་པ་མཐོང་། མདའ་དཔོན་གྱིས་དཔལ་མོ་འི་ཨ་སྟག་ལ་ཟེརས། ཨ་མ་དཔལ་མོ་འི་ཨ་སྟག་ལེ། ཨ་མ་རང་ལ་ཨང་གར་ལྷུངས་པ་ལེན་ཐུབ་ན། ལྷུགས་ཐག་ངས་བཅད་ཐུབ་ཡིན་ཟེརས། དཔལ་མོ་འི་ཨ་སྟག་གིས་ཁྲུབ་ཡིན་ཟེར་དེ་ལེནས་པ། མདའ་དཔོན་གྱིས་ལྷུགས་ཐག་དེ་བཅད་བཏངས་པ། ཨང་གར་ལྷུངས་པ་ཡང་དཔའ་བོ་འི་ཁྲི་ལ་བསྐྱིབ་སོང་། དེ་ནས་ཛེ་ཛེས་ཇོར་གྱི་གོས་གོན་དེ། སྐྱུལ་མགོ་མ་ཆབ་རྒྱུན་ནང་དུ་ཆང་ཁུར་དེ་ཆང་གི་ནང་དུ་དུག་ཛས་མང་པོ་བཏང་སྟེ། ཀལ་ཙེར་རོན་དེ་ཁུར་ནས། གླིང་པའི་དཔའ་བོ་འི་མདུན་ལ་སོངསྟེ་བླུ་འདི་ལྟར་བཏངས་སོ།

ངའི་གླིང་གི་དཔའ་བོ་ཀུན་དངོས་ལ་ཉོན་ལེ།
གླིང་གི་དཔའ་བོ་ཚང་ཀས་བདག་ལ་གསན་ལེ།
ང་ཕྱི་གླིང་ཡུལ་ལ་ཡོད་ཙ་ན་གླིང་ཡུལ་ལི་གོས་ཡོད་པིན།
དག་ས་ཇོར་ཡུལ་ལ་བསྐྱིབ་པ་ཇོར་གོས་གོན་དགོས།
ང་ཕྱི་གླིང་ཡུལ་ལ་ཡོད་ཙ་ན་གསུའི་སློག་པ་ཡོད་པིན།
དག་ས་ཇོར་ཡུལ་ལ་བསྐྱིབ་པ་ཇོར་དེབ་གོན་དགོས།
ངའི་ཕྱི་ལ་དཔའ་བོ་ཀུན་ལ་འོབ་རྒྱལ་ཞིག་མཐོང་ལོ།
སྐྱུལ་མགོ་ཆབ་རྒྱུན་ནང་དུ་སྐྱེམས་ཤིག་ཡོད་ལོ།

ང་ཡིས་བཅོས་མཁན་མེན་བཙལ་མཁན་ཞིག་ཡིན་ལོ།
ཉེ་ཞ་སྐྱེམ་སྤེ་ཡོད་ན་སྐྱེམས་བྲང་ཞིག་འདོན་ལོ།

དེ་ཟུག་ཟེརས་པ་སང་། མགོང་མ་ནོ་ནོས་ཀོ་རེ་ཕིངས་པ། དེ་ཚུག་པ་མདའ་དཔོན་མགོང་མ་ལ་དུག་ཡོད་ཅེས་ཞེས་དེ་ཟེརས། ཛོ་ཛོ་ལི་སྤོན་ལ་སྟེང་ལྷ་ཡུལ་ལ་ཕྲུལ། དེ་ཉིང་ན་བར་བཙན་ཡུལ་ལ་ཕྲུལ། དེ་ཉིང་ན་འོག་ཀླུ་ཡུལ་ལ་ཕྲུལ། ཕས་ལྷ་ཀིར་ཟེང་སྐྱན་པོ་ལ་ཕྲུལ། མས་ལྷ་བཀར་དམན་རྒྱལ་མོ་ལ་ཕྲུལ། གླིང་ཀ་སར་རྒྱལ་པོ་ལ་ཕྲུལ། ཟེར་དེ་མདའི་མགོ་དང་ཕངས་བཏངས་པ། ས་དོ་གོམས་གནམ་ལ་སོང་། གནམ་དོ་གོམས་ས་ལ་བབ། དེ་ནས་དཔལ་ལེ་རྒོད་པོ་ལ་སྤྲོ་ཡོང་སྟེ་ཛོ་ཛོ་ཟུམ་སྟེ་གླུ་འདི་ལྟར།

ཨོ་ཧོ། དཔལ་ལེ་ངའི་གྲི་ལ་གྲིབ་ཤད་ཅིག་ཡོད་ལོ།
རྒོད་པོའི་གྲི་ལ་གྲི་བཤད་ཅིག་ཡོད་ལོ།
ལོ་གསུམ་སྟེང་གི་ལྷ་ཡུལ་ལ་བོད་པ་ཡིན།
ལྷ་འཁོར་གསུམ་བརྒྱ་དྲུག་བཅུའི་ལྷ་གྲིས་ཤིག་འཕོག་པིན།
ལོ་གསུམ་བར་གྱི་བཙན་ཡུལ་ལ་བོར་པ་ཡིན།
བཙན་ཨ་མ་སྐྱབས་དུན་མའི་བཙན་གྲིས་ཤིག་འཕོག་པིན།
ལོ་གསུམ་འོག་གི་ཀླུ་ཡུལ་ལ་བོར་པ་ཡིན།
ཀླུ་གསུམ་བརྒྱ་དྲུག་བཅུའི་ཀླུ་གྲིས་ཤིག་འཕོག་པིན།
ལོ་གསུམ་གངས་ཀྱི་དཀྱིལ་ལ་བོརས་པ་ཡིན།
གངས་ཀྱི་གངས་ངར་ཞིག་འཕོག་མཁན་ཞིག་ཡིན་ལོ།

ལོ་གསུམ་བྲག་གི་དཀྱིལ་ལ་བོར་མཁན་ཞིག་ཡིན་ལོ།
བྲག་ཕི་བྲག་ངར་འཕོག་མཁན་ཞིག་ཡིན་ལོ།
ལོ་གསུམ་སའི་མཐིལ་ལ་བོར་མཁན་ཞིག་ཡིན་ལོ།
སའི་ས་ངར་འཕོག་མཁན་ཞིག་ཡིན་ལོ།
ལོ་གསུམ་ཆུའི་མཐིལ་ལ་བོར་མཁན་ཞིག་ཡིན་ལོ།
ཆུའི་ཆུ་ངར་འཕོག་མཁན་ཞིག་ཡིན་ལོ།
བྱང་ཚ་ཁ་ནས་ཚ་ཞིག་ཁྱོངས་པ་ཡིན།
ཤ་བ་རི་དྭགས་ཀྱི་ར་གོ་ཁྱོངས་པ་ཡིན།
ལུག་རྡོ་མོའི་རུ་ཅོ་ཁྱོངས་པ་ཡིན།
བྱ་ཁྲ་ཡུག་རྒྱལ་པོ་འི་ཤོག་པ་ཞིག་ཁྱོངས།
མཚོ་མོའི་མཐིལ་ནས་ཆུ་གྲང་མོ་ཞིག་ཁྱོངས།
སྟག་ལོ་པ་བཅོ་བརྒྱད་ཀྱིས་ཐར་ངད་དངས་པ་ཡིན།
འབྲུག་ལོ་མ་བཅོ་བརྒྱད་ཀྱིས་སྐྱིད་པ་ཞིག་ཐུས་ཡིན།
དེ་ཟླུག་ཐར་ངད་དྲག་པོ་ཞིག་བདངས་ཡིན།
ངའི་གྲི་མ་ཐིངས་པ་ནམ་ཐིངས་ལོ།
གྲི་ཐིངས་པ་ནས་ཐར་ལ་བསད་ཅེས་དེ་མེད་བ་མི་འདུག་ལོ།
ཁོག་སྟོད་ཁྲེ་རི་སྙིང་མཁར་ལ་ཕང་ཡིན།
ཁོག་སྨད་ཁྲེ་རི་ཀླུ་ཡུལ་ལ་ཕང་ཡིན།
སྐྱིད་པ་ཁྲེ་རི་བར་བཙན་ཡུལ་ལ་ཕང་ཡིན།
ཁྱོད་ཡབས་སྟན་པའི་བུ་མོ་ཁ་དམར་མོ་ཡིན་ནོག།

ཡུམ་སྔོན་མོའི་བུ་མོ་ལྷེ་དམར་མོ་ཡིན་ནོག།
ཞིམ་པོ་ཟེར་བའི་ཚིལ་སོགས་མོ་ཡིན་ནོག།
ལགས་མོ་གོན་པའི་སྣང་འཁྲིང་མོ་ཡིན་ནོག།
ཁྱེད་རེ་ཟུག་མེད་ན་གླིང་མཁར་ཤཱ་ལ་མ་ལ་སྐྲུངས་ས།
དེ་ཟུག་མེད་ན་གླིང་གི་ཟན་སྐྱིང་མར་སྐྱིང་ཚར་ར།
ཁྱེད་རེ་ཟུག་མེད་ན་ནོ་གཅིས་འབུ་དམར་བསདས་ས།
ཁྱེད་རེ་ཟུག་མེད་ན་པོ་ལད་གྲུད་གཞུ་རྟེར་ཡུལ་ལ་བཏངས་ས།
ཁྱེད་རེ་ཟུག་མེད་ན་ཏ་པོ་ཁ་ལ་མེ་འབར་རྟེར་ཡུལ་ལ་བསླེབ་བ།

དེ་ཟུག་ཟེར་ཏེ་དཔལ་ལེས་ལག་པ་གཡོན་པ་དང་འབྲུག་གུ་མའི་མགོ་སྤྱུ་ལ་འཐམས། ལག་པ་གཡས་པ་དང་རྣོ་ཆོད་མའི་རལ་གྲི་ལ་འཐམ་སྟེ་ཕྱིངས་པ། གོང་མའི་བུ་ཚ་དང་། ཁ་རྒྱན་གཉི། མདའ་དཔོན་གོང་མ། ཚང་ཀ་ཡོང་སྟེ་རལ་གྲི་བདང་མ་བཙུགས། དེ་ནས་ཇོ་ཇོ་རྨ་ཁར་ལ་སོང་སྟེ། གུར་དཀར་ལ་གནས་ཚུལ་ཚང་མ་ཟེརས་པ། དེ་ནས་ཕར་ལ་མགར་ཕྲུག་སེང་གེ་དོན་ལྡན་མཁར་ལ་ཡོང་མ་བཙུགས་པས། ཡང་མི་སྤུའང་ཡོང་མ་བཙུག་པར། ཇོ་ཇོ་དང་གུར་དཀར་རྒྱལ་པོ་བྲུ་གུ་ཀུན་ཚང་ཀ་འདུགས། དེ་ནས་གོང་མ་བུ་ཚ་མཁར་ལ་ལྷ་སྐོར་ལ་སོང་བས། ཇོ་ཇོ་འབྲུ་གུ་མ་མཁར་གྱི་ཁ་ཐོག་ལ་ཡོད་ཚུག། གོང་མ་བུ་ཚས་ཇོ་ཇོ་ལ་གླུ་ཞིག་བཏངས།

ཨ་ཅེ་ཇོ་ཇོས་དངོས་ལ་ཉོན་ལོ།
ཇོ་ཇོ་སོ་མས་བདག་ལ་གསན་ལོ།

ཨཁར་གྱི་མགོ་ལ་པེན་ཞིག་ཙོས་ལ།
དེའི་ཁ་གཡུའི་ཆོག་བྲུ་ཞིགཙུག་ལོ།
དེའི་ཁ་ཙུ་རུའི་ལག་པ་ཞིག་ཙུག་ལོ།
དེའི་ཁ་སྦུ་དིག་གི་ཀ་གུ་ཞིག་བོར་ལོ།
དེའི་ཁ་མེ་ལོང་ཞིག་བོར་ལོ།
དེའི་ཁ་ཀྲུ་ལོང་ཞིག་བོར་ལོ།
དེའི་ཁ་ཀྲུ་ཁབ་ཅིག་བོར་ལོ།
དེའི་ཁ་ཤུང་དཀར་ཞིག་བོར་ལོ།
དེའི་ཁ་ཧ་ཏྲག་ཅིག་བོར་ལོ།
བྲུ་ཚ་ང་རང་གིས་མདའ་ཞིག་བཏང་ཡིན།
འཕོག་ཡིན་ན་མི་འཕོག་ཚོད་ཅིག་རང་ལྟེན་ལོ།

དེ་ཟླུག་ཟེརས་པ་སང་། ཛོ་ཛོས་ཟེར་མཁན་ནང་ལྟར་བཙོས་པ། གོང་མ་བྲུ་ཚས་མདའ་ཞིག་བཏངས། དེ་ཚང་མའི་དཀྱིལ་ལ་ཕོག་སྟེ། ཚང་མ་ས་ལ་འགྱུར་སོང་། དེ་ནས་ཛོ་ཛོ་མགྱོགས་པ་ཡོང་སྟེ། གུར་དཀར་ལ་ཟེརས། གུར་དཀར་འཛིགས་སྟེ། དམག་སྐྱུལ་བཏང་སྟེ་གླིང་པ་དང་འཐབ་མོ་བཏངས། ཧོར་གྱི་དམག་ཚང་མ་གླིང་པས་ཅིག་ཀྱང་མེད་མཁན་བཙོ་སྟེ་བསད་བཏངས་པས། གུར་དཀར་དང་ཛོ་ཛོས་ཟེརས། ད་ཅི་བཙོ་ཡིན་ཟེརས་པ། གུར་དཀར་གྱིས་མགར་བྲུག་སེང་གེ་དོན་ལྡན་ལ་ཡོང་ཟེར། ཟེར་དེ་མི་བཏངས། དེ་ནས་མགར་བྲུག་ཡོངས། གུར་དཀར་གྱིས། ལྷ་མགར་བྲུག་སེང་གེ་དོན་ལྡན། གླིང་པའི་དམག་གིས་ཧོར་གྱི་དམག་གཅིག་ཀྱང་མེད་མཁན་བཙོས། ད་ཁྱོ་རང་ལ་འཁྲུད་

ཅིག་ཡོད་ན་ཅོས་ཟེརས་པ། མགར་ཕྲུག་གིས་གྲོ་རས་ལ་ང་ཉན་ནོག་ག་ལྟེན་ཟེརས་པས། གུར་དཀར་འཕྲད་སོང་། དེ་ནས་མགར་ཕྲུག་དེ་ལོག་སྟེ་ཡོང་སྟེ། མཚན་ལ་གླིང་པའི་དམག་འབྲང་ལ་སོང་སྟེ་དཔའ་བོ་ཀུན་ལ་ཟེརས་པ། ལྷ་དཔའ་བོ་ཀུན་གྲོ་རས་ལ་ང་ཧོར་གྱི་དམག་བཅོ་སྟེ་ཁྲེ་ཞ་རང་ལ་འཐབ་མོ་བཏང་ཡིན། ངས་ཤིང་གི་རལ་གྲི་ཞིག་ཁུར་སྟེ་རེ་རེ་བཏང་ཡིན། ཁྲིད་ཀུན་གྱིས་ཤི་རྫུན་ཅོས། དེ་ནས་མཚན་སོང་བ་དང་ཡངས་དེ་གླིང་ཡུལ་ལ་སོང་ཤིག། ཛོ་ཛོ་ང་རང་གཅིག་ཅིག་ལ་ཉན་ཡིན་ཟེརས། དེ་ནས་ཁོ་ལོག་སྟེ་ཡོངས། གྲོ་རས་ཚུག་པོ་ལ་ཁོ་མཁར་ལ་སོང་སྟེ། ཧོར་གྱི་ཁྲབ་རྨོག་གོན་དེ་རལ་གྲི་ཁུར་དེ། ཧོར་གྱི་འཁྲུལ་ཧ་ཀང་གསུམ་ལ་ཞོན་དེ་གླིང་པའི་དམག་འབྲང་ལ་སོང་སྟེ་འཐབ་མོ་བཏངས། རལ་གྲི་དེ་ཤིང་ལ་འཁྱུར་བཙུག་སྟེ་གླིང་པའི་དཔའ་བོ་ཚང་མ་ལ་རེ་རེ་བཏངས་པ་སང་། དཔའ་བོ་ཚང་མ་མལ་མལ་ལ་ཤི་རྫུན་བརྒྱབས། ཧོར་གྱི་འཁྲུལ་ཧ་ཀང་གསུམ་དེ་ཤི་མཁན་བཅོ་སྟེ་གླིང་པའི་དམག་འབྲང་ལ་བོར་དེ། ཁོ་རང་མཁར་ལ་ཡོངས་པ། ཛོ་ཛོས་ཁོ་ཡོང་མ་བཙུགས།

No. 8.

དེ་ནས་ཁོ་མགར་ཁང་དུ་ཡོང་སྟེ་འདུགས། གླིང་པ་ཚང་མས་མཚན་སོང་བ་སང་། ཧོར་གྱི་འཁྲུལ་ཧ་ཀང་གསུམ་ཁྲིད་དེ་གླིང་ཡུལ་ལ་སོང་། དེ་ནས་མགར་ཕྲུག་ཐང་ཆེན་གྱིས་ལྕགས་ཀྱི་སྒམ་ཞིག་བཅོ་འིན་འདུགས། ལྕགས་ཀྱི་སྒམ་དེ་འགྲུབ་སྟེ་ན། ཞག་དང་ཞུགས་པ་བིང་བ་བཅོ་འིན་ཞིག་འདུགས། ཨ་བས་ཟེརས། ལྷ་བུ་ཚ་ཟ་ཅེས་ལ་ཡོང་། དེ་ནང་ན་ཅི་འདུག་ཟེརས་པ། བུ་ཚས་ཟེརས། འདི་ནང་ན་ལྷ་ཡུལ་དང་མི་ཡུལ་མཐོང་འདུག་ཟེརས་པ། ཨ་ཞས་ང་

གཅིག་ཞུགས་ཡིན་ཟེརས་པ། བུ་ཚས་རྒྱལ་ཟེར་དེ་ཨ་བ་སྐམ་མི་ནང་དུ་བཏང་སྟེ་ཀ་ལིག་སློབ་དེ་བཙུགས། ཨ་བས་ཟེརས། ལྷ་བུ་ཚ་འདི་འདི་ནང་ན་ཅང་མཐོང་བ་མི་འདུག་ཟེརས་པཾ། བུ་ཚས་ཅ་བིག་སྦྱིང་སྟེ་ནས་མཐོང་ཡིན་ཟེར་རིན་ཞིག་རྐྱིད་བུ་བཅོ་སྟེ་སྐམ་དེ་བཀལ་དེ་མེ་ཕུ་སྟེ་སྤྲུད་པ་བཏངས། དེ་ནས་ཨ་བ་ལ་ཚན་དེ་ཚོར་དེ། ལྷ་བུ་ཚ་ཅི་བཅོ་འདད་ཟེརས། བུ་ཚས་ཨ་བ་རང་ལ་ལྷ་ཡུལ་དང་མི་ཡུལ་མཐོང་བཙུག་གེད་ལེ་ཟེརས། དེ་ཚུག་པ་ལྟུགས་སྐམ་ཚ་སྟེ་ཚན་དེ་སོང་བ་སང་། ཨ་བ་ལ་ཤེས་དེ་ཟེརས། ལྷ་བུ་ཚ་ང་བསད་མ་བསད་ཟེརས་པ། བུ་ཚས་ཟེརས། ངས་ཟེར་མཁན་བཅོ་ཡིན་ན། ཨ་བས་ཁྱེད་ཀྱིས་ཅི་ཟེར་མཁན་ངས་བཅོ་ཡིན་ཟེརས། བུ་ཚས་གསེར་པོ་འི་གསེར་མཁར་གྱི་ཁ་ཐོག་ལ་སླེབ་ཅས་སི་ལྟུགས་ཐག་བཅོ་ན་ཕྱུད་ཡིན་ཟེརས་པ། ཨ་བས་བཅོ་ཡིན་ཟེརས། དེ་ནས་སྐམ་མི་ནང་ནས་ཕེངས། དེ་ནས་ཁོང་གཉིས་ཀས་ལྟུགས་ཐག་བཅོས། མཚན་ཉི་མ་བཅོས་པ་བཅོ་ཚར།

དེ་ནས་མགར་ཕྲུག་གིས་ལྟུགས་ཐག་ཁྲུར་དེ་གསེར་པོ་འི་གསེར་མཁར་གྱི་རྩ་ལ་སོང་སྟེ། སྐེ་མོ་ལ་ཕྱུར་ཚ་ཞིག་བཏག་སྟེ་མཁར་གྱི་ཁ་ཐོག་ལ་ཐངས་པ། ཕྱུར་ཚ་དེ་ཁ་ཏོག་ལ་འཁད་དེ་སློན་དེ་སོང་བས། ཁོ་ལྟུགས་ཐག་ལ་འཁྲིལ་དེ་སོང་སྟེ་ཕྱེད་ཟམ་ལ་བསླེབ་པ་སང་། ནམ་མཁའ་ནས་བྱ་དཀར་ཞིག་དང་བྱ་ནག་གཅིག་འཁྲིལ་ལེན་ཡོངས་པ། བྱ་དཀར་དེ་བུད་དེ་ཡོངས་པ། དེ་དང་མཉམ་བོ་ཁོ་ཡང་བུད་སོང་། དེ་ནས་ཨ་ནེ་བཀུར་དམན་མོས་ཟེརས་པ། ལྷ་ཀེ་སར་ཁྱེད་ལ་མགར་གྲིབ་ཐོག་སྟེ་ཡིན་ནོག་ཟེར་དེ། ཨ་ནེས་ཁྲུས་མང་པོ་བཏང་སོང་། དེ་ནས་ཁོ་སོང་སྟེ་སྨོན་ལམ་བཏབ་སྟེ་ན་འཁྲིལ་དེ་སོང་བ། མཁར་གྱི་ཁ་ཐོག་ལ་བསླེབ་སོང་

ངས། ཁོས་པི་ཅོ་ཁ་ཅིག་བྱིངས། པི་ལ་ཞིག་བྱིང་སྟེ། གུར་དཀར་རྒྱལ་པོའི་མ་ལ་ཙའི་ནང་བདང་སྟེ་པི་ཅོ་ཤོར་བཅུགས། པི་ལ་འདེད་བཅུགས། གུར་དཀར་ལ་གཉིད་ཡོང་མ་བཅུགས། ཐོ་རངས་ཚུགས་པོ་ལ་ཁབ་པོན་གྱི་གཅིག་ཁུར་དེ་ཁོ་རང་སོང་སྟེ་གསེར་རལ་ཅན་དང་གཡུ་རལ་ཅན་གྱི་གཟུགས་པོ་ལ་བཙུགས་སྟེ་མཚན་མོ་རེ་གཉིད་ཡོང་མ་བཅུགས། གནམ་ལང་སྟེ་ན། དཀར་ཁུང་ནང་ནས་ནུ་མེན་ནི་ཛ་ལའི་ཁ་གསེར་གདུབས་པོ་ཕངས་བཏངས་པ། ཛོ་ཛོའི་མཛུ་གུ་ལ་འཁོད་སོང་བས། ཛོ་ཛོས་ད་ཀི་སར་བསླེབ་ཚར་རྫོར་ངན་བྱོད་ལོངས་ཟེརས་པ། རྫོར་དེ་ལང་སྟེ་གོན་ཅེས་གོན་ཚར་ར་དང་། ཀི་སར་བིང་སྟེ་འཁྲིལས། དེ་ནས་ཨ་ནེ་བཀུར་དམན་མོས་ལྷ་ཛོ་ཛོ་འབྲུ་གུ་མ། ཀི་སར་གྱི་ཁང་ཡོག་ལ་རྣལ་ལི་བག་ཕེ་དོང་། རྫོར་གྱི་ཁང་ཡོག་ལ་ལྕུགས་ཀྱི་སྨན་མ་དོང་ཟེརས་པ། ཛོ་ཛོས་ཀི་སར་ནི་མདའ་དར་དཀར་མོའི་གྲོགས་ཡིན། གུར་དཀར་རྒྱལ་པོ་ནི་བྱ་སྐྱེས་སི་གྲོགས་ཡིན་ཟེར་དེ་གཉིས་ཀ་སྲི་སྟེ་གཡོགས་བཏངས་པ། ཨ་ནེ་བཀུར་དམན་མོ་བྱ་ཞིག་ལ་ཛུསྟེ་ལྕུགས་ཀྱི་སྨན་མ་བསྐྱུ་སྟེ་རྫོར་གྱི་ཁང་ཡོག་ལ་བཏབས། རྣལ་ལི་བག་ཕེ་བསྐྱུ་སྟེ་ཀི་སར་གྱི་ཁང་ཡོག་ལ་བཏངས་པ། རྫོར་གྱིས་སྦུ་ཟ་གོན་དེ་ཡོད་པ་སང་། ལྕུགས་ཀྱི་སྨན་མའི་ཁ་ན་འདྲེད་ནས་ས་ལ་གྱེལ་སོང་བས། ཀི་སར་རྫོར་གྱི་བྲང་ངི་ཁ་བིང་སྟེ། བདུག་པ་ཅན་གྱི་ཕིངས་པ། རྫོར་གྱིས་སྦྱུ་བཏངས།།

རྒྱལ་ལྷམ་ཀི་སར་གྱིས་ངའི་དངོས་ལ་ཉེན་ལོ།
ལྷའི་བུ་ཀི་སར་གྱིས་བདག་ལ་གསན་དང་།
ང་ལ་མ་ཤེས་པ་རིག་སོང་ལོ།
ང་ལ་མི་མགས་པ་རིག་སོང་ལོ།

ཉིད་ཀྱིས་བག་སྒྲིས་ཞིག་རྣམས་འང་རྒྱལ་ལྷམ་ཆེན་མོ།
ཉིད་ཀྱིས་བག་སྒྲིས་ཞིག་རྣམས་འང་སྤྲུལ་པའི་རྒྱལ་པོ།
གླིང་ཡུལ་བསིལ་མོ་རིག་ཡིན་ལོ་དབྱར་ས་རིག་བཙོ་ཡིན་ལོ།
ཧོར་ཡུལ་གྲོན་མོ་རིག་ཡིན་ལོ་དགུན་ས་རིག་བཙོ་ཡིན་ལོ།
ང་མ་བསད་རྒྱལ་ལྷམ་ཆེན་མོ་བག་སྒྲིས་ཞིག་རྣམས་ལོ།

དེ་ཟླུག་ཟེར་ཅེས་འཕྲོང་སྟེ་ཀ་སར་ལ་སྙིང་རྗེ་ཆོར་དེ་མི་བསད་བསམ་པ། ཨ་ནེ་བཀུར་དམན་རྒྱལ་མོས་ཟེརས་པ། ལྷ་སྟང་ཅན་ནི་སྟངས་མེད་ཀ་སར་རྒྱལ་པོ། གླིང་མཁར་ཞབ་མ་བསྒྲུརས་པའི་ཡིད་དུ་ཡོང་བ་མི་རག་ག། གླིང་གི་ཞ་སྙིང་མར་སྙིང་ཟན་སྙིང་ཚང་མ་ཚར་བཙུགས། ཧོར་བུ་རིགས་ཚང་མ་ཧོར་ཡུལ་ལ་བསྐྱེབ་བཙུགས་པའི་ཡིད་དུ་ཡོང་བ་མི་རག་ག། གྲི་གུ་སོར་གསུམ་འགུལ་བ་མི་རག་ག། ཇོ་ཇོ་འབྲུ་གུ་མ་བཀོགས་པའི་ཡིད་དུ་ཡོང་བ་མི་རག་ག། དེ་ཟླུག་ཟེརས་པ། ཀ་སར་གྱིས་དུག་པ་ཅན་གྲི་གུ་དང་ཧོར་གྱི་གྲོད་པ་དེ་ཞགས། དེ་ནས་ཀ་སར་ཆོལ་གྱི་ནང་དུ་ནུབ་སྟེ་སོང་བས། ཨ་ནེ་བཀུར་དམན་མོས་གསོལ་མཆོད་ཅིག་བཏང་སྟེ་གླུ་ཞིག།

སྟེང་ལྷའི་དབང་པོ་རྒྱབ་བཞིན་ལ་མཆོད་དོ།
བར་བཙན་གྱི་ཨ་མ་སྐྱབ་མདུན་མ་ལ་མཆོད་དོ།
འོག་ཀླུའི་ཀླུ་རྒྱལ་ལྡོགས་པོ་ལ་མཆོད་དོ།
མཉམ་པོ་སྐྱེས་པའི་ལྷ་དགུ་ལ་མཆོད་དོ།
མཉམ་པོ་སྐྱེས་པའི་ཀླུ་དགུ་ལ་མཆོད་དོ།
ཕས་ལྷ་ཀར་ཟོང་སྟན་པོ་ལ་མཆོད་དོ།

མས་ལྷ་བཀུར་དཔན་རྒྱལ་མོ་ལ་མཆོད་དོ།

ཁྱེད་རྣམས་ཀྱིས་ཧོར་གྱི་ཤ་ཟོལ་འདོན་དགོས་ལོ།

དེ་ཟུག་ཟེརས་པ་ཧོར་གྱི་ཤ་ཟོལ་ཚང་མ་སྦྱིབ་ཅིག་ལ་ཚར་སོང་བས། རྣས་པ་ཁ་ཅིག་ལུས་པ། ཡང་གར་ཞིག་བཅོ་སྡེ་བོརས། དེ་ནས་གསེར་རལ་ཅན་དང་གཡུ་རལ་ཅན་གཉིས་ཀ་ལ། གླིང་ཡུལ་ལ་གྱུལ་ཟེརོས་པ། མི་ཆ་ཟེརས། དེ་ནས་གསེར་པོ་འི་གསེར་མཁར་དང་། ལྟགས་ཀྱི་གྲུང་སྐོར་ཚང་མ་ཤིགས། ནོར་བྱ་ཚང་མ་ཁྱིངས། གསེར་རལ་ཅན་དང་གཡུ་རལ་ཅན་བོར་དེ། ཇོ་ཇོ་དང་ཀེ་སར་ཡོངས།

No. 9.

དེ་ནས་བྲག་ཚའུ་དུང་དུང་མགྲོང་བ་སང་། ཀེ་སར་ལ་ཡིད་དུ་ཡོང་སྟེ་ཟེརས། ངའི་རྟ་ལྟུག་དེ་ལུས་དོག་ང་འཁྱོང་བ་ཆེན་ཟེརས་པ། ཇོ་ཇོས་ཟེརས། ཉེ་རང་གིས་ངའི་ཕྲུ་གུ་ཀུན་བསད་པ་ཡིན་ནོག་ཟེར་དེ་ཆ་མ་བཙུགས་པས། ཀེ་སར་གྱིས་ཟེརས། ང་རལ་གྲི་དང་མི་བསད་དུ་བག་མི་བཏང་ཟེརས་པ། ཇོ་ཇོ་བདེན་ཆེ་སྟེ་ཆ་བཙུགས། དེ་ནས་ཀེ་སར་ཕྲུ་གུ་ཀུན་གྱི་སྒོ་ལ་བསྐྱིབ་སྟེ་ཟེརས། ལྷ་གསེར་རལ་ཅན་དང་གཡུ་རལ་ཅར་གཉིས་ཀ། ངའི་རྟ་ལྟག་དེ་ལུས་དོག་དོང་ཟེརས་པ། ཕྲུ་གུ་གཉིས་ཀས་ཨ་པཱའི་ཀ་ལེ་ལ་ཆ་ཅིས་ལ་ཤུ་གུའི་མི་ནང་གང་བཅོ་སྟེ་ཡོད་ཚུག། ཁྱོང་རང་གིས་དུ་བག་གི་སྨན་བཅོ་འིན་ཞིག་ཡོད་ཚུག། ཀེ་སར་ལ་ཟེརས། ཉེ་རང་ལེན་བ་ཡོང་། ང་ཞལ་ལོང་མེད་ཟེརས་པ། ཀེ་སར་གྱིས་ཡང་དོང་ཟེརས་པ། ཁྱོང་གིས་བལྟས་པ་རྟ་ལྟུག་དེ་མ་ལྷིན་དེ་ཞིག་ཡོད་ཚུག།

ཁྱོང་གཉིས་ཀཱ་ཤ་ཡ་མ་དུ་ཀཱི་ པ་ཁྱིང་སྟེ་སྒོ་ལ་བསྐྱིབ་པ། ཀ་སར་གྱིས་བསམ། ཁྱོང་མཆོན་ཆ་དང་བསད་ན། ངས་མཉའ་བོར་མཁན་ཡིན། དེ་སང་ཧ་ལྷུག་དང་བསད་ཡིན་བསམ་སྟེ། ཧ་ལྷུག་དང་ཁྱོང་གཉིས་ཀའི་མགོ་ཀུན་བཅད་དེ་ཁུར་དེ་ཁྱིངས། དེ་ནས་ཇོ་ཇོ་བྲག་ཚའུ་དུང་དུང་ལ་བསྐྱིབ་སྟེ་ཡོད་ཚུག། ཀ་སར་ཇོ་ཇོའི་མདུན་ལ་ཙ་བིག་མ་བསྐྱིབ་པ་ཟེརས། ལྟོས་ཇོ་ཇོ་ངས་བྲག་ཚའུ་དུང་དུང་ལ་ལྟ་སྟེ་གྲ་ཕོག་ཅིག་བདང་ཡིན་ཇེརས་པ། ཇོ་ཇོས་བལྟས་པ། གསེར་རལ་ཅན་དང་གཡུ་རལ་ཅན་གཉིས་ཀའི་མགོ་ཀུན་ལ་གྲ་ཕོག་བདངས། ཇོ་ཇོ་ལ་དེ་ཟུག་ཤེས་དེ་སྨུན་སོང་བས། ཡང་ཇོ་ཇོས་ཟེརས་པ། ཀྲ་ཀ་སར་ཕོད་པ་ཅན། ད་ནས་ཕར་ལ་ཁྱེད་དང་ངའི་བར་ལ་བྲུ་གུ་མ་སྐྱེས་ཤིག་ཟེར་དེ་ནས། ཁྱོང་བྲག་སྒོ་ནས་བིང་སྟེ་སོང་། དེ་ནས་སྔོན་ལ་སྨ་ལུ་ཡོད་པའི་ས་ཁྲུད་ལ་བསྐྱིབ་སོང་། དེ་ནས་ཕར་ལ་ཇོ་ཇོ་ཧའི་ཟ་མ་ལ་བདག་སྟེ་བཀྲུད་གྱིན་ཞིག་ཁྱེརས། གླིང་ཡུལ་ལ་བསྐྱིབ་སྟེ་མཁར་ལ་སོང་སྟེ། ཇོ་ཇོ་གླིང་ཡུལ་ལ་མཐོང་ཀོ་ལ་ལོ་གསུམ་བདངས། ལོ་གསུམ་མགོ་འི་ཁ་འོལ་བདབ་སྟེ། མཛོ་དང་རྨོས། ལོ་གསུམ་ཕྱུགས་མོ་ལ་ཀོ་བ་བདབ་སྟེ་མཁར་གྱི་ལས་ལ་བཀོལས། ལོ་གསུམ་སྨྲག་པའི་ར་རྫི་བཅོས། ལོ་གསུམ་སེན་རིག་གི་འོ་མ་ཞོ་བཙུགས། དེ་ཟུག་གིས་ལོ་བཅོ་ལྔ་བུད་སོང་། མཁར་ལ་ཞིག་གསོབ་བཅོ་བ་ལ་ལོ་གཅིག་སོང་། དེ་ནས་ཀ་སར་གྱིས་ཇོ་ཇོ་འབྲུ་གུ་མ་སྔོན་མའི་ མཚོགས་སེ་ཇོ་ཇོ་བཅོ་སྟེ་མཚན་གསུམ། ཉིན་གསུམ་དུག་བག་སྟོན་བདང་ངེན་ཞིག་བདེ་སྐྱིད་སྤྲུན་གསུམ་ཚོགས་མཁར་དུ་འདུགས་སོ།།

།། མཐའ །།

TALE No. VII.

DEFEAT OF THE KING OF HOR.

ABSTRACT OF CONTENTS.

1.

Kesar was alone on the way to Hor. He found the road blocked by thorns, *lonicera*, mother-willows and tamarisks. All these obstacles were overcome with the assistance of helpers from *gLing*, who were called there through prayers. When Kesar lay down for his night-rest, at the Srar-pass, *Ane bkur dmanmo* showed him a terrifying spectacle of nature, to try his courage. He heard wolves and foxes howl, and dry manure and little stones were blown about by the storm.[1] He became quiet when he knew that *Ane bkur dmanmo* had caused the storm. Then he ate the magic food, received from her in a nut-shell, which could never be consumed. On the ascent, Kesar sang a song of all the animals which lose their strength on the pass,[2] and asked *Ane bkur dmanmo* to assist him. She sent him a fox to lead him across.

After seven days Kesar met an outpost of dwarfs who were playing at dice. They had put up a hat on a post, and this hat used to whirl round whenever a person drew near. Although Kesar had put on his invisible cap, the hat began to whirl, and the dwarfs, who could not see anybody, became angry. They said: "The hat does not like us to play all day long, and therefore moves about." Then they took the hat down, and Kesar showed his true self. He played at dice with the dwarfs and lost everything, for a female dwarf had taken her seat inside one of the dice.[3] When Kesar had to stake his life, *Ane bkur dmanmo* advised him to bore with his needle into one of the dice. When doing so, the dwarf-woman left the dice, and Kesar played on with his own dice. Now he won and said, he would take the life of the dwarfs which he had gained. To reconcile him, the dwarfs ordered their stick which had the power of providing everything, to bring the most precious goods from all the surrounding countries. When they had arrived, Kesar asked all the gods, etc., who were born with him, to devour the goods

---

[1] The same scene we find in the Sheh-version before Kesar's start to the north.

[2] Compare Ladakhi Songs, No. XXV.

[3] This reminds us of Nala's story.

at once. Now Kesar threatened to take the lives of the dwarfs if they would not become his guides on the way. To this they agreed.

2.

The dwarf and Kesar arrived at the rock *Thsau dung dung*. This was a door of rocks which closed and opened at the request of the dwarfs. When the dwarf, who showed Kesar the way, asked the door to open for him, Kesar rode through it as quickly as he could. But the door, recognizing Kesar, closed at once and caught the tail of Kesar's horse. This was not given free, until Kesar had promised to bring the heads of the two children of the King of Hor on his way back. Then they arrived at a place where stones flew about between heaven and earth, and later on before the yak 'brown sugar.'[1] The dwarf told this yak that Kesar would play tricks on him, and the yak devoured Kesar at once. After Kesar had remained inside the yak for some time, he was advised by *Ane bkur dmanmo* to use his knife to make a way out. Thus the yak was killed.

Kesar was angry with the dwarf and threatened to use him as a riding-yak with a nose-ring. But the dwarf assured Kesar that the rest of the road was not dangerous, and therefore he was sent home.

Then Kesar arrived at a place where nine bridges were tied together, and where 100 soldiers of Hor had to keep watch. Kesar took the shape of a young lama, and caused much rain to fall. He made friends with the soldiers and built a house for them, the roof of which rested on a single post. One night when much rain fell, he tied a silk cord to the post, went outside, and tore the post down. All the soldiers were slain by the falling roof.

When Kesar arrived on the height of the *Asalsal*-pass, he had 100 riders in front of him and 100 riders behind him ; when he came to the *Along*-plain, he had one rider in front of him, and one rider behind him. He turned up his sleeves three times, and the golden castle of Hor shook three times. Then he met the goat-herds of Hor, whom he told a

---

[1] I am very much inclined to explain the door of rocks which opens and closes of its own accord, as a development from the opening and closing of the ice on rivers and lakes in winter. I am lead to this explanation by the fact that in connection with the gate also hail-stones (the stones flying about between heaven and earth), and perhaps a block of ice, the yak 'brown sugar,' are mentioned. The lakes and rivers are the gates to the underworld, the realm of the *klu* ; and also in other mythologies we find a similar gate at the entrance to the underworld or realm of the dead.

sad story about the ruin of Kesar and his family. When the herdsmen, who had been stolen from *gLing*, cried, he showed them his true self.

3.

Kesar arrived in the land of Hor in the disguise of a beggar. There were four wells, one for the King of Hor, of gold; one for the Hor-lama, of copper; one for *a'Bruguma*, of turquoise; one for the smith of Hor, of iron. He soiled them all with old shoes, old cups, etc., and lay down in the road. At first the king's water-bearer arrived at the well. She had to jump over Kesar, because he would not make way. Next *a'Bruguma's* water-bearer came to fetch water, and the beggar dropped a ring in her water-vessel. This ring went on *a'Bruguma's* finger, when she was washing her hands. Then *a'Bruguma*, having put on her dress of *gLing*, went before the beggar to ask him about her friends in *gLing*. The beggar said that Kesar had died, and gave a full description of the stûpa erected in his memory, and of the rewards given to the lamas He also said, that her father's corpse was left on a plain, and that her mother was asking alms. *'aBruguma* was sorry on account of this news but thought that the beggar was Kesar.

Finally, the water-bearer of the smith Himis came to the well. She recognized in the beggar the same man whom she had seen riding across the *Asalsal*-pass with a retinue, and who had caused the castle of Hor to shake by waving his sleeves. Kesar told the girl that there had been 100 lice in front of him, and 100 behind him, and that he had waved his sleeves only because he was so pleased to see a village after the desert. He also said that he was the son of smith Himis, but the latter, when arriving at the well, denied the fact.

4.

One day, when the smith's daughter went to the pea-field, she saw the same beggar in it, eating peas and vomiting what he had eaten. She went to tell her father, who came carrying the huge hammer and a pair of tongs. However, the beggar had already restored everything, and the field was more beautiful than it had been before. The father, believing his daughter to be a liar, tore out her cheeks with the tongs, and beat her with the huge hammer.

The smith said to Kesar, the beggar: "If you are my son really, you will be able to recognize my tools among the tools of 100 other smiths." The boy was able to do so, because *Ane bkur dmanmo* helped him by sitting down in the shape of a golden fly on every tool which was Himis' property. According to her advice the boy said: "The big hammer and the big tongs are missing!" This was actually the case, and Kesar was accepted as the smith's son.

One day lady *'aBruguma* went to the smith to have a golden ornament made. The new boy of the smith went before her dandy, having taken his cap off. He was blamed for this by the smith, but replied, that whoever takes off his hat in *gLing* receives a piece of white cloth.[1] There were, however, no coals ready, and Kesar and the smith's daughter were sent together to the wood, to make charcoal. They were ordered not to cut any wood from the holy forest of the king of Hor. Kesar destroyed the whole holy forest of the King of Hor, and on his way home, when crossing a brook, he said: "The shoes of the donkeys (who carried the charcoal) will become wet," and cut the hoofs off. Again the girl ran to her father to complain; but because everything was in good order on his arrival, the girl received a punishment once more.

On the next day lady *'aBruguma* went again to the smithy, and Kesar caused the golden ornament to get lost. Then he caused it to be found underneath lady *'aBruguma.* Now he made a great noise, calling her a thief. *a'Bruguma's* maid-servant gave him a box on the ear for his impudence, so that his cap fell down. There the mark on his head could be seen,[2] and *'aBruguma* recognized Kesar. He said that he would make the ornament, and did so, calling all the gods to his assistance.

5.

Then *'aBruguma* and the king of Hor agreed to call together all the heroes of Hor and let them try the famous bow. If the boy of smith Himis would be able to bend it, there would be no doubt that he was really Kesar. To prevent the boy from going to the tournament, Himis gave him a great number of arrow-heads to sharpen. The boy, however, finished this work in no time, and went to the assembly, where the minister "Nine-lives" had just been able to bend the bow as much as a barley-corn's breadth. The boy prayed that the famous bow might go to *gLing* and another bow be given him. [This took place apparently.] Then Kesar bent the bow in such a way that it broke and its fragments killed the heroes of Hor, whilst the bow-string caught the king of Hor's neck so that he was almost choked. Only Kesar was able to release him from it.

---

1 This is the custom at burials and at weddings. A white cloth is worn on the cap. At weddings it is perhaps due to the idea that at the wedding the virgin dies. White is apparently the colour of mourning.

2 Does this mark on the crown of his head show the influence of Buddhist art?

On the next day there was a great wrestling match, and the strongest wrestler was the minister "Nine-lives." The smith, who wished to keep the boy at home, gave him a great number of needles to sharpen. The boy finished this work in no time, wrestled with the minister and killed him.

On the third day all the people assembled to see who would be able to ride on the horse *Khula me 'abar.* It was so high, that nine stirrups lead up to its back. The smith told his boy to watch the house, to prevent him from coming. The boy brought the whole house on his shoulders to the sporting place and said, he would watch it there. He at once mounted the horse, rode on it head to tail, and up to the sky to the *gLing* land. There he exchanged it for an ordinary horse, rode up to the sky again, and let the horse drop so that it was smashed.

Now the lama of Hor had a dream, foreboding the death of the king and other sad events. Before the king and *'aBruguma* had finished their council about the dream, the Agus of *gLing* arrived on the *Srar*-pass, and Agu *dPalle* shot an arrow which hit the beam, that was the king of Hor's heart-artery. Nobody was able to extract the arrow, except the young smith (Kesar), and he did it only after *'aBruguma* had prayed for the destruction of the king of Hor. This arrow, after having broken all the arrows of Hor, went back to *dPalle's* quiver.

6.

The king of Hor wished to send a spy to see if the army of *gLing* was approaching. As he liked the smith's boy (Kesar) very much, he sent him. The daughter of the smith went to warn the king, but was sent home in disgrace. Therefore she told Kesar to destroy the altars of white, red, and black colour on the road, because they were the altars of *Lhayul*, *Barbtsan*, and *Kluyul*, and to honour a brown (*smugpo*) altar, because that was the altar of Hor! He did exactly the opposite. At a certain place the road was very narrow and the 40 men of Hor, who accompanied him, could hardly walk. There Kesar put on his invisible cap, and threw all the forty into the river.

The seven Agus had arrived on the *Srarsrar*-pass. Kesar sent them a letter with his horse. Then he remained hidden, so that only the tip of his hat, an end of his bow, and an arrow-notch could be seen. First of all he was discovered by Agu *lTaba miggi rab*, but Agu *dPalle* would not believe. When Agu *dPalle* finally saw him, Agu *Gongma buthsa* was sent against the spy of Hor. Kesar, taking the shape of a pigeon, fled, and *Gongma buthsa* pursued him, taking the shape of a falcon. Suddenly Kesar took the shape of a mouse, and went into a hole of the ground, the Agu following him in the shape of a weasel. But *Gongma buthsa,* having become tired, went back to the encampment.

Then *dPalmoi astag,* the female Agu, went off to catch the spy of Hor. Kesar took the shape of a deer, and the Agu followed in the shape of a dog. Then Kesar fled in the shape of a fish, and the Agu followed in the shape of an otter. Again Kesar took the shape of a goat, and the Agu that of a wolf.[1] After all, the horse of the Agu, being tired out, threw her off, when she was beating him. Then she mounted *rKyang rgod dbyerpa,* against the advice of the other Agus. When she came riding on his own horse, Kesar showed his true self. The Agu, however, was in bad temper and gave Kesar a lesson, saying, that through his forgetfulness great misery had come to the land of *gLing.*

7.

Kesar went back to the king of Hor, and told him to prepare for war. The seven Agus, *dPalle, Gani, Gongma buthsa, lTaba miggi rab, rNa γyu rna rtsal, mDā dpon gongma* and *dPalmoi astag,*[2] arrived seven days after Kesar, riding on horses, and leading horses behind them. The king of Hor wished to buy the horses and to take the men in his service. When *aBruguma* told him that the apparent horse-merchants were the heroes of *gLing,* he would not believe. Therefore he released Agu *Angar ltsangspa* from prison and asked him the same question. When the Agu gave the same answer, the king became angry and put the Agu in an iron cage, which was hanging down from the castle to half the height of the walls. Then *mDā dpon gongma* divided the rope with an arrow, and *dPalmoi astag* received the cage with the Agu when it fell down.

Now *aBruguma* tried to poison the Agus with poisoned beer, but *mDa dpon gongma* knew at once that it was poisoned; therefore he threw the vessel with his arrow up to the sky. Then a piece of earth flew up to the sky, and a piece of sky fell down to the earth (as a sign that it was poison). Then *dPalle rgodpo,* after having praised his arms, advanced to kill *'aBruguma,* but was hindered by three of the Agus. *'aBruguma* went to the castle, and told the king all what had happened.

---

1 A similar scene we find in Ladakhi Songs, No. XXVI.

2 This set of seven Agus is probably a more original set of them than the set of 18 Agus, as we have it in the preface. These seven Agus seem to be of a somewhat similar type of figures to the helpers in such folk-lore as "Sechse Kommen durch dil ganze Welt."

Then they resolved not to leave their castle again, and not to allow the son of the smith to enter it. *Gongma buthsa* (probably *mDa dpon gongma* originally) told *'aBruguma* who was on the top of the castle, to pile up a heap of articles with a horse-hair on the top. He then sent an arrow into the middle of all of them and destroyed them all.

Then the men of *gLing* killed the whole army of Hor. When the young smith (Kesar) was sent against them, there was a sham-fight with wooden swords. Kesar once more sent the Agus home, saying, that he alone would be able to retake *'aBruguma.*

8.

The boy went back to the smithy and made a box, into which he kept jumping in and out. Himis asked why he was doing so, and the boy said that from inside the box *lhayul* and *miyul* could be seen. The father wished to try, but as soon as he had got into the box, the boy locked it and lit a fire underneath.[1] He did not open, until Himis had promised to assist him in making an iron rope, which could be thrown to the top of the Hor castle.

Then Kesar carried the rope to the castle of Hor and threw it up. The iron hook caught hold, and Kesar climbed up. When he had reached about half the height of the castle, he saw a white and a black bird fight with each other. The white bird was defeated, and together with him Kesar fell down to the ground. *Ane bkur dmanmo* knew that several stains from the smithy, left on Kesar's body, were the reason of his misfortune. She washed him and sent him up again. He succeeded, and then he caught mice and a cat which he sent into the king of Hor's bed, to prevent him from sleeping. During the next night he pricked the children of the king with needles and kept the whole family awake. Next morning he let his ring drop, and it went by itself on *a'Bruguma's* finger. Then *a'Bruguma* called up the king, and he rose to wrestle with Kesar. *Ane bkur dmanmo* told *a'Bruguma* to throw hard peas under the king of Hor's feet, and pap under Kesar's feet, but *'aBruguma* would not do so because, although Kesar was her legal spouse, she had borne children to the king of Hor. *'aBruguma* had mixed peas and pap, but *bkur dmanmo* in the shape of a fowl separated them again, and the king of Hor was defeated.

He asked Kesar to spare his life, and offered all his land instead. Kesar was willing to let him live, but *Ane bkur dmanmo* reminded him

---

1 According to the Khalatse-version (continuation of the Sheh-version) he threatens to throw the box in the water.

once more of all the sins of Hor, and therefore he was killed with a poisoned knife. When he was stabbed, a tremendous amount of fat came pouring out of him, and Kesar would have been drowned in it, had not *Ane bkur dmanmo* offered it all to the gods, etc. The children of the king of Hor would not accompany Kesar, although the castle was destroyed and all the treasures carried away.

9.

When Kesar and *'aBruguma* arrived at the door *Tsau dung dung*, Kesar remembered that the heads of the two children were required to induce the door to open of its own accord. He went back, cut off the heads of the children, and threw them towards the gate like a polo-ball. The door opened, and Kesar and *a'Bruguma*, though she had fainted, rode through it. *'aBruguma* said that she would not bear any more children to Kesar. Now she was punished in the following way: From the land of the dwarfs to *gLing* she was tied to the tail of the horse and dragged along. Then she had to be everybody's servant for three years, for three years lucerne was sown on her head and ploughed with *Dzos;* for three years she had to serve in the castle with leather round her knees; for three years she had to tend stone-partridges; for three years she had to milk the *Senting*-bird.[1] In this way fifteen years had elapsed. Then one year was required to repair the *gLing* castle. Now *'aBruguma* was made a lady again. The wedding lasted three days and three nights, and they lived in perfect happiness.

---

[1] Is this perhaps a similar expression to the German "Die Sonne zieht Wasser"?

VOCABULARY.

I.

གཅིག་པོ་ཙེ། *γcigpotse*, alone, solitary.

སོལ་བ་བསད་ཅས། *solba bsadcas*, 'kill the coal,' make charcoal.

ཕང་ཤིང་། *phang shing*, spindle-stick.

མ་ལྕང་། *ma lcang*, mother-willow, large kind of willow.

ཁུམ་བུ། *khumbu*, originally *khombu*, shell [of a wall-nut]. Assimilation to second syllable.

ཚེ་རེ། *thsere*, all the time; *mthsan thsere*, all through the night.

ཅུ་རུམ། *curum*, imitates the sound of chewing.

བརྒྱལ་ཅས། *brgyalcas*, said of the voice of foxes; 'howl.'

གཡའ། *γyā*, slate or flat stones.

ཤོག་སྒྲ། *shog sgra*, whistling sound; the Sheh-version has *shugs sgra*.

རྐང་ར། *rkang ra*, = *rkang sgra*, a noise such as is caused by the feet, when walking or jumping. Lad. Grammar, Laws of Sound, No. 3.

འོ། *'o*, exclamation.

མི་ངན། *mi ngan*, not bad.

ཟོད། *zod*, about so much, related to *thsod*; compare *thsam* and *zam*.

དེན་ན་ཟོད། *denna zod*, just as much.

མཇུག་རྡུམ། *mjug rdum*, = *mjug lzum*, bushy-tailed.

ཅུང་ཁ། *cung kha,=skyung kha,* raven.

སྦལ་ལུ། *.ballu,* originally 'frog'; is here understood to mean 'dwarf.'

སེམས་རྐུ་བཅོ་ཅས། *sems rku bcocas,* 'steal the soul,' *i.e.,* make other people to like me.

རྒྱ་མ་ལན། *rgyama lan,* rare occasion.

ཁྲོལ་འཛོམ་མོ། *khrol 'adzommo*
ཁྲོལ་ལེ་མོ། *khrollemo,* } name of a female dwarf.

རྩི་བི་ཏིང་། *rtsibiting,* explained as meaning 'artery.'

ཨོ་ཧོ་ཧོ། *ohoho,* exclamation.

ཁྲ་སུག། *khrasug,=khrabo,* many-coloured.

འབྲུག་འབྲིས་མ། *'abrug 'abrisma,* 'thunder-written,' name of Chinese silk with the pattern of clouds and dragons.

ཡར་ཁྱེན། *yar khyen,* Yarkand.

གྲོང་གྲོང་། *grong grong,* high-headed (of horses).

ཧལ་མན། *halman,* good (of dried apricots).

བལ་ཁོལ་མ། *bal kholma,* wool-spinner, name of the maid-servant of Hor.

མེན་ཟེ། *menze,* clean, beautiful.

ཨོལ་ལོ། *ollo,* clean, good.

སྐྱབ་མདུན་མ། *skyab mdunma,* instead of *skyabs bdun;* in this form the name would mean 'help in front of [you].'

དུང་དུང་། *dung dung,* shell-coloured; also, in Tale No. III the dwarfs are called white.

2.

བྲག་ཚའུ་དུང་དུང་། *brag thsau dung dung* (probably *rdung rdung*), name of the door of two rocks which continually open and shut again.

རྡོ་བ་ས་ཕར་ནམ་ཕར་། *rdoba sa phar nam phar*, stones which continually fly about between earth and sky; parallel to the preceding.

ཀ་ར་ཁམ་བ་། *kara khamba*, 'brown sugar,' name of a wild yak in the service of the king of Hor.

ནག་བསྟན་ཅས། *nag* [*nags*] *bstancas*, to behave basely.

རྨིད་པ། *rmidpa*, = *midpa*, devour.

སྟེབ་ཆུང་། *steb chung*, little axe.

སྟུབ་ཅས། *stubcas*, mince [meat].

རྩིབ་ལོག། *rtsiblog*, side of the ribs.

བོལ་མོ་། *bolmo*, soft.

ཐུད། *thud*, united [the nine bridges].

གན་དྲེ། *gandre*, a coat of many layers of cloth, sewn one on another.

སི་ཀྱིམ། *sikyim*, silk [perhaps from Sikkim).

ཁྲག་པ། *khragpa*, the wide sleeves.

3.

ལྩང་ཅས། *ltsangcas*, beg.

སྐྱང་ཅས། *skyangcas*, probably more correct than *rgyangcas* in previous tale; 'to fill.'

རྨུག་བླ་མ། *rmug blama*, probably *smug blama*, the brown lama; the lama of Hor.

རྒྱུན། *rgyun*, ribbands to fasten shoes.

ལམ་གག། *lam gag*, said to mean 'cross-way.'

གོམ་ཅས། *gomcas*, step over.

ཞབས་རྡོན། *zhabs rdon*, = *zhabs rdo*, sockle. Lad. Grammar, Laws of Sound, No. 5.

སྙན་དར། *snyan dar*, melodious silk; name of the prayer-flags on the top of a *mchod rten*.

འབུལ་ཡ། *'abul ya*, respectful for wages.

ལྕམ། *lcam*, 'wife,' name of the smith's daughter; another name of the same girl is *choron;* in the Sheh-version her names are *Bhag 'adzommo* and *chorol*.

4.

ཅེ་མ་འབུམ། *cema 'abum*, is also spelled *byema 'abum ;* people are doubtful about this word. Some think it is a spoon, others a head-ornament.

པལ་ཀྱི། *palkyi*, palanquin.

ཧེ་མིས། *Himis*, name of the smith of Hor, the pronunciation seems to vary, sometimes it is *Hemis*.

ཐང་རྙེད། *thang rnyed*, Kesar's name as a smith; is explained as 'the boy found on the plain'; should it not be a corruption of *thar rnyed?* Later on Kesar receives the name *Sengge don ldan*.

ལྷབ་ཚས། *lhab thsas*, garden dedicated to the gods (*lha*); the *b* I cannot explain.

བུང་བུ། *bungbu*, for *bongbu*, assimilation to the second syllable.

བལ་ཐོད། *bal thod*, turban.

པ་པུ། *papu*, cloth-shoes.

འབང་བ། *'abangba*, become wet; intransitive of *sbangba*, make wet.

ར་གོ། *rago*, hoof.

ལམ་ཅས། *lamcas*, be diligent, ready for work.

ཡད། *yad*, excellence.

ལྫོངས་ཅས། *ldzongscas*, examine.

ནོ་རོ། *noro*, nobleman.

མགོ་ལྕད། *mgo lcad*, box on the head.

རྨེ་བ། *rmeba*, here explained as meaning the 'crest on the head,' which is also an attribute of Buddha.

5.

ཁྲུབ་ཅས། *khrubcas*, Lower Ladakhi for *thubcas*, be able.

ཡི་ནཱམ། *yinām*, recompense, Urdu.

ཚགས་མ། *thsagsma*=*thsagma*, sieve.

དྲང་ཁུང་། *drang khung*, said to mean 'bow.'

མིན་བ། *minba*,=*menba*, besides.

འཐམས་ཅས། *'athamscas*, is here used for 'wrestle.'

ཞུབ་སྟེ། *shubste*, softly (of speech).

ཤོལ་ཅས། *sholcas*, disperse, go away.

འབྲུའི་ཀ། *'abrui ka*, the 'pillar which is the heart-artery' of the king of Hor. The Khalatse version has *'abrussi ka;* the *s* is probably due to the other formation of the genitive, see Lad. Grammar.

6.

ཡལ། *yal,*=*yar,* a small piece of butter.

གར་ཆ་ཆོ་རོན་མོ། *garcha choronmo* [or *choronemo*], a name of the smith's daughter; *choron,*=*chos sgron,* Lad. Grammar, Laws of Sound, No. 3.

དཔུང་གཏད། *dpung γtad,* helper.

ཁར་ཇི། *khar ji,* provisions. (Urdu.)

དམག་རྩས། *dmag rtsas,* armour.

ལྗག་རེས། *ljag res,* turn to go to fight.

གོང་མ་བུ་ཚ། *gongma buthsa,* the boy from the upper [place]; name of an agu.

ལྟ་བ་མིག་གི་རབ། *ltaba miggi rab,* name of the agu who is famous for his sharp eyes.

ས་བི་ཙེ། *sabitse,* mouse.

གཡའ་སེབ། *γyā seb,* hole between loose stones.

རྟ་ནག་ཁྲ་གློ་རིངས། *rta nag khra glorings,* the horse 'black and piebald, having long (lasting) lungs.'

རྣ་གཡུ་རྣ་རྩལ། *rna γyu rna rtsal* (in the Preface he was spelled *'athal*); name of the agu who is famous for his sharp ears.

ག་ནི། *gani,* another spelling for *dgāni;* the agu may have received his name on account of his armour (*gani*)

7.

ཞིབ་དཔོན། *zhib dpon*, officer at the Ladakhi court, who has to provide flour.

མེ་ར། *me ra*, = *me sgra*, roaring of fire.

ཆར་ལ། *charla*, explained as meaning 'till the middle' of a house.

སློག་པ། *slogpa*, sheep-skin worn by women.

བྱ་ཁྱུ་ཡུག། *bya khuyug*, = *khuyu*, the 'hornless bird,' name of the sun-bird; perhaps because he is never of the shape of a horn, in opposition to the moon.

ཐར་ངད་བཏང་ཅས། *thar ngad btangcas*, do the work of a smith.

པེན། *pen*, probably *dpen*, sign; Lad. Grammar, Laws of Sound, No. 5.

རྒྱ་ལོང་། *rgya long*, a mirror brought from China.

རྙག། *rnyag*, a single hair.

8.

པུར་ཆ། *purcha*, peg.

མལ་ཙ། *mal tsa*, = *mal sa*, bed.

པོན་གྲོ། *pon gro*, bunch, bundle.

ནུ་མེན། *numen*, is also a name of a lapis lazuli.

གདུབས། *ɣdubs*, = *ɣdub*, ring.

ཛ་ལ། *ala*, plaster.

རྣ་ལི་བག་ཕེ། *rnali bag phe*, pap

མུ་ཟ། *muza*, Yarkandi boots; related to Urdu *moza*.

རྣམས་ཅས། *rnamscas*, accept.

9.

གྱང་སྐོར། *gyang skor*, wall round the castle.

ཡ་མ་དུ་ལི་ལ། *yamadulila*, together.

གྲ་ཕོག། *gra phog*, the first blow in a polo-game.

བཀྲུད་ཅས། *bkrudcas*, to drag along.

པུགས་མོ། *pugsmo*, knee.

སེན་ཏིག། *sentig*, a yellow bird; (here the name of the sun-bird?).

སྤྲུན་གསུམ་མཚོགས། *spun ysum mthsogs*, 'like the three brothers' (sons of *dBangpo rgyab zhin?*). This is the Lower Ladakhi rendering of *phun sum thsogs*, perfect.

A LOWER LADAKHI VERSION OF THE KESAR SAGA.

LIST OF PERSONAL AND LOCAL NAMES, AND OTHER PROPER NOUNS OCCURRING IN THE KESAR SAGA

The following contains a list of all the proper nouns found in those Chapters of the Kesar Saga and kindred literature, which have been published by me till 1912. Besides the 'Lower Ladakhi Version of the Kesar Saga', the following works must be mentioned:

I.—'The Paladins of the Kesar Saga,' a collection of Sagas from Lower Ladakh, J.P. A.S.B., New Series, Vol. II, 1906, pp. 467 ff, Vol. III, pp. 67 ff, Vol. III, 1907, pp. 261 ff. This collection consists of the following five tales.

(1) The Tale of Kesar's beloved Mon.
(2) The Tale of *sKya-ba-rgod-po.*
(3) The Tale of *Shel-li-bu-zhung.*
(4) The Tale of *Gong-ma-bu-thsa's* boy and *rGyal-sa-dkar-po.*
(5) The Tale of *gSer-ri-bu-zhung.*

II.—Der Frühlings- und Wintermythus der Kesarsage, Mémoires de la Société Finno-ougrienne No. XV, Helsingfors, 1902. An English translation of the spring-myth (Frühlingsmythus) is found in the Indian Antiquary, Vol. XXXI, 1902. It consists of the following nine tales:

(1) of the Agus.
(2) of *dBang-po-rgyab-bzhin's* three sons.
(3) of *Don-grub's* fitting out for the land of *Gling.*
(4) of *Don-grub's* birth on earth.
(5) of *Khro-mo* who sought to harm Kesar.
(6) of the maiden *'aBru-gu-ma.*
(7) of *'aBru-gu-ma* who became Kesar's bride.
(8) of Kesar who teases *'aBru-gu-ma.*
(9) of the wedding.

The winter-myth consists of the following tales:

(1) Kesar's departure for the north.
(2) Kesar's arrival before the devil's castle in the north.
(3) Kesar's victory over the devil of the north.
(4) Kesar's return to *Gling.*
(5) Kesar's journey to *Hor.*

(6) Kesar's doings with the smith of *Hor*.
(7) Kesar's preparations for the combat with the King of *Hor*.
(8) Kesar's victory over the King of *Hor*.
(9) Kesar's return to *Gling*.

III.—The Ladakhi Pre-buddhist Marriage Ritual, Text and Translation published in the Indian Antiquary, Vol. XXX, 1901, pp. 131ff. The first nine songs only of this hymnal have been published; they treat principally of the 'tree of the world.'

IV.—The *Gling-glu* of Khalatse is a hymnal of nine songs, sung at the occasion of the spring—or Kesar—festival at Khalatse. It is found in Ladakhi Songs, Songs No. XXI–XXIX. Indian Antiquary, Vol. XXXI, 1902.

The *Gling-glu* of *Phyi-dbang* is a similar hymnal from the village of *Phyi-dbang*. It was published under the title 'A Ladakhi Bonpa Hymnal' in the Indian Antiquary, Vol. XXX, 1901, pp. 359 ff.

V.—The seven sagas contained in the Lower Ladakhi Version of the Kesar Saga contained in the present volume, are as follows:

(1) Prologue to the Kesarsaga, pp. 1–29.
(2) The Story of Kesar's birth, pp. 30–83.
(3) The Story of 'aBru-gu-ma's marriage to Kesar, pp. 84–138.
(4) Kesar's Journey to China, pp. 139–163.
(5) Kesar's Victory over the giant of the north, pp. 164–199.
(6) Capture of 'aBru-gu-ma by the King of Hor, pp. 200–255.
(7) Defeat of the King of Hor, pp. 256–321.

In the following list are included all the proper nouns occurring in:

1. 'A Lower Ladakhi Version of the Kesar-Saga,' (S).
2. 'The Paladins of the Kesar-Saga,' (P).
3. 'Der Frühlings- und Wintermythus der Kesarsage, (La, Lb).
4. The *Gling-glu* of Khalatse, and the *Gling-glu* of Phyi-dbang, (Gl. Kh.; Gl. Ph.).
5. The Ladakhi Pre-buddhist marriage-ritual, (M.R.).

Nos. 2–5 are all reprinted as *Appendices*. Large numerals refer to the parts of each work, and if followed by a small numeral connected by a hyphen, the latter indicates the subsection as the part.

ཀ།

ཀ་བུ་ལུ། *Ka-bu-lu*, (unintelligible), a goat killed and sacrificed by Kesar, before leaving for China. S. 4-1.

ཀ་རོག་ཡང་འཛིན། *Ka-rog-yang-'adzin,* (unintelligible), commander of the smiths of *Gling*, S. 6-7. He assists Kesar on the road to *Hor*, S. 7-1. Mentioned in P. 3. The sccond half of the name means in Ladakhi 'Seirer of joy.'

ཀ་ལ་ཀོལ། *Ka-la-kol,* (unintelligible) first cc untry of the world, S. 1.

ཀ་ལི་སྨཱན་ནི་མེན་ཏོག་གི་ཇོ། *Ka-li-mān-ni-men-tog-gi-jo,* 'Lord of the Kali-mān-flower,' a name of Kesar, Gl. Kh. 8.

ཀུན་བྱུང་ཐར་རྙེད། (or corrupt:.... ཐང་རྙེད) *Kun-byung-thar-rnyed,* 'he who finds delivcry for all creatures.' Kesar's name as smith in *Hor*. Lb. Compare *mGar-phrug-thang-rnyed*.

ཀུན་ལ་མཛེས་པའི་ཀུན་མཛེས་རོལ་མ། *Kun-la-mdzes-pai-Kun-mdzes-rol-ma,* 'Tārā, more beautiful than all,' nickname of Maiden *Go-chod*, P. 3.

ཀེ་སར། *Ke-sar,* King of *Gling*, son of *Gog-bzang-lha-mo*, S. 2 ff. Principal figure of the Kesarsaga. He is generally called *Gling-rgyal lham-Ke-sar*. He makes men of bones in S. 5-3. He does not allow the ogres to eat human flesh or horse flesh. He makes rain in S. 7-2. He takes the shape of a crow in P. 3 and calls *dPal-moi-a-stag* to assist *rGyal-sa-dkar-po*. There he is called *A-bā Kesar*, 'father Kesar.' See also P. 4-5 and Gl. Kh. 1. Compare *Gling-rgyal-lha*, etc.

ཀེར་ཟོང་སྙན་པོ། *Ker-zong-snyan-po* or *Pha-lha-skyer-rdzong-snyan-po* Kesar's father-god (*pha-lha*), S. 2. See under *Pha-lha*, etc.

ཀྱལ་ཀྱིལ། *Kyal-kyil,* a well. P. 4. (*'akhyil* means 'whirl.')

ཀྱེ་སར། *Kye-sar,* see *Ke-sar*. This spelling is found in S. 3-1. It is explained as *skye-gsar*, the 'reborn one.' The name is said to refer to Kesar's rebirth on earth after his death in heaven. The spelling *Kye-sar* is in correspondence with the popular pronunciation of this name in Lahoul, Zangs-dkar, and other tracts.

ཀྲ་ཕུས་སེ། *Kra-phus-se*, (unintelligible) a rat born to *Gog-bzang-lha-mo* in the forest, La. N.

ཀླུ་རྒྱལ་ལྗོགས་པོ། *Klu-rgyal-ljogs-po*, (*ljogs-po*=*lcog-po*), the 'lower Nāga-king.' (Compare *ljam*=*lcam*, spouse.) S. 2. He is connected with the colours black or blue, S. 5-2. He has a black sheep on his shoulder which is explained as a lotus-flower, P. 3-4. Offerings to him M.R. 1.

ཀླུ་སྐྱིན། *Klu-skyin*, 'Nāga ibex,' he asks Kesar to protect all the ibexes. S. 3-5.

ཀླུ་རྟ་སྔོན་ཆུང་། *Klu-rta-sngon-chung*, the 'little blue Nāga-horse' name of the horse of King *lCog-po*, La. 7.

ཀླུ་མོ་དར་གྱི་གོ་ཆོད་མ། *Klu-mo-dar-gyi-go-chod-ma*, the 'clever Nāgī, one of the ice,' she lives in a lake, she is the only being who is able to read Kesar's letter. S. 6-7.

ཀླུ་མོ་དར་གྱི་མཐོང་མཛེས་མ། *Klu-mo-dar-gyi-mthong-mdzes-ma*, the 'Nāgī of the ice, beautiful to look at,' P. 1.

ཀླུ་མོ་དར་གྱི་ཡང་མཛེས་མ། *Klu-mo-dar-gyi-yang-mdzes-ma*, the 'Nāgī of the ice, beautiful in her play,' P. 1.

ཀླུ་ཡུལ། *Klu-yul*, 'the land of the Nāgas,' the lowest of the three empires of the world. It has 18 towns. P. 1. The many riches, children, and cattle of the *Klu*, Lb. 5, 16, 17. It is covered by the roots of the tree of the world.

དཀར་ཐིག་མ། *dKar-thig-ma*, 'the white-spotted one' (?), the eldest daughter of the forefather *mGar-ba* at *Gling*-castle. S. 1. She is called *Gog-bzang-lha-mo's* younger sister, in S. 1. *A-ne-bkur-dman-mo* takes her shape in S. 2 and La. 4. Mentioned in P. 4.

དཀར་པོའི་དངུལ་རི། *dKar-poi-dngul-ri*, the 'white silver-hill.' It is formed out of the ogre's heart (creation-story). S. 1.

དཀར་མོའི་སྟོང་ཤོང་། *dKar-moi-stong-shong,* the 'white hold a-thousand,' the chief of all bags, probably a metaphor for the cloud. It is brought from the castle *Pa-chi-dpal-ldong,* S. 1. It is called *skye-mo-dKar-moi-stong-shong* in S. 2. There it is the mother of *Phad-khra-bo.* (*skye-mo,* a mistake for *sgye-mo.*)

བཀའ་བློན་ལྡན་པ། *bKā-blon-ldan-pa,* 'the minister, the owner' the fifteenth of the eighteen *agus;* he has a man's head, S. 1. He acts as the traitor among the Agus in P. 1. He seizes *'aBru-gu-ma* and the *Gling* castle, when Kesar is in *Klu-yul.*

བཀའ་བློན་ལྡན་པ། *bKā-blon-ldan-pa,* 'the minister, the owner,' or 'minister *lDan-pa,*' son of *bDud-lha-cin,* Kesar's enemy, S. 2-9.

བཀུར་དམན་རྒྱལ་མོ། *bKur-dman-rgyal-mo,* the 'honourable female, the queen,' name of *dBang-po-brgya-byin's* wife. She takes the shape of *dKar-thig-mo.* Called *bKur-dman-mo* in La. 4, or *A-ne-bkur-dman-mo* in Lb. 1. Gl. Kh. 2-5.

བཀུར་འཛོམས། *bKur-'adzom,* 'collected honour,' name of the maid-servant of the smith of *Hor.* Lb. 6.

བཀྲ་ཤིས། *bKra-shis,* 'happiness,' name of the forefather, S. 1. Compare *mGar-ba-bKra-shis.*

བཀྲ་ཤིས། *bKra-shis,* 'happiness,' name of the smith of *Gling,* P. 4. Perhaps identical with the preceding.

རྐང་རྐང་རིངས། *rKang-rkang-rings,* 'long leg'; the thirteenth of the eighteen agus; he has a foot instead of a head. S. 1. He is one of the seven agus accordirg to P. 2. He carries the water from the sea to the castle of *Gro-yul,* P. 2. A *Be-da-rKangs rings* is mentioned in S. 6-7.

རྐྱང་ཁྲ་མེ་ལོང་། *rKyang-khra-me-long,* the 'kiang, the falcon, the mirror,' name of the horse of *rGyal-sa-dkar-po.* P. 4. A flame is seen burning on its head. It is opened and closed with a key.

རྐྱང་རྒོད་དབྱེར་པ། *rKyang-rgod-dbyer-pa*, compare *rKyang-byung-dbyer-pa*. The meaning of *dbyer-pa* is uncertain. The first part of the name means 'wild Kiang,' or 'born from a Kiang.' S. 1 ff. Kesar's horse. It is sent back from the north, whilst Kesar goes to *Gliṅ*. Together with its arrival spring sets in. S. 6-7. The hair of this horse is plucked and placed on the head by the people, as a sign of blessing, P. 3-4. It is killed with a sling by *mDā-dpon-phru-gu*, when he obtains *rKyang-khra-me-long*, as his horse. See also La, Lb.

རྐྱང་བྱུང་ཁ་དཀར། *rKyang-byung-kha-dkar*, 'Offspring of the Kiang, white-mouth,' the horse born to *Gog-bzang-lha-mo*, La. N.

རྐྱང་བྱུང་དབྱེར་པ། *rKyang-byung-dbyer-pa*, Kesar's horse, identical with *rKyang-rgod-dbyer-pa*, born to *rGod-ma-thsa-langs*, S. 2-8, La. 3.

སྐད་སྙན་གླིང་བུ། *sKad-snyan-gling-bu*, the 'flute of sweet sound,' a place (probably) made of the ogre's nose, (account of the creation) S. 1.

སྐྱ་དང་ཟར་བུ་དོལ་ཐོག་རོལ་མ། *sKya-dang-zar-bu-dol-thog-rol-ma*, 'Tārā of the soup-spoon, ladle, and stone-pot'; nickname of maiden *Go-chod*, P. 3.

སྐྱ་བ་དཀར་པོ། *sKya-ba-dkar-po*, 'white ladle,' son of *sKya-ba-rgod-po*, P. 2.

སྐྱ་བ་རྒོད་པོ། *sKya-ba-rgod-po*, wild ladle, the fifth of the eighteen agus. He has a ladle instead of a head. S. 1. The story of his son see P. 2. He is eaten by a Yak and delivered from the Yak's stomach by his son. P. 2.

སྐྱིན་ཆེན་བ་རྒན། *sKyin-chen-ba-rgan*, 'the big ibex, the old cow,' born to *Gog-bzang-lha mo*. S. 2-7.

སྐྱེ་སེར་རླུངས་པོ། *sKye-ser-rlungs-po*, 'the wind, the producer of coolness.' He created the upper and lower valleys. M.R. 3.

ཁ།

ཁ་རྒན་[ད]གའ་ནི། *Kha-rgan-[d]-gā-ni, Kha-rgan* means 'old mouth,' the third of the 18 Agus. He has a white beard. S. 1. He goes to *lJang-yul*, P. 4; to the horse-market in *Hor*. Lb. 6.

ཁ་ཅུལ། *Kha-cul,* Kashmir. It is famous for its rice. S. 7-1. P. 3, reads *Kha-chul.*

ཁ་ར་གུ་རམ་སྦྲང་རྩི་རོལ་མ། *Kha-ra-gu-ram-sbrang-rtsi-rol-ma,* 'Tārā of sugar, syrup, and honey,' nickname of *Go-chod.* P. 3.

ཁ་ལ་མེ་བར། *Kha-la-me-bar,* 'Fire burning in his mouth,' name of the principal of all stallions (*rTa-pho*) S. 1. This horse was robbed by the King of Hor. S. 6-4. It is able to fly through the air. Kesar brings it back to *Gling* after a riding contest in *Hor.* P. 3.

ཁུང་འབྲུག། *Khung-'abrug,* the 'thunder-dragon.' Killed by Kesar in his fifth year. Lb.

ཁྱ་བ་ལག་རིངས། *Khya-ba-lag-rings,* see *Khyab-pa-lag-rings* S. 5-1. P. 4.

ཁྱབ་པ་ལག་རིངས། *Khyab-pa-lag-rings,* 'coverer, long-hand,' a name of the devil in S. 5-1, 3. Probably the husband of *Dze-mo-bam-za-'abum-skyid.* Killed by Kesar. He roars in his grave. Kesar mutters certain mystic formulas over him, to keep him in his grave. He was killed by Kesar in Kesar's sixteenth year, see Gl. Kh. 3.

ཁྱི་གུ་ཁྲ་ཆུང་། *Khyi-gu-khra-chung,* the 'little piebald dog.' He will be *Khyi-mo-ltom-dkar-mo's* comfort, when *Khyi-pho-gser-lings* goes to the north. S. 5-1.

ཁྱི་ལྗག། *Khyi-ljag,* 'dog-sling,' name of *'aBru-gu-ma's* sling. P. 1.

ཁྱི་ཕོ་གསེར་ལིངས། *Khyi-pho-gser-lings,* the 'dog golden-hunt,' born to *Khyi-mo-dkar-mo,* S. 2-8. He goes to the north. S. 5.

ཁྱི་མོ་དཀར་མོ། *Khyi-mo-dkar-mo*, the 'white bitch,' the mother of all dogs, brought from *Pa-chi-dpal-ldong*-castle. Compare *Khyi-mo-ltom-dkar* in S. 5-1. She is the mother of *Khyi-pho-gser-lings*, S. 2-8. According to La. N., *Khyi-mo-dkar-mo* is the mother of *Drum-bu-brang-dkar*.

ཁྱི་མོ་ལྟོམ་དཀར། *Khyi-mo-ltom-dkar*, the 'bitch with a white belly,' compare *Khyi-mo-dkar-mo*, with whom she may be identical. She wails on account of *Khyi-pho-gser-ling's* departure to the north. S. 5-1. She takes his place whilst he is away, S. 6-2.

ཁྱུ་མ་ཚ་ལངས། *Khyu-mo-thsa-langs*, 'mother of many, envy raising' horse of *Seng-chen-rgyal-lham* Lb. 6.

ཁྱེམ་བུ་པང་ཀ་ཏོག་ཙེ་རོལ་མ། *Khyem-bu-pang-ka-tog-tse-rol-ma*, 'Tārā of the shovel and pick-axe,' nickname of *Go-chod*. P. 3.

ཁྲ་སྐྱ་དཀར་པོ། *Khra-skya-dkar-po*, the 'white falcon.' Her nest is on the sixth bough of the tree of the world. She has an iron egg M.R. 8. Kesar takes her shape Gl. Kh. 6. Gl. Ph. 6.

ཁྲ་མིག་ཡང་ཤན། *Khra-mig-Yang-shan*, 'piebald eye full of joy,' a lady-friend of *dPal-moi-a-stag*, in *dPal-yul*, P. 4. *Yang shan* is *Yangs-can*.

ཁྲའི་མགོ་ཁྲའི་ཐུང་། *Khrai-mgo-Khrai-thung*, 'falcon-head, three years old'; the fourth of the eighteen agus. He has a falcon's head, S. 1. In S. 2 he is called *Khrai-mgo-Khru-thung*. In S. 3-2, where the spelling *Khrai-thung* is again found, we read that he was made the head of the land of *Gling* and was supposed to receive *'aBru-gu-ma* as his bride. In S. 4-1, Kesar sends him to China in his place. When Kesar goes to China, the agu makes himself King of *Gling* during the former's absence. Kesar kills him on his return from China, S. 4-4. During Kesar's journey to *Byang* he resides at *lDem-ldem-mi-ldem-mkhar*. He makes a weak attempt to deliver *'aBru-gu-ma* from the King of *Hor*, but is frightened by the voices of the Turks, S. 6-3. He kills *'aBu-dmar-lam-bstan* by roughly pulling the arrow out of his wound. Kesar punishes him for this by placing a heavy load on his back on the way to *Hor*, S. 6-7. He is frightened by two Nāgīs. P. 1. He is one of the group of seven agus according to P. 2. In P. 4 we read that *'aBu-dmar-lam-bstan* forgives him his faults.

ཁྲི་རྒྱ་མཚོ་ཆེན་མོ། *Khri-rgya-mthso-chen-mo*, the 'great occan of the throne'; *rGyal-sa-dkar-po* goes there. P. 3-4.

ཁྲོ་མོ། *Khro-mo*, the name seems to mean 'anger.' One of *gSer-ri-bu-zhung's* followers in P. 5. He is called *Agu-Khro-mo* in L. 1. His character is bad. He tries to kill the child *Ke-sar*. But he is thrown against a rock, and one side of his body is burnt. La. 5. According to La. 8, he kills the devil-bird.

ཁྲོམ་ཆེན་མོ། *Khrom-chen-mo*, the 'great market.' The place where Kesar's wedding is celebrated. S. 3-7.

འཁྲུལ་རྟ་རྐང་གསུམ། *'aKhrul-rta-rkang-gsum*, the 'three-legged magical horse.' It belongs to the heroes of *Hor*. S. 6-2, S. 7-7.

ག།

གངས་སྟོད་མཐོན་པོ། *Gangs-stod-mthon-po*, the 'high glacier,' the home of *Seng-ge-gYu-ral-can*, S. 5-1.

གངས་རི་དཀར་པོ། *Gangs-ri-dkar-po*, the 'white glacier,' Kailāsa, Lb. 1.

གུར་དཀར་རྒྱལ་པོ། *Gur-dkar-rgyal-po*, 'King of the white tent,' the real name of King *Hor-pa-hal-de* S. 6-2. His altar (*lha-tho*) is of a brown or violet colour. It is destroyed by Kesar. S. 7-6. When he is killed by Kesar, the latter is almost drowned in his fat. S. 7-8. He is called *Gur-dkar-lde-hor* in Lb. 6. He is also mentioned in Lb. 3 and P. 4.

གུར་གུམ་ཚས། *Gur-gum-thsas*, 'garden of calendula flowers.' The garden of Kesar's horse. Lb. 1.

གུར་རྨུག་བླ་མ། *Gur-rmug-bla-ma*, 'priest of the brown tent,' the priest of the King of *Hor*. S. 7-3.

གོ་ཆོད། *Go-chod*, the 'clever one,' servant-girl of *Shel-ldang-lha-mo*. She was given to nine peasants in turn as a bride; but could not agree with any of them. P. 3.

གོ་ཞེན་དང་ཡུག་དར་དཀར་རོལ་མ། *Go-shen-dang-yug-dar-dkar-rol-ma*, 'Tārā of velvet and white silk.' Nickname of *Go-chod*. P. 3.

གོག་ཟ་ལྷ་མོ། *Gog-za-lha-mo*, compare *Gog-bzang-lha-mo*, Kesar's mother on earth. La. 4.

གོག་བཟང་ལྷ་མོ། *Gog-bzang-lha-mo*, (unintelligible), earthly mother o King Kesar. S. 2. She lived in the cold valley (*Grang-ngi-lung-pa*). *Pa-sang-ldan-rva-skyes* was her husband, but not Kesar's father. According to P. 4 she was the third daughter of smith *bKra-shis*.

གོང་མ་བུ་ཚ། *Gong-ma-bu-thsa*, the 'upper boy,' belongs to the group of seven agus. He is sent out to catch Kesar, who appears as a spy from *Hor*. S. 7-6. He takes the shape of a falcon and of a weasel. In S. 7-7, he is called *Gong-ma-no-no*. His horse is called *Dung-gi-dar-dkar*. He is a great archer, see S. 7-7. He goes to *lJang-yul*, see P. 4.

གྲང་ངི་ལུང་པ། *Grang-ngi-lung-pa*, 'cold valley,' near *Ka-la-kol* S. 1. Place of agu *Pa-sang-ldan-rva-skyes* S. 2. Spelt *Drang-gilung-pa* in P. 1.

གྲི་གུ་སོར་གསུམ། *Gri-gu-sor-gsum*, 'Knif: of a length of three fingers,' Kesar's knife; perhaps identical with *Dug-pa-can-gri-gu* mentioned in P. 1. See Lb. 8.

གྲུ་གུ་གཡུ། *Gru-gu-gYu*, a country. The nyo-pas of the King of that country go to ('*a*)*Gro-yul*, P. 3.

གྲེ་ཞ་སྤུན་བདུན། *Gre-zha-spun-bdun*, 'the seven *Gre-zha*,' killed by Kesar in his second year, Lb. 8. They are probably identical with *Dre-zha-Kham-ba*, Gl. Kh. 4.

གྲོ་མ་ཐང་། *Gro-ma-thang*, the 'plain of *Gro-ma* roots.' S. 1-2. La. 6.

གྲོ་ཆེན་རྒྱལ་པོ། *Gro-chen-rgyal-po*, the 'great King of *Gro-yul*.' P. 2.

གྲོ་མོ་སོ་དཀར། *Gro-mo-so-dkar*, 'lady of *Gro* [land] with white teeth,' daughter of the King of *Gro-yul*. Her name is also spelt *Gro-mo-so-gar*, P. 2.

གྲོ་ཡུལ། *Gro-yul*, 'land of wheat,' or 'land of creatures,' a mythological country. The name is also erroneously spelt *'aGro-yul*, P. 2. This country is called *bDud-yul*, 'devil's realm' in P. 3-4.

གླག་མོ་མཁལ་དཀར། *Glang-mo-mkhal-dkar*, 'eagle white kidney,' name of the bird whose nest is found on the fourth bough of the tree of the world. She has a silver egg. M.R. 8.

གླིང་། *Gling*, the earth; or *gling-dkar*, the 'white earth.' S. 1. *Gling-bzhi*, the four continents, mentioned in S. 2-9. *Gling-bzhi-gru-brgyad*, the four continents with eight corners. S. 5-1. See also La. 1.

གླིང་མཁར་རྩེ་དགུ། *Gling-mkhar-rtse-dgu*, 'castle of *Gling* with nine pinnacles,' S. 1-2. It contains the stores of old meat and old butter. S. 6-3. It is destroyed by King *Gur-dkar* of *Hor*. On its top, *'aBu-dmar-lam-bstan's mchod-rten* is built. P. 4. See also Lb. 3.

གླིང་གི་མགོ་རི། *Gling-gi-mgo-ri*, 'chief-mountain of *Gling*,' name given to Kesar, after his victory over *Bya-nyi-ma-khyung-rung*, S. 3.—7. V. 1.

གླིང་རྒྱལ་ལྷམ་ཀེ་སར། *Gling-rgyal-lham-Ke-sar*, 'Kesar, the divine King of *Gling*.' The principal figure of the Saga. His birth, his marriage to *'aBru-gu-ma*, his victory over the giant of the north name victory over the Ḳing *Gur-dkar* of *Hor*; his journey to China. In S. 5.2, he is connected with the colour green (*ljang-khu*). His ugly shape is connected with hail and storm; his beautiful shape is connected with sunshine.

དགའ་ནི་གོང་བ། *dGā-ni-gong-ba*, (or: *Ga-ni-gong-ba*) perhaps: 'the highest collar,' name of the eleventh of the 18 agus. He has a collar instead of a head. S. 1. *'aBru-gu-ma* asks him to cast lots; he is Kesar's rival as a suitor for *'aBru-gu-ma*. S. 3.4. He is called *dGā-ni* in La. 1. According to La. 6 he sits on a golden throne. In La. 8 we find him connected with gold and copper. In Lb. 3 he is called *dGā-ni-mgon-po*. *Agu-Ga-ni* is one of the seven agus of the saga. S. 7.7.

དགུང་ཕྲུག་ཁྲ་སྐྱ། *dGung-phrug-khra-skya*, 'child of the midday, light-coloured falcon'; name of an agu, mentioned in Lb. 6.

དགུང་སྟོད་མཐོན་པོ། *dGung-stod-mthon-po*, 'the high zenith,' compare *gNam-stod-mthon-po*, Gl. Kh. 6.

མགར་ཆ་ཆོ་རོན། *mGar-cha-cho-ron* (=*chos-sgron*), 'Portion of the smith, light of virtue,' name of the smith's daughter in *Hor*. S. 7.5. Compare *Chos-ma-sgran*.

མགར་ཕྲུག་ཐང་རྙེད། *mGar-phrug-thang-rnyed*, 'child of the smith, found on the plain.' Kesar's name when he was an apprentice to the smith of *Hor*. S. 7.7. Compare *Kum-byung-thar-rnyed*.

མགར་ཕྲུག་སེང་གེ་དོན་ལྡན། *mGar-phrug-seng-ge-don-ldan*, 'child of the smith, possessing the qualities of a lion.' Name given to Kesar by the King of *Hor*, when he delivered him from the bow-string. S. 7.5.

མགར་བ་བཀྲ་ཤིས། *mGar-ba-bkra-shis*, 'smith-happiness,' or *A-pho-bkra-shis*, 'forefather happiness.' Name of the forefather who resided at the *Gling*-castle. S. 1.

མགར་མོ་ལྕམ། *mGar-mo-lcam*, 'the female smith, the wife,' name of the water-carrier or wife of smith *He-mis*. Kesar calls her his sister. S. 7.3.

མགར་ར་ཧི་མིས། *mGar-ra* (=*mgar-ba*)-*hi-mis*, 'smith *Hi-mis*,' smith of the King of *Hor* S. 7. Kesar pretends to be his son. He assists Kesar in making the iron rope, by which Kesar climbs up to the top of the *Hor* castle.

མགོ་བོ་ལྡད་དཀར། *mGo-bo-ldad* (=*glad*)-*dkar*, 'white head,' name of a bird whose nest is found on the third bough of the tree of the world. '*aGro-yul*, a mistake for *Gro-yul*. She has a pearl-white egg. M.R. 8.

རྒོད་པོ་འི་དཔལ་ལེ། *rGod-poi-dpal-le*, see *dPal-le-rgod-po*, S. 3-3.

རྒོད་མ་ཚ་ལངས། *rGod-ma-thsa-langs*, the mare 'Rising of envy.' The first of horses. S. 1. She is the mother of *rKyang-rgod-dbyer-pa*. S. 2-7, S. 5-1. La. N. *Shel-li-bu-zhung* rides on her. P. 3. She is called *Thsa-ldang* in La. N.

རྒྱ་གར་ཡུལ། *rGya-gar-yul* (=*rGyal-dkar*), 'the white expanse,' India. '*aBru-gu-ma* says that she has seen it. Some people assert that she came from India. Gl. Ph. 8. M.R. 5.

རྒྱ་སྟག་ཁྲ་བོ། *rGya-stag-khra-bo*, 'the many-coloured rope,' probably the rain-bow, the chief of ropes. S. 1. It was brought from the castle *Pa-chi-dpal-ldong*. It is the mother of *Thag-bu-khru-gang*.

རྒྱ་དར་རྩེ། *rGya-dar-rtse*, 'summit of extensive ice,' name of a village. P. 4.

རྒྱ་ནག། *rGya-nag*, the 'black expanse,' China. S. 4. It is covered with leprosy S. 4-3. The leprosy disappears on Kesar's arrival. S. 4-4. It is famous for its silk-cloth showing patterns of dragons. S. 7-1, P. 3. The *ngo-pa* from *rGya-nag* go to *Gro-yul*. P. 3.

རྒྱ་ནག་ཁྲི་སྐོར་གསུམ། *rGya-nag-khri-skor-gsum*, the three provinces of China. S. 4-2.

རྒྱ་ནག་རྒྱལ་པོ། *rGya-nag-rgyal-po*, 'King of China.' Kesar sends illness to him. He sends a bird to Kesar as a messenger; after that he sends a man formed of earth and his own blood as a messenger. Kesar comes and heals him from leprosy. S. 4. The son of the King of China carries off *Shel-ldang-lha-mo* of *Gro-yul.* P. 3.

རྒྱ་བོང་ཁ་དཀར། *rGya-bong-kha-dkar,* the 'chief donkey with a white mouth.' He goes to the north. S. 5.1. Compare *Nag-po-kha-dkar.*

རྒྱབ་རྟེན་ཕོ་ལོང་། *rGyab-rten-pho-long,* the 'back-leaning rock,' a rock made out of the ogre's kidneys. S. 1.

རྒྱལ་ལྕང་། *rGyal-lcang,* the 'royal willow,' the willow of the world. Its roots are in *gYog-klu,* and its highest branches in *sTang-lha.* It has six boughs. S. 3.7. MR.

རྒྱལ་ལྕང་ལྕང་གི་ལྕང་སྟོད། *rGyal-lcang-lcang-gi-lcang-stod,* the 'upper part of the royal willow' (willow of the world). Name of a place in *Gling* S. 3.7. The gods walk about there. Gl. Kh. 1.

རྒྱལ་བུ་རྒྱལ་ས། *rGyal-bu-rgyal-sa,* 'Prince grandson (?)' a name of *Shel-li-bu-zhung* or of *rGyal-sa-dkar-po* P. 3. He fights against the heroes of *Gro-yul,* but runs away before *Ri-bo-blon-chen.* He is saved by *dPal-moi-a-stag.* He is also called *rGyal-bu-shel-dkar.* P. 4. (*rgyal-sa=rgyal thsa,* royal grandson).

རྒྱལ་ཚ་ཞལ་དཀར། *rGyal-thsa-shel-dkar,* Kesar's son, killed by *Gur-dkar* of *Hor,* Lb. 4.

རྒྱལ་ལམ་ཆེན་མོ། *rGyal-lam-chen-mo,* 'great King,' name given to Kesar by the wild sheep. P. 3, Gl. Kh. 1. Compare *Gling rgyal lham,* Kesar.

རྒྱལ་ས་དཀར་པོ། *rGyal-sa-dkar-po,* the 'white prince,' name of Kesar's son who fights against *lJang-yul,* P. 4.

རྒྱུ་མ་རོང་། *rGyu-ma-rong,* gorge made of the ogre's intestines (Creation of the world). S. 1.

སྒེ་མོ་དཀར་མོ་འི་སྟོང་ཤོང་། *sGe-mo-dkar-moi-sTong-shong*, 'white bag holds a thousand,' the cloud. S. 1-9. Compare *dKar-moi-stong-shong*.

ང །

དངུལ་གྱི་རི། *dNgul-gyi-ri*, 'silver-hill.' It is situated on the road to *Dri-mo-dgu-chod*. S. 3-4.

སྔོ་རོག་པོན་པོན། *sNgo-rog-pon-pon*, 'blue-black, with a curled mane,' name of *dPal-le's* horse, S. 2; received from mother *sKyabs-bdun*. It takes the place of *rKyang-rgod-dbyer-pa*, when Kesar goes to the north. S. 6. In P. 4 it is the name of agu *Ga-ni-gong-ba's* horse. Mentioned in Lb. 6.

སྔོན་པོ་འི་གཡུ་རི། *sNgon-poi-gYu-ri*, the 'blue turquoise hill,' mentioned in S. 2. P. 4.

ཅ །

ཅུ་རུ་ལུ་གུ། *Cu-ru-lu-gu*, (*lu-gu* perhaps = *Klu-dgu*, 'nine nāgas') name of *Khyab-pa-lag-rings*, the devil. S. 5-1. Lb. 1-3. Name of a '*aBrong* or wild yak in P. 4. Killed by Kesar in his eighth year. Lb. 8.

ཆ །

ཆུ་མིག་ཚང་ཡ། *Chu-mig-thsang-ya*, a well, made of the ogre's eyes (Creation of the world). S. 1-2.

ཆུ་སྲམ་ཀ་མ། *Chu-sram-ka-ma*, the 'whitebreasted otter'; it is also called *Chu-sram-brang-dkar*, Gl. Kh. 6.

ཆོ་རོན། *Cho-ron*, see *Chos-sgron-ma*. Lb. 7.

ཆོས་སྒྲོན་མ། *Chos-sgron-ma*, 'lamp of religion (dharma)' name of the daughter of the smith of *Hor*. She is also called *mGar-cha-cho-ron.* Lb. 7.

ཆོས་སྒྲོལ། *Chos-sgrol*, 'delivery by religion (dharma),' name of the smith's wife, La. N. *Cho-rol* in La. 6 is *'aBru-gu-ma's* mother. *Cho-rol* is the same as *Chos-sgrol.*

ཇ།

ཇོ་ཇོ་འབྲུ་གུ་མ། *Jo-jo-'abru-gu-ma*, (*'abru-gu* means a 'little grain'). *Jo-jo* means 'lady.' Kesar's wife. At first she was to be given to agu *Khrai-thung*. S. 3-2. She is turned out, and sent into a black tent, when Kesar goes to China. Her hill is of blue colour. S. 5-2. According to S. 6-2 *'aBru-gu-ma's* upper half was of gold, her lower half of turquoise; but according to S. 5-2, her hair was very black, and her teeth and nails of the whitest. She fights against King *Gur-dkar*, but is frightened by the loud roar of his attendants. Then she becomes his wife. S. 6-3. As she is guilty of having caused the death of *'aBu-dmar-lam-bstan*, she is punished by Lucerne being grown on her head for three years. S. 6-4. In P. 4 we read that she inserted medicine in the horse's ear. In Gl. Kh. we read that thunder is caused by her walking in heaven. Compare *'aBru-gu-ma* and *aBrug mo*. She is of milk-white colour. Gl. Ph. 4.

ལྗང་ཡུལ། *lJang-yul*, the 'green country.' It is situated beyond the frontier of sun and moon. P. 4. Kesar's son makes war against it; he marries the princess of this country.

ལྗང་ས་གཡུའི་ཆོ་རོན་མ། *lJang-sa-gYui-cho-ron-ma*, the 'turquoise light of religion (dharma), daughter (?) of *lJang*,' name of the daughter of the King of *lJang-yul*. She is gained by Kesar's son *rGyal-sa-dkar-po*. P. 4. Abridged *lJangs-cho-ron*.

ལྗངས་སི་དམ་རྒྱལ་པོ། *lJangs-si-dam-rgyal-po*, (*si-dam* ?), name of the King of *lJang-yul*. P. 4.

ཉ།

ཉ་མོ་གསེར་མིག། *Nya-mo-gser-mig*, the 'female fish golden-eye,' name of the fish, born to *Gog-bzang-lha-mo*, S. 2.7. La. N. Lb. 1. *'aBru-gu-ma* takes her shape. Gl. Kh. 6. It is also called *Khyu-ru-nya-mo.*

ཉི་མ། *Nyi-ma*, the sun, born to *Gog-bzang-lha-mo*; his home is *gNam-stod-mthon-po*, the high zenith. S. 2.7. In S. 6.7, the *nyi-ma-spun-bdun*, the 'seven sun-brothers,' are mentioned. This seems to refer to the calendar of the seven agus. In MR. 3, the sun is called *Khri-gdugs-nyi-ma*, the 'throne-umbrella,' and also 'creator of east and west.'

ཏ།

ཏི་བང་བང་། *Ti-bang-bang*, name of a mountain in Upper *Gling* (*Gling-stod*). There the treasures obtained from *Bya-nyi-ma-khyung-rung* are distributed. S. 3.7.

ཏི་སུར་རུ། *Ti-sur-ru*, name of a high mountain in *Gling*, from the top of which the three realms of the world can be seen. From here Kesar's letter is read to all by Nāgī *Dar-gyi-go-chod-ma*. S. 6.7. Also *rGyal-bu-rgyal-sa's* wedding is proclaimed from the top of this hill. P. 3.

ཏོམ་ལྗག། *Tom-ljag*, name of a jewel which has the power to keep everybody motionless in a certain place. It is broken to pieces by mice.

གཏོར་བ་ནག་པོ། *gTor-ba-nag-po*, 'black oblation' (?), name of the Nāga who lives at the feet of *Shel-ldang-lha-mo* in *'Gro-yul*. He is mistaken for a donkey. P. 3.

བརྟན་འཛིན་དམར་པོ། *brTan-'adzin-dmar-po*, the 'red holder of the earth' (?), name of a giant (?). La. 3.

ལྟ་བ་མིག་གི་རབ། *lTa-ba-mig-gi-rab*, 'seer good-eye,' name of one of the seven agus who is able to see at a tremendous distance. S. 7.6. Also called *lTa-ba-mig-gi-rab-l[h]a*. He accompanies *rGyal-sa-dkar-po* to *lJang-yul*. P. 4.

ལྟོང་དཀར་མ། *lTong-dkar-ma*, 'white notch,' name of Kesar's arrow.

སྟ་རི་ཟླ་བ་དཀར་པོ། *sTa-ri-Zla-ba-dKar-po*, 'hatchet white moon,' the moon. S. 1.9.

སྟག་གཟིག། *sTag-gzig*, the Tajiks, Eastern Persian tribes. Persia, the *nyo-pa* from this country go to *'Gro-yul* to ask for the hand of the princess. P. 3.

སྟང་ལྷ་ཡུལ། *sTang-lha-yul*, the 'upper land of the Gods,' one of the three parts of the world; heaven; it is of white colour, also called *sTeng-lha*, etc. S. 1.2. La. 1. The *nyo-pa* from *sTang-lha* go to *'Gro-yul*, to ask for the hand of the princess. P. 3.

སྟེང་ལྷ་ཡུལ། *sTeng-lha-yul*, see *sTang-lha-yul*.

ཐ།

ཐག་པ་རྒྱ་སྟག (=ཐག་ཁྲ་)བོ། *Thag-pa-rgya-stag(=thag)-khra-bo*, 'rope many-coloured,' the rainbow. S. 1.9. See *rGya-stag-khra-bo*.

ཐག་བུ་ཁྲུ་གང། *Thag-bu-khru-gang*, 'rope one full yard in length,' name of a rope, born to *rGya-stag-khra-bo*. S. 2.8.

ཐང་དཀར་མགོ་དཀར། *Thang-dkar-mgo-dkar*, the 'white-headed white falcon,' he looses his strength on the *Srar*-pass. Gl. Kh. 5.

ཐང་སྟོད་མཐོན་པོ། *Thang-stod-mthon-po*, the 'high plain,' the home of the wolf *Shang-ku-mjug-rdum*. S. 5.1.

མཐོ་བ་རྟ་མགོ་མ། *mTho-ba-rta-mgo-ma*, the 'hammer [of the size of] a horse's head,' name of the hammer of the smith of *Hor*. Lb. 5.

དར་དཀར་ཙེ། *Dar-dkar-tse*, 'summit of white ice,' the home of *rGyal-sa-dkar-po* P. 3.

དར་སིང་། *Dar-sing*, 'the ice-lion,' name of the glacier. Compare *Seng-ge-dkar-mo*. M.R. 2.

དར་ལྷ་གོ་ཆོད་མ། *Dar-lha-go-chod-ma*, the 'clever goddess of the ice (or of the silk),' name of *'aBru-gu-ma's* maid-servant. P. 4. Compare *Go-chod*. La. 6, Lb. 1.

དུག་གི་མཚོ། *Dug-gi-mthso*, 'poisonous lake,' a lake situated in *Grang-gi-lung-pa*, P. 1. The Rakas. Tal is called by that name.

དུག་པ་ཅན་གྲི་གུ། *Dug-pa-can-gri-gu*, 'poisonous knife,' Kesar's Knife. He uses it to cut his way out of the stomach of the Yak which had swallowed him. S. 7-2. The King of *Hor* is killed with it. S. 7-8.

དུག་ཤ་ཕོ་ལོང་། *Dug-sha-pho-long*, 'rock poison-flesh.' A rock on the road to the 'land of the birds.' S. 3-6. It seems to be a yak according to P. 3. It is subdued by Kesar in his sixth year. Lb. 8.

དུང་གི་སྒྱིད་བུ། *Dung-gi-sgyid-bu*, 'hearth-stone of shell,' one of the treasures of *Gling-mkhar*, carried off by King *Gur-dkar*, S. 6-4. P. 3.

དུང་གི་དར་དཀར། *Dung-gi-dar-dkar*, 'silk-white' or 'ice-white,' 'being [made] of shell,' name of a horse given to *Gong-ma-bu-thsa*. S. 7-6. P. 3. It is to be given to Kesar's servant-boy *Byang-phrug*. Occasionally the name is spelt *Dung-ri-dar-dkar*. According to P. 4, it is agu *dPalle's* horse.

དུང་གི་བ་རི། *Dung-gi-ba-ri*, (bari ?), name of teacher *rTse-dgu's* monastery. P. 3.

དུང་སྦལ་དཀར་པོ། *Dung-sbal-dkar-po*, 'pearl white cell,' 'white frog of shell,' born to *Gog-za-lha-mo*, in *Bar-btsan*. La. N.

དེག་བུ་ཁ་དམར། *Deg-bu-kha-dmar*, 'pot with a red mouth,' perhaps the sun. The chief of utensils brought from the castle *Pa-chi-dpal-ldong*. S. 1, 2-8.

དེག་བུ་སྐྱེ་རིངས། *Deg-bu-skye-rings*, 'pot with a long neck,' born to *Deg-bu-kha-dmar*. S. 2-8.

དོང་གསུམ་མི་ལ་སྔོན་མོ། *Dong-gsum-mi-la-sngon-mo*, the, 'blue one, three faces to a man,' name of the son of forefather *bKra-shis*. He killed the dragon, out of whose body the world was built. S. 1.

དོན་གྲུབ་དཀར་པོ། *Din-grub-dkar-po*, 'the white Siddhārtha,' name of the third son of the King of heaven. He dies in heaven and is reborn as King Kesar on earth to *Gog-bzang-lha-mo*, after she had eaten a hail-stone. S. 1-3. His flesh becomes iron. S. 2. Mentioned in P. 3. He is called *Don-grub* in La. 1, Gl. Ph. 3-6.

དོན་ལྡན། *Don-ldan*, 'having a purpose,' name of the eldest son of the King of heaven. S. 1-2. La. 1. P. 3.

དོན་ཡོད། *Don-yod*, 'having a purpose,' name of the second son of the King of heaven. S. 1-2. La. 1. P. 3.

དོན་ཡོད་གྲུབ་པ། *Don-yod-grub-pa*, Amoghasiddha, guardian King of the North. Offerings to him in M.R. 1.

དྲག་ལྷ་རྒྱལ་མོ། *Drag-lha-rgyal-mo*, the 'terrible queen of the gods'; she takes the place of *Ma-lha-bkur-dman-rgyal-mo*, when Kesar is in the north. S. 6-2.

དྲང་གི་ལུང་པ། *Drang-gi-lung-pa*, the 'straight valley,' identical with *Grang-gi-lung-pa*. P. 1.

དྲང་གེ། *Drang-gè*, the 'true one,' name of one of Kesar's servants. S. 3-5.

དྲི་མོ་དགུ་ཆོད། *Dri-mo-dgu-chod*, said to mean 'smell of dung,' name of the valley, where *Pa-sang-ldan-ru-skyes* and *Gog-bzang-lha-mo* are sent to. S. 3-2.

དྲུམ་བུ་བྲང་དཀར། *Drum-bu-brang-dkar*, 'lascivious, with a white breast,' name of a little dog, born to *Khyi-mo-dkar-mo*. La. N.

དྲེ་ཞ་ཁམ་བ། *Dre-zha-kham-ba*, 'brown mules,' tended by Kesar. Gl. Kh. 4.

དྲོ་མོ། *Dro-mo*, the mother of all sheep. La. N. brought from *Pa-chi-dpal-ldong*. She will be ***Ma-mo-kham-ba's*** comfort, when *Pho-lags-mgo-gser* goes to the north. S. 1, 2-5. *Dro-mo* is a mistake for *gro-mo*, brown.

དྲོང་གེ། *Drong-ge*, name of one of Kesar's servants. S. 3-5.

བདུད་ཅུ་རུ་ལུ་གུ། *bDud-cu-ru-lu-gu*, the devil *Cu-ru-lu-gu*, a name of *Khyab-pa-lag-rings* as well as of the King of *Hor*. S. 2, 3-6, 5-2. Compare *Cu-ru-lu-gu*.

བདུད་བྱ་ར་བྷན་དྲེ། *bDud-bya-ra-bhan-dre*, 'devil-watchman, the [Buddhist] priest,' name of a devil subdued by the horse *rKyang-byung-dbyer-pa*. P. 3.

བདུད་རྩིའི་ཆུ་མིག། *bDud-rtsii-chu-mig*, 'well of nectar,' literally: 'of the devil's honey,' name of a spring which has its origin underneath *dBang-po-rgya-byin's* throne. S. 2. Perhaps identical with *bDud-rtsi-'o-mai-chu-mig*, 'well of nectar and milk,' found in the land of the devil. Lb. 4. It has medical properties.

བདུད་ཡུལ། *bDud-yul*, 'land of the devil,' in the north. S. 5-2. Lb. 4. The ogres *Mon-pa* and *Mon-sring* are sent there, after they have given trouble in *Klu-yul*. They go there to eat poisonous snakes. P. 1.

བདུད་ལྷ་ཅིན། *bDud-lha-cin*, (= gcin ?) 'urine (?) of the gods,' name of a devil. S. 2.9. The name *lha-cin* seems to be corrupted from *lHa-byin*, pronounced *lHa-jin*, Devadatta.

མདའ་དཀར་པོའི་ལམ་བསྟན། *mDā-dkar-poi-lam-bstan*, 'arrow, white way-leader,' name of an arrow. It takes the place of *mDā-mo-gser-mdā-mjug-rings*, when Kesar goes to the north. S. 6.2. Agu *dPal-le* shoots with this arrow and hits the heart-artery of the King of *Hor*. Only Kesar is able to save the king. S. 3.5. It is also used by *rGyal-sa-dkar-po*. P. 3. P. 4.

མདའ་དཔོན་གོང་མ། *mDā-dpon-gong-ma*, 'high captain of the archers,' name of the seventh of the eighteen agus. He has an arrow blade instead of a head. S. 1. He belongs also to the group of seven agus. S. 7.7. He delivers captive *Ang-gar-ltsangs-pa*, by cutting the rope of his cage with his arrow. S. 7.7. He finds out that poison was put in *'aBru-gu-ma's* beer. S. 7. He dies when *Ri-bo-blon-chen* is killed by *dPal-moi-a-stag*, when he is crushed to death by the thumb of the falling giant. P. 3. He is advised to take rebirth in *sTang-lha*. P. 3. He is *Gong-ma-bu-thsa's* father. P. 4.

མདའ་མོ་ནག་པོའི་སྲོག་ཆོད། *mDā-mo-nag-poi-srog-chod*, 'black arrow, taker of life,' name of one of *rGyal-sa-dkar-po's* arrows. P. 3.4.

མདའ་མོ་དམར་པོའི་ཁྲག་ལྡགས། *mDā - mo - dmar - poi - khrag - ldags*, 'red arrow, blood-licker,' name of one of *rGyal-sa-dkar-po's* arrows. P. 3.4.

མདའ་མོ་གསེར་མདའ་མཇུག་རིངས། *mDā-mo-gser-mdā-mjug-rings*, 'golden arrow, long tail,' name of Kesar's arrow. It accompanies him to the north. S. 6.2.

མདུང་དཔལ་འཇམ་རིང་མོ། *mDung-dpal-'ajam-ring-mo*, 'glorious, smooth and long spear.' Name of Kesar's spear. It is also called *dPal-'ajam-sngon-mo*, 'glorious, smooth and blue.' P. 3. S. 2.

རྡོ་ཆོད་མ། *rDo-chod-ma,* 'stone-cutter,' name of a sword. Used by agu *dPalle* ii. S. 2, 6.4; by Kesar in S. 5.1. It is also called *rDo-ba-chod-ma.* S. 6.2.

རྡོ་རྗེ་སེམས་དཔའ། *rDo-rje-sems-dpā,* Vajrasattva, guardian King of the East; an offering to him mentioned in M.R. 1

ལྡེམ་ལྡེམ་མི་ལྡེམ་མཁར། *lDem-ldem-mi-ldem-mKhar,* 'shaky castle,' name of a castle. It wails, when the *Gling-mkhar* goes to the north. S. 2, 5.1. It takes the place of *Gling-mkhar,* when the latter goes to the north. S. 6.2. Kesar goes there for meditation. P. 1, 4.

སྡང་མ་སྤྱང་ཁྲ། *sDang-ma-spyang-khra,* 'angry wolf-falcon,' apparently the name of one of the agus. Lb. 3.

སྡིག་པ། *sDig-pa,* 'sin,' 'sinful,' name of the giant-devil. La. 3.

སྡིག་པའི་གྲི་གུ་སོར་གསུམ། *sDig-pai-gri-gu-sor-gsum,* 'knife three fingers long of the sinful,' Kesar's knife. Lb. 2.

སྡིག་སྤྱོད་རྒྱལ་པོ། *sDig-spyod-rgyal-po,* 'King of sinful behaviour,' name of the minister of the King of *Hor.* Lb. 5.

ན།

ནག་ཁྲ་གློ་རིངས། *Nag-khra-glo-rings,* 'black falcon, long lungs,' name of *dPal-moi-a-stag's* horse. S. 7.6. P. 4.

ནག་ཐིག་མ། *Nag-thig-ma,* the 'black-spotted woman (?),' name of the second daughter of forefather *mGar-ba.* S. 1. She is called a younger sister of *Gog-bzang-lha-mo* in S. 2. Mentioned in P. 4.

ནག་པོ་ཁ་དཀར། *Nag-po-kha-dkur,* 'black with a white mouth,' name of the first of all donkeys. It is brought from *Pa-chi-dpal-ldong-mkhar.* S. 1. The mother of *Bong-bu-kham-pa.* S. 2.8.

ནག་ཤང་ཤང་། *Nag-shang-shang*, 'the clever black man (?),' name of the smith of *Hor*. Lb. 5.

ནང་གོང་། *Nang-gong*, Bàltistan; it is blessed with sweet apricots. P. 3.

ནུབ་ཕྱོགས་ཨུ་རྒྱན་གླིང་། *Nub-phyogs-u-rgyan-gling*, 'Udyāṇa of the west,' mentioned in M.R. 9.

གནམ་ཁྱེད་མ་ཕ་ལི་། *gNam-khyed-ma-pha-li*, 'shield comprising the sky,' name of Kesar's shield. S. 5-1.

གནམ་སྟོད་མཐོན་པོ་། *gNam-stod-mthon-po*, 'the high zenith,' the 'home of sun and moon,' S. 5-1. *'aBru-gu-ma* goes there, Gl. Kh. 6.

རྣ་གཡུ་རྣ་རྩལ་། *rNa-gYu-rna-rtsal*, 'turquoise of the ear, sharp ear,' name of the 17th of the group of 18 agus. S. 1. He belongs also to the group of seven agus. S. 7-7. He is also called *rNa-gYu-rna-'athal*. According to P. 4, he is *mDā-dꝑon-gong-ma's* son and identical with *Gong-ma-bu-thsa*. He has a turquoise instead of a head.

སྣང་བ་མཐའ་ཡས་། *sNang-ba-mthā-yas*, Amitābha, guardian King of the West. Offering to him in M.R. 1.

པ །

པ་ཆི་དཔལ་དོང་། *Pa-chi-dpal-dong*, 'castle of treasures' (?). From this castle the most useful animals, seeds and treasures are brought. S. 1.

པ་ལེ་། *Pa-le*, probably identical with *dPal-le-rgod-po*. P. 5. He has a red tent.

པ་སང་ལྡན་རྭ་སྐྱེས་། *Pa-sang-ldan-rva-skyes*, 'possessing the Friday, horns-growing,' name of the first of the 18 agus. He has a goat's head. S. 1. He is weaving in *Grang-gi-lung-pa* S. 2. *Me-me-rTse-dgu* calls him 'Kesar's father.' This is a lie. S. 3. His wife is *Gog-bzang-lha-mo*.

པན་ཆུང། *Pan-chung*, or *Pan-jung*, 'little Paṇḍit,' a name given to Kesar in S. 3.4.

པི་དབང་རྒྱལ་ཆེན། *Pi-dbang-rgyal-chen*, 'great king of the mice' (*pi-tse*) name of the king of the mice. P. 4.

པི་དབང་བློན་ཆེན། *Pi-dbang-blon-chen*, 'great minister of the mice,' name of the minister of the mice. P. 4.

པི་མོ་གསེར་རལ་ཅན། *Pi-mo-gser-ral-can*, 'mouse with golden locks,' name of *gSer-ri-bu-zhung's* wife. P. 5.

པི་ཙེ་ཡུལ། *Pi-tse-yul*, 'land of mice.' P. 4.

པེ་ནག། *Pe-nag*, 'black *Pe* (?),' name of the commander of the Mons of *Gling*. S. 6.7.

དཔལ་མའི་ཨ་སྟག། *dPal-mai-a-stag*, 'glorious *A-stag* (?),' S. 2, name of the female agu. She takes *'aBru-gu-ma's* place, when Kesar is in the north. S. 6.2. She is called Kesar's wife (*bTsun-mo*) in P. 3. She is the commander of the women of *Gling*. S. 6.7. She fights with a spear, S. 7.1, and belongs to the group of seven agus. S. 7. She is sent after the spy of *Hor* who in reality is Kesar. S. 7.6. Kesar reveals himself to her. She receives *Ang-gar-ltsangs-pa* in her arms, when he comes dropping down in his cage. A description of this heroine is given in P. 3. She has long hair, long teeth, and long breasts. She fights against *Ri-bo-blon-chen*, the hero of *Gro-yul*. and delivers *rGyal-sa-dkar-po*. P. 3. She is given as bride to the wazir of China, and at the occasion of the dance begins to kill the Chinese. P. 4.

དཔལ་ཡུལ། *dPal-yul*, 'glorious country,' the home of *dPal-mai-a-stag*. P. 4.

དཔལ་བོ་ཡུལ། *dPal-bo-yul*, 'glorious country,' perhaps identical with *Bal-po-yul*, Nepal. *'aBru-gu-ma* knows it from hearsay. Gl. Ph. 8.

དཔལ་ལེ་རྒོད་པོ། *dPal-le-rgod-po* (*rgod-po* = *rgad-po*), 'the old glorious one,' name of the 16th of the 18 agus. He has an old man's head. S. 1. He is called the son of a smith's daughter; she could not walk at first. Then he became a great archer. S. 6.2. He kills *'a-Bu-dmar-lam-bstan's* murderer, *Shang-kra-mi-ra*, but forgets to save the latter's life. S. 6.4. He is called the commander of the heroes of *Gling*. S. 6.7. P. 2. He belongs to the group of seven agus. P. 2. He hits the heart-artery of the King of *Hor* with his arrow. S. 7.5. He almost kills *'aBru-gu-ma* in his rage. He goes to *lJang-yul*. P. 4. According to La. 6 he sits on a throne of shell. He is connected with shell and lead. La. 8. He also kills the devil-bird in assisting *dBang-po-brgya-byin*, and asks the latter to send Kesar to earth. He also brings the treasures from *Pa-chi-dpal-ldong* to Gling. La. 1. S. 1.

དཔལ་ལེ་པ། *dPal-le-pa*, the 'glorious ones,' or perhaps better *Pal-le-pa*, 'frying-pans,' for their lives are contained in frying-pans. Name of seven ogres (*srin-po*). P. 5.

སྤང་སྟོད་མཐོན་པོ། *sPang-stod-mthon-po*, 'the high meadow,' the home of *'aBrong-chen-kham-pa*. S. 5.1.

སྤོ་མཐོ་ནང་མ། *sPo-mtho-nang-ma* (or *sPro-mtho*, etc.), 'inner place of high pleasure,' name of the hunting place which was made out of the ogre's little stomach.. See the account of the creation of the world. S. 1, 2. P. 4.

སྤྱང་ཀུ་མཇུག་ཟླུམ། *sPyang-ku-mjug-zlum*, 'the bushy-tailed wolf.' He looses his strength on the *Srar*-pass. Gl. Kh. 5.

སྤྱན་མིག་བཟང་། *sPyan-mig-bzang* (= *Mig-mi-bzang*), Virūpāksha, guardian King of the West. M.R.' 4.

ཕ།

ཕ་ལྷ་སྐྱེར་རྫོང་སྙན་པོ། *Pha-lha-sKyer-rdzong-snyan-po,* 'the father-god the well-sounding (speaking ?) *sKyer-rdzong* (?),' name of the highest Tibetan God, who is often identified with Indra. S. 2. P. 3-4. In S. 6-2, we find the spelling *Phas-lha* (= *pha-sla*)-*Ker-zong-snyan-po.* He is called *Pha-lha-snyan-po* in M.R. 1.

ཕད་ཁྲ་བོ། *Phad-khra-bo,* 'the many coloured bag,' (a cloud ?), born to *dkar-moi-stong-shong.* S. 2-8.

ཕས་ལྷ་རབ་ལྷ། *Phas-lha-rab-lha* (= *Pha-sla-rab-lha*), 'father-god, real god'; he takes the place of *Pha-lha-skyer-rdzong-snyan-po,* when Kesar is in the north. S. 6-2.

ཕོ་རོག་ནག་ཆུང་། *Pho-rog-nag-chung,* 'the little black crow,' it looses its strength on the *Srar*-pass. Gl. Kh. 5.

ཕོ་རོག་འབྱང་ཤེས། *Pho-rog-'abyang-shes,* 'crow of pure wisdom,' name of two crows of the King of *Hor.* S. 6-1. They are killed by *'aBu-dmar-lam-bstan.*

ཕོ་ལགས་མགོ་གསེར། *Pho-lags-mgo-gser,* the 'yellow-headed ram,' name of a ram. It goes to the north with Kesar. S. 5-1.

ཕོ་ལད་གྱད་གཞུ། *Pho-lad-gyad-gzhu,* the 'hero's bow of steel,' name of Kesar's bow. S. 2. It was robbed by King *Gur-dKar* of *Hor.* S. 6-4. P. 3. The heroes of *Hor* try in vain to bend it. Kesar alone is able to do so. The King of *Hor* is caught with its string. S. 7-5.

ཕོ་ལད་དི་སྟེ་པོ་རང་ཆོད། *Pho-lad-di-ste-po-rang-chod,* 'steel-axe which cuts of itself,' name of an axe, born to *Zla-ba-dkar-po.* S. 2-8. It may be identical with *Pho-lad-dkar-poi-steb-chung,* mentioned in S. 7-2.

འཕགས་སྐྱེད། *'aPhags-skyed,* Virūḍhaka, guardian King of the South. Mentioned in M.R. 4.

བ།

བ་ལུ་ཏུང་ཏུང་། *Ba-lu-tung-tung*, the 'white dwarf'; he makes arrangements for Kesar's and *'a-Bru-gu-ma's* marriage feast. S. 7-3. (*Ba-lu* = *rBa-lu*.)

བན་ཆུང་སྲོང་པོ། *Ban-chung-srong-po*, the 'little priest-vagabond,' name given to Kesar by the people of *Gling*. P. 3.

བར་བཙན། *Bar-btsan*, the 'firm place in the middle,' name of the earth. Its colour is red. Compare the Indian Baghwa colour. S. 2. The *nyo-pas* from there go to *Gro-yul*. P. 3.

བལ་ཁོལ་མ། *Bal-khol-ma*, 'wool-servant' (?), servant girl of the smith of *Hor*. S. 7-5.

བི་ལ་ཁྲ་སུག། *Bi-la-khra-sug*, the 'many-coloured cat,' born to *Bi-la-nag-mo*. She wails on account of *Bi-la-nag-chung's* departure for the north. S. 5-1.

བི་ལ་ནག་ཆུང་། *Bi-la-nag-chung*, the 'little black cat'; he accompanies Kesar to the north. S. 5-1.

བི་ལ་ནག་མོ། *Bi-la-nag-mo*, the 'black she-cat,' the mother of all cats. S. 1. She was brought from *Pa-chi-dpal-ldong* castle. The mother of *Bi-la-khra-sug*. S. 2-8.

བུ་རངས། *Bu-rangs*, Purang; a Tibetan province east of Guge; the name *bu-hrangs* seems to mean 'children only.' It is blessed with beautiful girls. P. 3.

བུ་རིག། *Bu-rig*, Purig, province between Lower Ladakh and Kashmir. The name seems to mean 'clever boys.' It is blessed with white wheat and flowers. P. 3. It is famous for its white wheat. S. 7, and 1.

བེ་ད་རྐང་རིངས། *Be-da-rkang-rings*, the '*Be-da* with long legs'; he is in command of the *Be-da* (a low caste) of *Gling*. He may be identical with *rKang-rkang-rings*. S. 6.7. P. 3.

བེན་པོ། *Ben-po*, 'pitcher (?),' 'pestilence (?),' name of a *Bon-po* priest who ran a race with a Buddha on mount *Ti-se*. P. 3. Compare a similar tale in *Mi-la-ras-pa*.

བེར་ཀ་ཚོམ་ཤིང་ཁྲུ་སུག། *Ber-ka-thsom-shing-khru-sug*, the 'many-coloured stick of gay colours,' (*khru-sug* = *khra-sug*) name of a stick belonging to the dwarfs. It has the power to provide every thing its possessor wants to get. S. 7.1.

བོང་ཐིལ། *Bong-thil*, 'middle part of a donkey,' name of *'aBru-gu-ma's* sling. P. 1.

བོང་ནག་ལྡུམ་བུ། *Bong-nag-ldum-bu*, 'black ass, lettuce,' name of the 14th of the 18 agus. He has a donkey's head. S. 1. He goes to the horse market. See Lb. 6.

བོང་བུ་ཁམས་པ། *Bong-bu-kham-pa*, 'brown ass,' name of a donkey, born to *Nag-po-kha-dkar*, S. 2.8. Apparently identical with *Bong-mo-kham-ba*, S. 5.1.

བོང་མོ་ཁམས་བ། *Bong-mo-kham-ba*, the 'female brown donkey.' She wails on account of *rGya-bong-kha-dkar's* departure for the north. S. 5.1.

བོད་ཡུལ། *Bod-Yul*, Tibet, mentioned in M.R. 5.

བོར་གར། *Bor-gar*, Bulgaria, a country famous for its leather, (Russian leather). S. 5.1. Apparently identical with *Bo-gar*, mentioned in P. 1, as a country famous for its powder.

བྱ་ཁུ་ཡུག་རྒྱལ་པོ། *Bya-khu-yug-rgyal-po*, 'bird cuckoo, the king,' name of the grandfather of the sun-bird. S. 1.

བྱ་ཁྲུང་ཁྲུང་དཀར་མོ། *Bya-khrung-khrung-dkar-mo,* the white storks, name of the birds that were sent to fetch Kesar back from *bDud-yul.* S. 6.4. These birds are white storks or cranes.

བྱ་རྒྱལ་རྒོད་པོ། *Bya-rgyal-rgod-po,* the 'wild (or: old ?) king of the birds'; he is born to *Gog-bzang-lha-mo,* S. 2.7. La. N. Lb. 1. His nest is found on the second bough of the tree of the world. He has a turquoise egg. M.R. 8.

བྱ་ཆེན་ཁྱུང་། *Bya-chen-khyung,* the 'great bird *Khyung*' (garuḍa); her nest is on the first bough of the tree of the world. She has a golden egg. M.R. 8.

བྱ་ཉི་མ་ཁྱུང་རུང་། *Bya-nyi-ma-khyung-rung,* the 'sun-bird.' S. 1. Kesar cuts off his wing. S. 3.6. A description of this bird is given in P. 3, ps. 290, 291. The spelling *Khyung-dkrung* is also found.

བྱ་ཕྲན་ཤོག་ཐོག། *Bya-phran-shog-thog,* the 'little bird with wings,' born to *Gog-bzang-lha-mo.* S. 2.7.

བྱ་དབང་ལྡན་དབང་ཕྱུག། *Bya-dbang-ldan-dbang-phyug,* 'bird, rich in powder'; the father of *Shel-ldang-lha-mo.* P. 3.

བྱ་མོ་དཀར་མོ། *Bya-mo-dkar-mo,* the 'white hen,' (probably the moon), the wife of *Bya-nyi-ma-khyung-rung,* S. 3.6. Kesar lives with her for one month. According to L, No. 9, she is the wife of the sun-bird.

བྱ་མོ་ལྡོ་རེ། *Bya-mo-ldo-re,* 'bird *lDo-re* (?),' a bird sent to Kesar by the Chinese. S. 4.1.

བྱ་ཚང་མའི་ཡུལ། *Bya-thsang-mai-yul,* the 'land of all the birds,' or *Bya-yul,* 'bird-land'; the home of *Bya-nyi-ma-khyung-rung.* S. 3.6.

བྱ་འོང་ལྡོ་རེ། *Bya-'ong-ldo-re,* 'bird *'Ong-ldo-re,*' the father of the sun-bird. S. 1. Compare *Bya-mo-ldo-re.*

བྱ་ཤོག་ཐོག། *Bya-shog-thog*, the 'bird with wings.' He wails, when the woods go to the north. S. 5.1. Compare *Bya-phran-shog-thog*.

བྱ་སོ་མིག་དམར། *Bya-so-mig-dmar*, 'bat red-eye,' the younger brother of the sun-bird. S. 1. He must guard the way of the sun. S. 3.6. Kesar kills him with his arrow, before killing *Bya-khyung-rung-nyi-ma*. S. 3.6.

བྱང་ཐང་། *Byang-thang*, 'northern plain,' the steppe-district, north-east of Ladakh. It is blessed with salt and wools. P. 3.

བྱང་ཕྲུག། *Byang-phrug*, 'child of the north,' name of the tiny servant-boy of *Gling*. He rides on *Dung-ri-dar-dkar*. He may be identical with *Gong-ma-bu-thsa*. P. 3.

བྱིལ་ཕྲུག་རྒན་ཛར། *Byil-phrug-rgan-jar*, the 'naked little bird'; he is born to *Gog-bzang-lha-mo* in the field. La. N.

བྲག་སྟོད་མཐོན་པོ། *Brag-stod-mthon-po*, 'the high rock.' It is the home of *sKyin-chen-la-rgan*. S. 5.1.

བྲག་ཚན་དུང་དུང་། *Brag-thsan-dung-dung*, (= *rdung* ?) the 'clapping rocks (?),' the opening and shutting rocks. (Scylla and Charybdis.) S. 7.1, 2. The tail of *rKyang-rgod-dbyer-pa* is caught in this door. On Kesar's return journey this door opens only, when the heads of *'aBru-gu-ma's* children are thrown against it. S. 7.9. Lb. 8.

བྲག་བཟངས་པོ། *Brag-bzangs-po*, 'good rock,' or is it 'copper rock'? The home of the nine-headed ogre. S. 1.

བློན་པོ་མིག་དམར། *Blon-po-mig-dmar*, 'minister red-eye,' name of a minister of *lJang-yul* (apparently). He is killed by *rGyal-bu-shel-dkar*. P. 4.

བྷག་འཛོམས་མོ། *Bhag-'adzom-mo*, the 'assembled private parts,' name of a maid-servant of the King of *Hor*. Lb. 5.

དབང་པོ་རྒྱབ་ཞིན། *dBang-po-rgyab-zhin* (or *rgya-bzhin,* originally *brgya-sbyin*), Śatakratu, Indra. Name of the highest god. S. 1. P. 4. La. 1. M.R. 1. He was identified with the old Tibetan god *sKyer-rdzong-snyan-po.* Compare *lka-yi-dbang-po-rgyab-bzhin.*

དབུས་གཙང་། *dBus-gtsang,* name of the two principal provinces of Central Tibet. They are famous for their tea. S. 7-1. P. 3. M.R. 5.

འབུ་དཀར་ལྡུམ་བུ། *'aBu-dkar-ldum-bu,* 'white (round ?) worm,' name of one of the dragons, killed by Kesar. S. 4-3.

འབུ་ཁང་། *'aBu-khang,* 'house of dragons,' the greatest sight in China. S. 4-3.

འབུ་ནག་ལྡུམ་བུ། *'aBu-nag-ldum-bu,* 'black round (?) worm,' name of one of the dragons, killed by Kesar in China. S. 4-3.

འབུ་དམར་ལམ་བསྟན། *'aBu-dmar-lam-bstan,* 'red worm, way-leader,' name of the ninth of the 18 agus. He has a worm's or insect's head. S. 1. He is of the size of a thumb; he will be *'aBru-gu-ma's* comfort, when Kesar goes to the north. S. 5-1. Then he takes Kesar's place. S. 6-1. He is in possession of a *rib-shing* (Nebelkappe), to make himself invisible. He is a great archer. S. 6-2. His body is of steel, but underneath his shoulder there is a piece of flesh of the size of a mirror. He is killed by *Shankramiru's* arrow, when he was drinking water at a mill. S. 6-4. He is called a father in P. 3. Also mentioned in Lb. 8.

འབུ་གསེར་ལྡུམ་བུ། *'aBu-gser-ldum-bu,* 'golden round (?) worm,' name of one of the dragons, killed by Kesar in China. S. 4-3.

འབུམ་ཁྲི་རྒྱལ་པོ། *'aBum-khri-rgyal-po,* 'King of 100,000 thrones,' name of the King of the gods. Gl. Ph. 5.

འབུམ་ཁྲི་རྒྱལ་མོ། *'aBum-khri-rgyal-mo,* 'queen of 100,000 thrones,' name of the queen of the gods. Gl. Ph. 5.

འབྲི་གུ་མ། *'aBri-gu-ma,* 'Yak-cow,' one of the names of *'aBru-gu-ma,* S. 1, 3.7. Compare Lb. 5.27, 28, where *'aBru-gu-ma* is called *'aBri-mo,* 'yak-cow.'

འབྲུ་གུ་མ། *'aBru-gu-ma,* 'a little grain,' or if it was developed from *'aBri-gu-ma,* by assimilation of the vowel of the first syllable to that of the second 'little yak-cow,' name of Kesar's principal wife. S. 2. She was carried off by the King of *Hor* and regained by Kesar. S. 5, 6. She was instructed by lamas and received the name of *Shes-can-lha-mo* 'goddess of wisdom,' Gl. Ph. 4. She is the mother of *gSer-ri-bu-zhung.* P. 5. Compare *Jo-jo-'abru-gu-ma* and *la-Brug-mo.*

འབྲུག་མོ། *'aBrug-mo,* 'female thunder,' probably a contracted form of *'aBru-gu-ma.* Lb. 4.

Mr. Van Manen kindly favours me with the following important note in his letter of the 8-10-25. In my Hor-gling MS. quite in the beginning I find this important passage, occurring in the part relating the birth of *'aBrug-mo*:—

ཡ་སྟོན་གུང་ནས་འབྲུག་གཅིག་གྲགས།

དོགས་མོ་ས་ལ་ལྷམ་གཅིག་སྐྱེས།

དཀར་ཡག་གངས་ལ་སེང་གེ་འགྲིངས།

སེང་ལྷམ་འབྲུག་མོ་ཉེ་ནས་ཐོགས།

From the centre of the heavens a peal of thunder sounded.
On the narrow earth a lady was born.
On the white good ice a lion strutted.
Hence she was given the name of Lion-Lady-Thunder.

འབྲུས་སི་ཀ། *'aBrus-si* (= *kyi*) *ka,* 'carved pillar,' name of a pillar in the castle of *Hor.* It was the heart-artery of the King of *Hor.* Lb. 6.

འབྲོང་ཀ་ར་ཁམ་པ། *'aBrong-ka-ra-khum-pa,* 'brown wild yak of sugar,' name of a huge yak which guards the road to *Hor*; (a cloud or an avalanche (?)). He devours Kesar and his horse. He is killed by Kesar who cuts his entrails. S. 7-2.

འབྲོང་ཀ་ར་རིན་ཆེན། *'aBrong-ka-ra-rin-chen*, 'wild yak, precious sugar,' apparently a name of *Lag-dmar-blon-chen*. P. 3.

འབྲོང་ཀར་རལ་རིལ། *'aBrong-[d]kar-ral-ril*, 'wild yak with long white (?) hair,' name of a yak, killed by Kesar in his seventh year. Lb. 8.

འབྲོང་ཆེན་ཁམ་པ། *'aBrong-chen-kham-pa*, the 'big brown yak,' name of a yak born to *Gog-bzang-lha-mo*, S. 2-7, identical with *'aBrong-chen-ri-ri*.

འབྲོང་ཆེན་རི་རི། *'aBrong-chen-ri-ri*, 'big yak'; *ri-ri* is an exclamation used when tending yaks. S. 3-5. Identical with the preceding.

འབྲོང་བྱུང་རོག་པོ། *'aBrong-byung-rog-po*, 'wild offspring of the wild yak,' born to *Gog-za-lha-mo*. La. N. Lb. 1.

སྦང་ཆར་ཟིལ་བུ། *sBang-char-zil-bu*, the 'dewy soaking rain'; he is the creator of height and depth. M.R. 3.

སྦལ་ཁང་གྲུ་བཞི། *sBal-khang-gru-bzhi*, the 'four-cornered house of the dwarfs,' (*sba-lu* = dwarf), name of the castle of the dwarfs. As it is warm in winter, it is offered to Kesar as a winter-retreat. S. 7-1.

སྦལ་ཏི། *sBal-ti*, Baltistan. The name seems to be connected with *sBa-lu*, dwarf.' It is praised on account of its apricots. S. 7-1.

སྦལ་མོ་ཁྲོལ་འཛོམ་མོ། *sBal-mo-khrol-'adzom-mo*, 'female dwarf, splendour united'; name of the female dwarf who entered one of the dice. S. 7.1.

སྦལ་མོ་ཁྲོལ་ལེ་མོ། *sBal-mo-khrol-le-mo*, 'female dwarf of splendour.' Name of a lady-dwarf. S. 7-1.

སྦ་ལུ་དུང་དུང། *sBa-lu-dung-dung* (= *rdung*?), 'dwarf beater' (?), name of the dwarf who has power over the opening and shutting door of rock, over the stones, flying about between heaven and earth, and over the yak *'aBrong-ka-ra-kham-ba*. S. 7.1.

སྦ་ལུའི་ལམ་སྲངས། *sBa-lui-lam-srangs*, 'street of the dwarfs.' Kesar passes by it on his way to *Hor*. S. 7.1.

སྦི་ཆུ་རབས། *sBi-chu-rabs, (sbi = spyi ?)*, 'general ford (?),' name of the chief of all fords. S. 2. The best part of it given to Kesar. S. 3.2.

མ།

མ་གོག་བཟང་ལྷ་མོ། *Ma-gog-bzang-lha-mo*, third daughter of forefather *mGar-ba* of *Gling*. S. 1. See *Gog-bzang-lha-mo*.

མ་ཐེ་མ་བདག། *Ma-the-ma-bdag*, (unintelligible) name of an unknown country; the *nyo-pas* from there go to *Gro-yul*. P. 3.

མ་ཕང་། *Ma-phang*, instead of *Ma-'apham*, 'unconquered,' the Manasarowar lake. Lb. 1.

མ་མོ་ཁམ་པ། *Ma-ma-kham-pa*, the 'brown ewe.' She wails on account of *Pho-lags-mgo-gser's* departure for the north. S. 5.1.

མ་སལ་སལ། *Ma-sal-sal*, name of a pass on the road from *Gling* to *Hor*. S. 7.

མ་ལྷ་བཀུར་དམན་རྒྱལ་མོ། *Ma-lha-bkur-dman-rgyal-mo*, 'Mother-goddess, honourable queen'; or *Ma-sla Mas-lha*, etc.; name of the queen of heaven. S. 2. Compare *bkur-dman-rgyal-mo*. The protecting mother-deity of Kesar. He prays to her, when he is in danger, hardly ever to his paternal deity *Pha-lha-skyer-rdzong-snyan-po*. P. 3-4. S. 5.2.

མི་དབང་རལ་ཆུང་། *Mi-dbang-ral-chung*, 'ruler of men, little lock [of hair],' name of a hero of king *lHo-krab-rgyal-po*. He is called *bDud*. P. 4.

མི་དབང་རལ་ཆེན། *Mi-dbang-ral-chen*, 'ruler of men, large lock [of hair],' name of a hero of King *lHo-krab-rgyal-po*. P. 4.

མི་ཡུལ། *Mi-yul*, 'land of men,' identical with *Bar-btsan 'aDzam-bu-gling*, etc. S. 2.9. Gl. Kh. 1.

མི་ཡུལ་ལ་མེད་པའི་གྲོད་པ་ཆེ། *Mi - yul - la - med - pai - grod - pa - che*, 'great stomach, as is not found in the land of men.' Name of one of the seven Agus. He eats 100 sheep at a sitting. P. 2.

མིག་དམར། *Mig-dmar*, see *Blon-po-mig-dmar*.

མིག་སི་རི་རལ་གྲི། *Mig-si-ri-ral-gri*, 'sword glory of the eye,' name of a sword which takes the place of *rDo-chod-ma*, when Kesar is in the north.

མེ་མེ་མཚམས་པ། *Me-me-mthsams-pa*, 'grandfather hermit,' name of *Yabs-thon-pa's* uncle; possibly identical with *Slob-dpon-rtse-dgu*. S. 4.1.

མོ་ངན་ནི་སྲོང་ཕྲུག། *Mo-ngan-ni-srong-phrug* (*Mo-Mon*, Indian) 'the bad Mon, street child,' name of Kesar in his ugly form. Abridged *Srong-po*. S. 3, 2, 4. La. 5.

མོན་རྐང་ཁྱིལ། *Mon-rkang-khyil*, the '*Mon* round (oval ?) legs.' Name of the principal *Nyo-pa* (bride-bidder) of the Mons. P. 3.

མོན་གཅེས་པ། *Mon-gces-pa*, the 'dear Mon,' Kesar's friend. He is killed by the Agus, and two children, *Mon-va* and *Mon-sring*, come out of his stomach. P. 1.

མོན་པ། *Mon-pa*, 'the Mon' (Indian); name of the male ogre that came out of *Mon-gces-pa's* stomach. P. 1.

མོན་སྲིང་། *Mon-sring*, 'sister of the *Mon*'; name of the female ogre that came out of *Mon-gces-pa's* stomach. P. 1.

ཙ།

ཙེ་ཙེ་ངང་དམར། *Tse-tse-ngang-dmar*, 'goat red-duck,' name of the goat that causes Kesar's death in heaven. La. 3. According to La. N. she is the mother of all goats.

བཙན་རྟ་དམར་ཆུང་། *brTsan-rta-dmar-chung*, 'firm horse, little red one,' name of mother *sKyabs-mdun's* horse. La. 7.

རྩིད་བུ་སྐྱེ་དམར། *rTsid-bu-skye-dmar*, the 'red-necked he-goat.' He goes to the north. S. 5-1. Compare *Ra-skyes-skye-dmar*.

རྩུག་རྣ་རིན་ཆེན། *rTsug-rna-rin-chen*, (*gTsug-sna*?), 'various precious sciences (?), name of a Nāga; Kesar plays at dice with him. P. 1.

རྩེ་དགུ། *rTse-dgu*, 'nine summits,' name of an old hermit in *Grang-gi-lung-pa*. S. 1. Kesar asks him who is his father. S. 3-1. He is the commander of the lamas of *Gling*, S. 6-7. See also P. 1, 4.

རྩེ་ལྷ་སྙན་པོ *rTse-lha-snyan-po*, 'melodious (well-speaking?) god of the summit.' An offering brought to him. M.R. 1.

ཚ།

མཚལ་མིག། *mThsal-mig*, 'red eye,' name of the little sheep, born to *Dro-mo*. La. N.

མཚོ་མོ་མ་པང་། *mThso-mo-ma-pang*, see *Ma-phang*. P. 4.

མཚོམ་སྟོད་མཐོན་པོ། *mThsom-stod-mthon-po* 'the high lake,' the home of *Nya-mo-gser-mig*, S. 5-1. Gl. Kh. 6.

ཛ།

ཛེ་མོ་བམ་ཟ་བུམ་སྐྱིད། *Dze-mo-bam-za-bum-skyid*, 'hundred-fold happiness,' name of *Cu-ru-lu-gu's* wife. She becomes Kesar's wife, when he kills the devil. A daughter is born to them. S. 5. Lb. 2, 3. *Dze-mo* is an abbreviaticn of *mDzes-mo*, beautiful lady.

མཛོ་ཕོ་རྐང་དཀར། *mDzo-pho-rkang-dkar*, 'male *mdzo* white foot,' name of Kesar's *mdzo* used for ploughing. He was born to *mDzo-mo-ru-yon*. S. 2-8. S. 5-1.

མཛོ་མོ་རུ་ཡོན། *mDzo-mo-ru-yon*, the 'female *mdzo* with crooked horns,' the mother of all cattle. S. 1, 2-8; 5-1.

འཛམ་བུ་གླིང་། *'aDzam-bu-gling* (or *'aDzam-gling*), Jambudvīpa, the same as *mi-yul*. S. 2-9. Gl. Kh. 1. It is covered by the leaves of the tree of the world.

ཝ།

ཝ་མོ་འབྱོལ་ལི། *Wa-mo-'abyol-li*, the 'vixen who is clever in hiding.' She lives in the *Lung-pa-chen-mo*. Identical with *Wa-tse-'abyol-mo*. S. 5-1.

ཟ།

ཟ། *Za*, perhaps *za-ba* originally; 'the eater,' name of an agu or giant. La. 3.

ཟངས་དཀར། *Zangs-dkar*, 'white copper,' name of a province south-west of Ladakh. It is blessed with red yaks (or yak-butter ?). P. 3.

ཟངས་བུ་ཁ་ཆོད། *Zangs-bu-kha-chod*, 'kettle with a cover,' born to *Zangs-bu-kha-yon*. S. 2-8.

ཟངས་བུ་ཁ་ཡོན། *Zangs-bu-kha-yon*, 'copper-kettle with the crooked mouth,' perhaps the moon, the 'chief or utensils.' It is brought to *Gling* from *Pa-chi-dpal-ldong*. S. 1-9.

ཟམ་པ་དགུ་ཐུད། *Zam-pa-dgu-thud*, (= *'athud*) 'ninefold prolonged bridge.' Name of a bridge on the road to *Hor*. S. 7-2.

ཟླ་བ། *Zla-ba*, 'the moon,' born to *Gog-bzang-lha-mo*. His home is *gNam-stod-mthon-po*. S. 2-7. In M.R. 3, he is called *Zla-mthsan-dkar-po*, the 'white moon.' He is the creator of north and south.

ཟླ་བ་དཀར་པོ། *Zla-ba-dkar-po*, the 'white moon,' name of the eighteenth of the 18 agus. He has a white shell instead of a head. S. 1. According to P. 3 he is *Zla-ba-bzang-po's* son.

ཟླ་བ་དཀར་པོ། *Zla-ba-dkar-po*, 'the white moon,' the principal of all axes or hatchets. It is brought to *Gling* from *Pa-chi-dpal-ldong*. S. 1.

ཟླ་བ་བཟང་པོ། *Zla-ba-bzang-po*, 'good moon,' name of the sixth of the 18 agus. He has a moon instead of a head. S. 1. He is in charge of the horses of *Gling* and is 1,050 years old. P. 3.

འ།

འོ་མ་རིགས་ཀྱི་མཁའ་འགྲོ་མ། *'O-ma-rigs-kyi-mkhā-'agro-ma*, 'milk-white-fairy'; a name of *'aBru-gu-ma*. Gl. Ph. 4.

འོག་ཀླུ། *'Og-klu*, the 'lower Nāgas,' name of the realm of the Nāgas. It is of blue or black colour. S. 2. The *Nyo-pas* go from there to *Gro-yul*. P. 3.

འོལ་ལ་དར། *'Ol-la-dar*, 'black silk (?),' name of *Gur-dkar's* and *'aBru-gu-ma's* son. Lb. 6.

ཡ།

ཡབས་མཐོན་པ། *Yabs-[m]thon-pa*, 'high father,' name of *aBru-gi-ma's* father. Occasionally he is called *Yabs-brtan-po*, 'firm father.' S. 1, 2, 3.

ཡབ་བརྟན་པ། *Yab-brtan-pa*, or *Yab-bstan-pa*, see above. S. 4, 7-2. La. 6.

ཡར་ཁྱེན། *Yar-khyen*, Yarkand. It is famous for its 'high-headed' horses. S. 7-1.

ཡུམ་སྔོན་མོ། *Yum-sngon-mo*, 'blue mother,' name of *'aBru-gu-ma's* mother. S. 1, 2, 3-4.

ཡུལ་འཁོར་སྲུང་། *Yul-'akhor-srung*, Dhṛtarāshṭa, King of the east. M.R. 4.

ཡུལ་མཇུག་གི་ཨ་བི། *Yul-mjug-gi-a-bi*, 'grandmother from the end of the village,' name of the grandmother who gives advice to *dPal-le* as well as to *Gur-dkar*. S. 6-4.

ཡུལ་ཚ་སྙན་པོ། *Yul-thsa-snyan-po*, 'melodious (or: well-speaking) village-idol (?).' An offering to it in M.R. 1.

གཡའ་ནང་གི་ལ་ཏིར་ར། *gYā-nang-gi-la-tir-ra*, 'weasel of the inner slate,' name of the weasel that will be *Bi-mo-khra-sug's* comfort, when *Bi-la-nag-chung* goes to the north. S. 5.

གཡུ་ལྕང་སྔོན་མོ། *gYu-lcang-sngon-mo*, the 'blue turquoise-willow,' a metaphor for the tree of the world. M.R. 5.

གཡུ་ཉ་ཟུངས་གཅིག། *gYu-nya-zungs-gcig*, a 'pair of turquoise fishes,' they belong to those treasures of *Gling-mkhar* which are carried off by King *Gur-dkar*. S. 6-4.

གཡུ་འབྲུག་ལྷ་ཁང་། *gYu-'abrug-lha-khang*, 'temple of the turquoise thunder,' name of Kesar's hermitage. Also *'aBrug-mo* goes to this place for meditation. Lb. 5.

གཡུ་སྦལ་སྔོན་པོ། *gYu-sbal-sngon-po*, the 'blue turquoise frog,' born to *Gog-za-lha-mo* in *gYog-klu.* La. N. He is called Kesar's younger brother in S. 2.

གཡུ་མ་ཕོ་རོན། *gYu-ma-pho-ron*, the 'turquoise pigeons'; they loose their strength on the *Srar*-pass. Gl. Kh. 5. *'aBru-gu-ma* takes the shape of one of them. Gl. Kh. 6. Gl. Ph. 6.

གཡུ་རལ་ཅན། *gYu-ral-can*, 'possessing locks of turquoise colour,' name of the daughter of minister *Mig-dmar* of *Gro-yul.* P. 3.

གཡུ་རལ་ཅན། *gYu-ral-can*, 'possessing locks of turquoise colour,' name of a child of *'aBru-gu-ma* and the King of *Hor.* S. 7-2. Lb. 6.

གཡུའི་དཀོན་མཆོག་མོ། *gYui-dkon-mchog-mo*, 'turquoise jewel,' name of the daughter of the King of China. S. 4-3.

ར།

ར་གན་གྱི་རི། *Ra-gan-gyi-ri*, 'hill of brass.' It is situated on the road to *Dri-mo-dgu-chod.* S. 3-4.

ར་མ་དཀར་མོ། *Ra-ma-dkar-mo*, 'white goat,' the mother of *Ra-skyes-skye-dmar*; she is brought from *Pa-chi-dpal-ldong.* S. I. S. 2-8. She wails on account of *rTsid-bu-skye-dmar's* departure for the north. S. 5-1.

ར་སྐྱེས་སྐྱེ་དམར། *Ra-skyes-skye-dmar*, 'Kid red-neck,' name of Kesar's goat, born to *Ra-ma-skye-dmar.* S. 2-8.

ར་དབྱུག། *Ra-dbyug*, 'goat-sling,' name of *'aBru-gu-ma's* sling. P. 1.

རི་དཀར་པོ་ནག་པོ་དམར་པོ་གསུམ། *Ri-dkar-po-nag-po-dmar-po-gsum*, 'the white, black, and red hill, the three.' Kesar goes there for meditation, before going to China. S. 4.1.

རི་གུ་ཁ་སྔོན། *Ri-gu-kha-sngon*, 'Kid blue-mouth'; he will be *Ra-ma-dkar-mo's* comfort, when *rTsid-bu-skye-dmar* goes to the north. S. 5.1.

རི་རྒྱལ་བློན་ཆེན། *Ri-rgyal-blon-chen*, 'King of the mountains, great minister.' He is killed by Kesar in his 12th year. Gl. Kh. 3.

རི་བོ་བློན་ཆེན། *Ri-bo-blon-chen*, 'mountain, great minister,' name of a giant hero of *Gro-yul*. P. 3. He drinks the water of the ocean at a gulp.

རི་བྱ་གོང་མོ། *Ri-bya-gong-mo*, the 'superior snow-partridge'; her nest is on the fifth bough of the tree of the world; she has a coral egg M.R. 8.

རི་ཝ་བློན་ཆེན། *Ri-wa-blon-chen*, see *Ri-bo-blon-chen*.

རིན་ཆེན་བྱུང་ལྡན། *Rin-chen-byung-ldan*, 'producer of jewels,' Ratnasattva, name of the guardian King of the South. M.R. 1.

རོ་ཉའི་རི། *Ro-nyai-ri*, 'hill of lead'; it is situated on the road to *Dri-mo-dgu-chod*. S. 3.4.

རོང་ཡུལ། *Rong-yul*, 'place of defiles,' name of the Indus valley above *Sle*. It is famous for its rifles. S. 5.1. P. 1.

རོན་བཙན་ཁྲོ་མོ། *Ron-btsan-khro-mo*, 'hot anger' (?), one of Kesar's enemies. La. N.

ལ།

ལ་དྭགས། *La-dvags*, 'pass, game,' (?) name of the district of *Sle*, map, *Leh*, it is famous for its jewels. S. 7.1. It is blessed with tiger-like heroes. P. 3.

ལག་དམར་བློན་ཆེན། *Lag-dmar-blon-chen*, 'Great minister red-hand,' name of one of the ministers of *Gro-yul.* He rides on a blue-black horse, and has fire in his mouth. He is called *bdud* (devil). He is killed by *Gyal-sa-dkar-po.* P. 3.

ལག་ལག་རིངས། *Lag-lag-rings*, 'Long hand,' name of the twelfth of the 18 agus. He has a hand instead of a head. S. 1. He belongs to the group of seven agus according to P. 2. Together with *rKang-rkang-rings* he constructs a watercourse and leads the water of the sea to the castle of *Gro-yul.* P. 2.

ལུག་དྲོ་མོ། *Lug-dro-mo*, see *Dro-mo* (*Gro-mo*).

ལུག་པོར་ཟེ། *Lug-por-ze*, 'sheep golden mouth,' name of the sheep, born to *Lug-dro-mo.* S. 2-8.

ལུང་པ་ཆེན་མོ། *Lung-pa-chen-mo*, 'great valley,' the home of *Wa-mo-'ajol-li* (or *'abyol-li*). S. 5-1.

ཤ།

ཤ་རན་དྲེ་བ་རན་དྲེ། *Sha-ran-dre-ba-ran-dre*, the words *shar*, 'East' and *ban-dhe*, 'Buddhist priest' are apparently contained in this word. Name of the three devils of the east who try to kill young Kesar. S. 2.

ཤང་ཀུ་མཇུག་རྡུམ། *Shang-ku-mjug-rdum*, the 'wolf with the bushy tail.' His home is *Thang-stod-mthon-po.* S. 5-1.

ཤང་མོ་འདུར། *Shang-mo-'adur*, the 'trotting female wolf,' name of a pass on the road from *Gling* to *Hor.* S. 6.

ཤན་ཀྲ་མི་རུ། *Shan-kra-mi-ru*, a general of the *Hor* army (apparently not Tibetan). He kills *'aBu-dmar-lam-bstan*, when the latter drinks water at a well. Then he is killed by *dPal-le-rgod-po*, who flays him and fills his skin with sand. S. 6-2, 4.

ཤར་གངས་རི་དཀར་པོ། *Shar-gangs-ri-dkar-po*, the 'white ice-mountain of the east'; name of the place, where a race was run by *rGyal-sa-dkar-po* and *Mig-dmar*. P. 3.

ཤར་ཕྱོགས་བདེ་ཆེན་གླིང་། *Shar-phyogs-bde-chen-gling*, the 'happy land of the east,' mentioned in M.R. 9.

ཤར་རི་ཨན་དྷེ་བན་དྷེ་བདུན། *Shar-ri-an-dhe-ban-dhe-bdun*, the 'seven [Buddhist] priests of the east,' compare the *Shar-ran-dre-ba-ran-dre*, above. (The spelling *An-dre-ba-ran-dre* is also found.) La. 5. Lb. 8. Eighteen of them are born together with Kesar. Three of them are killed by Kesar in his 8th year. Gl. Kh. 3.

ཤིང་རྒྱལ། *Shing-rgyal*, 'King of trees,' possibly a name of the tree of the world. It is planted before *dBang-po-rgya-bzhin's* house. S. 2.

ཤུག་པ་ཁན་ཏྲེ་ཏིག་ཏྲ་རོལ་མ། *Shug-pa-khan-tre-tig-tra-rol-ma*, 'Tārā of the bitter juniper-tree and of the Gentiana'; nickname of *Go-chod*. P. 3.

ཤེལ་དཀར། *Shel-dkar*, 'white crystal,' name of Kesar's son. He is killed by the king of *Hor*. Lb. 4.

ཤེལ་མཁར། *Shel-mkhar*, name of the castle of *Gro-yul*, Princess *Shel-ldang-lha-mo* is born there. P. 3.

ཤེལ་ལྕམ་འབྲུ་གུ་མ། *Shel-lcam-'abru-gu-ma*, ''aBru-gu-ma the crystal wife'; a name of Kesar's wife. S. 2. She is walking in heaven, Gl. Kh. 1, and famous for her wisdom, Gl. Ph. 2.

ཤེལ་ལྗམ། *Shel-ljam*, see *Shel-lcam*.

ཤེལ་ལྡང་ལྷ་མོ། *Shel-ldang-lha-mo*, (*ldang* = *ldan* ?) the 'crystal goddess,' name of the princess of *Gro-yul*. P. 3. When she is born, the world is filled with light. Kesar is called her father (father-in-law ?). She is robbed by the prince of China and brought back by *dPal-moi-a-stag*, the female *agu*. She offends *Shel-li-bu-zhung* by asserting that he belongs to the low caste of smiths. P. 4.

ཤེལ་ལི་བུ་ཞུང་། *Shel-li-bu-zhung* (*Shel-gyi-bu-chung*), 'Little boy of crystal,' name of the 10th of the 18 agus. He has a concave mirror instead of a head. S. 1. His tale in P. 3. He is a child without a father (supposed to be Kesar's child). He is identical with *rGyal-bu-rgyal-sa*. P. 3. He destroys the garden of the old women by fire and restores it again. According to P. 5 he is identical with *gSer-gyi-bu-chung*. See also Lb. 6.

ཤོལ་དང་ཉ་ཤིང་ཆུ་ཐུག་རོལ་མ། *Shol-dang-nyă-shing-chu-thug-rol-ma*, Tārā of the plough, yoke and leather-strap. A nickname of *Go-chod*. P. III.

ས །

ས་རི་ཅན་ལ། *Sa-ri-can-la*, 'pass of the mountains of the earth,' name of the pass, to which Kesar sends lightning. Gl. Kh. 9.

སང་སང་ལྷ་འབྲོག *Sang-sang-lha-'abrog*, (*sang* = *gsang*?), 'secret oasis of the gods,' name of Kesar's watch-hill. P. 1.

སངས་རྒྱས། *Sangs-rgyas*, Buddha; he ran a race on mount Kailāsa with a Bon-po priest. P. 3. A knife to stab Buddha is mentioned in La. 3.

སི་ཀྱིམ། *Si-kyim*, Sikhim; a rope from *Si-kyim* is mentioned in S. 7-2.

སི་ཏར་རཱམ། *Sitar-rām*, Sitā and Rāma, mentioned as inhabitants of *lHa-yul*. Gl. Kh. 7.

སིང་ཆེན་རྒྱལ་པོ། *Sing-chen-rgyal-po*, the 'King, the great lion,' a name of Kesar. Gl. Ph. 2.

སིང་ཕྲུག་ལེགས་མོ། *Sing-phrug-legs-mo*, the 'good child of the lion,' name of the child of *Seng-ge-dkar-mo-gyu-ral-can*. S. 2, 9.

སེང་གེ་དཀར་མོ་གཡུ་རལ་ཅན། *Seng-ge-dkar-mo-gyu-ral-can*, the 'white lioness with the turquoise locks'; the glacier; born to *Gog-bzang-lha-mo*. S. 2, 7. La. N. Lb. 1.

སེང་ཆེན་རྒྱལ་ལྷམ། *Seng-chen-rgyal-lham*, the 'great and divine lion-king,' a name of Kesar. Lb. 6.

སོག་བཅིངས་སོག་མ་བཅིངས། *Sog-bcings-sog-ma-bcings*, 'straw-binder (?),' name of a girl, given to *gSer-ri-bu-zhung* by the ogre *dPal-le-pa*. After the battle he drowns her in the pond of blood. P. 5.

སྲག་པ་ཅུན་དྲུ། *Srag-pa-cun-dru*, the 'earless partridges'; they loose their strength on the *Srar*-pass. Gl. Kh. 5.

སྲར་གྱི་ལ། *Srar-gyi-la*, 'rigorous pass,' name of a difficult pass on the road to *Hor*. S. 7.1. For Kesar's prayer on that pass see Gl. Kh. 5. Compare *A-srar-srar-gyi-la*.

སྲིན་གཞུ་སྔོན་པོ། *Srin-gzhu-sngon-po*, the 'blue bow of the ogres,' name of Kesar's bow. La. 3.

སྲིན་པོ་མགོ་དགུ། *Srin-po-mgo-dgu*, 'ogre with nine heads,' name of the ogre with nine heads, out of whose body the world (*Gling*) is formed. S. 1.

སྲིན་པོ་རག་ཤ། *Srin-po-rag-sha*, 'ogre rākshasa,' name of an ogre. S. 4.1.

སྲིན་རོ་ནེ་མོ། *Srin-po-ro-ne-mo*, 'ogress corpse eater,' name of an ogress, famous for her red cheeks. S. 4.1. In Lb. 8 her name is spelled *Srin-mo-ro-ne-mo*.

སྲུབ་ལྷ། *Srub-lha*, name of a festival. P. 4. (Harvest-festival.)

སྲོག་དགུ་པ། *Srog-dgu-pa*, 'man of nine lives,' name of a minister of the king of *Hor*. S. 7.2.

གསེར་གྱི་མེ་ཏོག་མཁར། *gSer-gyi-me-tog-mkhar*, 'castle of golden flowers,' name of the castle of minister *Mig-dmar* of *Gro-yul*. P. 3.

གསེར་གྱི་ཨ་རག་ཇོ་ཇོ། *gSer-gyi-a-rag-jo-jo*, 'lady of the golden arack,' name of the wife of minister *Mig-dmar* of *Gro-yul*. P. 3.

གསེར་ཉ་ཟུངས་གཅིག། *gSer-nya-zungs-gcig*, a 'pair of golden fishes'; they belong to the treasures of *Gling-mkhar*, carried off by king *Gur-dkar*. S. 6.4.

གསེར་པོའི་གསེར་མཁར། *gSer-poi-gser-mkhar*, 'golden castle,' name of the castle of the king of *Hor*. It begins to shake, when Kesar turns up his sleeves. Lb. 6.

གསེར་རལ་མཁན། *gSer-ral-mkhan*, 'having golden locks,' name of a son of minister *Mig-dmar* of *'aGro-yul*. P. 3. Lb. 6, 4.

གསེར་རལ་ཅན། *gSer-ral-can*, 'having golden locks,' name of a child, borne by *'aBru-gu-ma* to the king of *Hor*. It is killed at the rock *(brag)-Thsau-rdung-rdung*. S. 7.2.

གསེར་པོའི་གསེར་རི། *gSer-poi-gser-ri*, 'golden hill'; it is made out of the ogre's lungs (creation of the world). S. 1. It is situated on the road to *Dri-mo-dgu-chod*. S. 3, 4. P. 4.

གསེར་སྦལ་གསེར་པོ། *gSer-sbal-gser-po*, 'Golden frog,' name of Kesar's elder brother. S. 2. He is born to *Gog-bzang-lha-mo* in *sTang-lha*. La. N.

གསེར་རི་བུ་ཞུང། *gSer-ri-bu-zhung* (*gSer-gyi-bu-chung*), 'golden son.' P. 5. He is also called *Shel-li-bu-zhung*.

བསམ་ཕེལ། *bSam-phel*, 'increaser of thoughts,' name of one of the jewels, brought from *lJang-yul* by *rGyal-bu*. P. 4.

ཧ།

ཧེ་མིས། *He-mis*, (*hem* = 'snow' in Dard), name of the smith of *Hor*. Lb. 7.

ཧོར་ངན། *Hor-ngan*, 'the bad Turkoman,' name of the king of *Hor*. He is killed by Kesar in his 18th year. Gl. Kh. 3.

ཧོར་པ་ཧལ་ལྡེ། *Hor-pa-hal-lde*, (unintelligible) name of the king of *Hor*, identical with *Gur-dkar-rgyal-po*. S. 5-2, 6-1, 2. He carries off *'aBru-gu-ma* and is killed by Kesar. Lb. 6.

ཧོར་ཡུལ། *Hor-yul*, 'land of the Turkomans.' It is famous for its horses, and warm in winter. S. 6-1. P. 3, 4. Lb. 5. Gl. Ph. 9.

ལྷ་སྐྱིན། *lHa-skyin*, 'divine ibex'; he asks Kesar to protect the ibexes. S. 3, 5.

ལྷ་རྟ་ངང་པ། *lHa-rta-ngang-pa*, the 'light-bay divine horse,' name of *dBang-po-brgya-byin's* horse. La. 7.

ལྷ་ཡུལ། *lHa-yul*, see *sTang-lha-yul*. S. 2.

ལྷའི་དབང་པོ་རྒྱབ་བཞིན། *lHai-dbang-po-rgyab-bzhin* (= *brgya-byin*), Śatakratu, Indra, the king of the gods. S. 1, 2. He was identified with the old Tibetan god *sKyer-rdzong-snyan-po*. He is seated on a sun. S. 2, 4. He is connected with the colour white. S. 5-2. Steam rises from his shoulder. He is compared to the rising sun; a treasury of jewels. P. 3. Compare *dBang-po-rgyab-zhin*.

ལྷ་མོ་ཧི་ལིའི་བ་ཟར། *lHa-moi-lii-bazār*, the 'bazār of the gods, of bell-metal,' (*li*, 'bell-metal,' may be a parable for ice). Name of a place in *Gro-yul*. P. 3. *rGod-ma-thsa-langs* could not walk on it. It is broken to pieces by *rKyang-rgod-dbyer-pa*.

ལྷོ་ཀྲབ་རྒྱལ་པོ། *lHo-krab-rgyal-po*, 'king of *lHo-krab*'; he robs *lJang-sa-gYui-cho-ron-mo*. P. 4.

ཨ །

ཨ་གུ། *A-gu*, dialectical for *a-khu*, 'uncle,' the ordinary title of the heroes of the Kesar Saga.

ཨ་ནེ་བཀུར་དམན་མོ། *A-ne-bkur-dman-mo*, see *bkur-dman-rgyal-mo*.

ཨ་མ་སྐྱབས་བདུན། *A-ma-skyabs-bdun*, (or: *skyabs-mdun*), 'mother seven helps,' or 'help-mate'; name of the queen of the earth. S. 2. She is connected with the colour red. S. 5.2. She has a poisonous snake round her waist which is explained as a metaphor of the crooked land of men. P. 3.4. Offerings presented to her. M.R. 1.

ཨ་ལ་ཅོང་གོལ། *A-la-cong-gol*, (unintelligible), name of the eighth of the 18 agus. He has a sole of a boot instead of a head. The spelling *jong-gol* is also found. S. 1.

ཨ་ལོང་ཐང་། *A-long-thang*, 'ring-plain,' name of a plain on the road to *Hor*. S. 7.2. Gl. Ph. 3.

ཨ་སལ་སལ། *A-sal-sal*, (unintelligible), name of a pass on the road to *Hor*. S. 7.2. Lb. 5.

ཨ་སྲར་སྲར་གྱི་ལ། *A-srar-srar-gyi-la*, (unintelligible), name of a pass on the road to *Hor*, probably identical with *Srar-gyi-la*. S. 7.6.

ཨང་གར་ལངས་པ། *Ang-gar-ltsangs-pa*, (*ltsangs-pa* means 'lizard'), name
ཙ
of the second of the 18 agus. He has a lizard's head. S. 1. He is carried off captive by the king of *Hor*. S. 6.3. P. 3. He is put into a cage and suspended from the top of the castle. *mDā-dpon-gong-ma* cuts the suspending rope with his arrow, and *dPal-moi-a-stag* receives the falling agu in her arms. He belongs to the group of seven agus. P. 2. He is the chief *Nyo-pa* (bride-bidder) of the agus.

APPENDICES

(By A. H. Francke)

[1]

THE SPRING MYTH OF THE KESAR SAGA (I).[1]

Translated from the *Mémoires de la Société Finno-Ougrienne*, No. XV, 1900, by George R. Heath.[2]

Preface.

In the following pages one of the **Kesar Sagas**, which are commonly related by the people throughout **Western Tibet**, is introduced to the public, and a service thereby rendered to science, which will perhaps be of no insignificant worth. Various travellers and Tibetan explorers have often reported that so-called Kesar Sagas enjoy great popularity among the Tibetan people; but no one, as far as I know, has told us what the subject of these Sagas is. Even Waddell, who mentions a mythical **King Kesar** several times in his epoch-making book, *The Buddhism of Tibet*, can give no satisfactory information about his person and significance.

These pages will, I hope, prove the high scientific value of the Kesar Sagas, by shewing that they are one of the chief sources from which knowledge of the **pre-Buddhistic religion of Tibet** may be drawn.[3]

---

[1] Reprinted from the *Indian Antiquary*, Vol. XXX, 1901, pp. 329–341.

[2] All the numbers are in accordance with those of the Tibetan original. The latter may be obtained at the Depot de la Société Finno-Ougrienne, Helsingfors, Finland.

[3] There are sources of a very different character, from which Dr. Laufer is drawing his knowledge of the Pre-Buddhistic Religion of Tibet. I have had great pleasure in studying the following of his writings: *Klu 'abum bsduspai snyingpo*, *Mémoires de la Société Finno-Ougrienne*, No. XI, 1898.—*Über ein tibetisches Geschichts-werk der Bonpo, Toung-Pao*, Serie II, Vol. II, No. 1.—*Denkschriften der kais. Akademie der Wissenschaften*, Wien, Phil. His. Classe, Band XLVI, No. VII, *Ein Suhngedicht der Bonpo.* All these publications show a very far advanced type of the Pre-Buddhist Religion; they shew especially in the long lists of *klu-s* or *nāgas*, what a body of priests has been able to make of it. From the Kesar Myths we

An attempt has often been made to learn something about **Kesar** by setting about the translation of the long famous epics which bear this title. But up to the present no one has produced a complete translation. Such a work might well occupy a whole lifetime. If a translation of the whole should in the end be made, it would be of infinite value. Partial translations are not necessarily so, as the Buddhistic cast, which may be clearly discerned in the epic, renders the recognition of the mythological features unusually difficult. From a complete translation of the epic, a confirmation of the mythological ideas contained in the popular sagas may be expected. Until we have one, we are depended on the sagas alone. That is not, however, to be regretted at the commencement; for the popular sagas are short, clear, and free from Buddhistic influences.

The study of the **Spring Myth** leads quite naturally to the desire of becoming acquainted with the corresponding **Winter Myth.** I have now succeeded in discovering this also, and I hope soon to submit it in a German translation.

It has been already mentioned by others that the sagas treated here exist among the people in oral form. In this case, however, the question is not one of a free narration, which runs the risk of being altered in passing from mouth to mouth; but rather of matter learnt by heart, at the recitation of which (according to the respective versions) scarcely a word is altered. A girl of about sixteen years of age, in whose family the stories of Kesar are held in high esteem, related the following sagas slowly, so that the master of the Mission School she attended was enabled, under my supervision, to take them down word for word. This **First Manuscript** is the foundation of the accompanying Tibetan text almost throughout. In the comparison and confirmation of the text, as well as in the addition of some new features, a **Second Manuscript** has also been of great service. This was prepared for me by another Ladakhi who is able to write, and who went to the **Bedas** (a caste of musicians and popular entertainers), and wrote down literally what they related. The two manuscripts deviate a little from one

---

may learn, on the other hand, what this religion has been to the ordinary man. It would certainly not be right to consider the Kesar Sagas as mere fairy-tales, told for the amusement of the people. This is shown most plainly by a comparison with the Ladakhi Wedding Ritual and the popular Bonpa Hymnal (*gling glu*), which run on the same lines as the Kesar Sagas and are both of a distinctly religious cast.

another both in the form of the narrative and in the wording of the songs, but agree perfectly in everything essential.

Something remains to be said on the poetical form of the songs, which are interspersed in the narrative. We find in them different kinds of rhythm as well as of rhyme. The rhythms are almost always formed of trochees, which corresponds to the monosyllabic character of the language. Dactyls, however, also occur, especially when a suffix is added to a dissyllabic compound. **The sentence-rhyme peculiar to Tibet** is the one which occurs in almost all the songs (i.e., two or three sentences are formed in exactly the same manner, but different words are placed in the corresponding positions). I have tried in the translation to imitate the sentence-rhyme as far as possible. With regard to the rhythms I have allowed myself greater freedom.[1]

Finally, it should be pointed out that the language of the Tibetan text is not the classical but the Ladakhi dialect.

An Abridged Episode from the Kesar Saga.[2]

Translation.

I.

The first Tale is the Tale of the Agus (heroes).

1. In the land of **gLing** there were once **the wild Agus dPalle** and **Khromo** and **dGani**. Because there was no king in the land of gLing, deep sorrow came over Agu dPalle. Agu Khromo was a bad man; he rejoiced at the unhappiness of the land. One day the wild Agus went to tend goats. 2. Then **dBangpo-rgyab-bzhin** also came from the upper kingdom of the gods to tend goats. All at once the black devil-bird appeared, and wanted to carry off the goats. 3. dBangpo-rgyab-bzhin changed himself into the white god-bird, and both fought. 4. The thought occurred to all the Agus:—'The black bird seems to be the devil-bird.' 5. Then **Agu dPalle** seized the sling, and sang this song:—

6. Oh Sling, thou many-coloured sling,
7. (My) mother spun thee in her time,
8. (My) mother plaited thee in her time,

---

[1] This sentence-rhyme is the same type of parallelism as has become known from Chinese popular poetry.

[2] The division into nine parts is my own. (A. H. Francke.)

9. I carried it when I was a boy,[1]
10. Oh come, oh come thou oblong stone,
11. Hit sure, be there no escape!

12. So singing, he slung (the stone), and hit the black devil-bird on the wing (or shoulder-blade), so that he died. 13. At this **dBangpo-rgyab-bzhin** rejoiced greatly, and in order to shew love to the Agus, he sang:—

14. Men of gLing, kindly are ye come,
15. dPalle, dGani, kindly are ye come,
16. A cow and a calf will I give you a hundredfold,
17. Foal and horse will I give you a hundredfold,
18. A laden pack-sheep will I give you a hundredfold,
19. Goat and kid will I give you a hundredfold,
20. A saddled horse will I give you a hundredfold,
21. A yak with the nose-ring will I give you a hundredfold!

22. When he had sung this song, the Agus said:—'All that is not necessary.' 23. To Agu dPalle this thought occurred:—'The King of Heaven **dBangpo-rgyab-bzhin** has three sons; it would be good if he sent one son to the land of gLing as King.' Therefore he asked:—24. 'O give a child as chief to the chiefless land.' When dBangpo-rgyab-bzhin heard that, he went back quickly to the upper kingdom of the gods.

II.

The second Tale is the Tale of dBangpo-rgyab-bzhin's Three Sons.

1. **The king of the gods, dBangpo-rgyab-bzhin, had three sons, Donldan, Donyod and Dongrub.** Because their father loved them very much, he did not like to send even one to the land of gLing. 2. When therefore he came back to the upper kingdom of the gods, he ate nothing and sat there in anger. 3. Then his son **Donldan** brought his tea and his food, but the father ate nothing. Donldan said:—

'Father!

4. Has the wolf got at the sheep?
5. Has the crow got at the breakfast (or midday meal)?
6. Was the sling lost at the hunt?'

---

[1] Lit.: Carrying was at the time when I was a boy.

The father said:—

7. 'The wolf has not got at the sheep,
8. The crow has not got at the breakfast,
9. The sling was not lost at the hunt.

10. But thou, my son, wilt thou go as chief to the chiefless land of gLing? If thou goest, I will take the tea and the food!' 11. The son said:—'I shall not go!

12. If the dog is angry, the soup is left (uneaten),
13. If the king is full of wrath, the roast is left (uneaten)!'

14. Then came the son **Donyod** and said:—15. 'Father, eat the food and drink the tea!' 16. The father said:—'Thou, my son, wilt thou go as chief to the chiefless land of gLing?' 17. The son said:—'I shall not go!

18. If the dog is angry, the soup is left (uneaten),
19. If the king is full of wrath, the roast is left (uneaten)!'

20. Then came **Dongrub**, the smallest of all, and asked:—

'Father!

21. Has the wolf got at the sheep?
22. Has the crow got at the breakfast?
23. Was the sling lost at the hunt?'

The father said:—

24. 'The wolf has not got at the sheep,
25. The crow has not got at the breakfast,
26. The sling was not lost at the hunt!
27. My son, wilt thou go as chief to the chiefless land of gLing!'

28. The son said: 'If I do not listen to the word of father and mother, to whose word shall I listen? I shall go!' 29. Then the father took the tea and the food. Again great sadness came over the father, and he sang:—

30. (My) son Donldan, he is the heart of my thinking;
31. I am not able to tear out one's heart and to give it to another!
32. (My) son Donyod, he is the tongue of my speaking.
33. It is not right to tear out one's tongue and to give it to another!
34. (My) son Dongrub, he is the eye of my seeing;
35. It is not right to tear out one's eye and to give it to another!'

36. Then spake the father:—'Before Dongrub goes to the land of gLing, all you (my) sons must have a race on horseback one day in the morning, 37, at midday play at dice, 38, and in the evening shoot arrows.' 39. So they all had a horse-race in the morning, and the youngest son Dongrub won it. 40. At midday they played at dice, and the youngest son Dongrub won. 41. In the evening they shot arrows, and the youngest son Dongrub won. 42. Then came the time when the son Dongrub was to go to the land of gLing.

III.

The third Tale is the Tale of Dongrub, who is fitted out for the land of gLing.

1. Before the son Dongrub went to the land of men, the high mother gave him a lesson, the high father gave him a lesson. Both said thus:—'Thou needest

2. A horse that always knows the way back,
3. A horse that knows how to fly high,
4. A knife to stab the wicked people,
5. **A knife to stab Buddha,**
6. An arrow that always knows the way back!'

7. Then said the mother:—'O yes, it is hard for Dongrub to go to the land of men!

8. **rKyangbyung-dbyerpa** is certainly
9. A horse that always knows the way back,
10. A horse that knows how to fly high.
11. The knife "Three-fingers-long" is certainly
12. A knife to stab the wicked people,
13. A knife to stab Buddha.
14. The blue **Srinγzhu** is certainly
15. A bow whose arrow flies back.' This is the lesson of the high mother:—
16. 'rKyangbyung-dbyerpa, the high horse,
17. And moreover Srinγzhu, the blue bow,
18. Thou wilt find at the house of Uncle **brTandzin** the Red.
19. **Tsetse-ngangdmar** is on the pass;
20. Upon her, O Dongrub, thou wilt spring well
21. And of that, O Dongrub, thou wilt die.'

22. So then the son went to fetch the horse, the knife, and the bow, and arrived before the house of brTandzin the Red. 23. There he saw the horse, whose four legs were fastened with chains. When the horse heard a man coming he sprang up. 24. Dongrub spake:—'Uncle, all hail! Give me the horse rKyangbyung-dbyerpa and the blue bow Srinγzhu! I, the son Dongrub, am going to the land of men. I have come here to greet my uncle!' 25. The uncle said:—'The horse rKyangbyung-dbyerpa is here; lead him away! the blue bow Srinγzhu is not here, but in **Agu Za's** land!'. 26. When he heard that, he went to Agu Za's house, leading the horse. 27. In the middle of the way was a white and a black pool. 28. As he was washing his hands in the black pool, another hand came out of the water, seized Dongrub's hand and held it fast. 29. Then said Dongrub: 'Who is it that seizes my hand?' 30. Out of the water a voice answered:—'Why art thou washing thy hands in our water?' 31. When he heard that, Dongrub spake:—'Please, please let my hand go! I am in haste. I am going in order to become the chief of the chiefless gLing-Land and want to fetch the blue bow Srinγzhu from Agu Za.' 32. Then it was said out of the water:—'As soon as thou cryest, saying, "Agu Za", (the giant) will swallow thee. Therefore I tell thee this: In Agu Za's body is the knife and the bow. So take the knife in the right hand and his heart in the left. Then if thou stab his heart, he will cry, "Come out!"' 33. Then (he, she, it?) let Dongrub's hand go, and vanished in the water.

34. When Dongrub arrived at Agu Za's house, the Agu put his hand out at the window, seized Dongrub and ate him up. 35. So Dongrub sat in the body (of the Agu), and seized the knife with the right hand. In the left he took the heart, and stabbed. 36. Then Agu Za cried:—'Who is in my body? Come out!' 37. Dongrub said:—'My good Agu, am I not the son of the king of heaven, **rGyabbzhin**? When I am going as chief to the chiefless land of gLing and want to greet Agu and ask him for the blue bow Srinγzhu, the Agu seizes me and swallows me.' 38. Then spake the Agu:—'O my heart, all hail! I feel ill! Come out!' Dongrub answered:—39. 'My good Agu, wilt thou listen to my word? If thou listen to it, I will give thee sun and moon to eat for a year. Is that enough?' 40. The Agu said:—'It is enough, O my eye!' 41. Dongrub spake:—'Then I will come out through the Agu's pineal gland, and bring the whole brain out on to the head!' 42. The Agu requested:—'O my eye,

please come out by the way thou wentest in!' 43. 'Then I will come out at the Agu's sole.' 44. 'O my eye, rather than that come out by the way thou wentest in!' 45. Then Dongrub came out at the pit of the neck, and had the bow and the knife in his hand. He gave sun and moon to the Agu to eat for a year.

46. While he was going to the chiefless land of gLing, he arrived at the foot of a mountain, and saw the **goat Tsetse-ngangdmar** lying there. He sprang on to it. 47. The goat was frightened, and carried him on to the summit of three mountains. There it threw him down, and **Dongrub** died.

IV.

The fourth Tale is the Tale of Dongrub's birth on the earth.

1. **When Dongrub had died,** he changed himself into hail, and came down **to the land of gLing.** 2. There **he was born to Gogzalhamo.** 3. Although he was the high king of the land of gLing, he was born in lowly form. 4. His mouth was as large as a well, and (his) eyes black and ugly. 5. On the pillow of (his) mother there was some bad meal. The child suddenly got up, (and) went and ate some of the meal. 6. The mother said:—'He does not give himself time to grow, but eats meal (already)!' She clothed it with a piece of ass's sackcloth, tied a goat's hair string around it, and put a stone upon it. 7. For the mother was ashamed of the child's lowly form. 8. At the same time **the spouse bKur dmanmo** from the kingdom of the gods changed herself into **the mother dKar thigmo** and went to prepare some soup for Gogzalhamo. 9. Mother dKar thigmo said:—'Well, Gogzalhamo, what has been born to you?' Gogzalhamo spake:—10. 'Of all that which was or was not born to me there is nothing left. It was born with ugly black eyes and a mouth like a well, and it ate meal without giving itself time to grow. I have clothed it with a piece of ass's sackcloth, and put a stone on it. There it is, under the stone!' Mother dKar thigmo took the child from under the stone, and the child said:—

12. 'Kinder art thou than water, O Lady dKar thigmo, now listen!
13. Kinder than even (my) mother, O Lady dKar thigmo, now listen!
14. After the manner of men, a bowl should be filled with butter;

15. Gogzalhamo, however, threw to me buckwheat.
16. After the manner of men, the child should be put in the child-sack;[1]
17. Gogzalhamo, however, put sackcloth around me.
18. A son is born to the mother! says he,
19. A son is born to Gogza! says he,
20. And he blows white bands up to the sky.
21. A son is born to the mother! says he,
22. A son is born to Gogza! says he,
23. And he blows red bands across the earth.
24. A son is born to the mother! says he,
25. A son is born to Gogza! says he,
26. And he blows blue bands down to the waters.'

V.

The fifth Tale is the Tale of Khromo, who sought to harm Kesar, the King of the Gods.

1. While this was going on, **Agu Khrọmo** heard that **Kesar, the king of the gods, had been born to Gogzalhamo.** 2. Therefore he said to seven priests from the east:—'In that cottage there is a child. If you can kill the child, I will give you half of (my) castle and land.' 3. Then the priests from the east disguised themselves as beggars and went to Gogzalhamo's cottage. 4. Gogzalhamo thought:—'These seven men are beggars;' filled a golden and a silver plate for them, and brought it out. 5. The seven spiritual beggars said:—'We need neither a golden nor a silver plate. Give us the child! We want to teach it religion.' Then **Gogzalhamo gave them the child.** 6. Then came Mother dKar thigmo, and cried:—'Gogzalhamo, to whom have you given the child away?' 7. Gogzalhamo answered:—'Seven priests, who said, "We want to teach it religion", have carried it off.' 8. Then spake Mother dKar thigmo:—'How could you give the child away!' and Gogzalhamo ran to get back the child, till she met the seven beggars. 9. The beggars had bound the child's arms and legs with chains, had laid fire on his heart, and were pouring boiling water into his mouth. 10. When

---

[1] In Ladakh, it is a sack filled with dry horse-dung to keep the child warm. In this way baby linen, etc. is spared. (Francke's note.)

the mother saw that, she came before the seven beggars, and cried:—'Give me my child!' The child said:—

11. 'Fourfold I lie here not bound:
12. In four directions four enemies will fall.
13. On my breast I feel no flame:
14. It is a sign of flaming happiness.
15. Hot water I do not feel on my head:
16. It is a sign of tea, beer (and) milk to come.'

17. As he sang this, the child said:—'*Hung* one, *hung* two!' broke the chains and ran to his mother. Then Gogzalhamo carried the child home. 18. But the seven priests from the east changed themselves into beetles and devoured the ashes of the fire.

19. Sc when Agu Khromo knew that the child was not yet conquered, he said:—'I will go myself;' (and) came and asked Gogzalhamo:—'Where is the child? Has he grown big?' 20. The child said:—'My good Agu, I am here!' Whereupon Khromo took the child out of the bed and carried him off. 21. There was a rock of poison there. Upon it he wanted to throw the child. But although Agu Khromo was able to whirl him round, he could not throw him on to the rock. 22. The child said:—'Swing me round, good Agu, do! Throw me off, do!' 23. The Agu said:—'I am tired, I cannot any longer!' 24. Whereupon the child cried:—'Now the Agu's time for whirling (me) round is past; now it is my turn!' (and) saying this, he threw the Agu on to the poisonous rock. 25. As the rock was of fiery poison, one side of Khromo's body got burnt.

26. One day **Agu dPalle, Agu dGani and Agu Khromo** went hunting together, and killed a wild yak. To the place where they killed it the child came also. 27. The Agus said:—'Go, carry a whole leg at once to thy mother!' The child bit his teeth into a tendon of the leg, carried it off, gave it to his mother, and came back. 28. Then the Agus said:—'Take all the intestines and the inwards also to (thy) mother!' and sent him way. The child wrapped it all up in his hip-cloth, bit with (his) teeth into the upper end of the incestines, and carried it home to (his) mother. Then he returned. 29. Agu Khromo became angry, threw the wooden poker (at him), and hit the child on the mole at the back of the neck, so that he fainted and fell to the ground. 30. Then said Agu dPalle to Khromo:—'He is also a member of our father's brothers. They will avenge him on thee!' Then Agu Khromo was frightened, and spake to the child:—31. 'Listen, **Street-boy**; get up, please! I will

give thee the chief ford of a hundred fords.' 32. The child asked:—'Wilt thou give it (to me), my good Agu?' and got up. 33. When the **Street-child** had received the chief ford of a hundred fords, it allowed no one to cross it. 34. One day as Agu Khromo was coming through the water at that chief ford, the Street-child cried:—35. 'Who is coming through the water there?' and threw a stone at Khromo. 36. Agu Khromo said:—'Ow, it is I!' and the child cried smilingly:—'Why didst thou not say that before, my good Agu?' 37. The Street-boy became very powerful. If no part of the mourning-feast was given to him, he let no funeral procession pass; and if no part of the marriage-feast was given to him, he let no marriage procession cross. All that he carried away, and gave it to Gogzalhamo.

VI.

The sixth Tale is the Tale of the Maiden 'aBruguma, whom the Street-child met.

1. Now at that time the Street-child went to the upper *Groma*-field to gather *groma*[1] roots, and met there **the maiden 'aBruguma** and her handmaid **Darlhagochodma**. 2. The Street-child found as many roots as a horse's head or yak's head is great, and made a loaf for himself out of them. 3. Maiden 'aBruguma and Darlhagochodma found only one dry root each. 4. As they found no more, the handmaid said to the **Street-child**:—'Give our Lady 'aBruguma a piece of root-bread too!' 5. The Street-child answered:—'No, little sister, I must nourish my mother!' 6. Then he ate some of the root-bread before the two girls, and spake, '*Sindiremalag*!' While he said that, the loaf grew whole again, and he began to eat once more. 7. Then spake he:—'Now Maiden 'aBruguma shall also eat some. But as much as she eats must be brought back again. There, eat some!' 8. Maiden 'aBruguma ate half of the loaf and said, '*Sindiremalag*!' But although she said that, nothing came back. The mark of the teeth remained. 9. Then spake the Street-child:—'O thou daughter of **Father brTanpa**, O thou daughter of **Mother Chorol**! Give me back my bread! If I see a dog, the dog shall hear of it; if I see a man, the man shall hear of it!' 10. When Maiden 'aBruguma heard that, she thought he was angry, and spake to the Street-boy:—'To-morrow we are going to have a feast,

---

[1] *Groma* is a species of *potentilla*.

and thou shalt take part in it!' 11. The Street-child asked:—'Shall I take part, little sister?' and 'aBruguma said:—'Yes thou shalt be there.' 12. On the next day the Street-child went earlier than all (the rest) to 'aBruguma's house, and hid himself behind the upper door-beam. 13. So when all the people had come together to the feast, 'aBruguma said:—'Are we all here? Shut the door before the Street-child comes!' 14. Then the Street-child called out from the beam:—'I have already arrived, little sister!' 15. 'aBruguma spake:—'And I had just said that he had not come yet!' 16. He called out laughing:—'So I just heard (my) little sister say! If I see a dog, the dog shall hear of it; if I see a man, the man shall hear of it!' 17. Then spake 'aBruguma:—'Listen, Street-child, to-morrow we are going to give a friendly beer-banquet. All the Agus are going to come to it. Wilt thou also be there?' 18. He spake:—'Little sister, wilt thou listen to my word?' The maiden said:—'I will listen to it.' 19. He spake:—'Then thou must say this to Agu dPalle and the others:—

20. Who takes a drink of the beer of life, let him have children beyond measure!
21. Who takes a drink of the beer of blessing, let his life be like that of the gods!
22. Drink without touching the ten finger-tips,
23. And without wetting the silk of the tongue, [1]
24. Nor may'st thou knock the pearls of the teeth; [2]
25. Drink with the soul,
26. Yea, drink with the heart!'

27. So the next morning, when all the Agus had come together, 'aBruguma brought the beer of friendship, came before Agu dGani, and said:—

28. 'Hail, on (thy) golden throne, O Agu dGani, now listen!
29. See this vessel, filled with thoughts and nine-fold buttered. [3]

---

[1] *Literally:* And without tasting with the silken knots of the tongue.

[2] *Literally:* Not knocking the teeth like milk, like a rosary, like pearls.

[3] A small pica of butter (called *yar*) which is smeared round the edge of a vessel with the thumb to honour a guest. Dr. Laufer asks for an analysis of this sentence. The Tibetan text is properly *bungpa bsampas don sgrubla mis brgyabs dgu brgyabs shig yod.* This means literally: 'A vessel furnished with thoughts according to the meaning (*don*), smeared by men, smeared ninefold, such it is'; *brgyabs* is said instead of *yar brgyabs*, it is smeared with butter.

30. Who takes a drink of the beer of life, let him be blessed with many children!
31. Who takes a drink of the beer of blessing, let his life be like that of the gods!
32. Drink without touching the ten finger-tips,
33. And without wetting the silk of the tongue,
34. Nor may'st thou knock the pearls of the teeth;
35. Drink with the soul,
36. Yea, drink with the heart!'

Then spake Agu dGani:—

37. 'Not wetting the tongue,
38. Not filling the stomach,
39. Not touching the hands,
40. How then shall I drink it? Away with the bowl!'

41. Because he spoke so, the girl carried the vessel to Agu dPalle:—

42. 'Hail on (thy) throne of shell, O Agu dPalle, now listen!
43. See this vessel, filled with thoughts and nine-fold buttered!
44. Who takes a drink of the beer of life, let him be blessed with many children!
45. Who takes a drink of the beer of blessing, may he live as long as the gods!
46. Drink without touching the ten finger-tips,
47. And without wetting the silk of the tongue,
48. Nor may'st thou knock the pearls of the teeth;
49. Drink with the soul,
50. Yea, drink with the heart!'

Then spake Agu dPalle:—

51. 'Not wetting the tongue,
52. Not filling the stomach,
53. Not touching the hands,
54. How then shall I drink it? Away with the bowl!'

55. Then 'aBruguma said to the Agus:—'Shall I ask the Street-child also?' 56. The Agus spake:—'He is also a member of our father's brothers' (clan). Ask him also, do!' 57. And 'aBruguma addressed him:—'Yes, listen, Street-child, give me thy bowl!' 58. The Street-child spake:—'Yes, certainly, little sister, just as thou hast said to the Agus, speak also to me!' So 'aBruguma sang:—

59. 'Thou on (thy) wooden chair, thou Street-boy there, now listen:
60. See this vessel, filled with thoughts and nine-fold buttered!
61. Who takes a drink of the beer of life, let him be blessed with many children.
62. Who takes a drink of the beer of blessing, may he live as long as the gods!
63. Drink without touching the ten finger-tips,
64. And without wetting the silk of the tongue,
65. Nor may'st thou knock the pearls of the teeth!
66. Drink with the soul,
67. Yea, drink with the heart!'

68. Thereupon the Street-child said:—'Little sister, wait a little!' Then he threw the vessel towards the sky with his stick studded with dog's teeth, and drank the beer out of the sky. 69. While he drank it, he said:—'I feel how the Lord of Heaven, **rGyabbzhin**, is giving me a drink of the beer of friendship!' Then all the Street-folk shouted:—'Now our Street-boy has got Lady 'aBruguma as bride! Hurrah for Love [1]!'

VII.

The seventh Tale is the Tale of 'aBruguma, who becomes Kesar's bride.

1. The Sovereign of Heaven had heard the shouting of the Street-child, and he came with the whole retinue of heaven and the retinue of the water-spirits, and held a horse-race with all the Agus. 2. The handmaid Darlhagochodma took Lady 'aBruguma to the race-course, and put her on a rock. 3. The handmaid said:—'To-day listen to my word: Upon whose horse thou canst jump at the race, his bride thou wilt be!

4. Listen to-day to the word of the servant,
5. Listen to **Darlhagochodma's** word!
6. To-day will the skin be pulled over thy ears; [2]
7. Father **brTanpa's** daughter will receive blows!'

---

[1] *Yashaho!*—shouted at weddings.

[2] Dr. Laufer asks for an analysis of this sentence. The Tibetan has: *rkyab rlon ni bumola rkyal shus btang yin.* The literal translation is: 'To the girl who is like a wet leather-bag, will be given a peeling off of the skin.' In my translation I made use of the corresponding German idiom.

8. Then **the king of Heaven, rGyabbzhin,** came riding along, and **'aBruguma** spake:—

9. 'I know neither the man that is riding,
10. Nor even the swift horse underneath.'

Thereupon the handmaid said:—

11. 'If thou knowest not the man that is riding,
12. Know, that is the King of Heaven;
13. And the swift steed underneath
14. **Is the god's horse, called the Bay.**
15. Man and horse touch not, let them go! If thou jumpest now, then thou committest a great sin against the gods!'

So 'aBruguma did not jump.

16. Then **the Earth-Mother, sKyabsbdun** came riding along. Lady 'aBruguma spake:—

17. 'I know neither the man that is riding,
18. Nor even the swift horse underneath.'

The handmaid said:—

19. 'If thou knowest not yet the man that is riding,
20. See, it is sKyabsbdun, the Earth-Mother;
21. And the swift horse underneath,
22. That is the red earth-horse.
23. Rider and horse touch not, let them go! If thou jumpest now, then thou committest a great sin against the earth!'

So 'aBruguma did not jump.

24. Then **lCogpo, the King of the water-spirits,** came riding along, and 'aBruguma spake:—

25. 'I know neither the man that is riding,
26. Nor even the swift horse underneath.'

The servant said:—

27. 'If thou knowest not yet the man that is riding,
28. See, it is lCogpo, the Water-king;
29. And the swift steed underneath,
30. That is the blue water-horse.
31. Rider and horse touch not, let them go! If thou jumpest now, thou committest a great sin against the water-spirits!'

So 'aBruguma did not jump.

32. Then all **the Agus of the land of gLing** came riding past, and 'aBruguma did not jump. 33. Last of all **the Street-child** came riding along. He had put off his humble form. He had a reddish-violet crown, [1] and (his) horse a short, reddish-violet mane. On the man's right shoulder the sun was rising, (and) on left the moon. 'aBruguma spake:—

34. 'I know neither the man that is riding,
35. Nor even the swift horse underneath.'

Then said Darlhagochodma:—

36. 'If thou knowest not yet the man that is riding,
37. See, it is **Kesar, of gLing the King**;
38. And **the swift steed** underneath,
39. It is the noble **rKyangbyung dbyerpa**.

40. Now if everything is well carried out, then all people will call me **Gochodma** (that is: She that fulfils). If it is not carried out well, then I shall call myself **Gomichod** (that is: Unfulfilled). Man and horse let not pass; seize them.' 41. So when Kesar came riding on, the Maiden 'aBruguma suddenly jumped on to the horse. 42. As the maiden jumped, Kesar put on his humble form again, caused a strong smell of lice, and changed the horse into a female *Dzo* with broken horns. 43. Then all the street-folk shouted:—'Hurrah for love! Lady 'aBruguma is our Street-boy's bride!' Then 'aBruguma made the Street-child her bridegroom, and took him home.

VIII.

The eighth Tale is the Tale of Kesar, who teases 'aBruguma.

1. One day 'aBruguma's mother spread the carpet out the wrong way round, so that it had the front edge towards the wall. 2. The Street-boy said:—'Where the front edge of the carpet is, there the face of the guest must also be,' and sat down with his face turned to the wall. 3. Then spake **Father brTanpa** to 'aBruguma:—'The boy is nine times too clever; he will run away yet.' 4. Therefore the maiden covered the Street-boy with a pot, turning it upside down. [2] 5. Now

---

[1] Tuft of hair (according to Dr. Laufer and Jäschke's *Dictionary*).

[2] Dr. Laufer's translation, 'she put him in a pot with his face underneath', is impossible; *kha* is the opening of the pot.

although the handmaid and the maiden herself sat before it keeping watch, the Street-child escaped without letting either hear anything. 6. Before the door he tore his upper garment in pieces near the place where the dogs were kept, killed a goat and poured its blood out. The entrails of the goat he wrapped round the teeth of the dogs. Then he fled into the innermost part of the valley. 7. When Father brTanpa saw that (before the door), he said to 'aBruguma:—'My daughter, go and look for him! The dogs have surely not eaten him!' Then 'aBruguma went to look for him all around on a hundred, (yea) a thousand mountains, and did not find him. 8. The maiden's dress tore right up to the collar. (Her) shoes tore from the sole right up to the top. 9. As she did not find him yet, she went to **Agu dPalle** and **Agu dGani,** and spake:—

10. 'Thou on (thy) golden throne, Agu dGani, now listen!
11. Early in the morning I began to climb, and came on to the golden hill;
12. In the evening I descended, and came to the copper-field.
13. Did he then come for copper? I would now like to ask the Agu!'

Agu dGani spake:—

14. 'If the dogs have devoured the Street-child,
15. Then will the skin be pulled over thy ears,
16. Then indeed will blows be laid on brTanpa's daughter!'

So 'aBruguma went to Agu dPalle, and spake:—

17. 'Thou on (thy) throne of shell there, Agu dPalle, then listen!
18. In the morning I began to climb, and came on to the silver hill;
19. In the evening I descended, and came to the lead-fields.
20. Did he then come for lead? I would like to ask the Agu.'

Agu dPalle said:—

21. 'If the dogs have devoured the Street-child,
22. Then will the skin be pulled over thy ears,
23. Then indeed will blows be laid on brTanpa's daughter!'

24. Then spake 'aBruguma:—'Everybody says that!' and went to look for him again. Then she took a stone which had a hole (in it), looked through (it), (to see) whether she could see him, and caught

sight of him in the innermost corner of the valley. 25. And he had the reddish-violet crown on, and (his) horse (had) the reddish-violet mane; he had put off his humble form, and was dancing around merrily. 26. Then the maiden ran as fast as ever she could, and reached place where he was. 27. He said:—'Well, girl, from where hast thou come? and gave her, in a piece of a broken cup, a loathsome lump of bad meal, which he had kneaded together. 28. He spake:—'If thou eatest this, I will run off again!' 'aBruguma ate it and said:—'Then go, good King, do!' He spake:—29. 'And thou, the rich daughter of a rich man, hast eaten up the whole bad dough. 30. If I meet a dog, the dog shall hear of it. 31. If I meet a man, the man shall hear of it!' 32. Then they both went back to Mother **Gogzalhamo.**

33. One day as the Street-boy was preparing a feast, he slaughtered many sheep and goats. 34. One skinned animal he hid in 'aBruguma's cloak, and said:—35. 'One skinned animal is missing! Who is the thief? Mother, thou hast surely not stolen it?' 36. The mother answered:—'Would I then take anything besides what thou hast given me?' 37. He spake:—'Handmaid, thou hast surely not stolen it?' 38. The handmaid answered:—'Would I then take anything besides what the king has given me?' 39. Then he spake to 'aBruguma:—'And thou wilt surely steal nothing, thou rich child of a rich man? Stand up now, and shake (yourself)!' 40. 'aBruguma said:—'Would I then take anything besides what the king has given me?' All at once she stood up, and as she shook (herself), it dropped out of her cloak. 41. The Street-child said:—'And thou has stolen it, thou rich child of a rich man! I will not go with thee!' In this way he teased her.

IX.

The ninth Tale is the Tale of the Wedding.

1. **Mother Gogzalhamo** spread out three carpets, one blue, one red and one white. Then she hung up three ribbons, one white, one red and one blue. 2. She spake to 'aBruguma:—'Shut (thy) eyes tight, take one out of all these ribbons, and go and sit down on one of the carpets! I shall wait for a dream.' 3. So 'aBruguma shut (her) eyes tight, took a ribbon and went on to a carpet. 4. She took a blue ribbon, and came on to the blue carpet. 5 (Her) mother said:—'Now is **Kesar, the King of the gods,** thy portion. Later on the white tents of Yarkand will be thy portion!' This she spake prophesying. 6. In the same

moment the Street-child had put on (his) lowly form again. 7. 'aBruguma spake to (her) mother:—'Give me back the man who was just here!' 8. (Her) mother said:—'I will go (and look for him) with thee.' 9. The Street-child had been brought to the glorious castle, and been stripped of (his humble body by (his) father's brothers. 10. Maiden 'aBruguma arrived before the castle and saw **the horse rKyangbyung dbyerpa.** 11. The horse spake:—'Lady 'aBrugu, enter!' 'aBruguma said:—'I have lost my former husband.' 12. Then the horse took the maiden up with his teeth and threw her into the glorious castle. 13. Then **King Keṡar,** got a golden throne, and 'aBruguma a throne of turquoise. 14. Now they were happy, and became stout. Three nights long they celebrated their wedding, and three days long they gave feasts. The tale and the story is at an end.

THE SPRING MYTH OF THE KESAR SAGA (II.)[1]

(By Rev. A. H. Francke)

Additions to the Saga from other Versions.

Preliminary Note.

The Kesar Saga is told differently in different villages. To arrive at a final solution of the question, as to whether the oral tales **(kha sgrungs)** or the Kesar Epic **(dPe sgrungs)** are the original source with regard to Ladakh, it will be necessary to arrange something like a **Kesar-survey of Ladakh,** i.e., in every village the following material will have to be collected:—(1) the version of the Kesar Saga, (2) the **gLing glu** (Hymnal of the Kesar Saga), (3) the marriage ritual of the village. All this material will have to be compared with the Kesar Epic.

List of Additions.

The following list of additions is not, in the least, claimed as a full one.

1. At the place where the Agus ask for a king, the following request is also added: 'Send us nine kinds of corn-seed, and also horses, oxen and many four-footed animals.'

2. First detailed version of the story of the birth:—**Gogzalhamo** sat spinning in her room while the hail was falling. As she was hungry just then, she ate some hail-stones, and soon after conceived. When the hail came, all the horses fled: the mare **Thsaldang** was the last. All the dogs also fled, the she-dog **dKarmo** was the last; all the sheep fled, and the ewe **Dromo** was the last; all the goats fled, and **Tsetse-ngangdmar** was the last. Then came **Agu dPalle** and brought food to the animals that were with child. Thereupon the mare Thsaldang gave birth to the foal **rKyang-byung-dbyerpa,** the she-dog dKarmo to the puppy **Drumbu-brang-dkar,** the ewe Dromo to the lamb **mThsalmig,** the she-goat Tsetse-ngangdmar to the kid **Tsetse-ngangdmar.**

---

[1] Reprinted from the *Indian Antiquary*, Vol. XXXI, 1902, pp. 32–40.

3. Second version of the story of the birth:—Mother **Gogzalhamo** heard within her a voice, which said: 'I must be born in the lofty sky; please go to the lofty sky!' So she went, and gave birth to (the) sun and moon. Then it said: 'Sun and moon I am not; I must be born on the lofty mountain; please go on to the lofty mountain!' So she went, and gave birth to the white ice-lion. Then it said: 'The white ice-lion I am not; I must be born on the lofty rock; please go on to the lofty rock.' So she went, and gave birth to the wild bird-king. In this way the narrative progresses, and Gogzalhamo gives birth to the horse **rKyangbyung-khadkar** in the midst of the steppe; in the midst of the sea to the little fish Gold-eye; in the midst of the meadow to the yak **'aBrong byung rogpo**; in the midst of the forest to the rat **Kraphusse**; in the midst of the field to the little bare bird; also, in **Stanglha** to a golden frog; in **Barbtsan** to a white frog; and in **Yogklu** to a blue frog. After all that to her child also.

4. Third version of the story of the birth:—Over the whole earth it was dark; but at **Gogzalhamo's** house appeared a bright light. The child teased the mother in the same way as **Dongrub** did the giant in III. 34–45. Finally, it came out between the ribs, without causing the mother any pain. The child was very beautiful, and had golden hair and wings; yet the mother could see nothing of its beauty. At its birth the fire blazed up of itself; grand dishes were cooked in the oven; sweet fragrance filled the room, and jewels came raining in. The child grew in a day as much as others in a month.

5. To V. There came eighteen **Andhe Bandhe,** who put the child in a kettle, in order to boil it. The unintended effect was that the child came out much stronger and more hardened than it had been before.

6. The young folk of gLing have gone hunting, and have killed nothing. Thereupon the Street-child goes out with the sling, and drives a whole herd of game into the cattle-pen, where he kills the animals with (his) knife, and cuts off their heads. Now appear the Lamas from the monastery, and reproach him for killing animals. **Kesar** asks if they never ate meat. They say: 'Only (that) of animals which have died a natural death.' He says, '*Diridir*', and snaps his fingers. All the animals come to life, and look for their heads. In doing so, they take the wrong heads in their hurry, so that large animals get small heads, and *vice versa*. Then the whole herd runs away, and

the Street-boy says to the Lamas: 'Be sure not to forget to fetch the animals and eat them when they have died.'

7. The Agus institute an archery-contest. The one who hits in the middle shall be king. The Street-boy comes, and hits a tiny mark at an enormous distance; but vanishes again completely immediately after.

8. According to another version, it is **Agu Khromo**, and in one case the husband of Gogzalhamo, who is said to have killed the devil-bird; but this gives no logical coherence.

9. (To III.) Advice for the journey to the earth:

If **Bya khyung dkrung nyima** troubles thee,
Call **Byamo dkarmo** to thy help:
If **'aDre lha btsan bog** troubles thee,
Call **Dzemo 'aBamza 'aBum skyid** to thy help.

10. **a'Bruguma, a donkey's mother.** This story is told after *Spring Myth* No. VI. 16. All the guests, being drunk, had gone to sleep. Kesar silently left the room and went to a neighbour's she-ass, that was with child. He caused her to give birth to a young ass at once by giving her very cold water to drink. The foal he carries to the banqueting hall and puts it in the lap of the girl, who is nearest the door. When she awakes, she puts it into her neighbour's lap, and so on. Last of all 'aBruguma awakes, sees the foal in her lap and tries to hide it, because the Street-boy has entered the room. She succeeds in hiding it in her sleeve. The Street-boy says: 'You will certainly be scolded, because you are late for breakfast!' 'Oh no,' she replies, 'it is only the poor people, who have their breakfast early in the morning, we do not belong to them!' Then by witchcraft he caused the foal to fall out of the sleeve and said: 'Look there, you have given birth to a little donkey!' The girl is ashamed and wishes to keep him still; therefore she prays him to come to another banquet. Of this we hear in *Spring Myth* No. VI. 17–69.

11. To be inserted *Spring Myth* No. II. 36: He who is beaten in the contest, will have to go to the land of gLing.

The Mythology of the Kesar Saga.

General Notes.

Up to the present, when editing **Ladakhi folklore of a non-Buddhistic character**, I have made use of the terms 'Pre-Buddhistic' and 'Bonpo' indifferently, because I did not expect to meet with more than a single non-Buddhistic religion in Ladakh. Dr. Laufer's latest publications of Bonpo MSS., however, make it **advisable to separate Bonpo mythology from the mythology of Ladakhi folklore;** because, although both of them may have much in common, there appear to be fundamental differences between them. In future, therefore, when speaking of the mythology embodied, for instance, in the Kesar Saga, I shall make use of the term **'gLing-chos'**, i.e., **mythology of gLing.**

The material, from which I draw my information on the gLing-chos, has increased a great deal since the first publication in German of the first half of the Kesar Saga; but I do not wish my ideas on the subject to be taken for more than a theory. At present, the existence of the gLing-chos can only be supposed for Ladakh; but it may hereafter become evident that the same or similar systems of mythology were known in Tibet and many parts of Asia.

Sources of Information.

(1) **The Kesar Saga.** It is related in four parts:—

- (*a*) **Prelude to the Kesar Saga,** which tells of the creation of the world and of the birth of the eighteen ages.
- (*b*) **First half of the Kesar Saga (Spring Myth),** which tells of Kesar's birth in gLing, his wooing and marriage to 'aBruguma.
- (*c*) **Second half of the Kesar Saga (Winter Myth),** which tells of Kesar's journey to the north, the killing of the giant-devil, marriage of the devil's wife to Kesar, and of 'aBruguma's deliverance out of the hands of the King of Hor, who had abducted her.
- (*d*) **Kesar's Journey to China,** which is a different **version of the Winter Myth,** and tells of Kesar's marriage to the King of China's daughter.

(2) **The Ladakhi Marriage Ritual.** This was published *ante*, Vol. XXX, 1901, pp. 131ff.

(3) **Songs of the Nyopa** on their way to the bride's house.

(4) **The drinking song,** which is of a similar character to the marriage ritual.

(5) **The gLing-glu.** This has entirely the character of a **hymnal of the gLing-chos.** It is sung at the time of the Kesar Festival each spring. So far, the gLing-glu of only two villages has been collected, i.e., of Phyang and Khalatse. It will, perhaps, be easy to collect a large number of these songs, which appear to be of the greatest value for a proper understanding of the character of Kesar.

The Cosmology of the gLing-chos.

In nearly all of the above-mentioned sources three large realms are spoken of. Compare: *Spring Myth* No. IV. 20, 23, 26; *Marriage Ritual* No. I. B. 1, 2, 3; *gLing-glu* of Khalatse No. XXVII; *gLing-glu* of Phyang No. 1.

1. **sTang-lha, Heaven** (lit., 'the upper gods' or 'gods above'; no etymology is wanted, because the word is colloquial Ladakhi). Of this realm we hear in *Spring Myth* No. II; *Winter Myth* No. V. 8–13; *gLing-glu* of Phyang No. V; *gLing-glu* of Khalatse No. XXI, No. XXVII. 1, 2. From all these sources the following information can be drawn: A king reigns in sTang-lha, called **dBangpo-rgyabbzhin** (according to Dr. Laufer **rGya-byin,** compare under 'Names'). He is also called **sKyer-rdzong-snyanpo** and **'aBum-khri-rgyalpo.** The name of his wife is **bKur-dman-rgyalmo, Ane-bkur-dman-mo** or **'aBum-khri-rgyalmo.** Both are called 'Almighty': Compare *gLing-glu* of Phyang No. V.

They have three sons, **Donyod, Donldan, Dongrub.** The youngest is the most prominent figure. Lightning flashes from his sword out of the middle of the black clouds (*gLing-glu* of Khalatse No. XXIX). Thunder seems to be caused by the walking of the gods (*gLing-glu* of Khalatse No. XXI). Dongrub descends to the earth and becomes **King Kesar of gLing.**

The life of the gods is an idealised form of man's life. They form a state according to the *Winter Myth* No. V. 8–13. Besides a king there are ministers, servants and subjects. They live in perfect happiness and become old without illness. They tend goats, called *lhara*, apparently on the earth (*Spring Myth* No. I). Kesar later on discovers many of the stolen *lhara* in the devil's realm.

The king and the queen often change their shape. The king becomes a white bird (*Spring Myth* No. I. 3); the queen takes the shape of a woman (*Spring Myth* No. IV. 8), of a *Dzo* (*Winter Myth* No. I. 53).

2. **Bar-btsan, the Earth.** (No etymology is wanted, the name is colloquial Ladakhi for 'the firm place in the middle'.) Other names are: **Mi-yul,** Land of Men (compare *Spring Myth* No. III. 7); **gLing,** Continent (in colloquial Ladakhi). It is remarkable that neither the Spring Myth nor the Winter Myth tells us of beings, which entirely look like men. That the eighteen Agus are something different, is shown by their attributes.

The principal deity of the earth is mother **sKyabs-bdun** (*Marriage Ritual* No. I. B 2; *Spring Myth* No. VII. 19). It is probable, that she is identical with **brTanma,** the goddess of the earth (compare Jäschke's *Dictionary*), but at present nothing can be said for certain; nor do we know, if father **brTanpa** is her spouse and **'aBruguma** her daughter. All this will, perhaps, become plain with the publication of the Prelude to the Kesar Saga. Mother sKyabs-bdun rides a horse, called **bTsan-rta-dmar-chung** (*Spring Myth* No. VI. 22).

2. **Yog-klu, the Underworld** (lit., **the Nāgas** below). Of this realm we hear in *Winter Myth* No. V. 14–17; *gLing-glu* of Khalatse No. XXVII. 3, 4. Like sTang-lha, Yog-klu also seems to be a kingdom. There is a **king,** called **lCogpo** (*Marriage Ritual* No. I. B 3; *Spring Myth* No. VII. 24, 28); there are his servants and subjects, famous for their large number of children. The **Klu-mo or Nāginīs** are famous for their beauty; Kesar is warned not to fall in love with them.

According to all the material, which has accumulated so far, it is impossible to prove a distinct antagonism between the gods and the Nāgas. According to popular superstition, girls have to take care not to go near a well, where a male Nāga resides. **All the Nāgas have become protectors of the Buddhist faith** and show great enmity to all non-believers, if they can reach them.

The Colours of the three Realms.

They are mentioned in *Spring Myth* No. IV. 20, 23, 26; No. VII. 22, 30; No. IX. 1; *Winter Myth* No. II. 21, 22, 23. The colour of **sTang-lha** is white: it is perhaps the colour of the light; **Bar-btsan** is red: perhaps on account of the reddish colour of the ground; **Yog-klu** is blue: this may be due to the deep-blue colour of many West-Tibetan lakes. It may be in connection with this system of colours, that at the present day often three *mchod-rten* are erected, which are painted blue, white and red. Also most of the *lhatho* show the white colour.

In how far this system of colours may have influenced the pantheon of Lamaism, with its blue, white, red, green and golden-faced occupants, cannot yet be shown.

The King of Hor, called Gur-dkar is referred to in the prophesy (*Spring Myth* No. IX. 1–3), when 'aBruguma takes a blue ribbon and sits down on a blue carpet. This fact seems to suggest that he may be connected with Yog-klu in some way or other.

The Devil bDud.

In the *gLing-glu* of Phyang No. 1, to the three realms of the world, as described above, a fourth is added, **the Land of the Devil bDud.** We hear of the devil in *Spring Myth* No. I. 2–12, where he tries to carry away the heavenly goats and is killed. Apparently he comes to life again; for the first half of the *Winter Myth* tells of Kesar's victory over him. The devil is in possession of great treasures (*gLing-glu* of Phyang No. III.) and of a girl, who is kept in an iron cage (*Winter Myth* No. III.). As regards his size, appetite and stupidity, he closely resembles the giants of European mythology and folklore. The colour of the devil is black (*Spring Myth* No. I. 2; *Winter Myth* No. II 25). At first I was inclined to believe in a certain connection between the black and blue colours, because the hair of the Ladakhi girls is called 'turquoise' in some popular songs; however, this expression may refer to the actual turquoises, which are worn on the head. But also Kesar's pigtail, which is certainly without turquoises, is called blue; and the pool of the *klu* mentioned in *Spring Myth* No. III. 27, is called black.

Other names of the devil bDud are: **Srinpo** (*Winter Myth* No. III. 2); **Curulugu** (*Winter Myth* No. III. 8); **'aDre-lha-btsan-bog** (*Spring Myth*, Additions, No. IX); **sDigpa** (*Winter Myth* No. III. 26).

Of a very similar nature is Agu **Za** in *Spring Myth* No. III. 34–45. He devours not only Kesar, but also the sun and moon. He is in possession of the *srin γzhu*, the bow of the giants.

The devil bDud lives in a castle in the north (*byang*). There can be no doubt, that the word *byang* means actually the north, because everybody understands it in this sense. Near the castle there is the well of nectar (*bdud-rtsi*) and milk (*Winter Myth* No. IV. 17).

The Agus.

Dr. Laufer in his criticism tells me that the word *akhu*, from which the word *agu* may have developed, means 'uncle' in Tibetan. A I said before, it will be safest to look at the Ladakhi version of the Kesar Saga from a Ladakhi point of view; and in Ladakhi the word 'uncle' is never expressed by *akhu* or *agu*, but by *azhang*.

With regard to this word, I can only repeat what I said in my German Edition of the Kesar Saga: In Ladakhi the word *agu* serves to express (1) a husband in general, (2) from a child's point of view, one of the principal husband's younger brothers, who is more than an uncle to the principal husband's children; he is something like their step-father, as the principal husband's wife is his wife too.

Thus the word *agu* may be a variation of the word *pha-spun*, father-brothers (*Spring Myth* No. V. 33, VI. 56) of Kesar. At present the word *pha-spun* is always used in the sense of 'undertaker'. The *pha-spun* have to burn the dead; but it is possible that in ancient times the relatives of the dead had to take care of this office.

It is quite true that neither the *Spring* nor the *Winter Myth* tells us anything of a possible relationship between Kesar and the Agus. The 'Prelude to the **Kesar Saga**' will probably throw some light on the question. The latter contains a list of all the eighteen Agus with their characteristic marks. Many of them seem to possess more than a single name. This list is given below. As far as I can see, their attributes point to an ancient zodiac and to the days of the week. A picture, showing all the eighteen Agus, can, as I am told, be seen at Phagspa-gonpa, Lahoul, and at Hemis, Ladakh.

According to the Prelude of the Kesar Saga, the **Names of the Eighteen Agus** are the following[1] :—

(1) **Pasang ldan ru skyes,** possessing the Friday, horns growing. *Characteristic mark*: a goat's head.

(2) **Anggar rtsangspo, Anggar,** the lizard. *Char. m.*: a lizard's head.

(3) **Khra mgo khra thung,** falcon's head, short falcon. *Char. m.*: a falcon's head.

(4) **Kha rgan dgani (nyi),** old mouth, day of joy. *Char. m.*: a white beard.

(5) **sKya rgodpo,** wild soup-spoon. *Char. m.*: a soup-spoon instead of a head.

(6) **zLaba bzangpo,** good moon. *Char. m.*: a moon instead of a head.

[1] As given by Francke in the *Indian Antiquary*, 1901, p. 564.

(7) **mD'a dpon gongma,** the high headman of bowmen. *Char. m.*: an arrow blade instead of a head.

(8) **Ala jong gol** (this means, so I am told, the sole of a boot, the stupid one). *Char. m.*: the sole of a boot instead of a head.

(9) **'aBu dmar lamstan,** red vermin, way leader. *Char. m.*: a worm's head

(10) **Shelgyi buchung,** little boy of glass (or crystal). *Char. m.*: a concave mirror instead of a head.

(11) **dGani (nyi) gongba,** day of joy, the collar. *Char. m.*: a collar instead of a head.

(12) **Laglag rings,** long hand. *Char. m.*: a hand instead of a head.

(13) **rKang rkang rings,** long foot (or leg). *Char. m.*: a foot instead of a head.

(14) **Bongnag ldumbu,** black ass (*ldumbu* = a plant ?). *Char. m.*: a donkey's head.

(15) **bKa blon ldanpa,** the state-minister, the possessor. *Char. m.*: a man's head.

(16) **dPalle rgodpo,** wild splendour, glory. *Char. m.*: an old man's head.

(17) **rNa γyu rna 'athal,** turquoise earring. *Char. m.*: a turquoise instead of a head.

(18) **zLaba dkarpo,** white moon. *Char. m.*: a white shell instead of a head.

To these **Kesar or Kyesar** has to be added as their leader, he is the nineteenth. **Holy numbers** in the Pre-Buddhist religion of Ladakh are 3, 7, 9 and 18; but it is remarkable, that, whilst the first three of these numbers are always quoted without a following number, the 18 is always followed up by 19. For example: 'They digged a pit of 18, 19 yards', 'there appeared 18, 19 priests.'

If we take **Kesar,** the supposed **sun** hero, into the account, it is not difficult to identify **six of the nineteen Agus with six of the seven days of the Tibetan week.** Then the question remains: What could be the probable origin of the remaining 12? Their number seems to point to the Months of the Year, or to the Zodiac; but as I have no means available to compare their characteristic marks with those of other lunar calendars, I should be very glad, if competent scholars would offer an opinion on the subject.

As far as I can see, some of the Agus do not possess only a single name, but several, though the characteristic mark will probably remain the same.

The **representatives of the weekdays** are probably the following :—

No. 19, Sunday; No. 6, Monday; No. 9, Tuesday; No. 12, Wednesday; No. 7, Thursday; No. 1, Friday.

The Spring Myth of the Kesar Saga.

This is the portion of my mythology, that has met with the greatest opposition. Not taking the names into account, there were two reasons in particular, which induced me to believe in the possibility of a *Spring Myth*: (1) The two forms of Kesar. One of them is ugly and in this Kesar is born (*Spring Myth* No. IV. 3, 4, 5). The other is beautiful, and its attributes are the sun and moon (*Spring Myth* No. VII. 33). These two forms he changes continually, as is shown by the *Spring Myth*. (2) Kesar's ability to disappear altogether (*Spring Myth* No. VIII. 5, No. IX. 6, 7; Additions No. 7).

According to Dr. Laufer's criticism, the Kesar Myths, as related above, are very abrupt, and do not explain the motives for certain actions. They are repetitions of certain passages of the **Kesar Epic,** in which important ideas were forgotten. He gives an example: The story told in *Spring Myth* No. VIII. 33–41 is according to his conception a weak reflection of a passage of the Kesar Epic, given in Additions No. 10. With regard to this example, I must say that it does not hit the point. The Ladakhis themselves distinguish between the two stories. There is no more similarity between the two than there is between the story of Dongrub's descent to the earth through hail and the story of Zeus's descent in the golden rain. There is an endless variety of versions of the *Spring Myth* as well as of the *Winter Myth*, changing sometimes considerably from one village to the next. Most of them are matter learnt by heart. But all this material is never learnt by consulting the Kesar Epic. These are stories handed down in those villages from time immemorial. They are a necessary supplement to the *gLing-glu*, which would be unintelligible without them. Now the story, given in Additions No. 10, is not only a portion of the Kesar Epic (*dPe-sgrungs*), but is a portion of many oral tales as well (*Kha-sgrungs*). (The Ladakhis themselves distinguish emphatically between *dPe-sgrungs* and *Kha-sgrungs*). In one of my MSS. of the *Kha-sgrungs*, the story, given under Additions No. 10, is told at the end of the story of the banquet, that is, after *Spring Myth* No. VI. 16, and the story *Spring Myth* No. VIII. 33–41 in its usual place. Thus one and the same MS. contains both of them.

If it be a characteristic mark of the Kesar Epic to give motives for all the sudden disappearances of Kesar, that would not induce me to believe in the previous origin of the Epic; it would confirm my belief that there are fundamental differences between the epic and the oral tales. All the oral tales agree on this one point, that Kesar is capricious to the utmost extent. He comes and goes without a given reason, and likes nothing better than teasing.

That the form of the oral Kesar-stories, as we find them in the different villages, is not the original, is shown by their conglomerate character. They do not exhibit the labours of an editor but tell the same story several times according to different versions. Examples are:—

(1) *Spring Myth* No. II. 1–28. The father asks his sons, who would like to go to the country of men, and Dongrub decides to go. Now this story ought there to come to an end. However, the same tale continues (compare Additions No. 11; *Spring Myth* No. II. 36–42; *gLing-glu* of Phyang No. VII) that he shall go who loses in the contest.

(2) The full stories of Kesar's birth on the earth (Additions No. 2, 3, 4) were told in the following way: The first MS. relates the birth-story (Additions No. 2), and then, without any break or preceding notice, continues with Additions No. 3. The second MS. at first tells Additions No. 4, and then continues with Additions No. 3. Thus the child is born twice in the same tale.

(3) *Spring Myth* No. VI and No. VII are two different versions of the engagement story, told one after the other in the same oral tale.

Now, if the oral tales (*Kha-sgrungs*) are repetitions of the Kesar Epic in spite of all this, it remains a wonderful fact, that all those stories of wars and armies, which form the larger portion of the epic, are never repeated in the oral tales. As will be seen in the *Winter Myth*, the defeat of the Giant of the North, as well as that of the King of Hor, has nothing to do with armies and battles. The killing of both of them is a private affair of Kesar. Nor do the oral tales ever tell us much of human subjects of Kesar. The animals occupy a much more prominent place. A number of animals are born together with Kesar (Additions No. 2, 3), and another number of animals lament over Kesar's departure for his journey towards the north (*Winter Myth* No. I. 39–44). Looking at this passage, it is remarkable, indeed, that 'aBruguma is the only human being who mourns on account of Kesar's departure. I do not wish to offend anybody, but I must say, that I am simply unable to understand a passage like that without accepting the possibility that it is meant to express the mourning of Nature over the departure of the sun.

I am far from believing that every incident in the Kesar Saga ought to be explained on the ground that the whole of it is a Spring and Winter Myth; and I may have gone too far in my first outlines of the Kesar mythology; but I am afraid my critics are making the same mistake, if they will not even accept the possibility of a Spring and Winter Myth in the Saga.

In this connection it is also of some interest, that sun and moon are attributes of Kesar's beautiful shape, and that according to *gLing-glu* of Khalatse No. XXVIII. Kesar is compared with a flower, blooming on all the high passes, and according to No. XXIX in the middle of the black clouds lightning flashes from the godly king Kesar's sword.

The Loka-pālas.

There is some likelihood that the *gLing-chos* of Ladakh had four deities, corresponding to the Indian **Loka-pālas**. Up to the present I have met with them only in the marriage ritual (compare Song No. I. B 4–7). This is **the list of them:**

Tibetan.	English.	Sanskrit (Dhyānibuddha).	Region.
Donyod-grubpa ..	Fulfiller of the aim, he has.	**Amogha-siddha**	North.
rDorje-sems-dp'a	Thunderbolt, courageous soul.	**Vajra-sattva**	East.
Rinchen-byungldan	Great price, possessing creatures.	**Ratna-sambhava**	South.
sNangba-mth'a-yas	Eternal light ..	**Amitābha**	West.

This list shows that the Tibetan and Indian names correspond to a great degree. We shall, perhaps, be obliged to accept the theory of a mutual influencing between North India and Ladakh in pre-Buddhist times. Dr. Laufer for instance **identifies dBangpo-rgya-bzhin with Indra.** Also the name of the glacier, **Sengge-dkarmo-γyu-ral-can,** the white lioness with the turquoise locks (*sengge = siṁha*) may be mentioned.

What induces me to believe in the originality of the Tibetan names, is the fact that two of them, **rDo-rje-sems-dp'a** and **Rinchen-byung-ldan** (the pronunciation of the latter is not **Jung-ldan, but Byung-ldan** in Lower Ladakh), contain more meaning in Tibetan than in Sanskrit. I only wish to mention this fact. This subject was treated more fully in the *Globus*.

The Tree of the World.

We hear of it in *Marriage Ritual* No. V–VIII; *gLing-glu* of Khalatse No. 1. Its roots grow in Yog-klu, its top touches Stang-lha; it has six branches.

Animism in the gLing-Chos.

Here I should like to mention the following personifications: *skyeser*, the wind; *sbang-char-zilbu*, the rain; *sengge-dkarmo-γyuralcan*, the glacier; *bya-khyung-dkrung-nyima*, the sun; *byamo-dkarmo*, the moon. With *γnyan*, living in rocks and trees, I have met only in the wedding songs of *Tagmacig*.

It is remarkable that several of these personifications are mentioned together with the representatives of the animal world. Compare Additions No. 3; *Winter Myth* No. I. 39–44.

The Pre-Buddhist Origin of the Kesar Saga in Ladakh.

In my German edition of the Kesar Saga I tried to make it probable that the Kesar Saga was in existence in Ladakh at the time of the introduction of Buddhism into Ladakh. Dr. Laufer tells me that I had better fix the culture-historical epoch of the Kesar Saga. He makes the following suggestions: In *Spring Myth* No. I. 5–12 the use of the sling as a weapon is mentioned, and in No. IV. 14, the use of a stone vessel. To this I may add that according to *Winter Myth* No. III. 25, a stone sword is mentioned side by side with rifles and other weapons. This suggestion of the stone age may be very useful under European conditions, but is not of any use for fixing the age of a Tibetan tale. The reason is that the stone age has lasted in Ladakh up to the present day. I wonder how many stone vessels there are in use in my own private household! The sling of Agu dPalle is no more a weapon than that of David, because dogs are not used here for tending goats. Goats and sheep are called back with the help of stones thrown at them. I myself have seen a stone axe in use, and in side valleys near Lamayuru a stone hatchet, called *kalam*, is still in general use, so I am told. Pottery and iron ware are well known in Ladakh; however, want of wood makes both these articles extremely expensive, and side by side with pottery and iron ware, stone ware cannot be dispensed with.

I therefore stick to what I said before: that apparently the Kesar Saga was existent in Ladakh at the time of the introduction of Buddhism into Ladakh. The lines in *Spring Myth* No. III. 5 and 12, *sangs-rgyas la btangbai gri*, a knife to stab Buddha, were probably inserted at the time, when enmity against Buddhism became general. The passage in *Winter Myth* No. III. 26 and other researches have shown me plainly that the passages, in *Spring Myth* No. III. 5 and 12, can only be translated as I did.

In my German paper I had also mentioned the fact that Kesar is not at all scrupulous as regards the killing of animals. Dr. Laufer tells me that this fact does not in the least prove the non-Buddhistic character of the Kesar Saga, because animals have been killed and are still killed all over Tibet. I can only repeat what I said some time ago, that although the Ladakhis are very fond of eating meat, it is very difficult to find persons who are ready to kill animals. Most of the meat eaten by Ladakhis is taken from animals which have died a natural death. The fact that every body is simply swarming with lice is due to the fact that nobody wishes to kill these animals.

I hope the publication of the different *gLing-glu*, the Marriage Ritual, the *Winter Myth* and *Prelude to the Kesar Saga*, will justify my attempt to draw the outlines of the mythology of the *gLing-chos*. Whether the material of the Kesar Saga is originally Ladakhi, or whether it was introduced into Ladakh from some other part of Asia,[1] whether materials

---

[1] In one of my former papers on the Kesar Saga (*Globus*, Vol. LXXVI, No. 20) I made a mistake in saying that the Ladakhi versions of the Kesar Saga were entirely different from the Mongolian epic. This mistake was caused by a misunderstanding. As I had no means of comparing my Ladakhi MSS. with the Mongolian epic, I asked a friend to look up the latter in the Strassburg University Library. He apparently got hold of the wrong book; for what he told me of woodmen and other mythological beings could not well be reconciled with what I knew from the Ladakhi version. Dr. Laufer, starting from my mistake, proves a long demonstration of about 10 pages, that the subject in both is the same.

contained in the folklore of Ladakh are the original, or whether they are borrowed from the epic,—all this does not alter the fact, that in Ladakh this material has taken the shape of a religion, which exercises its influence up to the present day. I do not see why I should not write down the outlines of a religion, whose influence cannot be denied by all who have lived in Ladakh for some time.

General Position of the gLing-chos.

As has been stated, the Kesar Saga is not only known to Ladakhis, but is recited in a great number of countries all over Asia. Until it has been studied in all of them, it will be impossible to decide where is the original home of the Saga, nor by which road it has travelled from one country to the other. European folklore and mythology also contains many parallels to the Kesar Saga, as has been shown by Schott, Ersch, Gruber, Grimm, Jülg and Potanin (according to Dr. Laufer's criticism). There are certain mythological ideas which seem to be existent in a very large territory all over the globe. Dr. Laufer mentions the frequent use of number 9; great power of the hero; quick growth of the hero when a boy; two rocks, knocking against each other; a smith, teaching the hero:—all of which occur in the Kesar Saga.

If future researches should enable us to see the route, which all of these stories have followed in their wanderings, the question still remains, why just these stories, which do not appear to be particularly amusing, have travelled all over the earth. I could well imagine that solar mythologies, grown, perhaps, out of animism (and if stones were considered to be animated, why not the sun?), many have arisen in different places of the earth. These mythologies may have prepared the road for certain mythological tales; and the relationship of the different mythologies may rest in the fact that their originator, the Sun, is everywhere the same.

Note :—A third Article on the *Spring Myth of the Kesar Saga* by Francke appeared in the *Indian Antiquary*, Vol. XXXI, 1902, pp. 147–157. This is not printed again. It consists of 'Philological Notes' on the names of the Kesar Saga, and a 'Tibetan Alphabetical List of Proper Names' which are all given in the List of Proper Names already printed in this edition (pp. 323–371). Besides there are English translations of Francke's German Notes on some words and expressions in the Tibetan Text which appeared in the Helsingfors publication: a few of these, including Dr. B. Laufer's emendations, have been incorporated in the reprint. [S. K. Chatterji.]

[2]

THE WINTER MYTH OF THE KESAR SAGA.[1]

(English Translation by Dr. Batakrishna Ghosh and Dr. Suniti Kumar Chatterji of the German Rendering from the Ladakhi Tibetan Original by A. H. Francke.)

I.

1. **Kesar** the God-king of **gLing** was a strict hermit in the temple of **γYu 'abrug** (= 'Turquoise Thunder': Blue Lightning ?). He had joined it in the third month of the third year. 2. When about two or three months had elapsed, **Ane bKur dmanmo** the Queen of the Gods was having only bad and evil dreams. For that reason she went to the door of the hermitage and prayed there in the following way:

3. 'O thou my grandson, ah yea, hear my voice!
4. O dreaming boy, ah yea, hear my voice!
5. Ah, already for three nights I am having only evil dreams,
6. (I) saw the upper valley swept by a high flood,
7. Amidst the water, the King's castle, standing up, destroyed.
8. (I) saw in the lower valley a fire burning,
9. Over the flames, the King's castle, standing up, destroyed.
10. (I) saw **Curulugu**,[2] the devil, flying to Heaven,
11. King Kesar, however, creeping on the earth.
12. This year the fire strikes **Curulugu**, the devil.
13. This year the water strikes Kesar, the God-king.
14. If water is poured on the fire, then there will be a death.

15. Therefore do not go this year to bring ruin on the devil; it will suffice if next year he comes to the land of **gLing**. O thou my grandson, thou noble one, hear, hear!' 16. Thereupon Kesar answered to the Queen **Ane bKur dmanmo** :

---

[1] This English version is published for the first time. A few of Francke's notes are incorporated. The Tibetan Text and Francke's German Translation appeared in the *Suomalais-ugrilaisen Seuran Toimituksia XV* (Memoirs of the Finno-Ugrian Society XV), Helsingfors, 1902.

[2] **Curulugu** = Devil of the North: **lugu** = **Klu dgu** 'Nine Nāgas' ?

17. 'Gracious Nene (=Aunt), ah yea, just hear me now,
18. **Ane bKur dmanmo**, ah yea, be well disposed towards me!
19. I prepared a sacrificial cake, so *big*, on the hill to the right
20. I prepared a sacrificial cake, so *small*, on the hill to the left.
21. I shaped flowers out of butter like the rising sun and moon.
22. The whole I then painted with five colours of the rainbow.
23. Also I offered corn and bread offering in heaps.
24. I filled an overflowing lake of holy water.
25. I burnt a sacred lamp lighting up the darkness.

26. Therefore if possible give me leave for three years. If that cannot be done, give me leave for seven months. In the worst chance, give me in any case seven days!' 27. Then the goddess **Ane bKur dmanmo** thought: 'My grandson (at all events) has grown up in the virtues of Religion.' Thinking thus she again went away. 28. Thereupon the Crystal wife **'aBrugmo ('aBruguma)** said to the maid **Darlhagochodma**:

29. 'Prepare food as much as an Ice Mountain!
30. Prepare strong drink (in quantity) like the **Maphang** lake!
31. Then prepare heaps of the best (*lit.* strongest) yak flesh!
32. Similarly (flesh) of the fattest yak cow!
33. Also prepare goat's flesh which melts in the mouth!
34. Similarly lamb's meat which increases strength!
35. Also prepare a well-grown young sheep!
36. So go then, outside struggling for breath, yea, struggling (i.e. go out in breathless haste)!
37. So go then inside, bowing thyself low, yea, bowing!'

38. After she had said that they prepared the foodstuffs. Then **'aBruguma** sang the following song:

39. 'If Kesar the God-king does not stay on and goes towards the North,
Who is then possibly the hope of **'aBrugmo,** the loving wife?
40. If he does not stay on in the blue zenith and goes towards the North,
Who is then possibly the hope of the Sun and the Moon?
41. If he does not stay with the high glacier and goes towards the North,
Who is then possibly the hope of the white lioness?

42. If he does not stay on with the high rock and goes towards the North,
Who is then possibly the hope of the wild eagle?
43. If he does not stay on in the deep lake and goes towards the North,
Who is then possibly the hope of the gold-eyed one, the small fish?
44. If he does not stay on in the high mountain-pasture and goes towards the North,
Who is then possibly the hope of the wild yak?'

45. As the loving wife **'aBruguma** could not however separate herself from the King, she kept him on for one month. 46. One day **Ane bKur dmanmo** came about midnight and said:

47. 'The wise man is without wisdom,
The clever one is without cleverness!

48. King Kesar, when wilst thou go?'—speaking thus she rebuked him out. 49. When the next day broke, he felt himself unhappy, he was full of fright, vacillating and restless. 50. By sun-rise he fetched the foal **rKyang rgod dbyerpa** out of the garden of the round flowers, and put the saddle-trappings on him. 51. Then the loving wife **'aBrugmo** came with all her maids and the maidens of the neighbourhood who brought out burning cedar twigs and beer jugs garnished with many bits of butter, and they all accompanied him. 52. For a half-day's march Kesar accompanied (his wife), and then again (back) homewards, and **'aBruguma** again accompanied back (outwards): while they were going backwards and forwards in this way, evening fell. 53. Then **Ane bKur dmanmo** came again who had transformed herself into a female *Dzo* with crooked horns and gave the foal **rKyang rgod dbyerpa** a lusty thrust. 54. The King became angry, and cried out: 'How is that, that at the start of my journey thou female *Dzo* dost poke at my horse **rKyang rgod dbyerpa**?' Although however he emptied a whole quiver of arrows on the *Dzo*, not a single one of them struck him (= her). 55. Thereupon the Sun disappeared as also the female *Dzo*, and **'aBrugmo** came back home with her following.[1]

---

[1] In his *Notes*, Francke connects 55 with the proverb *'abrong dang nyima laru 'abud nachung bomo rtunla lus* 'the wild *yak* and the sun disappear on the pass, then the young woman, the maiden, stays on with her quern', i.e. to her remains nothing but the common hard labour.

II.

1. The God-king, both man and horse, stayed back at the entrance of the three valleys. During the night **Ane bKur dmanmo** showed a big and fearful nightmare:

2. In the upper valley the wolves howled,
In the lower valley the foxes growled.
3. The reed without lungs took to piping,
The dung without feet took to dancing.
4. The round dung at the side then sprang,
A storm on the pass, a frightful one, began.

5. In order to know whether Kesar could complete the journey to the north or not, she frightened him in this way. 6. Then Kesar was very much disturbed, and wept; on the next morning, however, all (i.e. the terrifying things) disappeared. **Ane bKur dmanmo** came and offered him the shell of a nut full of flour and the shell of a nut full of beer for his food. 'If thou prayest to the gods, then wilt get food of good taste, of a taste which one can only imagine,' so said she, and gave a saddle cloth for the horse which (looked) like a grass mat. 8. Then she brought as guide a female fox of pearl-white colour, and gave the following exhortation:

9. 'When the little fox creeps forward slowly, slowly,
Both, horse and king, then creep slowly after!
10. When the little fox flies forward, swiftly, swiftly,
Both, horse and king, then do like that!
11. When the little fox winding zigzagwise marches forward,
Both, horse and king, do like that!
12. When the little fox lays herself down to sleep,
Both, horse and king, then sleep peacefully!
13. When the little fox rises quickly from her sleep,
Both, horse and king, up! and hasten therefrom!'

14. Then they journeyed across a plain land, the ridge of a hill, and through a sheet of water, and when the sun went down, they made a halt in a desert and empty valley. 15. [Kesar] felt hungry and thought, 'I want to eat something!'. But as there was nothing but the cold dish of the shell of the nut, he thought: 'How can I satisfy my hunger (with this)? There is not even a single bite and a single sip!' and felt disturbed in his mind. 16. [But] the horse **rKyang rgod**

dbyerpa devoured the saddle cloth of grass mat, and throughout the whole night made the sound *curum curum*. 17. As even before the morning grey the King raised his head and looked [around himself], (he saw that) the colt had eaten enough, and had dropped much heavy dung: yet the grass mat (saddle-cover) was just as it was before. 18. Then Kesar thought, 'Who knows! should not also what I am eating come back again?' When he ate and (found the food) tasty as butter-meal, sugar and syrup. However much he ate, it all came back again. 19. 'That shows the kindness of my gentle mother!' thought he, and regained courage. Then they travelled over nine passes, nine valleys and nine high plateaux. 20. There on three passes stood three altars, of red, white and blue colours. To these three altars (Kesar) offered the following prayer:

21. 'A red altar stands on Red Pass,
A red altar is there raised.
Allow me to offer a piece of red scarf,
While I thought of the altars of **gLing**-land!
Grant me fulfilment of my thoughts (wishes)!
22. A white altar stands on White Pass,
A white altar is there raised.
A white scarf do I offer here,
While I thought of the altars of **gLing**-land!
Help me for fulfilling my thoughts!
23. A blue altar stands on Blue Pass,
A blue altar is there raised.
A blue scarf I wish to offer here,
While I thought of the altars of **gLing**-land!
Grant me the fulfilment of my thoughts!
24. Be mindful of (this) prayer and offering,
O ye God-kings all!'

25. Then he travelled through a black valley and a black plain and saw a big black altar (standing) on a black pass. As (Kesar) thought that that was the altar of the Devil-king, 26. he destroyed everything from its foundation. The fragments he threw into water, the dust he gave to the winds, and left no trace of it behind.

27. There a goatherd of the Devil-king was tending (his flock) in the valleys on this side and that. The King sought the heavenly sheep out of all the flocks of sheep and goats, he bound them, took

them with him and slaughtered them. The skins he stuffed and bound them together with a rope of goat's hair. 28. Then the King asked him (the goatherd) all about the Devil; but the latter said: 'Who art thou, what art thou?' and did not tell the truth. Then the King cried out: 'Wherefrom hast thou got these heavenly goats?' and seized (the herdsman) by the collar and struck him with the right hand three times on the cheek. 29. 'O gracious King, I knew not that thou art Kesar, the God-king of **gLing**! Please, procure me deliverance in this and in that life! I shall also tell you everything about the Devil! 30. At present the Devil has gone to the west to spy about. The **Dzemo 'abamza 'abumskyid** is sitting imprisoned in an iron cage. If thou now goest (thereto), thou wilt find only dead giants at the eastern, southern, western and northern gates of the Devil's castles, which are stuffed. They are set on horses and elephants, and are furnished with sword and flint. 31. They are however all empty; therefore do not be afraid:' saying thus, he instructed him. When the king went forward, he (however) felt afraid. It was as if his life would be taken. While going he shot arrows, and here and there dust whirled up.

III.

1. Then the King went forward and opened the nine gates in order. The innermost main gate was of gold. When he opened that he saw the **Dzemo 'abamza 'abumskyid** sitting in an iron cage. 2. The **Dzemo** said: 'Who art thou then?

Man that hast lost the way, this is a giant's nest!
Youth that hast lost the way, this is a giant's nest!

3. How wilt thou come out here again?' 'I am Kesar, the God-king of **gLing**! do thou just come out!' inasmuch as he said that, he drew her out of the iron cage, and for that reason the **Dzemo** showed the God-king much love, veneration and readiness for service. 4. When about 15 or 20 days had passed, then only came a strong wind, and then the whole area trembled and quaked. For that reason Kesar was afraid (and cried out), 'What is this? What do I hear? Tell me that, **Dzemo**!'. 5. The **Dzemo** answered: 'The King himself is now returning back home!' 'Where should we two, man and horse, then stay?' 'He will not arrive still within ten to fifteen days! Don't be anxious!' said she. 6. When about ten days had passed, there came more wind and earthquake, as on that occasion, so that Kesar was afraid and asked, 'What's

the matter now?' 'Now he has covered half the way,' answered she. 7. Then the **Dzemo** brought out of her right pocket seven little bones, and seven cowrie shells out of her left pocket. Then she said: '*Haha, huhu, hrum, hrum*,' and transformed the little bones into seven youths, the seven cowrie shells however into seven maidens. Then she had two pits of eighteen and nineteen fathom deep dug and put into them the King and the horse.

8. Then the King **Curulugu** (the Devil) appeared and said, **Dzemo!**

I smell human flesh,
I smell horse flesh!'

9. The **Dzemo** gave the following answer: 'There comes the King carrying on his right shoulder hundred carcasses of horses and on his left hundred human corpses, while he is still chewing an eight-year old child. How shall I then come out and see from the iron cage a human being or a horse?' 10. The Devil said, 'Then fetch my book! Don't hold it under your body, but offer incense, and bring it carrying it on the head'. The **Dzemo** went, held (the book) under the body, stepped on it, and burnt dog's dung as incense, and brought it. 11. Out of the book he said: 'The God-king Kesar of **gLing**, the man with the horse, has come and is sitting nine *rimpa* deep under a lake and three hills!' The lake and the hills are surely a symbol for the water of the copper-vessel and the three hearth-stones. 12. 'The book I know not!' said the Devil, and threw it into the fire. When half of it was burnt, the **Dzemo** drew it out again and said, 'It may yet once again be necessary for us!'

13. Then the giant shouted: '**Dzemo**, now I am hungry! Prepare the meal!' Thereupon the **Dzemo** prepared shovels of flour, cut to pieces hundred dead horses, donkeys and human beings, made a sauce and gave him (all that). 14. '**Dzemo**, now I shall sleep!' 'Very well,' said she, and made (the bed) with pillows for the head and the carpet. He asked: 'Shall I only have a little sleep like the birds, or shall I have a regular deep sleep?' Thereupon the **Dzemo** replied: 'When one is on a journey, one should take only a little sleep like the birds; now that you have come home, sleep well!' 15. '**Dzemo**, how much truth has (just) been uttered!' Then he fell asleep. When he had slept well, he did not well wake up before one year. When sleeping he was snoring loudly. 16. But the **Dzemo**, as before, fetched the seven little bones and the

seven *cowrie* shells, laid aside the copper vessel and the hearth-stone, and had the God-king, man and horse, dug out again. 17. The Devil snored on, and when he blew out the wind, the God-king, man and horse were pressed to the wall; when, however, he took in the breath, both horse and man flew up to his nostrils. 18. Then the God-king got afraid and could do nothing. The **Dzemo** however rode on the horse **rKyang rgod dbyerpa,** and although they several times ran about on the body of the Devil up and down, he did not betray by any sign that he was aware of it. 19. Then the God-king Kesar took courage and also ran about twice or thrice, riding on **rKyang rgod dbyerpa** (on the Devil).

20. The Devil had nine lives. (Kesar) cut off all of them one by one in order. First he cut off the nose, then he knocked out the two big corner-teeth · thereupon he cut off the right as well as the left hand. 21. When he tore out both the eyes, (the Devil) said: 'Who art thou?', (and) raised himself a little and laid himself down on the other side. 'I am **dPalle rgodpo**!' 'Oh, I shall not die at the hand of **dPalle rgodpo**.' said (the Devil). 22. And when (Kesar) cut out his tongue, he cried out, 'Ah woe, who art thou?' 'I am **dGani mgonpo of gLing**!' 'Oh, at his hand I shall not die!' 23. When both the ears were cut, (the Devil) cried up, 'Oh, woe! who art thou?' 'I am **sDangma spyang Khra** (= 'the angry Wolf-Eagle', name of one of the **Agus**) of **gLing**!' 'Oh, I shall not die at your hand!' Thereupon the God-king Kesar spake:

24. '**sKyer rdzong snyanpo**, O godly Father, praise to thee!
bKur dman rgyalmo, O godly Mother, praise to thee!
Send me nine of the gods born with me!
To-day come to my help, [ye highly honoured ones!],
To my most eager wish, give success!'

25. When he had spoken thus, he raised the stone sword in order to slit the throat (of the Devil). Then came **Ane bKur dman**, the God-queen, and cried:

'The wise one is without wisdom,
And the clever one without cleverness.

All (thy) thoughts are uprooted! O God-king Kesar! Do not kill (the Devil) with the stone sword! Hurry up with the knife "Three-finger-long" for the sinful one!' 26. Then he hastened with the dagger 'Three-finger-long' for the sinful one, and (the Devil) said: 'Art thou the God-king Kesar of gLing? At thy hand must I die! This year fire strikes me, and water strikes thee! I am laid low under thy hand!'

With that he died. 27. Then (Kesar) threw the pieces (of the Devil) into the water, the dust he threw away to the winds, and left no trace (of him).

IV.

1. The Dzemo 'aBamza 'abumskyid gave (Kesar) the food and drink of forgetfulness, and (thus) made him forget the land **gLing** and **'aBrugmo**, the castle and all people. Then whole day long they played at dice and shot arrows; in this way she kept him content. In this way three years passed.

2. King **Gur dKar** was leading along an army,
And broke asunder the nine towers of **gLing** castle.
3. He killed **Shel dKar**, the King's offspring,
And led away **'aBrugmo** the queen.
4. Of all this she wrote with blood in a letter,
And sent it forward by little birds in the house.

5. The latter flew once hither and once thither, but did not find the God-king Kesar (did not meet him). Their eyes were aching (from the search), the strength of their wings became lame; and they flew back again. 6. **Ane bKur dman** the Queen gave them a god-bath and a god-cleansing, let them have rest, and sent them out again in the search. When they were away, Queen **Ane bKur dmanmo** transformed herself into a dove, and as she showed them the way they arrived in the land of the Devil. 7. When just the God-king and the **Dzemo** were sitting at the game of dice, the birds of **gLing** let their voice resound down from the sky. In order not to let (Kesar) hear anything the **Dzemo** made noise. Kesar, however, said, 'Just hear, just hear, O **Dzemo**, I hear a voice like that of my birds of **gLing** coming?' 8. 'You are struck at present—

Já pará sugú
Shára rí sirí!' [1]

so she made noise. For that reason Kesar seized the **Dzemo** by her plait of hair and listened. 9. Then he spread out a white carpet and laid upon it the body of a freshly killed (animal). Also a black carpet he spread out and upon it he placed the carrion of a dead (animal). He said, 'If ye bring good news, then seat yourselves on the white carpet,

---

[1] *Já* = 12, *pará* = $\boxed{\times}$, *sugú* = 3, *shára* = 8, *rí* = 7, *sirí* = 3: these terms are used at the game of dice.

and set upon the fresh meat! If however ye bring bad news, then seat yourselves on the black carpet and set upon the carrion!' 10. Thereupon all the birds seated themselves on the black carpet and set upon the carrion. The big bird however loosened from his neck the letter and offered it. Therein was written the news of all that had happened hitherto.

11. Now when Kesar sought his horse **rKyang rgod dbyerpa**, it had vanished. He did not understand whither it could have run away, and whither not. When he asked the **Dzemo** about it, she said: 'Who knows? Nothing is known to me!' 12. Then King Kesar went out to seek it, and came up on three hills and down into three valleys. Finally, he saw it on the boundary between the loose rocks (moraines?) and the ice. It had a wounded back and wounded shank. Kesar was overpowered by sympathy and sorrow, and he called out to the horse. 13. Then the horse came to him (and said): 'Ah, thou thoughtless King Kesar!

14. Formerly I abided with **'aBrugmo**,
In the morning I used to get flour, butter and milk.
In the evening cakes and syrup of sugar.
When she came down, she used to fondle me;
When she went up, she patted me,
Saying, "my horse, how lean thou hast become!"

15. For three years I stood before the door of **Dzemo**.
In the morning I used to get ten loads of wood,
In the evening I used to get ten loads of sand.
When she got up, she used to kick me with her foot,
When she got down, with her fist she used to strike me,
Saying, "Thou horse, thou art much too fat!"

Then I had my fill of weeping.' 16. Kesar replied: 'Thou art quite right. The **Dzemo** has turned my head too. We should now go to the upland of **gLing**! But how should your wounds be healed?' 17. The horse said, 'In my right ear there are three good medicaments which my mother **'aBruguma** has placed there; in the left ear is a sharp little knife. Lead me to the spring of nectar and milk and wash me, cut with this small knife and apply the medicine; then I shall be healed'. 18. (Kesar) did as the horse had instructed him, and the latter became more fiery and better than he was before.

19. A child, a girl, was born to Kesar and the **Dzemo**; it was still young and a suckling. 20. Kesar followed the **Dzemo** and said:

'As the child is so small, thou cans't not come (with me). In one year I shall come (again) in order to fetch the mother and the child.' Yet (the **Dzemc**) did not listen, became proud (angry), and cried: 'I shall (nevertheless) go with you!' 21. Then the horse gave counsel: 'Let her sit behind on my back and side. When we come in the midst of a river, I shall give her a kick (push), so that she will reach the other bank.' Saying thus, he (the horse) let her sit behind on his back and carried her. 22. Then he gave her the push and threw her on the other bank. For that reason she was very angry, brought the unweaned child (the suckling), and said to Kesar, 'As thou, the father, art of a noble lineage, eat up the upper half (of the child)! As I am of lower lineage, I shall eat the lower half!' Then she made two parts of the child at the hips and sat there chewing the lower half. 23. Kesar however burnt the upper half, and arranged the bones which were left in the form of a picture of saints [1] and erected a little *mchod-rten* (stūpa) and went further on.

V.

1. On the way to the frontier between **Hor** and **gLing**, (Kesar) wrote a letter on the upper part of his saddle, (supported) on the stirrups, and sent it up to the castle of **gLing**. (In conformity with this letter, evidently, there came to meet him hundred faithful riders.) 2. Thus he arrived at the frontier of **Hor**, and rode from the **Asalsal** pass in the company of hundred riders; from the **Masalsal** pass he rode in the company of ten riders; and from the **Shangmo 'adur** (= 'Running She-wolf') pass he rode, man and horse, quite alone.

3. In the spring from which the drinking water for the King **Gur dKar** of **Hor** was drawn, he sank a big and dirty cup encircled with straw. Then he wetted his torn shoes therein, and himself put on a very torn and much patched-up coat, and threw himself back foremost into the spring. 4. Then the maid from **Hor** came, (named) **Bhag 'adzommo**, to fetch water, (and cried): 'This beggar and tramp has defiled our drinking water! Who art thou then? Thou bad, repulsive vagabond!' Thus she said, and abused him lustily. 5. Kesar replied: 'Oh, I am a vagrant man come here from far away; I am tired, exhausted and breathless!

---

[1] I.e. by mixing the powdered bone-fragments with earth and stamping them with figures of saints (Francke's note).

If thou art in hurry, then step over me!
If thou art not in hurry, go around me!'

So said he, and did not get up. 6. The maid went back to the castle without drawing water, and related to the beloved wife **'aBruguma** the whole incident; **'aBruguma** related the matter to King **Gur dKar.** 7. King **Gur dKar** appeared before (Kesar), and asked what it signified. Kesar replied, (by singing the following) like a song with its melody:

8. 'Did I go away as a monk, or did I not go?
9. Yet I went up, came into the realm of the gods.
10. King **rGya bzhin** himself I met there,
11. Lord, Servant, Son, Wife, Maid, are all in good health there.
12. Every subject waxed there and flourished,
13. Grew old without pain, and lived in eternal happiness.
14. Did I go away as a monk, or did I not go?
15. Yet I went down, came into the underworld.
16. King **lCogpo** himself I met there.
17. Everybody was there rich in children, and glad.
18. Did I go away as a monk, or did I not go?
19. Yet I ascended, came to the castle of **gLing.**
20. King Kesar died in the land of the Devil.
21. Sumptuous food and presents there are in heaps!
22. If a Lama is big, there are well ten thousand,
23. If he is not so big (*barpa*), then still a thousand coins.
24. If a Lama is small, there is still a hundred.
25. Each monk (*drvapa*) gets moreover yak and horse.
26. I, as a monk, received a black little sheep!
27. Previous year a yak-cow (*'abrimo*) disappeared from **gLing.**
28. This year a yak calf was born in **Hor,**
29. To see whether it is so, I a monk came hither.'

30 The King of **Hor** spake: 'Monk, thou art only a disguised monk!' and bound (Kesar) fast to a pillar. After a short while he freed himself loose, went away and was no more there.

31. Kesar went into the pea-field of the smith **Nagshangshang** (='the Clever Black One') and ate them (the peas) for food. Then **Chos sgron ma** (= 'Light of Dharma') the daughter of the smith went out, seized him and brought him (in). 32. When he came within the house of the smith, Kesar said, 'I am the son of the father (i.e. of the smith)! At the time when the army of **Hor** was led into the land of

gLing, my mother taught me and said, "Thy father is also of the land of **Hor**". 33. All children of the same condition had said, "Thou art one who hast no father—a bastard! Thou art not equal to us". Then my anger blazed out, and I related this weeping to my mother. Then my mother instructed me'. 34. The smith spoke: 'If thou art really my child, then thou must show (me) all (my) working tools (i.e. pick out from a heap of mixed tools those belonging to the smith **Nag-shangshang**)'. Kesar replied: 'To-morrow I shall pick them out;' and during the night cried to **Ane bKur dmanmo**. 35. The **Ane** remained invisible (without body), and said: 'From morning to midday when all tools have been put in a heap, I shall transform myself into a turquoise fly and sit upon all the tools belonging to the smith. Then be mindful and say, "the hammer big as a horse's head is not there".' 36. When (Kesar) acted according to the speech of the **Ane**, he was believed, and (they) handed over to him all the tools, and he remained there learning a smith's work.

37. **'aBruguma** did not love at all (the King of) **Hor**, fled and concealed herself continually. Then **'aBrugu** said (to the King): it was like a song:

38. 'Almost every one keeps a dog as his watcher, keeps as watcher!
But **'aBrugmo** keeps a wolf as her watcher, keeps as watcher!
If thou bringest an old wolf, fie on the animal, fie on the animal!
If thou bringest a small wolf, the poor animal, the poor animal!
Seek out a strong wolf, and stay one year, stay one year!

39. Almost every one keeps a yak as his draught animal, as his draught animal!
But **'aBrugmo** keeps a *brong* (= a wild yak) as her draught animal, as draught animal!
If thou bringest an old *brong*, fie on the animal, fie on the animal!
If thou bringest a small *brong*, the poor animal, the poor animal!
Seek out a strong *brong*, and stay one year, stay one year!

40. Almost every one keeps a mule as a riding animal, as a riding animal!
But **'aBrugmo** keeps a *kiang* (= wild horse) as her riding animal, as riding animal!

If thou bringest an old *kiang*, fie on the animal, fie on the animal!
If thou bringest a small *kiang*, the poor animal, the poor animal!
Seek out a strong *kiang*, and stay one year, stay one year!' [1]

41. 'Kesar will come back in three years,' thought *'aBruguma*; but although she waited (so long), there came no news of his coming. Then spoke **sDig spyod rgyalpo** (= 'King Sinful Conduct'), the minister of *Hor* (to the King):

42. 'Thou art not the King **Gur dKar** (= White-tent), O no, a white ox!
A young white ox whose horns can hardly be seen!
One has to cry *Riri*, otherwise he will not be led,[2]
One has to cry *Khyo khyo*, and also strike lustily.[2]
Some hundred beautiful fairies there are in the kingdom of the Gods.
Let us fetch at least one! so I said to thee long ago.
What **'aBrugmo** takes for food, that we give her then,
What **'aBrugmo** clothes herself with, that we put upon her,
We also call her **'aBrugmo**—that I advised thee already long ago.'

43. The King of Hor replied:
'The old King **sDig spyod,** he was a great hero.
But now our **sDig spyod** is only an old man.
Now he takes gladly to the spindle and sits by the fire-place.' [3]

44. **sDig spyod** spake:
'Thou art not King White-tent, a white donkey only;
It is a pity that thy ears are not a bit longer!
Some hundred beautiful *nāgis* there are in the underworld.
Let us fetch at least one! so I said to thee long ago.
What **'aBrugmo** takes for food, that we can give her then.
What **'aBrugmo** clothes herself with, that we put upon her.
We also call her **'aBrugmo**—that I advised thee already long ago.'

---

[1] The above was **'aBruguma's** ruse to gain time from the King of **Hor** for three years.

[2] *Riri* and *Khyo khyo* are terms used in driving cattle.

[3] *Gog ltag* = the raised place at the side of the ashes.

45. The King of **Hor** answered:
'The old King **sDig spyod,** he was like unto a lion!
But now our **sDig spyod** is no better than a fox.
Now he seeks old leather and carries it to his den.'

46. Then **'aBrugmo** stayed about a month in the hermitage **γYu 'abrug,** and did not at all go out. (Living) among the Lamas, clothed in cowl and coat, she stayed there and acted as if she knew nothing,—like a monk. Then the King of **Hor** made quite a fine device and led her away from there.

VI.

1. After about a year had again passed, there came all the heroes from **gLing** disguised as horse-dealers to the land of **Hor. Agu dGāni mgonpo, dPalle rgodpo, dGung Phrug Khra skya,**—which three embarked on their first transaction, each riding on a horse and leading another horse. King **Gur dKar** of **Hor** saw them, and being very much pleased, he sang (this) song:

2. 'Yea, during the father's time there came no dealer,
O no, during **Gur dKar's** time horses were not offered cheap.
As a son is born to me, now come here dealers.
Now that **Ollader** (= *Olba dar*, 'Black Extension'[1]) is born, horses are held cheap.
Now I buy all the horses for the benefit of my son,
Now I buy all the slaves for the benefit of my son.'

'*Yagshikhob, Yagshikhob*[2]', shouted he. 3. **'aBruguma** spake: 'All of these are the heroes of **gLing**: they have come to spy on you!' **Gur dKar** did not believe it, and said, 'No, no'.

(The second MS. from Khalatse)

4. **'aBrugmo** said to **Gur dKar** of **Hor**: 'The foremost horse is Kesar's horse **rKyang byung dbyerpo**; that thou shalt not get! The next one is **sNgorog pon pon**; that, too, thou shalt not get! The following one is **Khyuma thsa langs**, of the God-king, the great lion: that, too, thou

---

[1] The name of the son of **Gur dKar** and **'aBruguma.**

[2] A shout of joy, which can be heard among the Yarkand traders. The expression is believed by the Ladakhis to be Russian—but it is not Russian in any case.

shalt not get. 5. The foremost Agu is Agu **Bongnag ldumbu**; him thou shalt not get. The next one is **dPalle rgodpo** of **gLing**; him, too, thou shalt not get. The following one is **Kha rgan dgani**; him, too, thou shalt not get.'

6. King **Gur dgar lde hor** believed it and went into the castle. While he stayed, the three men of **gLing** went back to their battle camp, and **dPalle rgodpo** gave to the arrow which had the power to come back of itself (the following) instruction: 7. 'Thou must (now) fly into the castle of **Hor** and strike the decorated wooden columns. Do not come back without bringing a mouthful of the flesh of the King **Hor pahalde!**' So saying he shot the arrow to the castle. 8. Then the arrow struck the decorated wooden column, and because it was the heart-vein of (the King of) **Hor**, the latter was overcome with great pain. No one could draw out the arrow, and the son of the smith **Hemis** was called, the young smith **Kun byung thsar rnyed** (= 'He who finds liberation for all creatures'). 9. The latter called out to the maid named **bKur 'adzom**: 'Bring the big pair of tongs! Bring the big hammer! An arrow from **gLing** struck into the decorated columns of the King **Pahalde.** Great pain in the heart is come upon King **Gur dKar!**' So he said, and sent away the maid. 10. When he had waited a little, he went with the maid to the castle. Reaching there he taught the noble **'aBruguma** a charm '**'aBruguma**! recite a prayer!

11. May the golden gold-castle pass away!
May the castle with nine towers remain!
12. May γ**Serral** and γ**Yural** be disinherited!
May **Shelli búzhung** have the heritage![1]
13. May the King **Pahalde** be wife-less!
May King Kesar have the wife!

Weep while speaking thus', said he. 14. Then the young smith drew the arrow out and stuck it into a twig of the altar.[2] After waiting a little, (the arrow) extracted out of the breast of the King of **Hor** a mouthful of flesh, and also took away the altar-traveller from there, made a hole in the wall, and sped away from there. Then it went back to **dPalle.**

---

[1] γ**Ser-ral** = 'Golden-lock', name of a girl, and γ**Yu-ral** = 'Turquoise-lock', were the children of **'aBruguma** by **Gur dKar**; **Shelli búzhung** = 'the Small Son of the Mother-of-Pearl', was the son borne by **'aBruguma** to Kesar.

[2] A bower, if possible of cedar, is dedicated to the gods; twigs from this are stuck on the house or on the *lha-tho* erected outside.

15. **dPalle** of **gLing** feared that the arrow was tricky (naughty), and concealed it under a big rock. The arrow (however) came back into the quiver, while a fire burnt in its groove, and it carried a mouthful of the flesh of the King of **Hor**. 16. Thereupon the young smith **Thar rnyed** went to the camp of the men from **gLing** and said: 'Go back again to the land of **gLing**! I shall gradually conquer the King of **Hor** by stratagem!' For that reason all the men of **gLing** went to **gLing**-land.

VII.

1. Thereupon the young smith went back home and spoke to his father, the smith **Hemis**: 'I shall now go to fetch charcoal.' On which the father replied: 'Don't go into the valley to the right! It is the garden of the Gods, of the **Pahalde** of **Hor**! Go into the valley to the left, extinguish the coals and bring them.' 2. The young smith **Thar rnyed** and the smith-girl **Choron** (= *chos-sgron*), both (however) went into the Gods' garden of **Gur dKar lde**, and although the smith-girl **Choron** said, 'It is a Gods' garden, don't cut anything'. The young smith showed his might and spake:

3. 'Ye Gods, go ye all to the kingdom of the Gods!
Ye *Nāgas*, go ye all to the kingdom of the *Nāgas*.
4. More than a hatchet can is struck without a hatchet!
More than an axe can is struck without an axe!
More than fire can is performed without burning!
Akani nikani acini manidl!'

5. After he had uttered this prayer he felled wood. The coals were extinguished and laden on the donkey. Then they went, and when they came in front of the big water, the young smith **Thar rnyed** said: 'The hoofs of the donkey will get wet,' and broke into pieces the hoofs of the donkey on a stone. 6. The girl cried out, 'Art thou mad? Thou hast in fact smashed the feet of my father's donkey!' He said, '(Otherwise) the boots of the donkey would get wet'. Thereupon the smith-girl **Choron** ran home and related this to the father, the smith **Hemis**: 7. 'Father, he has laid fire to the Gods' garden of our King **Gur dKar**. And when he came to the ford, he said, "the boots of the donkeys will get wet!" and he smashed all their hoofs on a stone. O, the father has got an evil child!' 8. As she spoke thus, the father, the smith **Hemis**, got angry, seized the big iron hammer and the big pair of tongs, and went towards

the son in order to thrash him. When the father struck the son, all the donkeys were laden with coal and their hoofs were in the most beautiful (condition). 9. The father spoke to the son: 'Thou hast (thus) laid fire to the Gods' garden of King **Gur dKar**!' and scolded him away. The son spoke: 'Father, thy daughter has cavilled me! If fire has been laid to the Gods' garden, then let the father himself look to that! If the hoofs of the donkeys are broken, then let the father himself look to that!' 10. When the father looked into it, the Gods' garden was green as before, and the hoofs of the donkeys in the most beautiful (condition). Then father and son reached home arranging the coals. 11. Then the father said to the daughter: 'Thou liar!', struck her with the big hammer, tore out her flesh with the big pair of tongs, and did her much injury.

12. As the son then continually went on working on an iron chest, the father one day spoke: 'Hey, young man! do for once a (proper) bit of work! What art thou doing day after day making only that chest?' 13. The son replied: 'Oh, if one sits in this chest, one can see the kingdom of the Gods as well as the kingdom of men!' The father spoke: 'How so? I shall once see, indeed!' Thereupon he let the father go into the chest. 14. When he was therein, the son closed the lid and turned the lock and carried (the chest) away from there on his back. The father cried out of the chest, 'Whither art thou carrying me now? Hey, young man, thou bad son!' 15. The son replied: 'I am carrying the father away in order to throw him into the water!' Whereupon the father begged: 'O son! throw me not into the water! Hullo! I shall do what thou wilst tell me to!' 16. The son spoke: 'If thou makest me a wire-rope with which one can come up to golden castle of King **Gur dKar**, then I shall release the father! 17. Take an oath on the Gods' kingdom! And when thou takest an oath also on the land of men, I shall let thee out!' In this way (he) loaded him with oaths, and let him out. Then the two of them worked day and night on the wire-rope and finished it.

VIII.

1. Then the son bathed seven days long in milk in order to cleanse himself of the spots of the smithy. Now he went, carrying the wire-rope into the castle, threw up (the rope) and its end remained hanging above. 2. Then he firmly seized the rope, and as he climbed up there came from heaven a white and a black raven, which were fighting with each other.

The white raven succumbed. After the black one had conquered, he threw down the white one. Then **Ane bKur dmanmo** spake:

> 3. 'The wise one is without wisdom,
> The counseller is without counsel!

4. Even now a spot from the smithy has not been removed from thee! Wash thyself once more thoroughly in the milk-bath!' 5. After Kesar had come back, he washed himself again thoroughly in the milk-bath, and remained (therein) some seven days. Then he came again, carrying the wire-rope, into the castle. 'If my father and my mother are honourable people, then may the wire-rope remain hanging up on the castle!' So he spoke, flung the rope, and it remained hanging. 6. When he again climbed by the wire-rope, there came again a white and a black raven, which were fighting with each other. This time the white raven won and the black one fell down defeated on to the earth. 7. 'I shall win!' he thought, firmly seized the rope, and came up on to the castle. When he looked down out of the window, (he saw that) King **Pahalde** of **γSerralcan** and **γYuralcan** carried both of them (in his arms) and slept. 8. The noble **'aBruguma** was spinning threads white as mother-of-pearl on a golden spindle. As the turquoise-blue chalk-stone was like a lake to see, Kesar could not go (down), and threw down the golden finger-ring. 9. 'Touch the finger of the noble **'aBruguma**!' said he, and the golden ring rolled about on the chalk-stone (of the floor-planks) and then struck the finger of the noble **'aBruguma**. 10. **'aBruguma** thought: 'Ah, now Kesar has arrived!' Then Kesar came down from the window, and changed himself into a cat. He slipped into the bed of the King of **Hor** and pricked them both, **γSerralcan** and **γYuralcan**, with the poisoned dagger. 11. Both the children cried. Then the father spoke: '*Alolo!*

> A hundred people should seek all the lice with sharp eyes!
> A hundred people should seek all the lice with sharp nails!'

12. **'aBruguma** thought (at that): 'He has already come who will seek out thy lice!' When thereupon the King of **Hor** had waked up, he (began) to fight with Kesar. The Queen **Ane bKur dmanmo** said: 'Oh **'aBruguma!**

> 13. The wise one is without wisdom,
> And the woman of counsel is without counsel!
> 14. So do thou put paste under Kesar's feet,
> So do thou put iron (i.e. hard) peas under **Gur dKar's** feet!'

'aBruguma spoke:

15. 'I am the consort of Kesar, betrothed with the white band!
The sustainer of the clan to **Gur dKar**, to whom she (i.e. herself) has borne a son.'

16. Then she mixed the flour-paste with the peas and strew them (about). Then came **Ane bKur dmanmo**, transformed herself in a dove, gathered the peas and placed them under the feet of the King of **Hor**. Also she gathered the paste and put it under the feet of Kesar. 17. As the King of **Hor** had put on boots, he fell on the hard peas. Kesar's foot stuck on the flour-paste; he did not fall, remained (erect), and won. 18. Then he bound the beard of the King of **Hor** to the pillar, knelt on his breast, and the King of **Hor** besought Kesar for mercy:

19. 'Not knowing what I was doing, I had formerly destroyed the **gLing** castle.
Not knowing what I was doing, I had formerly carried off **'aBrugmo.**
20. Kill me not now, O God-king, thou great one!
I indeed wish to serve you, O God-king, thou great one!
21. It is warm in **Hor**, here should you live in winter;
In **gLing** it is cold, there should you live in summer!'

When he had pleaded thus, Kesar spoke:

22. 'I was one year old when I struck the **Andhe bandhe** out of the east;
A boy, I triumphed over them all!
23. When I was two years old, I killed the seven spirits;
A boy, I triumphed over them all!
24. When I was three years old, I killed the man with nine heads;
A boy, I triumphed over them!
25. When I was four years old, I killed the corpse-eating giantess;
A boy, I triumphed over this!
26. When I was five years old, I killed **Khung 'abru**[1];
A boy triumphed also over this!
27. When I was six years old, I struck 'Poison-flesh' the rock:
A boy triumphed also over this!

---

[1] A kind of winged dragon which moves about the clouds and produces thunder. (According to another view, thunder is heard when the gods move in the sky.)

28. When I was seven years old, I killed **Ralril** (='the Long-haired One'), the white yak bull:
A boy triumphed also over this!
29. When I was eight years old, I killed **Curulugu** the Devil:
A boy triumphed also over this!
30. But **Gur dKar**, thou base one, whom hast thou killed?'
31. Thereupon spoke **Ane bKur dmanmo**: 'What art thou then doing now? **'aBu dmar lam bstan**[1] of former times, does he not come into thy mind?
The abducted **'aBrugmo**, does she not come into thy mind?
Does not any louse bite in thy socks?'

32. When she spoke thus, Kesar drew out the knife 'Three-finger-long' and struck it into the body of the King of **Hor**. Then so much fat came out that Kesar's body was drowned in it. 33. **Ane bKur dmanmo** came, but although she plied hither and thither with shovel and spade, she could not succeed, and Kesar offered a prayer-offering:

34. 'May this disappear, before the nine Gods born with me!
May this disappear before the nine spirits born with me!
May this disappear before the eighteen **Andre barandre** (= **Andhe bandhe**) of the East!'

35. After he had spoken, they all came and did away with the flesh, blood and fat of **(Pahalde)**. The King of **Hor** was not yet dead, and as he still had the death-rattle, Kesar went into all the upper rooms in order to search. 36. There was somebody in the temple who was praying with covered head. Him Kesar seized and threw down from the tower of the castle. When he then came and examined, the King of **Hor** was dead and gone.

IX.

1. Kesar spoke to **'aBruguma**: 'Now, thou widow, come now with (me)!' and **'aBruguma** said to the two children: 'If ye two will come with me, then bite into this milk-cake! and if ye do not wish to come with me, then bite into this blood-cake!' 2. She kneaded a milk-cake and blood-cake, offered them to the two children, and the children spoke: 'We shall not go to the land of **gLing**! we shall stay in the land of **Hor** to

---

[1] 'Red Worm Path-shower', an Agu who accompanied Kesar on his journey to China.

avenge our father!' and ate the blood-cake. 3. Then Mother **'aBruguma** gave the children sweet-tasting food, and travelled with Kesar to the land of **gLing**.

4. In the middle of the way there was a rock gate named **Brag thsan rdung rdung** (= 'the Striking Rock'). When Kesar (once formerly) had come there, he had said to the rock gate: 'I shall bring (thee) the heads of both **γSerralcan** and **γYuralcan**!' 5. For that reason Kesar spoke to **'aBruguma**: 'Something has been left behind!' and went back. **'aBruguma** said: 'Thou wishest to go to kill my children!' and did not let Kesar go. 6. Then Kesar replied: 'I shall not kill them!', went back and came before the castle of **Hor**. He called the two children: 'Hey, **γSerralcan** and **γYuralcan**, ye two! The mother has sent you a message! Just look out of the window!' 7. The two children answered: 'We have no time to look out! Whoever that may be, may he come in!' 'Look out, only for a moment! I must go farther (i.e. I cannot wait)!' The two looked for a moment out of the window. 8. Then Kesar tore away with the ends of his bow their heads and brought them. He (now) kneaded much flour and butter, and put the heads in the midst of it, and carried them away. 9. When he then came to the noble **'aBruguma**, the army of **gLing** was (assembled) at the rock gate. Kesar said to **'aBruguma**: 'When thou wert (still) in the country of **gLing**, thou wert clever! If thou art clever even now, then distribute this flour with butter to the whole army! 10. Do not let anything remain! Neither finish it too (soon)!' **'aBruguma** distributed to the whole army, and it happened in equal measure. Then came out of the middle of the flour and butter the heads of the two children. 11. **'aBruguma** fainted a little; (but) Kesar offered the heads of the two children to the rock gate. 12. Then they went out of the rock gate, and Kesar and **'aBruguma** together with the army went to the land of **gLing**. They arrived in **gLing**, and remained (i.e. lived) there.

[3]

A LADAKHI BON-PA HYMNAL.[1]

By REV. A. H. FRANCKE.

INTRODUCTION.

It has become evident, that **the ancient religion of Tibet, known as Bon-chos**, is not yet extinguished, even in those parts of the country which are professedly Lamaist. In such places Lamaism has become the religion of the clergy, but Bon-chos has continued to live among laymen.

In all the Ladakhi villages each spring the Kyesar festival is held, when the male population exercises itself in archery. On this occasion the village band has to play and **the gling glu** is sung.[2] The *gling glu* seems to be a remnant of the hymnal of the ancient Bon-chos, and I have been so fortunate as to come into possession of **the gling glu of two villages, Phyang and Khalatse.** They are entirely different from each other, although the subject in each is the same, but it is to be remarked that they both consist of **nine songs.** It is probable, that in ancient times more than nine songs were known in a village; but as nine is the number which predominates over everything, the people were careful to sing neither more nor less than nine songs at a time.[3] And so it has happened that, when many of the ancient songs were forgotten, nine remained living in the minds of the people, simply because a Kyesar festival could not be allowed to pass by without the usual set of nine hymns.

These hymns are perfectly unintelligible to anyone who has not previously studied the **Kyesar Myths.** But Ladâkhî laymen, who know nothing of the life of Buddha, Padmasambhava or Tsongkhapa, know the life-story of Kyesar very well.

It is worth noticing, that **in Phyang** the Spring-hero's name is pronounced **Kyesar, not Kesar.**

---

[1] Reprinted from the *Indian Antiquary*, Vol. XXX, 1901, pp. 359–364.

[2] A reference to this festival we have in VI. 5, 6 below.

[3] The people will always play nine sets of Polo, to finish a game.

THE HYMNS.

Phyanggi gling-glu rnams yin

THESE SONGS ARE THE GLING-GLUS OF PHYANG.

I.

Kyesar, Conqueror of the World.

1. **steng nang lha yul kun nonpari**
   amala bu zhig ltams.
   A son, conquering the land of the gods in the heights,
   Was born to the mother.

2. **yog nang klu yul kun nonpari**
   gogzalhamola lha phrug rig ltams.
   A godly child, conquering the land of the lower water spirits,
   Was born to **Gogzalhamo.**

3. **bar nang btsan yul kun nonpari**
   amala bu zhig ltams.
   A son, conquering all the lands of the earth,
   Was born to the mother.

4. **bdud nang bdud yul kun nonpari**
   lha phrug cig ltamssed lei.
   A godly child, conquering all the lands of the devil,
   Is born, hurrah!

TEXT NOTES.

1. *etc.*, the termination *pari* is a dialectical form of the participle and corresponds to *mkhanni.*
2. *gogza* may be *gogsa*, a parallel case is *dagsa*, 'now', the *s* of which is often pronounced like *z*.
3. The word *bar btsan*, earth, was separated by *nang* only for the reason to form a sentence corresponding to the others.

TRANSLATION NOTES.

1. Is said to refer to Kyesar's victory over his two brothers, see *Kesarsage* II. 36–42. 4. refers to Kyesar's victory over the giant of the North, who is called **bDud.**

II.

Lullaby to the Young Kyesar.

1. **stod nang stodna, rgyallham chenmoi stangspola stod.**
When you praise, praise the ingenuity of the great godly king.

2. **alodalotsele, singchen rgyalpoi stangs nang grospola stod.**
Alodalotsele, praise the ingenuity and advice of the king, the great lion.

3. **stod nang stodna lei shellcam 'abrugumai mdzangspola stod.**
When you praise, praise the learning of **'aBruguma,** his crystal wife.

4. **alodalotsele, shellcam 'abrugumai shes nang mdzangspola stod.**
Alodalotsele, praise the wisdom and learning of 'aBruguma, his crystal wife.

Text notes.

1 and 3. *nang*, in; thus, if you praise in a praise; about *rgyallham*, see *Kesarsage*, notes 2 and 4. *alodalotsele*, lullaby. *nang*, within = mixed = together = and.

Translation notes.

It is remarkable how well the intellectual capacities of man and woman are characterised in this song: man as being productive, woman as reproductive.

III.

The Giant's Treasures.

bKur dman rgyalmos:
bKur-dman-rgyalmo says:

1. **lungpai phushedna norbu chechung tsam 'adug.**
How many treasures there are in the upper end of the valley!

2. **lungpai phushedna norbu chechung tsam 'adug.**
How many treasures there are in the upper end of the valley!

3. **norbu chechebo sgola mi shongces yod lei.**
The larger ones do not fit in the door.

4. **norbu chungchungbo pangla mi shongces yod lei.**
The smaller ones do not fit in the lap.

Dongrub kyis:
Dongrub says:

5. **den 'adrai norbu buthsa ngarangla sal lei.**
Such treasures give, please, to me (thy boy)!

6. **den 'adrai khyad norbu lagspai dongrubla sal lei.**
Such treasures give, please, to good **Dongrub**!

7. **alongthang γcigcig, buthsa ngarang γcigcig.**
There is one solitary Alongplain: there is myself, one solitary boy!

8. **alongthang γcigcig, lagspai dongrub γcigcig.**
There is one solitary Alongplain: there is one solitary dear Dongrub!

9. **buthsa ngarangla 'agrulbai 'agrullam cig sal lei.**
Show me, thy boy, please, a way to walk along!

TEXT NOTES.

3, 4. The reiteration of *che* and *chung* is due to the metre. 5, 6. The *n* of *den* is the initial silent *'a* of *'adra*, which is pronounced as a nasal with the preceding syllable. 6. *lagspa* = *legspa*. 7, 8. *alongthang* = ring-plain. The mountains of Tibet and the Himalayas are supposed to be the centre of the earth: the navel, these hills are surrounded by a ring of plains. 5, 6, 9. *sal* = *stsal*, give, respectful.

TRANSLATION NOTES.

In the first part of the song the mother describes the treasures to arouse Dongrub's covetousness. Then Dongrub starts in search of them and loses his way. In his difficulty he says the prayer, which forms part 2. According to the Winter Myth the giant of the North is in possession not only of a girl, but also of great treasures. It is remarkable that in the eyes of his heavenly mother **Kyesar remains always Dongrub.**

IV.

Praise of 'aBruguma.

1. **blama bzangpos chos salbas**
As the good Lama taught (her) religion,

2. **ngai shescan lhamo cila men**
Why should my wise goddess not be (wise)?

3. **blamas thamscad mkhyen mdzadpas**
As the Lama made her know everything,

4. **ngai mdzangscan 'aBruguma cila men**
Why should my learned 'aBruguma not be (learned)?

5. **yari'shes nang mdzangspo lei**
Thy wisdom and learning

6. **alam mdun nyad kunla ngonned lei**
Is known to all, who are before thee!

7. **'oma rigskyi mkh'an 'agroma**
Oh, thou milk-white fairy!

8. **yari shes nang mdzangspo lei**
Thy wisdom and learning

9. **alam mdun nyad kunla thsa langssed lei**
Is envied by all, who are before thee!

10. **'oma rigskyi mkh'an 'agroma**
Oh, thou milk-white fairy!

Text notes.

2. *men* = *ma yin*, is not. 5. *yari* = *yaranggi* = *nyidranggi*, you, thou. 6. *alam*, all, a Purig word. *mdun nyad* is perhaps *mdun yad* = *yado*, companion or people. 7. The *n* in *mkh'an* is the nasally pronounced *'a* of *'agroma*. 9. *thsa langsces*, rising of envy.

Translation notes.

Without doubting the historical character of **Srong-btsan-sgampo**, as well as that of his two wives, I feel inclined to believe that Bonpa mythology has added some fresh colour to their characters. Srong-btsan-sgampo's two wives remind us of **Kyesar's two wives**, above all, as regards their colour. **'aBruguma** has lent her colour to **the white Tārā**; **Bamza 'abumskyid**, the wife, first of the Giant, then of Kyesar, to **the green Tārā**. There is another parallel (within the two groups) as regards intellectual capacities. In both of them the husband is famous for his ingenuity, the wives for their learning.

In this connection I wish to draw attention to the following: (1) In J.A.S.B., Vol. LX, Part I, No. 3, 1891, Karl Marx, *History of Ladakh*, p. 116, note 13, we read the following interesting statement: 'In the *Gyalrabs*, Gesar (= Kesar) is referred to as one of the suitors of Konggo, the Chinese princess, who afterwards became the wife of *Srong-btsan-sgampa*'.

(2) Grünwedel, *Mythologie des Buddhismus*, note on *Abb.* 116; 'the crown of the green Tārā often shows the Dhyānibuddha Amoghasiddha. Amoghasiddha is the Tibetan Dongrub. Dongrub is the name of Kesar whilst dwelling in the North. It was in the North, where Kesar married his second wife'.

V.

The Almighty God-Father and God-Mother.

1. **phred de γzarpoi 'ona rbab dela shorthabs rig 'adug**
   There is a means of escape from a rolling rock on a steep path,
2. **phred ni γzarpoi rbabla shorthabs rig 'adug lei**
   Yes, there is a means of escape from a rolling rock on a steep path.
3. **yabchen ababai 'ona bk'a stsalnas shorthabs rig med**
   But there is no means of escape from the commandments of the Great Father.
4. **'abum khri rgyalpoi bk'a stsalnas shorthabs rig med lei**
   There is no means of escape from the commandments of the king of the 100,000 thrones.
5. **chu de chenmoi 'ona rabschenla bingthabs rig 'adug**
   There is no means of escape on the ford of the great waters.
6. **chu ni chenmoi rabschenla rgalthabs rig 'adug lo**
   Yes, there is a means of escape on the ford of the great waters.
7. **yumchen amabai 'ona bk'a stsalnas shorthabs rig med**
   But there is no means of escape from the commandments of the Great Mother.
8. **'abum khri rgyalmoi bk'a stsalnas shorthabs rig med lei**
   There is no means of escape from the commandments of the queen of the 100,000 thrones.

Text notes.

3, 7. The concluding *ba* in *ababai* and *amabai* was added only for the sake of the metre.

Translation notes.

This song shows that the originally physiological deities have become ethical deities.

VI.

Kyesar, Returning to 'aBruguma.

1. **γserri eranla sga bstadde**
nyemi chibs bsusla chen lei
Having saddled the golden steed,
I will ride off to meet my friend.

2. **dkarpoi glangpochela sga bstadde**
nyemoi rta bsusla chen lei
Having saddled the white ox,
I will ride off to meet my friend.

3. **khra skya dkarmola brdzuste**
nyemoi barbanla chen lo
Being changed into a white falcon,
I will go to the house of my friend.

4. **γyumai phoronla brdzuste**
nyemoi rab γsalla chen lo
Being changed into a turquoise crow,
I will go to the hall of my friend.

5. **khyogthong md'a phangs rtsebabo**
darung yod nang lei
The boys playing at arrow-shooting,
Well, they are still here.

6. **dohela nachung zurri kha ldingmabo**
darung da yod nang lei.
The girls, high on the edge of the roof,
They are still here, hallo!

Text notes.

1. *eran,* a horse from Iran, Persia. 2. *glangpocne,* literally 'large ox', is used nowadays for 'elephant'. In this connection it is probably a 'riding Yak'. 3. *barban,* the inside of a house; for *lo* see *yserri buzhung.* 4. *phoron = phorog,* crow; *rab ysal,* in Ladakhi not a balcony, but a large fine hall. 5, 6. *nang lei,* a concluding exclamation like *lei* and *lo.* 6. *dohela,* hallo! *ldingmabo,* means originally 'soaring'.

Translation notes.

Kyesar is still undecided, in which of the four ways he ought to travel. The song proper is finished with v. 4; v. 5 and 6 are later additions. They express the idea, that in spite of Buddhism and Mohamedanism the Bon Religion is not yet extinguished and the Kyesar festival is still in vogue. At this festival the girls watch the boys at archery from the roofs of the houses.

VII.

Kyesar, a Voluntary Saviour.

1. **nono rang miyulla skyodpa rig dgossug lei.**
The youngest son himself must go to the land of men.

2. **bu dongrub rang miyulla skyodpa rig dgossug lei.**
The son **Dongrub** himself must go to the land of men.

3. **sngamoi thasangna ngatanggis byaphran rig rtse yin lo**
In the early morning we will have a little tournament.

4. **nyiyi sngashar nang byaphran cig rtse yin lo**
At the early rising of the sun we will have a little tournament.

5. **rgyalla rig songna cila rig chen lo**
If I should be victorious, why should I go?

6. **ngatang phamse ring songna mi cha nang kha med rig yin lo**
If I am beaten, there is no sense in saying 'I will not go!'

7. **ngatang rgyalces mannas pham mi shes lo.**
But we do not know anything except being victorious: we do not know what it is to be beaten!

Text notes.

1. *dçossug* = *dgos 'adug*. 3. *byaphran*, a little deed, i.e. sham fighting. 5. *rgyalla* = *rgyalba*, conquér. 6. *phamse*, probably *phamste*; *khamed*, no sense.

Translation notes.

This song refers to *Kesarsage* II. 36–42. The three sons of the king of heaven have to fight each other. He who is beaten, must go to the earth. Dongrub, the youngest, in spite of his being victorious, goes of his own accord.

VIII.

'aBruguma's Innocence.

1. **ngazha rgyagar yulli mthong shescan yin lo**
   om kyenang kyele
   We know India from having seen it,
   Om kyenang kyele!

2. **ngazha dpalbo yulli nyan shescan yin lo**
   om kyenang kyele
   We know Nepal from having heard of it,
   Om kyenang kyele!

3. **ngazhas ma them menne gomparig mi shes**
   om kyenang kyele
   We do not know a step further than the threshold,
   Om kyenang kyele!

4. **ngazhas mazho rig menne thungba rig mi shes**
   om kyenang kyele
   We do not know any beverage besides mother's milk,
   Om kyenang kyele!

5. **sula phanba rig menne γnodpa rig co mi shes**
   om kyenang kyele.
   We do not know of doing any harm, if it be not for somebody's advantage,
   Om kyenang kyele!

Text notes.

The refrain of all verses *'om kyenang kyele* was explained to me to have been in the original *om mkhyen 'ang mkhyen lei*, which might mean: Oh do take notice of this! 3. *ma them*, the 'mother threshold', it is the one belonging to that part of the house, which is called *makhang*. *menne* = *mannas*, besides.

Translation notes.

1. **India** is considered by some people to be **'aBruguma's fatherland**. In this case the history of **Srong-btsan-sgampo's wives** may have influenced 'aBruguma's history. This song should be placed before 'aBruguma's marriage to Kyesar. Some people place it after Kyesar's return from the north; but in that case there would not be much left of 'aBruguma's innocence; as she gave birth to two children by the king of Yarkand!

IX.

The King of Yarkand's Entreaty for his Life.

1. **ngatang gling yulla chen dola gling yulla chen.**
We will go to the **land of gLing**: holloa, we will go to the **land of gLing** !

2. **dbyarla gling yulla bsilmo rig yod dola rgyallham chenmo.**
There it is cool in summer: holloa, great godly king!

3 **dgunla ngati horyulla drosa rig yinpas**
Because our **land of Hor** is warm in winter,

4. **ngatang horyulla chen dola sprulpai rgyalpole**
We will go there then: holloa, incarnated king!

5. **m'as shespa rig songna nyidkyis bagsris shig snams dola rgyallham chenmo**
If you are very wise, you will accept a present: holloa, great godly king!

6. **m'a shespa dang m'a mkhaspa songna nyidkyis bagsris shig mdzad 'ang mkhyenpai rgyalpo !**
If you are very wise and very clever, you will also give me a present, oh acknowledged king!

Text notes.

3. *drosa*, a warm place. 4. *le*, respectful termination. 5. *bagsris* = *bakhshish*, gift; the *r* in *sris* is never pronounced, and no reason whatever can be given for this way of spelling the word. 6. *mkhyen* is used very frequently to honour a person, for instance *Sahib mkhyen*.

Translation notes.

When this song is sung by **the king of Hor**, Kyesar is kneeling on his breast and ready to kill him. The king of Hor pretends to be in good spirits all the same, for which reason he repeatedly sings *dola*, holloa! He cannot yet give up telling lies, for in Hor it is not warm in winter. Originally **Hor** seems to have been **Mongolia**; but now it is generally supposed to be **Yarkand.** In 5 the king of Hor offers his hidden treasures, and the present, which he hopes to receive in exchange of them, in 6, is his life.

[4]

LADAKHI SONGS.[1]

By the Rev. A. H. Francke, Leh.

(*With the aid of the Rev. S. Ribbach and Dr. E. Shawe.*)

Khalatsei gling glu rnams yin

These songs (i.e. Nos. XXI–XXIX) are the gling glu[2] of Khalatse.

Song No. XXI.—Heavenly Voices.

1. **amai bu zhung bltamspari dusla**
   When mother's little boy was born,
2. **mi yulbo 'oddis 'ang khyangs**
   All the land of men was filled with light.
3. **lhayi bu Kesar kun bltams tsana**
   When Kesar and the (other) sons of the gods were born
4. **'adzambu gling 'oddis khyangs.**
   All 'aDzambugling was filled with light.
5. **rgyal lcang lcanggi lcang stodna**
   On the top of the willow of the world
6. **lha phrug γsum skyod 'adug lei**
   There are walking three sons of the gods.
7. **lha skad cig diriri**
   There is a hum of heavenly voices.
8. **rgyal lham chenmo kun skyod tsana**
   When all the great godly kings are walking
9. **lha skad cig diriri**
   There is a hum of heavenly voices.

---

[1] Reprinted from the *Indian Antiquary,* Vol. XXXI, 1902, pp. 304–311.

[2] *gLing glu* are the songs sung at the Spring or Kesar Festival, when everybody practises archery. The *gLing glu* of Khalatse and the *gLing glu* of Phyang may be usefully compared. This song was included (*ante,* Vol. XXX, pp. 359 ff.) in 'A Ladakhi Bonpo Hymnal'.

10. **lhayi bu kesar kun skyod tsana**
When Kesar and the (other) sons of the gods are walking,

11. **lha skad cig diriri**
There is a hum of heavenly voices.

12. **rgyal lcang lcanggi lcang stodna**
On the top of the willow of the world

13. **lhamo kun skyodded lei**
There are walking three goddesses.

14. **lha skad cig diriri**
There is a hum of heavenly voices.

15. **jojo 'abruguma skyod tsana**
When the noble **'aBruguma** is walking,

16. **lha skad cig diriri**
There is a hum of heavenly voices.

17. **shel lcam 'abruguma skyod tsana**
When 'aBruguma, the crystal wife, is walking,

18. **lha skad cig diriri**
There is a hum of heavenly voices.

Text notes.

1. *bltamspari,* for participles ending in *pari,* compare Song No. XVII, Note on 6. 2. 4. *khyangs*; just as *khyabpa* was derived from *'agebspa, khyangpa* was derived from *'agengspa.* 3. *kun,* for *kun,* in the sense of 'and so on', compare *ante,* 'Spring Myth of the Kesar Saga', Philological Notes, No. VI. 19. 5. *rgyal lcang,* originally probably *rgya-lcang,* the willow with far-spreading (branches). The prefixed *l* of the second syllable was sounded with the first. It is the tree of the world, mentioned in Ladakhi Wedding Ritual, Songs Nos. V, VI, VII, and VIII. 8. *rgyallham,* for the addition of final *m,* compare *ante,* 'Spring Myth of the Kesar Saga', Philological Notes, No. V. 1. 13. *skyodded* = *skyoddad,* see *Ladakhi Grammar,* present tenses.

Translation notes.

If I am not altogether mistaken, this hymn contains an explanation of the phenomenon of **thunder**. It is thought to be caused by the walking of the gods. The word *lhaskad,* which I translated by 'heavenly voices', may be taken for any sound, caused by the mouths, hands or feet of the gods. The idea of thunder is not so very far-fetched, if we consider that, according to Song No. XXIX, lightning is called 'Kesar's sword', and that the word *diriri* may have been originally *ldiriri*, which is used to express the rolling of thunder.

Song No. XXII.—Dedication of the Arrows.

1. **thangka bdemoi kha mdā shing legsmo rig yod.**
   On the beautiful plain there is a fine arrow-tree,
2. **thang de bdemoi kha mdā shing legsmo rig yod.**
   On that beautiful plain there is a fine arrow-tree.
3. **mdā shing ringmobo agui mdā shing zhig yin lo**
   The long arrow-shaft is an arrow-shaft of the Agus.
4. **dezuggi mdā shingbo agubai lagtu phul**
   Such arrow-shafts offer to the hands of the Agus!
5. **dezuggi mdā shingbo agu drungbabai lagtu phul lei**
   Such arrow-shafts offer to the hands of those who are before the Agus!
6. **mdā shing chung chungbo jojobai phang shing rig yin**
   The short arrow-shaft is a spindle-stick of the ladies
7. **dezuggi phang shingbo aneyi lag de la phul**
   Such spindle-sticks offer to the hands of the wife (of the heavenly king)!
8. **dezuggi phang shingbo ane bkur dmanmoi lag de la phul lei**
   Such spindle-sticks offer to the hands of **Ane bKurdmanmo !**

Text notes.

5, 6, 7 the syllable *ba* in *agubai*, *drungbabai*, *jojobai* was inserted only for the sake of singing. 7. *jojo*, the reiterated form, is always used with the feminine, *jo* with the masculine.

Translation notes.

All the arrows, used at the Kesar Festival, are to be considered as being dedicated, the longer ones to the Agus, the shorter ones to **the heavenly queen Ane bKurdmanmo.**

Song No. XXIII.—Kesar's Four Victories.

1. **buthsa ngarangngi dgung lo brgyadpoi nangdu**
shar ande bandhe γsum btulpa yin
buthsa de kunni kha 'agying 'agying rig 'agyingspa yin

When I, a boy, had reached my eighth year,
I subdued **the three Andebandhes of the East.**
The boy has been triumphing over all of them.

2. **buthsa ngarangngi dgung lo bcu γnyispai nangdu**
ri rgyal blon chen kun btulpa yin.
buthsa de kunni kha 'agying 'agying rig 'agyingspa yin.

When I, a boy, had reached my twelfth year,
I subdued all the great ministers of the hills.
The boy has been triumphing over all of them.

3. **buthsa ngarangngi dgung lo bcu drugpai nangdu**
bdud khyabpa lagring kun btulpa yin
buthsa de kunni kha 'agying 'agying rig 'agyingspa yin

When I, a boy, had reached my sixteenth year,
I subdued the devil **Khyabpa lagring** and his men.
The boy has been triumphing over all of them.

4. **buthsa ngarangngi dgung lo bco brgyadpai nangdu**
hor ngan kun btulpa yin
buthsa de kunni kha 'agying 'agying rig 'agyingspa yin.

When I, a boy, had reached my eighteenth year,
I subdued all the bad Yârkandıs.
The boy has been triumphing over all of them.

Text notes.

1. For the *Andebandhes* of the East, compare *Kesar Saga* No. V. 1–8. There we have seven of them. 2. *Kun,* compare Note No. 1. 3. 3. *Khyabpa lagring* means 'coverer longhand'. This is perhaps another name of **Agu Za** in *Kesar Saga* No. III.

Translation notes.

In this song we have probably the four victories, which were prophesied in 'the Spring Myth of the Kesar Saga', No. V. 11–16.

Instead of the word 'Yârkandîs' in 4 'Mongolians' may be said, compare Jäschke's *Dictionary*.

Song No. XXIV.—Kesar and the Mules.

1. **buthsa ngai ngosla nyon dang wa drezha khampa**
   Oh, you brown mules, listen to me, to a boy!
2. **buthsa ngai bdagla γsan dang wa drezha khampa**
   Oh, you brown mules, please, listen to me, to a boy.
3. **rtsvakha nang gar bzangpo za chogpa 'adug**
   There is quite enough of good pasture;
4. **drezha khampa khung khungbo cila bco 'ad lei**
   Oh, you brown mules, why are you crying *khung khung?*
5. **chu mig gar bzangpo 'athung chogces 'adug**
   There is quite enough of good wells:
6. **drezha khampa khung khungbo cila bco 'ad lei**
   Oh, you brown mules, why are you crying *khung khung?*
7. **sa ljab bdemoi kha 'adug chogees yod**
   You have been (long) enough on good pasture;
8. **drezha khampa khung khungbo cila bco 'ad lei**
   Oh, you brown mules, why are you crying *khung khung?*

Text notes.

4, 6, 8. *Khung khung* imitates the voice of the mules, *bo* is the emphatic article. 7. *saljab*, means the name as *sacha*, pasture ground.

Translation notes.

This song is to be placed after Kesar's return from **Hor**. Then he found that the mules had taken **the King of Hor's** part. It is almost certain that the word *'adre*, a certain spirit, was mixed up with the word *dre*, mule, and thus the original spirits became animals.

Song No. XXV.—On the Srar Pass.

1. **srargyi lai stengna thang dkar mgo dkar kun chadde luste 'adug**
   ane bkur dman rgyalmos ngala rogs shig mdzad

On the Srar Pass the strength of the White-headed falcon is broken, and he remains behind!
Oh, queen Ane bKurdmanmo, come to my help!

2. **srargyi lai stengna phorog nag chung kun chadde luste 'adug ane bkur dman rgyalmos ngala rogs shig mdzad**

On the Srar Pass the strength of all the little black crows is broken, and they remain behind.
Oh, queen Ane bKurdmanmo, come to my help!

3 **srargyi lai stengna γyuma phoron kun chadde luste 'adug ane bkur dman rgyalmos ngala rogs shig mdzad.**

On the Srar Pass the strength of all the turquoise pigeons is broken, and they remain behind!
Oh, queen Ane bKurdmanmo, come to my help!

4. **srargyi lai stengna shangku mjug zlum kun chadde luste 'adug ane bkur dman rgyalmos ngala rogs shig mdzad**

On the Srar Pass the strength of all the bushy-tailed wolves is broken, and they remain behind.
Oh, queen Ane bKurdmanmo, come to my help!

5. **srargyi lai stengna sragpa cundru kun chadde luste 'adug ane bkur dman rgyalmos ngala rogs shig mdzad.**

On the Srar Pass the strength of all the earless stone-partridges is broken, and they remain behind.
Oh queen Ane bKurdmanmo, come to my help!

Text notes.

chadde, in all the verses, means originally 'is cut off'. *rogs* = *grogs*, *Lad. Gr.* Laws of Sound 3. 3. *phoron* = *phugron*, pigeon. 4. *shangku* = *scangku* = *spyangku*, *Lad. Gr.* 1. of s. 1; 5, *cundru*, earless, derivation not known.

Translation notes.

This song is a prayer rendered by Kesar, which he addressed to the queen of the gods, when crossing the difficult Srar Pass. This pass he had to cross on his journey to the North.

Song No. XXVI.—Kesar, Returning to 'aBruguma.

1. **γyuma phoronla rdzuste**
γnam stod mthonpola 'agyingba chana
khra skya dkarpola rdzuste
γyuma phoronni sna skyilla chen lei.

If she, taking the shape of a turquoise dove,
Should go to soar in the highest skies,
I, taking the shape of a white falcon,
Will go to take her home again.

2. **γyuma phoronla rdzuste**
dgung stod mthonpola shorna
khra skya dkarpola rdzuste
γyuma phoronla 'adedpa chen lei.

If she, taking the shape of a turquoise dove,
Should go to flee into the highest zenith,
I, taking the shape of a white falcon,
Will go to follow after her.

3. **nyamo γser migla rdzuste**
mthso stod mthonpola 'agyingba chana
chu sram kamala rdzuste
nyamo γser miggi sna skyilla chen lei.

If she, taking the shape of the fish 'goldeye',
Should go to float in the deepest ocean,
I, taking the shape of a whitebreasted otter,
Will go to take her home again.

4. **nyamo γser migla rdzuste**
mthso rgyan mthongpola shorna
chu sram brang dkarla rdzuste
nyamo γser migla 'adedla chen lei.

If she, taking the shape of the fish 'goldeye',
Should go to flee into the wildest ocean,
I, taking the shape of a whitebreasted otter,
Will go to follow after her.

Text notes.

1. *phoron* = *phugron*, dove; *sna skyil*, literally 'hinder the nose', i.e., 'meet from the front'. 3. *Kama*, said to mean the same as *brang*

dkar, whitebreasted. 4. *rgyan* = *rgya*, wide. *Lad. Grammar*, Laws of Sound 5.

TRANSLATION NOTES.

Kesar, after having taken the food and drink of forgetfulness, had forgotten 'aBruguma. Now, that the birds, coming from the South, brought him a message from her, decides to win her again by all means; actually there was no need to use the transformations mentioned in the above song.

Song No. XXVII.—'aBruguma's Farewell to Kesar.

me ma khrulli Kesar!

O Kesar, who never lettest the fire fall!

1. **stangscanni rgyalpo nyerang**
steng nang lha yulla skyod zana
lha yulli lhamo kun mthongse
mi yulli jojo ning rjed ma rjed.

Oh, my clever King!
When thou wilt go to the upper land of the gods,
And seest all the fairies of heaven,
Then do not forget thy wife from the land of men.

2. **stangscanni jo nyerang**
steng nang lha yulla skyod zana
lhamo nang sitarrām kun mthongse
mi yulli 'abruguma 'aphang ma 'aphang.

Oh, my clever Lord!
When thou wilt go to the upper land of gods,
And seest all the **Sitarrāms** among the fairies,
Then do not reject 'aBruguma from the land of men.

3. **stangscanni rgyalpo nyerang**
yog nang klu yulla skyod zana
klu yulli klumo kun mthongse
mi yulli jojo ning rjed ma rjed.

Oh, my clever King!
When thou wilt go to the lower land of the snakes,
And seest all the *Nāginī* of it,
Then do not forget thy wife from the land of men.

4. **stangscanni jo nyerang**
yog nang klu yulla skyod zana
klu yulli klumo kun mthongse
mi yulli grogs skal 'aphang ma 'aphang

Oh, my clever Lord!
When thou wilt go to the lower land of the snakes,
And seest all the *Nāginī* of it,
Then do not forget thy helpmate from the land of men.

Text notes.

1. *stangscan* means 'clever in strategies'; *zana* = *tsana*, when; *mthongse* = *mthongste*, seeing. 2. (*sitarrām* seems to be a reference to Sītā and Rāma the heroine and hero of the *Rāmayāṇa*, looked upon as a 'fairy', the combination of the male and female names of allied deities which is common enough in India, being regarded as a single name.)

Translation notes.

As the Kesar Myth tells us, Kesar forgot 'aBruguma all the same, after having taken the food and drink of forgetfulness.

Song No. XXVIII.—Young Kesar.

1. **la khala yaspabo**
lagsmobai mentog cig yassed lei.
A flower, blooming on the pass,
Oh, a pure flower is in bloom!

2. **la stod nang mthonpo kunla**
γzugscanni mentog cig yassed lei.
On all the high passes
A flower of fine shape is in bloom!

3. **darung yaspai sgang zhig yod lei**
sngamo yaspai mentoggi jo.
Thou art but half opened,
Oh Lord (who art) like a flower of the morning!

4. **darung yaspai sgang zhig yod lei**
kalimānni mentoggi jo
Thou art but half opened,
Oh Lord (who art) like a *kalimān* flower!

TEXT NOTES.

3 and 4 may be translated just as well 'Oh Lord of the flower of the morning; oh Lord of the *kalimān* flower' The *kalimān* flower is not of a beautiful appearance, but has a very sweet scent.

TRANSLATION NOTES.

This song refers to the supposed spring hero, who has carried spring up to the high passes. All the same he has not yet displayed his full glory (the flower is only half opened).

Song No. XXIX.—Kesar, the God of Lightning.

1. **saricanni la mgona**
nagpoi sprin cig yongnged lei.
On the height of the Sarican Pass
Black clouds are gathering.

2. **saricanni la mgona**
dum dum sprin cig yongnged lei.
On the height of the Sarican Pass
Torn clouds are gathering.

3. **nagpo sprinpoi dkyil dena**
jo lagsmoi snamralla glog 'abarred lei.
In the middle of the black clouds
Lightning flashes from our good Lord's sword.

4. **nagpo sprinpoi dkyilpona**
rgyal lham kesarri snamralla glog 'abarred lei.
In the middle of the black clouds
Lightning flashes from the godly King Kesar's sword.

TEXT NCTES.

3, 4. *snamral*, respectful for *ralgri*, sword.

TRANSLATION NOTES.

This song furnishes us with one of the strongest arguments to prove Kesar's nature-origin.

Song No. XXX.—The Nyopa's Carpet: A Wedding Song.

A.—Nangmas:—

PEOPLE OF THE HOUSE ASK:—

1. **nam stod mthonpo de**
   su dang ganggi stan.
   The high sky,
   Whose and what carpet is it?

2. **gangs stod mthonpo de**
   su dang ganggi stan.
   The high glacier,
   Whose and what carpet is it?

3. **brag stod mthonpo de**
   su dang ganggi stan.
   The high rock,
   Whose and what carpet is it?

4. **mthsom stod mthonpo de**
   su dang ganggi stan.
   The high ocean,
   Whose and what carpet is it?

5. **mkhar stod mthonpo de**
   su dang ganggi stan.
   The high castle,
   Whose and what carpet is it?

6. **sa 'og phon che de**
   su dang ganggi stan.
   The wide earth,
   Whose and what carpet is it?

7. **khrom zed kha sngon de**
   su dang ganggi stan.
   The blue-bordered saddle-cloth,
   Whose and what carpet is it?

8. **sha stan sebo de**
   su dang ganggi stan.
   The grey deer-skin,
   Whose and what carpet is it?

9. **rtsva shing nags thsal de**
   su dang ganggi stan.
   Those meadows and woods,
   Whose and what carpet is it?

10. **snambu yug ring de**
    su dang ganggi stan.
    That long piece of woollen cloth,
    Whose and what carpet is it?

B.—Nyopas:—

THE NYOPAS SAY:—

1. **nam stod mthonpo de**
   nyi zla γnyiskai stan.
   The high sky
   Is the carpet of sun and moon.

2. **gangs stod mthonpo de**
   sengge γyu ralli stan.
   The high glacier
   Is the carpet of the lion with the turquoise mane.

3. **brag stod mthonpo de**
skyin chen ba rganni stan.
The high rock
Is the carpet of the mountain goat, the old ox.

4. **mthsom stod mthonpo de**
nyamo γser miggi stan.
The high ocean
Is the carpet of the fish 'golden eye'.

5. **mkhar stod mthonpo de**
mi chen gongmai stan.
The high castle
Is the carpet of great men.

6. **sa 'og phol che de**
rgya nag rgyalpoi stan.
The wide earth
Is the carpet of the King of China.

7. **khrom zed kha sngon de**
agu dpallei stan.
The blue-bordered saddle-cloth
Is the carpet of **Agu dPalle.**

8. **sha stan sebo de**
agu khru btungngi stan.
The grey deer-skin
Is the carpet of **Agu Khru btung.**

9. **rtsva shing nags thsal de**
bya dang byigui stan.
Those meadows and woods
Are the carpet of the great and little birds.

10. **snambu yug ring de**
nyo 'am spun bdunni stan.
That long piece of woollen cloth
Is the carpet of the Nyopas the seven brethren.

Text notes.

A. 4. *mthsom* = *mthso*, lake. 6. *phonche* or *pholche*, much, in this connection 'much land'. 7. *khrom zed* = *khromme zed*, 'glittering brush', used for velvet. 10. *yug* means 'not sewn', I am told; thus 'a long woven piece of cloth'.

B. 3. *ba rgan*, old ox; compare Song No. XV. 29. 8. Agu *Khru btung* (the spelling of the name is doubtful) has not a human, but a falcon's head.

Translation notes.

This song shows clearly the general character of the wedding songs. It is not in direct connection with the rest of the wedding songs, but forms a scene by itself. After the Nyopas (*lit.*, 'buyers' of the bride) have entered the house, they are not allowed to sit down on a carpet, until they have answered the questions, which form the first half of this song. (This custom seems to be allied to the world-wide 'impossible riddle' of Folklore, which is a variant of the idea of the 'impossible task' as a supernatural method of identifying of the expected hero. The root idea here would seem to be that the Nyopas have to prove that they really are Nyopas before being received, and the proof is in the Folklore method of answering certain formal riddles, as one of the 'signs' of the coming hero.—Editor, *Indian Antiquary*.)

THE LADAKHI PRE-BUDDHIST MARRIAGE RITUAL.[1]

(Translation and Notes.)

By A. H. Francke, Ladakh.

Some time ago I published in *Mémoires de la Société Finno-ougrienne*, Helsingfors, some translations in German of folktales and of extracts from a Tibetan MS. relating to the **Kesar-Myths of Western Tibet.** The publication of the **Marriage Songs of the Ladakhis** now undertaken is another step in the same direction. My object in these publications is to present means to the scientific world for unveiling the hitherto hidden treasures of the **Pre-Buddhist Religion of Tibet.** I was fortunate indeed to get hold of these wedding songs, just before they had vanished altogether. In Central and Upper Ladakh only mere reminiscences, are left of them, although the gorgeous dress of the **Nyopas** and the scene before the house are still in vogue. In Lower Ladakh the songs have been preserved much better, but a large portion of them have ceased to be intelligible to the people. Thus whilst the first nine of the songs I collected were, certain passages excepted, generally understood by the ordinary man, the latter half of the collection consists more or less of a succession of unintelligible sounds. The reason may be, that the wedding ritual proved too hard a trial on the patience of the party and was cut short in many cases.

The method of reading has been as follows. All the songs were dictated slowly by **the leader of the Nyopas** to the village Munshi of **Khalatse, Yeshes Rig 'adzin,** who wrote them down according to the actual sound. This copy proved to be very useful as far as Yeshes Rig 'adzin himself had understood the words. For disentangling the more obscure passages, however, the assistance of the mission schoolmaster of **Leh, Shamuel aByorldan,** and of other Ladakhis, possessed of commonsense, had to be requisitioned. In this way, the first half of the collection has become fairly intelligible, whilst the latter half is still full of obscure passages.

---

[1] Reprinted from the *Indian Antiquary*, XXX, 1901, pp. 131–149.

It is necessary for the proper comprehension of these songs to direct the attention of the readers to the fact that **the four points of the compass** play a rather important *rôle* in the wedding songs, as well as in other Pre-Buddhist literature (*vide Ladakhi Songs* No. XV). This is very natural, for as has been pointed out in the paper on the Kesar-Myths, **the Pre-Buddhist Religion must have been a system of Sun and Nature Worship.** Now it is the sun, who creates the four points of the compass. All of them are different manifestations of the sun and hence the importance attached to them in a physiological religion. This fact suggests a solution to the difficult problem of explaining **the ancient mystic emblem of the Bon Religion, γyungdrung 卐**. This emblem was in my view invented to represent the sun as the creator of East, South, West and North, the little mark at the end of each line indicating the inclination of the sun to proceed from one point to the other.

It is not an easy matter to give a satisfactory explanation of the word **γyungdrung**, but I dare to offer one, in favour of which there is at least some probability. In the Kesar Myths **an old name of the Sun, bya Khyung dkrung nyima,** occurs. This means literally 'the bird *Khyung*, the disc, the sun'. In course of time the name **Khyung dkrung** may have degenerated to become **γyungdrung**, especially at a time when the idea of the emblem had ceased to be generally understood. Laws of sound cannot be of much avail here, because we are dealing with a proper noun. A few suggestions, however, might be made in favour of this derivation:—(1) a word *γyung* is absolutely non-existing and cannot be found in any dictionary; (2) there exist a few cases of *k* being dropped when preceding *y*, thus *kyang* = *yang*, *kyi* = *yi*, *kyin* = *yin*; (3) there is only a very slight, hardly perceptible, difference in the pronunciation of *dkrung* and *drung*. Of course, this explanation of the emblem rests on the theory, that it is always the same sun, which appears in the East every morning, and is in opposition to the theory shown in Song No. I. B. 7, *post*, p. 135. However, the study of other physiological religions has proved plainly that the most contradictory theories may dwell in them side by side.

While on the point of derivation; in regard to the change from *khyung* to *γyung*, it may be compared also to the following corresponding words in Jäschke's *Tibetan Dictionary: khyabpa-yabpa*, both 'cover' in Ladakhi; *'akhyarba-yarba*, both 'go astray'; *'akhyampa-yamyom*, both 'be unsteady'; *akhyigspa*, 'to fetter'; *γyigspa*, 'to be hindered'; *akhyurba*, 'to be separated'; *yurba* or *yurma*, 'pull out' (weeds, *etc.*);

'akhyompa, 'to wave'; *yompa*, 'be swinging', swing. The γ of *γyung* and *γyigspa* is a silent prefixed letter and is often omitted in writing.

In the figures *a* and *b* below is shown the *γyungdrung* in both positions: the natural and the reversed. The Rev. A. W. Heyde of Ghoom tells me that the *γyungdrung* as a monogram is said to be composed of the two syllables  *su* and  *ti, suti* = *svasti.*

卐 卍

a *b*

According to Waddell, *Lamaism in Tibet*, both the established Buddhist church and the adherents to the Bon Religion have a *γyungdrung* of their own, the one under *a* being the emblem of Lamaism, that under *b* of the Bon Religion. It is most natural that *a* alone should correspond to the actual course of the sun, for it is probably the older one. Indian Buddhist missionaries may have fought in vain against the use of the symbol, and finally agreed to introduce it into their own system by regarding it as a monogram, containing the three syllables *su asti* in Indian characters. Afterwards in opposition to Buddhism and at a time when the leading ideas of the once physiological religion had vanished, Bon priests made the emblem turn the other way; just as the custom of circumambulation was altered by the Bonpas from right to left.

In the above drawings showing the γ**yungdrung** as an ornament in Native houses in Khalatse, Lower Ladakh, it will be seen turned both ways.

However all this may really be, on the whole I feel obliged to say, that my explanation of the γyungdrung must not be taken for more than a mere guess at its interpretation from a Tibetan point of view. I have no means in this remote land of collating these speculations with the mass of literature on the *svastika*.

The γyungdrung is thought to be of great importance at the wedding ceremony, and both bride and bridegroom have to sit on carpets showing the emblem. It is indeed in universal use in this connection, for in a copy of the wedding songs, which I received a few days ago from Phyang the γyungdrung is used for punctuation instead of the full stop.

Song No. I.[1]

bagma btangtsana nyopas sgola btangcessi glu'i[2] dpecha yin.

This is the book of the songs, which are sung at the door by the *Nyopas*, when the bride is given.

om bkrashispar gyurcig, bkrashis bdeblags dang ldanpar gyurcig.

nangmas btang 'adug.

Om, may you be blessed! May the blessing come unto you speedily! The people of the house say:

A.

I. A. 1.	**duba sngonmo de**	**stengdu rgyugpa ci'i don.**
	That blue smoke,	Rising upwards, what does it mean?
2.	**duba sngonmo de**	**bardu rgyugpa ci'i don.**
	The blue smoke,	Hanging over the ground, what does it mean?
3.	**duba sngonmo de**	**'ogtu rgyugpa ci'i don.**
	The blue smoke,	Falling to the ground, what does it mean?
4.	**duba sngonmo de**	**sharla rgyugpa ci'i don.**
	The blue smoke,	Spreading towards East, what does it mean?

---

1 The orthography of the songs has been brought in accordance with that of Ladakhi letter writing. In all doubtful cases, however, the spelling of the first MS. will be given.

2 A *chungba* is indicated by an apostrophe.

5. **duba sngonmo de** **lhoru rgyugpa ci'i don.**
The blue smoke, Spreading towards South, what does it mean?

6. **duba sngonmo de** **byangdu rgyugpa ci'i don.**
The blue smoke, Spreading towards North, what does it mean?

7. **duba sngonmo de** **nubtu rgyugpa ci'i don.**
The blue smoke, Spreading towards West, what does it mean?

8. **duba sngonmo de** **mkhardu rgyugpa ci'i don.**
The blue smoke, Rising to the castle, what does it mean?

9. **duba sngonmo de** **yulla rgyugpa ci'i don.**
The blue smoke, Spreading over the country, what does it mean?

10. **duba sngonmo de** **grongdu rgyugpa ci'i don.**
The blue smoke, Spreading over the village, what does it mean?

B.

I. B. phyimas landu.

People outside (the *Nyopas*) answer:

1. **duba sngonmo de stengdu rgyugpa de**
lhai dbangpo rgya bzhinla rgolba ma zhus sam
bsang shug phulba'i don.

The blue smoke Rises upwards,
I think, that the Lord of Heaven, **dBangpo rgyabzhin's** anger may not be provoked,
It is an offering to him.

2. **duba sngonmo de bardu rgyugpa de**
btsan ama skyabs bdunla rgolba ma zhus sam
bsang shug phulba'i don.

The blue smoke Is hanging over the earth,
I think, that the Earth-Mother **Skyabsbdun's** anger may not be provoked,
It is an offering to her.

3. **duba sngonma de 'ogtu rgyugpa de**
klurgyal lcogpola rgolba ma zhus sam
bsang shug phulba'i don.

The blue smoke Is falling to the ground,
I think, that the Water-King **lCogpo's** anger may not be provoked,
It is an offering to him.

4. **duba sngonmo de shardu rgyugpa de**
shar rdorje sems dp'ala rgolba ma zhus sam
bsang shug phulba'i don.

The blue smoke Is spreading towards East,
I think, that the eastern **rDorje sems dp'a's** anger may not be provoked,
It is an offering to him.

5. **duba sngonmo de lhoru rgyugpa de**
lho rinchen byung ldanla rgolba ma zhus sam
bsang shug phulba'i don.

The blue smoke Is spreading towards South,
I think, that the southern **Rinchen byungldan's** anger may not be provoked,
It is an offering to him.

6. **duba sngonmo de byangdu rgyugpa de**
byang donyod grubpala rgolb ma zhus sam
bsang shug phulba'i don.

The blue smoke Is spreading towards North,
I think, that the northern **Donyodgrubpa's** anger may not be provoked,
It is an offering to him.

7. **duba sngonmo de nubtu rgyugpa de**
nub snangba mth'ayasla rgolba ma zhus sam
bsang shug phulba'i don.

The blue smoke Is spreading towards West,
I think, that the western **sNangba mthyas'** anger may not be provoked,
It is an offering to him.

8. **duba sngonmo de mkhardu rgyugpa de**
rtselha snyanpola rgolba ma zhus sam
bsang shug phulba'i don.

The blue smoke Is rising to the castle,
I think, that **rTselha snyanpo's** anger may not be provoked,
It is an offering to him.

9. **duba sngonmo de yulla rgyugpa de**
yulthsa snyanpola rgolba ma zhus sam
bsang shug phulba'i don.

The blue smoke Is spreading over the country,
I think, that **Yulthsa snyanpo's** anger may not be provoked,
It is an offering to him.

10. **duba sngonmo de grongla rgyugpa de**
phalha snyanpola rgolba ma zhus sam
bsang shug phulba'i don.

The blue smoke Is spreading over the peasants' (houses),
I think, that **Phalha snyanpo's** anger may not be provoked,
It is an offering to him.

NOTES ON THE TIBETAN TEXT.

Nyopa, buyer, because the bride was bought in ancient times. The salutation in classical language **Om bkrashispar**, *etc.*, is exchanged after each strophe, but will not be repeated in these pages.

I. A. In all verses *ci'i don* means literally: it is the meaning of what? II. B. As regards the meaning of names and general position of the heads of the Pre-Buddhist cosmology, see my paper on the Kesar Myth in *Mémoires de la Société Finno-ougrienne*, 1900, No. XV. The syllable *sam* I was first inclined to translate by 'or', but people told me, that they understood it to mean 'think', in favour of which might be pointed to the people's response: Well thought, you mighty friends. In v. 4, 5, 6, and 7 the gods, who govern the four directions, are mentioned.

They are the properly Tibetan *Lōka-pālas.* In Lamaism three of them have become *Dhyānibuddhas,* whilst *rDorje sems dp'a* has become their president. That their relationship to the four points of the globe has not yet quite been lost in Lamaism, is shown by the *Padmàthanyig,* see Grünwedel, *Mythologie des Buddhismus,* pp. 98, 99.

The names in literal translation mean:—

4. 'The thunderbolt with the courageous soul.' 5. 'The producer of great price.' 6. 'Fulfiller of the aim, he has.' 7. 'Eternal light.' With the exception of 6, all the names point plainly to the different manifestations of the sun. 7 in particular goes back to the idea, that the West is the receptacle of all the suns, which have been imported from Persia. Instead of *ma zhus* the original rendering was probably *ma zhu*, the imperative being used for the optative. 8. *rTselha*, god of the summit. 9. *Yulthsa*, village idol. 10. *Phalha*, god of the fathers, i.e. family.

Notes on the Translation.

It might be well to say a few words about the scene, which forms the background of the songs. The *Nyopas* (i.e. friends of the bridegroom, who were sent to buy the bride) come on horseback and clad in gorgeous dress [1] before the house of the bride and ask for entrance. This is refused to them unless they are **able to answer certain questions.** All the people of the house are armed with sticks and the *Nyopas* are beaten unmercifully as soon as they fail to prove their respectable origin by answering the questions satisfactorily. The people of the house light a fire of the wood of the pencil cedar and concerning tne smoke of this the first questions are asked.

After the questions regarding the principal deities have been settled, in 8, 9, and 10 the local deities come in. Though in ancient times idols do not seem to have had a place in the Bon Religion, we can see how the idea gradually crept in. As we know from the Kesar Myths, the **lha's** or gods used to visit the earth frequently. High hills became known as places of the gods' descent, and to honour them properly, white altars were erected. By and by these altars or **lhatho's** were considered as being the dwelling places of certain *lha's* and at last the idea was developed, that wherever a *lhatho* was erected, a *lha* would soon take his seat. So we have a *lha* on the hill (near the castle) in 8, and the family (father) *lha* in 10. In 9 the word *thsa* might point to a rough idol; compare Jäschke's *Dictionary*, *thsathsa*. All of them have the epithet *snyanpo* = 'well-sounding'.

---

[1] With the article as published orginally in the *Indian Antiquary* there is a coloured plate, facing p. 136 (IA., XXX, 1901). in which the dress of the *Nyopas* is depicted.

Song No. II.

A.

II. A. legs bsams dbangi nyebo nangmas.	Well thought, you mighty friends. People of the house say:
1. phuru yar γzigs 'ang	Look over there to the upper valley!
gangs chu dkarpo de	That white glacier water,
su dang ganggi chang.	What and whose beer is it?
2. γyasla yar γzigs 'ang	Look over there to the right!
γy'a chu khral khrol de	That foaming water among the stones.
su dang ganggi chang.	What and whose beer is it?
3. mdoru yar γzigs 'ang	Look over there below!
γtsang chab sngonmo de	That blue river water,
su dang ganggi chang.	What and whose beer is it?
4. γyonla yar γzigs 'ang	Look over there to the left!
chumig kyal kyil de	Those wells here and there,
su dang ganggi chang.	What and whose beer are they?
5. sbrulmgo ma chabrkyan nangdu	And in this large jar with the snake's head
yang dkar̃ naskyi chang su	The beer (made) of white barley,
dang ganggi chang.	What and whose beer is this?

B.

Nyopas landu. The *Nyopas* answer:

II. B. 1. phuru yar γzigs 'ang
gangs chu dkarpo de
dar sing γsoba'i chang.

Look over there to the upper valley!
That white glacier water
Is the beer, nourishing the ice-lion.

2. γyasla yar γzigs 'ang
γy'a chu khral khrol de
shaphran γsoba'i chang.

Look over there to the right!
That foaming water among the stones
Is the beer, nourishing the young deer.

3. **mdoru yar γzigs 'ang**
γtsang chab sngonmo de
nyaphran γsoba'i chang.

Look over there below!
That blue river water
Is the beer, nourishing the little fishes.

3. **γyonla yar γzigs 'ang**
chumig kyal kyil de
ma zhing γsoba'i chang.

Look over there to the left!
Those wells here and there
Are the beer, nourishing the mother-fields.

5. **sbrulmgo ma chab rkyanla**
yang dkar naskyi khuba de
nyo 'am spun bdungyi chang.

And in this large jar with the snake's head,
The fluid (made) of white barley
Is the beer of the *Nyopas* or the seven brethren.

Text Notes.

A. 2. *γyachu*, this word is used here, so people tell me, for water with stones, not for stagnant water, *khralkhrol*, noisy. 4. *kyal-kyil* scattered about. 5. *ma*, mother, used for everything large, here the large jar.

B. 4. *ma zhing*, motherfield, a very fertile field. Instead of *kyalkyil-parpur* is also used in the same sense.

Translation Notes.

A. 5. The mouth of the jar is formed like a snake's head. B. 1. The ice-lion with the blue locks (or mane) was originally the glacier itself, later on it developed into a fabulous being, which was thought to live there. 5. The number of the *Nyopas* ought to be seven.

Song No. III.

A.

III. A. **snyan γsanpar mdzodcig.**
Now listen with your ears!

1. **dgung dang dbyibskyi mjalthsul de**
su dang ganggis byas.
The existence of the high heaven and of the forms (plants, animals),
By whom and how was it created?

2. **shar dang nubkyi mjalthsul de**
su dang ganggis byas.
The existence of East and West,
By whom and how was it created?

3. **lho dang byanggi mjalthsul de**
su dang ganggis byas.
The existence of South and North,
By whom and how was it created?

4. **steng dang 'oggi mjalthsul de**
su dang ganggis byas.
The existence of height and depth,
By whom and how was it created?

5. **phu dang mdoyi mjalthsul de**
su dang ganggis byas.
The existence of an upper and a lower valley,
By whom and how was it created?

6. **mkhar dang yulgyi mjalthsul de**
su dang ganggis byas.
The existence of castle and village,
By whom and how was it created?

7. **γzhis dang γnaskyi mjalthsul de**
su dang ganggis byas.
The existence of hearth and home,
By whom and how was it created?

8. **phyi dang nanggi mjalthsul de**
su dang ganggis byas.
The fact, that some people are outside and some inside,
By whom and how was it created?

B.

phyimas landu.

The *Nyopas* answer:

III. B. 1. **dgung dang dbyibskyi mjalthsul de**
nyi zla γnyiskyis byas.
The existence of the high heaven and of the forms
Was created by sun and moon.

2. **shar dang nubkyi mjalthsul de**
khri γdugs nyimas byas.
The existence of East and West
Was created by the sun the umbrella of the throne.

3. **lho dang byanggi mjalthsul de**
zla mthsan dkarpos byas.
The existence of South and North
Was created by the Moon, the whitener of the night.

4. **steng dang 'oggi mjalthsul de**
sbang char zilbus byas.
The existence of height and depth
Was created by the dewy soaking rain.

5. **phu dang mdoyi mjalthsul de**
skyeser [1] rlungpos byas.
The existence of an upper and a lower valley
Was created by *skyeser*, the wind.

6. **mkhar dang yulgyi mjalthsul de**
rgyal dang blongyis byas.
The existence of castle and village
Was created by the king and the ministers.

---

[1] Having been questioned meanwhile by Regierungsrat Dr. E. Schlagintweit about the equation *Kesar* = **skyegsar**, I wish to state the following facts: This equation was not worked out by myself, but received ready made from the natives, who explain the name in this way. According to a letter from Rev. Fr. Peter, Kyelang, the popular pronunciation of the same name is *Kyesar* in Lahoul. In a collection of popular songs which I received from Phyang three days ago, the king's name is invariably spelled *Kyesar*. In Leh ordinary people pronounce the name *Kesar*, but educated people, who know the myths from the epos, pronounce it *Gesar*, All the changes from *Kyesar* to *Gesar* can be accounted for, see my *Ladakhi Grammar*, Introduction, *Kyirmo* = *girmo*.

7. **γzhis dang γnaskyi mjalthsul de**
γnyendrung rnamskyis byas.
The existence of hearth and home.
Was created by you, our friends.

8. **phyi dang nanggi mjalthsul de**
nyo 'am spun bdungyis byas.
The fact, that some people are outside and some inside,
Was created by the *Nyopas*, the seven brethren.

Text Notes.

In the original *mjalthso* is given instead of *mjalthsul*, which is unintelligible. See more examples for elision of *l* at the end of a syllable in my *Ladakhi Grammar*, laws of sound 4. *dbyibs* is a word, not so easily understood, two kinds of *dbyibs* are mentioned in XIII, they are *nammkha*, sky, heaven, and *chos*, religion. B. 5. *skyeser*, name of the wind god. May be either *skyegsar*, the reborn one, see Kesar Myth, or *skyebser*, producer of coolness.

Translation Notes

A. 8. This question refers to the scene created by the arrival of the *Nyopas*. B. 2. The sun is often called an umbrella on account of his circular shape. 3. Though the moon as representative of the night can be made to account for the North, it is difficult to see her relation to the South.

B. 4. Perhaps on account of the fact, that clouds show great varieties of altitude. 5. A strong draught is felt in every valley.

Song No. IV.

A.

byonrabs yin.
This is about the origin (of the *Nyopas*).

IV. A. 1. **'adir byon rnams shargyi glingnas yongstsana**
shar phyogs rgyalpo suzhig bzhugs
bran dang 'akhor γyog cila dkar
dbyibs dang chalugs cinda 'adra.
When you came here from the eastern country,
Who was king there in the East?
Why may we call his subjects and servants white?
What is their shape and custom like?

2. **lhoyi phyogsnas yongstsana**
lho phyogs rgyalpo su zhig bzhugs
bran dang 'akhor γyog cila dkar
dbyibs dang chalugs cinda 'adra.

When you came here from the southern country,
Who was king there in the South?
Why may we call his subjects and servants white?
What is their shape and custom like?

3. **kyed rnams nubkyi glingnas yongstsana**
nubphyogs rgyalpo su zhig bzhugs
bran dang 'akhor γyog cila dkar
dbyibs dang chalugs cinda 'adra.

When you came here from the Western country,
Who was king there in the West?
Why may we call his subjects and servants white?
What is their shape and custom like?

4. **kyed rnams byanggi glingnas yongstsana**
byangphyogs rgyalpo su zhig bzhugs
bran dang 'akhor γyog cila dkar
dbyibs dang chalugs cinda 'adra.

When you came here from the northern country,
Who was king there in the North?
Why may we call his subjects and servants white?
What is their shape and custom like?

B.

phimas landu.
The *Nyopas* answer:

IV. B. 1. **ngacag nyebo rnams shargyi glingnas yongstsana**
sharphyogs rgyalpo yul 'akhor srung
bran dang 'akhor γyog chosla dkar
dbyibs dang chalugs bdelegs 'adug
sharna khri γdugs nyima mchis
skad cig 'adrina dela dris.

When we came here from the eastern country,
Yul 'akhor srung was king there in the East.

For the sake of their religion we may call his subjects and servants white.
Their shape and custom are good.
In the East there dwells the sun, the umbrella of the throne,
If you want to hear some news, ask him!

2. **nga nyebo lhoyi glingnas yongstsana**
lho phyogs rgyalpo 'aphags skyed bzhugs
bran dang 'akhor γyog chosla dkar
dbyibs dang chalugs bdelegs 'adug
lhona 'abru sna 'adzommo dg'a
skad cig 'adrina dela dris.

When we came here from the southern country,
'aPhagsskyed was king there in the South.
For the sake of their religion we may call his subjects and servants white.
Their shape and custom are good.
In the South they enjoy all kinds of grain,
If you wish to hear some news, ask that!

3. **nga nyebo nubKhyi glingnas yongstsana**
nub phyogs rgyalpo spyan mig bzang bzhugs
bran dang 'akhor γyog chosla dkar
dyibs dang chalugs bdelegs 'adug
nubna sman sna 'adzommo 'adug
skad cig 'adrina dela dris.

When we came here from the western country,
sPhyanmig bzang was king there in the West.
For the sake of their religion we may call his subjects and servants white.
Their shape and custom are good.
In the West there are all kinds of medicines.
If you wish to hear some news, ask them!

4. **ngacag nyebo rnams byanggi glingnas byongstsana**
byang phyogs rgyalpo 'aphags skyed bzhugs
bran dang 'akhor γyog chosla dkar
dbyibs dang chalugs bdelegs 'adug
byangna thsos sna 'adzommo 'adug
skad cig 'adrina dela dris.

When we came here from the northern country,
'aPhagsskyed was king there in the North.
For the sake of their religion we may call his subjects and servants white.
Their shape and custom are good.
In the North there are all kinds of dyes,
If you wish to hear some news, ask them.

TEXT NOTES.

A. 1. *etc. cin da,* ought to be spelt according to the views of Ladakhis *ci mda, mda* (or perhaps *'ada*) meaning 'about'. The names of the kings mean, B. 1. protector of the country. 2 and 4. the high-born one. 3. good eye. Very likely the original name of 4 had been lost and that of 2 was inserted instead. Each verse may also have a seventh concluding line: *ngacag nyebo rnamsla skadcha bshadrgyu med,* we friends do not know any news; *'adzommo = 'adzompo,* plentiful. Instead of *bdelegs* the original has *bdelags.*

TRANSLATION NOTES.

A. 1, etc. White is the colour of the **lha's** and of all good things. B. As regards the products of the different countries, they are mentioned in about the same manner in *Ladakhi Songs* No. XV, Harvest festival at **Skyurbuchan.** They are perhaps more of a practical than of a mythological interest.

The three names, given in this song, do not seem to be of Tibetan origin. They are probably the Tibetan names of the Indian *Lōkapālas.* Though there can be no doubt as to the pre-Buddhist origin of this song as a whole, the names of the kings may be later Lamaist interpolations. I am rather inclined to believe, that an ancient version of this song had the names of those kings, who actually reigned in the respective regions many years ago. In this connection it may be added, that in Song No. X, where the four points of the compass come in again, actual geographical kingdoms, for instance China and India, are mentioned. Regarding the names, given in IV, compare Grünwedel, *Mythologie des Buddhismus,* p. 181; *spyanmig bzang,* instead of *mig mi bzang,* is probably a corruption, as it does not correspond to the Indian *Virūpāksha.*

Song No. V.

A.

berrabs yin. This is about the sticks.

phyimas. The *Nyopas* say:

V. A. 1. **shing stagpa skyerpa shugpa γsum.**
The birch, the alp-willow and the cedar,

2. **de γsum shing dang ma rdungshig.**
With sticks of these three kinds of wood do not beat us!

3. **de γsum shing dang rdung zerna**
If you beat us with these three kinds of wood,

4. **mgoyi ldem 'achagna ldem 'achag stong dang len**
Breaking our helmets, you must return them a thousandfold,

5. **luskyi phe ralna pheral stong dang len**
Hurting our body, we shall return it a thousandfold,

6. **snyangyi γyu 'achagna γyu 'achag stong dang len**
Breaking our earrings, you must return them a thousandfold,

7. **'oggı sga 'achagna sga 'achag stong dang len.**
legs bsams dbanggi nyebo.
Breaking our saddles, you must return them a thousandfold!
Well thought, you mighty friends!

B.

nangmas landu People of the house say:

V. B. 1. **bdaggi lagtu yodpai shing γyu lcang ldempa 'adi**
This elastic stick of the turquoise willow, which is my hand,

2. **'akhrungsa rgyagar yuldu 'akhrungs**
Arose in India, its birth-place.

3. **thsarsa bodyul dbussu thsar**
It grew in **dBus** in Tibet, its growing place.

4. **lcugstod serpo γserla yod**
Its flexible yellow upper half looks like gold.

5. **rtsemo sngonmo γyula byas**
Its blue tip was made of turquoise.

6. **lhayi dbangpo rgya bzhinnas**
By the king of the gods, **rGya bzhin,**

7. **lcags rgyabpai bk'a khrol cig**
(There was issued) an order to beat (with it).

8. **'adila bk'alung yang dagpa zhig γnang zerna**
If you ask, what holy prophecy he gave regarding it,

9. **nyi zlai buzhig 'abrangs**
'A son of sun and moon may follow (you)!

10. **zla skar mdundu mchis**
The moon and the stars may be before (you)!

11. **don ngan phugssu 'akhrugs**
Bad speech ought to be blamed.

12. **phu ngan duba che**
If (the fire) is badly blown, there is much smoke.

13. **mgron ngan ringdu mchis**
A bad guest be far away!'

14. **rinchen dbyugpas char cig phob**
Now let go down a rain (of blows) with the costly sticks,

15. **nam bz'a rincangyi ldurcig phob.**
Beat them on their costly dress!

Text Notes.

A. 4. *ldem,* said to be the golden hat of the *Nyopas,* is called *ldem* either on account of its stiff shape or because of its being an emblem (allegory) of the sun. As will have been noticed in the preceding songs, the *Nyopas* have to play the part of the sun god. 5. *phe* = *phye*, perfect tense, of *'abyedpa,* to open, thus 'if you beat an opening of the body', 'a wound', the verb being used as a noun.

B. 3. *thsarsa,* finishing place, when applied to men, it is the country, where maturity is attained. 4. *γserla yod,* it belongs to gold. 5. *γyula byas,* it was made (turned) into turquoise. 9. *'brangs* = *'abrengs,* imperative tense. 10. Instead of *mdundu* the original has *dondu,* instead of *mchis* it has *ches* and *che*; the same must be said of *mchis* in B. 13. *nambz'a,* Ladakhi for *nabz'a. ldur* perhaps the same as *ldur ldur* in Jäschke's *Dictionary.*

Translation Notes.

Because at the end of each verse in IV. the *Nyopas* failed to give a satisfactory account of the four countries, this is taken as a sufficient cause to beat them. For their defence they recite V. A., VI. A., and VII. A., and find fault with the sticks. On the other hand, the bride's party praise their sticks as having been approved of by the king of heaven V. B., ꜀ king of the earth VI. B., and the king of the underworld (waters) in VII. B.

B. 9 and 10 is said to refer to the procession of the wedding party.

Song No. VI.

A.

phyimas. The *Nyopas* say:

VI. A. 1. **shing grama glangma lcangma γsum**
The furze, the hill willow and the house willow

2. **de γsum shing dang ma rdungshig**
With sticks of these three kinds of wood do not beat us!

3. **de γsum shing dang rdung zerna**
If you beat us with these three kinds of wood.

4. **mgoyi ldem 'achagna ldem 'achag stong dang len**
Breaking our helmets, you must return them a thousandfold.

5. **luskyi phe ralna pheral stong dang len**
Hurting our body, we shall return it a thousandfold,

6. **snyangyi γyu 'achagna γyu 'achag stong dang len**
Breaking our earrings, you must return them a thousandfold!

7. **'oggi sga 'achagna sga 'achag stong dang len.**
legs bsams dbanggi nyebo.
Breaking our saddles, you must return them a thousandfold!
Well thought, you mighty friends!

B.

nangmas landu People of the house answer:

VI. B. 1. **bdaggi lagtu yodpai shing γyu lcang sngonpoi**
Of this green stick of the turquoise willow, which is in my hand,

2. **skyedpa sngonpo γyula byas**
The blue middle was made of turquoise.

3. **lo 'adab 'adzamgling mi yul khyab**
The leaves of the tree cover all **'aDzamgling** the country of men.

4. **rje sabdag rgyalpo bzhinnas**
By the king, the owner and lord of the earth.

5. **lcags rgyabpai bk'a khrol cig.**
(There was issued) an order to beat (with it).

6. **'adila bk'alung yang dagpa zhig γnang zerna**
If you ask, what holy prophecy he gave regarding it,

7. **rgyalpoi bu zhig 'abrangs**
'A son of the king may follow (you)!

8. **zlaskar mdundu mchis**
The moon and the stars may be before (you)!

9. **don ngan phugssu 'akhrugs**
Bad speech ought to be blamed,

10. **phu ngan duba che**
If (the fire) is badly blown there is much smoke!'

11. **mgron ngan ringdu mchis**
A bad guest be far away!

12. **rinchen dbyugpas char cig phob**
Now let go down a rain (of blows) with the costly sticks,

13. **nam bz'a rincangyi ldur cig phob.**
Beat them on their costly dress.

Text Notes.

In E. two lines seem to have been lost, because for all the rest this song is in conformity with V. B. or perhaps V. B. 2, 3 are later additions. In 4 the king is mentioned as representative of the earth, an older version may have had Mother **sKyabs bdun**, compare Song No. I. B. 2, *ante*, p. 134.

Translation Notes.

B. 3. **'aDzamgling** or **'aDzambugling**, comprised originally Tibet and India, later on all Asia or the whole earth, in the latter sense it is to be taken here. It is the Indian *Jambu-dvīpa*.

Song No. VII.

A.

phyimas The *Nyopas* say:

VII. A. 1. **shing starbu 'umbu thserbu γsum**
The walnut-tree, the tamarisk and the thorn,

2. **de γsum shing dang ma rdungshig**
With sticks of these three kinds of wood do not beat us!

3. **de γsum shing dang rdung zerna**
If you beat us with these three kinds of wood,

4. **mgoyi ldem 'achagna lden 'achag stong dang len**
Breaking our helmets, you must return them a thousandfold,

5. **luskyi phe ralna pheral stong dang len**
Hurting our body, we shall return it a thousandfold,

6. **snyangvi γyu 'achagna γyu 'achag stong dang len**
Breaking our earrings, you must return them a thousandfold,

7. **'Oggi sga 'achagna sga 'achag stong dang len.**
Breaking our saddles, you must return them a thousandfold!

B.

nangmas People of the house say:

VII. B. 1. **bdaggi lagtu yodpai shing γyu lcang sngonpoi**
Of this green stick of the turquoise willow, which is in my hand,

2. **rtsaba dkarpo dungla byas.**
The white root was made of a shell.

3. **sbathag 'og phyogs kluyal khyab**
The roots (of the tree) cover all the lower underworld.

4. **klurgyal lcogpo m'a gros zilchennas.**
By the wise and glorious lCogpo, King of the Underworld,

5. **lcags rgyabpai bk'a khrol cig**
(There was issued) an order to beat (with it).

6. **'adila bk'alung yang dagpa zhig γnang zerna**
If you ask, what holy prophecy he gave regarding it,

7. **klu phranbu zhig 'abrangs**
'A young **kLu** may follow (you)!

8. **yul thsa mdundu mchis**
The village idol may be before (you)!

9. **don ngan phugssu 'akhrugs**
Bad speech ought to be blamed.

10. **phu ngan duba che**
If (the fire) is badly blown, there is much smoke.

11. **mgron ngan ringdu mchis**
A bad guest be far away!'

12. **rinchen dbyugpas char cig phob.**
Now let go down a rain (of blows) with the costly sticks,

13. **nambz'a rincangyi ldur cig phob.**
Beat them on their costly dress!

Text Notes.

VII. A. 1. *'umbu* = *'ombu*, tamarisk. B. 7. *phran* is generally used only of young animals. In II the original has *song*, go, instead of *mchis*, be. This fact is perhaps the best justification for my putting *mchis* in the place of *che* and *ches* of the original.

Translation Notes.

If we look at V. B. 4, VI. B. 2, and VII. B. 2, we see, that the stick of the turquoise willow is identified with the tree of the world, which we find in so many mythologies. The roots of this tree cover the underworld, VII. B. 3, the leaves cover the earth VI. B. 3, and the top reaches *stanglha*.

Song No. VIII.

A.

phyimas. The *Nyoγas* say:

VIII. A. 1. **skyaba zanthsan dang 'ulu thsigs**
bcad dang yogpa snanag dang
The soup-spoon, the gravy-spoon and the black-nosed poker,

2. **de γsum shing dang ma rdungshig**
With these three sticks do not beat us!

3. **de γsum shing dang rdung zerna**
If you beat us with these three sticks,

4. **mgoyi ldem 'achagna ldem 'achag stong dang len**
Breaking our helmets, you must return them a thousandfold,

5. **luskyi phe ralna pheral stong dang len**
Hurting our body, we shall return it a thousandfold,

6. **synangyi γyu 'achagna γyu 'achag stong dang len**
Breaking our earrings, you must return them a thousandfold,

7. **'oggi sga 'achagna sga 'achag stong dang len.**
Breaking our saddles, you must return them a thousandfold!

B.

nangmas lan ma shespas yang phyimas

Because the people of the house do not know what to answer, the *Nyopas* say:

VII. B. 1. **nged nyebo rnamsla rdungbai shing zhig yod**
shing hala ldempai shing zhig yod
shing hula ldempai shing zhig yod
shing rtsaba γcigla rtsemo γsum
rtsemo γsumla yalga drug.

A wood to beat us, friends, does exist.
It is a wonderfully elastic wood,
It is a marvellously elastic wood.
There is a tree, the root of which has three stems
These three stems have (together) six boughs.

2. **yalga dangporu**
bya chen khyunggi thsangs
γser sgong ma bcagpa
bya thsangs ma bshigpa
bya de ma 'agrogspa
shing de snamnas byon
de dang rdung mdzod cig
de dang rgyob mdzod cig
de dang rdung mdzodna
mgoyi ldem 'achagnayang
ldem 'achag stong meddo
luskyi phe ralna

pheral stong meddo
snyangyi γyu 'achagnayang
γyu 'ạchag stong meddo
'oggi sga 'achagnayang
sga 'achag stong yańg med.

On the first bough
There is the nest of the huge bird **khyung.**
Not breaking the golden egg,
Not destroying the bird's nest
Not frightening the bird,
Take a stick and come!
With this stick do beat us!
With this stick do whip us!
If you beat us with this stick,
Breaking our helmets,
You need not return them a thousandfold.
Hurting our body,
We shall not return it a thousandfold.
Breaking our earrings,
You need not return them a thousandfold.
Breaking our saddles,
You need not return them a thousandfold!

3. **yalga γnyisparu**
byargyal rgodpoi thsangs
γyu sgong ma bcagpa
bya de ma 'agrogspa
bya thsangs ma bshigpa
shing de snamnas byon
de dang rdung mdzod cig, etc.
(See v. 2.)

On the second bough
There is the nest of the wild eagle.
Not breaking the turquoise egg,
Not frightening the bird,
Not destroying the bird's nest,
Take a stick and come!
With this stick do beat us! etc.
(See v. 2.)

4. **yalga γsumparu**
mgobo ldad dkar thsangs
dung sgong ma bcagpa
bya thsangs ma bshigpa
bya de ma 'agrogspa
shing de snamnas byon
de dang rdung mdzod cig, etc.

On the third bough
There is the nest of the bird 'white head'.
Not breaking the pearl-white egg,
Not destroying the bird's nest,
Not frightening the bird,
Take a stick and come!
With this stick do beat us! etc.

5. **yalga bzhiparu**
glagmo mkhal dkar thsangs
dngul sgong ma bcagpa
bya thsangs ma bshigpa
bya de ma 'agrogspa
shing de snamnas byon
de dang rdung mdzod cig, etc.

On the fourth bough
There is the nest of the eagle 'white kidney'.
Not breaking the silver egg,
Not destroying the bird's nest,
Not frightening the bird,
Take a stick and come!
With this stick do beat us! etc.

6. **yalga lngaparu**
ribya gongmoi thsangs
byur sgong ma bcagpa
bya thsangs ma bshigpa
bya de ma 'agrogspa
shing de snamnas byon
de dang rdung mdzod cig, etc.

On the fifth bough
There is the nest of the snow partridge.
Not breaking the coral egg,

Not destroying the bird's nest,
Not frightening the bird,
Take a stick and come!
With this stick do beat us! etc.

7. **yalga drugparu**
khraskya dkarmoi thsangs
lcags sgong ma bcagpa
bya thsangs ma bshigpa
bya de ma 'agropspa
shing de snamnas byon
de dang rdung mdzog cig, etc.

On the sixth bough
There is the nest of the white falcon.
Not breaking the iron egg,
Not destroying the bird's nest,
Not frightening the bird,
Take a stick and come!
With this stick do beat us! etc.

Text Notes.

A. I. The expressions given here are colloquial Lower Ladakhi for soup-spoon, table-spoon and poker. B. 1. *hala* = *halas, hula* the same as *hala*, *rtsemo* means originally 'top'. 2. *sgong* = *sgonga*, egg. The termination *pa* in *bcagpa, bshigpa* and *'agrogspa* is Ladakhi for *par*, the supine being used here in a gerundial sense. 5. *mkhal dkar*, white kidney, i.e. the feathers over the kidney are white. 6. *ribya*, another name of the same bird is *lhabya*.

Translation Notes.

This song seems to contain a further description of the tree of the world. It is remarkable that the tree of the world is said to have **six boughs, for I have not yet met with the number six in other books relating to Bonpa Mythology.** In this connection I should like to mention that according to the *Edda* there are six animals (a goat and five stags) feeding on the leaves of the tree of the world, and that the *Edda* (not *Simrock*) speaks of six worlds.

Song No. IX.

A.

IX. A. 1. **khyed nyebo me ma khrul**
Now, friends, do not let the fire fall down!

2. **da nang yongba gangnas yongs**
Now, you, who enter, from where do you come?

3. **'agroba nyidcag gangdu 'agro**
Then, where will you go to?

4. **sdodpai bde lce gangna yod**
Where will you be pleased to sit down?

5. **dgospai skudon sula yod**
For whose sake do you come?

6. **γzhungyul 'adriru cila byon.**
Why did you come here into the middle of the village?

B.

phyimas. The *Nyopas* say:

IX. B. 1. **yong da ngazha sharphyogs bdechen glingnas yongs.**
We come from a happy country in the East.

2. **'agro da ngazha nubphyogs urgyan glingdu 'agro**
We go to the country of the paradise in the West.

3. **sdodpai bdelce de sa γnas 'adina yod**
We shall be pleased to sit down here.

4. **dgospai skudon ni γzhungyul 'adina yod.**
legs bsams dbanggi nyebo.
Our aim is here in the middle of village.
Well thought, you mighty friends!

Text Notes.

A. 1. *me ma khrul,* do not let the fire fall down, proverbial expression, for 'do not break down now, show your ingenuity!'. 4. The original has *sula* instead of *gangna*, the lines 4 and 5 having been confounded. B. 2. **urgyan,** here in Lower Ladakh is understood to mean either **Padmasambhava** or the **'Western Paradise'.** 1 and 2 again show, plainly, that the *Nyopas* have to play the part of the sun.

Translation Notes.

This song IX is generally the conclusion of the scene before the house, the *Nyopas* are invited to enter and tell the name of the girl. Then the bridal party, the *Nyopas* and the whole village, sit down for a great feast, when the **Chang glu** (the continuation of the wedding song given above) is sung. On the following morning a Buddhist Lama appears and reads a scripture portion from an orthodox Buddhist book. People tell me that he may read anything he likes, because neither the Lama nor the bride is able to grasp the meaning, and the chief thing is the correct pronunciation. Then the bride and the *Nyopas* mount their horses and ride to the house of the bridegroom, where another feast is given.

Conclusion.

Having thus arrived at the end of the first intelligible half of the wedding ritual, it will be as well to add a few words about the other less intelligible half, though the latter is not yet ready for publication. After a study of the verses contained in it, which can be understood fairly well, I have come to the conclusion that the so-called **second half of the ritual** is not the continuation of the first but a composition apart. It is in reality a **new ritual dating from the time of the introduction of Buddhism into Ladakh,** and is an attempt to replace the ancient Bonpa ritual by another, which, though not entirely Lamaist, tries to introduce Buddhist ideas by placing them side by side with Bonpa ideas. That this compromise has proved a failure, is shown by the fact that people have never been able to grasp it in full and are now on the point of abandoning it altogether.

As might have been expected, my interpretation of the Kesar Myths has been criticised[1] as being unscientific. There can be no doubt that there are no scientific means available to prove the solar origin of many a hero. It is so much easier to prove the descent of all of them from great ancestors. However, a certain amount of commonsense, now and then speaks in favour of a solar descent. In my notes to Wedding Song No. I, I said that the name of the northern **Lokapāla Donyodgrubpa** could not well be explained as a manifestation

[1] This remark refers only to private letters from certain professors; if I had had the pleasure of seeing Prof. Dr. Grünwedel's most interesting review of the *Kesar Myth* (published in the *Globus,* August, 1900), I should certainly have modified my expressions.

of the sun, but my critics have helped me to bring him into the system. From the Kesar Myths we learn, that **Kesar,** the supposed spring-hero, had a different name before his birth on earth, that is, during winter. Then, whilst in heaven, he was called **Dongrub,** 'the fulfiller of the aim'. This name is, so to say, a prophecy, it indicates the future doings of the hero. There can be no doubt that the year and the day have certain parallels, and the winter of the year corresponds to the night of the day. Is it wonderful then, that the **Lokapāla** of the north (i.e. the place where the sun is during night) should have the same name as the spring-god during winter? **Donyodgrubpa** means 'the fulfiller of the aim, he has'. The original name **Dongrub** was changed into a four-syallabled one simply to bring it into accordance with the four-syllabled names of the other **Lokapālas.** Thus we see, that the name of the supposed spring-hero **Kesar,** before his entering into action is in accordance with the name of the sun before his starting his day's work. Does this fact not suggest a possible solar origin of Kesar?

Hitherto certain school especially have considered it scientific to compare the mythologies of certain nations only with those of such nations as are related to them by language. However, religion overleaps the barriers of linguistic relationship, and there is no necessity to believe that a solar mythology had been worked out by a single nation and was carried to others by her missionaries. On the contrary, solar mythologies may have arisen in many countries and later on the different nations have borrowed one from the other.[1] The existence of the *Nibelungensage* not only among the Uigurs, but also among the Tibetans is an established fact. Compare G. N. Potanin: *Vostocnyje motivy v srednevĕkovym jevropejskim eposĕ*, Moscow, 1899.

[1] Just like the *Wundermärchen*.

THE PALADINS OF THE KESAR-SAGA. A COLLECTION OF SAGAS FROM LOWER LADAKH.

By A. H. Francke.

Preface.[1]

The following tales, which I call **Sagas of the Paladins of the Kesar-saga**, were dictated slowly by the same man who dictated the 'Lower Ladakhi Version of the Kesar-saga', and were written down by the Munshi of Khalatse, *Yeshes rig 'adzin.* The sagas contained in the present collection are not considered by the people to be of the same importance as the Kesar-saga proper; but they are interesting enough to the European student of Tibetan folklore as throwing new light on the Kesar-saga, According to my conception, the present sagas constitute parallels to the Kesar-saga, as were told in side-valleys. Some of the Agus appearing in them look exactly like Kesar himself under a new name. When these tales were united with the principal saga, Kesar under a different name (i.e. the Agu) had to become a son or servant of Kesar under his own name. In the first of the tales, however, we find Kesar under his own name, and the tale reminds us in many parts decidedly of Kesar-saga, Tale No. V, Kesar's defeat of the giant of the North.

Tale No. 1.

The Tale of Kesar's Beloved Mon.

Abstract of Contents.

Kesar had a Mon (low-caste man) whom he loved more than anybody else. The Agus became jealous and killed the Mon on the occasion of a hunting party which they had undertaken in his company, by pushing him from a high rock. Kesar went to find him and heard a voice speaking out of his corpse. Therefore he opened the Mon's belly with a knife, and out of the corpse came two Mons, a male and a female one which

---

[1] Extract from the *Journal and Proceedings of the Asiat. Soc. Bengal,* Vol. II, 1906. pp. 467–469. The Tibetan Texts are not reprinted.

he carried home in his loin cloth. Both were some sort of devils who required a great amount of food. At first the Agus had to feed them, but when their supplies were finished, the Mon-devils were entrusted to grandfather *rTse dgu*. This old hermit gave them much work and little food. Once they found a lump of gold and a turquoise of the size of a hearth-stone. These treasures they presented to the hermit, asking him to increase their food and give them less work. He, however, did the opposite, as he was of opinion that they would find him more treasures if he was hard on them. Then the two devils fled to a poisonous lake in which they bathed, with the result that their appearance became perfectly diabolic. One of their teeth grew down to the earth and another up to the sky, and they received locks of blood-red colour. They attacked the hermit in his house, but Kesar was sent to rescue him. When they had told their tale to Kesar, the latter advised them erroneously to go to the land of the Nāgas and devour its inhabitants. This was a slip of the tongue, for he had intended to send them to the land of the devil. When the misery of the Nāgas became very great, they were advised by their sorcerers to send two of their ladies, *Dargyi yang mdzesma*, and *Dargyi mthong mdzesma*, to Kesar, to ask him to come to their assistance. These two Nāginī went towards the land of *gLing* and put up 100 black and 100 white tents. First of all, Agu *Khrai mgo khrai thung* was sent against them. The ladies took the shape of bears, and the Agu ran away before them, wounding his horse with his own sword in his fright. Then Agu *dPalle* was sent, but he also fled before the bears. Still he found out that they were females. Therefore he gave the advice that *'aBruguma* ought to be sent to the tents. She was well accepted and asked by the Nāginī to send King Kesar to them for some time. Kesar agreed to that, saying that *'aBruguma* would probably repent her promise. Then *'aBruguma* was ordered to fetch Kesar's horse from the cold (or straight) valley. But the horse behaved awkwardly and would not come. By throwing a stone at it with a sling, she succeeded after all in mounting it. But then the horse went off in the most extraordinary way, carrying her up to the sky, and then dragging her along mountain ridges, *'aBruguma* spending most of the time below the belly of the horse, with the result that, when they arrived after all in the stable, the back of the horse was sore. Then *'aBruguma* went to her father and mother, angry. Kesar healed the horse with the medicines which were always ready for use in the horse's ear, and took *'aBruguma* back to the castle. There she had to clean all the harnesses and other armature which Kesar intended to take along with him on his expedition.[1] Then *'aBruguma* sang a song in which Kesar is praised as a being from whom light, dew, and flowers proceed. Kesar answered with a song in which he said that, although leaving as a young man, he would return as an old man. Kesar was led by a fox to the land of the Nāgas. He punished the two Mon-devils and sent them to the land of the devil to eat there all the poisonous snakes. Then he played at dice with the brother of the two Nāginī, *Yang mdzesma* and *mThong mdzesma*. Thus nine years elapsed. But then the Nāga had a difference with Kesar and called him, 'Forgetter of *gLing*'. That very night Kesar saw his horse in his dream. He went to look after him the next day and found him after a long time. The horse advised him not to accept the food which was to be offered to him by the Nāginī, as it was poisonous, and they rode off in the direction of *gLing*. Two days before arriving there, Kesar took the shape of a wolf, and soon met with Agu *dPalle* who had taken the shape of a sheep. But the latter recognized Kesar and blamed him for not hurrying home, as *bKā bloṅ ldanpa* had taken possession of the castle of *gLing* and *'aBruguma*, and killed Agu *mDa dpon gongma*. Therefore Kesar took the shape of a begging monk and went to the *gLing* castle to ask alms. He told *'aBruguma* that he had heard news of Kesar's death in the land of the Nāgas. *'aBruguma* liked that news and gave him a little room to sleep in. At night Kesar surprised *'aBruguma* in the company of *bKā blon ldanpa*. The latter was suspended in a cage, but released when he made over his property to Kesar. Also *'aBruguma* was forgiven and re-accepted.

Tale No. II.[2]

The Tale of Skyaba Rgodpo.

Abstract of Contents.

Agu *Skyaba rgodpo* of *gLing* went a-hunting and met with the great king of *Groyul*. They became friends and arranged that their children were to marry each other. Both their wives were with child, and, one day, when *Skyaba rgodpo* found a golden bow and arrow, and the king of *Groyul* a mother-of-pearl spindle, they knew that the former was to get a baby-boy, and the latter a baby-girl. They agreed that

---

[1] There is a very similar passage to this in Kesar-saga, Tale No. V, Kesar's victory over the giant of the North, *Bibliotheca Indica.*

[2] Extract from the *Journal and Proceedings of the Asiat. Soc. Bengal*, Vol. III, 1907, pp. 67-68.

the names of their children were to be *Gromo so dkar* (black brown with white teeth) for the girl, and *Skyaba dkarpo* (white ladle) for the boy. Then they played at dice for seven days about their children, to find out who of the two was to become the master of the house.[1] The result was that *Skyaba rgodpo's* boy was to be master, and that the girl was to accept him, even if he shold be very poor. Then the whole contract was written by *Skyaba rgodpo* with his own blood and hidden beneath his saddle. On his way home, *Skyaba rgodpo* was swallowed by a wild yak, and the horse arrived in the stable alone.

When *Skyaba rgodpo's* boy was born and grown up, he decided to leave his home and go to find his father. He saddled his horse and discovered the marriage contract. From a high hill he saw a yak grazing and asked him what kind of food he liked best. The yak replied that he liked the flesh of men and animals best of all, and that he would not eat grass unless he could not get the former. Next morning the boy killed the yak with seven arrows and opened his belly. Out of it came a number of men whom the yak had devoured, and also the boy's father. The latter, however, died soon. His corpse was burnt over three arrows and deposited in a *spur khang* (corpse house).

Then the boy decided to go to gain his bride from *Groyul*. In a counsel with king Kesar, the following Agus received orders to accompany the boy, *dPalle rgodpo, Khrai mgo khrai thung, Anggar ltsangspa*; [*Mi yulla medpai*] *Grodpa che*; *Lag lag rings*; *rKang rkang rings*. Before arriving in *Groyul*, they came to a great lake. Agu *dPalle* made a great dumpling of one bushel of flour and sat down on a boulder to eat it. Then a beautiful girl with a golden water-pot appeared on the opposite shore, and Agu *dPalle* asked her where the castle of the king of *Groyul* was, and whether the expected daughter had been born to him or not. The girl asked in return what he wanted to do with the king and his daughter and advised him to fly across the water or to swim through it. *dPalle* went wading through it, but a short distance before reaching the shore, he pretended to be carried away by the current, and the girl ran to his assistance. She said that she was the daughter of the king of *Groyul*, but that she was not willing to show the way to the castle, as she was afraid he would revenge himself on her (for having been unkind to him). *dPalle* spent the night in the house of two field labourers, and when all the Agus had arrived, he went with them before the king

[1] The question is whether the boy is to be a *bagpo* who provides a wife for himself, or a *magpa* who is asked by the girl, whilst she remains master in her father's house.

of *Groyul*, and demanded his daughter as bride for *Skyaba rgodpo*. The king said that he would give her to him who was able to point her out, when she was in the company of one hundred other girls. Agu *dPalle* was able to do that, for *Ane bkur dmanmo*, the Queen of Heaven, who had taken the shape of a golden fly, descended on the forehead of the king's daughter. Thus showing whom he must point out. The king of *Groyul*, however, was not yet ready to part with his daughter, and said, he would give her to him who could eat one hundred carcasses at a sit down. This feat was performed by Agu *Grodpa che* (great stomach) who even ate the bones of the animals. Then the king said, he would give his daughter to him who was able to carry one hundred jugs of water from the sea to the castle within a day. This was done by the Agus *Lag lag rings* (Long hand) and *rKang rkang rings* (Long leg). Then there was still a delay; for the wedding was postponed, until the uncle of the bride had arrived and the Nyopas [1] were brought together. The uncle arrived after thirty days and the Nyopas spent seven days with singing the Ritual and three days with singing the Drinking Song.[2]

Before the Agus started with the bride, Agu *dPalle*, in a song, demanded the bridal presents which were presented. Also the treasures of the castle followed after the bride, but a portion of them was returned to her relations. In the desert, Agu *dPalle* provided the party with water, which he dug out of a moist spot. Agu *Khrai mgo khrai thung* was sent in advance to prepare the people of *gLing* for the event. They came with many Nyopas to meet the bride. Then there was a second wedding feast, and the country remained in a happy state.

Tale No. III.[3]

The Tale of Shelli Buzhung.

Abstract of Contents.

When Kesar was old, there was a little boy in the castle of *gLing* called *Shelli bu zhung* ('the little boy of Crystal') who had no father.[4]

---

[1] Nyopas are the honorary buyers of the bride: see 'A Lower Ladakhi Marriage Ritual', *Indian Antiquary*, 1901.

[2] See 'The Drinking Songs of Khalatse', Tibetan Text, printed at Leh, 1901.

[3] Extract from the *Journal and Proceedings Asiat. Soc. Bengal*, Vol. III, 1907, pp. 261–263.

[4] Just as Kesar had no human father, his boy was also supposed to have none. Compare 'A Lower Ladakhi Version of the Kesar-saga', Tale No. II.

It was found necessary to provide a bride for him, and as the hermit *rTse dgu* was the only person likely to know a suitable bride, a little servant-boy was sent to ask his advice. The boy received a letter authorizing him to ride on the horse *Dunggi dar dkar*, which was in the care of Agu *Zlaba bzangpo.* This Agu was 1,050 years old and had a son called *Zlaba dkarpo. Zlaba dkarpo* could not believe that the horse was to be entrusted to the little servant-boy, and went before king Kesar together with the boy, to make special enquiries. But Kesar gave the same order once more, and the child was carried by the horse before the hermit's house, after it had jumped with him so close to the sun that the boy got almost burnt. The hermit, however, was offended, because Kesar had sent a little boy instead of a proper Agu. But the boy was carried by dragons directly before the hermit's house. Then he made a bow and arrow and frightened the old man. The latter read Kesar's letter and said that the bride of Kesar's son, *rGyalsa dkarpo*, was to be born to the king of *Groyul*, whose castle was on the top of the three realms of the world. She was to be born together with many powerful jewels. He gave the advice to make friends with the grandmother who took care of the garden below *Groyul*; and prophesied that the bride would be obtained, although one of the Agus would lose his life in the task (*mDā dpon gongma*). When the answer of the hermit was brought to the castle of *gLing*, *'aBruguma* did not like the news, and entreated Kesar to select a bride from the daughters of the country. He, however, went off with his son. When they arrived half-way to *Groyul*, they met with the Nyopas (buyers of the bride) of many countries who wished to gain the daughter of the king of *Groyul* for themselves. They took night-quarters at the grandmother's house. The son first frightened the grandmother by burning her garden down, and then appeased her by restoring everything in a miraculous way. During night, when the daughter of the king of *Groyul* was born, the earth was filled with light. But the boy had a bad dream and believed that the daughter of an ogre had been born. However, the grandmother comforted him, saying that the daughter was a fairy, and that the Nyopas of many countries had already arrived, desirous of gaining her. Also the new-born daughter of the king of *Groyul* had a dream, in which she saw two men and an ogress (the female Agu *dPal moi astag*) of terrible shape, arrive, and carry her off by twisting her hair round a spear. But her mother comforted her, saying that it was a good dream, and that she was to become the wife of king Kesar's son.

The boy *rGyalbu rgyalsa* wished to ride to and break the bazaar of *Groyul*, which consisted of bell-metal; but did not succeed. He therefore asked his father to lend him the horse *rKyang rgod dbyerpa*. Riding on him, he broke the bazaar of bell-metal to pieces. This was the signal for the people of *Groyul* to send their army against the men of *gLing*. The first whom *rGyalbu rgyalsa* met was *Lag dmar blon chen*. Although *Lag dmar blon chen* was on the opposite shore of a lake, he was killed by a miraculous war dance of the boy, when the drums used for the dance went off suddenly and entered into the body of the giant. The second hero of *Groyul* was *Mig dmar*. He went to fight the boy of *gLing* in spite of his wife's warnings. He tumbled into the water which was between the combatants, on account of the strong wind produced by the horse *rKyang rgod dbyerpa* with his wings. Then they decided on a contest in arrow-shooting. The heavy arrow of the giant split the rocks asunder; but the light arrows of the boy caused so much wind that the giant was thrown into the water a second time. Then the giant and the child rode a race. The giant arrived at the goal first and cooked some tea. But the boy, although he arrived a little later, had his tea sooner ready. Then they rode a race to the top of a mountain. On the same day also a Buddha and a Bonpo priest had betted who would be first on the top of the same mountain. The Buddha and the boy of *gLing* both arrived there first. From the top of this mountain the child pronounced a blessing, according to which the countries were to be filled with what they are famous for in the eyes of the Ladakhis: China with silks of the dragon pattern; Central Tibet with tea; Yarkand with horses; the West Tibetan lake-district with salt and wool; Purangs with beautiful girls; Ladakh with tiger-like heroes; Zangskar with yaks; Purik with *Gro dkar* flowers; Baltistan with apricots; Kashmir with rice! Then the boy killed the giant by snipping with his finger against the giant's forehead, and ordered him to be reborn to a female *Kyang* of fifty years of age.

Kesar went with his son to the engagement-beer of the King of China's daughter and sat down on a throne of sticks. The maid-servant, *Gochod*, offered the beer and told the guests to drink it without touching the pot.[1] As the honoured guests, who sat on thrones of gold and silver, were unable to perform the task, she considered it superfluous to ask

---

[1] The same scene occurs in 'A Lower Ladakhi Version of the Kesar-saga', Tale No. III.

the two men of *gLing* to try. However, the boy prayed her to offer the beer to him and gave her a new name. Then he threw the pot towards the sky with his stick, and the beer was consumed by the 360 gods and nāgas. Thus the girls were won by the men of *gLing*. But when the boy exhibited his great power, the heroes of *Groyul* would not give him the princess and sent the giant *Riwa* (or *Ribo*) *blon chen* against him. The boy fled before the giant, as a partridge flies before a falcon. Therefore Kesar took the shape of a crow and asked *dPalmoi astag* (the female Agu) to come to his assistance. She went to fight the giant and asked Agu *mDā dpon gongma* to come also. The giant was defeated by the woman in a great arrow and spear contest; but when he fell down, *mDā dpon gongma* happened to come under the giant's thumb and was smashed.

During this combat, the son of the King of China (*rGyanag*) had carried off the bride to his own country. Therefore Kesar, his son, and the Agus, went to China. A grandmother made the arrangement that on the day of the prince of China's wedding to the princess of *Groyul*, *dPalmoi astag*, who had taken a beautiful shape, was to be married to the minister of China. But when the wedding dance was performed, *dPalmoi astag* started a war-dance, followed by Kesar and the other men of *gLing*. During this dance, they killed the king of China and all his men, and the female Agu put her spear in *Shel ldang lha.no's* hair, which she twisted round it, and dragged the girl out of the castle on the road to *gLing*. Only after long entreaties by the whole party and the gods was she willing to let the girl ride on the horse of her bridegroom.

Then a message was sent to *gLing* with two doves, and a great wedding was celebrated on the hill *Tisuru* (Kailasa).

Tale No. IV.[1]

The Tale of Gongma Buthsa's Boy and rGyalsa dKarpo.

Abstract of Contents.

Old Kesar went to a hermitage and left the government to his son *rGyalsa dKarpo*. The latter had a difference with his wife *Shel ldang lhamo*. To find out who was wrong, Kesar sent two storks to watch the couple. The latter heard *Shel ldang lhamo* abuse the family of Kesar

---

[1] Extract from the *Journal and Proceedings Asiat. Soc. Bengal*, Vol. III, 1907, pp. 321–323.

by calling them 'descendants of a smith'.[1] When they brought this news to Kesar, *Shel ldang lhamo* was turned out of the castle and Agu *Khrai mgo khrai thung*, who wished to mend his bad repute by a good deed, was sent to the hermit *rTse dgu* to ask him from whence to get another wife for *rGyalsa dKarpo*. The hermit answered that a suitable princess could be obtained from *Ljang*, which country is situated on the frontier between sun and moon, and advised the Agu to circumambulate round *mDā dpon gongmā's* stūpa, until a lizard would appear and nod with the head. This he might take as an assurance that his sin in killing the Agu was forgiven. When the hermit's answer was brought to *gLing*, *rGyalso dKarpo* and the Agus started for *Ljang*.

mDā dpon gongma's son, called *Gongma buthsa*, wished to accompany the heroes and went first of all to find his horse called *rKyang Khra melong*. He found it in a valley and recognized it by a flame which proceeded from its forehead. It refused to come, until he threw stones at it with a miraculous sling. He threw three stones at a time. The first broke the horn of the wild yak *Curulugu* to pieces, the second killed the mother mare and the third made a hole in the foal's ear.

After a feast had been given, the boy, riding on *rKyanq Khra melong*, followed *rGyalsa dKarpo* and the Agus, he himself riding in the sky. The first who saw him come was Agu *Miggi rab lha*, but Agu *dPalle* would not believe until the boy arrived. The boy had at once a difference with Agu *dPalle*, but the two combatants were separated by *rGyalsa dKarpo*. Soon king *Lho krab* arrived on his way to *Ljang*, as he also wished to gain the princess of that country. He had two heroes with him; one's name was *Mi dbang ral chen* and the other's *Mi dban ral chung*. The latter was sent first to fight against the men of *gLing*. He was opposed by *Gongma buthsa*; but the boy was hit twice by *Mi dbang ral chung's* spear, first in the head and then in the breast. He was healed by *Ane bKur dmanmo* who extracted the spear. Then he prayed to his father *mDā dpon gongma* and received from him good advice. in particular, which arrows to use. With these arrows he killed *Mi dbang ral chung*. In consequence of this defeat, king *Lho krab* with his followers went off to his own country.

To conquer *Ljang*, however, the assistance of the female Agu was necessary, and Agu *dPalle* was despatched to fetch her. He found her

---

1 Compare 'A Lower Ladakhi Version of the Kesar-saga', Tale No. I. The present tale proves beyond doubt that forefather *bKrashis* and Smith *bKrashis* are identical.

sporting in *dPal yul* (Nepal) together with a friend. After some trouble he persuaded her to come. Two yaks, mother and daughter, who offered themselves as food to the ladies, were advised to go to *dPalmoi astag's* valley in the North-West, as they would be safest in that valley.

The army of *gLing* went before the castle of *Ljang*, but could not induce the men of *Ljang* to fight. Therefore *mDā dpon gongma's* son, who is suddenly called *rNa jyu rna rtsal*, went off to find a means. He discovered a girl crying in a hut below the castle of *Ljang* and asked her why she cried. She said, the reason was that both her husbands *bLonpo mig dmar* and *Mi dbang ral chung* had been killed by men of *gLing*. She added that it would be possible to induce the men of *Ljang* to fight, if the servant-girl who carried the water to the castle was killed. In acknowledgment of this good advice *rNa jyu rna rtsal* in a miraculous way caused the girl to be re-united with *bLonpo mig dmar* in a castle on a far-off plain.

When in the morning the water-carrying girl came (apparently from the castle of *Ljang*, the passage is not quite clear), the boy killed the girl. The people of *Ljang* came in search of the murderer and the boy betrayed himself by showing the jewel which he had taken from the girl. He was thrown into prison. Once three fishes which had been offered to the king, laughed; and the boy pretended to know the reason why. He said the fishes had laughed because the queen was in secret union with the king of the Nāgas. When this was found out to be untrue the boy was condemned to death. Then the men of *Ljang* could not agree with regard to the kind of death. Therefore the boy proposed to them to fetter him and burn him alive.

Whilst preparations for the execution were made, the men of *gLing* became troubled where *mDā dpon gongma's* son remained, and, to find him, sent to his younger brother[1] who took the shape of a crow. When *mDā dpon gongma's* son in his fettered condition saw his younger brother, he asked him to tell *Ane bkur dmanmo* to send his horse. The horse arrived and remained unseen to the men of *Ljang*. Suddenly the boy mounted it and killed many men of *Ljang*. Then he returned to the army of *gLing* and admonished it to advance.

The daughter of the king of *Ljang*, who was married to the king of *Lho krab*, advised her father to use the power of the jewel *Tom ljag*, by which, everybody could be kept motionless in that very place and position, which he just occupied. Thus the whole army of *gLing* was

[1] Apparently, the passage is not quite clear.

kept bound by unseen fetters. Agu *Khrai mgo khrai thung* was accidentally away, and, therefore, escaped the magic spell. By stealing he provided food for his fettered companions and kept them alive by feeding them in their helpless positions. Then he took the shape of a cat and went into a mouse-hole, where he found the mice celebrating the wedding of their king. He seized the king and minister and was attacked by all the mice who ate his flesh. But although nothing but bone remained he did not release his captives, till the mice restored his flesh and promised to steal the jewel *Tom ljag*. Thus the whole army of *gLing* was delivered. On their way back to *gLing*, *mDā dpon's* son said he would go to *Lho krab* and fetch the princess. He placed a firebrand in the tail of a fox and threw the fox into the *Lho krab* castle, which consisted of sealing wax and melted. Thus the princess of *Ljang* was gained and united with *rGyalsa dKarpo.*

At the celebration of the wedding the princess' food was restored in a miraculous way, whilst the prince's was not. Kesar took this as proof that the girl was of better character than his son, became angry and left the couple alone in the wilderness. Then the two separated, the girl going back to *Ljang* and the boy to *gLing*. But as the latter did not cease to deplore the loss of his new bride, he was once more allowed to go and fetch her. He took service in the *Ljang* castle; but whatever work he did, as cow-herd, dog-herd, etc., it was accompanied by much blessing. Once he saw in a picture of a miraculous *mchod rten*, how much he was missed by the people of *gLing*, and the couple decided to run away. Through a spell he caused the treasures of *Ljang* to adhere to his body and carried them off. The couple was followed by the army of *Ljang*, but *rGyalsa dKarpo* beat them and made a pond of blood which he surrounded with a wall of bones. Then a crow was sent to *gLing* to give news of the arrival of the couple and a great wedding was celebrated.

Tale No. V.[1]

Appendix.

The Tale of γSerri buzhung.

Note.

The tale of *γSerri buzhung* being extremely similar to the last part of the tale of *Gongma butisa's* boy and *rGyalsa dKarpo*, I do not consider

[1] Extract from the *Journal and Proceedings Asiat. Soc. Bengal,* Vol. III, 1907,

it necessary to give the Tibetan text, as it shows again how far certain versions of the Kesar-saga may differ from one village to another. The tale of *γSerri buzhung* represents the Sheh version. It was told by Zarra of Sheh, and written down by Shamuel Joldan of Leh. It has not yet been published in its original form. A small number of copies of it were printed in an arranged form, suitable for school use.